MANAGEMENT

THEORY, PROCESS, AND PRACTICE

FIFTH EDITION

MANAGEMENT
THEORY, PROCESS, AND PRACTICE
F I F T H   E D I T I O N

RICHARD M. HODGETTS

Florida International University

HARCOURT BRACE JOVANOVICH, PUBLISHERS

San Diego   New York   Chicago   Austin   Washington, D.C.
London   Sydney   Tokyo   Toronto

To Steven

Preface

In this century human progress may be characterized by technical and scientific prowess, but it is accounted for by managerial expertise. Without the ability to formulate objectives, to devise plans, and to coordinate people and materials in a synergistic fashion, Henry Ford would never have built his production line, Neil Armstrong would never have walked on the moon, and the microcomputer revolution would never have come about. In many undertakings, management, the process of getting things done through people, is the key to success or failure.

The purpose of *Management: Theory, Process, and Practice* is to familiarize readers with basic modern management concepts and to acquaint them with the present status and future of this growing field. I have assumed that readers of this fifth edition are newcomers to the study and practice of management. Therefore, the book can be used effectively in an introductory undergraduate management course. In addition, it can be employed in professional training courses and is useful to practicing executives who wish to update their knowledge of the field.

I have attempted to present the concepts of modern management in a readable, interesting style through the use of the following special features.

DISTINGUISHING FEATURES

Organization

The book is divided into five major parts. Part 1 introduces and examines the challenge of management and the evolution of management thought. Part 2 traces the development of modern management theory and emphasizes and explains the process school of management thought, which is so important to today's practicing manager. Part 3 discusses the quantitative school of management thought while Part 4 examines the behavioral school of management. Part 5 takes an overview of current management theory and a look at some critical dimensions on today's management scene including business's social responsibilities, international business, and the future of management.

Exhibits

Numerous tables, charts, and illustrations highlight important concepts in the clearest possible manner.

Biographical Sketches

Chapter 2 discusses a number of important contributors to early management thought. To provide the reader with a better understanding of these individuals, pictures and biographical sketches of a number of them are included.

Short Cases

Students too often learn theories without understanding their practical applications. For this reason, four short cases appear at the end of each chapter. These cases give readers many opportunities to apply the principles, processes, and practices presented in the individual chapters, and thus, reinforce the major concepts introduced.

Comprehensive Cases

Parts 2, 3, 4, and 5 conclude with a comprehensive case. The purpose of these cases is to provide readers with an opportunity to integrate and apply many of the ideas contained in the preceding chapters to a realistic situation.

INSTRUCTOR'S RESOURCE MANUAL

An *Instructor's Resource Manual* has been designed to accompany the text. This supplementary teaching aid contains a synopsis of the goals and material in each chapter. In addition, it includes answers to the review and study questions at the end of each chapter, answers to the questions associated with the cases at the end of each chapter, and a large pool of true-false and multiple-choice questions for testing purposes.

FIFTH EDITION CHANGES

Since this book was first written, a number of major changes have occurred in the field of management. Some of the most exciting topics of today—strategic planning, women in management, organizational culture, computer technology, developments in international management—were of little importance to newcomers to the field twenty years ago. Today this has changed, and no basic textbook in the area would be complete without consideration of these topics. In addition to focusing on these major changes, I also have identified six major key result areas that will greatly influence the success of organizations: social responsibility, ethics, intrapreneurship, technology, internationalism, and communications. These topics are covered within specific chapters, but they are so important that I have also woven them throughout the text. Each chapter contains two boxed examples that illustrate how key result areas influence or are affected by the major topic under discussion.

I have also tried to bridge more completely the gap between management theory and process and management practice by incorporating "real-life interviews" with key management personnel and by writing a new real-life, end-of-the-chapter case for each chapter.

My overall objective in writing this book is to integrate management theory and process with management practice, hence the title I have chosen. Every student of management needs to know why things are done the way they are (theory), the systematic arrangement used in doing them (process), and how to actually carry them out (practice). In this latest edition, I have attempted to strengthen the theory and practice sides by putting greater focus on why and how things are done as they are.

In the final analysis, however, you, the reader, will be the ultimate judge of how well these goals have been attained. I hope you find the material to be interesting, insightful, enjoyable, and, most importantly, useful.

ACKNOWLEDG-MENTS

Many individuals have played a decisive role in helping me write this book. In particular, I would like to thank Fred Luthans, of the University of Nebraska, who provided me with many helpful suggestions and ideas. Ronald A. Greenwood of GMI and Jane W. Gibson of Nova University provided important insights. I would also like to thank those who have read, reviewed, and commented on portions of the text, in particular: C. Kendrick Gibson, Hope College; Joseph Gray, Nassau Community College; Dan Madison, California State University–Long Beach; Ken Keiser, Western State College; Norma Givens, Fort Valley State College; Peter Everett, Des Moines Area Community College; Ed Borgens, San Diego Mesa College; Eugene Britt, Grossmont College; Ron Herrick, Mesa Community College; Steve Popejoy, Central Missouri State University; Martha Crumpacker, Washburn University; Stephen D. Schuster, California State University–Northridge; Furman Penland, University of North Carolina at Greensboro; E. M. Teagarden, Dakota State College; Steve Clapham, Vincennes University; and Randy Joyner, Wilkes Community College.

I want to express special appreciation to my colleagues at Florida International University: Dean Charles Nickerson of the College of Business Administration; Dana Farrow, Karl Magnusen, and Enzo Valenzi. I am also grateful to Henry Albers, former Dean of the University of Petroleum and Minerals in Dhaharan, Saudi Arabia. Sincerest thanks to the people at Harcourt Brace Jovanovich for their professional efforts. Finally, thanks go to Ruth Chapman for typing the manuscript.

Contents

1

DEVELOPMENT

OF

MANAGEMENT

THEORY

The first part of the book introduces the reader to the field of management. Particular attention is given to three objectives: (1) explaining what management is, (2) setting forth some of the challenges that will confront the manager during the 1990s, and (3) studying the evolution of management thought from antiquity to the middle of the current century.

Chapter 1 explains the nature of management and where it is heading. Chapter 2 provides the background necessary for studying the field and determining how to meet the challenges that Chapter 1 describes. Chapter 3 focuses in some detail on particular modern management theories and practices.

The beginning of Chapter 1 discusses what management is and is not. It highlights the role of the manager as a person who works through other people. Then it examines the changing world of work, and the challenges that will confront the manager of the future.

Chapter 2 traces the emergence of management thought from the Sumerians, the ancient Romans, and the Roman Catholic Church through the Industrial Revolution and finally up into the twentieth century. Along this time continuum many thinkers contributed to the foundations of modern management; this book pays particular attention to the work of the scientific managers, the administrative management theorists, and the early behavioral researchers. After the contributions of these three groups are examined, they will be placed in a contemporary critical perspective by means of analyses of both their strong and weak points.

Chapter 3 reviews the development of modern management theory. Many people made contributions to early management thought. A few of the major contributors are, for example, Frederick W. Taylor, who turned interest toward time-and-motion study; Henri Fayol, the early management theorist; and Elton Mayo, one of the early theorists in the sociopsychological aspects of working. The writing of these scholars continues today to exert influence on management theory; therefore, they and other significant early theorists appear in the chapter for historical and present-day reasons. Chapter 3 basically develops the concepts of three types of early modern management theory: scientific management, administrative management, and behavioral observation.

The overriding objective of Part 1 is to familiarize the reader with management by looking at both future challenges and past accomplishments in the field. The book then proceeds logically to the study of modern management theory and practice.

The
Challenge
of
Management

Management has been popularly defined as getting things done through people. In more complex terms, it is the process of setting objectives, organizing resources to attain these predetermined goals, and then evaluating the results for the purpose of determining future action. Whatever definition is used, management has for thousands of years been the key to success for individuals and civilizations alike. In this century effective management practices have helped raise the United States to a position of world power. Effective management has also played a key role in the success and development of giant corporations such as General Motors, American Telephone and Telegraph, and IBM. Today, as countries with opposing political theories seek détente, effective management will be needed to bring the sides together. Thus, whether one is examining the prerequisite for world prominence, corporate growth, or international peace, management must be considered.

The first goal of this chapter is to look at the nature of management by examining this process in action. The second goal is to study the changing world of work. The third is to examine the specific challenges that are going to confront the modern manager because of the most recent changes in the work environment.

When you are finished reading this chapter, you should be able to:

1. Define and describe what is meant by the term *management*.
2. Explain the principles on which industrialism rested.

3. Relate the challenges that will confront the manager of the 1990s.

4. Explain why the study of management requires attention to the past and the future, as well as the present, for a solid grounding in the subject.

THE NATURE OF MANAGEMENT

The overall purpose of this book is to examine the field of management. In doing so, it is helpful to first discuss what a manager *is* and what a manager *is not*. The key characteristic which distinguishes managers from others is that managers get things done *through* other people. Consider the following individual, Sam Begley:

> Sam is the manager of a sales force for a medium-sized hardware manufacturer. Salaries for all salespeople are a direct percentage of sales. Sam's basic salary, however, is guaranteed although he also receives a 1 percent override on everything his people sell and a 15 percent commission on everything he personally sells. Except for Monday mornings, which he spends in the office answering correspondence and talking to his sales staff, Sam spends his entire week in the field, selling merchandise. "I don't have to motivate my people," says Sam. "They know what to do. My job is simply to take care of the office work and then get out and try to supplement my salary through sales activity."

Is Begley a manager? Not in the true sense of the word. There is very little he is doing *through* other people. Basically, he is an entrepreneur who is working for his own account. His job is very similar to that of the salespeople. Of course, he does carry out some managerial tasks, such as planning and organizing the office work, and undoubtedly he is responsible for controlling overall operations. However, these are really secondary to his sales efforts. In the final analysis, Begley does not represent the type of individual who would frequently use the information contained in this text. On the other hand, consider the case of Sharon Eaton:

> Sharon is in charge of the commercial loan department at a major bank. Her job is to maintain current commercial accounts while trying to obtain even more. There are sixteen people in the department, and her job requires her to spend a great deal of time in the office. However, she is also responsible for visiting with customers, entertaining them at lunches and dinners, helping them analyze their banking needs, and providing the services they require. Much of this activity is actually handled by her assistants in the department because she has other functions that also require time. Included in this group are discussing job-related matters with subordinates, assigning tasks to them, attending bank meetings, projecting departmental needs in terms of both personnel and budget and seeing that these are forwarded to higher

management, and evaluating the overall performance of the personnel and offering suggestions for improvement.

Managers work through other people.

The job Eaton performs is much more managerial in nature than Begley's. It is certainly not the case that everything she does is through others; she performs many tasks herself. However, she is not entrepreneurial in the sense that Begley is.

When management in action is examined, it is important to remember that there are two parts to the picture. First is the work to be done. Second is the people who will be doing the work. An effective manager is work-oriented but also concerned with personnel. There is a *blend* of work and people. No effective manager can emphasize one to the exclusion of the other. In short, management is the process of getting things done through others, and this process puts emphasis on both the objectives to be attained and the people who will be pursuing them.

This book will undertake a close examination of the management process. Before getting to that, however, it is important to understand the kinds of challenges management is going to be facing in the decades ahead. Conditions will continue to change, and the manager must be prepared to respond to these new developments. What will the future look like? This question is best answered by first examining the past, present, and future waves of change.

THE CHANGING WORLD OF WORK

Throughout the course of human history the world of work has continually changed. Early prehistoric man lived in small groups, which often migrated throughout a given region foraging for food. Fishing, hunting, and herding were the basic forms of work needed for survival. Between 8000 and 3000 B.C. the agricultural revolution greatly changed the way people lived. Farming and livestock breeding continued to develop reaching new heights after the Middle Ages. However, the world of work changed even more dramatically with the advent of industrialism.

The Rise of Industrialism

Around 1800 A.D. the Industrial Revolution began. Industrialism was characterized by the harnessing of power to machinery. Beginning in Europe and then America this development gradually gained a major foothold and changed the world of work. Industrialism brought with it important rules or principles that greatly affected the behavior of people at work.[1]

One of these was *standardization*. Industrialization made it possible to produce identical goods in millions of units. The result was a general increase

---

[1]For more on this see Alvin Toffler, *The Third Wave* (New York: William Morrow, 1980).

When goods were standardized.

in volume and a corresponding decrease in price. People did not seem to mind standardization because they felt the convenience of it was worth the sacrifice of uniqueness.

Jobs were specialized.

A second characteristic was *specialization.* In the workplace it became necessary to have large numbers of people performing a series of predetermined rote tasks. Each worker became a specialist at a particular job; their specialization in turn helped workers increase the number of units they could produce. The basic idea was carried over to Henry Ford's assembly line, where sixty cars an hour were being produced by the mid-1920s. And this trend toward specialization was not restricted to manufacturing. It began to dominate many areas, including the professions. Specialists moved in to monopolize fields of knowledge, and these fields became specialized. There were now producers and consumers. The producers were those who provided the service; the consumers were those who used it. In the medical profession doctors provided health care, and the general public used it. In academia, teachers produced the education, and students consumed it.

Work elements were synchronized.

A third basic characteristic of this revolution was *synchronization,* a coordination or blending of all elements in the workplace. For example, since it made no sense for job orders to wait while machinery needed repair, schedules of preventive maintenance were set up so that the machinery was ready to operate and the orders could be quickly processed when the workers were on site. This characteristic even affected the work lives of the employees, for now there were set time periods during which they had to be on the job. Synchronization brought a new kind of time element into the workplace and, combined with standardization and specialization, resulted in the rise of an industrial complex.

Resources were concentrated.

A fourth characteristic was *concentration,* which took two forms. In the first type of concentration, people left the farms and concentrated wherever the factories were located, often in the cities. In the second type, business began to concentrate when major companies started acquiring large inventories of the raw materials and other resources needed to dominate their respective industries. The giant corporations of today have resulted from such action. Consider the fact that as early as the mid-1960s there were only four large American manufacturers of automobiles still in existence. In Europe the situation was the same. Four German automakers accounted for 91 percent of auto production; in France Renault, Citroen, Simca, and Peugeot turned out virtually all of the country's cars; and in Italy, Fiat alone accounted for over 90 percent of all auto production. The same pattern held in education. At the turn of the century, major universities' student bodies were no larger than 5,000; most were much smaller. Today a university of this size is considered quite small. In fact, within many universities there are now colleges with more than 5,000 students!

Maximization was emphasized.

A fifth characteristic was *maximization.* Bigness began to be synonymous with efficiency. Business firms attempted to increase their market shares, their returns on investment, and their overall sales by annual increases of 10 to 15 percent. Any slippage was regarded as inefficient. In this race to maintain growth, acquisition and merger were used. Medium-sized firms combined their assets to become large. Larger firms often bought out smaller, more profitable ones in other industries, thus turning themselves into multi-industry conglomerates with high returns on capital.

And operations were centralized.

Finally, there was *centralization.* Operational decisions were often pushed down the line while overall financial control was maintained at the top. Following the adage that the individual who controls the purse strings controls everything, large firms sought to hold a tight rein on operations. This particular characteristic was noticeable as early as a century ago in the railroads, when management carefully synchronized operations through centralized decision making. Railroad lines extending hundreds of miles from headquarters were run by home office managers.

These six principles characterized industrialism. To a large degree they were responsible for the growth of the United States as an industrial power; and their use in other countries helped account for the rise of such industrial giants as Germany, England, France, Japan, and the Soviet Union.

If managers were going to operate solely within the framework of these six principles during the 1990s, the challenge of management would not be very great. There would be basic guidelines to help, and the past would provide sufficient examples of what to expect in the future. However, this will not be the case. Currently, a series of changes are presenting new challenges and opportunities. No student of management can seriously study the field without having a fundamental understanding of what these latest changes are and how they are likely to affect the world of work.

Modern Management Changes

Dramatic new changes are occurring.

Current changes are affecting much of the environment in which many modern organizations operate. New developments are taking place in many different areas, and while it is still too early to relate their overall impact on U.S. industry, it is possible to identify some of the changes that are occurring.

Before looking at them, one point requires emphasis: The future will *not* be a mere extension of the past. Dramatic changes are in sight. The management challenge for the upcoming decades will be one of anticipating what is likely to happen in the future and planning a proper response. For many businesses this is a new phenomenon because it strikes at the very heart of the traditional belief that things will remain about the same, a philosophy that has been fundamental to the thinking of many:

> Most people—to the extent that they bother to think about the future at all—assume the world they know will last indefinitely. They find it difficult to imagine a truly different way of life for themselves, let alone a totally new civilization. Of course they recognize that things are changing. But they assume today's changes will somehow pass them by

and that nothing will shake the familiar economic framework and political structure. They confidently expect the future to continue the past.[2]

But the future appears very unlikely to replicate the past. Recent evidence suggests that managers of the future will have to cope with a great many changes and challenges. Tom Peters, of *In Search of Excellence* fame, notes that the successful firm of the 1990s and beyond will have to be: (1) quality conscious; (2) service conscious; (3) more responsive to changes in the environment; (4) able to innovate rapidly; (5) oriented toward producing products that are differentiated from their competitors; (6) able to create market niches; (7) capable of producing high value-added goods; (8) characterized by an organization structure that has fewer levels in the hierarchy; (9) populated by autonomous units that have the authority to make decisions without having to clear everything with higher-level management; and (10) staffed by highly trained, flexible people.[3]

In meeting these challenges, there are nine areas with which managers will have to be concerned: the technological environment, information handling, the world of work, organizational loyalty, organizational structures, redefinition of organizational purposes, intrapreneurship, communications, and multinationalism.

Technological Environment

New sources of energy are being discovered.

Technology will continue to advance. The result will be both opportunities and challenges for business. The management of energy is an excellent example. During the next few decades there will be further development of both renewable and exhaustible sources of energy.

The result is going to be a large number of different energy sources, in contrast to the present small number. Besides the expansion of energy options, there will be less energy waste, since society will match the types and quality of energy being produced to its increasingly varied needs. The challenge for management will be one of determining how to most efficiently purchase and use this energy.

Genetic engineering is another example of technology that will affect business. Information on genetics is now doubling every two years, and major firms are currently using commercial applications of this "new biology." There is now talk of placing enzymes in automobiles; the enzymes would monitor exhausts and send data on pollution to microprocessors in the car, which would then adjust the engine. Other scientists are studying the possibility of using bacteria capable of converting sunlight into electrochemi-

---

[2]Ibid., p. 5.

[3]Tom Peters, "Facing Up to the Need for a Management Revolution," *California Management Review*, Winter 1988, pp. 30–33.

cal energy. Some scientists are also considering whether life forms can be bred to replace nuclear power plants.

A new agricultural revolution is occurring.

There is even a new agricultural revolution taking place. This bioagricultural movement is aimed at reducing the dependence on artificial fertilizer. The result will be high-yielding crops that will grow well in sandy or salty soil and also be able to fight off pests. It will be possible to create entirely new foods and fibers along with more effective energy conservation methods for sorting and processing foods. The result of all this should be the end of widespread famine anywhere on earth.

Of course, these are only speculative conclusions. However, scientists are convinced that technology is moving in these general directions. More importantly, technology is going to affect the way things are done in the workplace (see Technology in Action: Shaking Up the Industry).

TECHNOLOGY IN ACTION: Shaking Up the Industry

Until recently, American Express cardholders received a packet with their monthly bill. The packet contained individual paper receipts for each purchase made in the previous month. Now, thanks to modern technology, a radical new system of billing is being used. Today an image processing camera copies the receipts onto laser-printed sheets with as many as eight receipts per page. The results are lower billing and storage costs for the firm because there is no need to keep copies of individual receipts. American Express had reduced its billing expenses by 25 percent.

This development has given the firm a jump on the competition. However, American Express is not stopping there. The firm now plans to track individual purchases in order to identify each cardholder's business habits and lifestyle. Using this information, the company will then work with business to custom-tailor advertising to the cardholder's monthly billing package. For example, if 15,000 customers regularly go to London the company will team up with a London hotel and advertise the hotel's services. If 25,000 cardholders regularly use health facilities, American Express will try to sell them exercise equipment. The advertising options are endless once the computer is able to identify the particular goods and services that a customer regularly purchases with the American Express card.

The company is also installing a computer system based on artificial intelligence. This system will help handle routine charge card authorizations and provide detailed guidance to operators in handling more complex transactions. The firm hopes to extend its technological expertise to eventually include speech recognition, electronic mail services, and individual credit analysis. For American Express, technology is more than a way of lowering labor costs; it is becoming a means of creating new services and gaining a sustainable advantage over the competition.

Source: John Markoff, "American Express Goes High-Tech," *New York Times,* July 31, 1988, pp. 1, 6.

Information Handling

*Paperwork will di-
minish.*

The modern manager is a decision maker. As such, he or she requires up-to-date information from which to make choices. Computer technology provides managers with such information more efficiently than was possible in the recent past. File cabinets and massive paperwork have largely given way to computer storage facilities. Terminals link managerial offices, and memos are sent electronically. Meanwhile, any information the manager wants from the file is retrieved from data banks.

At the secretarial level, word processors have virtually made even the most advanced typewriters obsolete. Their TV-like screens allow the writer to revise, rearrange, underline, insert, and delete before the material is printed out. The use of word processors is widespread and increasing.

With these technological advances has come the inevitable fear of change. How will this new gadgetry affect people's jobs? There is a certain degree of calm and safety associated with being able to see and touch file copies of memos and papers. When information is stored in a data bank, however, many people feel that they are at the mercy of technology. It is the manager's job to deal with this conflict and resolve it to the satisfaction of both workers and the organization.

The World of Work

*White-collar employ-
ment will increase.*

One of the first questions asked by those who study emerging technology is what effect all of this will have on the work force. Will computers eventually replace 50 percent of the people in every major accounting department? Will "thinking" machines take over the entire assembly line in Detroit? How will technology affect employees? While no final answer is clear yet, recent research shows that mechanization and automation do not bring unemployment. For example, as the blue-collar segment of the American work force has shrunk, the white-collar segment has increased dramatically. Today over 50 percent of the labor force is accounted for by white-collar workers. These people work in three main types of occupations. The first consists of professional and technical occupations, such as engineers, medical technicians, personnel and labor relations specialists, nurses, and social workers. The second is made up of clerical occupations, such as bookkeepers, cashiers, secretaries, stenographers, office machine operators, and bank tellers. The third comprises service occupations, including waiters, waitresses, policemen, practical nurses, cooks, and beauticians. The membership of these white-collar occupations has risen while blue-collar jobs, such as craftsmen, operators, and laborers, as well as farm workers, have declined.

Furthermore, as the United States continues to advance technologically, occupational jobs will change. There will be more room for professional, technical, and managerial people, while laborers, operatives, craftsmen, and first-line supervisors will decline in number. This new work force composition will present a variety of new challenges to the modern manager.

Specifically, life in the workplace will change—but not necessarily for the worse. Recent findings show that many people are dissatisfied with their current jobs. At the lower levels of the hierarchy, many workers report that they will be changing their occupation in the next five years. However, as one goes up the hierarchy, this expectation diminishes. Only one in four professionals feel that they will change their occupation in the next five years. There will therefore be both changes and stability in the personnel ranks during the 1990s.

How else will the workplace change over the next few decades? One way, as has been noted, is through the introduction of still newer technology. New machinery and equipment will make the work easier to perform. Another trend will be toward a higher quality of work life. Many workers are demanding that they be allowed more control over their working schedules. With this *flextime* approach they will be able to come to work at, say, 11:00 A.M. and leave at 7:00 P.M. rather than working the typical 9 to 5 schedule of earlier years. This means that people will be able to mesh their biological rhythms with their work demands. Someone who is basically an "afternoon" person will be able to show up around noon and work into the evening. If the person is a "night" person, and the work does not require daytime attendance, it is possible for the worker to come in at 6:00 P.M. and work until 2:00 A.M. Of course, there may be times when the individual has to coordinate activities with the manager or other workers, in which case it will be necessary to work certain times or days of the week. For the most part, however, individual workers will have increased control over their work time schedules.[4]

The use of flextime will increase.

Additionally, time clocks will be eliminated in many cases, and people will not be confined to specific work locales. They will be allowed to move to other work locations during the day. This same type of freedom will extend to the way people dress and the pace at which they work. All of this may sound quite revolutionary and threatening to the authority of the manager. However, managers are already finding that the old days of bureaucratic control are starting to disappear. Employees are beginning to put up with less organizational control. They are demanding, and in most cases getting, more authority in their work lives.

Compensation packages will change.

This trend is also spreading to the area of employee compensation. In the past, most people were paid a fixed salary and a benefit package on top. In the future, workers will be given more control over what this compensation package looks like. Some employers, like TRW Inc., are now offering their employees a smorgasbord of such fringe benefits as medical benefits, pensions, optional holidays, and insurance. Individuals can tailor the package to their own personal needs. It is becoming evident that money alone does not motivate modern employees. They also want to feel important and

---

[4]For more on flextime see: Barney Olmsted, "(Flex)Time is Money," *Management Review*, November 1987, pp. 47–52; James E. Bailey, "Personnel Scheduling with Flexshift: A Win/Win Scenario," *Personnel*, September 1986, pp. 62–67; Jean B. McGuire and Joseph R. Liro, "Absenteeism and Flexible Work Schedules," *Public Personnel Management*, Spring 1987, pp. 47–59; and Donald J. Petersen, "Flexitime in the United States: The Lessons of Experience," *Personnel*, January–February 1980, pp. 21–31.

to like their jobs. The workplace is becoming "a better place in which to live." Based on his analysis of postwar work trends and future prospects, Kalleberg has concluded that:

> The challenge for the future is to match the organization's needs for efficient production of goods and services with the needs and values individuals seek to fulfill through their work activity. Successful matching of organizational and individual requirements presents many problems. Some of these problems are due to impersonal market and economic forces beyond the control of individual firms. Some of these poor fits, however, are produced by personnel and employment practices that are at odds with workers' needs and goals. These can be partly alleviated through the efforts of managers or individual companies. A greater attention to the problems and needs of labor is essential for creating the kind of world in which human fulfillment and material production are both realized.[5]

Organizational Loyalty

Loyalty will decline.

Another development of the 1990s is a continuing decline in organizational loyalty. Companies find that their employees are well motivated and eager to pursue organizational objectives only if there is some personal payoff. Work which offers challenge, increased responsibility, and a feeling of accomplishment is vigorously pursued because these things attach a personal reward to the job. Rote, monotonous, boring tasks are accepted only by those who badly need work or for whom the pay is better than what they could earn elsewhere. However, since no strong motivators are attached, those individuals who must do this kind of work will be likely to continue to see their work as "just a job."

Innovative redesign of the work will take place. People will once again become masters of the job rather than slaves to it. The workplace will evolve into an extension of the individual's social life. Thus, loyalty and camaraderie among employees will increase while organizational loyalty will decline. Interpersonal relations and commitment to objectives will replace blind organizational affiliation. The company as an economic entity will not become a socioeconomic institution. People will like and respect their organizations, but they will not fear them.[6]

Organizational Structures

Bureaucratic designs will continue to give way to more adaptive structures. The classical industrial bureaucracy, with its hierarchical, mechanistic designs, was well constructed for repetitive jobs and decision making in a stable

---

[5]Arne L. Kalleberg, "Work: Postwar Trends and Future Prospects," *Business Horizons*, July–August 1982, p. 84.

[6]For more on this topic see William B. Werther, Jr., "Loyalty at Work," *Business Horizons*, March–April 1988, pp. 28–35.

environment. Today, however, these designs are being complemented by less top-heavy structures that are flatter and more flexible.

Adaptive structures will increase in use.

Many of these adaptive designs allow for the free flow of ideas up and down the line. A more democratic, participative approach is employed. Bureaucracy is giving way to *adhocracy*, or temporary structures. Rather than construct hierarchical arrangements that will last indefinitely, some firms now put departments, groups, or teams of employees together for the sole purpose of attaining one specific objective. Once this is done, the unit is disbanded and allowed to flow into other departments, groups, or teams which come together to pursue still other objectives.

Many of these adaptive structures make use of the matrix organization, in which employees often have two or more bosses. While representing a sharp break with earlier management practices, the matrix structure is being found a highly effective design for handling certain types of projects.

Redefinition of Organizational Purposes

Many major corporations today are undergoing a kind of identity crisis. Top management is being forced to examine the organization's basic purposes. In particular, business firms are beginning to realize that there are many groups to which they have obligations.

Social responsiveness will increase.

The result is that the modern corporation is no longer just a profit-making or goods and services producing institution. It is responsible for dealing with ecological, moral, political, and social problems as well. The corporation, responding both to external and internal pressure, is becoming a multipurpose institution. Examples are abundant. Amoco, the oil giant, in choosing a plant location, now supplements its economic evaluation with a detailed look at the impact of the plant on the physical environment, local employment conditions, and public facilities. Where alternative locations are similar in economic terms but different in social impact, the latter affects the final choice. Control Data has a similar approach. In fact, this firm has built its new plants in the inner-city areas of Minneapolis, St. Paul, and Washington, D.C., in order to help revive urban centers and provide employment to minorities. The corporation states its basic mission as improving the quality, equality, and potential of people's lives.

Other companies are rewarding their managers for meeting affirmative action targets, such as hiring the hardcore unemployed, minorities, and women. At Pillsbury, the giant food corporation, each of its three product groups now has to present not only the customary annual sales plan but a plan for hiring, training, and promoting women and minority group members. Social goals are as important as economic ones. AT&T also evaluates its employees on the attainment of social goals, and at the Chemical Bank in New York, 10 to 15 percent of a branch manager's performance appraisal is tied to such areas as hiring and upgrading minorities, making loans to not-for-profit companies, and participating on community agency boards.

In the future we are likely to see more attention paid to the area of social objectives. This will be reflected in company efforts to meet them and in

INTERVIEW WITH CHRIS GILSON

Chris Gilson is a partner and the creative director at Beber Silverstein, a nationally known, Miami-based advertising agency. His creative talents have been instrumental in helping his agency gain accounts with Avis, Citicorp, Ford Motor, Scandinavian Airlines, and *Rolling Stone* magazine, to name but five. Chris is also a highly creative author and a consultant to companies seeking to increase the creative abilities of their personnel.

Q.   *What is going to be one of the major challenges facing management during the 1990s and how will the challenge have to be met?*

A.   The major challenge I see that is that managers are going to have to be more creative in their approach to dealing with both problems and people. This isn't going to be easy. In many cases managers have been penalized for being creative or taking chances. As a result, many of them tend to be risk-aversive and have become accustomed to operating in an environment of compromise and consensus. Quite often they find that it's more important to make zero errors than to be associated with a high-risk venture that doesn't pay out. Who wants to take a chance on a creative solution when a more mundane one will be just as acceptable and far less risky? Managerial creativity is often a function of the environment and those corporate cultures that discourage creativity will ultimately drive out those individuals who are creative. It's as simple as that.

Q.   *How can organizations encourage their employees to become more creative?*

A.   I can tell you in one word: rewards. People will do things for which they are given money, praise, or whatever other forms of rewards they feel are motiva-

---

reports of the results to stockholders and the general public[7] (see Ethics in Action: Business Responds).

Intrapreneurship

Intrapreneurship is entrepreneurial activity that occurs *inside* an enterprise. Today more and more firms are coming to realize that they must capture this entrepeneurial spirit within their organizations if they hope to be competi-

---

[7]LaRue Tone Hosmer, "Adding Ethics to the Business Curriculum," *Business Horizons*, July–August 1988, pp. 9–15; and Archie B. Carroll, "In Search of the Moral Manager," *Business Horizons*, March–April 1987, pp. 7–15.

tional. Additionally, management has to start structuring creativity as carefully as it structures other management tasks. For example, I've found that it's productive to provide a creative time when managers can get together and brainstorm without the inhibiting factors of criticism and second-guessing. A creative task can be structured as follows: First, make some wishes—a very blue sky, for example. Second, define some of the wishes more carefully into objectives. What can you do to meet these objectives in a perfect world? Third, allow each person 15 minutes for purely free associative brainstorming with no one being allowed to say "that won't work because . . ." Fourth, wrap things up by realistically scaling down these ideas and pruning out those that are attainable. The problem for many firms is that they do not encourage creativity because they are continuing narrowing their field of focus to those things they believe will work. You can't reach the stars unless you can dream. Those who operate only within their current reach can never hope to extend their grasp.

Q. *Does creativity really pay off in terms of the bottom line?*

A. Creativity really does pay off in bottom-line results. Let me give you just a few brief examples. First, consider the case of Fred Smith, founder of People's Express. He had this seemingly inane notion that an overnight parcel from Los Angeles to San Francisco would go faster if routed through Memphis. And he believed that people would pay for this service. Most of the people to whom he tried to sell this idea scoffed at him. Or consider Post-it® notes, made famous by the 3M Company. This product is now one of its most profitable lines, and it was developed thanks to the creativity and ingenuity of its scientific and marketing staff. At 3M those guys think creatively 24 hours a day. But creativity is not limited to big firms. Look at the local home mortgage markets around the country. Who is gaining this market share? Those with strong market-driven strategies that are willing to put together creative packages that help people buy and refinance their homes. The markets of the 1990s will belong to those who have the ability and daring to be creative!

Intrapreneurship is entrepreneurial activity within the organization.

tively innovative, creative, and adaptive. One of the most common intrapreneurial approaches is to encourage and reward individual and group activity in the development of new goods and services. Some companies do this informally, others make it part of the formal process. General Electric employs the latter approach.

The company selects young, high-technology people with only a few years' work experience, and often no formal management education, and literally sets them up in their own businesses. Basically, General Electric gives these new entrepreneurs a product line and a time period, and then asks them to make the company grow. They must compete against each other for allocation of funds and resources, and they must

Business ethics has recently become a major area of concern for many organizations. One reason is because so many companies have been charged with unethical practices. For example, Rockwell International was fined a record $5.5 million for defrauding the Air Force. TRW agreed to pay back the government for overcharges on military work. Hertz, the auto rental firm, overcharged users and insurers $13 million for repairs to damaged rental cars before making restitution. Ocean Spray Cranberries was indicted by a federal grand jury for pollution.

How can business clean up its act? There are a number of steps being taken. Chemical Bank runs many of its senior people through a two-day seminar on company values. The managers analyze cases dealing with issues such as loan approvals, branch closings, and staff reductions. They also learn the company's code of ethics and violations of the code often result in dismissal.

Xerox publishes handbooks and policy statements emphasizing integrity and provides its employees with orientation on values and policies. Anyone who commits a major violation of ethical practices is fired; those committing minor infractions such as petty cheating on expense accounts can also expect to be dismissed.

At Boeing, there is an ethics committee that reports directly to the board of directors. The firm also provides training to its line managers, and if anyone in the company wants to report a violation, there is a toll free number.

General Mills has developed detailed guidelines for its people to use in dealing with vendors, competitors, and customers. It also encourages employees to become active in social affairs. As one executive put it, "It's hard to imagine that a person who reads to the blind at night would cheat on his expense account."

Despite these types of efforts, unethical practices still occur. Battles may be continually won, but the war goes on. As one ethics expert noted, "You have to keep renewing the effort." Many firms are doing just this.

Source: John A. Byrne, "Businesses Are Signing Up for Ethics 101," *Business Week,* February 15, 1988, pp. 56–57.

learn to assess markets and prioritize and deploy resources. This process is enhanced through the active support of the supervisors who regularly meet with their intrapreneurs. Finally, at the end of the time period, these venture managers are assessed by how well they have attained their objectives and how much money they have made. Compensation is related to this contribution.[8]

Not all intrapreneurial activity is venture-oriented. In many cases managers are allowed to run their units or divisions as if they were independent businesses. The autonomy and authority to make important decisions

[8]Donald D. Kuratko and Richard M. Hodgetts, *Entrepreneurship: A Contemporary Approach* (Hinsdale, IL: Dryden Press, 1989), p. 553.

TABLE 1-1
Satisfaction with MBA Communication Skills

	Percentage Satisfied with	
	Oral Communication Skills	Written Communication Skills
Fortune "500" presidents	48%	47%
Fortune "500" personnel directors	56	40
1978 MBA alumni from a variety of nationally accredited schools	44	37
Faculty from nationally accredited business schools	29	20
Deans of nationally accredited business schools	25	9

Source: Roger L. Jenkins, Richard C. Reizenstein, and F. G. Rogers, "Report Cards on the MBA," *Harvard Business Review*, September–October 1984, p. 26.

without having to clear them with senior-level management often results in faster, more accurate, and more profitable decisions. This is one of the major reasons why intrapreneuring is going to be a major trend of the 1990s.[9]

Communications

Effective managers speak and write well.

Effective managers are good communicators. They speak well and they write well. During the decade of the 1990s, greater attention is going to focus on this topic because organizations are finding that many new hires, including college graduates, do not have the requisite communication skills. Table 1-1 shows the satisfaction reported by business and faculty of individuals with masters degrees in business (MBAs). If these individuals do not communicate well, one can imagine the state of affairs among those with even less formal education.

Oral communication is becoming more important because so much business is done over the phone and face to face. Additionally, managers increasingly are required to speak to groups ranging from small organizational units to large company gatherings. The ability to communicate verbally is critical to management success especially at the upper levels of the hierarchy.

Written communication is important because of the number of memos, letters, and reports that must be prepared by managers. Additionally, as computer systems are integrated and electronic mail becomes more prevalent, the importance of written communications will increase. New software developments designed to provide spelling and grammar assistance will prove helpful, but they will not replace the need to develop effective writing skills. The successful manager of the 1990s will have to be an effective communicator.

[9]For more on this topic see W. Jack Duncan, Peter M. Gintger, Andrew C. Rucks, and T. Douglas Jacobs, "Intrepreneurship and the Reinvention of the Corporation," *Business Horizons*, May–June 1988, pp. 16–21; and Kenneth Labick, "The Innovators," *Fortune*, June 6, 1988, pp. 50–64.

Multinationalism

Multinational management will be important.

Multinational corporations emerged in the post-World War II era, and today they are responsible for much of the trade that occurs between nations. A few examples of U.S. multinationals are IBM, GM, IT&T, Ford Motor, and Exxon. One noted writer remarked that, in contrast to a hundred years ago, the sun today does set on the British Empire—but it does not set on the scores of global corporate empires of the multinational corporations. Yet their impact on international trade cannot be measured solely in terms of geographic dispersion. Their economic size is astounding. The largest have annual sales revenues that are larger than the gross national product of all but about ten nations of the world! Their assets are also vast.

The challenge of managing these giant corporations is as great as any that faces a chief executive of a country. Customs, language, culture, and values vary by nations. Managers in the United States may be making decisions that affect the firm's holdings in Brazil. Decisions by the branch manager in Amsterdam may affect the sales of the company's subsidiary in Belgium. In short, the multinational corporation is an interdependent, interactive body which transcends national boundaries. While the job of the overseas manager may appear to be the same as that of a colleague stationed stateside, the overseas job is more demanding because of the effects decisions can have on other overseas affiliates and branches. Additionally, there is the need to interact and fit in with the host country. For years IBM has done this in France by being one of the nation's largest exporters. Regardless of method, the multinational corporation must find ways to work within the framework of the country where it is doing business while also being responsive to the directives of the home office.

DEALING WITH MANAGEMENT CHALLENGES

The 1990s will present new challenges to management. These can be grouped into ten categories:

The challenges.

1. Forecasting and planning for the future.
2. Designing effective organization structures.
3. Controlling operations.
4. Making effective decisions.
5. Communicating, motivating, and leading personnel.
6. Designing human resource programs for developing people's abilities and talents and encouraging intrapreneurship.
7. Understanding the role and impact of technology on the organization.
8. Being aware of and prepared to respond to social and ethical challenges.
9. Having basic understanding of management in the international arena.
10. Having basic knowledge of where the field of management is going and the new challenges that will complement or replace those noted here.

This book specifically addresses these ten challenges:

Challenge	Chapters
Planning	4
Organizing	5, 6
Controlling	7
Decision making	8, 9, 10
Communicating, motivating, and leading	12, 13, 14
Designing human resource programs	15
Understanding the role and impact of technology	11, 16
Social challenges	17
International management	18
Future of management	19

Of course, this study of management will do more than merely present the topics that constitute modern challenges. A comprehensive framework brings all these topics together in a unified composite in which the reader will see the relationships among the various functions the manager performs. And many topics not yet mentioned will be addressed by way of providing a comprehensive, up-to-date introduction to the field of modern management. While addressing the challenges of the third wave, this text also provides a great deal of additional practical management information.

AN INVITATION TO MANAGEMENT

Although they require a well-thought-out approach, the managerial challenges of the 1990s are not beyond solution. This book will provide such an approach by means of a systematic analysis of the field.

From the Past

The past provides foundation.

The foundations of modern management are to a large degree found in the past. The work of early civilizations and the experiences of managers in the Industrial Revolution were important in forming the basic foundations of modern management theory and practice.

During the past century, contributions from individuals in the areas of factory management, administrative levels of the hierarchy, and behavioral sciences all helped mold modern management, and these contributions will be examined in Chapter 2.

To the Present

Management theory has three major lines of approach.

Management theory today has three major themes, or lines of approach, which need to be studied if one is to fully understand the field of management. These will be investigated in Chapters 3 through 16 of this book, in which modern management theory is thoroughly explored. Such key areas as planning, organizing, controlling, decision making, quantitative methods, communication, motivation, leadership, and human resources development will all be studied. Attention will also be given to current management theory and where it appears to be heading.

To the Future

The future holds new challenges.

Finally, this text will direct attention to changes that will confront management throughout the remainder of this century. Particular focus will be placed on technology, the management of personnel and talent, social responsibility, international management, and corporate democracy. Consideration will also be given to the topic of careers in management. While some of this material will be covered in Chapters 5 through 16, most will be addressed in Chapters 17 through 19.

Readers who have finished this book will know where management has been, where it is today, and where it will be going. More importantly, they will have a basic understanding of the challenges that will be confronting the manager during this decade and will also know some of the tools, techniques, and approaches for dealing with these challenges.

In order to understand the present and predict the future, it is often best to begin with a review of the past. As the great historian Will Durant has noted, "The present is the past rolled up for action, and the past is the present unrolled for understanding."[10] To fully comprehend management theory, process, and practice, it is necessary to know how modern management thought evolved. The managerial challenges of tomorrow will be too important to be handled by expedient decisions. Sound fundamental concepts will have to serve as the basis for effective decision making. Accordingly, no student of modern management will be able to ignore the past. Nor should one wish to, for there is a wealth of basic information that can serve as knowledge that propels one forward to meet the challenges of tomorrow.

■ SUMMARY

Management is the process of getting things done through other people. Some individuals carry the title of manager but are not managers in the true sense of the word. They may have people reporting to them, but they tend to work alone, seeming to manage their subordinates as an afterthought. Such individuals are basically entrepreneurs, and it is likely that they will find themselves unable to cope with the dynamic changes now confronting modern organizations.

---

[10]Will Durant, *The Reformation* (New York: Simon and Schuster, 1957), p. viii.

Industrialism began in the early eighteenth century. This period was characterized by standardization, specialization, synchronization, concentration, maximization, and centralization.

Today there are even more dramatic changes and challenges. Some of the major factors which affect the modern manager's job are changes in the technological environment, new methods of information handling, new employee demands in the world of work, a decline in organizational loyalty, the evolution of adaptive organizational structures, a redefinition of organizational purpose, communications, intrapreneurship, and multinationalism. The impact of these events on the modern manager will be studied throughout this book, with attention directed toward explaining how these changes can be handled. A past-present-future framework will be used.

■ REVIEW AND STUDY QUESTIONS

1. In your own words, tell what is meant by the term *management*. Compare and contrast managers and nonmanagers. How do their roles differ?

2. What are the six characteristics of industrialism? Identify and explain each of them.

3. In your own words, explain what is meant by the following statement: "Most people, to the extent that they bother to think about the future at all, assume the world they know will last indefinitely."

4. During the next decade, what kinds of changes can be expected in the technological environment? In information handling? How will these changes affect employment? What will be their impact on the world of work?

5. What is meant by the term *flextime?* How likely is it that this concept will increase in use during the current decade? Defend your answer.

6. What is happening to organizational loyalty? Is it increasing or decreasing?

7. What changes are likely to take place in many bureaucratic designs?

8. How are businesses likely to redefine their organizational purposes? What role will ethics and social responsibility play in this definition? Explain.

9. Are college graduates good communicators? Should they be? What relevance do your answers have for effective management?

10. What is *intrapreneurship?* Why is it of value to management? Explain.

11. How important is an understanding of the multinational corporation to the study of basic management? Why should these organizations be included in one's examination of the field? Support your answer.

■ SELECTED REFERENCES

Albert, Michael, and Murray Silverman. "Making Management Philosophy a Cultural Reality, Part 1: Get Started." *Personnel,* January–February 1984, pp. 12–21.

Byrne, John A. "Businesses Are Signing Up for Ethics 101." *Business Week,* February 15, 1988, pp. 56–57.

Drucker, Peter F. *The Concept of the Corporation.* New York: New American Library, Mentor, 1964.

Duncan, W. Jack, Peter M. Gintger, Andrew C. Rucks, and T. Douglas Jacobs. "Intrepreneurship and the Reinvention of the Corporation." *Business Horizons,* May–June 1988, pp. 16–21.

Grant, Philip C. "Why Employee Motivation Has Declined in America." *Personnel Journal,* December 1982, pp. 905–909.

Harris, Philip R., and Dorothy L. Harris. "Twelve Trends You and Your CEO Should Be Monitoring." *Training and Development Journal,* October 1983, pp. 62–69.

Hosmer, LaRue Tone. "Adding Ethics to the Business Curriculum." *Business Horizons,* July–August 1988, pp. 9–15.

Kalleberg, Arne L. "Work: Postwar Trends and Future Prospects." *Business Horizons,* July–August 1982, pp. 79–84.

Koprowski, Eugene J. "Exploring the Meaning of 'Good' Management." *Academy of Management Review,* July 1981, pp. 459–67.

Kuratko, Donald D., and Richard M. Hodgetts. *Entrepreneurship: A Contemporary Approach.* Hinsdale, IL: Dryden Press, 1989.

Luthans, Fred, Richard M. Hodgetts, and Kenneth A. Thompson. *Social Issues in Business,* 5th ed. New York: Macmillan, 1987.

Macmillan, Ian C., and Patricia E. Jones. "Designing Organizations to Compete." *Journal of Business Strategy,* Spring 1984, pp. 11–26.

Olmsted, Barney. "(Flex)Time is Money." *Management Review,* November 1987, pp. 47–52.

Peters, Tom. "Facing Up to the Need for a Management Revolution." *California Management Review,* Winter 1988, pp. 30–33.

Sloan, A. P., Jr. *My Years with General Motors.* New York: MacFadden-Bartell, 1965.

Smith, Adam. *The Wealth of Nations.* 1776. New York: Random House, Modern Library, 1937.

Toffler, Alvin. *The Third Wave.* New York: William Morrow, 1980.

Veiga, John F. "Do Managers on the Move Get Anywhere?" *Harvard Business Review,* March–April 1981, pp. 20–27.

Watson, Craig M. "Leadership, Management, and the Seven Keys." *Business Horizons,* March–April 1983, pp. 8–13.

Werther, William B. "Loyalty at Work." *Business Horizons,* March–April 1988, pp. 28–35.

■ CASE: We Told You So

A large eastern insurance company recently brought in one of the nation's major computer firms to see if something could be done about the mass of paperwork confronting lower-level insurance personnel. After analyzing the needs of the company, the consulting firm recommended the purchase of a giant computer. The proposal was based on a cost-saving estimate of $3 million spread over the expected ten-year life of the machine.

After a series of top-level conferences, the insurance management decided to make the purchase. Managers then passed this information on to lower-level managers, who, with the help of their own people and some systems department staff, started revising job assignments. Most of the routine paper-processing tasks were to be reassigned to the computer. The rest of the work was to be handled by the regular clerical personnel. The problem, however, was that under this plan over 60 percent of the work was to be allocated to the computer. Not surprisingly, the staff was concerned about its continued employment.

Management tried to allay these fears by categorically stating that all efforts would be made to find work in other departments for any displaced employees. In making good on this promise, within the first month the firm transferred 30 percent of its personnel to other units. However, this move simply increased anxiety among the remaining workers. As one of them said, "You mark my words. There just aren't enough jobs in the company to absorb everyone. So it's just a matter of time before the company announces that it will be laying some of us off."

The statement seemed to reflect the sentiments of other employees because at just about this time, management noticed a decline in cooperation from these people. Both the managers and the systems engineers who were revising the work schedules found many of the workers unwilling to answer questions about their work assignments. Those who would answer provided only minimal information. One manager described the workers as "downright hostile." Another said, "They think they're going to be fired, so they're doing everything they can to screw us up." The result of this series of events was that it took three weeks longer than anticipated to get everything straightened out and transferred to the computer. Meanwhile, what about the clerical personnel? As it turned out, none of them was laid off. Work was found for all.

Questions

1. How common is it today to find technology having an effect on workers' jobs?

2. How much of a problem did the introduction of the computer present to the management team in this company?

3. If you had been in charge, how would you have tried to alleviate the fears of the employees who thought they would be replaced by the computer? Explain thoroughly.

■ CASE: Jack Dangrath's Evaluation

Jack Dangrath is the newly appointed head manager of an industrial complex located in the Northeast. He took over as head of operations two weeks ago, and his task is clear: Management wants more output and greater efficiency. The Northeast complex has been one of the organization's least efficient. It lost money for the five years preceding Dangrath's appointment.

Since arriving and analyzing the situation, Dangrath has learned a number of things about operations. Some of them follow:

1. The factory work force is inefficient because, among other things, it needs new equipment. The competition has better, more efficient machinery as a result of some key technological breakthroughs by machine manufacturers.
2. Some of the assembly jobs could be done more efficiently if each person assembled more parts—in other words, with less specialization of labor.
3. A recent in-house survey shows that most of the employees would like to try a flextime working hours schedule.
4. A new computer has been installed in the accounting department, and there is a lot of talk about this department starting to lay people off.
5. Most department and unit managers, feeling that there is too much specialization, want more decision-making authority delegated to them.

Questions

1. Which of the characteristics of industrialism appear to be present in Jack Dangrath's new organization? Explain.
2. What new challenges are now appearing in the organization? Describe them.
3. What would you recommend that Dangrath do in regard to each of the five listed developments? Make your answer as complete as possible.

■ CASE: Same Old Stuff

As part of honors convocation week, Bill Whitling, vice-president of a large bank, had been asked to talk to a group of graduating seniors in the college of business at State University. He was delighted to do so, as he wanted an opportunity to speak about the dynamic environment in which his firm operated. Whitling felt that the challenges facing his bank's managers typified those that new managers would soon meet. At one point in his talk, he said:

> Today, our management people are being confronted with new problems, and we have to come up with brand new solutions. Managers in our company certainly find that a business education is helpful. But there's a tremendous adjustment that has to be made in moving from the halls of academia to those of industry. Quite frankly, we've never before faced a similar situation; the challenges and problems are brand new.

During the question and answer session that followed, one student asked Whitling, "Aren't modern managers confronting the same basic problems that their counterparts in antiquity had to face? The way I see it, whether we're building the Great Pyramid or Chicago's Sears Tower, the management problems are virtually the same. Oh sure, the problems or issues may be more complex, but our forebears in the Roman Empire or other early civilizations probably wrestled with similar problems. After all, there's nothing new under the sun. Is there?"

Questions

1. Are modern managers facing totally new problems or the same old problems as always? Explain.
2. What problems do today's universities create for managers? Have these problems changed with time? Explain.
3. How can the study of management help modern managers do their jobs more effectively? Explain.

■ CASE: Giving It a Management Flavor

Years ago Peace Corps volunteers used to be liberal arts majors or retired people who wanted to contribute their time toward helping people in other countries. Quite often they would be assigned to teach English or set up a library or advise farmers on conservation techniques. However, today all of this has changed. The Peace Corps of the 1990s has more profit-oriented goals and is recruiting business-oriented people. The salary is still not very much ($200 a month plus room and board), but many of the challenges lend themselves to business solutions.

One of the primary goals is to promote economic development, and there are plenty of people who want to help. In fact, there are five applications for every position and many recruits come from nontraditional quarters including executives who are looking for midcareer adventure, financially secure retirees who are enlisting in the war on hunger, and yuppie dropouts.

During the 1970s and 1980s the Peace Corps had trouble getting funding from Congress. The conservatives wanted to see more economically measurable results from the agency; the liberals wanted to see greater attention to dealing with poverty and hunger. During the mid-1980s the Corps' focus changed and began to combine both of these concerns. As a result funding between 1986–88 increased by 20 percent to $146 million. One of the main reasons is because the Corps is now focusing, among other things, on microenterprises. These tiny businesses are designed to be run on a shoestring, and many of them make money. In the Dominican Republic, for example, $1.2 million in loans has resulted in 4,674 microenterprises that have created 6,000 jobs. Moreover, less than 2 percent of the loans are nonperforming.

The Peace Corps is also trying to get American businesses to give people paid leaves of absence so they can work overseas for a year or two. However, even if it is not successful in this endeavor, the number and type of individuals who are now applying for positions with the Peace Corps is ensuring that the agency will continue to be a more effective organization than it has been in the past. Thanks to the influx of management talent, the Corps is showing that it can provide assistance in both the public and the private sector.

Questions

1. How has the Peace Corps redefined its basic purpose?

2. Why is the organization able to attract so many talented people? Explain.

3. How important is management to overall success of the Peace Corps? Be complete in your answer.

Source: Pete Engardio and Steve Askin, "The Peace Corps' New Frontier," *Business Week,* August 22, 1988, pp. 62–63.

■ SELF-FEEDBACK EXERCISE: **What Do You *Really* Know about Management?**

Why is it useful to study management formally? One reason is because "getting things done through people" involves a great deal more than just common sense and good intentions. A lot of what people "know" about how to manage others is not correct. The following 15 statements are either true or false. Circle the T or F for each and then check your answers with the key provided at the end.

T   F   1.   The management of large corporations is becoming so efficient that it is driving small businesses out of the economy.

T F   2. Most people report that such things as a feeling of accomplishment or pride in a job well done are more motivational to them than is money.

T F   3. When communicating with another person, the major challenge is to get the individual's attention.

T F   4. Women have a stronger work ethic than men.

T F   5. The work ethic in America is dying.

T F   6. Assembly-line workers hate the monotony of the line and would prefer to assemble cars the way they do in Sweden by using teams of workers collectively to put together the auto.

T F   7. On average, most managers are more work-centered and less people-centered than they should be.

T F   8. Managers in industry report that business school graduates are well trained in quantitative methods, but the individuals have poor verbal and written skills.

T F   9. Effective organizations seek to eliminate all traces of bureaucracy.

T F 10. Most of what we know about effective management is a result of research conducted since 1970.

T F 11. In well-run firms, the organization first formulates its strategy and then designs its structure rather than vice versa.

T F 12. In high-tech industries organization structures are much more flexible than they are in low-tech industries.

T F 13. Successful enterprises are more interested in being efficient than in being effective.

T F 14. The quality of many American products is much higher today than it was five years ago thanks to improved management and operations techniques.

T F 15. Most firms strive to promote creativity among their employees.

Answers

1. False. The number of small businesses is on the rise, while large enterprises are currently cutting back personnel.

2. True.

3. False. The major challenge is achieving understanding of the message.

4. True.

5. False. It is alive and well.

6. False. They feel the Swedish approach would require them to work too hard.

7. True.

8. True.

9.   False. They still use some basic principles of bureaucracy, but they minimize the red tape.

10.   False. A great deal about management was known prior to 1970.

11.   True.

12.   True.

13.   False. It is just the opposite.

14.   True.

15.   False. Most firms actually discourage creativity.

How many did you get right? If it was less than 15, do not be upset. After you have finished reading this book, you will know all of the answers—and more.

CHAPTER 2

The Evolution of Management Thought

GOALS OF THE CHAPTER

Management is not a new concept; it has been practiced for thousands of years. The primary goal of this chapter is to examine the evolution of management thought. The first part of the chapter illustrates some effective management practices from early organizations. Then the focus changes to more recent times and to the emergence of the factory system, the scientific management movement, early management theory, and behavioral beginnings. Finally, the chapter focuses on modern management thought in a comprehensive historical perspective. When you are finished reading this chapter, you should be able to:

1. Discuss the contributions to management of the Sumerians, the Romans, and the Roman Catholic Church.

2. Relate the importance of the Industrial Revolution in the development of management thought.

3. Identify the contributions of Frederick Taylor, Frank Gilbreth, Lillian Moller Gilbreth, Henri Fayol, Elton Mayo, and Chester Barnard to the development of modern management thought.

4. Discuss the value of the Hawthorne studies to the behavioral approach to management.

5.   Compare and contrast the contributions and shortcomings of the scientific managers, the administrative management theorists, and the behaviorists in modern management thought.

MANAGEMENT IN ANTIQUITY

A managerial control process was developed.

One of the earliest civilizations known is that of the Sumerians, whose culture is famous for the development of a written language. From 3000 B.C. onward, priests in the Sumerian city of Ur (the site of which is now in Iraq) kept business, legal, and historical records on clay tablets. Some of these tablets relate the management practices of Sumerian priests, the most influential class in the civilization. The priests were of such importance, in fact, that it appears highly likely that the Sumerians developed a written language in response to their need for a *managerial control process*.[1]

Empire structure was reorganized.

The ancient Romans also provided numerous illustrations of effective management. Perhaps the most famous is the emperor Diocletian's reorganization of his empire. Assuming his position in A.D. 284, Diocletian soon realized that the empire had acquired an unmanageable form. There were far too many people and matters of importance for the emperor to handle individually. Abandoning the old structure, in which all provincial governors reported directly to him, Diocletian established more levels in the hierarchy. The governors were pushed farther down the structure and, with the help of other administrators, the emperor was able to more effectively manage this vast empire.

Administrative principles were developed.

The Roman Catholic Church also made important contributions to early management thought. One was the Church's wide use of job descriptions for its priests, bishops, presbyters, and other religious workers. Everyone's duties were clear, and a chain of command that extended from the pope to the laity was created. A second Roman Catholic contribution to management was that of *compulsory staff service*, the requirement that certain members of the church hierarchy seek the advice of other hierarchs before making particular kinds of decisions. A third was the use of *staff independence*, the assignment of certain advisors to key church officials. Since these advisors were not removable by the official they could give the advice they considered best, without fear of reprisals from superiors.[2]

THE INDUSTRIAL REVOLUTION

Although early civilizations and the Church provide illustrations of effective management practices, the technological innovations of the Industrial Revolution had a more dynamic impact on managerial thinking than anything

---

[1]Will Durant, *The Story of Civilization, Part 1, Our Oriental Heritage* (New York: Simon and Schuster, 1954), p. 131.

[2]James D. Mooney and Alan C. Reiley, *Onward Industry!* (New York: Harper & Bros., 1931), p. 246.

that had occurred previously. This is clearly seen in the history of Great Britain between the years 1700 and 1785, when major changes occurred in the basic organization of production.

First in the century came the *domestic system*, in which people produced goods in their own homes. These were then taken to the local fair and sold. Soon, however, entrepreneurs entered the picture and offered to provide families with necessary production materials and pay them a fixed amount for each unit of output they provided. This was known as the *putting-out system*, and it was characterized by the entrepreneur's putting out the raw materials and then paying for the finished goods. Finally came the *factory system*, characterized by the placing of power-driven machinery under one roof. When significant numbers of people came to a central locale to work, the putting-out system was dead.

The factory system eventually emerged.

Management in the factory system was first characterized by strict control of operations. The owners of the enterprises were most concerned with making the greatest possible profit from their investment. A great deal of interest was therefore focused on streamlining operations, eliminating waste, and motivating workers to increase their output. (The motivation came in the form of money.) These developments led to the emergence of the scientific management movement.

THE SCIENTIFIC MANAGEMENT MOVEMENT

The factory system caused management to focus on developing the most scientific, rational principles for handling its people, machines, materials, and money. This challenge took two major forms: (1) how to increase *productivity* (output/input) by making work easier to perform, and (2) how to motivate workers to take advantage of new methods and techniques. The individuals who developed approaches for meeting these challenges helped lay the foundation for what is known as *scientific management*.

Frederick W. Taylor

The need to increase productivity followed the Industrial Revolution from Europe to the United States. The individuals who made scientific management a household word in the United States were, for the most part, trained mechanical engineers. Their major emphasis was on the management of *work*, and to a large degree they saw the worker as merely an adjunct of the machines. The most famous scientific manager in America was Frederick Winslow Taylor.

Bethlehem Steel Experiments

In 1898 Frederick Taylor went to work for the Bethlehem Steel Company. While there, he conducted several important studies, the most significant in the area of pig-iron handling.

Frederick W. Taylor
(1856–1915)

Frederick W. Taylor, often referred to as the Father of Scientific Management, is the best known of all the scientific managers. Born in Germantown, Pennsylvania, in 1856, he spent many of his early years attending school in Germany and France and traveling on the European continent. In 1872 he enrolled in Phillips Exeter Academy to prepare for Harvard College. Although he passed the Harvard entrance exams with honors, poor eyesight prevented him from attending the college. In late 1874 Taylor entered the pattern making and machinist trades, in a small company owned by family friends. In 1878, employment in the machinist trade was difficult to obtain, so Taylor went to work as a laborer at the Midvale Steel Company. Within eight years he rose from ordinary laborer to chief engineer of the works. Meanwhile, continuing his education through correspondence courses and home study, he managed to complete all requirements for a mechanical engineering degree at Stevens Institute.[3]

This experiment involved a group of about seventy-five men who loaded ingots (called pigs) of iron into open railroad cars. When Taylor arrived at Bethlehem Steel, each laborer was loading an average of 12.5 long tons a day. (A long ton is 2,240 pounds.) Taylor decided to experiment with the job to see whether he could increase the output. His research showed that a worker ought to be able to load 47 long tons a day, working 42 percent of the time and "free of load" for the other 58 percent. In order to test the validity of this theory, Taylor chose one of the workers, to whom he gave the pseudonym Schmidt, and began supervising the man very closely. By early evening of the first day, Schmidt had loaded 47.5 long tons. Other men in the group were then gradually trained to load this amount.

The experiment in pig-iron handling was only one such experiment by Taylor at Bethlehem Steel. Another dealt with the shoveling of iron ore and rice coal. After determining that an average scoop load of 21 pounds would result in maximum output, Taylor did away with the practice of workers bringing their own shovels. Instead, the company provided shovels, all designed to carry a 21-pound load. As a result of this experiment, the firm was able to reduce the number of yard laborers from 600 to 140, increase each laborer's average number of tons per day from 16 to 59, and cut the average cost of handling a ton of coal from 7.2 to 3.3 cents. At the same time, the average earnings per man per day rose from $1.15 to $1.88.

Work tools were provided.

Taylor's Writings and Philosophy
In 1885 Taylor joined the American Society of Mechanical Engineers (ASME). He eventually presented two papers before its membership. The

---

[3]Harlow S. Person, foreward to *Principles of Scientific Management,* by Frederick W. Taylor (New York: Harper & Bros., 1911), p. ix.

Wages were tied to output.

first paper, presented in 1895, was entitled "A Piece Rate System." In it, Taylor expressed concern over some of the incentive payment schemes then being used in industry. As an alternative he recommended a differential piece-rate system. For each job in which it was to be employed, a time-and-motion study would first be conducted. On the basis of the results a standard for a fair day's work would be ascertained. A worker who produced less than standard would receive a certain price for each piece produced. A worker who reached or surpassed the standard would be paid a higher per-unit piece rate. For example, if standard was 100 pieces a day, with the low rate being 1.1 cents per piece and the high rate being 1.8 cents per piece, a worker producing 90 pieces would receive 99 cents whereas a worker turning out 102 pieces would receive $1.84.

In 1903 Taylor presented a second paper, entitled "Shop Management," to the ASME. This time the emphasis was on his philosophy of management. Taylor pointed out the need to provide high wages and attain low per-unit production costs. This, he felt, would entail the scientific selection and training of workers coupled with management-*employee* cooperation.

The audiences for both these papers failed to understand Taylor's emphases, thinking money to be of greater concern than systematic managerial work in scientific management. When Taylor put forth his ideas in his 1911 book, *Principles of Scientific Management,* he outlined four principles, the scope of which was greater than time-and-motion study. The *four principles of scientific management* represented a combination of mechanical, conceptual, and philosophical ideas:

- First.   Develop a science for each element of a man's work, which replaces the old rule-of-thumb method.

- Second.   Scientifically select and then train, teach, and develop the workman, whereas in the past a workman chose his own work and trained himself as best he could.

Principles of scientific management were developed.

- Third.   Heartily cooperate with the men so as to insure all of the work being done in accordance with the principles of the science which has been developed.

- Fourth.   There is an almost equal division of the work and the responsibility between the management and the workmen. The management take over all work for which they are better fitted than the workmen, while in the past almost all of the work and the greater part of the responsibility were thrown upon the men.[4]

These principles help pinpoint Taylor's two major contributions to modern management. First, he separated the planning function from the operating function. Second, he pointed out the need for a complete change in attitude,

---

[4]Ibid., pp. 36–37.

almost a revolutionary shift, on the part of both workers and managers toward their jobs. Each had to work in harmony with the other.

In recent years, some researchers have questioned Taylor's contributions. For example, Wrege and Perroni contend that Taylor did not actually conduct the pig-iron experiments;[5] and Wrege and Stotka claim that Taylor plagiarized most of his *Principles of Scientific Management* from a manuscript written by Morris Cooke, a colleague.[6] On the other hand, after carefully reviewing these criticisms, Locke argues that "most of the criticisms that have been made of Taylor are unjustified. Taylor's genius has not been appreciated by many contemporary writers."[7] In large degree, this situation is unfortunate, for, as seen in Table 2-1, many of his ideas and techniques are still being used by modern managers. Additionally, he commonly is known as the father of scientific management, a title that was a result of the fame he acquired from his remarks to a congressional committee in 1912. In fact, scientific management and Frederick Taylor become synonymous terms. In some quarters, the system of shop management that he advocated became known as the Taylor system. However, as he stated in his testimony before the House, he was only one of many people instrumental in developing this system. Another, to whom he gave specific credit, was Frank Gilbreth.

Frank and Lillian Gilbreth

Bricklaying techniques were developed.

Frank Gilbreth was a contractor who developed an early interest in the various motions used by bricklayers. Could any extraneous motions be eliminated, thereby reducing the time and effort necessary to lay bricks? After much experimentation, he was able to reduce the number of hand motions required to lay exterior brick from 18 to 4.5 and interior brick from 18 to 2. He also developed an adjustable stand to eliminate the need for stooping to pick up the bricks. Likewise, he had workers use mortar of proper consistency to eliminate "tapping." He was thus able to increase the number of bricks a worker could lay in an hour from 120 to 350.

In 1904 Lillian Moller and Frank Gilbreth, who became known as the father of motion study, were married. Lillian Gilbreth had a strong background in management and psychology, and the two combined their talents for the purpose of developing better work methods. One of their most famous techniques was the use of motion pictures. By filming the individual at work and then playing back the film, they could analyze the person's motions *(motion study)* and determine which, if any, where extraneous.

---

[5]Charles D. Wrege and Amedeo G. Perroni, "Taylor's Pig-Tale: A Historical Analysis of Frederick W. Taylor's Pig-Iron Experiments," *Academy of Management Journal*, March 1974, pp. 6–27.

[6]Charles D. Wrege and Anne Marie Stotka, "Cooke Creates a Classic: The Story Behind F. W. Taylor's Principles of Scientific Management," *Academy of Management Review*, July 1978, pp. 736–49.

[7]Edwin A. Locke, "The Ideas of Frederick W. Taylor: An Evaluation," *Academy of Management Review*, January 1982, p. 14.

	Valid?	Now Accepted?	Manifested in (Outgrowths):
TABLE 2-1 Status of Taylor's Ideas and Techniques in Contemporary Management			
Philosophy			
Scientific decision making	Yes	Yes	Management science: operations research, cost accounting, etc.
Management-labor cooperation	Yes	Partly	Greater management–labor cooperation (but conflict not eliminated)
Techniques			
Time-and-motion study	Yes	Yes	Widespread use; standard times
Standardization	Yes	Yes	Standardized procedures in many spheres; human engineering
Task	Yes	Yes	Goal setting, MBO, feedback
Bonus	Yes	Increasingly	Proliferation of reward system, Scanlon Plan, Improshare, need to consider money in job enrichment/OD studies
Individualized work	Partly	Partly	Recognition of dangers of groups, groupthink, social loafing, contextual theories of group decision making (but group jobs sometimes more efficient)
Management training	Yes	Yes	Management responsibility for employee training
Scientific selection	Yes	Yes	Development of fields of industrial psychology and personnel management
Shorter hours; rest pauses	Yes	Yes	40-hour (or less) work week; common use of rest pauses

Source: Edwin A. Locke, "The Ideas of Frederick W. Taylor: An Evaluation," *Academy of Management Review,* January 1982, p. 22. Reprinted with permission.

Since the cameras in those days were hand cranked, Frank Gilbreth invented the *microchronometer,* a clock with a large sweeping hand that records time to 1/2000 of a minute, and placed it in the field of work being filmed. (Today, unless the camera contains constant-speed electric motors, the microchronometer is still used in photographing time-and-motion patterns.) Following its invention, the Gilbreths could analyze the individual's motions while determining precisely how long the work took *(time study).* In addition, they went so far as to categorize all hand motions into only seventeen basic motions (such as "grasp," "hold," and "position"), which they called *therbligs*—Gilbreth spelled backward with the "t" and the "h" transposed. These ideas proved useful throughout industry. They also gained popularity in the medical profession, specifically in hospitals.

Frank Gilbreth
(1868–1924)

Lillian Gilbreth
(1878–1972)

Frank Gilbreth, born in 1868, passed the entrance exams for the Massachusetts Institute of Technology but decided instead to go into the contracting business. Beginning as an apprentice bricklayer, he quickly became interested in the different sets of motions that were used in training bricklayers. First, the laborer was taught how to lay bricks; then he was taught how to work at a slow pace; finally, he was trained to work at a fast pace. Gilbreth wondered whether any of these three sets of motions could be eliminated in the interest of efficiency. From here he extended his time-and-motion study interests to many other areas of work. His wife Lillian was a constant companion and co-partner, in addition to becoming a renowned authority and international lecturer in the field of management.

Lillian worked closely with her husband, and after his death she spread the Gilbreth message throughout the United States and abroad. Her writings and talks were on topics that even today would be of interest: applying scientific management to setting up a household and bringing up a family; the effects of mechanization on worker satisfaction; why women succeed in management; how to save time and energy. Her concepts of applied psychology, coupled with her worldwide tours, helped to earn her the title of "First Lady of Management."[8]

EARLY MANAGEMENT THEORY

The scientific managers concentrated on the people on the operational level of the organization and their work became of interest to enterprises throughout the world. For example, in Poland, Karol Adamiecki (1866–1933) pioneered scientific management, using techniques similar to those being discovered by Taylor and his associates.[9]

Russian-born Walter Polakov (1879–*) worked to get Soviet industry to employ the concepts of scientific management that he learned during his visits to the United States.[10] Yoichi Ueno (1883–1957) applied scientific management ideas in Japan; he even came to the United States to study under Gilbreth, he translated Taylor's works into Japanese, and he invited

---

[8]Ronald G. Greenwood, Regina A. Greenwood, and Jay Severance, "Lillian M. Gilbreth, First Lady of Management," *National Academy of Management Proceedings*, 1978, pp. 2–6.

[9]Zdzislaw P. Wesolowski, "The Polish Contribution to the Development of Scientific Management," *National Academy of Management Proceedings*, 1978, pp. 12–16.

*Management historians are unsure when Polakov died.

[10]Daniel A. Wren, "Scientific Management in the U.S.S.R., with Particular Reference to the Contribution of Walter N. Polakov," *Academy of Management Proceedings*, January 1980, pp. 1–11.

Henri Fayol
(1841–1925)

Henri Fayol is commonly referred to as the father of modern management theory. After receiving his degree from the French National School of Mines at St. Etienne at the age of nineteen, he entered the employ of a mining combine known as the Commentry-Fourchambault. There he remained for his entire career, attaining the position of general manager (essentially, president) in 1888 and holding it until 1918, when he became a director of the firm. Throughout these years, Fayol proved himself an outstanding administrator. When he assumed the position of general manager, the firm was in critical condition, but by 1918 its financial stability was excellent.

many of the most famous scientific managers to come to the Orient to discuss their ideas.[11] By 1930, scientific management was an international movement. The scope of these activities was restricted essentially to the workers and first-line supervisors. However, success at this level led to a change in the worker–manager ratio and eventually resulted in attention being focused farther up the hierarchy.

With more and more people entering the management ranks, the study of management soon began to receive attention. These early observers were interested in such questions as what management is, what organizational principles are, and the methods by which managers could more effectively do their jobs. The people who devoted attention to answering these questions helped formulate the basis of modern management theory. The most important of them was Henri Fayol.

Definition and Teaching of Administration

In 1916 Fayol wrote a monograph entitled *Industrial and General Administration,* attempting in it to synthesize his managerial experience and knowledge.[12] His overall goal was to elevate the status of administration by providing an analytical framework for management. One of the most important sections of this book dealt with the definition and teaching of administration.

Fayol wrote that all administrative activities and business undertakings could be divided into six groups:

---

[11]Ronald G. Greenwood, Regina A. Greenwood, and Robert H. Ross, "Yoichi Ueno: A Brief History of Japanese Management: 1911 to World War II," *National Academy of Management Proceedings,* 1981, pp. 107–15.

[12]Henri Fayol, *Industrial and General Administration,* trans. J. A. Coubrough (Geneva, Switzerland: International Management Institute, 1929).

1. Technical operations (production, manufacture).
2. Commercial operations (purchases, sales, and exchanges).
3. Financial operations (finding and controlling capital).
4. Security operations (protection of goods and persons).
5. Accounting operations (stocktaking, balance sheet, costing, statistics).
6. Administrative operations (planning, organization, command, coordination, and control).[13]

Managers need administrative ability.

Fayol analyzed these six operations, noting that the worker's chief characteristic is technical ability, the relative importance of which declines while that of administrative ability increases as a laborer goes up the organizational hierarchy.

> Technical ability is the chief characteristic of the lower employees of a big undertaking and the heads of small industrial concerns; administrative ability is the chief characteristic of all the men in important positions. Technical ability is the most important quality at the bottom of the industrial ladder and administrative ability at the top.[14]

Management can be taught.

In contrasting Henri Fayol with Frederick W. Taylor, one sees Fayol was far less concerned than Taylor with the operational level and much more interested in approaching the subject from a general management point of view. In so doing, he made one of his greatest contributions to management —the identification of the administrator's activities or functions: planning, organizing, commanding, coordinating, and controlling. A manager who could carry out these functions properly would be effective. Fayol believed that insufficient attention was given to these functions. Many people recognized them as important but believed they could only be learned on the job, as technical skills are. Fayol disagreed, pointing out that administration could be taught in a scholastic setting, if only a theory of administration could be formulated.

Principles of Administration

Noting that the administrative function was concerned only with the human part of an undertaking, Fayol hastened to explain in his monograph that he employed the word *principles*, not *laws* or *rules*, because of the flexibility required in applying such concepts to people. Since these principles are hardly ever used twice in the same way because of changing conditions, individual administrators must adapt them to their particular needs. The fourteen principles that Fayol felt he had occasion to use most frequently were:

---

[13]Ibid., p. 8.

[14]Ibid., p. 15.

Fayol's fourteen principles of administration.

1. **Division of Work.** By employing the classic concept of specialization of labor, increases in efficiency can be achieved.

2. **Authority and Responsibility.** According to Fayol, authority and responsibility went hand in hand. *Authority* was "the right to command and the power to make oneself obeyed."[15] *Responsibility* was a reward or penalty accompanying the use of this power. In later years this principle would be called parity of authority and responsibility, indicating that the two should always be equal.

3. **Discipline.** The essence of discipline is "obedience, diligence, energy, correct attitude, and outward marks of respect, within the limits fixed by the agreement between a concern and its employees."[16]

4. **Unity of Command.** Everyone should have one and only one boss.

5. **Unity of Management.** Not to be confused with unity of command, unity of management calls for one manager and one plan for all operations having the same objective.

6. **Subordination of Individual Interests to the Common Good.** The goals of the organization must take precedence over those of individuals or groups of employees.

7. **Remuneration of the Staff.** Fayol believed that all employees should be paid for their work and that the payment plan should: (a) ensure fair remuneration, (b) encourage keenness by rewarding successful effort, and (c) not lead to rewards beyond a reasonable limit.

8. **Centralization.** Fayol felt that centralization of authority was a natural tendency of organizations, since all major decisions were typically made by a few people at the top of the structure. In and of itself, this is neither good nor bad. It is, however, always present to some degree. The challenge is to ascertain what degree is best for the organization.

9. **Hierarchy.** The hierarchy, or *scalar chain,* as it is often called, is the order of rank that runs through the organization from top to bottom. In order to preserve the integrity of the hierarchy and to ensure unity of command, communications should follow this formal channel. However, Fayol recognized the problem of red tape in a large organization and the resulting inadvisability of always taking the long, formal route. In Figure 2-1, for example, if one followed the scalar chain, E would have to ascend the hierarchy to A and then descend it to K in order to pass the lateral message.

   To overcome this problem, Fayol prescribed his *gangplank principle.* People at the same level of the hierarchy should be allowed to communicate directly, provided that they have permission from their

---

[15]Ibid., p. 20.
[16]Ibid.

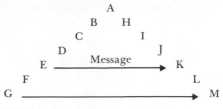

FIGURE 2-1   Fayol's Gangplank Principle

superiors to do so and that they tell their respective chiefs afterward what they have agreed to do. In this way, the integrity of the hierarchy is never threatened. Furthermore, Fayol remarked, if A made subordinates B and H use the gangplank principle and they did likewise for their subordinates, C and I, much greater efficiency would be introduced into the organization. Although it is an error to leave the hierarchical chain without a good reason, it would be a greater mistake to follow it when such a procedure would prove harmful to the undertaking.

10.   **Order.** ''A place for everything and everything in its place'' was the way Fayol described the principle of order.

11.   **Equity.** Equity results when friendliness is coupled with justice.

12.   **Stability of Staff.** It takes time for an able employee to settle down to a job and perform satisfactorily. Thus, organizations should encourage the long-term commitment of their employees.

13.   **Initiative.** Fayol defined *initiative* as the power to conceive and execute a plan of action.

14.   **Esprit de Corps.** Esprit de corps, or morale, depends upon harmony and unity among an organization's staff.

In conclusion, Fayol also pointed out that he had made no attempt to be exhaustive in his coverage of principles. He had merely described some of those he had used most often.

Elements of Administration

The second part of Fayol's book was devoted to a description of the five functions, or ''elements,'' as he called them, of administration: planning, organizing, commanding, coordinating, and controlling. He elaborated upon each as follows:

Planning. Planning requires a forecast of events and, based on the forecast, the construction of an operating program. Forecasts should extend as far into the future as the needs of the organization demand, although ten-year forecasts should be redrafted every five years.

Organizing. Organizing entails the structuring of activities, materials, and personnel for accomplishing the assigned tasks. This calls for effective coordination of all the firm's resources.

The functions of management are planning, organizing, commanding, coordinating, and controlling.

Commanding. Commanding encompasses the art of leadership coupled with the goal of putting the organization into motion. Setting a good example, making periodic examinations of the organization, eliminating incompetent personnel, and not getting bogged down with detail were some of the suggestions Fayol made for effectively carrying out this function.

Coordinating. Coordinating provides the requisite unity and harmony needed to attain organizational goals. One way of accomplishing this, Fayol believed, was through regular meetings of managers and subordinates. If this function were properly implemented, everything would flow smoothly.

Controlling. Controlling entails seeing that everything is done in accord with the adopted plan. This function must be applied to all segments of an activity—workers, materials, and operations alike.

Fayol's Contribution

Fayol's contribution to management theory cannot be overstated. First, he provided a conceptual framework for analyzing the management process. In the post-World War II era, when colleges of business began to flourish in the United States, it was Fayol's conceptual framework that provided the guidelines along which many management texts were written. Writers would identify a number of managerial functions and then describe each in depth. Some even went so far as to provide specific principles of management at the end of each section—for example, principles of planning and principles of organizing. These scholars and writers became known as the *management process school,* and there is no doubt that the basic framework originated with Fayol.

Second, the attention Fayol focused on the need and possibility of teaching management via the development of a theory of administration put him in the forefront of classical management theoreticians. Much of what was to follow in the development of management theory and practice constituted an extension and development of his basic ideas including a consideration of social responsibility (see Social Responsibility in Action: Being the Best).

BEHAVIORAL BEGINNINGS

At the time Henri Fayol and other administrative theorists were investigating the nature of management, interest in its behavioral aspects was generated, marking the beginning of the *human relations philosophy.* Three of the earliest contributors to behavioral and human relations studies were Elton Mayo, the Hawthorne studies researchers, and Chester Barnard.

Mayo's Mule Spinning Inquiry

Mayo's most famous early writings reported an experiment which took place in a Philadelphia textile mill in 1923 and 1924. Its purpose was to identify the

SOCIAL
RESPONSIBILITY
IN
ACTION:
Being
the
Best

Henri Fayol's principles were designed to help an organization be the best it could be. How does a company know when it is the best? In recent years *Fortune* magazine has polled top executives, outside directors, and financial analysts in an effort to determine America's most admired corporations. One of the latest poll shows the following to be the top ten:

1. Merck
2. Rubbermaid
3. Dow Jones
4. Procter & Gamble
5. Liz Claiborne
6. 3M
7. Philip Morris
8. J. P. Morgan & Co.
9. RJR Nabisco
10. Wal-Mart Stores

Fortune arrived at this list by rating firms on eight key attributes, four of which provide at least an indirect measure of social responsibility. These four are: (1) community and environmental responsibility; (2) the ability to attract, develop, and keep talented people; (3) the quality of product or services; and (4) innovativeness. In order for a firm to be one of the most admired, it has to rank high on most, if not all, of these measures of social responsibility. For example, when it comes to community and environmental responsibility, Procter & Gamble was one of the top three. Conversely, Financial Corporation of America, Texas Air, and Manville were ranked last on this criterion, and these same three firms overall ranked in the last ten of all 306 firms that were rated by *Fortune*.

When it comes to the ability to attract, develop, and keep talented people, Merck, Philip Morris, and J. P. Morgan were the top three. Financial Corporation of America, BankAmerica, and LTV were the lowest three in this category and they also ranked in the last ten of all firms rated by the magazine.

When it comes to quality of products or services, Merck, Dow Jones, and Rubbermaid headed the list while Texas Air, Financial Corporation of America, and Control Data were last here and in the last ten of all firms that were rated.

In the area of innovativeness, Merck, Liz Claiborne, and Rubbermaid were tops. BankAmerica, Bethlehem Steel, and Financial Corporation of America were rated last and again were also in the last ten of all companies that were rated.

Simply put, firms that ranked high in the social responsibility area were likely to rank high overall, and firms that ranked low in the social responsibility were likely to rank low overall.

Source: Ellen Schultz, "America's Most Admired Corporations," *Fortune*, January 18, 1988, pp. 32–49.

cause of high labor turnover in the mule spinning department, where workers made thread or yarn on mules, a type of spinning machine that was also called a mulejenny. Turnover in the company's other departments was between 5 and 6 percent a year, but in the mule spinning department it had risen as high as 250 percent.

Rest Periods

With rest periods, productivity rose.

Mayo decided to make some changes in the work pattern to see whether the situation would improve. He introduced two ten-minute rest periods in the morning and two more in the afternoon for one of the groups in the department—with astounding results. Morale improved, high turnover ended, and production, despite the work breaks, remained the same. Soon the entire department was included in the rest-period experiment, and output increased tremendously. Monthly productivity, which had never been above 70 percent, rose over the next five months to an overall average of 80 percent; and with this increase came bonus pay, which was given for productivity over 75 percent.

Analysis of the Results

What led to the high morale, high productivity, and virtual elimination of labor turnover? Mayo felt it was the systematic introduction of the rest periods, which not only helped overcome physical fatigue but reduced what he called pessimistic revery. Mayo extended the term *revery* to mean, basically, outlook on life. The reasoning was that a worker whose monotonous job led toward pessimistic revery would possibly be consumed by this attitude. The reduction of pessimism in the revery would therefore be presumed to increase energy and productivity.

Mayo and his associates drew some interesting physiological and psychological conclusions, but time and further research allowed for additional, more substantial, finds. The Hawthorne studies, which were done soon after Mayo's pioneering work, were notable among them.

Hawthorne Studies

The Hawthorne studies (1924–1932) had their roots in the logic of scientific management. The initial purpose of these experiments was to study the effect of illumination on output. Begun with that relatively simple goal, these studies at the Hawthorne Works of Western Electric's plant near Cicero, Illinois, would have four major phases: the illumination experiments, the relay assembly test room study, the massive interviewing program, and the bank wiring observation room study.

Illumination Experiments

No relationship between illumination and output was found.

The illumination phase of the Hawthorne studies lasted two and a half years. During this period, three different experiments were conducted, with notable improvement in experimental design as the tests continued. However, the researchers were unable to ascertain the relationship between illumination and output.

Even so, the company did not feel that the experiments had been unsuccessful. On the contrary, Western Electric management believed that it had gained invaluable experience in the technique of conducting research and was eager to push forward. The result was phase two of the studies, the

Elton Mayo
(1880–1949)

Elton Mayo was an Australian who taught ethics, philosophy, and logic at Queensland University and later studied medicine in Edinburgh, Scotland. While in Edinburgh, he became a research associate in the study of psychopathology. Then, under a grant from the Laura Spelman Rockefeller Fund, he came to the United States and joined the faculty of the Wharton School of Finance and Commerce of the University of Pennsylvania. In 1926, he joined the Harvard University industrial research faculty.[17] While he was best known for his participation in the Hawthorne studies, Mayo's writings on the human and social problems of an industrial civilization helped provide important early insights into human behavior in the workplace.

relay assembly test room experiment. Elton Mayo and a number of Harvard researchers entered at this stage in the program, though the Harvard group did not play a significant role until the third phase of the study, and Mayo, personally, spent only six days at the plant.[18]

Relay Assembly Test Room

In order to obtain more control over the factors affecting work performance, the researchers decided to isolate a small group of workers from the regular work force. Five assemblers and a layout operator (all women) were placed in a room with an observer who was to record everything that happened and maintain a friendly atmosphere. The six workers were told that the experiment was not designed to boost production but merely to study various types of working conditions so that the most suitable environment could be ascertained. They were instructed to keep working at the regular pace.

Once the impact of most of these new changes was noted, the researchers moved the experiment into its second stage. During this stage, rest pauses were introduced in order to determine what effect they would have on output. The result was an increase in productivity, leading to the initial hypothesis that the pauses reduced fatigue and thereby improved output. Applying this theory further, the researchers introduced shorter workdays and workweeks. Once again, output increased. However, when these changes were later terminated and original conditions reestablished, output still

---

[17]Daniel A. Wren, *The Evolution of Management Thought*, 2nd ed. (New York: Ronald Press, 1979), pp. 299–300.

[18]Ronald G. Greenwood, Alfred A. Bolton, and Regina A. Greenwood, "Hawthorne a Half Century Later: Relay Assembly Participants Remember," *Journal of Management*, Fall/Winter 1983, pp. 217–31.

remained high, indicating that the change in conditions was not the only reason for the increase in output. Some investigators hypothesized that the increases were related not to the rest pauses or shorter working hours but to the improved outlook that the workers had toward their work. But no one seemed able to answer the question of what the improved outlook could be related to.

After rejecting various hypotheses, the researchers concluded that the most likely cause was that changes in the social conditions and in the method of supervision brought about the improved attitude and production rates. In order to gather information on this idea, management decided to investigate employee attitudes and the factors to which they could be traced. The result was a massive interviewing program. This program started simply as a plan for improving supervision, but it actually marked the turning point in the research and for a time overshadowed all other aspects of the project.

The workers had an improved outlook toward their work.

Massive Interviewing Program

Over 20,000 interviews were conducted in the third phase of the studies. The interviewers began by asking employees direct questions about supervision and the work environment in general. Although the interviewers made it clear that answers would be kept in strict confidence, the responses to questions were often guarded and stereotyped. The approach was therefore changed from direct to nondirect questioning. The employees were free to choose their own topics. A wealth of information about employee attitudes resulted. The researchers realized that an individual's work performance, position, and status in the organization were determined not by that person alone but also by the group members. Peers had an effect on individual performance. In order to study this more systematically, the research entered its fourth and final phase, that of the bank wiring observation room.

A nondirective interviewing technique was employed.

Bank Wiring Observation Room

In choosing a department to study, the investigators decided to concentrate on a small group engaged in one particular type of work rather than to encompass many groups with dissimilar jobs. The department chosen for the study was the bank wiring department, which had an all-male staff. For the next six months, the work and the behavior of this group were observed.

The Group's Output.   One significant finding was that most of the workers were restricting their output. Why did the workers restrict output? One told the interviewer that if they did too much work, the company would raise the expected amount. Another felt they might work themselves out of a job simply by working too hard and doing too much. Others felt that a slow pace protected the slower workers, preventing them from looking bad. It should also be noted that management seemed to accept this informal rate, though there was no official notice of it.

Some workers restricted their output.

The workers treated the managers differently.

The Supervisory Situation.   Study of the supervisory situation in the room also provided human behavioral insights, for the manner in which the men treated their superiors differed. Most of the employees regarded the group chief as one of themselves. As a result, they thought nothing of disobeying him. The section chief fared a little better. The assistant foreman, on the other hand, received much different treatment. The same pattern existed in the case of the foreman. In fact, when he was present, the workers refrained from any activity that was not strictly in accord with the rules. Thus, the workers' respect for, and apprehension in the presence of, others seemed to increase as these others progressed up the organizational hierarchy.

Interpersonal relations were studied.

Group Dynamics.   Another aspect of the group that was closely observed was that of interpersonal relationships. The researchers gained a great deal of knowledge about the informal organization that existed in the room. For example, most of the workers engaged in various games, including baseball pools, shooting craps, sharing candy, and "binging." The latter, a device used to control individual behavior, consisted of hitting a worker as hard as possible on the upper arm. This person was then free to retaliate by striking back just as hard. Although the stated reason was to see who could hit the hardest, the underlying cause was often one of punishment for those who were accomplishing either too much or too little.

Job trading and the helping of one another provided further bases for studying the group's behavior. Some individuals sought help while others gave it, although such action was in direct violation of company rules. This led to interest in the development of friendships and antagonisms. Who liked whom and who disliked whom?

The researchers were able to identify social cliques.

Social Cliques.   By studying the types of games and other interactions of the participants, the investigators were able to divide the men into two groups, or cliques, which they labeled A and B. Several conclusions were drawn from the specification of these groups. First, location in the room influenced the formation of a clique. The A group was located in the front of the room. The B group in the rear. Second, some men were accepted by neither clique. Third, each clique regarded itself as superior to the other, with the opinions based on either the things clique members did or the things they refrained from doing. For example, Clique A did not trade jobs and did not "bing" as often as did Clique B. Conversely, the members of Clique B did not argue among themselves or engage in games of chance as often as did Clique A. Fourth, each clique had certain *informal group norms* or sentiments which anyone wanting acceptance into the groups had to subscribe to. F. J. Roethlisberger and William J. Dickson identified the first four of these, and George C. Homans later stated the fifth:

1. You should not turn out too much work. If you do, you are a "rate-buster."

2. You should not turn out too little work. If you do, you are a "chiseler."

Norms of behavior were also identified.

3. You should not tell a superior anything that will react to the detriment of an associate. If you do, you are a "squealer."

4. You should not attempt to maintain social distance or act officious. If you are an inspector, for example, you should not act like one.

5. You should not be noisy, self-assertive, and anxious for leadership.[19]

Findings and Implications of Hawthorne

The Hawthorne studies constituted the single most important foundation for the behavioral approach to management. The conclusions drawn from them were many and varied.

The restructuring of the social network was more important than rest periods.

Elimination of Mental Revery.   In Elton Mayo's opinion, one of the major explanations of the results rested with the elimination of what he had earlier called pessimistic revery. However, on the basis of the findings of the Hawthorne studies, Mayo now realized that rest pauses or changes in the work environment did not, of themselves, overcome this problem. Rather, the key was to be found in the reorganization of the workers. Thus, Mayo realized that the results were caused not by such scientific management practices as rest periods, but by sociopsychological phenomena, of which the restructuring of social networks is an example.

The novelty of the situation was important.

Hawthorne Effect.   A second finding, and probably the most widely cited, is the *Hawthorne effect*, which is simply the observation that when people know they are being watched, they will act differently than when they are not aware of being observed. Applying this concept to the increase in productivity in the relay room, many modern psychologists contend that it was not the changes in the rest pauses that led to increased output but the fact that the workers liked the new situation, in which they were considered to be of some significance. The attention given them led them to increase their output. The Hawthorne effect thus seemed to lead to the decline in revery, but further investigation indicated that it was apparently not the only factor involved.

Supervisory Climate.   The relay assembly test room work force did more work than ever before, but the bank wiring room workers restricted their output. There had to be more than a Hawthorne effect and a resulting decline in pessimistic revery.

The style of supervision was another critical factor.

What, then, accounted for the difference in output between the two rooms? The major difference may well have been the type of supervision. In the relay room the observer took over some of the supervisory functions, but in a supportive style. In the bank wiring room, however, the regular supervisors were used to maintain order and control. The observer was relegated to a minor role, having none of the authority of his relay room

[19]F. J. Roethlisberger and William J. Dickson, *Management and the Worker* (Cambridge, MA: Harvard University Press, 1939), p. 522; and George C. Homans, *The Human Group* (New York: Harcourt, Brace & World, 1950), p. 79.

Chester I. Barnard
(1886–1961)

Chester I. Barnard made a significant contribution to behavioral thought. Entering Harvard University in 1906, he studied economics and finished all the requirements in three years. However, he failed to receive his degree because he lacked a laboratory science. Since he had passed the course with distinction, he felt it was pointless to take the lab section. Upon leaving the university, he joined the statistical department of the American Telephone and Telegraph system. In 1927 he became president of New Jersey Bell and remained in that capacity until his retirement. In addition, he worked with numerous other organizations, including the Rockefeller Foundation, of which he served as president for four years, and the United States Organization, of which he was president for three years.

counterpart. This particular finding downplays the Hawthorne effect, which has probably received undue emphasis for far too long a time.

The Light from Hawthorne.   The illumination experiment at Hawthorne might be said to have lighted the way for the human relations research to follow. It was difficult for the original investigators of human relations studies to persevere in view of the various letdowns and surprises of the Hawthorne studies. But these researchers did continue and, as a result, reached two significant milestones.

First, the Hawthorne studies did yield insights into group and individual behavior. The researchers had laid important foundations, even though they realistically had to concede that they were further from the goals they had expected to achieve at Hawthorne than they might have hoped during the studies. Second, the Hawthorne studies had focused attention on the supervisory climate, providing an impetus for later research on leadership style.[20]

Another important behavioral contributor was Chester I. Barnard, who was interested in making a logical analysis of organizational structure, and who applied sociological concepts to management in his book *The Functions of the Executive.* His work has proved so influential to the study of management that one writer has credited him with having had "a more profound impact on the thinking about the complex subject matter of human organization than has any other contributor to the continuum of management

---

[20]For example, there were the pioneering studies conducted by Ronald Lippitt and Ralph K. White under Kurt Lewin at the University of Iowa. One of their best-known articles is "Patterns of Aggressive Behavior in Experimentally Created 'Social Climates,'" *Journal of Social Psychology*, May 1939, pp. 271–76.

thought."[21] His theory has been of major importance in the development of management theory.

Functions of the Executive

In *The Functions of the Executive,* Barnard pointed out that there had been no theory on the universal characteristics of organizations that seemed to correspond to his experience or to the implicit understanding shared by the leaders of any given organization. Much of what had been written, furthermore, seemed unrealistic and illogical. Using executive experience as his guide, Barnard sought to state two things: a description of the organizational process and a theory of cooperation.

He defined the formal organization as "a system of consciously coordinated activities of two or more persons."[22] Within this structure the executive is the most strategic factor, the person who must maintain a system of cooperative effort. The entire process is carried out through three essential executive functions.

There are three essential executive functions.

The first executive function is the establishment and maintenance of a communication system. It is the executive's primary job, and it is accomplished through careful employee selection, the use of positive and negative sanctions, and the securing of the informal organization.

The second executive function is the promotion and acquisition of essential effort from employees of the organization. It requires the recruiting of personnel and the development of an incentive program.

The third executive function is the formulation of the purpose and objectives of the organization. This calls for the skillful delegation of authority and development of a communication system for monitoring the overall plan (see Communication in Action: Improving One's Speaking Ability).

The Theory of Authority

The acceptance theory of authority is explained.

Throughout his book, Barnard emphasized the importance of inducing the subordinate to cooperate. Merely having the authority to give orders is insufficient, for the subordinate may refuse to obey. The result of this reasoning has become commonly known as the *acceptance theory of authority.* Authority, or the right to command, depends upon whether or not the subordinates obey. Naturally, one could reason that it is possible for the executive to bring sanctions, but this will not necessarily ensure acceptance

---

[21]Claude S. George, Jr., *The History of Management Thought,* 2nd ed. (Englewood Cliffs, NJ: Prentice-Hall, 1972), p. 140.

[22]Chester I. Barnard, *The Functions of the Executive* (Cambridge, MA: Harvard University Press, 1938), p. 73.

COMMUNICATION
IN
ACTION:
Improving
One's
Speaking
Ability

While Chester Barnard knew the importance of effective communication, many managers find it difficult to master this area, especially that of public speaking. They freeze up before giving a talk and are nervous while delivering their message. Fortunately, a great deal of research has been conducted regarding how to improve managerial speech making. Here are four of the most helpful guidelines.

First, videotape or audiotape the talk. This will provide you with feedback as to how well you present yourself, and is one of the most effective ways of identifying steps for improvement. Jot down these weaknesses and make it a point to work on them during the next talk.

Second, keep things simple. No matter how important the topic, focus on just two or three points. Do not attempt to cover too much territory because this will either confuse the audience or result in your glossing over everything too quickly. Instead, develop these few points and make them as interesting and informative as possible. In doing so, conduct some research on the audience and find out what they would like to know. Gear your presentation in this direction.

Third, learn how to make your hands and eyes work for you. Keep your hands waist-high or fold them lightly on top of each other. If you are at a podium, put your hands flat on the reading shelf. In this way you can use your hands to gesture and emphasize those points that are most important. Meanwhile continue to maintain eye contact with your audience and look from left to right and back again. Also remember to look at those directly in front of you as well as those in the back of the room. This eye-contact strategy makes everyone feel that you are talking directly to them.

Fourth, if you feel nervous before addressing the audience, modify your breathing. Inhale deeply and deliberately a few minutes before you stand up. Fill your lungs to capacity and hold your breath for a couple of seconds before exhaling slowly and fully. This will calm you down.

These steps will not make you an outstanding speaker; however, they will improve your speaking ability and make you a better communicator.

Source: Jack Franchetti and George McCartney, "How to Wow 'Em When You Speak," *Changing Times,* August 1988, pp. 29–31.

of the orders, for the employee may be willing to accept any fate dealt out by management.

The entire acceptance theory of authority would be quite threatening if this were all there was to it. Management might literally be at the mercy of the subordinates. However, Barnard realized that the consent and coopera- tion of subordinates are often easily obtained. First, the four conditions necessary for acceptance are generally present, so workers will regard a communication as authoritative. Second, each individual has what Barnard called a "zone of indifference." Orders falling within this zone are accepted without question. The others either fall on the neutral line or are conceived of as clearly unacceptable. The indifference zone tells the story, and it will be either wide or narrow, depending on the inducements being accorded the individual and the sacrifices the worker is making on behalf of the organization. The effective executive assures that all individuals feel they are receiving more from the organization than they are giving. This widens the indifference zone, and the subordinates agreeably accept most orders. Third, one person's refusal to obey will affect the efficiency of the organization. It will also threaten the other members. When this happens, co-workers will often pressure the individual to comply, and the result is general stability within the organization.

Barnard's Contribution

Barnard made several important contributions to management theory. First, he described executive functions in analytic and dynamic terms, in contrast to the descriptive writers who had preceded him. Second, he stimulated interest in topics such as communication, motivation, decision making, objectives, and organizational relationships. Third, he advanced the work of Fayol and others who had been concerned with management from the standpoint of principles and functions. Barnard, drawing upon his interest in the psychological and sociological aspects of management, extended these ideas to include the interaction of people in the work force.[23]

EARLY MANAGEMENT THOUGHT IN PERSPECTIVE

The scientific managers, early management theorists, and human relations researchers all made significant contributions to management, and all were complementary to one another. Frederick W. Taylor and his associates conducted important time-and-motion study research for forty years, 1880 to 1920. Then the early theorists in the years between 1915 and 1945 provided important information about the administrative side of management. From 1912 to 1955, the human relations researchers added a new level of sophistication to management thought. The objective of this part of the chapter is to place these three groups in perspective, first by examining some of the weaknesses and shortcomings of each group and then by reviewing the positive side of their contributions.

Scientific Management Shortcomings

Although the scientific managers made many important contributions to management, much of their work reflected a very limited understanding of

---

[23]Virginia B. Levsen, ''The Classical Barnard and the Management Theories of His Time,'' paper presented at the National Academy of Management Meetings, August 7–10, 1988.

REAL-LIFE MANAGERS:

INTERVIEW WITH RAYMOND SEMASKA

Raymond Semaska is a management consultant for a nationwide consulting firm. Ray has a bachelor's degree in industrial and systems engineering and a master's degree in business administration. He specializes in the health-care field where he provides expert assistance to hospitals and health-care institutions regarding how to more effectively apply management concepts and to provide the highest quality health care at the lowest cost.

Q.   *As a management consultant, how important is it to know the history of the organization with which you are working?*

A.   It's extremely important. In health care, for example, a doctor would not prescribe a treatment without first examining the patient. The same is true for consulting work. I have to look over the organization's past performance and find out how well they have been doing financially and operationally in a number of different areas relating to the delivery of health-care services. After I get this profile data, I can then identify and analyze problem spots and follow on with recommendations regarding how to improve things.

Q.   *What's the biggest challenge in health care today, and how does an understanding of management history help you do your job?*

A.   The biggest challenge in health care today is cost control. Over the last decade there has been a tremendous change in the way hospitals and health-care facilities operate, due to government cost controls and insurance company

the human element in the workplace. For example, most of the scientific management theorists seriously believed that money was the worker's prime motivation. This belief resulted in the development of various incentive payment plans such as Taylor's differential piece rate; if the employees worked harder, they would earn more money. Such thinking led these traditionalists to view the worker as an economic man.

Economic Man

The term *economic man* refers to an individual who makes decisions that maximize economic objectives. In the case of the worker, it is the individual willing to stay on the job from dawn until dusk in order to take home the biggest paycheck possible. Wage incentive plans are very important to this type of person because they provide economic opportunity.

coverages that limit payments and length of stay based on diagnosis. For example, when a person checks into the hospital for an operation such as an appendectomy, the hospital knows how long the individual will be staying barring some unforeseen problem. The hospital should have the patient back home in a matter of days. If they cannot, they end up having to absorb the costs associated with the individual's stay. Similarly, there are set prices for various medical procedures and the hospital is reimbursed by the insurance company or the government based on these predetermined rates. So the hospital has to be efficient if it hopes to be profitable. My knowledge of this information helps me pinpoint problem areas that warrant consideration.

Q. *When you review a hospital's operations, how do you know if the cost of various services or procedures is too high or too low? How do you know what they ought to do and not do?*

A. Part of the answer is found in historical information. I work in this industry full time, so I know what it costs other hospitals to provide various services and I know how much they charge. This helps me identify problem areas and recommend changes. Also, the health-care field has become much more market-driven in recent years. Advertising, providing additional services, and other marketing techniques are being used to attract people to the facilities. Through my consulting experience, I know which approaches have worked well and which have not done well, and this helps me formulate my recommendations for action. When you put a consultant's job in perspective, an understanding of management history and motivation is critical to effectiveness. If you don't know what has happened in the past and what is going on currently, both in the hospital and within the industry, you are not in a position to recommend substantive changes to your client. You have to have a fundamental appreciation of history in order to do this job well.

Economic men maximize economic objectives.

Lacking a solid understanding of human behavior, the scientific managers were unable to comprehend why not all employees took advantage of any chance to maximize their income. They failed to realize that some people might be happy merely to earn a satisfactory amount of money.[24]

The Irrationality of Rationalism

People are complex beings.

A second shortcoming complementary to the economic man theory was the scientific managers' view of the worker as a totally rational human being who would weigh all alternatives and then choose the one that would give the greatest economic return. This thinking, of course, completely omitted any consideration of social factors. Furthermore, as noted by sociologist Peter M.

---

[24]Herbert A. Simon, *Administrative Behavior*, 3rd ed. (New York: Free Press, 1976), p. xxix.

Blau, "To administer a social organization according to purely technical criteria of rationality is irrational, because it ignores the nonrational aspects of social conduct."[25] The word *complex* would have been much more appropriate than *economic*, for many factors besides money motivate the worker.

The Black Box

The scientific managers could have overcome these problems if they had concerned themselves with what is called the *black box concept*. For example, suppose that a company introduces a new incentive payment plan and productivity increases by 10 percent. Why does the increase in productivity occur? Is it brought about by the opportunity to earn more money? Is it caused by an increase in morale because the workers think management is interested in their well-being? Or is it caused by a third, as yet undemonstrated, reason? As Figure 2-2 shows, the answer rests in the black box, the transformation process that takes place between input and output.

The scientific managers did not analyze the transformation process.

To understand what goes on during this process, it is necessary to understand the importance of the human element. The Hawthorne researchers attempted to study this process by ascertaining, for example, why output increased in the relay room but did not increase in the bank wiring room. The scientific managers, however, were unconcerned with this line of thinking. They knew that workers produce more while working individually as opposed to working in groups, and they used this information to guide them in organizing the work force. Their basic approach to the management of people was simplistic, and this created limitations to their work.

Classical Management Deficiencies

The basic weakness of the classical theorists, especially Fayol, was that their statements on management principles were often too general to be of much help to the practicing manager. This problem is illustrated by the unity of command principle.

Unity of Command

The unity of command principle states that everyone should have one, and only one, boss. Luther Gulick, a classical theorist in the 1930s, indicated quite

[25]Peter M. Blau, *Bureaucracy in Modern Society* (New York: Random House, 1956), p. 58.

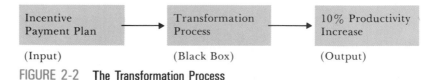

| Incentive Payment Plan | Transformation Process | 10% Productivity Increase |
| (Input) | (Black Box) | (Output) |

FIGURE 2-2   The Transformation Process

clearly the importance that early management theorists assigned to this principle:

> The significance of this principle in the process of co-ordination and organization must not be lost sight of. In building a structure of co-ordination, it is often tempting to set up more than one boss for a man who is doing work which has more than one relationship. Even as great a philosopher of management as Taylor fell into this error in setting up separate foremen to deal with machinery, with materials, with speed, etc., each with the power of giving orders directly to the individual workman. The rigid adherence to the principle of unity of command may have its absurdities; these are, however, unimportant in comparison with the certainty of confusion, inefficiency, and irresponsibility which arise from the violation of the principle.[26]

The unity of command principle seems to contradict the principle of specialization (or division of labor), which states that efficiency will be increased if one task is divided among the members of a group. Herbert A. Simon, the American economist who was awarded the 1978 Nobel Prize in economic sciences for his research into the decision-making process in economic groups, has noted:

> If unity of command, in Gulick's sense, is observed, the decisions of a person at any point in the administrative hierarchy are subject to influence through only one channel of authority; and if his decisions are of a kind that requires expertise in more than one field of knowledge, then advisory and informational services must be relied upon to supply those premises which lie in a field not recognized by the mode of specialization in the organization. For example, if an accountant in a school department is subordinate to an educator, and if unity of command is observed, then the finance department cannot issue direct orders to him regarding the technical, accounting aspects of his work.[27]

Unity of command is considered too inflexible a principle.

If unity of command were to be as vigorously enforced as Gulick suggested, specialization would be impeded. Realistically, it is necessary to introduce some flexibility into the interpretation of the principle. In so doing, however, other problems arise. The principle seems to lack some of its previous authority and may be less effective in solving administrative problems.

---

[26]Luther Gulick, "Notes on the Theory of Organization," in *Papers on the Science of Administration,* ed. Luther Gulick and L. Urwick (New York: Institute of Public Administration, 1937), p. 9.

[27]Simon, pp. 23–24.

The Problem with Principles

The classical theorists enumerated lists of principles in an attempt to make management more of a science and less of an art. This was an admirable objective, but in the process of implementing it, the theorists forced a rigidity into some principles, such as unity of command. In other cases, they were superficial in their attention.

Close analysis of classical principles reflects many shortcomings. Suffering the problems of both rigidity and vagueness, the theorists dealt with authority, responsibility, and other principles as concepts. However, when managers attempted to apply these ideas to the organizational structure, the outcome was far from satisfactory.

Inadequacy of the Human Relations Approach

The Hawthorne studies had a significant impact on management thought. One reason for this is that they complemented the work of the traditionalists. This is clearly seen in Figure 2-3, which applies the contributions of Taylor, Fayol, and Mayo to an organization chart. Taylor did the bulk of his work at the lower management–worker level; Fayol's contribution came at the administrative management level; the Hawthorne studies cut across the entire spectrum, providing information of value to all levels of management. Nonetheless, these studies and the resulting human relations movement had a number of problems.

The Scientific Method and Hawthorne

The research procedure is criticized.

One of the major criticisms of the human relations approach is directed at the very heart of the movement: Some researchers claim that the Hawthorne studies were not sufficiently scientific. These critics contend that the researchers had preconceived ideas and biases that affected their interpretation of the results. Others contend that the supporting evidence for the conclusions was just plain flimsy. Henry A. Landsberger, who made a systematic analysis of these studies in his book *Hawthorne Revisited,* criticized the studies further, challenging that the plant was not really typical because it was a thoroughly unpleasant place in which to work; that the researchers accepted management objectives, viewing the worker as a mere means of attaining these goals; and that the researchers gave inadequate attention to the personal attitudes people brought with them to the job, thus overlooking the effect of the unions and other extra-plant forces.[28]

The Human Relations Philosophy

Another criticism of the human relations movement is directed at one of its basic concepts, the idea that employee participation leads to job satisfaction

---

[28]Henry A. Landsberger, *Hawthorne Revisited* (Ithaca, NY: Cornell University Press, 1958).

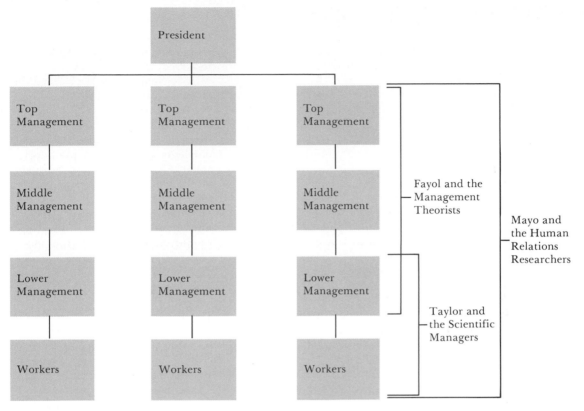

FIGURE 2-3 Contributions to Management Thought

Happy workers are not necessarily productive workers.

and job satisfaction brings about increased productivity. Recent research challenges the assumption that happy workers are productive workers. Job satisfaction is a multidimensional variable, impossible to explain in such simplistic terms. Output depends not only on a person's morale but also on individual goals and motivation within the work force. Still another criticism of the human relations movement was that it really did not offer an approach to managing workers that was much different from that of the scientific managers. Many modern researchers feel that the human relationists simply took the scientific management approach to people and candy-coated it. In any event, by the late 1950s the human relations movement was fading from the scene. It was replaced by what is known as a *human resources philosophy,* which contains a more viable interpretation of modern workers. Table 2-2 provides a comparison of the human relations and human resources theories. Notice from the table that the human relationists wanted to treat people well, while the human resources people attempt to use people well. There is a big difference between the two approaches.

TABLE 2-2

Partial Comparison of Human Relations Philosophy with Human Resources Philosophy

Human Relations	Human Resources
1. People need to be liked, to be respected, and to belong.	1. In addition to wanting to be liked, respected, and needed, most people want to contribute to the accomplishment of worthwhile objectives.
2. The manager's basic job is to make each employee believe that he or she is part of the departmental team.	2. The manager's basic job is to create an environment in which subordinates can contribute their full range of talents to the attainment of organizational goals. In so doing, he or she must attempt to uncover and tap their creative resources.
3. The manager should be willing to explain his or her plans to the subordinates and discuss any objections they might have. On routine matters, he or she should encourage participation by them in the planning and decision-making process.	3. The manager should allow participation in important matters as well as routine ones. In fact, the more important the dicision, the more vigorously he or she should attempt to involve the subordinates.
4. Within narrow limits, individuals and groups should be permitted to exercise self-direction and self-control in carrying out plans.	4. The manager should continually try to expand the subordinates' use of self-control and self-direction, especially as they develop and demonstrate increased insight and ability.
5. Involving subordinates in the communication and decision-making process will help them in satisfying their needs for belonging and individual recognition.	5. As the manager makes use of the subordinates' experiences, insights, and creative abilities, the overall quality of decision making and performance will improve.
6. High morale and reduced resistance to formal authority may lead to improved performance. They should at least reduce intradepartmental friction and make the manager's job easier.	6. Employee satisfaction is brought about by improved performance and the chance to contribute creatively to this improvement.

The Positive Side of the Picture

It should be noted that only the shortcomings and deficiencies of the scientific managers, classical theorists, and human relationists have so far been mentioned in the chapter, for the positive accomplishments have been outlined earlier. It is, after all, impossible to view a school of thought in proper perspective if one examines only the strengths.

Yet it would be unfair not to give credit to these three groups for their accomplishments. They made mistakes, but they were breaking new ground; and many of the facts known to us today remained mysteries to them. Still they persisted, gathering information that proved useful. The scientific management pioneers helped industry reach new heights of efficiency. Contributions from the early management theorists have helped train executives in the principles of planning, organizing, and controlling. Human relations research provided important insights into human behavior in the work environment; and as they went along, these researchers improved their research design. Some of the early Hawthorne experiments, for example, were redone because the researchers realized they were not controlling some of the causal variables. Their concern with formulating an adequate research procedure has carried over to the present day, as reflected in the high degree of importance currently assigned to the scientific method as a research tool. Although there is no universally accepted method, there is general agreement as to the basic steps, which follow:

1. **Identify the problem.** Precisely what is the objective of the entire investigation?

2. **Obtain preliminary information.** Gather as many available facts as possible about the problem area. Obtain background information.

3. **Pose a tentative solution to the problem.** State a hypothesis, which can be tested and proved to be either right or wrong, that is most likely to solve the problem.

Steps in the scientific method.

4. **Investigate the problem area.** Using both available data and, if possible, information gathered through experimentation, examine the problem in its entirety.

5. **Classify the information.** Take all the data that have been gathered and put them in an order that expedites their use and helps establish a relationship with the hypothesis.

6. **State a tentative answer to the problem.** Draw a conclusion regarding the right answer to the problem.

7. **Test the answer.** Implement the solution. If it works, the problem is solved. If not, go back to step 3 and continue through the process again.

This method is highly regarded by researchers. As Fred N. Kerlinger notes in his outstanding work, *Foundations of Behavioral Research:*

The scientific method has one characteristic that no other method of attaining knowledge has: self-correction. There are built-in checks all along the way to scientific knowledge. These checks are so conceived and used that they control and verify the scientist's activities and conclusions to the end of attaining dependable knowledge outside himself.[29]

The refinement of this procedure has played a key role in the development of modern management.

■ SUMMARY

Management is not a new concept. It has been employed for thousands of years, as seen in the practices of the Sumerians, the Romans, and the Roman Catholic Church. However, the emergence of the factory system presented management with a new challenge. With industrialization it became necessary to develop rational, scientific principles for handling workers, materials, money, and machinery. The scientific managers played a major role in helping attain this objective.

The primary goal of these managers was that of achieving the highest productivity possible by devising efficient work methods and encouraging employees to take advantage of these new techniques. In the United States, scientific management was made famous by people such as Frederick W. Taylor. His experiments at Bethlehem Steel illustrated the importance of time-and-motion study, and his differential piece-rate system provides students an insight into the types of wage incentive payment plans used during this period. Another important scientific manager of the day was Frank Gilbreth, renowned for his work in time-and-motion study and for a large body of work in management in which he collaborated with Lillian Gilbreth.

The success of the scientific managers brought about changes in the worker-manager ratio and moved the focus of attention farther up the hierarchy. The result was two distinct levels of inquiry about management. The first sought to identify generally the purview of management. The second sought to examine both individual and group behavior in organizations.

The most famous of the early management theorists was Henri Fayol. Fayol's outstanding contribution was the conceptual framework he provided for analyzing the management process. In the behavioral area, Elton Mayo studied group behavior in organizations. The Hawthorne studies, however, had an even greater impact on the field, and they became the single most important foundation for the behavioral approach to management. Meanwhile, Chester Barnard, whose acceptance theory of authority is still regard-

---

[29]Fred N. Kerlinger, *Foundations of Behavioral Research,* 2nd ed. (New York: Holt, Rinehart & Winston, 1973), p. 6.

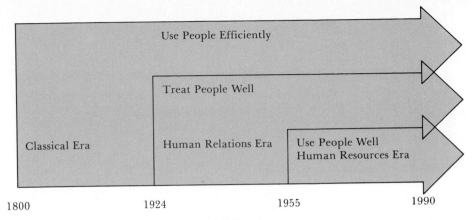

FIGURE 2-4   Time Frame of Managerial Philosophy

ed as a major landmark in the development of management theory, made the most memorable contribution to early behavioral knowledge.

In perspective all three groups—the scientific managers, the classical theorists, and the human relationists—had shortcomings. Yet it must also be realized that they complemented each other, helping to form the basis for modern management theory and practice. The efficiency goals of the scientific managers and classical theorists led to the human relations philosophy of treating people well, which in turn has been replaced, as seen in Figure 2-4, by a human resources philosophy of using people well.

■ REVIEW AND STUDY QUESTIONS

1. What contributions did the Sumerians make to early management thought? Diocletian? The Roman Catholic Church? Put these contributions in your own words.

2. What was the domestic system? The putting-out system? The factory system? Explain each.

3. Why is Frederick Taylor known as the father of scientific management?

4. Why is Frank Gilbreth known as the father of motion study?

5. Why is Henri Fayol known as the father of modern management theory?

6. Did the Hawthorne researchers find any relationship between illumination and output? Explain.

7. What were the norms to which the workers in the bank wiring room subscribed? Identify and describe them.

8. Of what significance to management were the Hawthorne studies? Explain.

9. According to Chester Barnard, what are the three essential executive functions? Explain each.

10. What is the acceptance theory of authority? Do you agree with it? Explain your answer.

11. What is meant by the term *economic man?*

12. In understanding human behavior, what is meant by the term *irrationality of rationalism?*

13. What is the major argument raised against classical management principles? Be specific in your answer.

14. Summarize the major criticism directed toward the Hawthorne studies.

15. How does the human relations philosophy differ from the human resources philosophy?

16. What is the scientific method? Outline the steps in the process.

■ SELECTED REFERENCES

Barnard, Chester I. *The Functions of the Executive.* Cambridge, MA: Harvard University Press, 1938.

Bolton, Alfred. "The Hawthorne Bank Wiring Observation Room: A Shop Floor View." Paper presented at the National Academy of Management Meetings, New Orleans, LA, August 9–12, 1987.

Breeze, John D. "Henri Fayol's Basic Tools of Administration." *National Academy of Management Proceedings,* August 1981, pp. 101–105.

Fayol, Henri. *General and Industrial Management.* Translated by Constance Starrs. London: Sir Isaac Pitman & Sons, 1949.

Franke, Richard H. "The Hawthorne Experiments: Empirical Findings and Implications for Management." Paper presented at the National Academy of Management Meetings, New Orleans, LA, August 9–12, 1987.

Gantt, Henry L. *Work, Wages, and Profits.* New York: Engineering Magazine, 1910.

Gilbreth, Frank B. *Motion Study.* New York: D. Van Nostrand, 1911.

Gilbreth, Lillian M. *The Psychology of Management.* New York: Sturgis and Walton, 1914.

Greenwood, Ronald G., Regina A. Greenwood, and Robert H. Ross, "Yoichi Ueno: A Brief History of Japanese Management: 1911 to World War II." *National Academy of Management Proceedings,* August 1981, pp. 107–115.

Greenwood, Ronald G., Regina A. Greenwood, and Jay A. Severance, "Lillian M. Gilbreth, First Lady of Management." *National Academy of Management Proceedings,* August 1978, pp. 2–6.

Jay, Antony. *Management and Machiavelli.* New York: Holt, Rinehart and Winston, 1967.

Landsberger, Henry A. *Hawthorne Revisited.* Ithaca, NY: State School of Industrial and Labor Relations, Cornell University Press, 1958.

Locke, Edwin A. "The Ideas of Frederick W. Taylor: An Evaluation." *Academy of Management Review,* January 1982, pp. 14–24.

Mayo, Elton. *The Human Problems of an Industrial Civilization.* Cambridge, MA: Harvard University Press, 1946.

Mee, J. F. *Management Thought in a Dynamic Economy.* New York: New York University Press, 1963.

Merrill, C. F., ed. *Classics in Management.* New York: American Management Association, 1960.

Milner, B. "Application of Scientific Methods to Management in the Soviet Union." *Academy of Management Review,* October 1977, pp. 554–60.

Mooney, J. D., and A. C. Reiley. *Onward Industry!* New York: Harper & Bros., 1931.

Munsterberg, H. *Business Psychology.* Chicago: LaSalle Extension University, 1915.

Parker, L. D. "Control in Organizational Life: The Contribution of Mary Parker Follett." *Academy of Management Review,* October 1984, pp. 736–45.

Pethia, Robert F. "Behavior of the Group Output Rate in the Relay Assembly Test Room Experiment: What Really Happened?" *National Academy of Management Proceedings,* August 1979, pp. 2–6.

Roethlisberger, F. J., and W. J. Dickson. *Management and the Worker.* Cambridge, MA: Harvard University Press, 1939.

Shepard, Jean M. "On Alex Carey's Radical Criticism of the Hawthorne Studies." *Academy of Management Journal,* March 1971, pp. 23–32.

Simon, H. A. *Administrative Behavior,* 3rd ed. New York: Free Press, 1976.

Taylor, Frederick W. *Principles of Scientific Management.* New York: Harper & Bros., 1911.

Urwick, L. *The Elements of Administration.* New York: Harper & Bros., 1943.

Wesolowski, Zdzislaw P. "The Polish Contributions to the Development of Scientific Management." *National Academy of Management Proceedings,* August 1978, pp. 12–16.

Wrege, Charles D. "The Efficient Management of Hospitals: Pioneer Work of Ernest Codman, Robert Dickinson, and Frank Gilbreth: 1910–1918." *National Academy of Management Proceedings,* August 1980, pp. 110–18.

Wrege, Charles D., Ronald G. Greenwood, Jacqueline Mundy, and William F. Muhs. "Hugo Munsterberg's Pioneer Studies of Managerial Decision Making." *National Academy of Management Proceedings,* August 1982, pp. 107–11.

Wrege, Charles D., Ronald G. Greenwood, and Matthew Major. "Copley's Reporting of Midvale in Taylor's Biography: A Case of Ignorance, Censorship and Plagiarism." Paper presented at the National Academy of Management Meetings, Anaheim, CA, August 7–10, 1988.

Wren, D. A. "Scientific Management in the U.S.S.R., with Particular Reference to the Contribution of Walter N. Polakov." *Academy of Management Review*, January 1980, pp. 1–11.

Wren, D. A. *The Evolution of Management Thought*, 3rd ed. New York: Ronald Press, 1987.

■ CASE: For a Few Dollars More

A national manufacturing firm recently received a number of large orders for industrial equipment. Realizing that it would be unable to fill the orders unless a dramatic increase in output could be achieved, the company instituted an incentive plan to supplement the current hourly wage. Under this new program, all increases in productivity would result in direct pay increases of similar magnitude. For example:

Old Hourly Wage	Productivity Increase	Productivity Bonus	New Hourly Wage
$8.00	10%	$ .80	$ 8.80
8.00	20	1.60	9.60
8.00	30	2.40	10.40
8.00	40	3.20	11.20
8.00	50	4.00	12.00

In addition, the company was willing to apply the same incentive scheme for Saturday work, which paid time and a half, and Sunday work, which paid double time. Top management indicated that it was shooting for a 40 percent increase in productivity across the board.

Within sixty days, however, it became evident to management that the plan was not working. On the average, productivity was up only 17 percent, and despite all management efforts to promote weekend work only 23 percent of the workers were willing to work on Saturday and 14 percent on Sunday.

In giving his opinion of the situation, one manager said, "What more do the workers want? Under this new pay scheme they can increase their pay way above what they would ordinarily earn. However, most of the workers I talked to say they're not interested in the extra money. One of them told me he spent the whole weekend working in his garden. Another took his kids fishing for two days. I just don't understand guys like that. They'd rather loaf than work. I guess the Protestant Ethic is dead."

One of the workers, however, gave a different reason for the unexpectedly low productivity increases: "Who cares about the extra money? I'm making more than enough now. What am I going to do with an extra $2,000? Better that I stay home and enjoy my family and watch television on Sunday. I'm not going to knock myself out for a few dollars more."

Questions

1. Why is the incentive scheme having so little effect?
2. How would Frederick Taylor interpret the results?
3. What suggestions would you make to management?

■ CASE: Technicians and Managers

A management consulting firm in New York City received a phone call from a local industrial machine manufacturer. The company's board of directors had just concluded its quarterly meeting and had decided that something had to be done to improve operations. For the sixth consecutive quarter, profits had declined. Sales were higher than ever, but costs were apparently out of control.

The consultants spent ten weeks examining the firm's operations. Everyone in the company was interviewed, from the chief executive officer to the janitor. When the team finished its analysis, it submitted a 212 page report to the board. One of its key findings follows:

> Since its inception, the company has had a policy of promoting from within. The prime criterion for these promotions appears to be technical competence. This is as true at the upper levels as at the lower ones. And it is not uncommon to find managers down on the machine floor examining and commenting on technical problems. Unfortunately, this leaves little time for managing. In fact, managerial functions such as planning, organizing and controlling are given almost no attention. What the company needs is an influx of outside management people who will place less attention on the technical side of the job and more on the management side.

Questions

1. How do these findings fit into Fayol's philosophy of management?
2. How common is it to find managers spending more time on the technical than on the managerial side of their job? Explain.
3. How can these problems be overcome?

■ CASE: The Firefighter

A fire broke out on the third floor of a machine shop on Long Island. According to the fire department, workers on the floor had apparently been throwing oily rags in the corner for three or four days. The maintenance crew had not picked up the rags. As a result, when someone flipped a lighted cigarette butt onto the rags, they immediately ignited.

As soon as the workers saw the blaze, most of them vacated the premises and gathered out in the parking lot. However, at least fifteen minutes passed before anyone turned in an alarm. This was done by Jaime Rodriguez, a new employee who was delivering some equipment to one of the work stations when he suddenly saw the blaze. Rodriguez pulled the fire alarm and then raced to the wall for a fire extinguisher. When the fire fighters arrived, they found Rodriguez vigorously fighting the blaze. Thanks to his assistance, the fire was quickly brought under control.

The first fire fighter on the scene told management: "Without that guy's quick thinking, you might have lost the whole building. He managed to confine the fire to one small area until we could get here and put it out." A thankful management gave Rodriguez a $10-a-week salary increase and a check for $500. Most of the workers, however, did not share management's point of view. Some of their remarks included:

"That guy Rodriguez is an idiot. He could have gotten his tail burned off. And for what? A crummy $500 and a piddly raise."

"My job around here is running a drill press. They don't pay me to fight fires or even to report them. It's not in my job description."

Six months later, Rodriguez quit the company. When asked why, he said: "I don't like working with these guys. Somehow we just don't get on."

Questions

1. Based on the information in this case, what conclusions can you draw about the norms and values of the workers? What is their code of expected behavior?

2. If you were told that there was a union in this shop, would that help explain the comments made by the workers? Would it be possible to draw any conclusions about worker–management relations? Explain.

3. Why do you think Rodriguez quit? Explain your opinion.

■ CASE: The Best in the World

In recent years overseas manufacturers have found the United States to be one of their primary markets. In every annual quarter, the American balance of payments has been negative as we have bought more from abroad than we have sold there. Will America become a marketplace for the world's goods while its own industries flounder? The answer is no. Unknown to most Americans, the United States competes very effectively in many international markets. One of the primary reasons for this success is that U. S. quality is beginning to increase dramatically, and there are some goods that America produces better than anyone else in the world. Here are a dozen such examples along with the manufacturer(s) of each:

Good	Manufacturer
Aluminum foil	Reynolds Aluminum
Ballpoint pens	A. T. Cross
Clothes dryers	Whirlpool
Dishwashers	General Electric
FM two-way radios	Motorola
Handbags	Coach Leatherware
Heating controls	Honeywell
Loaders and backhoes	Case IH
Minicomputers	Digital Equipment, Hewlett-Packard, IBM
Pianos	Steinway
Scotch S-VHS videotape	3M
Teflon	Du Pont

Overall, America dominates the world when it comes to agricultural equipment, aerospace products, computers, and pharmaceuticals. These goods are not only of high quality, they are durable and represent the height of innovation and technological development. Additionally, while some of these goods may be produced with parts provided by overseas suppliers, in every case at least half of the final product is made in America.

How has the United States managed to achieve all of this? Part of the answer is found in improved quality control. The cliche "do it right the first time" is becoming an operating philosophy in many American companies. A second reason is because enterprises are reorganizing their operations and eliminating bureaucratic red tape. A third is because American businesses are creating an environment in which employees can freely communicate with each other and work in harmonious fashion.

Questions

1. Are any of the ideas of the scientific managers being used by the firms in this case?

2. How are Fayol's concepts of value to American firms striving for high-quality output? Explain.

3. Are Chester Barnard's ideas of any value to the companies in this case? How?

Source: Some of the information in this case can be found in Christopher Knowlton, "What America Makes Best," *Fortune,* March 28, 1988, pp. 40–54.

■ SELF-FEEDBACK EXERCISE: Early Management in Perspective

Based on your reading of this chapter, you know a great deal about the history of management thought. See how well you can use this information to answer the following questions about other management history developments or conclusions.

T F **1.** Many of the basic ideas of Frederick Taylor are still in use today.

T F **2.** Frederick Taylor introduced an organizational approach that called for each worker to have a series of specialists who would provide expert assistance, and this concept (called functional foremanship) is still quite popular.

T F **3.** Frederick Taylor invented a golf putter that was so accurate that it is still used by some of the members of the Professional Golfers Association (PGA).

T F **4.** Frank Gilbreth was so devoted to reducing the time for completing projects that he used to lather his face using two brushes (one in each hand) and even tried shaving with both hands simultaneously.

T F **5.** In recent years Frank Gilbreth has emerged as a more important contributor to management thought than Frederick Taylor.

T F **6.** Henri Fayol's basic purpose in writing his book was to provide a framework for management scholars to use in developing principles of management textbooks.

T F **7.** Managers today rely very heavily on the use of formal management principles such as those espoused by Henri Fayol.

T F **8.** When Elton Mayo first started consulting in industry, he approached things more as a scientific manager than a psychologist or behavioralist.

T F **9.** In recent years the Hawthorne studies have been found to be much more scientific and analytical than was believed previously.

T F **10.** Many practicing managers feel that Chester Barnard's thinking is as relevant today as when he first wrote *The Functions of the Executive.*

Answers

1. True. Time-and-motion concepts are still important today.

2. False. Functional foremanship with its violation of the principle of unity of command proved too cumbersome and has been abandoned.

3. False. The putter was so accurate that the PGA outlawed it.

4. True. However, he eventually stopped shaving with both hands because he cut himself too often.

5. True.

6. False. It was not until years later that textbook writers began adopting Fayol's framework as a basis for principles of management texts.

7. False. Formal principles are regarded as too mechanistic and most managers modify them in practice.

8. True.

9. False. The studies have been further criticized as unscientific and biased.

10. True.

CHAPTER 3

Modern
Schools
of
Management
Thought

Since World War II, management research has been a very busy and productive field. The concepts of Taylor, Fayol, Mayo, and their associates have expanded as scholars have increased past knowledge about management. The result has been that, at least at the present time, management theory is in what can be called a schools phase, and any student who approaches the field without a basic understanding of these schools does so at a considerable disadvantage.

The schools represent viewpoints on what management is and how it should be studied. Obviously, not everyone in management can be placed in a particular school; some defy such simple categorization. Nevertheless, the background and training of management theorists and practitioners are reflected in their beliefs about management and, in most cases, make them candidates for one of the three schools of thought that will be examined in this chapter: the management process school, the quantitative school, and the behavioral school. The goal of this chapter is to examine each of these schools in depth. When you have finished this chapter, you should be able to:

1. State the basic beliefs and tenets of the management process school.

2. Identify the ideas to which advocates of the quantitative school subscribe.

3. Understand the philosophy and composition of the behavioral school.

4. Describe the weaknesses present in each of the three schools.

5. Discuss the possibility of synthesizing the three schools into a unified composite.

MANAGEMENT PROCESS SCHOOL

The *management process school*, which is sometimes called the classical school, traces its ancestry to Henri Fayol. Its primary approach is to specify the *management functions* such as: planning, organizing, commanding, coordinating, and controlling. Its proponents continue to view these functions as a process that is carried out by managers.

During the years immediately following World War II, the management process school flourished. The major reason for its acceptance can be traced to the outline it provides for the systematic study of management. A student who can identify management functions and then examine each in detail has a wealth of information about the field. Although modern management scientists (quantitative theorists) and behaviorists might take issue with this statement, some of the most prominent books in the field have been based on a process framework.

An Ongoing Framework

The process approach provides a skeletal design.

A major tenet of the process school is that the analysis of management along functional lines allows the construction of a framework into which all new management concepts can be placed. For example, a skeletal design of planning, organizing, and controlling emerges. Any new mathematical or behavioral technique that can improve managerial performance will fall into one of these three functional areas. The result is an enduring systematic design. Although this concept is now under attack, there is little doubt that the framework provided by the management process school has been the major reason for its acceptance by both students and practitioners. As Carroll and Gillen have noted:

> The classical functions still represent the most useful way of conceptualizing the manager's job, especially for management education, and perhaps this is why it is still the most favored description of managerial work in current management textbooks. The classical functions provide clear and discrete methods of classifying the thousands of different activities that managers carry out and the techniques they use in terms of the functions they perform for the achievement of organizational goals.[1]

[1]Stephen J. Carroll and Dennis J. Gillen, "Are the Classical Management Functions Useful in Describing Managerial Work?" *Academy of Management Review*, January 1987, p. 48.

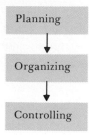

FIGURE 3-1   Noninterrelated Management Functions

Management as a Process

Management is viewed as an interrelated functional process.

Management process proponents see the manager's job as a process of interrelated functions. Consider, for example, the case of planning, organizing, and controlling. Figure 3-1 does not represent management as a process because the functions follow in sequential order; only an indirect relationship exists between planning and controlling. Everything seems to be rigidly predetermined. Figure 3-2 more accurately represents the process concept of management as consisting of interrelated functions that are neither totally random nor rigidly predetermined. They are, instead, dynamic functions, each one playing an integral role in a larger picture in which all the functions are integrated. The total is thus greater than the sum of its parts.

Management Principles

Another belief of process school advocates is that *principles of management* can be derived from an intellectual analysis of the managerial functions. Principles of each of the functions can therefore be extracted by dividing the manager's job into its components. For example, there is the *primacy of planning principle,* which states that planning precedes all other managerial functions. Managers must plan before they can organize and control. Under the organizing principle called *absoluteness of responsibility,* a manager cannot escape responsibility for the activities of individual subordinates. The

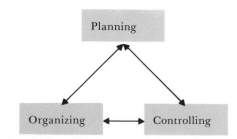

FIGURE 3-2   Interrelated Management Functions

manager can delegate authority but not responsibility. If something goes wrong in delegated work, the subordinate has made the error and may be responsible for whatever penalties the manager exacts; but the error is, overall, the responsibility of the manager. The *exception principle*, a principle of control, holds that managers should concern themselves with exceptional cases, not routine results. Under this principle, significant deviations, such as very good or very bad profit performance, merit the manager's time far more than average or expected results.

The process principles are designed to improve organizational efficiency. They must not, however, be looked upon as rules, since a rule is supposed to be inflexible. For example, a sign that says "No Smoking" is a rule: It demands a certain kind of action and allows no deviations. Conversely, a principle, as used here, is merely a useful guideline that does not require rigid adherence. Advocates of the management process school, therefore, view principles simply as general guidelines that must be constant focal points for research. If a particular principle proves invalid or useless, it should be discarded. But it must not be assumed that a principle will be useful at all times or under all conditions or that a violation constitutes invalidation. Since management is an art as well as a science, the manager remains the final arbiter in choosing and applying principles.

Universality of Management Functions

Advocates believe that the management process is universal.

Process school advocates also believe that basic management functions are performed by all managers, regardless of enterprise, activity, or hierarchical level. The manager of a manufacturing plant, the administrator of a hospital, and the local chief of police all carry out the same managerial functions. This is also true for their subordinate managers all the way down the hierarchy, although the percentage of time devoted to each function will, of course, vary according to the level. For example, again using planning, organizing, and controlling as illustrations, low-level managers, who are concerned with detailed and routine types of work, tend to do a great amount of controlling and less planning and organizing. However, as one progresses up the organizational chain, the work requires more creativity and administrative ability, resulting in an increase in the amount of time needed for planning and a decrease in that required for controlling. Figure 3-3 shows these proportional relationships.

A Philosophy of Management

A philosophy of management can be developed.

The process school also stresses the development of a management philosophy. This requires answering such questions as: Precisely what does a manager do? What kinds of values are important to management? What values are important to workers? The development of a management philosophy results in helping the manager understand and establish relationships between material things and human beings. Process school advocates

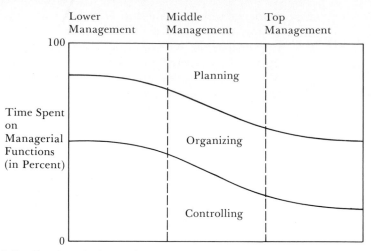

FIGURE 3-3   Functions Performed by Managers at Different Hierarchichal Levels

believe that managers can accomplish this feat more easily by following the management process theories, because then their activities revolve around certain functions. In carrying them out, managers employ the fundamental beliefs and attitudes to which they subscribe. The result is a modus operandi that links the management process with the fundamental ideals, basic concepts, and essential beliefs of the manager. The outcome is a philosophy that helps the manager win the support of subordinates in achieving organizational objectives. It also provides the groundwork for future action. Intrapreneurship in Action shows how a management philosophy can help firms increase their success in new ventures.

The process school has many advantages, the major one undoubtedly being the framework it offers for analyzing the field. Although viewed by many of its critics as simplistic and too static to be useful, it has been better received by practitioners and students than any of the other schools of management thought.

QUANTITATIVE SCHOOL

The *quantitative school,* which is also called the management science school, consists of those theorists who see management as a body of quantitative tools and methodologies designed to aid today's manager in making the complex decisions related to operations and production. Proponents of this school are concerned with decision making and, to a large degree, are modern-day adherents of Taylor's scientific management movement. They give a great deal of their attention to defining objectives and the problems that surround their achievement. This type of orderly, logical methodology is helpful in constructing problem-solving models. As will be seen later in the

INTRAPRENEURSHIP
IN
ACTION:
Creating
the
Right
Environment

Intrapreneurship has often been defined as "entrepreneurial activity within the firm itself." Companies that are teaching their people to think and act like in-house entrepreneurs are finding the idea highly profitable. This is particularly true in the consumer goods area where firms like Colgate, General Foods, and Scott Paper have been very successful with their intrapreneurial approaches. Here are a few examples.

Colgate-Palmolive has formed a company called Colgate Venture to provide assistance to in-house people with ideas for new products. This has led to entirely new product categories such as Fresh Feliners, a diaperlike pad for litter boxes, Teen Clean, a denture cleanser directed to the teenage market, and a mail-order catalog of educational toys and other products for kids. These new products, hopefully, will help ensure that Colgate remains market responsive.

General Foods has taken the intrapreneurial approach by creating a new unit to help develop refrigerated take-out food. A final example is Scott Paper which has set up a new venture group to sell products to the handyman, grease monkey, or home remodeler.

When companies establish these venture groups, they allow the participants to run the venture just as if it were their own company. The members of the small group champion the products, seek financing from the firm, conduct the market analysis, design the goods, and set up the distribution plan.

Many firms are finding that the first few products often do not work out well because the intrapreneurial group is still too inexperienced and sometimes promotes products that are initially well received but then fall flat. On the other hand, the companies are also coming to realize that these intrapreneurial groups are one of their best hopes for developing new product lines without having to go through the typical in-house bureaucratic process. As they begin to pay off, more firms are likely to follow suit.

Source: Ronald Alsop, "Consumer-Product Giants Relying on 'Intrapreneurs' in New Ventures," *Wall Street Journal,* April 23, 1988, p. 35.

book, the approach has been effective in dealing with inventory, materials, and production control problems.

In the post-World War II era, many management scientists came onto the business scene. Today, they go by various and sundry titles, from management analysts to operations researchers to systems analysts. However, they share a number of common characteristics: (1) the application of scientific analysis to managerial problems, (2) the goal of improving the manager's decision-making ability, (3) a high regard for economic effectiveness criteria, (4) a reliance on mathematical models, and (5) the utilization of electronic computers. For purposes of this discussion, all individuals meeting these criteria are collectively placed in the quantitative school. Two topics that have been of major interest to these people are optimization and suboptimization.

Management scientists share some common characteristics.

Optimization and Suboptimization

It is general managerial truth that most people do not maximize their goals. Instead, they satisfy them: For example, managers do not usually try to make all possible profit; they try instead to achieve a satisfactory level. However, it is possible sometimes, through the *optimization* of production (that is, the combining of all the resources in the right balance), to maximize profit. Maximization is a very difficult task, and to attain it, an approach called suboptimization is often used. *Suboptimization* means using less than the total of each input in order to maximize the total output, or profit. For example, consider a production setting in which materials are ordered, processed, and finished. A firm would try to suboptimize each of the three functions by using only the amount of each that would result in the greatest profit from each component. George R. Terry explains the process of achieving maximization through optimization and suboptimization in this way:

> Suppose our objective is to maximize production profits. To achieve this we consider the common portions of most enterprises to be (1) input, (2) process, and (3) output. Also, we optimize production, assuming all we can produce will be sold at a satisfactory market price. Since the totality—production—is to be optimized, its components of input, process, and output are optimized, as each relates to the totality. Common parlance for this is to suboptimize the components. Step No. 1: Input, or raw materials being received, are suboptimized. This will depend upon forecast demand, inventory carrying cost, and order processing cost. Likewise, Step No. 2: Process, or materials processed, are suboptimized by adequate consideration to production capacity, machine setup cost, and processing cost for each product. Last, Step No. 3: Suboptimization of output or products finished is obtained by considering product demand and transportation cost.[2]

Each step in the production process (ordering, processing, and finishing goods) is affected by suboptimization factors, as Figure 3-4 shows. The firm does not purchase all the raw materials it can; nor does it process or ship the total possible amount. Instead, it finds a balance that results in the ideal production level and the maximization of profit.

Mathematical Models

Problem solving via mathematical models is widely employed.

Optimization of resources is often achieved with the use of a mathematical model. The model can be a single equation or a series of equations, depending on the number of factors involved and the complexity of the situation. In the construction of these models, management scientists have found calculus to be one of the most useful branches of mathematics because

---

[2]George R. Terry, *Principles of Management,* 7th ed. (Homewood, IL: Richard D. Irwin, 1977), p. 30.

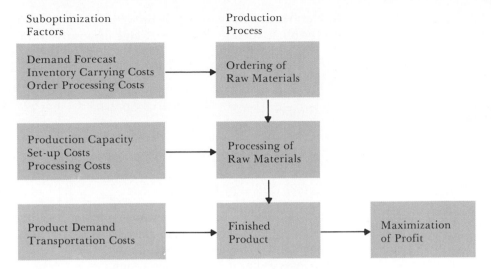

FIGURE 3-4   Optimization of Production and Maximization of Profit

it allows them to measure the rate of change in a dependent variable in relation to changes in an independent variable. For example, if a company increases the size of its plant and cost per unit declines, its management may want to learn the extent to which the production facilities can be expanded before the cost per unit will begin to increase. If the firm has a mathematical model constructed for this purpose, it merely has to determine at what point the cost per unit change moves from negative to either zero or positive, for at this point costs stop decreasing.

The same basic concept can also be used by many kinds of managers. For example, suppose an appliance store manager wants to know how many different product lines to carry. Assume that the individual then formulates the following mathematical equation:

$$Y = 16X - X^2$$

where Y = Maximum profit
X = Number of product lines carried

The equation states that maximum profit is equal to sixteen times the number of product lines ($16X$) minus the number of product lines squared ($-X^2$). By increasing the value of X, the manager can attain the respective values of Y. For example:

when $X = 0$
$Y = 16 \times 0 - 0^2$
$Y = 0;$
when $X = 1$
$Y = 16 \times 1 - 1^2$
$Y = 15.$

By constructing the entire table up to the point where Y again equals zero, it is possible to identify the entire range of positive profit values:

X (Product Lines)	0	1	2	3	4	5	6	7	8	9	10	11	12	13	14	15	16
Y (Profit)	0	15	28	39	48	55	60	63	64	63	60	55	48	39	28	15	0

Thus, the number of product lines that should be carried is eight, which will result in a maximization of profit.

Overview and Contributions

Although highly simplified, the above mathematical model is representative of the ones employed by management scientists. In fact, it is common to find adherents of this school relying strongly on such mathematical tools and techniques as linear programming, simulation, Monte Carlo theory, queuing theory, and game theory, topics that will be covered in Chapter 9. The quantitative school has gained many supporters in recent years. The increasing use of computers, accompanied by the development of more sophisticated mathematical models for solving business problems, accounts for many of the advances made by this school. In addition, the quantitative school has played an important role in the development of management thought by encouraging people to approach problem solving in an orderly fashion, looking more carefully at problem inputs and relationships. Figure 3-5 shows the ways in which this is accomplished. This school has also made clear the need for goal formulation and the measurement of performance.

BEHAVIORAL SCHOOL

The *behavioral school* grew out of the efforts of people who recognized the importance of the individual in the workplace and those who were interested in group processes. Today, it is common to find individuals in this school with training in the social sciences, including psychology, sociology, anthro-

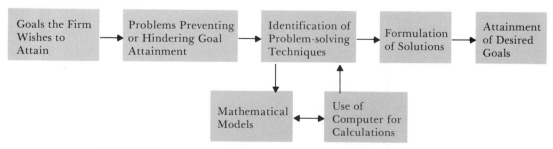

FIGURE 3-5   Problem Solving via a Quantitative Approach

pology, social psychology, and industrial psychology, applying their skills to business problems.

As one would expect, behavioral school proponents are largely concerned with human behavior. They contend that because management entails getting things done through people, the effective manager must understand the importance of such factors as needs, drives, motivation, leadership, personality, behavior, work groups, and the management of change; for all these are going to have a direct effect on the manager's ability to manage. All members of the behavioral school share this philosophy, but some emphasize the individual and others the group. The behavioral school, therefore, consists of two branches: the interpersonal behavior branch and the group behavior branch.

Interpersonal Behavior

Some behaviorists are interested in interpersonal relations and are oriented toward individual and social psychology. They belong to the *interpersonal behavior branch* of the behavior school.

Some focus primarily on individual behavior.

The writers and scholars in this school are heavily oriented to individual psychology, and, indeed, most are trained as psychologists. Their focus is on the individual, and his or her motivations as a sociopsychological being. In this school are those who appear to emphasize human relations as an art that managers, even when foolishly trying to be amateur psychiatrists, can understand and practice. There are those who see the manager as a leader and may even equate managership and leadership—thus, in effect, treating all "led" activities as "managed." Others have concentrated on motivation or leadership and have cast important light on these subjects, which has been useful to managers.[3]

Members of this branch believe that the individual, not just the work group, must be understood if the manager is to do an effective job.

Group Behavior

The other branch of the behavioral school, often confused with its interpersonal behavior cousins, consists of individuals who see management as a social system, or collection of cultural interrelationships. Known collectively as the *group behavior branch*, they are highly sociological in nature, viewing human organizations as systems of interdependent groups, primary and secondary alike:

Others are highly sociological in their approach.

---

[3]Harold Koontz, "The Management Theory Jungle Revisited," *Academy of Management Review,* April 1980, pp. 177–78.

This approach varies all the way from the study of small groups, with their cultural and behavioral patterns, to the behavioral characteristics of large groups. It is often called a study of "organization behavior" and the term "organization" may be taken to mean the system, or pattern, of any set of group relationships in a company, a government agency, a hospital, or any other kind of undertaking.[4]

Advocates of the group behavior branch see the manager as an individual who must interact and deal with groups. For this reason, they place great emphasis on the need to understand both the formal and the informal organization. International Business in Action illustrates how a knowledge of group behavior has been helping American firms in overseas markets.

Overview and Contributions

Although the interpersonal behavior branch stresses the importance of understanding the individual (psychology) and the group behavior branch places prime importance on the knowledge of group behavior (sociology), the two are actually interdependent. The group is made up of individuals, but the whole is actually greater than the sum of its parts. Both psychology and sociology are important to the behaviorists, regardless of the priorities assigned to each area in any given project.

Although the behavioral school lacks the type of framework used by management process advocates, it certainly does not lack structure. For example, communication, motivation, and leadership, a few of the school's basic concerns, are areas of major analysis. However, instead of working from functions to activities and principles, as do the management process advocates, the behaviorists work in the opposite direction; they start with human behavior research and build up to topics or functions. Thus, theirs is a much less rigid and more empirically based school of thought. Two prominent researchers in the field, Max S. Wortman and Fred Luthans, have enumerated several major contributions made by these behaviorists:

Behaviorists are highly empirical in their approach.

> (1) **conceptual,** the formulation of concepts and explanations about individual and group behavior in the organization; (2) **methodological,** the empirical testing of these concepts in many different experimental and field settings; and (3) **operations,** the establishment of actual managerial policies and decisions based on these conceptual and methodological frameworks. Since behavioral approaches have become widely disseminated throughout the management literature, there has been an increasing acceptance of the behavioral approach by management.[5]

---

[4]Ibid., p. 178.

[5]Max S. Wortman, Jr., and Fred Luthans, eds., *Emerging Concepts in Management* (New York: Macmillan, 1975), p. 190.

INTERNATIONAL

BUSINESS

IN

ACTION:

Storming

Foreign

Markets

Americans really do not know much about foreign business and are not very successful in doing business there, right? Wrong. A new breed of highly aggressive American firms is currently storming foreign markets and the trade walls are beginning to crumble. Moreover, a recent survey by McKinsey & Company reports that over two-thirds of midsize firms doing business overseas expect their international sales to jump 15 to 20 percent annually over the next five years.

These international firms take many different management approaches. For example, the Mead Corporation has set up a direct export program designed specifically with the needs of the overseas buyer in mind. The firm signed a marketing agreement with the Seibu Saison Group, a privately held retailer in Japan, to provide them with $20 billion of goods. This allows Mead to circumvent the expensive Japanese distribution system and sell directly to the retailer, thus ensuring profits for all parties involved including savings for the customer.

Not all firms are large manufacturers. Thorneburg Hosiery, a $10 million company in North Carolina, produces a line of athletic socks that are designed and padded for specific sports such as tennis and jogging. Showing its wares at an overseas trade show, the company president was pleasantly surprised to find five Japanese distributors competing for the right to represent the product. Result: the company will sell $1 million of its socks in Japan alone.

Or consider Guild Wineries & Distilleries of Woodbridge which has been selling medium-priced table wines in Denmark. Wine in Europe is fairly inexpensive because of the oversupply. However, Guild's secret is in the packaging. Its wines are placed in plastic-lined cardboard containers that look like milk containers. These packages lower the shipping costs, make the wine easier to pour, and have a long shelf life.

Another success has been reported by Tidy Car of Boca Raton, Florida. The firm sells cleaning and auto-polishing equipment for those who want to keep their car looking new. Realizing that there is a strong international demand for this product, the owner of the firm began licensing the product in Europe. Today there are 80 Tidy Car Total Appearance Centers in the Scandanavian countries and 50 more are planned for Belgium, the Netherlands, and Luxembourg. Japan and West Germany are next on the list.

Source: Christopher Knowlton, "The New Export Entrepreneurs," *Fortune*, June 6, 1988, pp. 87–102.

TOWARD A UNIFIED THEORY?

Is there really a legitimate basis for these three schools of management thought, or should a synthesis be immediately undertaken? Many writers in the field believe a coalescence of differing viewpoints can be achieved, but one of the key obstacles, in their view, is that of semantics. Everyone may say the same thing, but the use of different words can make it seem that the

There is still much disagreement.

subjects are also different. One group of authors believes that "as is so often true when intelligent men differ in their interpretations of problems, some of the trouble lies in key words."[6]

Another major barrier is identified as differing definitions of management. If the field were clearly defined in terms of fairly specific content, differences among the various schools of management might be reduced to the point where synthesis would be possible. Although the idea sounds plausible, chances for its implementation are not good at present.[7] One of the reasons is the current lack of research:

> The choice of a school or writer to follow presents a serious dilemma . . . "I don't know" remains the appropriate answer. When sufficient research has been compiled, the schools will fade of their own accord. That they have not faded is good evidence that the quantity of research to date is insufficient to render judgment.. . . No amount of argument between conflicting schools . . . is likely to achieve either consensus or truth.[8]

Advocates of each of the three schools believe strongly in their own point of view and resist attempts at theory synthesis or integration. Unlike the process school theorists, who have been vigorous in their attempts to bring the quantitative and behavioral people into their domain, the latter groups consider that their own contribution to management as too significant to be relegated to the kind of secondary position being advocated for them by the process people. Nor are they necessarily wrong, for each of the three schools has its weaknesses as well as its strengths, and currently, none of them possesses the characteristics necessary for a successful and meaningful integration of management theory.

At present, a great deal of management research is in progress. However, this research is splintered: The focus of each effort is toward a specific topic or issue—for example, leadership styles in nonprofit organizations, strategic planning in a high technology industry, or testing of a motivation theory to see if earlier findings can be replicated. Little interest in trying to blend all available management information into an overall theory currently exists. Management scholars and practitioners seem content to go their own ways, investigating pieces of the giant management theory puzzle. For this reason, the schools of thought discussed here continue to remain valid points of departure in the study of modern management.

---

[6]Harold Koontz and Cyril O'Donnell, *Management: A System and Contingency Analysis of Managerial Functions* (New York: McGraw-Hill, 1976), p. 66.

[7]W. Jack Duncan, "Transferring Management Theory to Practice," *Academy of Management Journal,* December 1974, pp. 724–38.

[8]John B. Miner, *Management Theory* (New York: Macmillan, 1971), p. 150.

THE WEAKNESSES OF THE SCHOOLS

All three schools have weaknesses. The following examines some of the shortcomings of each.

Process School Weaknesses

A static approach?

One of the foremost arguments against the process school is that it pays only lip service to the human element, regarding management as a static and dehumanized process. Although process advocates argue that this is not the case at all, behaviorists in particular remain unswayed.

Are management principles universally applicable?

Many also attack the school's foundation, claiming that management principles are not universally applicable. Such critics see the principles as most appropriate in stable production-line situations where unions are not very strong or where unemployment is high. When used in professional organizations, the principles often require modification, their application being contingent upon the specific situation. This is why Fayol and his associates, who operated under stable production-line situations, were able to use them effectively, whereas modern managers, operating under dynamic conditions, have trouble doing so.[9] In addition, principle proponents tend to formulate generalizations as principles even though they have not been empirically validated.

Is the management process universal?

A third argument, along the same lines, questions the universality of the management process. Do all managers perform the same basic functions? There is considerable controversy on this point. Research has revealed that although similarities exist among various positions within firms, the same is not true among firms. When professional organizations (law firms, research and development laboratories, architectural firms, hospitals, universities) and administrative organizations (manufacturing companies, retailing firms, insurance agencies, transportation companies) are compared, the latter tend to be more bureaucratic, emphasizing rules, policies, procedures, and hierarchical authority.[10] Conversely, in professional organizations, power and authority tend to shift from the managerial jobs to those of the nonmanaging professions.[11] For example, doctors in hospitals sometimes have as much

---

[9]Ibid., pp. 139–40.

[10]As used here, "professional organizations" are those which: (a) are recognized by society as having professional status, (b) are encouraged and influenced by a professional association or society, and (c) have a set of specialized techniques supported by a body of theory. For further information on this point, see John B. Miner, *The Management Process: Theory, Research and Practice,* 2nd ed. (New York: Macmillan, 1978), p. 324.

[11]See Richard H. Hall, "Some Organizational Considerations in the Professional-Organizational Relationship," *Administrative Science Quarterly,* December 1967, pp. 461–78; and Gerald D. Bell, "Predictability of Work Demands and Professionalization as Determinants of Workers' Discretion," *Academy of Management Journal,* March 1966, pp. 20–28.

INTERVIEW WITH JANE DUCOMB

Jane DuComb is president of Jane J. DuComb, Inc. of Phoenix, Arizona. Jane is in the travel business and her agency does approximately $2 million of business a year. About 70 percent of this business is air travel; the remainder comes from cruises, tours, and related travel arrangements. During the last eight years, Jane's business has grown dramatically and the future promises to be more of the past.

Q. *What is the most important part of your business? What determines whether you are going to be successful or fail?*

A. This is a people business. None of my clients have to buy their tickets or make their reservations through me. They can use another travel agent or call the airlines and buy the ticket over the phone. Personal relationships and service are the most important factors for success. If I can give people fast, efficient service, they're likely to come back to me. For example, when we book someone roundtrip from Phoenix to London with a change of planes at Kennedy International, we give the person all of the information he or she needs: the departure and arrival times, seating assignments, the confirmation number for the rental car, the name and address of the hotel where the individual will be staying, etc. I want my customer to know that we've taken care of all the travel-related items. In this business, the best way to distinguish your agency is on the basis of service.

Q. *How important is the computer to your work?*

freedom to make decisions as do top administrators. Nurses often have more freedom of action or discretion in carrying out their tasks than do certain middle managers.

Results such as these have led John Miner, a leading management researcher, to conclude that "when decision-making authority is dispersed . . . some very sizeable changes in managerial functions must occur, relative to administrative organizations."[12] He continues by noting that "analysis of professional versus administrative organizations once again leads to the conclusion that managerial functions are not universal. Not only do managerial jobs differ in their mix of functions depending on their level and the particular department involved, but they also differ from organization to

[12]Miner, p. 88.

A. We can't exist without it. Everything in this business is computerized. If I want to quote fares from Phoenix to anywhere in the world, I need a computer to provide me with this information and to show me the various routes that the individual can take. For example, if someone wants to go to from here to Montreal, I need to know the departure times on the date the person is leaving and whether the person will have to change planes. The old days of looking all of this up in a book and writing the tickets by hand are gone. Computerization is the only way to operate a multimillion-dollar travel business.

Q. *In this chapter the discussion focuses on behavioral and quantitative sides of management. You obviously need both in your business. But what about the general management side. Do you have to do any planning or can you depend on call-in and repeat business?*

A. I have to plan, and there are two parts to this activity. First, in the case of things like tours, I have to figure out those trips that people might enjoy taking and put together the package. Then I have to go out and sell the tour. This takes a lot of time and effort because there are so many facets to the operation. Additionally, I have to go along to ensure that everything goes well. I can't sell a tour and then wave goodbye to everyone at the airport. They expect me to come along and provide them with assistance throughout the trip. I might have someone on the other end who is going to take us on a tour of Great Wall of China, but I have to be there to coordinate the tour with that individual. There's a great deal of planning involved in running these tours. Second, planning is required in running the internal operations of the business. I have to plan monthly expenses and cash flows as well as decide how to organize the office. Assignment of duties and periodic reorganization of the work is critical to the overall success of the operation. Business does not run itself. It requires effective management!

organization. This interorganizational difference is particularly noticeable when administrative and professional types are compared."[13]

Quantitative School Weaknesses

Is it a tool or a school?

The quantitative school is attacked on the ground that it fails to see the complete picture. Is management a system of mathematical models and processes, or is this too narrow a view? Critics opt for the latter, calling management science a tool, not a school. They note that mathematics is used in physics, engineering, chemistry, and medicine, but it has never emerged as a separate school in these disciplines. Why should it do so in the field of

---

[13]Ibid., p. 93.

management? There is no doubt that the management sciences have supplied very useful tools for the manager to employ in solving complex problems. Inventory, material, and production control have all been eased by these quantitative contributors. However, what about human behavior? How does one write an equation that solves people problems? Both the process and behavioral schools attack the quantitative theorists on this point, and the latter appear hard pressed to refute the argument.

Behavioral School Weaknesses

The major argument lodged against the behaviorists is that they, like the management science people, do not see the complete picture. Psychology, sociology, and related areas are all important in the study of management, but there is more to the field than just human behavior. Some forms of technical knowledge are also needed. The process school provides an important structural framework within which to study human behavior. The quantitative school offers an objective, quantifiable approach to decision making. Without these supplemental elements, managers cannot adequately apply their knowledge of behavior.

Is there failure to see the complete picture?

To be an effective manager, one must have more than a mere working knowledge of the human, dynamic model. True, the people in the workplace constitute a continually changing social system, but managers must supplement their ideas about their own and workers' rational behavior by a full understanding of the prevalence of nonrationality in human beings. Critics argue that the behavioral school is only one segment, albeit an important one, of the total picture, and that in and of itself it is incomplete.

A CONCEPTUAL FRAMEWORK

As noted earlier, there is a need for further research if the three schools are ever to be synthesized. In addition, it should be realized that there are some who oppose any such action, contending that fundamental and inescapable differences among the various schools make a unified theory of management impossible.

Whether the three schools will ever come together is a matter of current debate. However, the student of management is well advised to travel all three roads—process, quantitative, and behavioral—for each makes important contributions to the study of management. In the process, important ideas such as systems management and contingency management will be interwoven into the discussion, showing that there is a good deal of common interest between the three.

■ SUMMARY

Modern management theory is currently in the schools phase. Three schools of management thought are the management process, the quantitative, and the behavioral schools.

The management process, or classical, school traces its ancestry to Fayol. One of its major tenets is that by analyzing management along functional lines, a framework can be constructed into which all new management concepts can be placed. This framework consists of a process of interrelated functions such as planning, organizing, and controlling. Another belief of the process school is that management principles can be derived through an analysis of managerial functions. A third tenet is that the basic management functions are performed by all managers, regardless of enterprise, activity, or hierarchical level. Additionally, the process school stresses the development of a management philosophy.

The quantitative, or management science, school consists of theorists who see management as a system of mathematical models and processes. Relying heavily on the application of scientific analysis to managerial problems, economic effectiveness criteria, and the use of computers, adherents of this school have promoted understanding of the need for goal formulation and the measurement of performance.

The behavioral school consists of two branches: interpersonal behavior and group behavior. The former is heavily psychological in orientation; the latter is heavily sociological. While this school lacks the type of framework used by management process advocates, it does not lack structure. However, there is a major difference in method. Instead of working from functions to activities and principles, as the management process advocates do, the behaviorists work in the opposite direction. They start with human behavior research and build up to topics or functions.

Today there is no unified theory of management. Several reasons can be cited, among them semantics, differing definitions of management, and lack of research. Advocates of each school claim that the others have serious flaws. The process school is seen as being too static; the quantitative school is seen as a series of useful tools but not a school; the behaviorists are attacked as failing to see the total picture.

It is still unclear whether the three schools will ever be synthesized. For this reason, the student of management is well advised to understand all three.

■ REVIEW AND STUDY QUESTIONS

1. What are the basic beliefs of management process school advocates?
2. How important are management principles to process school advocates?
3. Precisely what is meant by the term *universality of management functions?*
4. What background or training do management scientists have?
5. What is meant by the term *optimization? Suboptimization?*
6. What are some of the contributions made to management theory by the management scientists?

7. Identify and describe the two major branches of the behavioral school.

8. What contributions have the behaviorists made to management?

9. In your own words, what are the primary weaknesses of the process school? The quantitative school? The behavioral school?

10. Will the three schools of management ever be merged or synthesized? Give your reasoning as the main part of your answer.

■ SELECTED REFERENCES

Aggarwal, Sumer C. "Manager, Manage Thyself!" *Business Horizons*, January –February 1983, pp. 25–30.

Albers, H. H. *Principles of Management: A Modern Approach*, 4th ed. New York: Wiley, 1974.

Fayol, Henri. *General and Industrial Management*. Translated by Constance Starrs. London: Sir Isaac Pitman & Sons, 1949.

Gannon, Martin J. "Managerial Ignorance." *Business Horizons*, May–June 1983, pp. 26–32.

Gordon, P. J. "Management Territory: By Their Buzz Words Shall Ye Know Them." *Business Horizons*, February 1979, pp. 57–59.

Koontz, Harold, ed. *Toward a Unified Theory of Management*. New York: McGraw-Hill, 1964.

Koontz, Harold. "The Management Theory Jungle." *Academy of Management Journal*, December 1961, pp. 174–88.

Koontz, Harold. "The Management Theory Jungle Revisited." *Academy of Management Review*, April 1980, pp. 175–87.

Koontz, Harold, Cyril O'Donnell, and Heinz Weihrich. *Management*, 7th ed. New York: McGraw-Hill, 1980.

McGuire, Joseph W. "Management Theory: Retreat to the Academy." *Business Horizons*, July–August 1982, pp. 31–37.

Miner, J. B. *Management Theory*. New York: Macmillan, 1971.

Miner, J. B. *The Management Process: Theory, Research, and Practice*, 2nd ed. New York: Macmillan, 1978.

Strinivasan, A. V. "University of Management Principles: An Indian Version." Paper presented at the National Academy of Management Meetings, Chicago, IL, August 13–16, 1986.

Woolf, D. A. "The Management Theory Jungle Revisited." *Advanced Management Journal*, October 1965, pp. 6–15.

Wortman, M. S., Jr., and Fred Luthans, eds. *Emerging Concepts in Management*, 2nd ed. New York: Macmillan, 1975.

■ CASE: The Manager's Job

In gathering data for a term paper on the functions of the manager, Sam Crocker, a junior at a large eastern business school, decided to interview five executives from different organizations. He asked the same question of each: "In your view, what are the functions of a manager?" Some of the executives explained their answers at great length; others merely listed managerial functions.

At the end of each interview Crocker would review the executive's comments, telling how he was going to summarize the answers. All agreed with his summations. The result of the five interviews follows:

Functions	Manager 1	Manager 2	Manager 3	Manager 4	Manager 5
Planning	X	X	X	X	X
Organizing	X	X	X	X	X
Staffing			X		
Communicating		X			
Coordinating	X				
Motivating	X			X	
Directing			X		
Controlling	X	X	X	X	X

Questions

1. How do you account for the apparent discrepancies in the replies of the managers? Explain.

2. If you were told that one of the managers was from an insurance company and the others were from manufacturing firms, which of the managers would you identify as an insurance manager? Give your reasoning.

3. If you were told that one of the five managers was a hospital administrator, which would you expect to be the administrator? Give your reasoning.

■ CASE: The Advertising Budget

The importance of advertising was always something that Jay Hallen, owner of a retail store, wondered about. In 1984 his store had an advertising budget of over $90,000, an increase of 17 percent from the previous year, but Hallen was really not sure how much of this money was being wisely spent. Nevertheless, he knew advertising was important, so he followed a simple guideline, spending 6 percent of estimated sales for advertising.

In mid-1989 Hallen received an announcement about a one-week management seminar being sponsored by a local university. Realizing that he had some middle-level managers who could profit from this training, he sent two of his up-and-coming people. When they returned, he learned that one of the speakers was a university professor who had talked about the need for constructing mathematical models for decision-making purposes. One of the professor's major points was that many companies spend more money on advertising than they should. Unaware of where to draw the line, they spend more and more each year. In fact, the speaker noted, a large percentage of firms tend to tie advertising to their sales forecast. If they estimate sales at $1 million, they spend $100,000; if they project sales at $2 million, they spend $200,000. "Actually," said the professor, "this is a very simple, and generally erroneous, approach. The only way to really ascertain how much to spend on advertising is to measure previous expenditures and results."

Hallen liked the basic idea, so he called the university and asked the professor to consider undertaking a consulting assignment. The professor agreed and for the next week examined the company's past sales figures and advertising expenditures and conducted some computer analysis. At the end of that time the professor concluded that advertising effectiveness could be determined with the following formula:

$$Y = 10X - X^2 + \$50,000$$

$$\text{where } Y = \text{Total sales}$$
$$X = \text{Total advertising expenditures}/\$10,000$$

Questions

1. Using just the above formula, how much sales income will the store obtain with advertising expenditures (per $10,000) from $10,000 to $110,000?

2. Based on the above answers, how much advertising should this company do? Explain.

3. How useful are management scientists in the field of management? Explain.

■ CASE: A State of Confusion

"Bill," said Anita Tuner, training director at Willowby Insurance, "how would you like to attend a training session in New York City this coming week?"

"What's it going to be about?" Bill Jarvis asked.

"Since when have you gotten so particular? Usually, when the company intends to send a few people to a training session, you jump at it. I can remember that winter you talked me into sending you to Miami Beach. You were sure interested in going to seminars then," responded Tuner.

"Yeah, but that was when I only had a little work to do. Now I've got work piled up on my desk and I don't want to go running off to just any old training session."

Tuner spoke rather firmly as she said, "I wouldn't ask you to go to just any training session. Besides you know that I'm only asking you to repay a favor. Do you want to go or not?"

"Tell me what it's going to be about," Jarvis insisted.

"It's called 'Understanding Today's Worker,'" replied Tuner.

Jarvis answered, "Yeah, well, thanks, but I'm not interested." When asked why not, he said, "Because that last time you sent me to one of those behavioral seminars, I came away more confused than before. Look, a lot of research being conducted in the behavioral sciences is great research, but it has no real applicability. I mean, there is just no way to take it back to the job and use it."

Tuner was skeptical. "You mean those people never tell you how you can apply it?"

"Oh no, they do that. The problem is the way they explain it and the way it really works are two different things. The truth is, I really think I'm a lot better off just doing things my own way and not messing around with these new behavioral theories. They just leave me all confused."

Questions

1. Have the behaviorists really made any contribution to management? Explain.

2. How important is it to understand today's worker?

3. What does Jarvis mean by his statement that behavioral seminars have him confused? Explain.

■ CASE: Off and Running

When a good company is small, it will often grow very quickly. As the firm becomes larger, growth typically slows up. However, not every large firm finds it difficult to grow. Consider some of the fastest growing corporations:

Company	Principal Business	1983 Sales ($ millions)	1987 Sales ($ millions)	Average Growth Rate per Year 1983–1987
Reebok International	Shoe wholesaling	$ 13	$1,389	155%
Sun Microsystems	Computer manufacturing	9	538	127
Businessland	Computer retailing and wholesaling	10	600	127
Harvard Industries	Diversified manufacturing	27	559	83

continued

continued

Company	Principal Business	1983 Sales ($ millions)	1987 Sales ($ millions)	Average Growth Rate per Year 1983–1987
Compaq	Computer manufacturing	111	1,224	62
Seagate Technology	Computer accessory manufacturing	110	958	54
Emerson Radio	Electronics wholesaling	95	811	54
Home Depot	Building supply retailing	256	1,454	42
Price Co.	General merchandise retailing	634	3,323	39
M.D.C. Holdings	Homebuilding	155	751	37

What accounts for the rapid growth of these firms? The answer is effective management as reflected by such factors as high morale, outstanding product quality, effective organization design, and a willingness to be creative and innovative in their approach to business. For example, when a key development project at Sun Microsystems got bogged down, the president told the group to clear out of the headquarters and finish the job off site. The change in environment resulted in the project getting back on schedule. In another case, Compaq realized that its greatest competition would come from IBM, which sold computers through its own retail stores and through other retailers. Compaq decided on a daring strategy. It would market exclusively through dealers and would offer exclusive franchises and attractive profit margins. Result: the company won its distribution battle against IBM. In another case, Wal-Mart (not reported above) has been able to achieve a growth rate of 28 percent by offering quality merchandise at large discounts and supporting its network of operations with gigantic, strategically situated warehouses that can restock the company's over 1100 stores on a 24-hour basis.

Many large corporations are unable to maintain high rates of growth. However, there are many others that can do so year after year. These are the ones that truly understand what effective management is all about.

Questions

1. Do the firms analyzed in this case make use of a management process framework? Explain.

2. Where would a concern for quantitative school concepts be of value to fast growing corporations?

3. Would these firms be using any of the concepts espoused by the behavioral school? Explain.

Source: The material in this case can be found in Stuart Gannes, "America's Fastest-Growing Companies," *Fortune*, May 23, 1988, pp. 28–36.

■ SELF-FEEDBACK EXERCISE: Your View of Management

Rank each of the following 15 items by first looking over the entire list and determining those with which you *most* agree and those with which you *least* agree. Place a "15" next to the one with which you most agree, etc. until you have ranked all statements from first (15) to last (1). Remember that there are no right and wrong answers. When you have finished, enter all of the answers on the summary sheet at the back and total the three columns.

_____ a. One of the most important factors in designing jobs is ensuring that workers are given autonomy and the opportunity for feedback from the job.

_____ b. Most managers are not as quantitatively analytical as they should be.

_____ c. As organization size increases, it is usually most efficient for enterprises to begin taking on bureaucratic characteristics.

_____ d. Rules and procedures generally help an organization improve its efficiency.

_____ e. Management science is critical to effective decision making.

_____ f. Modern organization designs that are flexible and free-form in nature are better than most conventional designs.

_____ g. In designing an effective organization, external developments such as market changes are more important than internal factors such as the need for accurate job descriptions and well-defined chains of command.

_____ h. Profit and efficiency can often be improved through detailed financial and quantitative analysis of data.

_____ i. Enterprises that organize operations around their people do a better job than those that organize around functional areas such as production, marketing, and finance.

_____ j. Profit maximization is an important organizational objective.

_____ k. Organization design changes are more a result of changes in external environmental variables such as technology, customer demand, or competitive moves than they are changes in internal variables such as employee values, morale, and attitudes.

_____ l. All things considered equal, organization structures that have only a few levels in the hierarchy but many people at each level are preferable to those which have many levels but only a small number of people at each level.

_____ m. Computers are grossly underrated in terms of their value to organizational effectiveness.

_____ n. The most important function of a manager is communication.

_____ o. Market share and return on investment are more important objectives than are profit and cost containment.

Summary Sheet

Place your answers on the summary sheet below by matching the number (1–15) you gave to each letter. For example, if you gave answer "b" a "15," put a 15 next to the "b" in Column I. After you have entered all 15 answers, total each column and enter the answer above the double line.

I	II	III
_____ (b)	_____ (a)	_____ (c)
_____ (e)	_____ (f)	_____ (d)
_____ (h)	_____ (i)	_____ (g)
_____ (j)	_____ (l)	_____ (k)
_____ (m)	_____ (n)	_____ (o)
═══	═══	═══

Interpretation

The higher your column score, the greater your personal preference for one of the three schools of management thought. Column I represents a preference for the quantitative school philosophy, Column II represents the behavior school, and Column III represents the process school. There is no set of right answers to this exercise, but compare your responses to those of fellow students. You will find support for all three schools. This shows that there is no universally accepted approach to management. All three schools will continue in existence.

PART

2

THE
MANAGEMENT
PROCESS
SCHOOL
OF
MANAGEMENT

Chapter 4 is devoted to an examination of the planning process, including comprehensive, strategic, and operational planning. In the chapter consideration is given to such key topics as basic mission, objectives, evaluation of the environment, and the identification of propitious niches. The advantages and disadvantages of planning are also discussed. Planning is the first of the managerial functions, because without it the rest cannot be carried out. Once objectives are established and plans have been drawn up, the organization is then in a position to formulate its organization design.

Chapter 5 reviews the organizing process. This chapter presents the nuts-and-bolts ideas involved in integrating the personnel and the structure. Some of the major concepts covered in this chapter include: common forms of departmentalization; use of committees; the importance of span of control to effective organization design; authority, including line, staff, and functional; determinants of decentralization; the art of delegation; sources of power; and the informal organization and its value to management.

Chapter 6 discusses adaptive organization structures. Many organizations are finding that, because of advancing technology and other external factors, they must modify their designs to make them more responsive to the external environment. This chapter examines some of the most common forms of organization structure and the forces that determine the "best" design. In particular, consideration is given to bureaucracies and their shortcomings, technology and its impact on both personnel and organization structures, configurations of organization design, project and matrix structures and their value to modern enterprises, the nature of contingency organization design, and forces that help dictate the most efficient structure.

Chapter 7 reviews the controlling process. After the three basic steps in this process are presented and the requirements of an effective control system are analyzed, attention is focused on specific types of control. These include comprehensive budgeting, zero-base budgeting, break-even point analysis, the measurement of employee performance, the Gantt chart, Program Evaluation and Review Technique, milestone budgeting, financial techniques for measuring overall performance, and management audits.

The overall purpose of this part of the book is to provide a general framework for the management process approach to the field. In general terms this means a consideration of three functions: planning, organizing, and controlling.

The
Planning
Process

There is an adage in management: If you don't know where you are going, any path will get you there. However, when a person or a firm has objectives—and all businesses should—then planning is essential. The overriding goal of this chapter is to examine the planning process. This topic has received a great deal of attention in recent years. In particular, the area of strategic planning has become a subject of interest for both theorists and practitioners. One of the questions that both are concerned with answering is: What strategies are best under what conditions? A second area of interest is strategy implementation. Many firms complain that after paying a consulting team a great deal of money, the recommended plan did not work. Formulating a strategy is difficult work; implementing it can be just as demanding, especially if some of the assumptions on which the plan rested prove to be inaccurate.

The goals of this chapter are to study the planning process; define and observe comprehensive, strategic, and operational planning; and discuss the advantages and limitations of planning. Attention is also focused on some of the key issues that are addressed in effective plans.

When you have finished reading this chapter, you should be able to:

1. Describe what is meant by the term comprehensive planning.
2. Define the term *strategic planning.*
3. Identify the three foundations of a strategic plan.
4. Relate some of the most common ways of conducting evaluations of external and internal environments.
5. Explain how a firm goes about developing a market niche.

6. Describe how a planning organization can help a business carry out comprehensive planning.

7. Outline some of the basic advantages of planning.

8. Explain why planning can help but still may not be able to prevent or cure all future problems.

COMPREHENSIVE PLANNING

Comprehensive planning involves all levels of the organization.

Modern businesses operate in a highly dynamic environment where change is a constant factor, and where firms must continually strive to remain competitive. A recent survey by the *Harvard Business Review* reveals that most managers believe U. S. competitiveness is declining and it is management's responsibility to correct this situation.[1] They must rise to the challenge of tougher competition.[2] As a result, it has become more and more necessary for companies to determine their objectives carefully and then systematically to construct plans for attaining them. This has become a continuous process throughout every organization. Naturally, managers at the upper levels should be concerned with long-range or strategic planning, whereas the attention of those managers at the lower levels ought to be focused mainly on operational planning. Yet research indicates that some top managers have not been devoting sufficient attention to long-range planning. Rather, they tend to spend most of their time worrying about short-run goals and performance results. In fact, it is not uncommon to find some chief executive officers who believe that comprehensive planning is something that can be delegated to their subordinates. When the overall plan is completed, they breathe a sigh of relief and think they can now get back to their real work.

Fortunately, however, there has been a marked trend in recent years toward *comprehensive planning,* a process in which all departments of the organization identify their objectives and determine how they will be attained. William Lindsay and Leslie Rue conducted a two-stage survey of 199 corporations in 15 industrial classifications and found that firms tend to adapt a more complete long-range planning process as the complexity and instability of their environment increases.[3] In this process, each department ties its objectives to those units above and below it in the hierarchy. The result is an integrated plan in which all groups work toward the same basic objectives. Today comprehensive planning is used not only by large organiza-

---

[1]"Competitiveness Survey: HBR Readers Respond," *Harvard Business Review,* September–October 1987, pp. 8–12.

[2]G. David Wallace et al., "America's Leanest and Meanest," *Business Week,* October 5, 1987, pp. 78–84.

[3]William M. Lindsay and Leslie W. Rue, "Impact of the Organization Environment on the Long-Range Planning Process: A Contingency View," *Academy of Management Journal,* September 1980, pp. 385–404.

tions but by medium and small ones as well. In fact, smaller companies have begun to realize that, despite their limited resources, they have about the same fundamental planning requirements as larger companies.[4] This trend toward comprehensive planning on the part of large and small businesses alike will continue, and those firms that have not begun to take the requisite steps toward insuring well-coordinated overall plans will find themselves unable to maintain the pace.

STRATEGIC PLANNING

George Steiner has defined *strategic planning* as "the process of determining the major objectives of an organization and the policies and strategies that will govern the acquisition, use, and disposition of resources to achieve those objectives."[5] Strategic plans provide a firm with long-range direction and growth from three foundations, the first of which is the *basic socioeconomic purpose* of the organization: Why is the business in existence? However it is stated, a socioeconomic purpose always entails a consideration of company survival (profits) and societal needs (social functions). The second foundation is the values and philosophy of the top management. This composite of values and ideals influences the strategic plan because it helps determine the manner in which management will treat its customers and employees. The third basic foundation is the assessment of the organization's strengths and weaknesses in the context of the external and internal environment. These three foundations of strategic planning are interdependent, as Figure 4-1 shows.

Basic Socioeconomic Purpose

The basic purpose for existence must be identified.

More and more business firms are beginning to reevaluate the purposes of their existence. For example, years ago, when Henry Ford entered the automobile business, he saw his basic mission as one of providing people with a basic necessity—a form of transportation. People needed cars for mobility; Ford could provide them. General Motors later broadened this idea, viewing the automobile as a luxury as well as a necessity. As a result, the firm offered the customer more extras and a wider line, albeit at a higher price, and replaced Ford as the number one automobile manufacturer. The nation's privately owned railroads have done the same, restating their purposes for existence so that they are no longer in the passenger-carrying business but in

---

[4]For an excellent discussion of this area, see George A. Steiner, ed., *Managerial Long Range Planning* (New York: McGraw-Hill, 1963); and George A. Steiner, *Strategic Planning: What Every Manager Must Know* (New York: Free Press, 1979).

[5]George Steiner, *Top Management Planning* (New York: Macmillan, 1969), p. 34; and Henry Mintzberg, "The Strategy Concept I: Five Ps for Strategy," *California Management Review*, Fall 1987, pp. 11–24.

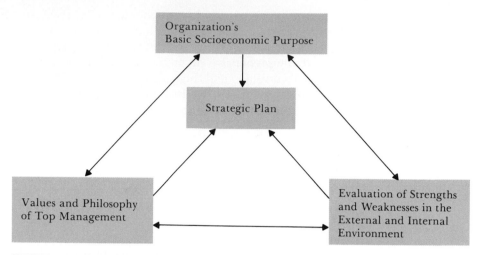

FIGURE 4-1   Basic Foundations of a Strategic Plan

the transportation business. Today, almost all railway profits are derived from freight. The movie industry has also redefined its basic mission: It is no longer merely in the movie business; it is now in the business of informing as well as entertaining its audience.

Furthermore, rather than talking about specific product lines, modern organizations tend to define their business in terms of *market definition*. The following lists of types of firms and market definitions provide some examples:

Type of Firm	Business It Is In (by Market Definition)
Copy machine	Office productivity
Oil	Energy
Cosmetic	Beauty
TV manufacturer	Entertainment
Computer	Information processing
Encyclopedia	Information development
Fertilizer	World hunger fighting

A critical fact about business, one which managers must remember, is that products change but basic markets remain. Autos may be replaced by electric bicycles, but the transportation market is still there. For this reason, the socioeconomic purpose is stated in terms of the market. From here, a basic mission statement can then be formulated. The following list illustrates this for some major firms:

1. Volkswagen's mission is to provide an economic means of private transportation.

2. American Telephone and Telegraph's mission is to provide quick and efficient communication capabilities.

3. IBM's mission is to meet the problem-solving needs of businesses.

4. Shell Oil's mission is to meet the energy needs of humanity.

5. International Minerals and Chemical Corporation's mission is to increase agricultural productivity to feed the world's hungry.[6]

Unless an organization can define its socioeconomic purpose and continuously redefine it as conditions change, it will lack a clear understanding of its basic mission and have great difficulty in constructing a strategic plan.

Management Values

In the 1980s, the idea of social responsibility received a tremendous amount of attention. Equal opportunity, ecology, and the various aspects of the consumer movement and its supporting legislation, which for convenience we can call consumerism, all became focal points for management consideration and action. Why did these issues come to the fore? Part of the answer rests with external actions, such as government legislation. However, even more significant (and generally overlooked) have been the social action programs proposed by businesses themselves. What led to them? The answer rests in the values and beliefs of the top management.

Management values will influence the strategic plan.

In every organization all the managers bring a certain set of values to the workplace with them, and every generation tends to have differing values. Most of today's top managers are in the forty-five to sixty age group. This means that most of the managers of the 1990s will have been born during the years 1940 to 1955. The older ones will have some memory of World War II and, less importantly for them, the 1950s and the cold war, which form the first memories of today's younger managers. During the traumas of these early years, the values of the managers of the 1990s will have been formed. How will these values differ from those of the managers' parents and grandparents? Generally, 1990s managers will be more socially conscious than earlier managers. They will tend to be more concerned also with quality of life, and will have a more participative leadership style. These values will predictably influence the managers' organizational strategic plans.

Evaluation of the Environment

Managers evaluate the external and internal environment to help identify organizational strengths and weaknesses. They can then formulate objectives based on the environmental studies. In evaluating the external environment, organizations rely most heavily on *forecasting*, the projection of future business conditions.

---

[6]Philip Kotler, *Marketing Management: Analysis, Planning, and Control*, 5th ed. (Englewood Cliffs, NJ: Prentice-Hall, 1984), p. 48.

INTERVIEW WITH TONY HAIN

Until recently Tony Hain was general director of corporate strategic planning for General Motors. In this capacity he helped the company develop its strategic plan by working with both central management and with the various divisions of the company. Using a "from the top down" approach coupled with a "from the bottom up" approach, he helped the company formulate and implement a strategic plan. Today Tony is general director for personnel planning, helping the company deal more effectively with one of its major strategic resources.

Q.   *How important is strategic planning? Is it a lot of hype or does it really have value?*

A.   It really does have value. The problem with strategic planning for a lot of firms is that they treat the whole process as a ceremonial ritual rather than as a process that has practical value. It took us almost a decade at GM before we got to the point where we learned how to put together a useful strategic plan. Today we can use a very decentralized approach and facilitate development and implementation of the planning process at the lowest levels. We help each division and plant manager do this and then, at the top, work to coordinate the overall plan. This helps us blend strategy formulation (where we want to go) with strategy implementation (how we're going to get there.)

Q.   *Does strategic planning really pay off or is it just an interesting process that has yet to generate any real bottom-line effects?*

External Environmental Forecasting

Forecasting the external environment can be done in a number of ways, depending on what the management would like to know. But there is one paradoxically constant variable: The environment is always changing. The greater the change, the more important it is for the organization to gather data about it.

The dynamic environment of the business world can be seen through a sales comparison of the twenty largest industrials over a ten-year period. The decade 1977–1987 has been chosen because during this period the economy went into a prolonged slump and then began to turn around. As Table 4-1 shows, eight of the ten top firms in *Fortune's* 500 in 1977 had maintained their positions in this elite group in 1987, the other two having fallen into the second or been reclassified, merged or acquired. Of the second group of ten,

A.   It pays off. No doubt about it. First of all, strategic planning provides the personnel with corporate vision. The process has become a very effective communication tool for integrating management direction and action. We used to have centralized people each formulating a strategic plan for their particular area such as finance, marketing, and production. However, there would be no integration of these ideas. That is all changed now. We have strategic planning guidelines and assistance providing from central management, but the operating managers are the ones who decide what will actually be done and how it will be done. Does this process pay off? I think so and so do our customers. The most recent J. D. Power independent survey on customer satisfaction found that Buick, Olds, and Cadillac are in the list of top ten cars in the world. The other seven consist of Japanese and European autos. A lot of this perceived satisfaction is the result of our strategic planning. A third way strategic planning helps is that it makes you more fluid and adept in responding to market demands, and this is going to be critical in the 1990s.

Q.   *What will be the future of strategic planning?*

A.   I think we're going to see American firms spending a lot more time focusing on strategy implementation. We're real good at formulating plans, but implementation tends to be our weak suit. This is in contrast to overseas companies such as the Japanese who are very strong in strategy implementation but do not give as much consideration to formulation. I think during the 1990s you'll see an increasing focus by firms on that side of strategic planning that they have been shortchanging, and there will be a more balanced approach to strategy formulation and implementation.

however, only four were still in that category. One had moved up, three had fallen back, and the other two were reclassified, merged, or acquired. The table illustrates that no firm is ever standing still; it must be moving forward, or it is falling behind. Table 4-2 shows this rather dramatically, comparing the last ten industrials in *Fortune's* 500 in 1977 and 1987.

If the nation's top firms have to withstand such dynamics, it stands to reason that smaller businesses must undergo even more notable changes, simply because they lack the size and financial strength of their giant counterparts. Thus, their need for forecasting change is even greater. The following examines some of the ways of conducting forecasts.[7]

[7]F. William Barnett, "Four Steps to Forecast Total Market Demand," *Harvard Business Review*, July–August 1988, pp. 28–37.

	Firm	1977 Rank	1987 Rank
TABLE 4-1 *Fortune's* Largest Industrials in 1977 and 1987 (on the basis of sales)	General Motors	1	1
	Exxon	2	2
	Ford Motor	3	3
	Mobil	4	5
	Texaco	5	7
	Standard Oil of California (Chevron)	6	11
	IBM	7	4
	Gulf Oil	8	*
	General Electric	9	6
	Chrysler	10	10
	ITT	11	45
	Standard Oil of Indiana (Amoco)	12	14
	Atlantic Richfield	13	18
	Shell Oil	14	13
	U. S. Steel	15	23
	Du Pont de Nemours (E. I.)	16	9
	Continental Oil	17	*
	Western Electric	18	*
	Tenneco	19	21
	Procter & Gamble	20	17

* Reclassified, merged, or acquired.

Source: Adapted from *Fortune*, May 1978 and April 1988.

Various types of economic forecasts can be used to project developments in the external environment.

1. **Economic Forecasting.** The most common type of external forecasting is the economic forecast. If the economy is in an upswing, many businesses find their positions improved; sales rise and returns on investments increase. Conversely, a downturn has a dampening effect. Much depends on the current state of the economy as reflected by *gross national product (GNP)*, which is the value of goods and services produced in the country in a year.

A. Extrapolation. The simplest form of economic forecast is that of *extrapolation,* which is simply a projection of the current trend into the future. If a firm sold $100,000 worth of goods in 1987, $200,000 in 1988, and $300,000 in 1989, it might estimate continual $100,000 growth increments for the next decade. Using extrapolation as a general method of business forecasting is, of course, dangerous, because it fails to take into account changing environmental conditions as reflected in economic cycles. However, in such cases as population growth or life expectancy, a long-term forecast based on extrapolation can be fairly accurate.

B. Leads and Lags. The National Bureau of Economic Research (NBER) has discovered that when the economy turns up or down, some indicators seem to precede the change, some coincide with it, and still

	Firm	1977 Rank	1987 Rank
TABLE 4-2 Changes in Selected Firms in *Fortune's* 500 Industrials between 1977–1987 (on the basis of sales)	American Hoist and Derrick	491	—
	Ruth Packing	492	—
	Tyler	493	300
	Monfort of Colorado	494	—
	Idle Wild Foods	495	—
	Koehring	496	—
	Butler Manufacturing	497	418
	Economics Laboratory	498	331
	Dennison Manufacturing	499	391
	McCormick	500	308

— *not listed*

Source: Adapted from *Fortune*, May 1978 and April 1988.

others follow it. There are thus a lead group, a coincident group, and a lag group.

Of greatest importance to forecasters are the *lead indicators*, for they tend to signal upcoming changes in the economic cycle. In all, there are twelve lead indicators on the NBER's short list, including average weekly hours worked, new business formations, new building permits, common stock prices, corporate profit after taxes, new orders for durable goods, and changes in consumer installment credit. Many forecasters place great value on these indicators, feeling they provide the best clues as to what is likely to happen.

Lag indicators are important because they follow the economic cycle, making it possible to anticipate changes. The NBER has six indicators on its short list, including business expenditures for plant and equipment, unemployment rate, bank rates on short-term loans, manufacturers' inventories, and common and industrial loans outstanding. If the economy is beginning an upswing, banks can expect manufacturers to begin increasing their loans and investing money in plant and equipment. If the economy is beginning a downturn, there will be a reduction in business borrowing and plant and equipment expenditures, as well as a general increase in the unemployment rate.

Unfortunately, the lead and lag method of forecasting is more than a matter of merely plugging various values into a mathematical equation. Qualitative judgments must also be made to determine the impact of the indicators. For example, if the number of residential building permits increases, orders for durable goods rise, and the average number of weekly hours worked goes up, then the GNP may start to rise. Do these occurrences indicate that the company should float a new stock issue? Supposedly, the price of industrial stocks will begin to rise, but there is no certainty of this. In short, the lead and lag method helps the forecaster predict the future, but in so doing the individual is only making an educated guess. There is no guarantee that the guess is correct.

C. Econometrics. Another forecasting technique that is widely employed today is *econometrics*, a mathematical approach in which the main variables are brought together in a series of equations. GNP can then be forecast on the basis of various assumptions arrived at through these equations. The econometric technique provides the forecaster with a picture of what to expect under various conditions. Three such conditions—the most optimistic, the most likely, and the most pessimistic—exemplify some of the commonest types of sought-after answers.

The results can be further analyzed by applying them to specific industries and companies. For example, if a firm estimates that the industry will sell between 12 and 14 million units (pessimistic and optimistic) and further estimates that it will capture between 6 and 7 percent of the market, then sales will range from 720,000 to 980,000 units inclusive. These data can be used to construct initial income statements, illustrating profit and loss at various levels of sales. It is also possible to estimate production and marketing costs at these levels. If the forecasters like, they can make changes in one area while leaving everything else the same. For example, what impact would a 15 percent increase in advertising have on industry and company sales? The value of the econometric model is not only that it assists the company in forecasting the future; it also helps management predict results of various changes in strategy.

2. **Technological Forecasting.** Many firms must use technological forecasting. There are two ways of conducting such forecasts: exploratory and normative.

    Exploratory forecasting begins with current knowledge and predicts the future on the basis of predictable technological progress. It is thus a rather passive process. Forecasters using this method tend to assume that current technological progress will continue at the same rate and that this advance will not be affected by external conditions. They can, if they wish, later speculate on how the forecast might be affected by the nontechnical environment (see Technology in Action: Planning for the Future).

    Electronics development provides an illustration of how this method can be used. Immediately after World War II, transistors were expensive and qualitatively unpredictable. Since then, however, their price has declined, their quality has improved, and their application has become widespread. If a business firm had decided to conduct an exploratory forecast right after World War II, it would have been possible to predict these events. Industrial firms in particular have found great value in this type of forecasting because the results can help companies in searching

Exploratory forecasting projects the future according to predictable technological progress.

TECHNOLOGY
IN
ACTION:
Planning
for
the
Future

Planning is important in every industry, but more so in those where there is long lead time between when a product decision is made and when the product comes to market. Automobiles are a good example. Next year's models have already been decided; the following year's models are being finalized right now; and those for three years from now are well on their way to completion on the designer's drawing board. Yet this does not mean that future cars will not have the latest technology. If anything, they will be very heavily technology-driven. Consider some of the changes that will be incorporated into automobiles over the next decade:

Collision avoidance. Front and rear radar systems will warn the driver of an impending crash as well as alert the driver to approaching vehicles.

Navigation system. A video screen will map the car's location and will plot the fastest route to the driver's destination.

Tire pressure sensors. Sensors will keep track of individual tire pressure and tell the driver when more air is needed.

Adaptive lights. If a rear turn signal burns out, the brake light will blink instead thus serving a dual role until the turn signal can be replaced.

Automatic lights. Headlights will be controlled by a sensor that will automatically turn them on at dusk and off in daylight.

Traction control. Tires will not spin on slippery surface thanks to special traction control.

Fuel economy. Electronics will replace mechanical linkages under the hood and connect the gas pedal and the throttle so as to boost fuel economy.

Active suspensions. Sensors will spot bumps and potholes in the road and the tire will be automatically lifted over the hole and set down on the other side.

Image enhancement. Instrument readings will appear to float in front of the hood so the driver will not have to look down to read the display panels.

At the present time these developments, and more, are being planned for cars of the 1990s. While this is good news, many drivers who have bought cars with state-of-the-art equipment have found that new technological developments often do not work properly. How will the cars of the future deal with this problem? The in-car computer will keep track of all sensors and high-tech equipment that does not function properly. When the mechanic works on the car, the individual will get this readout from the computer and use it to eliminate the malfunctioning equipment. In short, the driver will not have to keep track of what is going wrong, the on-board computer will do all of this thus ensuring that problem areas are accurately identified.

Source: William Hampton et al., ''Smart Cars,'' *Business Week,* June 13, 1988, pp. 68–74.

out clues as to market entry, potential competition, and ease of expansion into related product areas; and it has the added advantage of being rather easy to do.

Normative forecasting begins with an identification of some future technological objective—say, for example, the development of a space station by 2010. After the goal is set, the forecaster works back to the present, identifying the obstacles to be surmounted along the way. Attention is devoted to both technical and nontechnical factors. For example, when will the technical know-how for a space station be available, and how will this time estimate be affected by government allocations? (That is, will the government put a lot of money into the project and develop it quickly, or will the project take a longer time because of reluctance or lack of enthusiasm in Washington?) Normative forecasting is much more dynamic than exploratory forecasting.

Normative forecasting works from the future back to the present.

3. **Government Action.** Few companies escape government influence. Most businesses face a host of laws designed to prevent monopoly, promote competition, and encourage ethical practices. In addition, there is the ever-present concern with monetary action, whereby the federal government can regulate credit through the federal reserve banks and open market operations. This spurs the economy forward or, in the case of runaway inflation, help put on the brakes. Likewise, the federal government can pump money into the economy or draw it out through such fiscal action as higher taxes or a refusal to spend what has been currently collected. For these reasons, the government has a direct impact on business strategy.

The impact of government control must be evaluated.

4. **Sales Forecasting.** Businesses forecast the economy in general so as to set the stage for determining their own particular *sales forecasts*. Some use an econometric approach, but not all businesses have the expertise for employing such a sophisticated technique. For them, the questions of how many goods or services they will sell to whom, in which place, and by which methods, in light of economic projections, require a more down-to-earth sales forecast. In arriving at an answer, the first place a firm often turns to is its own sales records. A survey of current sales information will indicate what products are selling best in which areas and to what kinds of customers. Further sales forecast data can often be obtained from the United States Bureau of the Census, the Department of Commerce, local trade associations, and the Chamber of Commerce.

Sales forecasting can be conducted in a number of ways.

Another, and often supplemental, method of gauging sales is the *jury of executive opinion.* In this approach, various executives in the organization are brought together for the purpose of constructing the sales forecast. Sometimes they work independently of each other; other times they form a joint opinion. In both cases, there is an input to the sales forecast based on what these executives believe will take place. Another version entails the review and modification of the executive forecast by the manager of marketing research. The value of the jury of executive opinion approach is that it allows input from executives who are in a position to make intelligent guesstimates about the future.

Another supplemental approach, often called the *grass-roots method,* entails a survey of the sales force. Since salespeople are in the field on a continuing basis, they should have some general ideas about what will and will not sell. Their ideas are obtained by the sales manager, who compiles the results and sends them up the line. In the process, the composites from salespeople in all the districts and regions are aggregated and sent to central headquarters, where they are compared with the forecast constructed by a home office staff. Finally, changes are made based on management decisions regarding advertising, product line, price, and other such considerations. Then the forecast is reviewed and approved. The major advantage of the grass-roots method is that it obtains sales information from the people who do the actual selling.

A third supplemental approach is that of *user expectation.* A firm that wants to know how the customer feels about a product can gain valuable information simply by going out and asking the consumer. Although some customers may say one thing and do another, if the firm obtains a large enough sample, it is possible to negate the impact of such responses.

Internal Environmental Evaluation

A forecast of external environmental factors provides the organization with important planning information. However, these data must be supplemented with an evaluation of the internal environment, focusing particularly on the identification of the company's internal strengths and weaknesses. In making this evaluation, the manager must consider two factors:

Material resources such as cash, plant, and equipment must be evaluated.

1. **Material Resources.** The plant capacity plus the amount of cash, equipment, and inventory a company has on hand are important because they constitute the tools with which a strategic plan can be fashioned. Often these resources will help dictate a particular type of strategy. For example, a business with a large plant capacity will have a large fixed expense. However, if it can manufacture at capacity, the firm can spread these costs over many items, thereby reducing the cost per unit. This company will undoubtedly compete vigorously with a low price strategy. Conversely, a small manufacturer will not have so high a fixed expense but will also have fewer units among which to spread these costs. As a result, the small plant cannot meet the big manufacturer head-to-head in a price war. Therefore, it will devise a strategy that the larger competition cannot or will not effectively combat, such as high price coupled with a great degree of personal selling.

    A second reason for evaluating material resources is to ascertain the financial strength of the firm. If a company has $1 million in cash and $9 million in other assets, it can often maintain a strategic posture far longer than a firm with only a tenth of these assets. This raises the question of how long a firm should remain with a particular strategic plan. The answer is to stick with it until it pays off or until it becomes evident that the results are not going to justify the costs. Unfortunately, many firms adopt strategic plans that are not in accord with their material resources and as a result find themselves continually revising and modifying their plan. A strategic plan should always be tempered by the available material resources.

Personnel competencies must be identified.

2. **Personnel Competence.** In every organization workers will have a distinctive area of competence; there is something the work force does extremely well. For example, in a firm such as the *New York Times*, it is the ability to gather information from all over the world and compile it quickly, accurately, and in readable form. In contrast, many small papers use their people to gather local news happenings and rely upon wire sources to provide them with international news. Analogously, the ''Big Three'' auto manufacturers in America have the labor needed to mass produce and market cars, whereas Rolls Royce, in the same basic business, concentrates its efforts less on marketing and more on production quality. Because a strategic plan must draw upon the company's strengths, the competence of the workers is an important consideration.

DEVELOPING A PROPITIOUS NICHE

On the basis of the external and internal environmental analysis, the philosophy of the management, and the socioeconomic mission of the organization, long-range objectives can be formulated.[8] However, it should be noted that every strategic plan must be designed so as to develop or take advantage of a particular niche.[9] Every organization must find a thing, or some things, it does best and build a strategy around this strength. For example, the *New York Times* has a specific market niche, selling its papers to thousands of people every day. It is not, however, the largest selling newspaper in New York City; this position is held by the *New York Daily News*. Anyone who has ever read the two papers knows that the *Daily News* is a picture newspaper written in a very easy-to-read style. It is much more appealing to the mass market than is the *Times*. Yet it would be foolish for the *Times* to copy the style of its competition. To do so would mean abandoning a niche in which its competencies are best employed. The basic mission,

---

[8]Arie P. de Geus, ''Planning as Learning,'' *Harvard Business Review*, March–April 1988, pp. 70–74.

[9]Daniel J. Isenberg, ''The Tactics of Strategic Opportunism,'' *Harvard Business Review*, March–April 1987, pp. 92–97.

philosophy of management, and strength of the *Times* are all geared toward its current style of news coverage. This is what is known as *leading from strength*. Every well-formulated plan draws upon the organization's strengths in fashioning the most successful strategy possible.[10]

The firm must build a strategy that capitalizes on its strengths.

Surprising as it may seem, many businesses do not lead from strength. Instead, they tend to hold back and respond defensively to the environment. In fact, many managers spend an inordinate amount of time trying to straighten out little problem areas instead of boldly taking advantage of their strengths. They do not have a strategic, long-range plan. They spend most of their time on day-to-day matters, like chess players who seize poisoned pawns because the immediate capture of any enemy is given priority over the long-range development of their own pieces.

By identifying a niche in which its competencies can be effectively employed, an organization focuses on goals. In so doing, Peter Drucker, the world-famous management authority, has noted, the successful manager must never try to cover too much territory. Instead, the manager must milk a propitious niche for all it is worth, according to the following guidelines:

1. Economic results require that managers concentrate their efforts on the smallest number of products, product lines, services, customers, markets, distribution channels, end uses, and so on which will produce the largest amount of revenue. Managers must minimize the attention devoted to products which produce primarily costs, because their value is too small or too splintered.

2. Economic results require also that staff efforts be concentrated on the very few activities that are capable of producing truly significant business results—with as little staff work and staff effort as possible spent on the others.

3. Effective cost control requires a similar concentration of work and efforts on those very few areas where improvement in cost performance will have significant impact on business performance and results—that is, on those areas where a relatively minor increase in efficiency will produce a major increase in economic effectiveness.

4. Managers must allocate resources, especially high-grade human resources, to activities which provide opportunities for high economic results.[11]

These basic ideas are employed by a number of firms that handle their strategic business plans like investment portfolios—pruning the losing lines

---

[10]Michael E. Porter, "From Competitive Advantage to Corporate Strategy," *Harvard Business Review,* May–June 1987, pp. 43–59.

[11]Peter F. Drucker, "Managing for Business Effectiveness," *Harvard Business Review,* May–June 1963, p. 56.

and backing the successful ones through systematic analysis. In doing so, management first identifies the *strategic business units (SBUs)* which make up the firm. Each has the following characteristics:

1. Is a single business or collection of related businesses.
2. Has a distinct mission.
3. Has its own competitors.
4. Has a responsible manager.
5. Consists of one or more program units and functional units.
6. Can benefit from strategic planning.
7. Can be planned independently of the other businesses.[12]

SBUs share major characteristics.

Depending on the situation, an SBU can be an entire company division, a product line within a division, or a single product. Whatever it happens to be in a given company, the firm, on identifying the SBU, sets about evaluating its current and expected performance. While there are a number of ways of doing this, one of the most popular is that developed by General Electric, which has more than forty distinct businesses. Each must be rated on quantitative factors such as sales, profit, and return on investment, as well as hard-to-quantify factors such as market share, technology needs, employee loyalty in the industry, competitive stance, and social need. In conducting its annual planning review, GE has developed a strategic business planning grid, shown in Figure 4-2. On this grid are two dimensions, industry attractiveness and business strengths. Industry attractiveness takes into account such factors as market size, market growth rate, profit margin, and competitive intensity. Business strength includes relative market share, price competitiveness, product quality, and knowledge of the customer and the market. Depending on the combination of each (high, medium, or low), the firm will decide to: (a) invest and grow, (b) get further information because the business might go either way, or (c) reduce the investment.[13]

In Figure 4-2A industry attractiveness is medium and business strengths are high. In this case the company would opt to invest and grow. In Figure 4-2B industry attractiveness is low and business strengths are medium. In this situation the company would not invest further and would start to reduce or consolidate its holdings. Finally, in Figure 4-2C industry attractiveness and business strengths are both medium. The company would wait for further information before making a final decision.

A similar approach, pioneered by the Boston Consulting Group, classifies the SBUs into a *business portfolio matrix* such as that shown in Figure 4-3. On

---

[12]Kotler, p. 51.

[13]See "General Electric's 'Spotlight Strategy' for Planning," *Business Week,* April 28, 1975, p. 49.

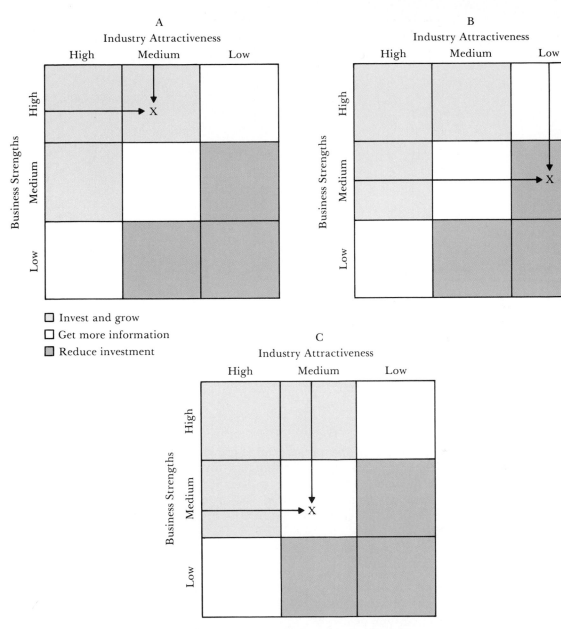

FIGURE 4-2   General Electric's Strategic Planning Grid

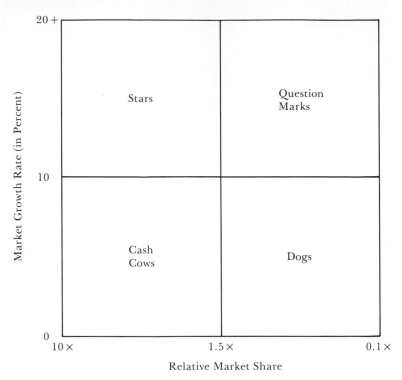

FIGURE 4-3   The Boston Consulting Group's Portfolio Matrix

the vertical axis is the annual market growth rate for each of the SBUs. Ten percent is the growth line dividing high and low growth. On the horizontal axis is the relative market share for each SBU in relation to the share held by the industry's largest competitor. The dividing line between low and high here is 1.5X, which means the SBU is 50 percent larger than its biggest competitor.

Each of the quadrants represents a distinct type of cash flow situation. The four classifications follow:

Stars. Stars have high growth, high market share SBUs. These need a lot of cash to finance their rapid growth. When this growth slows down, they will become cash cows.

Cows. Cash cows have low growth, high market share SBUs. These throw off a lot of cash to support other SBUs and help the firm meet its bills.

Question Marks. Question marks have low share SBUs in high growth markets. These require a lot of cash in order to maintain their share, let alone increase it.

The Boston Consulting Group made four business portfolio classifications.

Dogs. Dogs have low growth, low share SBUs. These may generate enough cash to maintain themselves but do not promise to be a large source of cash.[14]

After this evaluation, management must decide a strategy for each SBU. Typically, it will try to build those question marks which will become stars if their market share grows, hold on to and milk the market of the strong cash cows, harvest the weak cash cows and question marks whose futures look dim, and divest itself of the dogs.

Many companies use this portfolio planning approach. In fact, Philippe Haspeslagh, after conducting a survey of U. S. firms, has reported that, "Diversified companies, particularly the large ones, widely practice the art of portfolio planning; for most of them, it is indeed much more than an analytical tool. At the corporate level, 75% practice or are implementing . . . portfolio planning."[15]

In recent years a great deal of investigation has been conducted regarding the best strategies to follow with each of the four categories in Figure 4-3.[16] Are the recommendations set forth two paragraphs above accurate ones? Research shows that, in the main, they are.[17] Attention is also being focused on how to effectively manage SBUs.[18] These research trends show a growing interest in the area of strategic planning.

LONG- AND INTERMEDIATE-RANGE OBJECTIVES

A business formulates its long-range objectives on the basis of its socioeconomic purpose, the values of its top managers, and an analysis of its external and internal environments. For a manufacturing firm, as Figure 4-4 shows, some of the commonest goals have to do with manufacturing, finance, and marketing. However, in long-range perspective these goals are often insuffi-

---

[14]For more on this subject, see Charles W. Hofer and Dan Schendel, *Strategy Formulation: Analytical Concepts* (St. Paul, MN: West Publishing, 1978); George S. Day, "Diagnosing the Product Portfolio," *Journal of Marketing*, April 1977, pp. 29–38; and "Olin's Shift to Strategic Planning," *Business Week*, March 27, 1978, pp. 102–105.

[15]Philippe Haspeslagh, "Portfolio Planning: Uses and Limits," *Harvard Business Review*, January–February 1982, p. 63.

[16]Christopher K. Bart, "Implementing 'Growth' and 'Harvest' Product Strategies," *California Management Review*, Summer 1987, pp. 137–56.

[17]Ian C. MacMillan, Donald C. Hambrick, and Diane L. Day, "The Product Portfolio and Profitability—A PIMS-Based Analysis of Industrial-Product Businesses," *Academy of Management Journal*, December 1982, pp. 733–55; and Donald C. Hambrick and Ian C. MacMillan, "The Product Portfolio and Man's Best Friend," *California Management Review*, Fall 1982, pp. 84–95.

[18]Anil K. Gupta and V. Govindarajan, "Business Unit Strategy, Managerial Characteristics, and Business Unit Effectiveness at Strategy Implementation," *Academy of Management Journal*, March 1984, pp. 25–41.

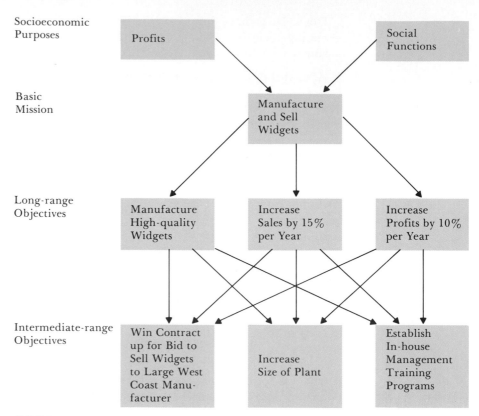

Socioeconomic Purposes

Profits

Social Functions

Basic Mission

Manufacture and Sell Widgets

Long-range Objectives

Manufacture High-quality Widgets

Increase Sales by 15% per Year

Increase Profits by 10% per Year

Intermediate-range Objectives

Win Contract up for Bid to Sell Widgets to Large West Coast Manufacturer

Increase Size of Plant

Establish In-house Management Training Programs

FIGURE 4-4   Interrelationships of Purposes, Mission, and Long- and Intermediate-Range Objectives

ciently clear. For example, consider this goal: Open Nashville plant in third quarter 1984. Such statements of objectives need to be reduced to intermediate-range objectives, thereby increasing the amount of specificity and making the goals more action-oriented. In the example of the Nashville plant, some intermediate-range goals might be: (1) send site evaluators to view best location options, (2) select most favorable location, and (3) let bids for contractors.

In Figure 4-4 the long-range objective is to increase sales by 15 percent a year. How can this be attained? First, the intermediate-range goals need to be clearly defined—in this case, to win a contract currently up for bid to sell widgets to a large West Coast manufacturer, to increase the size of the plant, and to establish in-house management training programs. In addition, all the long-range objectives convey the basic mission of manufacturing and selling widgets—that mission, in turn, being directly related to the socioeconomic purposes of the organization. The manufacture and sale of widgets will result in profits as well as the fulfillment of certain social functions, such as the

From long-range goals, intermediate-range objectives can be formulated.

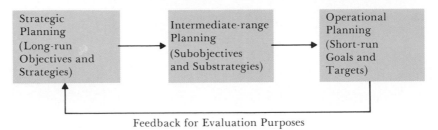

Feedback for Evaluation Purposes

FIGURE 4-5   Planning Structure

satisfaction of demand for this particular good. There is thus an interrelated *hierarchy of objectives,* and the strategic plan assists the firm in identifying its long-range objectives and formulating the derivative intermediate-range goals.

OPERATIONAL PLANNING

Operational planning is action-oriented.

The third type of planning is *operational planning.* Operational planning is short-range in contrast to strategic planning, and most low- and intermediate-level administrators spend a good deal of their time carrying out these short-range plans. Figure 4-5 shows the relationship between strategic and operational planning. Strategic planning can be viewed as the formulation of long-range objectives, whereas operational planning is the implementation of these decisions.

The time-lapse between the formulation stage and the implementation stage may be as great as a decade, although firms most often opt for a five-year plan. For example, one survey[19] of 420 companies revealed the following planning period distributions:

- No corporate plan   16%
- Under five years   6
- Five years only   53
- Five to ten years   8
- Ten years only   11
- Over ten years   6

Most operational plans are divided into functional areas. In a manufacturing enterprise, for example, they would appear as in Figure 4-6. This plan is much more specific than its strategic counterpart, with goals and targets spelled out in great detail. As an operational plan comes down the chain of command, the level of abstraction decreases and the degree of specificity

---

[19]Reported in Steiner, p. 22.

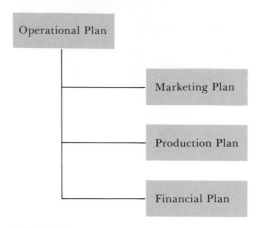

FIGURE 4-6   Partial Elements of an Operational Plan

increases. Marketing plans, production plans, and financial plans are typical examples of operational planning.

Marketing Plan

Selling current products and developing new ones are important marketing objectives.

Most marketing plans have two main objectives, selling current products and helping develop new ones. The former entails the setting of quotas and market shares for the various product lines. These objectives are translated into operational plans through advertising budgets, the maintenance of a sales force, the assignment of quotas, and the determination of product prices. Then at the end of the given period (for example, six months or a year), performance will be evaluated and goals or targets revised accordingly.

Concurrently, the marketing plan will entail some consideration of new product development. Every business knows that each product has a limited life cycle, as Figure 4-7 illustrates. Some goods will maintain their market position for years while others may never get off the ground, and today's big sellers may have no market demand five years from now.[20] For these reasons, product planning is necessary for generating new product ideas. Sometimes these will come from the research and development lab; other times they may be the result of suggestions from top management, salespeople, customers, or consultants. No matter where they come from, however, only about two of every one hundred ideas will ever materialize in the form of profitable products. The rest will either be screened out for technical, economic, or market test reasons (95 percent) or will just plain fail to sell, despite all initial signs to the contrary (3 percent).

---

[20]John E. Swan and David R. Rink, "Fitting Market Strategy to Varying Product Life Cycles," *Business Horizons*, January–February 1982, pp. 72–76.

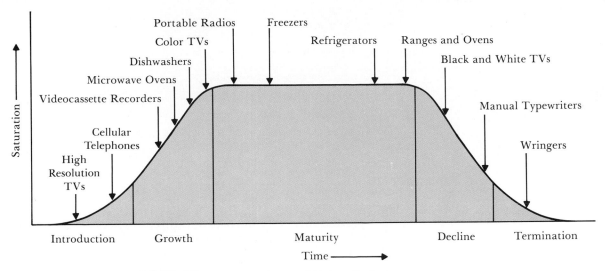

FIGURE 4-7   **Life Cycle Stages of Various Products**

Production Plan

The production plan is designed to satisfy consumer demand by turning out the desired amount of goods. Sometimes production capability will be greater than estimated demand; other times it will be necessary for the manufacturing department to go to a second or third shift to meet this demand. Both instances illustrate that marketing and production planning are actually intertwined. This relationship is illustrated in Figure 4-8.

The main production objective is to satisfy consumer demand.

The basic objectives of a production plan will entail the purchase, coordination, and maintenance of factors of production—specifically machines, material, and people. How much will it cost to manufacture a particular good? The answer depends on the costs associated with raw materials, merchandise, supplies, labor, and equipment. For this reason, the production plan starts with the desired number of units (the objective) and works backward, determining the amount of equipment and the number of people needed to attain these goals.

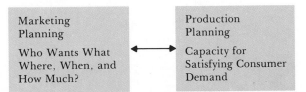

FIGURE 4-8   Interrelationships of Marketing and Production Planning

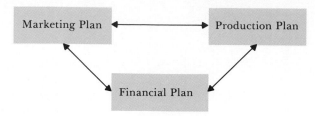

FIGURE 4-9   Interrelationships of Operational Planning Components

Financial Plan

The financial plan provides a quantitative basis for decision making and control.

The financial plan, as seen in Figure 4-9, is also interrelated with the marketing and production plans; each of the three influences the others. However, it should be noted that the financial plan is often given more importance than the other plans because it provides a quantitative basis for decision making and control. In an operational plan, managers want to know how well they are doing; financial data tell them. For example, in the production plan the vice-president of production will follow cost per unit very closely; at the same time, the marketing vice-president will be watching the sales curve. Both managers know that if things do not go well, the results will be reflected in the financial feedback.

Harmonizing Functional Plans

Budgets are useful in harmonizing plans.

One way in which firms combine these three functional plans (marketing, production, finance) is through the use of the budget. Many managers believe the budget is only a control technique. Instead, it is equally a planning tool: It provides a basis for action. Expected results can be expressed in numerical terms, cash flows can be projected, number of hours to be worked in the current period can be calculated, and units of production can be determined. Furthermore, research shows that when plans are linked to budgets, overall accuracy tends to be greater than when they are not.[21]

Another way in which management draws operational plans together is by setting financial objectives, such as return on investment (profit/assets), market share, growth rate, and profit. In fact when marketing, production, and finance plans are harmonized, it is common to find the financial plan being the fulcrum upon which the other two are balanced. As Figure 4-10 shows, if the marketing or production plans are in disequilibrium, the imbalance will be reflected in the financial data, and corrective action will be taken to reestablish the necessary balance.

---

[21]Richard F. Vancil, "The Accuracy of Long-Range Planning," *Harvard Business Review,* September–October 1970, p. 100.

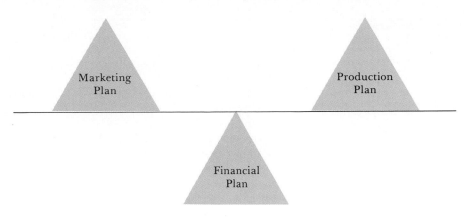

FIGURE 4-10   Functional Plan Fulcrum

Quite often the overall plan is brought together in the form of a written report. This is particularly true in the case of entrepreneurs or executives who want to raise money for expansion and must present their plan to investors. Communication in Action: Planning for Action describes this process.

USE OF A PLANNING ORGANIZATION

As noted previously, managers in many firms are most concerned with day-to-day problems. They do not have time to construct strategic plans; their interest rests in carrying out operational plans. For this reason, it is common to find departments drawing up their own budgets—with supporting justifications for any proposed capital expenditures—and forwarding these proposals to top management. The high-level managers then combine departmental plans into divisional plans, which they in turn review, modify as indicated, and finally approve.

A planning organization can help design a comprehensive plan.

The development of a comprehensive plan is never simple. It requires a tremendous amount of coordination. For this reason many firms, especially large corporations, have begun to develop their own *planning organizations*. Often five to eight years pass before this structure functions smoothly. (Table 4-3 shows how this time is typically spent.) Even though the process is lengthy, there are two important advantages to be gleaned from it. First, some companies lack a complete appreciation for planning at the highest ranks of the organization. A planning organization can surmount this lack of complete commitment. Second, many managers within the structure have never really been taught the concept of planning. A planning organization helps overcome this deficiency.

Organizational Metamorphosis

R. Hal Mason reports, as shown in the table, that a planning organization often begins at the top management level with the formation of a committee

	Phase	Action	Time Span	Total Time Elapsed
TABLE 4-3 Time Phases of a Planning Organization	1	Establish executive planning committee.	6–12 months	6–12 months
	2	Select director of planning and provide *ad hoc* staff committee.	About 12 months	18–24 months
	3	Director develops permanent planning staff at corporate level; division planning committees added.	12–36 months	30–60 months
	4	Appoint vice-president of planning and corporate development reporting to president and executive planning committee; select division planning coordinator.	12–24 months	42–72 months
	5	Specialize corporate development, planning, and evaluation functions; provide division planning staffs reporting to division heads but with relationship to corporate development and planning department.	12–36 months	60–108 months

Source: R. Hal Mason, "Developing a Planning Organization," *Business Horizons,* August 1969, p. 62. Copyright 1969 by the Foundation for the School of Business at Indiana University. Used with permission.

to identify and organize data on the firm and its industry position.[22] In Phase 1 attention is given to the development of a framework within which long-range planning can take place.

Phase 2 entails the formation of the first formal long-range plan. At best, it is often a rudimentary guide, lacking both depth and breadth. The plan is constructed by an executive planning staff at the upper divisions which acts as consultant to the rest of the organization.

Planning organiza-tions often go through five phases.

In Phase 3, which occurs about three years after the plan's inception, the planning organization prepares its first comprehensive five-year plan. This is done through the coordination and integration of the plans prepared by the major operating units. It is a "bottom-up" approach; the departments within each division or unit create plans and send them up the line. Thus the

---

[22]This five-phase metamorphosis comes from R. Hal Mason, "Developing a Planning Organization," *Business Horizons,* August 1969, pp. 61–69.

division carries the bulk of the total planning effort. During this phase, divisional planning committees will be added to the operating units to assist both the unit and the planning organization. These committees will assess reporting procedures and information generated about products, customers, and competitors. For its part, the planning organization will assist the committee in the design of the information and reporting systems.

By the time the committee reaches Phase 4, the annual preparation of a long-range plan will have become routine. Operating divisions have usually become attuned to developing plans that are in harmony with each other. At this stage it is also common to find that organizational planning takes on greater importance, and the head of the planning organization is often appointed to vice-presidential rank, reporting directly to the president.

In Phase 5, the final development step is reached. Mason describes the phase as follows:

> The activities of planning groups at all levels tend to shift their attention increasingly toward corporate developmental activities, which include the matching of opportunity to corporate capabilities and the development of those capabilities. The formal development of planning information has become routine in certain ways, and each division is aware of the types of data it must generate for planning purposes. An integrated set of plans is put together within a format, and corporate action is evaluated relative to plan. The machinery for developing plans and updating the corporate plan exists and is functioning. This frees the planning group so that it can devote a growing share of its total resources to searching the environment, evaluating corporate strengths and weaknesses, and identifying opportunities for corporate growth and profit improvement.[23]

This type of organization is being employed by an increasing number of firms which realize that intelligent planning requires a concerted effort on the part of the management.[24]

ADVANTAGES OF PLANNING

Planning gains a firm a number of important advantages. First, it forces a firm to forecast the environment. No longer does the management assume a wait-and-see attitude. Instead, the company begins evaluating conditions and formulating its own response. Passivity gives way to activity.

Second, planning gives the company direction in the form of objectives. Once the organization knows what it can and cannot do over the next one to

---

[23]Ibid., pp. 68–69.

[24]For more on this topic see R. T. Lenz, "Managing the Evolution of the Strategic Planning Process," *Business Horizons*, January–February 1987, pp. 34–39.

Many management experts like to point out the importance of "planning to plan." By this they mean that planning requires a conscious, deliberate effort to identify objectives and the steps that must be attained in reaching these goals. One of the most important parts of planning is getting the ideas on paper so that they can be communicated to others. This is particularly true in the case of entrepreneurs who are seeking funding from venture capitalists or banks. For these individuals, in particular, a well-written business plan is critical.

Effective business plans follow a number of useful guidelines. They are short, simple, and well organized. They also identify a target market, demonstrate the benefits of the company's good or services, and illustrate that the firm has the management team need to accomplish its goals. This approach helps convince investors that they are going to get their money back—and a lot more.

The ultimate success of the plan typically depends on how well the manager can prepare the document. Well-written business plans begin with an executive summary that provides a basic recap of the plan and can be quickly and easily read by potential investors. The remainder of the plan is divided into ten specific sections. The following briefly describes each.

1. **Background and purpose.** This section gives the reader a brief history of the firm, current products or services that are being offered, and the key factors that dictate the success of the business.

2. **Objectives.** In general terms, this section describes the company's overall goals.

3. **Market analysis.** This section provides an analysis of the overall market, the niche the firm is pursuing, the competitors in this niche, and other factors that will influence sales.

4. **Development and production.** This section highlights the various features related to researching, developing, and producing the basic product(s).

five years, it can begin setting goals. Day-to-day operational thinking gives way to more long-run designs.

Third, planning provides a basis for teamwork. When the goals are clearly defined, work assignments can be determined and everyone can begin to contribute to the fulfillment of these objectives. This often leads to improvements in morale; it also helps develop management talent. The manager can now delegate authority to subordinates and begin to evaluate performance. Without planning, such coordination would be a dream; with planning, it is a reality.

Finally, planning helps management learn to live with ambiguity. This is especially true in long- and intermediate-range planning. Management must realize that vagueness has its virtues. If management demands perfect clarity

5. **Marketing.** This section describes the marketing strategy that will be used to reach the potential market that has been described in section three.

6. **Financial plans.** This section provides projected financial statements, start-up costs, cash flow analysis, break-even point analysis, and a list of the amounts of money that will be needed from lenders or investors as well as when these funds will be needed.

7. **Organization and management.** This section provides an organization chart, a description of the tasks performed by key executives, and a general discussion of the workforce.

8. **Ownership.** This section discusses the legal form of business that is used and the implications of this form on the operation of the enterprise.

9. **Critical risks and problems.** This part of the report identifies the potential risks faced by investors and lenders and explains how these areas will be handled.

10. **Summary and conclusions.** This section briefly summarizes the key features of the report and provides a timetable for carrying out all of the important activities identified in the report.

A well-written business plan does not guarantee that the enterprise will get the funding it needs. However, the ability to concisely convey the objectives, scope, direction, and potential of the business often spells the difference between those who are able to secure the necessary financing and those who are not. Simply put, adequate financing is often a result of the ability of communicate the enterprise's plan of business.

Source: W. Keith Schilit, "How to Write a Business Plan," *Business Horizons*, September –October 1987, pp. 23–32.

beyond the point where such observations are possible, staff often refuse to do anything beyond operational planning.

PLANNING IS NO GUARANTEE

The development of the long-range plan and its integration with short-range plans are very useful. There is no guarantee, however, that a firm will be successful merely because it plans. Many things can go wrong, and they always, in one way or another, can be traced back to the premises on which the plan was formulated.

Sometimes information coming in from the field is erroneous. Salespeople may give strong endorsement to a particular modification of a current product, but the modified good may not sell very well. What potential customers say they are going to do and what they end up doing may be two different things, illustrating a problem inherent in marketing research.

A second basic problem is the economy. A plan predicated on a rising economy will run into trouble if a downturn is encountered. For example, during much of the ten-year period from 1980 to 1990, the economy expanded, and many organizational planners saw the future as more of the same. After all, it is far easier (and to many, more logical) to extrapolate the present than to wonder when the bloom will be off the rose. If a company has increased its sales by 25 percent a year for the last five years, it is very difficult for management to estimate the following year's increase at 15 percent. Psychologically, managers in this situation are taking a 10 percent cut. For this reason, many firms tend to extrapolate the economy during good times and estimate an upturn or leveling out during poor times. They design the economy to fit the plan instead of the proper reverse.

A third problem can be the company's financial position. A plan may rely heavily on strong advertising and personal promotion. If the company is then unable to finance this kind of campaign, the plan can fall flat. In fact, a downward spiral may occur with reduced promotional expenses leading to the nonmaterialization of sales, which results in the cutback of any further promotional effect. The publishing industry often faces this problem because of its small profit margin. For example, let us assume a textbook will be given an estimated sales price of $27.95 and an annual market potential of 5,000 copies. The advertising budget will be set at $10,000 for the first year and $5,000 for the second. However, if internal budgetary cuts require changes in the plan, the textbook price might be raised to $28.95 to help cover the publisher's in-house expenses. Yet such a move might also result in a decline in demand for the now-too-expensive book; perhaps only 3,500 copies would be bought. Revenue would then dip from an expected total of $139,750 to an actual total of $101,325. This, in turn, could lead the company to eliminate the follow-up advertising budget. Once the initial plan runs into trouble, everything goes awry because the plan is basically a sequence of cause-effect relationships that are supposed to work in particular ways. If the sequence of relationships is imperfect, every attempt to reestablish an equilibrium can lead to further problems.

A fourth common problem is lack of coordination. Even when the objectives are clear, the functional departments sometimes fail to synchronize their efforts. Sometimes this is caused by the staff's loss of enthusiasm for its own plan; more commonly, it results when the proposed plan is modified by higher authority. In either event, the human element comes into play, and plans are not implemented according to the previously determined schedule.

Planning does not lead to some future utopia in the life of any firm. Too many things can go wrong despite the most careful planning. Nevertheless, companies that plan do increase their chances for success, and it is that predictable benefit that leads intelligent managers to keep on planning.

■ SUMMARY

In this chapter comprehensive planning, which consists of strategic, intermediate, and operational plans, has been examined. Prime attention was given to long-run considerations, with the observation that most firms tend to be oriented too much toward the short run. The chapter also examined the roles played by the determination of the firm's basic socioeconomic mission, values of the top management, and analysis of the organization's strengths and weaknesses in the formulation of the strategic plan. The analysis of strengths requires accurate economic and sales forecasting coupled with a frank, honest evaluation of the company's material resources and personnel competencies. Only in this way can a firm identify a niche and formulate long-range objectives.

Although the long-range plan provides general direction, the intermediate-range and especially the operational plans are also important because they offer specific direction. The operational plan often consists of derivative functional plans such as marketing, production, and finance plans, designed to attain short-run objectives while harmonizing with the previously determined long-range goals. Such short-range plans provide management with a method for gauging progress, serving as a basis from which to adapt or modify current plans and construct future ones.

■ REVIEW AND STUDY QUESTIONS

1. What is meant by the term *comprehensive planning?* Why has there been a marked trend toward comprehensive planning on the part of many business firms?

2. What is meant by the term *strategic planning?* Put it in your own words.

3. How do companies go about determining their basic socioeconomic purpose? Cite three examples, including your local utility firm.

4. In what way do management values impact on strategic planning? Explain.

5. How does a firm conduct an external environmental forecast? What are some of the most common approaches? What kinds of considerations do these approaches address?

6. How does a firm evaluate its internal environment? What things does it consider in this evaluation? Explain.

7. How does a firm go about developing a propitious niche? What are some of the guidelines it should follow in doing so?

8.   What is a strategic business unit? Give a detailed example. Also, of what value are these SBUs in strategic planning? How are they used?

9.   In what ways are the General Electric strategic planning grid and the Boston Consulting Group's business portfolio matrix similar? In what ways are they different? Compare and contrast the two.

10. In formulating strategy for SBUs, what approach would be used with each of the following: stars, cash cows, question marks, dogs?

11. What is meant by the term *operational planning?* What is the difference between this type of planning and strategic planning? Explain.

12. In what way does the financial plan serve as the fulcrum for balancing the marketing and production plans? Give an example.

13. How can a planning organization be useful to management? Explain your answer.

14. What are some of the major advantages of planning? What are some of the major disadvantages? Explain.

15. What are some of the common problems that can cause a plan to fail? Identify and describe four.

■ SELECTED REFERENCES

Barnett, F. William "Four Steps to Forecast Total Market Demand." *Harvard Business Review,* July–August 1988, pp. 28–37.

Chrisman, James J., Charles W. Hofer, and William R. Boulton. "Toward a System for Classifying Business Strategies." *Academy of Management Review,* July 1988, pp. 413–28.

Day, George. "Gaining Insights Through Strategy Analysis." *Journal of Business Strategy,* Summer 1983, pp. 51–58.

de Geus, Arie P. "Planning as Learning." *Harvard Business Review,* March–April 1988, pp. 70–74.

Drucker, Peter F. *Management: Tasks, Responsibilities, Practices.* New York: Harper & Row, 1974, chaps. 5–10.

Gale, Bradley T., and Donald J. Swire. "Business Strategies That Create Wealth," *Planning Review,* March/April 1988, pp. 6–13.

Gupta, Anil K., and V. Govindarajan. "Build, Hold, Harvest: Converting Strategic Intentions into Reality," *Journal of Business Strategy,* Winter 1984, pp. 34–37.

Hambrick, Donald C., Ian C. MacMillan, and Diana L. Day. "Strategic Attributes and Performance in the BCG Matrix—A PIMS-Based Analysis of Industrial Product Businesses," *Academy of Management Journal,* September 1982, pp. 510–31.

Hamermesh, Richard G., and Roderick E. White. "Manage Beyond Portfolio Analysis." *Harvard Business Review,* January–February 1984, pp. 103–109.

Harrigan, Kathryn Rudie, and Michael E. Porter. "End-Game Strategies for

Declining Industries." *Harvard Business Review*, July–August 1983, pp. 111–20.

Hodgetts, Richard M., and Constance G. Bates. "In Search of Strategy: Lessons from History," *Strategy and Executive Action*, Spring 1984, pp. 2–5.

Horovitz, Jacques. "New Perspectives on Strategic Management." *Journal of Business Strategy*, Winter 1984, pp. 19–33.

Jauch, Lawrence R., and Richard N. Osborn. "Toward an Integrated Theory of Strategy." *Academy of Management Review*, September 1981, pp. 491–98.

Kiechel III, Walter. "Corporate Strategy for the 1990s." *Fortune*, February 29, 1988, pp. 34–42.

Lewis, Geoff, et al. "Big Changes at Big Blue," *Business Week*, February 15, 1988, pp. 92–98.

Lorange, Peter, and Richard F. Vancil. "How to Design a Strategic Planning System." *Harvard Business Review*, September–October 1976, pp. 75–81.

Mason, David H., and Robert G. Wilson. "Future Mapping: A New Approach to Managing Strategic Uncertainty." *Planning Review*, May/June 1987, pp. 20–29.

Mason, R. Hal. "Developing a Planning Organization." *Business Horizons*, August 1969, pp. 61–69.

Mintzberg, Henry, and James A. Waters. "Tracking Strategy in an Entrepreneurial Firm." *Academy of Management Journal*, September 1982, pp. 465–99.

Oliver, Alex R., and Joseph R. Garber. "Implementing Strategic Planning: Ten Sure-Fire Ways to Do It Wrong." *Business Horizons*, March–April 1983, pp. 49–51.

Pearce II, John A. "An Executive-Level Perspective on the Strategic Management Process." *California Management Review*, Fall 1981, pp. 39–48.

Rubin, Leonard R. "Planning Tiles: A CEO's Guide Through the Corporate Planning Maze." *Business Horizons*, September–October 1984, pp. 66–70.

Slevin, Dennis P., and Jeffrey K. Pinto. "Balancing Strategy and Tactics in Project Implementation." *Sloan Management Review*, Fall 1987, pp. 33–41.

Steiner, G. A. *Strategic Planning: What Every Manager Must Know*. New York: Free Press, 1979.

Swan, John E., and David R. Rink. "Fitting Market Strategy to Varying Product Life Cycles." *Business Horizons*, January–February 1982, pp. 72–76.

Taylor III, Alex. "Back to the Future at Saturn," *Fortune*, August 1, 1988, pp. 63–72.

Thompson, Arthur A., Jr. "Strategies for Staying Cost Competitive." *Harvard Business Review*, January–February 1984, pp. 110–17.

■ CASE: A Better Mousetrap

If you build a better mousetrap, it is said, the world will beat a path to your door. But will it really? The Woodstream Company had manufactured traps for catching all kinds of animals, from elephants to grizzly bears. One day, the firm decided to design and manufacture a streamlined mousetrap.

A product designer was brought in to design a trap that would look interesting enough for people to notice the change. The final product was made of plastic and looked like a sardine can with an arched doorway at floor level through which mice could enter. Any mouse coming through the doorway would trip a spring and be choked to death by a wire which, acting like an upside-down guillotine, would snap up from below.

The company called the new product "Little Champ" and priced it at 25 cents, in contrast to the wooden ones, which sold at two for 15 cents. Although the price was higher than average, the trap was easier to set, extremely efficient, and, perhaps best of all, could be cleaned and reused. It did not have to be thrown out with the mouse.

Looking forward to a booming demand, the company sent the traps out to hardware dealers across the nation. And the mousetraps just sat there on the hardware shelves, gathering expensive dust. Despite the changes in the traps' efficiency features, no one wanted them. Why? Apparently potential buyers, who thought nothing of throwing away the old wooden snap-trap, mouse and all, did not want to extract the dead mouse and clean the new plastic 25-cent trap.

The venture failed. Richard Woolworth, the company president, was unable to generate interest in the product, although he certainly tried. For example, during a New York City garbage strike, Woolworth wired the governor of New York, offering to ship a million rat traps for $144,000. But the governor was not interested, and the Woodstream Company finally gave up on the product.

Questions

1. What kind of planning should the Woodstream Company have done before manufacturing these traps?

2. Why was the company unable to sell the traps? Do you agree with the above analysis, or are there other reasons for the failure? Explain.

3. Is there anything the company can now do with the traps, or is the venture a total loss?

Source: Adapted from Stephen J. Fansweet, "Dick Woolworth Builds a Better Mousetrap—and Falls on His Face," *Wall Street Journal,* September 24, 1970, p. 1.

■ CASE: Milking the Cow

Marie Newsom had been president of Newsom Printing for five years, having left a high-paying job in sales for an eastern publishing firm to return to the family business. "We were on the verge of selling out," she told Willy

Chishilm, her management consultant. "My dad, who started the business, had died, and the other members of the family didn't want anything to do with it. That was when I began to look into the possibility of taking over and seeing what I could do. Well, you know the story. You've been here for a week now looking over operations and examining our financial statements. You know better than anyone how well we've done over the last four years."

Chishilm moved his chair closer to the desk and placed some papers on top of it. "Marie, you look just great on paper. I have absolutely no arguments with your technical operations. Some of the new machinery you purchased is going to save you a lot of money in the long run. And your staff morale is sky high. My management team has been talking to your people since Wednesday, and there hasn't been one negative comment about anything."

"Somehow, Willy, I don't think this is your way of telling me that everything is perfect."

"Right. It's my way of leading up to a plan of action that I want to recommend to you. You do have a problem here. You're too short-run oriented. You have no real idea of where you are going. You've got a couple of banks that you are supplying with printed material and a lot of walk-in business and that's all."

"Oh, I don't know about that. You can't forget that seventeen firms in town send all their printing orders to us also."

"Okay, them too. However, that's all you've got. You are tied directly into the orders you get from your local captive businesses and anyone coming in off the streets and that's it."

"So what's wrong with that? Look at our sales. In 1987 we did over $1.5 million of business. In 1988 we had sales of $1.75 million. This year we're anticipating $2.0 million, but at the rate we're going, it's going to be closer to $2.2 million. It seems to me we're in great shape."

"Financially speaking, you are. However, have you any idea where Newsom Printing is going to be in 1992? Or how about 1995? What are your long-range plans?"

"Willy, you know I don't mess with long-range planning. I don't need it. In this town there are two large banks. They send all their business to us. They always have. Besides them, we have those other seventeen companies, most of which are insurance firms that need an awful lot of printing done. All I have to do is keep worrying about the next three months. That's my long-range plan, ninety days into the future. As long as I know I have enough financing at the bank and my collections are taking place on time, I have a good cash flow. What else is there to running a successful business?"

"Marie, do you think the banks you print for got to be as large as they are by planning ninety days into the future?"

"No, but then I'm not a bank. My business has a number of companies that rely upon it exclusively for their printing. There is no company in town that can match my price on any job because I've got the best equipment and can offer higher quality and lower prices than any of them. So tell me why I need to worry about long-range planning. My whole plan consists of keeping the machines in working order and not letting the competition get any technological jumps on me. That's the only way I can get beaten out of a job, and it's just not going to happen. In a manner of speaking, I've carved a niche for myself. This niche is a very fat, profitable cow, and my job is to sit here and milk that cow for all it's worth. The last thing on my mind is long-range or, as you call it, strategic planning. Who needs it? When you've got a good thing going, enjoy it. What can long-range planning do for a business like mine?''

Questions

1. What are the advantages of long-range planning? Be specific.

2. What arguments should Chishilm raise in defense of his long-range planning proposal?

3. Can long-range planning really be of any value to Newsom Printing, or is the firm better off sticking with its current short-range planning approach? Defend your opinion.

■ CASE: Just Leave Us Alone

The Johnson Corporation was founded by Buzz Johnson in 1969. The going was rough in the early years, but by 1975 things had started to improve, and in the late 1970s, while the economy was dipping, Johnson's business was at its best. Sales and profits set new highs between 1984 and 1989, as seen in the listed company data:

Year	Sales	Net Profit
1984	$4,600,000	$ 400,000
1985	4,900,000	510,000
1986	5,300,000	636,000
1987	6,000,000	720,000
1988	7,850,000	1,020,000
1989	9,000,000	1,350,000

The firm's record was so outstanding, in fact, that a number of large corporations made offers to buy it. Finally, after careful consideration, Johnson accepted the offer of a large Eastern conglomerate. In addition to a very lucrative financial settlement, the conglomerate agreed that Johnson and his management team would remain at the helm, with business continuing as usual. The only major change was that all long-range and short-range performance goals (profitability, return on investment, sales, and the like) would have to be cleared with the planning organization at the conglomerate's headquarters so as to ensure overall organizational coordination.

Initially everything went smoothly, but by the end of the first year it was apparent things were not going well at all. Johnson called a meeting of his top people to see if things could be ironed out. He also persuaded the vice-president of corporate planning and his two staff assistants to fly in for the conference. Johnson sensed bad feelings between his people and the central planning group and decided it was time for both to air their gripes. The basic points of view presented by the two groups follow:

Johnson Group

Before we were purchased by the Eastern conglomerate, we used to run our own show around here. After all, who knows more about how to manufacture and sell our product than we do? But now we're asked to coordinate our plans with those of seven other companies. And sometimes our suggested plans apparently don't fit in because they're rejected or modified by the corporate planning department. We've had it with being told how to run our own end of the business. This concept of overall coordinated planning is having a drastic effect on the morale of our management team. Why don't you Easterners just leave us alone?

Corporate Planning Group

We have eight major companies in our conglomerate. The only way we can make these eight work as one is to coordinate their long- and short-range planning. We know people don't like to be told how to do their own job. And we don't mean to do that. But there has to be some harmony if we're to work as one big team. We can understand that managers don't like having their plans modified or revised, but this just can't be helped. And until the management of the Johnson Corporation realizes that it's part of a team, we're going to continue to have this problem. Big companies can't offer the personal touch that small ones can. When you become the member of a conglomerate, you have to be willing to give up a little autonomy. Perhaps the Johnson management should try seeing things from our point of view.

Questions

1. Can a conglomerate operate as what the planners called "one big team" without running into the kind of problems seen in this case?
2. Is the Johnson management right? Is the central planning organization indifferent to its problems?
3. How can this problem be solved? Present a feasible solution.

■ CASE: Thinking Smaller

The biggest auto producer in the world is General Motors, but over the past decade the firm has seen its market share diminish from 52 percent of the total North American market to less than 40 percent. What are the company's plans for the future? Will it recapture this lost market share and once again establish itself as the premier automaker in the world? GM spokespeople seem to think so, but they are in the minority. It appears that the future plans for General Motors will be to increase market share moderately in North America while increasing both production and plant utilization. This, in turn, will result in an increase in both return on equity and earnings per share. Here are some data contrasting 1987's results with 1992's projected position based on a forecast by industry experts:

	1987	1992
U. S. car market share	36.4%	37%
Plants	27	22
Car production	3,700,000	4,200,000
Capacity utilization	70%	95%
Return on equity	11.7%	15%
Earnings per share	$10.06	$22.00

The strategy for General Motors during the 1990s can be summed up in one word: downsizing. The firm will attempt to get more productivity out of fewer plants and, as a result, become more profitable. Will it be able to achieve these goals? This depends on a number of critical factors. One factor is how well it can protect its market share against imports from Germany and Japan as well as from local competition by Ford and Chrysler. Ford has been the big winner in gaining market share during the 1980s thanks to excellent design and quality improvements. Chrysler has been able to pull itself back from the brink of bankruptcy and increase its market share from a low of 9 percent during its bleakest period in the early 1980s to a high of around 14 percent by the end of this decade.

In fending off the competition General Motors will have to improve its quality, lower its cost per car (which has been the highest in the industry in recent years), and attract car buyers away from the competition. These are very ambitious objectives, but it is imperative that GM attain them. Failure to do so could result in the company slipping into second place in North America behind Ford Motor.

Questions

1. What is General Motors' basic socioeconomic purpose? Will it change as the firm downsizes? Why or why not?

2. How important are technological forecasting and sales forecasting to a company like GM? Explain.

3. In what way can a strategic planning grid such as the one presented in Figure 4-2 be of value to GM in attaining its future goals? Be complete in your answer.

Source: James Treece and Robert Ingersoll, "GM Faces Reality," *Business Week,* May 9, 1988, pp. 114–22.

■ SELF-FEEDBACK EXERCISE: Can You Recognize the Basic Mission?

Every organization has a basic mission or reason for existence. The following list of 25 firms are all sufficiently different so that it is possible to identify their basic mission from the answers provided on the right. Start by identifying those that you know and then complete the remainder by using an elimination process. Answers are provided at the end of the exercise.

Firm	Basic mission
1. 3M	_____ a. fast food
2. Liz Claiborne	_____ b. beauty
3. Florida Power & Light	_____ c. telecommunications
4. Philip Morris	_____ d. scientific and photographic equipment
5. IBM	_____ e. metals
6. AT&T	_____ f. pharmaceuticals
7. Harvard University	_____ g. instant photography
8. American Express	_____ h. food
9. PepsiCo	_____ i. energy
10. Wal-Mart	_____ j. health care
11. NBC	_____ k. publishing
12. Chrysler	_____ l. tobacco
13. Estee Lauder	_____ m. financial services
14. Polaroid	_____ n. motor vehicles and parts
15. Ryder Corporation	_____ o. electronics
16. International Telephone & Telegraph	_____ p. commercial banking
17. McDonald's	_____ q. agricultural productivity
18. Mt. Sinai Hospital	_____ r. entertainment
19. Delta Airlines	_____ s. truck rental
20. Deere	_____ t. education
21. Squibb	_____ u. discount retailing
22. New York Times	_____ v. soaps and cosmetics
23. Procter & Gamble	_____ w. air transportation
24. J. P. Morgan & Co.	_____ x. information processing
25. Bethlehem Steel	_____ y. apparel

Answers

1.	d	8.	m	14.	g	20.	q
2.	y	9.	h	15.	s	21.	f
3.	i	10.	u	16.	o	22.	k
4.	l	11.	r	17.	a	23.	v
5.	x	12.	n	18.	j	24.	p
6.	c	13.	b	19.	w	25.	e
7.	t						

CHAPTER 5

The Organizing Process

GOALS OF THE CHAPTER

Organizing entails the assignment of duties and the coordination of efforts among all organizational staff to ensure maximum efficiency in the attainment of predetermined objectives. The goals of this chapter are to examine the nature, purpose, and function of organizing.

When you have finished reading the chapter, you should be able to do the following:

1. Identify and describe the most commonly used forms of departmentalization.

2. Discuss the advantages and limitations of the committee form of organization.

3. Define the concept of span of control and relate its importance to effective organization design.

4. Describe the three types of authority used in organizational settings—line, staff, and functional—and relate their value in effective organizing.

5. Identify the determinants of decentralization and explain why some organizations are basically decentralized while others remain centralized.

6. Discuss the art of delegation, including some dos and don'ts.

7. Identify the five sources of power and the ways in which managers can increase their own power.

8. Describe the informal organization and discuss its importance to the modern manager.

FROM STRATEGY TO STRUCTURE

Strategy is a prerequisite for structure.

It has already been noted that the planning process encompasses strategic, intermediate, and operational plans. Our model can now be expanded, as in Figure 5-1, to include the organization structure, hence the often used phrase, from strategy to structure, which research has shown to be an accurate statement. Alfred D. Chandler, Jr., after conducting intensive studies of General Motors, DuPont, Standard Oil of New Jersey, and Sears, Roebuck and Company, showed that strategy is a prerequisite for structure.[1] Peter Grinyer and Masoud Yasai-Ardekani agree. After studying forty manufacturing firms that ranged in size from thirty-five employees to 17,000, they found a correlation between company size and both strategy and structure. This finding led them to conclude that as organizations became larger, greater attention was given to the strategy/structure linkage.[2] So while a small enterprise need be only minimally concerned with formal organization design, as it grows in size, a logical basis for organizing human efforts and material resources must be formulated. This chapter will be devoted to the various structures and concepts that can assist the manager in this process.

COMMON FORMS OF DEPARTMENT-ALIZATION

Perhaps the easiest way to grasp the function of organizing is to examine the mechanics of the process. By dividing the work and the work force into group activities, managers can form departments for the purpose of specialization. The three most widely used types of departmentalization are functional, product, and territorial.

Functional Departmentalization

Functional departmentalization is the most widely used.

Functional departmentalization, the most widely used departmentalization form, occurs when an enterprise organizes itself around the firm's major activities. In a manufacturing enterprise, in which the *organic functions*—those activities which are vital to the continued existence of a firm—are

---

[1]Alfred D. Chandler, Jr., *Strategy and Structure* (Garden City, NY: Anchor Books, Doubleday, 1966); see also Danny Miller, "Relating Porter's Business Strategies to Environment and Structure: Analysis and Performance Implications," *Academy of Management Journal*, June 1988, pp. 280–308.

[2]Peter H. Grinyer and Masoud Yasai-Ardekani, "Strategy, Structure, Size, and Bureaucracy," *Academy of Management Journal*, September 1981, pp. 471–86.

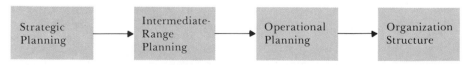

FIGURE 5-1   From Strategy to Structure

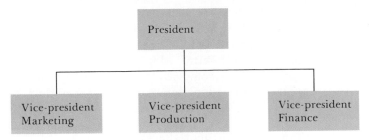

FIGURE 5-2   Typical Functional Organization Chart in Manufacturing

marketing, production, and finance, a typical functional organization chart is that shown in Figure 5-2. The figure shows also what an *organization chart* basically is—a diagram of an organization's departments and their relationships to each other.

In nonmanufacturing firms these functions differ. For example, in a large bank they often include comptroller, operations, legal, and public relations. In an insurance company it would be common to find actuarial, underwriting, agency, and claim adjustment. In a public utility organic functions would include accounting, sales, engineering, and personnel. All these are illustrations of major functional departments, which, in turn, can have *derivative departments*. For example, expanding Figure 5-2 to include second-level functional departments might result in the organization chart shown in Figure 5-3.

Similar charts could be drawn for all functionally organized enterprises, but the structure need not stop at the second level. Third-, fourth-, and even fifth-level departments may evolve, depending on the size of the enterprise.

Perhaps the major reason that functional departmentalization is so widely employed is the emphasis it places on basic activities, providing a logic and

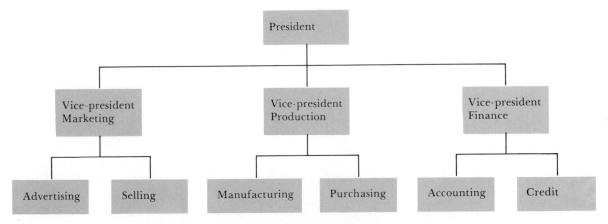

FIGURE 5-3   Derivative Functional Departments

framework for specialization. However, functional departmentalization also has some drawbacks. It can create a form of mental tunnel vision, in which functional specialists see nothing but their own areas of interest. Also, in some instances, firms adopt functional departmentalization because other companies are doing it. They decide to follow that kind of lead even if another form—departmentalization by product, for example—would actually be more beneficial for them.

Product Departmentalization

Product departmenta-lization is employed by many multi-line, large-scale compa-nies.

Product departmentalization has had increasing importance in recent years, especially among multi-line, large-scale enterprises. General Motors, DuPont, RCA, and General Electric all employ it. Many firms now organized by product were originally functional organizations which, as they grew, developed a need for a reorganization along product lines. Figure 5-4 is a simple illustration of a manufacturing firm reorganized along product lines. The organic functions of marketing, production, and finance can still be found in the structure, but prime attention now goes to the product lines, with all activities that relate to a particular product brought together.

Perhaps the main value of product departmentalization is that it facilitates coordination and allows for specialization. If the firm is large, this can be

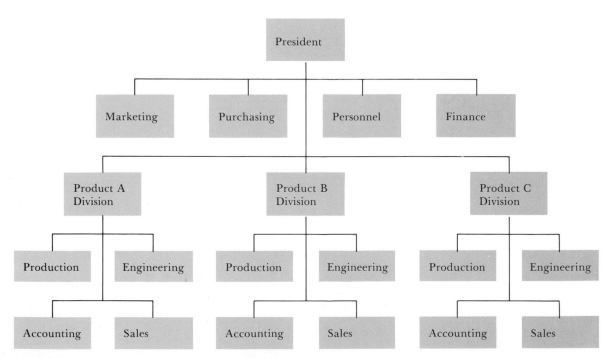

FIGURE 5-4   Product Organization Chart for a Manufacturing Firm

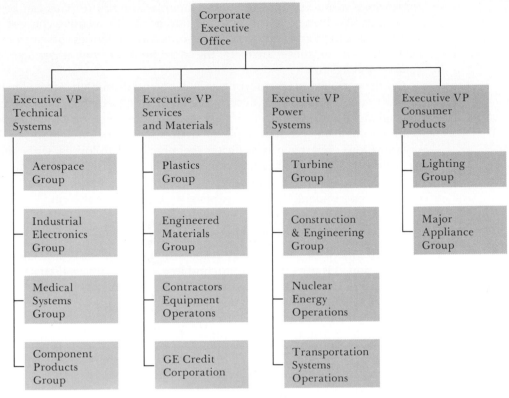

FIGURE 5-5   General Electric: Partial Organization Chart

Source: General Electric's *1983 Annual Report.*

especially beneficial. For example, General Electric in 1988 had seven major operating groups, each containing no fewer than six—and in some cases as many as twelve—divisions. Figure 5-5 shows some of these major groups. Had GE opted for functional departmentalization, the kind of massive coordination necessary in running such an enterprise would have proved impossible.

The product form of departmentalization can also aid in the measurement and control of operating performance. Since all revenues and costs can be differentiated and assigned to a particular product line, cost centers can be established, high-profit areas can be cultivated, and unprofitable product lines can be dropped.

Product departmentalization also provides an excellent opportunity for training executive personnel. Since the department or division is multi-functional, it often operates like a complete company, providing executives with a wealth of diversified functional experience that is useful in overcoming narrowness of interest and seasoning them for the future. This can be very important to a manager who will one day be chief executive charged with coordinating marketing, finance, and production activities. To overemphasize any one of these areas to the detriment of the others can have catastrophic results.

On the other hand, this form also has potential problem areas. First, the product divisions may try to become too autonomous, thereby presenting top management with a control problem. Second, because of its emphasis on semi-autonomism, product departmentalization works well only in those organizations that have a sufficient number of employees with general management ability. Third, it is common to find product divisions duplicating some of the facilities found at the top levels of the structure, making product departmentalization an expensive organizational form.

Territorial Departmentalization

When an enterprise is physically dispersed, as in the case of a large-scale organization, it is not uncommon to find *territorial departmentalization*, as seen in Figure 5-6. Contrasting the figure with that of product departmentalization (Figure 5-4) illustrates how similar the two forms really are.

The major advantage of a territorial organization is that of local operation. For example, a firm that manufactures close to the supply of raw materials

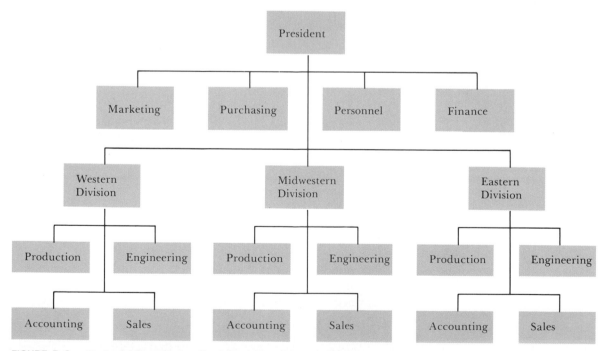

FIGURE 5-6   Territorial Organization Chart for a Manufacturing Firm

Geographically dispersed organizations often employ territorial departmentalization.

can produce its product at a lower cost per unit. Furthermore, employees in local sales departments can get to know their customers and markets much better than salespeople who live far away from their territories.

The disadvantages of territorial departmentalization are the same as those found in product departmentalization. It is often difficult for top management to control operations, and there is a tendency to duplicate services.

Other Types of Departmentalization

In addition, there are a number of other forms of departmentalization.

Functional, product, and territorial are only three types of departmentalization. There are numerous other forms, some of the most common being departmentalization by simple numbers, by time, by customer, and by equipment or process.

Departmentalization by simple numbers is used when the success of the undertaking depends exclusively on the amount of available labor. In community chest drives, for example, each manager is given a number of volunteers and a section of the city to canvass. Success depends to a great extent on the number of people available to ring doorbells. The U.S. military, in which portions of the infantry are still organized on the basis of numbers of people, provides another illustration. In the business setting, common labor crews are also organized this way.

Departmentalization by time is one of the oldest ways of grouping activities. For example, the division of the work force into three shifts—day, swing, and graveyard—is a common application of this form. Police and fire departments, hospitals, and other such emergency services all over the world still use this approach, as do industrial firms facing great demand for their goods.

Departmentalization by customer is used by organizations such as meat packers, retail stores, and container manufacturers. The meat packer's major departments are frequently dairy, poultry, beef, lamb, veal, and by-products; those of the retail store are often men's clothing, women's clothing, and children's clothing; the container company's major departments are likely to be drug and chemical, closure and plastics, and beverage industries. Educational institutions that offer both regular day courses on campus and extension courses at night or off campus in order to cater to the needs of different groups of students are another example. Departmentalization by customer helps organizations meet the special and widely varying needs of the customers they depend on.

Departmentalization by equipment (process departmentalization) is often used in manufacturing organizations—for example, in the establishment of an electronic data processing department. Similarly, it is common in many plants to find lathe presses or automatic screw machines arranged in one locale. The basic value of this organizational form is the economic advantages that such groupings bring about. By placing the machines together, the company can obtain greater efficiency.

All the basic departmentalization patterns examined thus far are common organizational forms. It should be noted, however, that every enterprise employs its own particular variation. Most organizations have some form of hybridization in their designs—for example, a basically functional organization with traces of product, equipment, process, customer, and territorial departmentalization. Organization charts are rarely specimens of pure functional, product, or territorial departmentalization.

COMMITTEE ORGANIZATIONS

Another common organizational form is the committee.

Another common organizational form, often used in conjunction with departmentalization, is the committee. Research indicates that committees are increasingly used in business. In general, there are two types. The most common is the *ad hoc committee*, a committee that is appointed for a particular purpose and then disbanded after it has analyzed a problem or conducted some research in order to give its recommendations. The other type, which does not disband, is often called the *standing committee;* many of these are also advisory, like the ad hoc committees. If a committee has the authority to order implementation of its recommendations, however, its members are working in a *plural executive* capacity. The most common illustration of a plural executive is a board of directors, but in large corporations it is not uncommon to find the high-level policy committees—for example, executive or finance—also serving in the plural executive capacity.[3] (see also Social Responsibility in Action: Shape Up or Ship Out).

Advantages of Committees

Committees have some important advantages to offer. Three of the most commonly cited are group deliberation, motivation, and coordination.

Group Deliberation

Two heads being better than one, a committee would be expected to have more knowledge, experience, and judgment than any lone individual. When an organization focuses the attention of a committee on a particular problem, the result is often a solution superior to that which could have been obtained from any one member working independently.

Motivation

Research has shown that when subordinates are permitted to participate in the decision-making process, enthusiasm for accepting and implementing the recommendations often increases. The work force supports the solution because its members had a hand in fashioning it. Committees can provide the basis for such action.

---

[3]J. Richard Harrison, "The Strategic Use of Corporate Board Committees," *California Management Review*, Fall 1987, pp. 109–125.

The stockholders are the owners of the company, and the board of directors is directly responsible to them. That is the way it is supposed to work, but in practice many boards of directors have been oblivious to the concerns and demands of the stockholders. That is all beginning to change. The 1990s are going to see much greater responsiveness from these boards. One reason is because stockholders are beginning to apply pressure and to sue when they feel the boards are not acting in accordance with the corporate charter. Here are some examples.

The board of directors at Allegheny International gave a $1 million salary to the president, put the man's son up in a $1 million apartment at company expense, and approved $30 million in personal loans to officers and directors at a 2 percent rate of interest. When this information became public, the shareholders sued the board for wasting corporate assets and making grossly improper business decisions.

Shareholders of the Trans Union Corporation sued the members of the board of directors personally. The court upheld the suit and found that the directors were negligent in their operation of the firm. In particular, the judge found that the board had not spent sufficient time determining the fair market value of a railcar-leasing company which it sold to another firm. As a result the directors settled the case for $23 million.

In a host of other cases shareholders have forced the company to put resolutions on the ballot ranging from doing business in South Africa to handling takeover attempts by outside raiders. Most of these resolutions have been defeated, but in many cases the vote has been razor-thin. This is a clear sign that the stockholders intend to play a major role in determining the company's long-range strategy and major operating decisions. The days when the board was voted into office and then did whatever it wanted are fast fading. Board members are finding that if they do not remain responsive to the shareholders, they will soon find themselves tossed out of the executive suite. For many of them it is becoming a matter of shaping up or shipping out.

Source: Stratford P. Sherman, "Pushing Corporate Boards to Be Better," *Fortune,* July 18, 1988, pp. 58–67.

Coordination

Committees are also useful in coordinating plans and transmitting information. The implementation of a major program, for example, often involves many departments, and a committee can help each to see where it fits in the overall plan. It can also obtain agreement on what each is going to do and when, thereby coordinating overall efforts.

Disadvantages of Committees

Despite all their advantages, committees are the butt of many jokes (for example, the one about a camel being a horse designed by a committee) because the drawbacks to using committees in the organizational design often outweigh the returns. Three of the most commonly cited disadvantages are waste of time, compromise, and lack of individual action.

Waste of Time

The adage that time is money can be well considered in evaluating the costs and worth of committees. Many of them are far too large, and many spend an excessive amount of time discussing trivial matters. On the issue of size, C. Northcote Parkinson has remarked that there is constant pressure to increase the number of people on a committee if for no other reason than to include more individuals with specialized knowledge.[4]

On the issue of time spent on trivial matters, Parkinson notes that complex issues often confound people, who, because they are unwilling to admit ignorance, adopt a policy of silence. The result is the dispatching of crucial decisions, such as the allocation of $1.2 billion for an atomic reactor, within a matter of minutes. However, on simple issues that are understandable to all, such as the construction of a $5,000 bicycle shed for use by the clerical staff, committee members come alive. Comprehending both the issue and expenses (and realizing they were lax in their participation in the atomic reactor topic), they spring into action with newfound vigor.[5] Parkinson attributes this phenomenon to the *law of triviality*, which states that "the time spent on any item of the agenda will be in inverse proportion to the sum involved."[6] If this is true, many committees may indeed not be worth the cost.

Compromise

Committees always pose the danger of inappropriate compromise. After haggling over an issue for a long time, the group may decide to mediate the matter. No one gets what anyone started out for, but the ultimate decision is one everybody can live with. Unfortunately, the result is often a mediocre decision, truly representing the least common denominator.

Lack of Individual Action

There are some things that are better accomplished by individuals than by committees. For example, one very famous American Management Association report found that although committees were considered useful in handling jurisdictional questions, such as interdepartmental disputes, many executives regarded them as ineffective in carrying out such functions as decision making, organizing, executing, and leading.[7] Instead, the respon-

---

[4]C. Northcote Parkinson, *Parkinson's Law* (Boston: Houghton Mifflin, 1957), chap. 3.

[5]Ibid.

[6]Ibid., p. 24.

[7]Ernest Dale, *Planning and Developing the Company Organization Structure*, Research Report No. 20 (New York: American Management Association, 1952), p. 92.

dents preferred individual action. People in management must recognize the times when committees do not perform as well as the individual manager.

How to Use Committees Effectively

There are five important guidelines for using committees effectively.

In view of their drawbacks, a manager working with committees should adhere to some important guidelines if committees are to be effectively employed. First, the objective of the group must be clearly stated. Second, participants must be carefully chosen so that they provide the expertise needed to attain the objective. Third, the size must be manageable, allowing for discussion and healthy disagreement without becoming too unwieldly in the process. Fourth, an agenda indicating the topics for discussion and analysis must be sent out beforehand so that everyone can be prepared to begin immediately. Fifth, the chair must be able to encourage participation while keeping the group headed toward the objective. Although these guidelines cannot ensure success, they have been found to improve committee performance markedly because they are designed to overcome specific common pitfalls.

SPAN OF CONTROL

Span of control, which refers to the number of people reporting to a given superior, is another important organizing concept. Many of the classical theorists believed the ideal span to be between three and six workers. Although this number is open to dispute, the span will certainly have a great deal of influence on the organizational design. For example, taking two companies with approximately the same number of employees, Figure 5-7

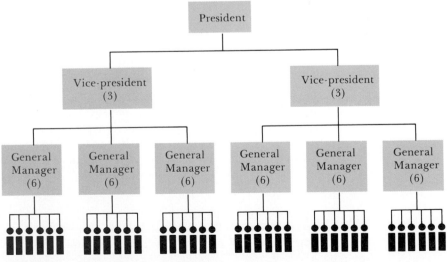

FIGURE 5-7   Narrow Span of Control

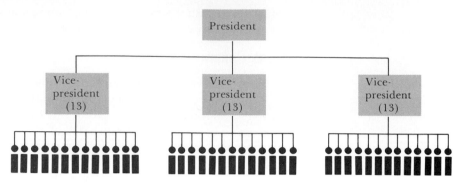

FIGURE 5-8   Wide Span of Control

illustrates how the structure would appear if a narrow span of control were employed, while Figure 5-8 shows a company with a wide span of control.

A narrow span of control requires that the organization have more levels in the hierarchy, and the structure therefore looks very much like a pyramid. Conversely, the organization with the wide span of control has fewer levels and a rectangular shape; it is shallow and wide. The organization chart for the firm with the narrow span of control is called a tall structure; the one for the firm with the wide span is called a flat structure.

Flat and Tall Structures

Classical bureaucratic organizations typically have very *tall organization structures*, characterized by narrow spans that allow the manager to exercise tight control. The manager has only a few subordinates and can therefore be aware of everything the subordinates are doing.

The most famous departure from the narrow span was made by Sears, Roebuck and Company and is often attributed to James C. Worthy, a management consultant and former vice-president of the company.[8] After experimenting with both conventional and flat structures, the Sears management concluded that on the basis of sales volume, profit, morale, and management competence, the flat design was superior. Several factors accounted for the results. First, having a large number of subordinate managers, the superiors found they had to delegate important decisions; they did not have the time to do everything themselves. In turn, by being forced to manage, the subordinates became better at their jobs. This led to increased

[8]James C. Worthy, "Organizational Structure and Employee Morale," *American Sociological Review*, April 1950, pp. 169–79; and "Factors Influencing Employee Morale," *Harvard Business Review*, January 1950, pp. 61–73.

morale and higher quality performance. It also made store managers more selective in choosing subordinates, because they knew they would have to delegate considerable authority to the people they hired. In addition, reducing the number of hierarchical levels improved communication. Such a structure helped overcome what Peter Drucker, one of the best known and most highly regarded authorities on management today, calls the major malorganization symptom, which he states this way:

> The most common and most serious symptom of malorganization is multiplication of the number of management levels. A basic rule of organization is to build the *least possible* number of management levels and forge the shortest possible chain of command.[9]

There are benefits to both flat and tall structures.

This does not mean, however, that flat structures are always superior. Research by Rocco Carzo, Jr., and John N. Yanouzas, for example, has shown that groups operating under a basically tall structure had significantly better results than those operating under a flat structure.[10] There are arguments to be made for each structure, indicating that the right span is a function of the situation, the manager, the subordinates, and the work itself.[11] Perhaps Robert J. House and John B. Miner have summarized this entire area best:

> The implications for the span of control seem to be that (1) under most circumstances the optimal span is likely to be in the range 5 through 10; (2) the larger spans, say 8 through 10, are most often appropriate at the highest policy-making levels of an organization, where greater resources for diversified problem-solving appear to be needed (although diversified problem-solving without larger spans may well be possible); (3) the breadth of effective spans of first line supervisors is contingent on the technology of the organization; and (4) in prescribing the span of control for specific situations consideration must be given to a host of local factors such as the desirability of high group cohesiveness, the performance demands of the task, the degree of stress in the environment, task interdependencies, the need for member satisfaction, and the leadership skills available to the organization.[12]

---

[9]Peter F. Drucker, *Management: Tasks, Responsibilities, Practices* (New York: Harper & Row, 1974), p. 546.

[10]Rocco Carzo, Jr., and John N. Yanouzas, "Effects of Flat and Tall Organization Structure," *Administrative Science Quarterly*, June 1969, pp. 178–91.

[11]For more on this topic, see Dan R. Dalton, William D. Todor, Michael J. Spendolini, Gordon J. Fielding, and Lyman W. Porter, "Organization Structure and Performance: A Critical Review," *Academy of Management Review*, January 1980, pp. 49–64.

[12]Robert J. House and John B. Miner, "Merging Management and Behavioral Theory: The Interaction between Span of Control and Group Size," *Administrative Science Quarterly*, September 1969, pp. 461–62.

AUTHORITY – RESPONSIBILITY RELATIONSHIPS

Concurrent with the formation of an organization structure exists the need for assigning specific duties to the employees. Often companies will construct position descriptions which outline the functions each individual is to perform, the authority and responsibility associated with the position, and the inherent organizational relationships attached to the position. (Such items as to whom the employee reports and is responsible and a statement of necessary employee interactions that the job sets up would be dealt with in this part of the description.)

Sources of Authority

Authority is the right to command. The *formal theory of authority*, which supports the organizational hierarchy, contends that authority comes from the top, as seen in Figure 5-9. Chester I. Barnard, however, argued that

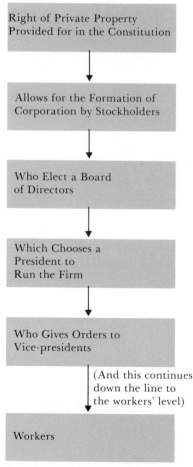

FIGURE 5-9   Formal Theory of Authority

authority actually comes from the bottom because no one has authority unless subordinates accept directives; this is the basis of Barnard's famous *acceptance theory of authority.*

There are several other theories of authority. One is the *authority of the situation.* For example, if a person hands a bank teller a note demanding all the money, the teller, by pressing the silent burglar alarm which calls the police for bank emergencies, has exercised the authority of the situation. This authority is limited to an occasion, but there is no doubt that the person who seizes it has the right to command. Crisis situations, which usually call for instant action, often impel those present to assume authority whether or not it has been formally delegated to them.

Another theory of authority is known as the *authority of knowledge.* The person who knows the most about the situation simply becomes the person in charge of the operation. For example, if the president of the United States is flying to Paris for an urgent summit conference and the plane encounters engine trouble twenty minutes into flight from Dulles International, the pilot will tell the president that they are turning back. As commander in chief, the president has the authority to countermand this order. However, none has ever done such a thing because the presidents have realized that their pilots know far more about this type of situation than they do. Superior knowledge gives the pilot the requisite authority.

Another exercise of this type of authority involved a particular president on a plane filled with confusion over whether city, county, state, or federal law allowed the plane carrying the body of President John F. Kennedy and also carrying the newly-sworn president, Lyndon B. Johnson, to leave Dallas's Love Field for its flight back to Washington on November 22, 1963. Johnson's decision to get the plane airborne resolved the arguments over jurisdiction; he did not, however, make a practice of ordering his jet to take off. His decision on this day was based on his knowledge of all four governments and of their rights and powers in addition to his awareness of the need for the president to be close to the seat of national power. He was the person on the plane with the greatest relevant knowledge; therefore, he made the accepted decision.

There are three major types of authority.

It is evident there is more than one source of authority. The acceptance theory in particular illustrates that the concept is dynamic, pointing the way to consideration of such topics as power and the role of the informal organization. Before taking up these subjects, however, this chapter will assess the three major types of authority: line authority, staff authority, and functional authority. Line authority and staff authority come from the departments that bear their names. *Line departments* carry out activities directly related to the accomplishment of the firm's major objectives, whereas *staff departments* carry out activities that are indirectly related to these objectives. For reasons that will develop clearly, it is necessary to defer the discussion of functional authority. But each of the three types of authority is an essential part of the basic framework of an organization's structure.

Although they are always modified in practice, as were the forms of departmentalization just examined, the three types are and will continue to be of central importance to an understanding of the organizing process.

TYPES OF AUTHORITY

Line authority is direct authority.

Line Authority

Line authority, the most fundamental type of authority, is often referred to as direct authority because it encompasses the right to give orders and to have decisions implemented. All superiors have line authority over their subordinates. The military provides a classic illustration. The general has line authority over the colonel, who has line authority over the major, and so on down the hierarchy. Analogously, as seen in Figure 5-10, the president of a company has line authority over the vice-presidents. In turn, the vice-president of production can give direct orders to the heads of manufacturing and purchasing, who are the immediate subordinates of the vice-president, and they, in turn, have direct authority over their respective subordinates. Line authority results in a chain of command, often called the scalar chain, which runs from the top to the bottom of the organization and establishes an authority-responsibility relationship throughout.

Staff Authority

Staff authority is auxiliary authority. Its scope is limited in one significant way: It does not provide the right to command. Rather, the nature of the staff

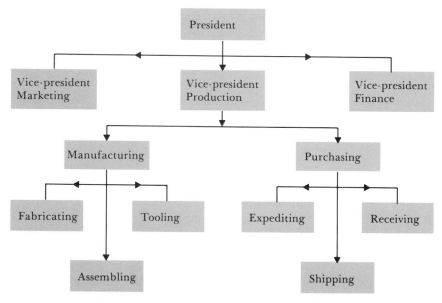

FIGURE 5-10   Line Authority

Staff authority is auxiliary authority.

relationship is supportive. Individuals with staff authority assist, advise, recommend, and facilitate organizational activities. As an organization grows in size, executives face increasingly complex problems. Line authority alone is inadequate, and as a result, staff relationships are created.

One of the most common examples of staff authority is the subordinate manager who provides auxiliary services for a superior in the form of recommendations or advice. Another example is the assistant to the president whose job is to counsel the chief executive. A third illustration is the lawyer charged with providing legal advice to the president of a company. Figure 5-11 provides an illustration of a line-staff chart.

Line-Staff Problems

It may well be considered that the line-staff authority relationship virtually created the need for functional authority. Therefore, before discussing the third fundamental type of authority, it will be necessary to discuss the line-staff relationship in some detail. Many firms have found that staff authority can be advantageous and can also lead to authority conflicts

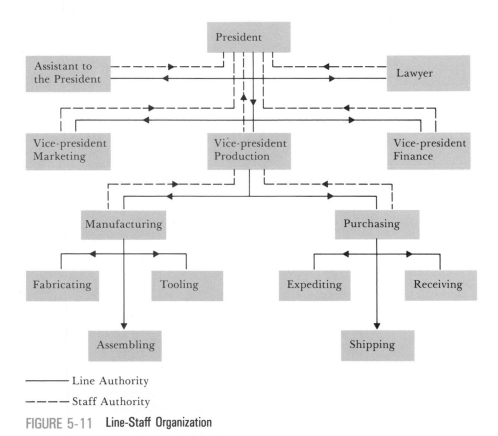

FIGURE 5-11 **Line-Staff Organization**

between line and staff executives.[13] One of the major causes rests in the attitudes of the two groups. For example, it is common to find that a line executive is an older person who came up the hard way. If this executive has a college degree (many do not), it may have been earned primarily through correspondence study or night classes. Conversely, the staff counterpart is often a younger person, perhaps with a master's degree in business, who may be bursting with bright ideas about how to improve operations. The line executive sees the young person as lacking in practical experience. The staff executive sees the older person as unwilling to try new ideas.

A second problem arises from the fact that line executives have ultimate responsibility for the decisions they make. If they accept a staff recommendation and the results are poor, they cannot pass the buck back upstairs. This makes them wary of staff advice. Conversely, staff people see hesitancy or refusal on the part of the line executives as indecisiveness and inability to recognize substantive recommendations. They feel the line should accept their expertise outright instead of having to be diplomatically persuaded to accept staff recommendations.

Some of the other common reasons for the line-staff conflicts are brought about by the following attitudes and philosophies:

Line	Staff
1. Highly action-oriented.	1. Concerned with studying a problem in depth before making recommendations.
2. High intuitive, in contrast to analytical staff.	2. Highly analytical, in contrast to intuitive line.
3. Often shortsighted.	3. Often too long-range-oriented.
4. Often ask the wrong kinds of questions.	4. Have answers and therefore spend time looking for questions.
5. Want simple, easy-to-use solutions.	5. Complicate the situation by providing esoteric data.
6. Accustomed to examining some of the available alternatives and choosing one of them.	6. Interested in examining all possible alternatives, weighing and analyzing them, then choosing the best, regardless of time or cost restraints.
7. Highly protective of the organization.	7. Highly critical of the organization.

Various causes of line-staff conflicts have been identified.

---

[13]See, for example, T. F. Cawsey, "Why Line Managers Don't Listen to Their Personnel Departments," *Personnel*, January–February 1980, pp. 11–20.

When line and staff attitudes and philosophies are in conflict, the organization will not achieve maximum benefit from the work force. However, it is not necessary for these conditions to exist. Various approaches can be used to improve line-staff relations.

Improving Line-Staff Relations

There are a number of steps for improving line-staff relations.

One of the most effective ways to bring about and foster line-staff cooperation is to get everyone to understand the nature of the authority relationships. If the line people realize that they are responsible for making operating decisions and that staff people are there to assist them, the line may obtain a greater appreciation of the staff. Likewise, staff people must understand that theirs is only an auxiliary function; they must sell their ideas to line supervisors. They cannot order implementation of their recommendations; they must persuade line managers to adopt them. That often means that staff presentations to line executives must be sufficiently persuasive to help the line supervisor sell the idea to line workers.

A second approach, which may seem obvious but unfortunately is not, is to encourage the line to listen to the staff. Chapter 2 showed how the Roman Catholic Church has used the concept of compulsory staff service for centuries, thus requiring the solicitation of staff advice. Although such a mandatory approach can have serious drawbacks in a business setting, line managers should at least be encouraged to listen to their staff. Many line executives have found that their proposals and plans are more readily accepted if they consult with the staff before submitting them. Such an approach ensures a united front when top management then asks the staff how they feel about the proposal.

A third method of forestalling line-staff relationship problems is keeping staff specialists informed about matters that fall within their province. It is impossible for assistants to help line managers who fail to relate the kind of information they need or to explain the types of decisions confronting them. A line manager who does keep an information flow open, however, paves the way for effective staff work.

Another useful method of dealing with line-staff relations is that of *completed staff work.* This concept involves studying the problem and presenting a solution or recommendation in such a way that the line executive can either approve or disapprove the action. Prior to presentation, the staff works out all details of a planned project. Although the approach can involve a tremendous amount of time on the part of staff people, it saves the line manager from being subjected to continual meetings and discussions. The entire project is assumed by the staff specialists, and the line people are not bothered with details until the entire issue is presented to them. This technique not only provides a basis for justifying the existence of staff; it also gives them an opportunity to sell their ideas to the line.

Functional Authority

Functional authority is the right to give orders in a department other than one's own.

As an organization grows in size, specialization increases. In addition to the use of line and staff authority, many firms also employ *functional authority,* authority in a department other than one's own. This authority is delegated to an individual or a department concerned with a specified policy, practice, or process being carried out by individuals in other units, and it can be exercised by managers in both line and staff departments. For example, as shown in Figure 5-12, in a product departmentalization structure, certain line managers can have functional authority over the product division managers. In such a case, a vice-president of finance may be able to require the divisions to keep particular kinds of accounting records. At the same time, the vice-president of marketing may be able to request from the departments the presentation of the weekly sales data in tabular form. In a manner of speaking, the vice-presidents in this sort of situation have a slice of line authority in the divisions. It should be stressed, however, that this is limited authority based on expertise and designed to improve organizational efficiency. For this reason, it is common to find functional authority limited to telling people how they are to do something and when it should be done. It seldom involves, where, what, or who, for this would seriously undermine the divisional manager's own line authority. Furthermore, the president will almost always tell the division heads that functional authority is going to be delegated to the vice-presidents of marketing, engineering, production, and finance, asking the division heads' opinions in the process. This method is used to ensure that power grabbing stays at a minimum.

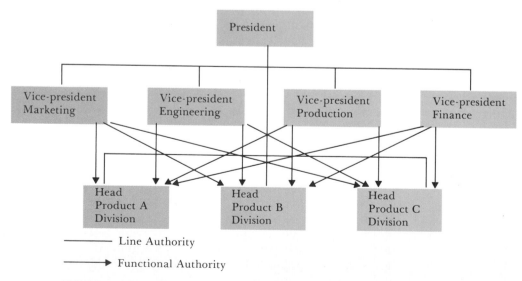

FIGURE 5-12   Line Departments with Functional Authority

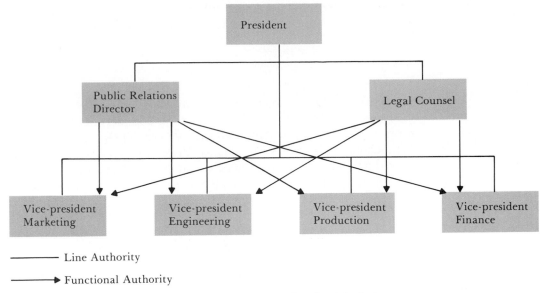

Line Authority

Functional Authority

FIGURE 5-13   Staff Departments with Functional Authority

Functional authority can also be delegated to staff specialists. For example, the president may have many auxiliary staff members, including a public relations director and legal counsel. In a pure staff situation, these people offer advice only in their own areas of expertise. However, the president may find it more efficient to delegate functional authority to these people. The president who works this way allows staff to issue their own directives, in their own areas of authority, to line managers, thus making it unnecessary for all communication to be cleared through the president. This situation is illustrated in Figure 5-13. A pure staff relationship no longer exists.

Problems with Functional Authority

Functional authority can undermine a manager's authority.

The major problem in employing functional authority is the danger of undermining the integrity of managerial positions. For this reason, it is important to indicate precisely who has functional authority and in what matters. Unfortunately, many organizations fail to do this. As a result, managers take wide latitude in their interpretation of the breadth of their functional authority, and confusion and anger ensue. In theory, functional authority is supposed to be limited, but in practice the reverse is often more accurate. Written definitions of functional authority are one means of reducing this problem. Another way is to limit the scope of such authority whenever possible, so that it does not extend more than one hierarchical level below that of the manager holding the functional authority. Such a rule prevents a top executive from undermining other managers in the structure by giving orders directly to their subordinates. Functional authority certainly has advantages for the organization; however, it should be employed with prudence.

DECENTRAL- IZATION OF AUTHORITY

For some time now many firms, especially large ones, have followed a policy of decentralizing authority. The term *decentralization* should not be confused with that of delegation. Although the two are closely related, *decentralization* is much more encompassing in nature, reflecting a management philosophy regarding which decisions to send down the line and which to maintain near the top for purposes of organizational control. All organizations have some degree of decentralization, since absolute centralization is virtually impossible. For this reason, decentralization must be viewed as a relative concept, not as an absolute. Ernest Dale, a well-known management writer, has described some conditions when decentralization is greater:

1. The greater the number of decisions made lower down the management hierarchy.

2. The more important the decisions made lower down the management hierarchy. For example, the greater the sum of capital expenditure that can be approved by the plant manager without consulting anyone else, the greater the degree of decentralization in this field.

Decentralization is a relative concept.

3. The more functions affected by decisions made at lower levels. Thus companies which permit only operational decisions to be made at separate branch plants are less decentralized than those which also permit financial and personnel decisions at branch plants.

4. The less checking required on the decision. Decentralization is greatest when no check at all must be made; less when superiors have to be informed of the decision after it has been made; still less if superiors have to be consulted before the decision is made. The fewer people to be consulted, and the lower they are on the management hierarchy, the greater the degree of decentralization.[14]

In recent years, there has been a trend toward decentralization, although in some industries, such as smelting and refining, centralized structures are still fairly common. The major question, of course, is whether decentralization is preferable to centralization in terms of job performance. Dan Dalton and his associates investigated this question by looking at the relationship between centralization and performance and concluded that "the limited evidence tends to support a negative relationship between centralization and

---

[14]Dale, p. 107.

performance for managers and professionals in studies using hard performance criteria. Otherwise little is known of the association between centralization and performance.[15] Findings such as these, coupled with American values that encourage a democratic approach to getting things done, undoubtedly help explain the growing degree of decentralization in many firms. What must be remembered is that this degree of decentralization will be tempered by a series of important determinants. The following paragraphs examine six of these.

Determinants of Decentralization

The degree of decentralization depends on a number of factors.

Many factors influence the decentralization of authority. Most are beyond control of the individual manager, hence the previous statement distinguishing this term from delegation, whereby the manager decides which duties to assign to a subordinate. Some of the most important determinants of the degree of decentralization follow.

Cost Factors

As a rule of thumb, the greater the cost involved, the more likely it is that the decision will be made at the upper levels. It is not uncommon to find a firm with a policy permitting all expenditures of $500 or less to be approved by an operating department while all others are decided upon by a centralized purchasing or finance committee. In this way top management is able to control major expenditures for such items as capital equipment. Many organizations, including General Motors, employ highly centralized controls in the financial area.

Uniform Policy

A desire for uniform policies is another cause for centralization of authority. Standardization of quality, price, credit, and delivery can be beneficial because it ensures that everyone will be treated alike. Similarly, standardization of financial and accounting records makes it easier to compare the performance of various units and analyze their overall efficiency. When the firm wants everything done in a particular, uniform way, centralization of policy is desirable.

Company Size

As a firm gets larger, it is impossible to maintain the old degree of centralization; top management cannot continue to hold such a tight grip on the reins. It is common to find such firms reorganizing and assigning more

---

[15]Dan R. Dalton, William R. Todor, Michael J. Spendolini, Gordon J. Fielding, and Lyman W. Porter, "Organization Structure and Performance: A Critical Review," *Academy of Management Review*, January 1980, p. 59.

authority to the various departments and operating units. In this way, the company reduces the expenses that often accompany growth. The units operate on a more autonomous basis, the top management concerning itself with tasks such as planning, financing, evaluating, and controlling the overall operations of the firm. Day-to-day activities are handled at the lower levels.

Philosophy of Top Management

Many firms are highly centralized, whereas others are highly decentralized simply because of the character and philosophy of their top management. Henry Ford's firm was highly centralized because that was the way he wanted it; Ford decided matters for the entire company. Conversely, General Motors has been highly decentralized for years because in 1920 A. P. Sloan was able to get his reorganization plan accepted by the board of directors. In essence, it called for decentralization of operating authority to the divisions while maintaining centralized control at the top levels. Ernest Dale described the two principles on which the recommendations rested in this way:

1. The responsibility attached to the chief executive of each operation shall in no way be limited. Each such organization headed by its chief executive shall be complete in every necessary function and enabled to exercise its full initiative in a logical development. (Decentralization of operations.)

2. Certain central organization functions are absolutely essential to the logical development and proper coordination of the Corporation's activities. (Centralized staff services to advise the line of specialized phases of the work, and central measurement of results to check the exercise of delegated responsibility.)[16]

Philosophy of Subordinate Managers

The philosophy of subordinate managers affects decentralization because these people can either encourage or discourage such a policy. If subordinates want decentralization, top management may feel there is little to be gained by maintaining all important decision making at the upper levels. The desire by the subordinates for independence and the willingness to assume increased responsibility may convince them to become more decentralized. Conversely, a shortage of lower-level managers that leaves the current group of subordinates with an excessive amount of work sometimes encourages top management to maintain a more centralized approach.

Functional Area

Some functional areas of enterprise will be more decentralized than others. For example, in a manufacturing firm, production will often be highly decentralized. As the size of the facilities increases, authority will be

---

[16]Ernest Dale, *The Great Organizers* (New York: McGraw-Hill, 1960), p. 87.

decentralized so that it rests at the operating level. This is so because the people who handle production operations tend to know them better than anyone else. Sales also will often be decentralized for this same reason. Of course, budgets and controls will still have a great deal of centralization, as will other areas in which overall control is necessary: pricing, advertising, and market research, for example. Finance will be highly centralized; top management will maintain that control over the entire organization. Although decisions on small expenditures may be made at the lower levels, those that seriously affect the company's profit or financial stability will be made at the top.

THE ART OF DELEGATION

Delegation is a process the manager uses in distributing work to the subordinates. The process encompasses three basic steps: the assigning of duties to the subordinates; the granting of authority to carry out these duties; and the creation of an obligation whereby the subordinate assumes responsibility to the superior to complete the task satisfactorily.

Delegation, like decentralization, is often a matter of personal preference on the part of the manager. However, while some will delegate so much work to their subordinates that they virtually abdicate their role as manager, it is far more common to find the reverse. Many managers hang on to everything, refusing to allow their subordinates to try their hands at anything. This unwillingness to let go is based on the assumption that the manager can do the job better than the subordinate. Delegation, to a manager like this, is at best a bother and at worst a personal threat. Unfortunately, this attitude is often self-defeating. It leads subordinates to the conclusion that they are not trusted by their superior. It also results in a failure to develop effective management talent. How can a junior executive ever be expected to fill the boss's shoes if the subordinate never gets the opportunity to try and to be observed?

These deficiencies can be overcome if the manager is willing to follow certain key steps. First, the manager must agree to try delegating authority and to do so in explicit terms. The subordinates must know exactly what they are to do and what kinds of results are going to be expected. Second, the person and the job must be carefully matched. Third, if there is a problem, the manager should have some form of open-door policy that encourages the subordinate to seek assistance. Fourth, broad, not narrow, controls should be established so that the manager knows when things are going well. At least initially, the manager should overlook minor problems and pay attention to significant deviations. The manager thus controls the situation without appearing to try to monitor everything. The subordinate should be expected to make some mistakes; beginners do, however great their potential. Fifth, when the job is done, the manager should praise the subordinate's performance in the areas in which good results were obtained and express a

The manager must take steps to improve delegation.

INTERVIEW WITH DAN EGGLAND

Dan Eggland is the chief executive officer of Metro Bank, a rapidly growing financial institution in Miami, Florida. The bank opened five years ago and has now expanded to three locations and has assets of over $55 million. This rapid growth has required careful structuring of activities and delegation of authority.

Q.   *As the bank continues its rapid expansion, will it be difficult to maintain managerial control of operations?*

A.   I don't think so, although rapid expansion usually results, if only temporarily, in some loss of control. However, if the organization structure is well planned, it can accommodate expansion and ensure that management continues to remain in firm control of operations. As we continue our rapid growth, we are continually looking at ways to centralize some functions and cut our costs while decentralizing other functions in order to provide even better services to our customers. It's impossible to grow as fast as we have without modifying the organization structure, but we have to do it in a way that helps us maintain our efficiency.

Q.   *Do you expect a great deal of decentralization at the bank over the next five years?*

willingness to work with the individual in improving the other areas. The manager can best do this by continuing to delegate tasks to the subordinate, indicating trust and confidence in the less experienced person.

Participative Management

Delegation is the basis for participative management, and there are some very important long-term results that can accrue from involving subordinates in the decision-making process. Burt Scanlan and Roger Atherton have described two of the major ones:

> First, it contributes to the process of authority being legitimized or gaining the consent of the people subject to authority. Second, . . . it serves to unleash the potential of people to make positive contributions. Since this is more likely to result in mental and emotional involvement, both motivation and commitment are heightened. *The important point to note is that by changing our approach to using authority we can begin to*

A. I certainly do. More and more important decisions are going to have to be made at lower levels, and for good reason. We're not just in the finance business; we're in the customer service business. A person who wants to borrow $15,000 to buy a car will find a lot of banks willing to make the loan. In differentiating ourselves from the competition, we have to provide service that will attract new accounts and keep old ones. By decentralizing authority, we increase our ability to be market-driven and that's the direction in which the banking industry is moving. Any financial institution can lend money, but not every institution knows how to market itself effectively so that the customer keeps coming back. A well-designed organization structure can help accomplish this objective.

Q. *Are you finding greater delegation of authority also taking place? If so, are there any problems associated with delegating?*

A. There is more delegation of authority. There has to be if we're going to operate efficiently. At the same time, we have to ensure that any delegation problems are dealt with quickly and effectively. There are a number of them that can prove troublesome. One is that our managers have to become accustomed to delegating authority and having faith that their people will do the right thing. A second is that the lower-level personnel have to learn to accept more authority and be willing to use their own judgment in getting things done. Delegation is a two-way street. One party has to be willing to let go of authority; the other has to be prepared to accept it along with the accompanying responsibility. However, I don't look on this as a problem but as an opportunity. If we can take advantage of this opportunity, we're going to continue to expand and grow.

employ more participation and gain the advantages associated with participation. Not the least of these advantages is participation's positive impact on achievement motivation.[17]

Do employees really want greater participation in decision making? Do managers really want to delegate the necessary authority? The answers to these two questions are yes and no, respectively. Most employees do want more opportunity to participate and play a role. William Halal and Bob Brown conducted a questionnaire survey in which they asked the respondents to relate the participative practices now occurring in their organization and the ones they would like to see.[18] They found that, except for self-pacing

[17]Burt K. Scanlan and Roger M. Atherton, Jr., "Participation and the Effective Use of Authority," *Personnel Journal*, September 1981, p. 702.

[18]William E. Halal and Bob S. Brown, "Participative Management: Myth and Reality," *California Management Review*, Summer 1981, pp. 20–32.

(working at one's own speed), the employees wanted more participatory practices. These included greater use of flextime (control over starting and ending work hours), MBO (Management by Objectives), incentive systems, and the selection of new coworkers.

On the other hand, Halal and Brown also found many managers unresponsive to a participative management style. The latter enjoyed directive leadership, found it hard to relinquish their control, and felt that subordinates really did not want to assume greater responsibility for their behavior. So while delegation certainly has its benefits, there are still a significant number of managers who find the art of delegation to be a difficult process to implement (see Intrapreneurship in Action: Making Bigger Better).

THE INFORMAL ORGANIZATION

Attention has thus far been focused exclusively on the formal organization as designed and implemented by management. No organization, however, actually operates solely along formal lines. The individuals in any structure tend to remake it, changing things to meet their own needs and strengths. Functional design theorists contend that an organization should initially be developed without regard for the human element, but it is never long before this theoretic ideal gives way to some more practical structure created by the actual firm within its various environments and with its individual assets and deficiencies. E. Wight Bakke called this a *fusion process*, stating that:

> When an individual and an organization come together in such way that the individual is a participant in, and a member of, the organization and the two are mutually dependent on each other, both are reconstructed in the process. The organization to some degree remakes the individual and the individual to some degree remakes the organization.[19]

The informal organization is not shown on the organization chart.

Consideration of this informal structure introduces a more dynamic view of the organization than is available from a mere analysis of the formal design. To obtain a mental picture of the *informal organization*, it is helpful to regard it as a structure superimposed on the formal one.

The organization chart cannot show all the informal relationships that exist in the organization. Just an attempt to depict functional authority, for example, would lead to a mass of lines running all over the page. It is probably impossible to draw the informal organization. Not only are the relationships varied, but they are continually changing. Sometimes an informal organization consists of members of the same work group. Other

---

[19]E. Wight Bakke, *The Fusion Process* (New Haven: Labor and Management Center, Yale University, 1953), pp. 12–13.

INTRAPRENEURSHIP
IN
ACTION:
Making
Bigger
Better

Over the past decade more and more firms have been trying to develop an intrapreneurial spirit within their firms. High-tech companies seem to have the least trouble because the nature of their business encourages intrapreneurial activity. Old-line firms have more problems making this transition because they are unaccustomed to doing business this way. A good example is found in the case of General Motors which has been continually losing market share. What can be done to correct this problem? Ross Perot, the self-made billionnaire and former member of the GM board of directors, has been particularly critical of the firm. Noting that GM is the largest auto company in the world, with the greatest research capability and largest manufacturing facilities, Perot has pointed out that the company fails to get the most out of its people because it does not develop the right environment for quality work. Many of his suggestions for improvement are based on intrapreneurial ideas. Here are five of them.

First, everyone in the company should be a full-time General Motors (GMer) employee. No one should hold jobs in other firms including members of the board of directors. The primary and sole interest of GM's personnel should be in making GM the premier auto firm in the world.

Second, in order to motivate people, everyone should be given only one form of financial incentive: GM stock. This will reinforce the need to make GM the best and, if this goal is attained, will result in the price of the stock going up.

Third, groups representing a cross section of the organization should be formed. This includes people from senior-level management down to newly hired factory trainees. These groups should analyze the company's overall plan and have the opportunity to recommend changes.

Fourth, the company should meet in small groups with GM dealers and find out how to improve the cars. The company should also visit with mechanics who repair these autos and find out what can be done to improve them. Additionally, meetings should be scheduled with stockholders so that the company leadership understands what the owners want.

Fifth, the leadership must strive to make GM such an exciting, rewarding place that GMers will look forward to coming to work and will be prepared to take on all competitors and beat them.

These basic intrapreneurial principles are used by many foreign auto manufacturers. In Perot's view, if GM employed these ideas the payoff would be even better because the company has more muscle to put behind its efforts.

Source: Ross Perot, "How I Would Turn Around GM," *Fortune,* February 15, 1988, pp. 44–48.

times it involves intergroup membership, as when formal lines are abandoned in the name of expediency and managers turn to unofficial channels in order to get things done.

Figure 5-14 provides an example, using a small portion of a larger formal organization. Notice in the figure that there are both formal and informal

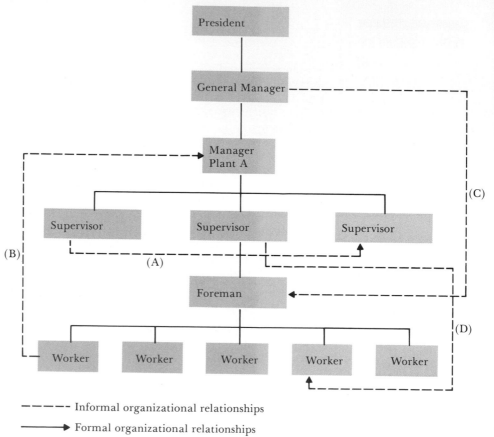

- - - - - Informal organizational relationships

———→ Formal organizational relationships

FIGURE 5-14   The Informal Organization

relationships. The informal relationships are accounted for by these actions: (1) one supervisor has called another to tell her about an interesting article that appeared in a current supervisory management journal; (2) a worker has contacted the plant manager to remind him that they are bowling for the league championship the following evening; (3) the general manager has called one of the foremen, who happens to be a neighbor, to ask for a ride home that evening because his car is in the shop; and (4) a supervisor in another department, who is looking for a new car, has come by to ask one of the workers where the latter bought his new auto and if he thinks the dealer will provide reliable service.

Authority and Power

Authority is formal power. The organization sanctions its use; however, effective managers must rely on more than just formal means to get things done. They must supplement their authority with informal sources of power. In all, there are five types of power.

Types of Power

John R. P. French, Jr., and Bertram Raven have identified five distinct types of power. They are:

Legitimate power. Legitimate power is vested in the manager's position and is given to all who hold that particular position.

Reward power. Reward power emanates from the manager's ability to reward those who comply with his or her orders and/or do their jobs well; this power is often used to provide economic rewards to subordinates.

There are five major types of power.

Coercive power. Coercive power is based on the manager's ability to control rewards that are valued by subordinates, as well as to punish those who do not comply with directives and formal procedures.

Expert power. Expert power is based on task-relevant knowledge as perceived by the subordinates; as long as the personnel see the manager as competent in his or her job, the individual has power or control over them.

Referent power. Referent power is based on the followers' identification with the leader; the subordinates are loyal to the individual because they identify with him or her and are influenced by the person's personality, reputation, charisma, and other leadership characteristics.[20]

Effective managers know that they must use power wisely if they are to lead their people. Which type of power is best? The choice depends heavily on the personnel. For example, some subordinates are highly committed to the organization. They are enthusiastic about carrying out requests and exercising maximum effort in accomplishing them. Other subordinates comply with orders but are not enthusiastic about carrying out such requests. Still others resist management efforts to lead and direct them. Table 5-1 shows the results of the latest research on the effectiveness of the five different types of power, with each of these types of subordinates.

---

[20]For more on this see John R. P. French, Jr., and Bertram Raven, "The Bases of Social Power," in Dorwin Cartwright, ed., *Studies in Social Power* (Ann Arbor, MI: Institute for Social Research, 1959), pp. 159–64.

	Power Source	Commitment	Compliance	Resistance
TABLE 5-1 **Outcomes Resulting from Different Types of Power**	Legitimate power	Possible	LIKELY	Possible
	Reward power	Possible	LIKELY	Possible
	Coercive power	Unlikely	Possible	LIKELY
	Expert power	LIKELY	Possible	Possible
	Referent power	LIKELY	Possible	Possible

Source: Reprinted, by permission of the publisher, from "The Effective Use of Managerial Power," by Gary Yukl and Tom Taber, *Personnel*, March–April 1983, p. 39. Copyright © 1983 by American Management Association, New York. All rights reserved.

When dealing with committed subordinates, leaders are most effective with expert and referent power, although legitimate and reward power can also provide satisfactory results. When dealing with subordinates who merely comply, legitimate and reward power are preferable. Finally, when dealing with subordinates who resist management efforts, coercive power is most likely to be effective.[21]

Gaining Power

Another major area of power and authority relates to the ways in which managers actually go about gaining power. Many people believe that the farther up the organization's hierarchy a person goes, the less need the individual has for personal power. The authority of the position provides all of the power that is needed. This view, however, is not correct.[22] There are many different tactics employed by managers in their efforts to increase personal power. Some of these include attacking or blaming others, image building, the use of power coalitions, development of associations with influential personnel, and the creation of obligations that call for reciprocity later on.[23] An even more interesting point is that research shows that even though managers may engage in organizational politics not all of them necessarily recognize their conduct as political activity. Drawing upon research among 428 managers, Victor Murray and Jeffrey Gandz found that over 90 percent believed politics was common in most organizations and that to get ahead it was necessary to play politics.[24] On the other hand, they also found that the higher the person's income the less politics he or she observed in the office, leading Murray and Gandz to note that, "These were interesting findings since . . . most . . . people felt that it was those in the top jobs who did the most politicking at work. Obviously those in top jobs don't see it that way."[25]

Given the fact that politics is a part of organizational life, managers must strive to build and maintain power. How can they do this? Numerous recommendations have been offered by researchers and practitioners. Some of the most useful are the following:

---

[21]Gary Yukl and Tom Taber, "The Effective Use of Managerial Power," *Personnel,* March–April 1981, pp. 37–44.

[22]Arnold Brown, "The Eroding Power of the CEO," *Business Horizons,* April 1980, pp. 7–10; David C. Calabria, "CEOs and the Paradox of Power," *Business Horizons,* January–February 1982, pp. 29–31.

[23]Robert W. Allen, Dan L. Madison, Lyman W. Porter, Patricia A. Renwick, and Bronston T. Mayes, "Organizational Politics: Tactics and Characteristics of Its Actors," *California Management Review,* Fall 1979, pp. 77–83.

[24]Victor Murray and Jeffrey Gandz, "Games Executives Play: Politics at Work," *Business Horizons,* December 1980, pp. 11–23.

[25]Ibid., p. 20.

1. **Create the perception of power.** Even if the manager does not have power, the individual should try to make others think he or she does.

2. **Draw upon the least costly form of power first.** If the manager has generous monetary resources, the individual should use reward power to increase his or her power; if there are few monetary resources, the individual should withhold these and rely on some other less costly forms, such as legitimate power.

3. **Make rewards and punishments contingent on actual behavior.** By rewarding those who do things well, the manager ensures that these people will be loyal. By punishing (or at least failing to reward) those who do things poorly, the manager ensures that these people will either improve their performance or be forced out of the organization. Most important, perhaps, is that this approach will help develop the manager's reputation for fairness and integrity and win the individual a following of qualified people.

4. **Use partial reinforcement for longer-lasting behavior change.** Effective managers know that they do not have to reward employees every time they do something well. By rewarding them on an intermittent basis, the manager increases the effectiveness of the reward.

Ways to gain power.

5. **Use the power strategy most likely to be effective with the individual to be influenced.** The approach should be tailored to the person. Some people respond best to reward power; others need to be coerced or prodded; still others perform best when the manager uses expert power, and so on.

6. **Use direct control of behavior as infrequently as possible.** Direct control takes a great deal of time and resources. Effective managers use it sparingly, preferring to employ direct control only when indirect methods will be inappropriate.

7. **Keep power exchanges in balance so that obligations are tipped in one's own favor.** Effective managers try to do favors for others so that the latter are obligated to them. They call the shots.

8. **Invest power wisely so that it pays off.** Successful managers take a cost/benefit approach to the use of power. When the return does not justify the effort, the individual does not become involved.

9. **Use power only within those domains over which one has control.** Effective managers do not waste time or effort trying to influence individuals who are outside their domain or who think that the manager lacks the right to influence them.

10. **Control the use of power, reevaluating it frequently to make sure it has the intended consequences rather than unintentional consequences that might well diminish it.** The successful manager follows

up and makes an evaluation of how well he or she is using power. Only in this way can the person determine if a change in strategy is necessary.[26]

Formal and Informal Organizational Relationships

The informal organization is an inevitable product of human social processes. Unfortunately, too many organizations view it as a destructive element that needs to be weeded out. Actually, the informal organization can offer some very important advantages. Primarily, it is a source of satisfaction for the members, often bringing about much higher morale than would otherwise be the case.

The informal organization can be very helpful to the company.

Early writings in the field pictured the informal organization as disruptive and the role of management as one of manipulating the group into accepting formal goals. Today, it is evident that such manipulation is seldom necessary. The goals of the formal and informal organizations are often mutually reinforcing. Of course, this has not always been true, but until management is quite certain that the informal organization is in irreparable conflict with the formal, all attempts should be made to nurture the relationship. It does management no good to try to form a clear-cut distinction between the two. They are interrelated parts of a complex system, and management's job must be that of creating an organizational climate in which the goals and expectations of both groups can be attained.

There is now an increasing need for more adaptive, less bureaucratic organizational structures that help organizations meet the varied demands of their environments. A great amount of new organization design research and the evolution of modern organization structures which often radically modify or extend the concepts presented in this chapter have resulted from this need. Management in the 1990s is continuing to respond to this vast and dynamic need.

■ SUMMARY

This chapter examined the nature, purpose, and function of organizing. Organizing involves the assignment of duties and the coordination of efforts among all organizational personnel to ensure maximum efficiency in the attainment of predetermined objectives. The process covers a broad area and offers the manager many alternatives in both routine and critical situations. The numerous forms of departmentalization include functional, product, territorial, simple numbers, time, customer, and equipment or process.

---

[26]These ideas can be found in: Vandra L. Huber, "The Sources, Uses, and Conservation of Managerial Power," *Personnel*, August–September 1981, pp. 70–71.

Another common organizational form, often used in conjunction with departmentalization, is committees. The two general types of committees are ad hoc and standing. The chapter showed that committees can be effectively used to complement the basic organizational structure.

Span of control is the phrase used to refer to the number of people reporting to a given superior. A wide span of control results in a flat organization chart, while a narrow span results in a tall organization chart.

There are three basic types of authority: line, staff, and functional. Line authority is direct authority, as illustrated by a manager who gives orders directly to a subordinate. Staff authority is auxillary authority that is supportive in nature, as in the case of the lawyer who has authority to advise the president on legal matters. Functional authority is authority in a department other than one's own, as in the case of the vice-president of finance who can give orders to the head of a product division in regard to financial matters.

The chapter devoted particular attention to problem areas such as line-staff conflicts, which show that organizing is certainly no mechanical function. For example, line people tend to be highly action-oriented, while staff people are concerned with studying problems in depth before making recommendations.

The last part of the chapter examined the topics of decentralization and the informal organization. Decentralization is influenced by a number of factors, including cost, uniform policy, company size, philosophy of top management, philosophy of subordinate managers, and the functional area in which one works. The informal organization is the organizational arrangement created by the individuals who work in the structure. Their informal relationships supplement formal authority. Authority thus consists of two factors: formal authority, which is delegated by one's superior, and personal power, which can be attained in a number of different ways, including experience, drive, and education.

With the introduction of the informal organization, it becomes obvious that organizing is a dynamic process. While this chapter has set forth some of the basic ideas every manager must know about organizing, new organization structures are now emerging. Drawing upon the ideas presented here, modern structures are now adapting these concepts to meet the demands of the external environment. The result has been the emergence of adaptive structures, the focus of attention in the next chapter.

■ REVIEW AND STUDY QUESTIONS

1. What is meant by the phrase *from strategy to structure?* Include in your answer a discussion of the planning process.
2. List the most widely used forms of departmentalization.

3. How does functional departmentalization differ from product departmentalization? How does it differ from territorial departmentalization? What are the advantages associated with each?

4. What are the common advantages and disadvantages of committees? Cite three of each.

5. How does a tall organizational structure differ from a flat one? Give an example of each.

6. What impact does the span of control have on the structure? Explain.

7. What is meant by the term *authority*? Where does authority come from? Be specific in your answer.

8. What is line authority? Staff authority? Functional authority? Explain by using an illustration of each.

9. What are some common line-staff conflicts? What gives rise to them? How can they be prevented or overcome?

10. How does decentralization differ from delegation? Give an illustration of each.

11. What are some of the factors that influence the degree of delegation that takes place in an organization? Differentiate between those that encourage it and those that discourage it.

12. List and discuss some of the key steps used to improve a manager's ability to delegate authority. Be sure to include recommended dos and don'ts.

13. How does the formal organization differ from the informal? Explain.

14. What are the five types of power? Identify and describe each.

15. How can managers go about increasing their power? Offer at least five recommendations, being sure to explain each.

16. Are the objectives of the formal and informal organization always in conflict? Defend your answer.

■ SELECTED REFERENCES

Allen, Robert W., Dan L. Madison, Lyman W. Porter, Patricia A. Renwick, and Bronston T. Mayes. "Organizational Politics: Tactics and Characteristics of Its Actors." *California Management Review*, Fall 1979, pp. 77–83.

Bhambri, Arvind, and Jeffrey Sonnenfeld. "Organization Structure and Corporate Social Performance: A Field Study in Two Contrasting Industries." *Academy of Management Journal*, September 1988, pp. 642–62.

Blackburn, Richard S. "Dimensions of Structure: A Review and Reappraisal." *Academy of Management Review*, April 1981, pp. 59–66.

Calabria, David C. "CEOs and the Paradox of Power." *Business Horizons*, January–February 1982, pp. 29–31.

Carter, Nancy M., and John B. Cullen. "A Comparison of Centralization/ Decentralization of Decision-Making Concepts and Measures." *Journal of Management*, Summer 1984, pp. 259–68.

Cawsey, T. F. "Why Line Managers Don't Listen to Their Personnel Departments." *Personnel*, January–February 1980, pp. 11–20.

Chandler, Alfred D., Jr. *Strategy and Structure.* Garden City, NY: Anchor Books, Doubleday, 1966.

Covin, Jeffrey G., and Dennis P. Slevin. "The Influence of Organization Structure on the Utility of an Entrepreneurial Top Management Style." *Journal of Management Studies*, May 1988, pp. 217–34.

Dalton, Dan R., William D. Todor, Michael J. Spendolini, Gordon J. Fielding, and Lyman W. Porter. "Organizational Structure and Performance: A Critical Review." *Academy of Management Review*, January 1980, pp. 49–64.

Grinyer, Peter H., and Masoud Yasai-Ardekani. "Strategy, Structure, Size and Bureaucracy." *Academy of Management Journal*, September 1981, pp. 471–86.

Halal, William E., and Bob S. Brown. "Participative Management: Myth and Reality." *California Management Review*, Summer 1981, pp. 20–32.

Hambrick, Donald C. "The Top Management Team: Key to Strategic Success." *California Management Review*, Fall 1987, pp. 88–108.

Harrell, Thomas, and Bernard Alpert. "The Need for Autonomy among Managers." *Academy of Management Review*, April 1979, pp. 259–67.

Huber, Vandra L. "The Sources, Uses, and Conservation of Managerial Power." *Personnel*, July–August 1981, pp. 62–71.

Jamison, Kaleel. "Competing with Peers—for Fun and Productivity." *Personnel*, September–October 1981, pp. 33–42.

Kerr, Jeffrey, and Richard A. Bettis. "Boards of Directors, Top Management Compensation, and Shareholder Returns." *Academy of Management Journal*, December 1987, pp. 645–64.

Kesner, Idalene F. "Directors' Characteristics and Committee Membership: An Investigation of Type, Occupation, Tenure, and Gender." *Academy of Management Journal*, March 1988, pp. 66–84.

Kets de Vries, Manfred F. R. "The Dark Side of CEO Succession." *Harvard Business Review*, January–February 1988, pp. 56–60.

Main, John G., and John Thackray. "The Logic of Restructuring." *Planning Review*, May/June 1987, pp. 5–7.

Montana, Patrick J., and Deborah F. Nash. "Delegation: The Art of Managing." *Personnel Journal*, October 1981, pp. 784–87.

Murray, Victor, and Jeffrey Gandz. "Games Executives Play: Politics at Work." *Business Horizons*, December 1980, pp. 11–23.

Scanlan, Burt K., and Roger M. Atherton, Jr. "Participation and the Effective Use of Authority." *Personnel Journal*, September 1981, pp. 697–703.

Urwick, Lt. Col. L. F. "V.A. Graicunas and the Span of Control." *Academy of Management Journal*, June 1974, pp. 349–464.

Vancil, Richard F. "A Look at CEO Succession." *Harvard Business Review,* March–April 1987, pp. 107–117.

Van Fleet, D. D., and Arthur G. Bedeian. "A History of the Span of Management." *Academy of Management Review,* July 1977, pp. 356–72.

Yukl, Gary, and Tom Taber. "The Effective Use of Managerial Power." *Personnel,* March–April 1983, pp. 37–44.

■ CASE: A New Switch

Fun-For-All is a national manufacturing firm that produces and sells toys and games. Prior to 1979, the company specialized in children's toys, but in the late seventies adult games began to gain acceptance, and Fun-For-All followed that market trend. The basic feature of the adult games is that they have no single, correct strategy and as a result require a great deal of thought on the part of the participant. For example, Monopoly, from Parker Brothers, has a basic strategy that often depends upon chance rather than skill. Players who are wise buy as much land as they can and start putting houses, and eventually hotels, on the property. However, true adult games, such as chess, are much more complex. There is no one right way to win a chess match; the outcome depends on what one's opponent does and also on one's own skill. The same is true for backgammon.

In 1988 Fun-For-All decided to market an expensive ($250) backgammon set. The company was convinced that despite the sluggish economy, demand for such a high-priced game would be sufficient to justify a 25 percent return on investment. By Christmas, thanks to timing and a strong advertising program, the firm had sold four times the number of sets it had initially forecast.

In 1989, because of growing sales, the management of Fun-For-All was considering reorganization. At the time, the firm was organized along functional lines, as in Figure 5-15. However, the president thought the

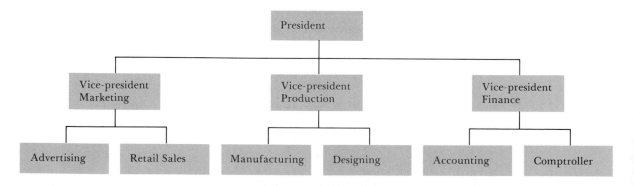

FIGURE 5-15   Fun-For-All, Inc., Organization Chart, September 1989

company might be wiser to change to product departmentalization, and some of the people in marketing also seemed to think that it would be a good idea. The production department, however, felt more was to be gained from functional departmentalization. The finance people seemed indifferent about the matter, but indicated they would make an analysis of the two structures if the president desired.

The president's reorganization plan was to set up three product divisions: boys' toys, girls' toys, and adult games. The first two divisions accounted for over 75 percent of the firm's sales, but the latter was growing rapidly and would, according to marketing estimates, account for over 50 percent of all sales by 1993.

Questions

1. Draw the proposed reorganization chart. Be as complete as possible.
2. In this company's situation, what are the advantages of product departmentalization over functional departmentalization?
3. What recommendations would you make to the president before deciding to switch from functional to product departmentalization? Explain.

■ CASE: A Matter of Opinion

Julian Bacal had been a production manager for over thirty years, and he knew virtually everything about production. Bacal's new assistant, Catherine Knowles, had great admiration for him. She felt she had learned more about how to handle workers and obtain increased output in her first four weeks on the job with Bacal than in her four years of undergraduate business school.

During this initial period, Knowles tried to keep her eyes and ears open; she was determined to learn as much about the job as possible. For example, she knew that Charles Jackson, another production manager, was a good friend of Bacal, and she had instructions that she should take care of any favors Jackson needed from Bacal if Bacal was not there to handle the request himself. Gradually, she also began to learn the names and positions of other people with whom the production department came in contact on a rather regular basis. One of these was Eileen Menger from the personnel department, who often visited Bacal. Knowles knew Bacal was interested in hiring some production supervisors and had asked Menger to take out some ads and to keep scouting the local colleges and universities when she went out recruiting.

About six months after Knowles had started, she knew her way around pretty well. At least she thought she did, until she walked into Bacal's office and was horrified to see that her boss and Eileen Menger were yelling angrily at one another. When they heard the door open, they immediately lowered their voices, but the situation was clearly tense. Knowles backed out the door. A few minutes later she noticed Menger leaving and went back in:

"I'm sorry, Mr. Bacal. I didn't realize you had anyone in here with you."

"That's okay. Come on in, Miss Knowles. I think it's about time you realized that not everyone around here agrees with everyone else all the time."

"But what conflict can you be having with Miss Menger? Isn't she in personnel?"

"Yes, but she screens all incoming people. Remember those tests you took as part of your application process?"

"Sure."

"Well, they're designed to find out something about your management potential. At least that's what Menger says. Supposedly, eight out of ten people who do well on them become good supervisory managers and the other two do not. Now our Miss Menger wants us to use that test as a screening device."

"And you don't want to?"

"Let's put it this way. I want to see an applicant face-to-face and talk. I know what to look for in a good supervisor; I don't need any test to tell me how a guy can handle himself. Two young fellows interviewed and tested for that job we have open. I want to hire the one that did poorly on the exam. He's going to work out. Miss Menger disagrees."

"Can she force you to use the test as a screening device?"

"No. Her entire job is to evaluate the applicants and give me her recommendations. I decide who gets hired in this department. The truth is, Menger's getting just too damn smart. She's supposed to be advising me and she winds up giving me orders. Imagine telling me that that young fellow I interviewed last week did poorly on the exam and I should forget about hiring him. Well, until the president decides that Menger has more savvy about how to run this department than I do, I'm going to make all the hiring decisions."

Questions

1. What kind of authority does Menger have? How do you know?
2. What kind of line-staff conflict is represented here? Explain.
3. How can these problems be prevented in the future? Make your answer specific.

■ CASE: I Did It My Way

Anyone who ever mentioned Shayling, Inc., was actually talking about a man more than a business—Peter Shayling, founder, owner, president, and chairman of the board. Shayling, Inc., was one of the largest television retail and repair stores in the city, with gross sales of over $10 million. Shayling delighted in telling customers how he had started out in a small shop on the outskirts of town and gradually increased the size of his business to where he could afford to move into his current modern, midtown facilities.

When his store was very small, Shayling and his wife, Linda, did everything, including keeping the books. The only outside assistance they had was an accountant who came in every three months to balance the ledgers and compute the taxes. Gradually, as volume increased, Shayling began hiring paid help. First, he brought in a television repairman; then he hired a salesman. In midyear 1985, fifteen people were working for Shayling, nine in the repair and delivery shop, six on the sales floor.

Although things appeared to be going well, Shayling admitted to his wife that he was disturbed by the large turnover in his sales staff; on an average, he was losing one salesperson a month. He was also losing an average of one repairer every other month. About this time Shayling received a call from a group of MBA candidates in a nearby college of business who were taking an upper division management course that required them to analyze a local concern. They wanted to know if Shayling would let them write their paper on his company. Although initially reluctant, he decided to take advantage of the students' offer of a list of recommendations, so he agreed. "It's like getting free consulting," he told his wife.

Six weeks later the team sent him a copy of its paper. The analysis and recommendations were of great interest to Shayling. He felt the team had done an admirable job, and he intended to implement many of the suggested changes. However, he disagreed strenuously with the following segment of the report:

> The high sales turnover can be directly attributed to the owner's failure to delegate authority. No salesperson is ever able to introduce a product to a customer or close a sale without Mr. Shayling getting into the act; he is everywhere. The result is a decline in morale brought about by the fact that the owner seems to lack faith in his own personnel. An analogous situation exists in the repair shop, although not to the same degree. In summary, Mr. Shayling should spend more time managing and less time looking over people's shoulders.

In defense of his actions, Shayling noted to his wife that the students undoubtedly lacked an understanding of the television repair business. "You've got to be on top of everything all the time," he said. "And far from getting in the way, I am really quite helpful to the sales force. After all, who knows more about how to sell than me? I built this store from nothing and I did it my way, which, it so happens, is the *right way!* And there's no substitute for success. In fact, if I change anything at all about the way I handle my sales crew, I'll get in there and mix it up with them a little more. They'd do an even better job if I spent more time helping them out. Why wouldn't they? After all, one of them is always new."

Questions

1. Is failure to delegate a cause of poor morale? Explain.
2. How is Shayling's action typical of many owner-managers? Explain.
3. How can Shayling overcome his problem? Be specific in your recommendations.
4. Could the report have been worded differently so as to sell the recommendation to Shayling? Explain, giving reasons for your opinion and methods for implementing it.

▪ CASE: Reorganization Comes to America

During the 1960s and 1970s large business firms grew rapidly. As these firms expanded the size and scope of their operations, thousands of new personnel were hired. Many of these became line personnel with direct control of operations and assumed positions such as product manager, plan superintendent, and vice-president of operations. Some of the new hires went into staff positions where they provided expertise in areas such as public relations, training, and development.

The 1980s began on a down note. The economy was weak and many firms found that their growth rate and profit levels were beginning to decline. By the middle of the decade it was becoming painfully obvious that there was only one solution—the firms had to downsize.

During the late 1980s many large companies began these downsizing efforts. This was not a surprise to most industry analysts who had been predicting that personnel cutbacks were in the works. What was a surprise to many was where the cutbacks came. In the past lower-level personnel were the ones who could expect the ax when things got bad. This time, however, it was the middle managers who were the target. In particular, management began reducing the number of people at the upper-middle ranks. There were three reasons for this decision. First, management felt that there were many people at these levels who were replaceable. The company could either eliminate these jobs or delegate them to others. Second, these upper-level managers were making large salaries ($50,000 to $80,000) which could be used to improve overall profit. Third, upper-level management would now have greater control over the operations because they would be closer to the operating level.

Many of the executives who lost their jobs found it hard to secure new employment. When they did, most wound up working for smaller companies in different industries and supervising fewer subordinates. However, this did not mean that they were unhappy in their new positions. Although almost half of them reported that they received more money than in their previous position, they liked the fact that they were able to spend more time interacting with their personnel and not having to worry about overcoming bureaucratic procedures in order to get things done.

Questions

1. After these upper-middle management executives were let go, what did the organization structure of the old firm look like? Describe it in terms of Figures 5-7 and 5-8.

2. Do the managers find that there is more participative management in the new firms? Do they like this? Explain.

3. Do you think these managers knew they were going to be let go before they received the formal announcement? Explain, being sure to incorporate a discussion of the informal organization into your answer.

Source: Some of this material can be found in Peter Nulty, "Pushed Out at 45—Now What?" *Fortune,* March 2, 1987, pp. 26–30.

■ SELF-FEEDBACK EXERCISE: What Do You Really Know about the Informal Organization?

Each of the following statements is either true or false. Circle the appropriate response. Answers are provided at the end of the exercise.

T F 1. Most information passed on by the informal organization is inaccurate.

T F 2. Most managers ignore the informal organization.

T F 3. In ideal organizations, an informal organization does not exist.

T F 4. Effective managers rely heavily on the informal organization to gather information on what is going on in the enterprise.

T F 5. Successful managers use the informal organization to help them network in the enterprise.

T F 6. The informal organization often conveys information faster than the formal organization.

T F 7. The informal organization carries only personal information not business-oriented information.

T F 8. Most information that is passed along by the informal organization is done so on a random basis.

T F 9. People who are members of an informal organization usually remain members of this group for an indefinite time.

T F 10. The informal organization is an excellent means of supplementing formal channels.

T F 11. As an organization becomes more profitable or efficient, use of the informal organization declines.

T F 12. The informal organization is a source of job satisfaction for many employees.

Answers

1. False. Much of it is accurate.
2. False. Most managers use the informal organization.
3. False. It is present in all organizations.
4. True. They gather a great deal of information this way.
5. True. It is an effective way of networking with others in the hierarchy.
6. True. The channel processes information very quickly.
7. False. It carries both personal and business-related information.
8. False. The information is passed along on a selective basis.
9. False. Membership in informal organizations often changes based on the information that is being passed along.
10. True.
11. False. Quite often the informal organization becomes even more important.
12. True.

Adaptive Organization Structures

Change—and adapting to and coping with it—is one of the greatest challenges facing the modern manager. Some change is brought on by conditions in the external environment; some is internally generated. In either case, the organization must be capable of meeting the demands of the situation. One way in which organizations are doing this is through the use of adaptive organization structures. Organizations find that with new, flexible designs, they are better able to interact with their external environment. These structures also encourage the use of effective motivation and leadership techniques. The goals of this chapter are to identify the five configurations of organization design, to examine the impact of technology on organization structure, to study some of the adaptive organization designs, and to learn what is meant by the term contingency organization design.

When you have completed this chapter, you should be able to:

1. Define the characteristics of an ideal bureaucracy.
2. Identify the five configurations of organization design.
3. Explain why bureaucratic structures are declining in importance.
4. Examine the effect of technology on the personnel and structure of organizations.
5. Describe what a project organization is and how it functions.
6. Compare and contrast project and matrix structures.
7. Describe the four models of matrix design that are in use today.
8. Discuss the differences between a free-form organization and a bureaucratic design.

9.   Explain what contingency organization design is.

10.   Identify and describe those forces that help determine the "best" organization structure.

ORGANIZATION CONFIGURATION

There are many types of organization design. Some are very useful in a stable environment; others are most efficient in dealing with a changing environment. Quite often, the term "bureaucratic" is used to describe the former and "adaptive" is employed to describe the latter. Each can offer benefits, although there are distinct structural differences between them.

The *bureaucracy* in its ideal form has five main characteristics. Max Weber, a German sociologist, made one of the earliest and best known studies of bureaucratic organizational design. Peter Blau has identified the Weber characteristics in this way:

1.   A clear-cut division of labor resulting in a host of specialized experts in each position.

The characteristics of an ideal bureaucracy.

2.   A hierarchy of offices, with each lower one being controlled and supervised by a higher one.

3.   A consistent system of abstract rules and standards which assures uniformity in the performance of all duties and the coordination of various tasks.

4.   A spirit of formalistic impersonality in which officials carry out the duties of their office.

5.   Employment based on technical qualifications and protected from arbitrary dismissal.[1]

Of course, no modern organization employs the bureaucracy in its ideal form; however, many use some version of it. The problem with these total organization structures is that, to a degree, they have proved unworkable. Quite simply, many of them lack the ability to cope with the stress, change, and tension of today's complex environment. This is particularly true in the case of organizations facing technological change.

On the other hand, there are *adhocratic structures* that are formed for the purpose of accomplishing a specific task and are then disbanded. These temporary organizational arrangements have proven very useful in helping modern enterprises cope with changing conditions. They are highly adaptive designs and, if placed on a continuum, would be at the opposite extreme from that of the bureaucracy (see Figure 6-1).

Adhocracy suits those organizations that face continual change. These structures are commonly employed in industries such as aerospace, petro-

[1]Peter M. Blau, *Bureaucracy in Modern Society* (New York: Random House, 1956), pp. 28–33.

FIGURE 6-1   An Organization Structure Continuum

Adhocracies are common in high-change industries.

chemicals, filmmaking, and think-tank consulting. These enterprises need to innovate; the simple structure is too centralized for them, and the bureaucratic design is too inflexible for their purposes. They need a structure that makes use of smoothly-functioning, creative project teams. Commenting on this organizational form, Mintzberg notes:

> Adhocracy is the most difficult of the five configurations to describe because it is both complex and nonstandardized. Indeed, adhocracy contradicts much of what we accept on faith in organizations— consistency in output, control by administrators, unity of command, strategy emanating from the top. It is a tremendously fluid structure, in which power is constantly shifting and coordination and control are by mutual adjustment through the informal communication and interaction of competent experts. Moreover, adhocracy . . . is emerging as a key structure configuration, one that deserves a good deal of consideration.[2]

In an adhocracy, experts coordinate their efforts to achieve results. Ordinarily, they work in small teams right alongside those who have been designated as managers. In this situation, power is based on expertise and line-staff distinctions evaporate.[3]

Adhocracies, in particular, face a number of major challenges. One of these is the impact that technology has on the personnel.

TECHNOLOGY AND PERSONNEL

Many modern organizations must keep up with technological developments. However, it is also important for management to keep in mind that these technological changes have an effect on both the personnel and the structure of an organization.

Technology, Tension, and Effectiveness

Bringing people and technology together can cause tension. For example, Figure 6-2 shows a relationship between effectiveness and tension. Up to Point B in the figure, some degree of pressure, accountability, responsibility,

---

[2]Ibid., p. 111.

[3]See, for example, Peter F. Drucker, "The Coming of the New Organization," *Harvard Business Review,* January–February 1988, pp. 455–63.

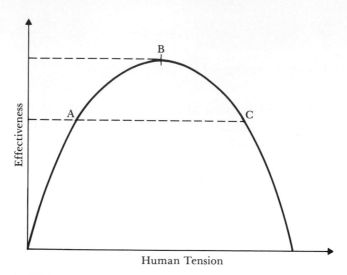

FIGURE 6-2   Relationship between Effectiveness and Tension

Technology can cause tension and impair effectiveness.

pride, and obligation is necessary. However, if tension is increased beyond this point (to Point C, for example), effectiveness can decline.[4]

The same is true in the case of technological capability and effectiveness, as seen in Figure 6-3. In this figure, the field to the left of Point E shows insufficient technological capacity for getting the job done; to the right of this point there is too much.

Figures 6-2 and 6-3 can be brought together and overlapped in three-dimensional style. As Henry M. Boettinger notes:

> If a brilliant technologist makes optimal provision of tools (Point E) to an inept manager who operates at Points A or C, he has wasted his time. If an ideal manager, carrying his people to Point B, has been furnished the wrong processes or equipment (points D or F), his people cannot catch rivals who have skilled technologists looking after their interests.
>
> One can compensate for bad technology, to some extent, with greater leadership, and for poor leadership with superb technology. But peak performance can never be achieved without peaks in *both* domains —the human and the technical.[5]

The challenge is thus one of introducing neither too much nor too little tension or technology, and this is not an easy task.

---

[4]For more on this topic, see Henry M. Boettinger, "Technology in the Manager's Future," *Harvard Business Review,* November–December 1970, pp. 4–14, 165.

[5]Ibid., p. 14.

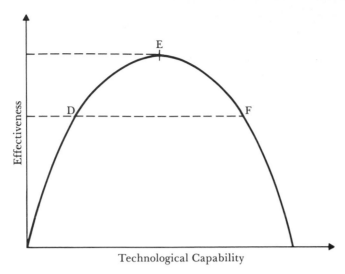

FIGURE 6-3 Relationship between Effectiveness and Technological Capability

Effect of Technology on the People

At the worker level, for example, technology can affect the social relationships among the people by bringing about changes in such human elements as the size and composition of the work group or the frequency of contact with other workers. E. L. Trist and K. W. Bamforth discovered this when they conducted research among post-World War I coal miners. The miners initially worked in small, independent, cohesive groups. However, advances in technology and equipment led to changes in the composition of these work groups, and the result was a decline in productivity. Only when management restored many of the social and small group relationships did output again increase.[6]

Technology can affect the psychosocial system.

It is perhaps the greatest fear of workers faced with new technology that the machinery will lead to the abolition of jobs or to the reduction of tasks to such simplistic levels that workers can hardly endure the stress of their new, extremely dull functions. Since the human being must be able to support one or more persons by means of work and since the mind resists its own belittling, such changes, brought about by advancing technology, have a profound effect on the psychosocial system. In order to prevent intolerable upheaval, management must be simultaneously and equally aware of the social (human) and the technical (operational) aspects and needs of the

[6]E. L. Trist and K. W. Bamforth, "Some Social and Psychological Consequences of the Longwall Method of Coal-getting," *Human Relations*, February 1951, pp. 3–38.

TABLE 6-1

A Comparison of Some of the Key Dimensions of Mechanistic and Organic Organization Structures

Systems and Their Key Dimensions	Characteristics of Organization Systems	
	Closed/ Stable/ Mechanistic	Open/ Adaptive/ Organic
Environmental Suprasystem		
General nature	Peaceful	Turbulent
Predictability	High certainty	High uncertainty
Technology	Stable	Dynamic
Degree of environmental influence on organization	Low	High
Overall Organizational System		
Emphasis of organization	On performance	On problem solving
Predictability of actions	Relatively certain	Relatively uncertain
Decision-making process	Programmable	Nonprogrammable
Goals and Values		
Overall values	Efficiency, predictability, security, risk averting	Effectiveness, adaptability, responsiveness, risk taking
Involvement in setting objectives	Primarily from the top down	Wide participation, including people from the bottom as well as from the top
Technical System		
Knowledge	Highly specialized	Highly generalized
Time perspective	Short-term	Long-term
Interdependency of tasks	Low	High
Structural System		
Procedures and rules	Many, often formal and written	Few, often informal and unwritten
Levels of the hierarchy	Many	Few
Source of authority	Position in organization	Knowledge of individual
Responsibility	Attached to position	Assumed by individual
Psychosocial System		
Interpersonal relationships	Formal	Informal
Personal involvement	Low	High

continued

	Characteristics of Organization Systems	
Systems and Their Key Dimensions	Closed/ Stable/ Mechanistic	Open/ Adaptive/ Organic
Motivation factors	Emphasis on lower-level needs	Emphasis on upper-level needs
Leadership Style	Autocratic	Democratic
Managerial System		
Content of communications	Decisions and instructions	Advice and information
Control process	Impersonal use of devices such as rules and regulations	Interpersonal contacts, persuasion, and suggestions
Means of resolving conflict	Superior uses the "book" in handling the matter	Group resolves issue with situational ethics

TABLE 6-1
continued

organization. Unless the impact of technology on the worker is considered, organizational effectiveness and efficiency will suffer.

Technology affects the managerial as well as the production staffs. Managers today are more specialized than ever before, as seen through the ever-growing number of public relations people, operations researchers, and other staff personnel in organizations. Previously, major consideration was given to breaking jobs into their component parts. Now, however, the emphasis is on integrating the work of the managers, especially in those industries in which technology plays a major role.

Tom Burns and G. M. Stalker, for example, undertook a study of a number of British and Scottish firms. The companies, which had operated in stable technologies and environments, were trying to move into the electronics field, which is characterized by rapidly changing technology.[7] The researchers found that as the companies made this transition, they underwent significant changes in their management systems. Initially, they had had *mechanistic organization structures*, characterized by formal job descriptions and a rigid overall structure. It was quite clear to everyone what all workers did and to whom they reported.

In the new environment, however, another managerial system developed —the *organic organization structure*. (See Table 6-1 for a comparison of some of

Technology can also lead to the replacement of mechanistic structures by organic ones.

[7]Tom Burns and G. M. Stalker, *The Management of Innovation* (London: Tavistock Publications, 1961).

the key dimensions of mechanistic and organic organization structures.) Management had to adapt to changing conditions, and the old mechanistic structure gave way to a more flexible one. Managers found themselves in more frequent interaction with each other; they also placed greater emphasis on lateral, rather than vertical, communication. In order to survive in this new, highly dynamic environment, the managers began to restructure the old line-staff relationships in favor of more flexible ones.

TECHNOLOGY AND STRUCTURE

Technology has been seen to have profound effects on people within a workplace. Its effects on organizational structure are equally powerful. One of the most significant studies evaluating the impact of technology on structure was conducted by Joan Woodward.[8] Her research, which covered a hundred firms in a London suburb, was designed to determine how structural variables affected economic success. She found the answer by analyzing the types of technology the firms were employing. There were three types in all:

1. **Mass and large batch production.** This type of technology is used for mass-production items, such as automobiles and television sets.

2. **Continuous process production.** This type of technology is employed in producing continuous-flow production items, such as in the manufacture of chemicals or the processing of oils.

3. **Unit and small batch production.** This type of technology is used for "one-of-a-kind" products or those built to customer specifications, such as spacecrafts and locomotives.

The appropriateness of the organizational structure, Woodward found, was dependent on the type of technology the firm used. If the company employed mass-production techniques, a mechanistic structure seemed to work best. Conversely, if the firm used continuous-process or unit production, in which technology plays a more significant role, an organic structure seemed to work best. Table 6-2 illustrates these findings.

In addition, Woodward found that the organic structures tended to be oriented more toward human relations than were the mechanistic ones.

---

[8]Joan Woodward, *Industrial Organization: Theory and Practice* (London: Oxford University Press, 1965).

TABLE 6-2
Woodward's Research Findings

	Mechanistic	Organic
	Mass production	Continuous process Unit production

Since Joan Woodward's initial study, other researchers have also attempted to evaluate the importance of technology on the organization. Perhaps the most widely known of these is William L. Zwerman, who, using fifty-five firms from the Minneapolis area, replicated Woodward's research in the United States.[9] In essence, he corroborated her basic findings,[10] concluding that the "type of production technology was most closely and consistently related to variations in the organizational characteristics of the firms."[11]

In a related study, Paul R. Lawrence and Jay W. Lorsch posed the question of which form of management is best under which conditions. Employing a sample of ten industrial organizations, they grouped them by degree of market and technological change.[12] The six in the plastics industry were categorized as operating in a highly dynamic environment; the two in the consumer foods industry were seen as being in an environment with an intermediate degree of change; the two in the standardized container industry were identified as being in a relatively stable environment. The researchers found that to be successful, those in the dynamic environment needed a flexible structure, whereas those in the stable environment were most effective with a mechanistic management system, and those in the intermediate environment needed to operate somewhere between the two extremes (see Technology in Action: Adapting to Change).

Numerous research studies have been conducted on the effect of technology on structure.

Marshall W. Meyer, studying the impact of automation on the formal structure, investigated 254 state and local government departments of finance.[13] He found that automation creates interdependency in the organization, and nonhierarchical (organic) structures are better able to deal with the situation than are rigid, hierarchical (mechanical) ones.

Other research further substantiates these findings.[14] The general pattern is already clear: Technology has a definite impact on organizational structure (see Table 6-3). It is thus possible to extend Chandler's thesis of "from strategy to structure"[15] by incorporating the technological factor in Figure 6-4 (see page 192).

One final point merits attention. Technology is not the only factor affecting structure; nor is it always the most critical. David J. Hickson's research team,

[9]William L. Zwerman, *New Perspectives on Organization Theory* (Westport, CT: Greenwood Publishing, 1970).

[10]Because of a lack of firms in continuous-process operations, however, he was unable to make any inferences about this particular group.

[11]Zwerman, p. 148.

[12]Paul R. Lawrence and Jay W. Lorsch, *Organization and Environment* (Boston: Harvard Graduate School of Business Administration, 1967).

[13]Marshall W. Meyer, "Automation and Bureaucratic Structure," *American Journal of Sociology,* November 1968, pp. 256–64.

[14]For example, see Edward Harvey, "Technology and the Structure of Organizations," *American Sociological Review,* April 1968, pp. 256–64.

[15]Alfred D. Chandler, *Strategy and Structure* (Garden City, NY: Anchor Books, Doubleday, 1966).

One reason that the old line-staff organization structure is being modified by more adaptive designs arises from the necessity for firms continually to adjust to environmental change. In the past, there was much less pressure for adaptation and adjustment; changes came very slowly. For example, in 1714 the first English patent for a typewriter was issued; however, 150 years passed before the machine was commercially available. Or consider the farm combine. In 1836 a machine was invented that mowed, threshed, tied straw into sheaves, and poured grain into sacks. The machine used technology that was already 20 years old, yet 90 years more elapsed before this combine was commercially marketed. In the twentieth century the time span between development and peak production has decreased dramatically. The Stanford Research Institute reports that for patents introduced before 1920 there was an average span of 34 years between introduction of the device and peak production. In the post-World War II era this time span has been shortened to 5–8 years. At the same time, the frequency with which American firms are introducing their new products into foreign markets is also increasing. One researcher recently reported the following findings:

Period of U. S. Innovation	Number of Innovations	Percent Produced in Foreign Markets	
		Within 1 year of U. S. Introduction	Within 5 years of U. S. Introduction
1945–1950	161	5.6	22.0
1951–1955	115	2.6	29.6
1956–1960	134	10.4	36.6
1961–1965	133	24.1	55.6
1966–1970	115	37.4	60.1
1971–1975	75	38.7	64.0*

These data indicate that multinational firms in particular are greatly increasing their overseas efforts. Since structure follows strategy, it is obvious that they must also adapt their organizational designs to accommodate their efforts in the market place. For many of them this means the use of some form of multidimensional matrix structure.

*Reported in Kathryn Rudie Harrigan, "Innovation Within Overseas Subsidiaries," *Journal of Business Strategy*, Spring 1984, p. 52.

	Organization Structure		
TABLE 6-3			
Research Findings Relating Technology and Organization Structure	Researcher	Mechanistic	Intermediate	Organic
	Woodward	Mass production		Continuous process Unit production
	Zwerman	Mass production		Unit production
	Lawrence and Lorsch	Stable environment	Intermediate degree of stability	Dynamic environment
	Meyer	Low degree of interdependency		High degree of interdependency

in fact, found it to be of significant importance only for small organizations.[16] Where it does play a role, it is the effect on such variables as span of control and manager-manager and manager-subordinate relationships that is important. As Joan Woodward has noted:

> Among the organizational characteristics showing a direct relationship with technical advance were: the length of the line of command; the span of control of the chief executive; the percentage of total turnover allocated to the payment of wages and salaries; and the ratios of managers to total personnel, of clerical and administrative staff to manual workers, of direct to indirect labour, and of graduate to nongraduate supervision in production departments.[17]

Thus, for reasons having to do with technology and other variables, new organization designs have been created. What forms are these new designs taking? There are many answers to this question. Some of the most common include the project organization, the matrix structure, and free-form organization designs, which will now be examined.

THE PROJECT ORGANIZATION

The use of the project organization has increased throughout the last decade. It is currently being employed in numerous and diverse undertakings from building dams and weapon systems to conducting research and development, choosing distribution center sites, and redesigning bank credit-card

---

[16]David J. Hickson, D. S. Pugh, and Diana C. Pheysey, "Operations Technology and Organization Structure: An Empirical Reappraisal," *Administrative Science Quarterly*, September 1969, pp. 378–97.

[17]Woodward, *Industrial Organization*, p. 51.

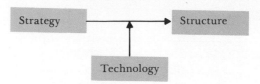

FIGURE 6-4   Impact of Technology on Structure

systems. The *project organization* can take various forms, but one overriding characteristic distinguishes it from the usual line and staff departments: Once the project has been completed, the organization is phased out. This is made clear by its very definition. Project management is "the gathering of the best available talent to accomplish a specific and complex undertaking within time, cost and/or quality parameters, followed by the disbanding of the team upon completion of the undertaking."[18] In a manner of speaking, the project manager and project staff work themselves out of a job. The group members then go on to another project, are given jobs elsewhere in the organization, or, in some cases, are phased entirely out of a firm.

The major advantage of the project form of organization is that it allows a project manager and team to concentrate their attention on one specific undertaking. The manager makes sure that the project does not get lost in the shuffle of organizational activities. In short, project managers act as focal points for their project activities.

Criteria for using a project structure are set forth.

Although the project structure has many advantages, its application is limited. For example, one writer has recommended criteria for the use of a project structure, stating that it should be: (a) definable in terms of a specific goal; (b) somewhat unusual and unfamiliar to the existing organization; (c) complex with respect to interdependence of activities necessary to accomplishment; (d) critical with respect to possible gain or loss; and (e) temporary with respect to duration of need.[19]

Planning the Project

Once it has been determined that a project organization will be used, the objectives must be set, the personnel drawn together, the structure formulated, and a control system designed for obtaining feedback. Although the organization will be more fluid than its conventional line-staff counterpart, there will still be the assignment of authority and responsibility. The structure is thus formalized to a degree. A project manager will be appointed to oversee the proceedings, and employees will report to this individual.

---

[18]Richard M. Hodgetts, "An Interindustry Analysis of Certain Aspects of Project Management" (Ph.D. dissertation, University of Oklahoma, 1968), p. 7.

[19]John M. Stewart, "Making Project Management Work," *Business Horizons*, Fall 1965, pp. 54–68.

Some of the workers will remain through the duration of the project while others may be involved for only a short period of time. The duties of the project group vary, naturally, with the objectives and the organizational structure.

Designing the Project Structure

Pure project structure is reserved for large undertakings.

Once project objectives have been ascertained, the project structure can be designed. The structure can take numerous forms, from simple to complex. In the simple project structure, shown in Figure 6-5, the project manager is put in charge of an undertaking and is also given direct authority over the team members. The project manager has all the resources needed for getting the job done, and the project structure departments are exact duplicates of the permanent functional organization. This type of design is often referred to as a pure, or aggregate, project structure. However, because of its duplication of facilities, the aggregate structure is one of the most expensive ways to organize a project, and its use is generally reserved for very large

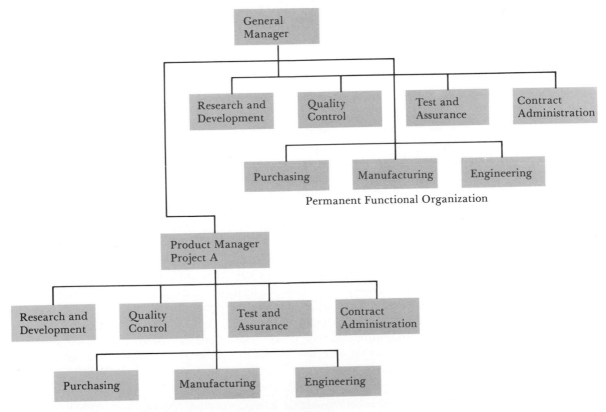

FIGURE 6-5   Pure Project Organization

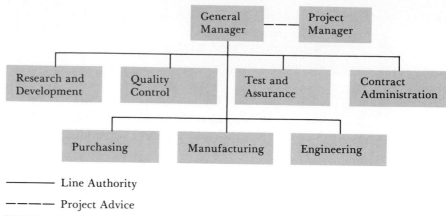

FIGURE 6-6   Functional Organization with Project Manager Serving in Advisory Capacity

undertakings. More common is the structure in which a project manager occupies the role of advisor to the general manager, who in turn administers the entire project within a functional organization hierarchy (see Figure 6-6 for an illustration of this). A third variation, the matrix structure, is the most common of all.

THE MATRIX STRUCTURE

Matrix structure is a functional and project organization hybrid.

A *matrix structure* is a hybrid organizational form, containing characteristics of both project and functional structures. Essentially, a matrix design allows operational responsibilities to be divided into two parts. One part contains all of the responsibilities associated with the management of a business and is given to an individual who can be aptly titled a "business-results manager." The other part contains all of the responsibilities related to the management of facilities, personnel, and other resources needed to get the job done. The person responsible for these is the "resource manager." "The matrix is built around a cooperative relationship between the 'business-results manager,' *who directs the work but who does not deploy the people,* and the 'resource manager,' *who does the hiring, training, paying, and terminating of the people who actually do the work, but who does not determine what work they do.'*[20] Thus, project staff members in a matrix structure have a dual responsibility. First, they are responsible to the head of their functional department, the person who has assigned them to the project. The functional department head is their line superior and will, despite the added matrix structure, continue to be so. But aside from that, the matrix project manager exercises what is called

---

[20]Allen R. Janger, *Matrix Organization of Complex Businesses* (New York: The Conference Board, Inc., 1979), p. 2.

project authority over the project staff. Thus, these employees report to two executives, one permanent, the other for the matrix project only. Figure 6-7 describes three project managers, each with project authority over personnel from departments supporting their respective undertakings.

Project authority flows horizontally.

When the concepts of functional and project authority are brought together, the result is an organization structure that is both vertical and horizontal. The vertical pattern is brought about by the typical line authority flowing down from superior to subordinate. The horizontal authority flow is caused by the fact that both the scalar principle and unity of command principle are violated, and in their place comes the need for close cooperation between the project manager and the respective functional managers (see Figure 6-8). All this is clearer following a detailed examination of the concept of project authority.

Project Authority

Project authority can be identified and described as follows:

Project authority is defined.

> One major problem has been cited consistently in studies made of the project [matrix] organization: while the functional managers have line or direct authority over their subordinates, the project managers must work through the respective functional managers, who supply the team personnel, in running their projects. The project managers have an "authority-gap" because they do not possess authority to reward or promote their personnel. They lack complete authority over the team and thus possess what is called "project authority." Because their responsibility outweighs their authority, the project managers must find ways of increasing their authority and thus minimizing their "authority-gap."[21]

This lack of complete authority means that the project manager cannot rely exclusively upon conventional line authority. Instead, this individual must work with the functional managers, convincing them that they should support the project by giving its manager the assistance needed to finish the undertaking within the assigned time, cost, and quality parameters. This persuasive bargaining calls for a horizontal relationship in which one manager coordinates activities with another. What is sometimes called legal authority, such as the hierarchical flow, position descriptions, and policy documents, is of little value to most project managers. Instead, they must rely upon reality authority, such as negotiation with their peers, the building of alliances with the functional managers, and the effective use of the informal

---

[21]Richard M. Hodgetts, "Leadership Techniques in the Project Organization," *Academy of Management Journal*, June 1968, p. 211.

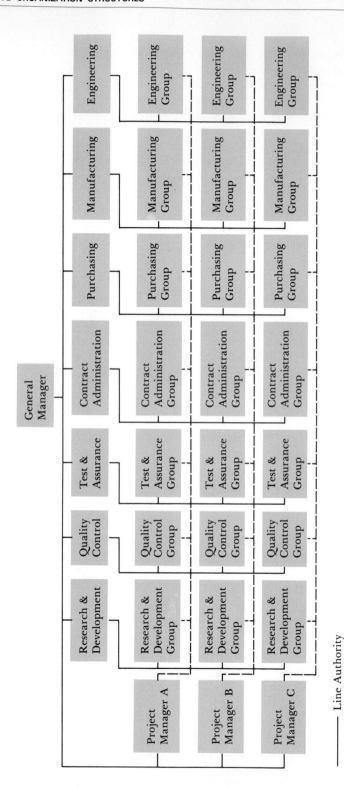

FIGURE 6-7   Matrix Organization

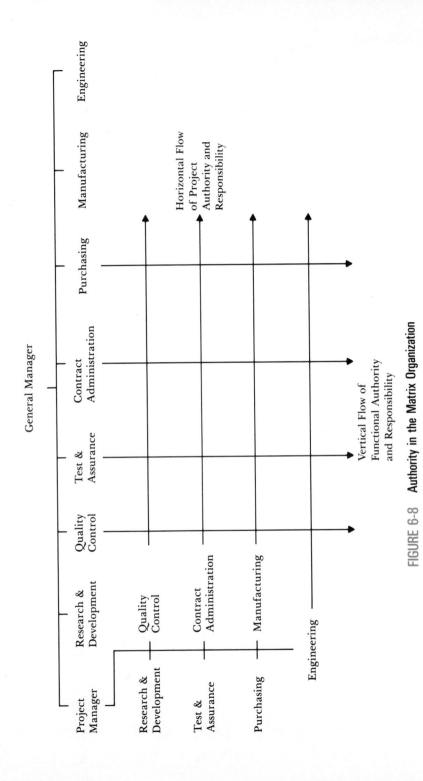

FIGURE 6-8 **Authority in the Matrix Organization**

	Phenomena	Functional Viewpoint	Project Viewpoint
TABLE 6-4 Comparison of the Functional and the Project Viewpoints	Line-staff organizational dichotomy	Line functions have direct responsibility for accomplishing the objectives: line commands, staff advises.	Vestiges of the hierarchical model remain, but line functions are placed in a support position. A web of authority and responsibility relationships exists.
	Scalar principle	The chain of authority relationships is from superior to subordinate throughout the organization. Central, crucial, and important business is conducted up and down the vertical hierarchy.	Elements of the vertical chain exist, but prime emphasis is placed on horizontal and diagonal work flow. Important business is conducted as the legitimacy of the task requires.
	Superior-subordinate relationship	This is the most important relationship; if kept healthy, success will follow. All important business is conducted through a pyramiding structure of superiors-subordinates.	Peer to peer, manager to technical expert, associate to associate relationships are used to conduct much of the salient business.
	Organizational objectives	Organizational objectives are sought by the parent unit (an assembly of suborganizations) working within its environment. The objective is unilateral.	Management of a project becomes a joint venture of many relatively independent organizations. Thus, the objective becomes multilateral.
	Unity of direction	The general manager acts as the head for a group of activities having the same plan.	The project manager manages across functional and organizational lines to accomplish a common interorganizational objective.

continued

	Phenomena	Functional Viewpoint	Project Viewpoint
TABLE 6-4 *continued*	Parity of authority and responsibility	Consistent with functional management, the integrity of the superior-subordinate relationship is maintained through functional authority and advisory staff services.	Considerable opportunity exists for the project manager's responsibility to exceed his or her authority. Support people are often responsible to other managers (functional) for pay, performance reports, promotions, and so forth.
	Time duration	Tends to perpetuate itself to provide continuing facilitative support.	The project (and hence the organization) is finite in duration.

Source: Reprinted from David I. Cleland, "Understanding Project Authority," *Business Horizons,* Spring 1967, p. 66. Copyright, 1966, by the Foundation for the School of Business at Indiana University. Used with permission.

organization. (See Table 6-4, which compares the functional and project organizations in detail.)

In investigating leadership techniques used by project managers to supplement their project authority and overcome their authority gap, the author discovered a general pattern. All project managers in the study indicated that personality and persuasive ability were important. In addition, some of them relied upon negotiation, competence, and reciprocal favors. The use of these approaches illustrates the importance that project managers assign to reality authority.

Each project manager's need for these techniques varies. On those projects where the manager is given little formal authority, the horizontal relationships will be of great importance. Conversely, in those cases where a great deal of authority has been delegated to the project manager, the structure is less a matrix organization and more a pure project organization. Research shows that smaller projects (those with less dollar size) tend to be more common than do larger ones, and their project managers tend to have less formal authority than do those who are overseeing larger undertakings.[22] This means that they have to rely more on a human relations than on a formal authority approach. For example, in forty-one of the firms surveyed, the author found that there was a continuum ranging from small project organizations to large ones. As an examiner progresses across the continuum,

[22]Ibid., pp. 211–19.

project authority declines in importance and formal authority replaces it. Informal leadership techniques such as negotiation, personality, persuasive ability, competence, and reciprocal favors are not as useful to the manager of a large project as they are to the manager of a small one. One project manager, involved in a multibillion-dollar undertaking, explained this phenomenon as follows:

> It would appear to be vital . . . that the organizational environment, into which the project manager is placed, be such that he need not depend entirely on negotiating ability, a dynamic personality, etc., to perform his most important job. For this reason the organization of a project, in a manner to give the project manager the control he needs over the area of budgeting, planning, and scheduling becomes a basic consideration. The organization must be so designed that the project manager indeed does control the people assigned to the project, in the sense they are responsible to him. Thus, the organization gives the project manager his authority so he can devote more of his time to obtaining the schedule, cost, and technical performance goals of the project.[23]

Additional research in these areas confirms the need of most project managers to rely on influence sources other than formal authority. For example, Edward J. Dunne, Jr., Michael J. Stahl, and Leonard J. Melhart, Jr., asked project managers why project personnel complied with their requests, asked project personnel why they complied with the project manager's request, and asked project personnel why they complied with orders from their immediate functional manager.[24] The responses are presented in Table 6-5. Notice in the case of both the project manager and the project group members that formal authority ranked in the bottom half, but when it came to responding to the functional manager, formal authority ranked close to the top. In short, influence sources are more important in project organization matters, and formal authority is more important in nonproject matters.[25]

Advantages of Matrix Organizations

Although the manager of a matrix organization faces many challenges, there are also numerous advantages to employing such a structure. David I. Cleland and William R. King identify the advantages as follows:

---

[23]Ibid., pp. 218.

[24]Edward J. Dunne, Jr., Michael J. Stahl, and Leonard J. Melhart, Jr., "Influence Sources of Project and Functional Managers in Matrix Organizations," *Academy of Management Journal*, March 1978, pp. 135–40.

[25]For more on this topic of influence see Jeffrey Barker, Dean Tjosvold, and I. Robert Andrews, "Conflict Approaches of Effective and Ineffective Project Managers: A Field Study in a Matrix Organization," *Journal of Management Studies*, March 1988, pp. 167–78.

TABLE 6-5

Influence Scores

Why Project Managers Believe Employees Comply with Project Requests		Why Project Staff Members Comply with Requests from Project Managers		Why Project Staff Members Comply with Orders from Immediate Functional Managers	
Source	Score*	Source	Score	Source	Score
Expertise	80	Position/ responsibility	79	Position/ responsibility	88
Position/ responsibility	74	Expertise	75	Formal authority	85
Friendship	65	Challenge	62	Expertise	81
Challenge	56	Friendship	54	Direct rating	80
Pressure/ penalize	30	Indirect rating	35	Challenge	74
Indirect rating	26	Formal authority	25	Indirect rating	62
Future work	25	Future work	22	Friendship	58
Formal authority	18	Pressure/ penalize	22	Pressure/ penalize	56
Direct rating	9	Direct rating	14	Future work	55

*The score range was 1–100, with higher ratings indicating higher importance.
Source: Reprinted by permission from Edward J. Dunne, Jr., Michael J. Stahl, and Leonard J. Melhart, Jr., "Influence Sources of Project and Functional Managers in Matrix Organizaitons," *Academy of Management Journal*, March 1978, p. 137.

Certain benefits are associated with the use of a matrix structure.

1. The project is emphasized by designating one individual as the focal point for all matters pertaining to it.

2. Utilization of manpower can be flexible because a reservoir of specialists is maintained in functional organizations.

3. Specialized knowledge is available to all programs on an equal basis; knowledge and experience can be transferred from one project to another.

4. Project people have a functional home when they are no longer needed on a given project.

5. Responsiveness to project needs and customer desires is generally faster because lines of communication are established and decision points are centralized.

6. Management consistency between projects can be maintained through the deliberate conflict operating in the project-functional environment.

7. A better balance between time, cost and performance can be obtained through the built-in checks and balances (the deliberate conflict) and the

continuous negotiations carried on between the project and the functional organizations.[26]

In recent years others have also sung the praises of matrix organizations. For example, Stanley M. Davis and Paul R. Lawrence, while noting that corporations such as Bechtel, Citibank, Dow Chemical, Shell Oil, and Texas Instruments all use matrix designs, have concluded that the biggest advantage to this structure is that "it facilitates a rapid management response to changing market and technical requirements."[27] On the other hand, they also note that there are drawbacks to the matrix organization and that managers should be aware of them.

Disadvantages of Matrix Organizations

Numerous drawbacks to the matrix organization could be cited, but the following five are probably the most significant. An examiner of these disadvantages must keep in mind that most of them are built into the use of the matrix. Managers cannot avoid them; they can only learn to deal more effectively with them.

There may be power struggles.

One of the primary disadvantages relates to power struggles. Since use of the matrix means use of dual command, managers often end up jockeying for power. Many project managers spend a lot of their time trying to get preferential treatment for their projects—even when it is unnecessary. The only way to deal with this problem is for the top functional manager to balance project needs with organizational resources and for project managers to place the overall organization ahead of the personal satisfaction associated with project completion.

Groupitis may develop.

Second, the matrix entails wide use of group decision making because group cooperation is required for project success. However, if the project manager is not careful, a syndrome called groupitis will develop, in which case every decision will be hammered out in large numbers of contentious meetings. The waste of time is obviously expensive. Moreover, such meetings can negatively affect the morale of project participants. The best way to overcome this problem is to make it a personal managerial policy to use group decision making as often as necessary and as little as possible.

There may be a severe layering of matrixes.

Third, if an organization has many ongoing projects, the result may be a severe layering of matrixes. Matrix projects mushroom everywhere, with some large matrix structures creating their own internal matrixes. As Davis and Lawrence note: "When this occurs, organization charts begin to resemble blueprints for a complex electronic machine, relationships become

---

[26]David I. Cleland and William R. King, *Systems Analysis and Project Management*, 2nd ed. (New York: McGraw-Hill, 1975), pp. 251–52.

[27]Stanley M. Davis and Paul R. Lawrence, "Problems of Matrix Organizations," *Harvard Business Review*, May–June 1978, p. 132.

unnecessarily complex, and the matrix form may become more of a burden than it is worth."[28] The best remedy is for the functional manager to whom the project head reports to insist that the structure be kept as simple as possible. Uncontrolled growth of matrix structures often results in power struggles between the managers; during such conflict, organizational efficiency suffers badly.

Matrix structures can be expensive.

Fourth, a matrix structure can be expensive. The dual chain of command may cause management costs to double. This is particularly true when the structure is being set up. As the matrix matures, these added costs should be offset by efficiency increases. Therefore, as long as the organization keeps its eye on cost control and carefully monitors the matrix through its growth period, things should turn out all right.

The matrix may be quickly abandoned.

Fifth, when there is an economic crunch and the organization has to cut back, matrix structures are often the first to go. This is often as it should be. In a weak economy, some projects may experience drastic turnabouts in customer demand and so have to be terminated. However, the drawback is that some companies blame the matrix for the decline in business. In these cases, the matrix is abandoned forever—an unfortunate outcome, since the matrix is not responsible for the economic setback. Management should have plans for handling economic declines. The matrix should not become a scapegoat for poor management. The way to avoid this pitfall is for top management to realize that while the matrix can help achieve new levels of efficiency, it is not a substitute for effective management.[29] In summing up their analysis of matrix organization pitfalls, Davis and Lawrence write:

> We do not recommend that every company adopt the matrix form. But where it is relevant, it can become an important part of an effective managerial process. Like any new method it may develop serious bugs, but the experience that many new companies are acquiring with this organization form can now help others realize its benefits and avoid its pitfalls.[30]

Matrix Structures In Action

There are many examples of matrix structures. For purposes of simplicity, however, they can be described in terms of four models.

There are four basic types of matrix structures.

One is the *project matrix* such as that used by Lockheed Missiles and Space Company, the Rocketdyne Division of Rockwell International, and other

---

[28]Ibid., p. 139.

[29]For more on the advantages and disadvantages of the matrix organization see: Thomas D. Rowan, C. Douglas Howell, and Jan A. Gugliotti, "The Pros and Cons of Matrix Management," *Administrative Management*, December 1980, pp. 22–24, 50, 59.

[30]Davis and Lawrence, p. 142.

organizations in the aerospace industry. These firms all employ matrix designs similar to that in Figure 6-7.

A second is the *product–function matrix* such as that used by consumer products companies who assign managers the responsibility for a product line. Sometimes the company using this matrix hopes to create product divisions but is currently too small to sustain the costs of divisionalization. At other times the firm has a product that will move through its life cycle from introduction to termination in a period of one to three years; thus it is handled the way a project is, the only difference being that the primary individual is given the title of product manager. At still other times the product is expected to be marketable for years to come, and the product manager's position is a permanent one.

Product managers are usually responsible for several related products, which they manage both individually and as part of an integrated product line. If planning and other management activities are devoted to bringing a single product to completion, the product manager usually has additional responsibilities for coordinating product lines. At General Electric, product managers are responsible for managing products related largely by "classes of consumer need." Products may also be grouped together based on common competition.

In each case, the product manager has a broad responsibility for meshing company capabilities and market needs in a way that will be profitable for the company. To do this, product managers may introduce new products or eliminate existing ones; they may plan and implement advertising and other marketing programs; they may, indeed, do most of the things that are commonly associated with the management of a business.[31]

The design of the product matrix is very similar to that in Figure 6-7. The major difference is that the position of project manager is replaced by that of product manager. The product manager is the business-results person and the functional department heads are the resource managers.

A third form of structure is the *product–region matrix*. This organizational arrangement arose out of the need of multinational manufacturers to achieve product–market emphasis. Philips, Siemens, and other large European multinationals first popularized these structures. Their worldwide regional subsidiaries used to produce, import, and sell company products for their particular region of the world. These divisions found, however, that they were unable to match the manufacturing and distribution costs of their U. S. competitors unless product planning, manufacturing, and distribution could be coordinated on a worldwide basis. As a result, the product division vice-presidents were appointed business-results managers. They became responsible for business and product planning related to their product lines. The heads of the regional subsidiaries became resource managers for the

---

[31]Janger, p. 29.

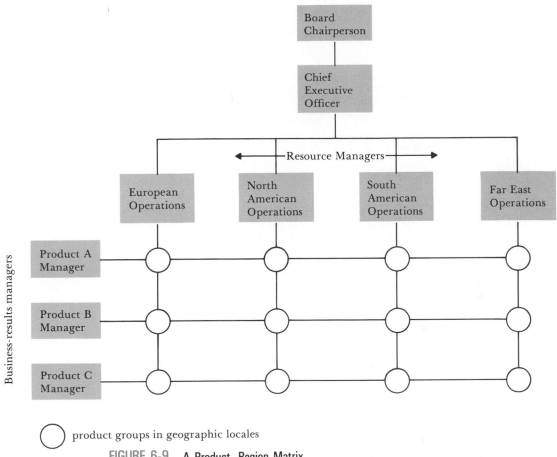

product groups in geographic locales

FIGURE 6-9   A Product–Region Matrix

portion of their plant output that was in international trade. So while the latter supervised company plants and manufacturing personnel in their regions, production planning, scheduling, and output were determined by the product division executive who was the worldwide business-results manager. Figure 6-9 provides an example of a product-region matrix.

A fourth form of structure is the *multidimensional matrix*. This design combines a number of different variables such as product, function, and geographic area. Also used by multinational enterprises, it is typified by that of Dow Corning, which has a 3-D type of arrangement combining businesses or product lines, functional support areas, and geographic areas. Figure 6-10 provides an illustration of this form. Notice that business profit centers are created in each geographic area of the world. Functional support is provided to each center, which is free to sell whatever company products are desired in the particular locale.

Multidimensional structures are also used by multinationals.

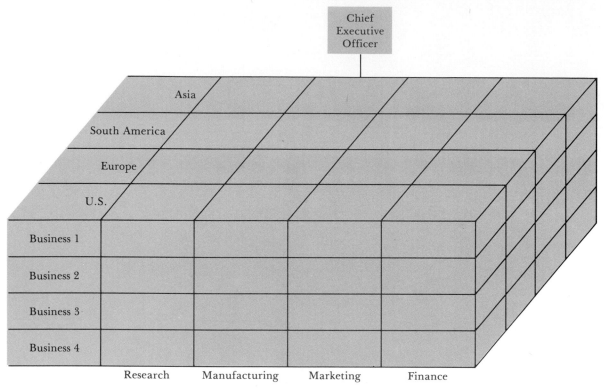

FIGURE 6-10   A Multidimensional Matrix Organization

Over the past two decades, the matrix structure has gained in popularity;[32] however, it has not proven to be an organizational design panacea. As a result, some firms have dropped their use of the matrix. Citibank of New York and Skandia of Stockholm are examples. Many others, including Chase Manhattan, TRW, and American Bankers Insurance Group, have adopted matrices because of the benefits they offer in managing complex undertakings. Another such design that is being employed by more and more firms is the free-form, or organic, organization structure.

FREE-FORM ORGANIZATIONS

The free-form organization structure (also called organic) has proved very useful in large-scale organizations, which suffer most severely from the negative effects of the bureaucratic process. The essence of this structure is in its name. The organization can take any form, but the objective is always the

Free-form structure discourages petty controls.

same: The design must help the executive manage change. For this reason, firms using a free-form structure tend to play down the organizational hierarchy, with its emphasis on departmentalization and job descriptions. Instead, all reasonable attempts are made to free workers from petty controls. In fact, some individuals have even suggested doing away with the traditional worker-boss relationship.

With rigid bureaucratic rules discarded, the manager is given freedom that is necessary to do a particular job. Many times the only controls top management employs are those related to profits or the allocation of scarce resources. In turn, it is common to find managers in these free-form organizations handling their subordinates with similar latitude. Reliance on consensus plays a major role, and two-way communication is encouraged. The organization operates as a team, as opposed to a department with a structured superior-subordinate relationship. In fact, at the upper levels there is sometimes *multiple* top management. The president alone does not make the final decisions on major matters; instead, decisions are made by a group of three or four key executives. The result is an "office of the president," staffed by more than one individual. A manager must remember, however, that this team approach at the top level has not worked well for every form. It should be used only after careful managerial consideration has been given to its advantages and disadvantages.

Synergy and Strategic Planning

Cooperative action is attained via strategic planning.

Another common characteristic of free-form structures is the emphasis on getting all departments, units, and subsidiaries to work together. Although some organizational forms (holding companies, for example) will have many separate, unrelated, semi-autonomous firms operating under one banner, free-form companies tend to have fewer such holdings, and they try to blend them in harmonious fashion. As a result of this cooperative action, or synergism, the total effect is greater than the sum of the individual parts working independently. To a large extent, this synergy is accomplished at the top level of the organization.

What happens is that the central management will draw up a strategic plan that is designed to obtain the greatest synergistic effect from its units. Resources are then allocated on the basis of the potential synergism. Although the units are encouraged to plan, top management makes the final decision on all strategic plans. In this way, the master plan for each division can be revised in light of overall enterprise commitments and objectives.

Emphasis is given to decentralized operation with centralized control.

The main synergistic ingredient is centralized control with decentralized operation. Additionally, strong emphasis is placed on organizing along the lines of profit centers. Further, managers are urged to take risks and to operate their units more from a human-behavior standpoint than ever before. Perhaps this is the reason why firms using free-form structures tend to stress the need for young, dynamic managers unshackled by outmoded assump-

INTERVIEW WITH KIRK LANDON

Kirk Landon is Chairman of the Board and Chief Executive Officer of the American Bankers Insurance Group. Over the last ten years the firm has had dramatic growth with revenues increasing from $196 to $712 million and the amount of life insurance that the company has expanding from $8 billion to over $30 billion. As president of a diverse insurance group, Kirk has found that a matrix structure has been particularly useful in helping the firm keep control of its expanding operations.

Q. *Many insurance companies don't use a matrix structure, yet you've been very successful with yours. Isn't a matrix a pretty difficult type of structure to operationalize?*

A. It can be, and the matrix structure we have in place today certainly is not the one we started out with. In the beginning we had a matrix that combined two elements: functions and markets. We had to learn how to live with this type of a structural arrangement before we could move on to something more sophisticated like our current matrix.

Q. *What does your current matrix structure look like? How sophisticated is it?*

A. We use a matrix structure that allow us to focus on markets and functions. For example, we have an auto insurance market and people from various functional

tions. It also accounts for the fact that free-form organizations are most widely used by firms whose operations are highly adaptive to products or services on the frontier of public use (for example, air pollution devices) and those meeting an essential and high-demand industrial, consumer, or military need (for example, electronic devices, lenses and frames, space-age hardware). Still another characteristic of these structures is their use of computerized performance evaluations, which determine whether a division or department is contributing to overall profitability. Units which do not do this are likely to be pruned from the organization.

The Challenges of Free-form Structures

Despite the successes free-form structures have led to, they are not without their drawbacks and challenges. The major challenge of the free-form structure is that it discards or de-emphasizes such management principles as unity of command and the scalar chain. In their place is a form of situational management in which individuals are encouraged to interact and work rather

Management principles are de-emphasized.

areas that staff this group. The group is looked on as a "business" and there is a business board that holds meetings and is charged with creating profits from that auto market. With the use of matrix, we're able to create small businesses within the overall structure. It's a fairly sophisticated arrangement, and it has taken time for us to learn how to operate efficiently with a matrix. However, for us at least, it's the best possible arrangement because it lets us focus on both our external markets and our internal functions.

Q. *What are the benefits and drawbacks of this type of matrix arrangement?*

A. There are two basic basic benefits to our type of matrix arrangement. First, it lets us drive profit responsibility down to the middle management levels, and that's where we want it to be. You can't have everything done at the top management levels. You need to get the rest of the people involved. Second, if their business does well, the personnel are rewarded for this success. So they have a stake in the operation and this tends to motivate them.

On the other hand, there are two major disadvantages. One is that it takes a reasonably long time to get the matrix structure into place. It took us almost five years before we had ours to the point where it works the way we want it to work. Second, the business boards have periodic meetings that the members have to attend to help plan and control operations. It can be time-consuming work, but it has to be done.

Overall, however, I'm pleased with our structure and the performance we've been able to achieve. I think a lot of our success has been a direct result of the effective use of matrix design.

unpredictably with other members of the organization. Operating within the profit-center concept, they are encouraged to carry out their strategic plans in an environment designed to deal with change. New technology may alter the nature of their work, but the organizational structure is able to take advantage of these changes. For the dynamic, mature manager, the new environment is a welcome relief; for the middle-of-the-road traditionalist, it is a nightmare that brings on tension, anxiety, and fear. The lack of rigidity disrupts the average individual's orientation, and many managers are unable to adapt to the new system.

Structures help manage change.

Second, free-form structures are designed to incorporate change. This is why they are found in firms operating in highly technical industries. Not all organizations, however, operate in this kind of environment. Thus, the structure can have limited value for some firms.

Free-form design encourages excellence.

Third, free-form structures encourage excellence. Managers are on their own and allowed to use the approach they feel works best in attaining the objective. And questions must arise:

But if free-form management can bestow such benefits, why don't more companies adopt it? Perhaps the major reason is that time-worn management methods and structures are also protective devices for assigning responsibility for failure. The point is sharply emphasized by Robert H. Schaffer: . . . "The easiest place to camouflage failures in obtaining goals," insists Schaffer, "is the well-fractioned organization where, as any veteran can testify, stalled performance almost always is attributable to 'the system,' to other departments or to forces that lie outside the control of any department."[33]

For a variety of reasons, the use of free-form structures appears to be increasing. First, managers are demanding more flexible organizations to meet current changes and challenges. Second, managers are more competent than ever before, so they can effectively utilize these new organizational structures. Third, new technological developments are putting pressure on companies to modernize their organizational designs. Fourth, bureaucratic super-structures will no longer do the job; too much dependence on organization charts and job descriptions stunts the growth of the enterprise. For many, free-form structures will prove to be the answer to a large number of old problems.

CONTINGENCY ORGANIZATION DESIGN

The right organization structure will depend on the situation.

The key word currently characterizing organization design is *contingency*. This word, and the theory it designates, means simply using whatever approach is most effective. Today, the development of structures in which minimum attention is given to the formal division of duties is resulting in increasingly flexible designs. Mechanistic structures are, in many cases, being replaced by organic ones.[34] Of course, each company has to evaluate its own situation, but as Jay W. Lorsch and Paul R. Lawrence note, a trend toward *contingency organization design* now seems important.[35]

Influencing Forces

Y. K. Shetty and Howard M. Carlisle echo statements by Lawrence and Lorsch about the need for contingency design, noting that the "best" organization structure must vary according to situation. In essence, structure is a function of forces in the managers, the subordinates, the task, and the

---

[33]William W. George, "Task Teams for Rapid Growth," *Harvard Business Review,* March–April 1977, pp. 71–80.

[34]For more on this see Henry L. Tosi, Jr., and John W. Slocum, Jr., "Contingency Theory: Some Suggested Directions," *Journal of Management,* Spring 1984, pp. 9–26.

[35]Jay W. Lorsch and Paul R. Lawrence, *Studies in Organization Design* (Homewood, IL: Richard D. Irwin, Dorsey Press, 1970), p. 1.

environment.[36] Forces in the managers are readily evident. A superior who feels that the work force is basically lazy will design a structure that reflects these views and will refuse to delegate much authority. Conversely, a manager who believes that the best method of managing depends on putting faith in the workers and sharing information and responsibility with them will be more prone to using a design that facilitates decentralization and delegation of authority. Forces in the subordinates would include motives such as a desire for autonomy and an opportunity to participate in decision making. If these factors are present, they will have an impact on the structure. Forces in the task are often reflected in technology. Shetty and Carlisle note: "Technology may determine the extent to which the job may be programmed, that is, employee behaviors may be precisely specified. The kind of organization required in a low task structure is not the same as that required in a high task structure."[37] Environmental forces include the availability of resources, the nature of the competition, the predictability of demand, and the type of products or services being provided by the company.

These four interacting forces influence the type of organizational design that will evolve, as Figure 6-11 shows. By employing this framework, a company can identify the conditions enhancing or impeding a particular structure. Sometimes it needs a more flexible design, other times a more structured one:

> The organization appropriate in one market-technology environment may be irrelevant or even dysfunctional in another environment. A firm producing a standardized product sold in a stable market may require a pattern of organization altogether different from a company manufacturing a highly technical product for a more dynamic market. There is

---

[36]Y. K. Shetty and Howard M. Carlisle, "A Contingency Model of Organization Design," *California Management Review*, Fall 1972, pp. 38–45.

[37]Ibid., p. 42.

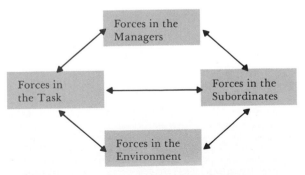

FIGURE 6-11   Forces Affecting Organization Structure

no one pattern of organization style that is universally appropriate. (See Intrapreneurship in Action: Keep It Simple.)[38]

A Matter of "Fit"

In essence, then, management must look for what is essentially the right "fit" among personnel, organizational characteristics, and task requirement. John J. Morse and Jay W. Lorsch illustrated this when they made an analysis of four business firms, two highly effective and two less effective. One of the highly effective firms was an Akron container manufacturing plant in which formal relationships were highly structured, rules were specific and comprehensive, and the time orientation was short-term. The other was a Stockton research lab where formal relations were less well defined, rules were minimal and flexible, and the time orientation was long-term. Table 6-6

---

[38]Ibid., p. 44.

TABLE 6-6 Differences in "Climate" Characteristics in High-Performing Organizations	Characteristics	Akron	Stockton
	1. Structural orientation	Perceptions of tightly controlled behavior and a high degree of structure	Perceptions of a low degree of structure
	2. Distribution of influence	Perceptions of low total influence concentrated at upper levels in the organization	Perceptions of high total influence, more evenly spread out among all levels
	3. Character of superior-subordinate relations	Low freedom vis-à-vis superiors to choose and handle jobs, directive type of supervision	High freedom vis-à-vis superiors to choose and handle projects, participatory type of supervision
	4. Character of colleague relations	Perceptions of many similarities among colleagues, high degree of coordination of colleague effort	Perceptions of many differences among colleagues, relatively low degree of coordination of colleague effort
	5. Time orientation	Short-term	Long-term
	6. Goal orientation	Manufacturing	Scientific
	7. Top executive's "managerial style"	More concerned with task than people	More concerned with task than people

Source: Reprinted by permission of the *Harvard Business Review*. Exhibit from "Beyond Theory Y" by John J. Morse and Jay W. Lorsch (May–June 1970, p. 66). Copyright © 1970 by the President and Fellows of Harvard College; all rights reserved.

Although matrix and free-form organization designs are used in industry, there are a large number of firms that do not employ them. In their best selling book, *In Search of Excellence*, Thomas Peters and Robert Waterman, Jr., report that none of the firms they found to be excellent were using the matrix. Companies like Boeing employed project management, but that was it. The authors explained the situation by noting:

> How have the excellent companies avoided this? The answer is, in a number of ways, but underlying it all is a basic simplicity of form. Underpinning most of the excellent companies we find a fairly stable, unchanging form—perhaps the product division—that provides the essential touchstone which everybody understands, and from which the complexities of day-to-day life can be approached. Clarity on values is also an important part of the underlying touchstone of stability and simplicity as well.*

Simply put, successful organizations try to meet changing, complex situations through the use of simple, flexible, and responsive designs that promote intrapreneurship. Rather than using a matrix, they stay with their product structure but decentralize authority to the point at which operating managers can make the necessary decisions. They ensure that everyone knows what to do and to whom to report. In this way there is less concern with the internal organizational relationships, allowing the manager to focus on business results. Johnson & Johnson is an example. The firm has over 150 independent divisions, of which 55 deal with consumer products. The latter are each responsible for their own research, marketing, and distribution. People in each division know what they are doing and, if necessary, can be transferred between divisions with almost no problem. They understand the consumer products business.

Another interesting fact about successful organizations is that they tend to have fewer people at the corporate level than do their less successful counterparts. Those who do work on that level spend more of their time dealing with problem solving than with supervision.

Does all of this mean that the matrix and free-form structures are a waste of time? Far from it. These designs can be very effective, but they must be used carefully. The ability of the matrix to respond to changing conditions is a very important asset. The ability of adhocratic designs to handle multiple pressures without creating new bureaucracies is a big advantage. On the other hand, when these structures are used simply for resolving temporary problems, they fail to provide the long-run value that an enterprise should expect from its organization design. In these cases, simpler structures are often superior.

*Thomas J. Peters and Robert H. Waterman, Jr., *In Search of Excellence* (New York: Harper & Row, Publishers, 1982), p. 308.

shows Morse and Lorsch's comparison of the two. Both firms, despite these differences, were successful because their structures brought the task and the people together in the right way. Conversely, in the two less effective plants they studied, these researchers found that the formal and informal organizational characteristics did not fit the task requirements as well as in the successful counterparts in Akron and Stockton. This indicates the importance of a correct task-organization-people fit.

> In arguing for an approach which emphasizes the fit among task, organization, and people, we are putting to rest the question of which organizational approach—the classical or the participative—is best. In its place we are raising a new question: What organizational approach is most appropriate given the task and the people involved?
>
> For many enterprises, given the new needs of younger employees for more autonomy, and the rapid rates of social and technological change, it may well be that the more participative approach is the most appropriate. But there will still be many situations in which the more controlled and formalized organization is desirable. Such an organization need not be coercive or punitive. If it makes sense to the individuals involved, given their needs and their jobs, they will find it rewarding and motivating.[39]

■ SUMMARY

The use of bureaucratic structures has begun to decline. One reason for this decline is that the inherent assumptions underlying bureaucracy are unrealistic. The organization cannot function with mechanical rules and regulations that have limited value in motivating and leading the modern worker.

In overcoming bureaucratic deficiencies, many firms are turning to adaptive organization structures, new designs based on a number of assumptions. One such assumption is that the organization operates in a dynamic environment. A second is that personnel, task, and environment are related and must be fit together properly for the best structure and output. This chapter initially directed attention to the impact of technology and its effect on organizational personnel, from the workers right up to the managers. At the worker level, technology affects social relationships as well as job content. At the managerial level, it encourages greater integration of colleagues and of planning effort.

Technology also affects the organization structure by causing changes in such factors as the length of the line of command, the span of control of the

---

[39]John J. Morse and Jay W. Lorsch, "Beyond Theory Y," *Harvard Business Review*, May–June 1970, p. 68.

chief executive, and the ratio of managers to total personnel. In addition, mechanistic designs tend to give way to organic ones, as has been seen in the research of Woodward, Zwerman, Lawrence and Lorsch, and Meyer, to name only five prominent researchers in the organization-study boom of recent times.

What do these new organic structures look like? How do they work? Exactly when are they used? These questions are answered through examinations of project, matrix, and free-form designs. The project organization form entails ''the gathering of the best available talent to accomplish a specific and complex understanding within time, cost and/or quality parameters, followed by the disbanding of the team upon completion of the undertaking.''[40] Project organization has been employed in numerous and diverse ways, from building dams and weapon systems to conducting research and development and designing bank credit-card systems. The major advantage of this organizational form is that it allows the project manager and team to concentrate their attention on one specific undertaking.

The matrix structure is a hybrid form of organization, containing characteristics of both project and functional structures. In a matrix design, employees are in a sense on partial loan to the matrix project manager. These employees, therefore, have a dual responsibility—to the line manager who lent them to the project and to the project manager for whom they work for the life of the project. The result is a uniquely horizontal and vertical flow of authority. Since the project manager has only project authority, this individual must rely on human relations assets and skills—for example, negotiation, personality, persuasive ability, the aura of competence, and the brokering of reciprocal favors. While the matrix structure has advantages, the organization considering its use must also weigh the disadvantages inherent in it. Only after considering both aspects of the matrix can an organization make an intelligent decision regarding its overall value.

Another adaptive organization design is the free-form, or organic, structure. This design can take any shape, but it always has two prime characteristics: the downplay of rigid bureaucratic rules and an emphasis on self-regulation. A number of conglomerates have adopted this organization form. There are four basic models of matrix structures: project, product–function, product–region, and multidimensional. Perhaps the greatest advantage of a free-form structure is its value to the manager who must cope with change.

What kind of structure is best? The question has no single right answer. ''Best'' depends on the situation. For that reason, the area of contingency organization design is currently very important. Some firms need a mechanistic structure; others work better with an organic one. The answer to the question thus depends on forces operating on managers, subordinates, task, and environment.

---

[40]Hodgetts, ''Interindustry Analysis of Certain Aspects of Project Management,'' p. 7.

This chapter has examined the ways in which organizations are redesigning their structures in order to adapt more effectively to their environments. However, the organizing process only helps bring together the workers and the work. Management still needs a basis for comparing the plan and the results. This subject is discussed in the next chapter.

■ REVIEW AND STUDY QUESTIONS

1. What are the characteristics of an ideal bureaucracy? Describe them.
2. Why is the bureaucratic form of organization declining today?
3. What impact can technology have on workers? On managers?
4. What is a mechanistic organization structure? Give an example, and explain how your example fits the structure definition.
5. What is an organic organization structure? Give an example, including in your discussion of it the aspects of the example that make it organic.
6. What effect does technology have on organization structure? Base your answer on recent research, particularly Joan Woodward's research in the London suburbs.
7. What is a project organization?
8. When can a project organization be used most effectively? Explain.
9. Explain this statement: A matrix structure is a hybrid form of organization, containing characteristics of both project and functional structures.
10. What is project authority?
11. Describe in your own words some of the advantages of a matrix structure. What are some of its disadvantages?
12. How are matrix structures being used today? In your answer, be sure to discuss the four models of matrix.
13. How is the free-form organization useful to large-scale organizations?
14. How do free-form organizations employ synergy in their strategic planning?
15. What is a contingency organization design?
16. What are some common guidelines for contingency organization designs? Explain the guidelines that you cite.
17. The research team of Y. K. Shetty and Howard M. Carlisle noted that the "best" organization structure is a function of four forces. Identify and explain all four.
18. Explain what John J. Morse and Jay W. Lorsch meant when they discussed the need for "fit" among task, organization, and personnel.

■ SELECTED REFERENCES

Barker, Jeffrey, Dean Tjosvold, and I. Robert Andrews. "Conflict Approaches of Effective and Ineffective Project Managers: A Field Study in a Matrix Organization." *Journal of Management Studies*, March 1988, pp. 167–78.

Brown, John L., and Neil McK. Agnew. "The Balance of Power in a Matrix Structure." *Business Horizons*, November–December, 1982, pp. 51–54.

Burns, Tom, and G. M. Stalker. *The Management of Innovation*. London: Tavistock Publications, 1961.

Child, John. "Predicting and Understanding Organization Structure." *Administrative Science Quarterly*, June 1973, pp. 168–85.

Cleland, David I. "Understanding Project Authority." *Business Horizons*, Spring 1967, pp. 63–70.

Davis, Stanley, and Paul R. Lawrence. "Problems of Matrix Organizations." *Harvard Business Review*, May–June 1978, pp. 131–42.

Drucker, Peter F. "The Coming of the New Organization." *Harvard Business Review*, January–February 1988, pp. 45–53.

Dunne, Edward J. Jr., Michael J. Stahl, and Leonard J. Melhart, Jr. "Influence Sources of Project and Functional Managers in Matrix Organizations." *Academy of Management Journal*, March 1978, pp. 135–40.

Fry, Louis W. "Technology–Structure Research: Three Critical Issues." *Academy of Management Journal*, September 1982, pp. 532–52.

George, W. W. "Task Teams for Rapid Growth." *Harvard Business Review*, March–April 1977, pp. 71–80.

Gerwin, D. "The Comparative Analysis of Structure and Technology: A Critical Appraisal." *Academy of Management Review*, January 1979, pp. 41–51.

Hickson, David J., D. J. Pugh, and Diana C. Pheysey. "Operations Technology and Organization Structure: An Empirical Reappraisal." *Administrative Science Quarterly*, September 1969, pp. 378–97.

Hodgetts, Richard M. "Leadership Techniques in the Project Organization." *Academy of Management Journal*, June 1968, pp. 211–19.

Janger, Allen R. *Matrix Organization of Complex Business*. New York: National Industrial Conference Board, 1979.

Johnston, Russell, and Paul R. Lawrence. "Beyond Vertical Integration—the Rise of the Value-Adding Partnership." *Harvard Business Review*, July–August 1988, pp. 94–101.

Kolodny, Harvey F. "Evolution to a Matrix Organization." *Academy of Management Review*, October, 1979, pp. 543–54.

Kolodny, Harvey F. "Managing in A Matrix." *Business Horizons*, March–April 1981, pp. 17–24.

Larson, Erik W., and David H. Gobeli. "Matrix Management: Contradictions and Insights." *California Management Review*, Summer 1987, pp. 126–38.

Lawrence, Paul R., and Jay W. Lorsch. *Organization and Environment*. Boston: Harvard Graduate School of Business Administration, 1967.

Lincoln, James R., Mitsuyo Hanada, and Kerry McBride. "Organizational Structures in Japanese and U. S. Manufacturing." *Administrative Science Quarterly*, September 1986, pp. 338–64.

Mills, Peter K., and Barry Z. Posner. "The Relationships Among Self-Supervision, Structure, and Technology in Professional Service Organizations." *Academy of Management Journal*, June 1982, pp. 437–43.

Mintzberg, Henry. "Organization Design: Fashion or Fit?" *Harvard Business Review*, January–February 1981, pp. 103–15.

Morse, John J., and Jay W. Lorsch. "Beyond Theory Y." *Harvard Business Review*, May–June 1970, pp. 61–68.

Pearson, Andrall E. "Muscle-Build the Organization." *Harvard Business Review*, July–August 1987, pp. 49–55.

Peters, Thomas J. "Beyond the Matrix Organization." *Business Horizons*, October 1979, pp. 15–27.

Powell, Walter W. "Hybrid Organizational Arrangements: New Form or Transitional Development." *California Management Review*, Fall 1987, pp. 67–87.

Rowen, Thomas D., C. Douglas Howell, and Jan A. Gugliotti. "The Pros and Cons of Matrix Management." *Administrative Management*, December 1980, pp. 22–24.

Sheridan, John H. "Matrix Maze: Are Two Bosses Better Than One?" *Industry Week*, June 11, 1979, pp. 77–81.

■ CASE: More Order, Not Less

When Sousa Incorporated started business in 1950, its three founders stated the firm's basic mission as one of "inventing and manufacturing sophisticated telecommunication equipment." Over the next thirty years the company prospered, thanks to the high degree of technical expertise possessed by the owners and the staff they hired. In 1987, however, the founders decided they had had enough. They wished to retire and spend the rest of their years in leisure. They therefore sold Sousa for $60 million to a large national conglomerate. This was the conglomerate's first venture into the communications industry; its initial success had come in manufacturing. Nevertheless, the board of directors liked Sousa's profitability picture and felt that the company was making an excellent acquisition.

Soon after the takeover, the Sousa work force was told that the conglomerate would make no radical changes; everything was to be "business as usual." But there was one exception: The conglomerate would be reorganizing the structure of the firm. The new owners preferred a line-staff organization. When asked about this, the new president of the firm said: "We feel Sousa is too disorganized. We want to create more formal lines of communication and authority-responsibility relationships. This way everyone will know what to do and to whom activities are to be reported. At present, this is not the case."

Within six months after the reorganization, however, Sousa's financial statement indicated that something was quite wrong. Instead of obtaining high profitability, the newly acquired company was reporting its first loss in years. The president and his advisors were unable to explain why. One of the board members put it this way: "We tried to straighten out the firm's chaotic nature by introducing some order into the structure. But instead of becoming more profitable, Sousa is now losing money. The president has talked it over with us and decided to call in a management consulting firm. Perhaps we need an even more formalized structure than we thought. In any event, something has to be done."

Questions

1. Explain why the new organization structure is not working.

2. Do you agree with the new president's comment about Sousa being too disorganized?

3. What recommendations would you make to this firm? Explain, bringing the topics of mechanistic and organic structures into your discussion.

■ CASE: The Glorified Coordinator

William Uyesugi, a graduate student of business at State University, was writing a paper on modern organization structures. As part of his research he interviewed project, matrix, and free-form organization managers in ten major corporations throughout the city. One of the managers worked in a consumer products firm. She explained her job as follows:

> I'm responsible for developing a consumer product. In order to get the job done, I've had people assigned to me from the various functional departments: research, design, manufacturing, and test. Of course, these people will stay within their own departments; but when I need them, they will work for me.
>
> I spent most of last week figuring out exactly when I'd need these people. I'm going to need the R&D people starting next week. Then, when they're finished with the project, I'll have it manufactured and tested. This will come in about two months. The reason I know the schedule so well is that this week I have to go around to the functional managers and ask them to assign people to me for the project. They'll want to see the time schedule and then they'll figure out who can work on my project. Of course, these people will continue to report to their functional boss, but they will be working on my project. Nevertheless, I suppose you'd be right if you called me a glorified project coordinator or

an expediter. After all, my only goal is to get everyone together and make sure the product is manufactured on time. Then it will be tested in various sections of the country; and if it catches on, the company will set up a new product department to handle it. Meanwhile, I'll go on to another project.

Questions

1. What kind of authority does the project manager have over the project personnel in this case?
2. Is this a project, matrix, or free-form organization? Give your reasoning.

■ CASE: Fly Me to the Moon

In his second State of the Union address to the Congress in May 1961, President John F. Kennedy stated, "I believe that this nation should commit itself to achieving the goal, before this decade is out, of landing a man on the moon and returning him safely to earth." The race to the moon was on.

The United States undertook three distinct projects: Mercury, Gemini, and Apollo. Mercury's primary objectives included investigating human capabilities in the space environment and developing manned space flight technology. Gemini's primary goals entailed subjecting two men and supporting equipment to long duration flights, effecting rendezvous and docking maneuvers with other orbiting vehicles, and perfecting methods of re-entry and landing. Apollo had three primary goals: to put two men on the moon, to allow them to carry out limited exploration, and then to return them safely to earth.

To achieve Apollo's goals, the United States needed a spacecraft to get the astronauts into and out of the moon's orbit and a lunar excursion module (LEM) to take them down to the moon's surface and return them to the spacecraft. In order to build these two pieces of equipment, the National Aeronautics and Space Administration (NASA) solicited contracts. The award for the spacecraft was given to North American Aviation while Grumman Aircraft received the LEM contract. In addition, NASA set up a project organization, known as the Apollo Spacecraft Program Office (ASPO), to monitor the contractors and see that the hardware was built on time and within cost and quality parameters. As the contractors built the spacecraft and the LEM, ASPO personnel would check to see that everything was going according to schedule. If there was a problem, for example, and the contractor wanted to change the design of the hardware, ASPO had to clear the change. In short, the Apollo program people were charged with seeing that contractors did their jobs correctly. ASPO headquarters were located in Houston, but the ASPO people were continually flying out to see contractors on site. They also had frequent reports made to them so they could ascertain that progress was being made and that the work quality was appropriate.

Questions

1. What kind of authority did the Apollo Spacecraft Program Office have over contractors? Explain your answer.
2. Was the ASPO a project, matrix, or free-form organization? Why do you think so?
3. Could NASA have gotten the moonshot launched and landed as efficiently as it did if it had used a different organization structure? Defend your opinion.

■ CASE: Here to Stay

How popular are matrix and free-form organization designs? Research shows that in some industries they are becoming common-place. An example is the publishing business. After researching the field, Walter Powell recently reported that:

> . . . successful editors enjoy freedom from corporate constraints, and authors enjoy the intimacy and closeness associated with smaller houses. These hybrid forms of organization allow an editor to rely on his or her own judgment and not have to appeal for higher-level approval. The large firm is able to keep top-flight editors content and, at the same time, give them a greater financial stake in the books they bring in.

In some cases publishing houses have even spun off subsidiaries that operate autonomously within the boundaries of the larger firm. This organizational arrangement allows for "a firm within a firm." Moreover, many editors actually feel greater responsibility to their authors and readers than they do to the enterprise. Yet, in order to hold on to the services of key editors, publishing houses are willing to tolerate this dual allegiance.

Nor are free-form enterprises restricted to the United States. The German textile industry is a good example. Because many companies in the industry specialize and thus depend on the support and assistance of other firms, medium and large textile enterprises in the industry are linked together. The industry has an elaborate system of subcontracting which keeps everyone in close contact with the others.

> Most textile producers are highly specialized and . . . the more distinctive each firm is, the more it depends on the success of other firm's products that complement its own. This production system depends on an extensive subcontracting system in which key technologies are

developed in collaboration. . . . These linkages allow textile makers to benefit from the subcontractors' experiences with customers in other industries, and the suppliers are, in turn, buffered from downturns in any one industry.

It seems that flexible organization designs may vary from one organization to another but, in general, they are here to stay.

Questions

1. Is the arrangement used in the publishing business an example of a project or a matrix structure? Explain.

2. Is the arrangement used in the German textile business an example of a project or a matrix structure? Explain.

3. What makes these forms of organizational design so effective? Defend your answer.

Source: Walter W. Powell, "Hybrid Organizational Arrangements: New Form or Transitional Development," *California Management Review,* Fall 1987, p. 69.

■   SELF-FEEDBACK EXERCISE: Identifying Your Ideal Organization

In what type of organization would you like to work? Read each of the following ten pairs of statements and decide with which you most agree: A or B. Then give yourself a score for each statement by using the following scales:

■ If the A statement is totally descriptive of the organization where you would like to work, give yourself 5 points.

■ If the A statement is much more descriptive of the organization for which you would like to work than is the B statement, give yourself 4 points.

■ If the A statement is slightly more descriptive of the organization for which you would like to work than is the B statement, give yourself 3 points.

■ If the B statement is slightly more descriptive of the organization for which you would like to work than is the A statement, give yourself 2 points.

■ If the B statement is much more descriptive of the organization for which you would like to work than is the A statement, give yourself 1 point.

■ If the B statement is totally descriptive of the organization for which you would like to work, give yourself 0 points.

When you are finished, enter your answers on the answer sheet. An interpretation of the results is provided at the end of this assignment.

1. A. An organization chart is important and it should be as detailed and complete as possible.
    B. Organization charts are unnecessary and the enterprise will run just as efficiently without them.

2. A. Everyone should have detailed job descriptions.
    B. People should be told what they are supposed to do, but job descriptions are unnecessary.

3. A. Authority should be determined by the individual's position with those in higher-level posts having more authority than those below them.
    B. Authority should be based primarily on knowledge and skill.

4. A. Objectives should be set from the top on down.
    B. Objectives should be set via a participative management approach that involves the subordinates.

5. A. Work should be as routine and repetitive as possible.
    B. Work should be as nonroutine and nonrepetitive as possible.

6. A. The environment should be as predictable as possible because this helps ensure stability and productivity.
    B. The environment should be highly unpredictable because this helps ensure profitability and rapid growth.

7. A. Control procedures should be highly impersonal in nature.
    B. Control procedures should be highly personal in nature.

8. A. Organizations should be most interested in efficiency and predictability.
    B. Organizations should be most interested in effectiveness and adaptability.

9. A. Motivation should come basically in the form of monetary rewards.
    B. Motivation should come basically in the form of internal, psychological rewards.

10. A. The organization should be most interested in bottom-line performance.
    B. The organization should be most interested in problem-solving.

Answers

1. _____   6. _____

2. _____   7. _____

3. _____   8. _____

4. _____   9. _____

5. _____   10. _____

Interpretation

0–10   You would feel most comfortable working for an organization that is highly organic in nature.

11–20   You would feel most comfortable in an organization that is basically organic in nature.

21–30   You would like it best working in an organization that is a blend of organic and mechanistic.

31–40   You would feel most comfortable in an organization that is basically mechanistic in nature.

41–50   You would feel most comfortable working in an organization that is highly mechanistic.

The
Controlling
Process

An organization that attains its objectives can formulate more ambitious ones. A firm that falls short of its goals must develop a revised plan. In both cases, the firms must conduct evaluations to assess their performance; the controlling process is the means whereby businesses evaluate plans and experiences.

The goals of this chapter are to examine the nature and process of control, with prime focus on traditional, specialized, and overall control techniques. This chapter shows a strong link between planning and controlling. The two are so entwined that it is sometimes difficult to determine where one leaves off and the other begins. And so it is within the chapter.

When you have finished this chapter, you should be able to:

1. Describe the three basic steps in the controlling process.
2. Discuss the requirements for an effective control system.
3. Relate how comprehensive budgeting and zero-base budgeting work.
4. Explain how the break-even point can be used for control purposes.
5. Describe some of the ways of measuring employee performance.
6. Present a brief description of the Gantt chart, PERT, and milestone budgeting, noting how they can help an organization control its operations.
7. Describe some of the most commonly used techniques for controlling an organization's overall performance.

THE BASIC CONTROLLING PROCESS

As Henri Fayol noted: "The control of an undertaking consists of seeing that everything is being carried out in accordance with the plan which has been adopted, the orders which have been given, and the principles which have been laid down. Its object is to point out mistakes in order that they may be rectified and prevented from occurring again."[1]

The *controlling process* has three basic steps: the establishment of standards, the comparison of performance against these standards, and the correction of deviations that have occurred. The latter two, of course, can only be attained through the establishment of effective feedback. This section will examine these three basic steps and the role of feedback in the controlling process.

Establishing Standards

Standards provide a basis against which performance can be measured. They are often a result of the goals the organization formulates during its planning phase. Sometimes they are very specific, expressed in terms of costs, revenues, products, or hours worked. Other times they are more qualitative in nature—for example, a desire to maintain high morale among the employees or to design a public relations program for gaining community goodwill (see Ethics in Action: Fraud and Bribery in the Defense Industry).

Comparing Performance with Standards

Ideally, management should design a control system that permits it to identify major problems before they occur.[2] For example, research shows that workers' attitudes toward their jobs decline before their productivity goes down. If management could identify the lead factor, it could begin taking steps to prevent the impending decline in output. However, since this is more often an idealistic wish than a practical solution, the next best step is to identify such deviations as early as possible. Most competent managers do so through use of the *exception principle,* which holds that attention should be focused on especially good or especially bad situations. Managers who work on this principle avoid the major danger of trying to control every deviation, great or small; they do not spread themselves so thin that they are inert when managerial attention and action are clearly indicated.

Some standards are not easily measured.

The major problem most managers encounter is how to measure actual performance. Some standards are easily measurable, but others require custom-made appraisals. Still others seem actually to defy objective evaluation. For example, how does one really measure worker motivation, since

---

[1]Henri Fayol, *Industrial and General Administration*, trans. J. A. Coubrough (Geneva, Switzerland: International Management Institute, 1929), p. 77.

[2]Georg Schreyogg and Horst Steinmann, "Strategic Control: A New Perspective," *Academy of Management Review,* January 1987, pp. 91–103.

ETHICS

IN

ACTION:

Fraud

and

Bribery

in the

Defense

Industry

Ethical standards are an important part of every business's operation. In recent years, however, it has become increasingly clear that some companies are lax in their enforcement of these standards. The defense industry is a good example. TRW recently admitted to fraud in overcharging the government for electronic gear. Rockwell was fined $5.5 million for double-billing the Air Force on navigational satellite contracts. Hughes Aircraft is currently under investigation for alleged payments to an Intelsat official to obtain information on projects that were up for bid. And Northrop is charged with falsifying test reports on components for the MX missile guidance system, as well as for allegedly bribing South Korean officials in an effort to sell the firm's F-20 fighter plane.

Many observers wonder whether defense contractors are sufficiently ethical in their business dealings. True, the industry is very competitive and, as Congress continues to trim the military budget, there are likely to be less dollars and fewer projects on which to bid. This increases the pressure on weapons contractors to win their bids for new jobs, and the steps that are taken to achieve these ends are not difficult to forecast: bribery, special payments, and industrial spying.

Of course, not all firms in the defense industry are guilty of unethical practices. Companies like General Electric, General Dynamics, and Grumman have good records, as do others. In fact, General Dynamics gives each of its employees a wallet card with a toll-free phone number to call if any employee has suspicions regarding fraud or waste. Congress is also trying to help promote higher ethical standards in the defense industry. There currently is a bill in committee that offers up to $250,000 to those who report fraud in defense contracting.

Regrettably, there are many in the industry who believe that these types of rewards are insufficient. A director of a Washington watchdog group, the Project on Military Procurement, contends that, "It won't stop until high executives of big companies go to jail. That's the only way people will take the law seriously." In any event, one thing is certain: the latest defense scandal involving bribery and fraud in the industry is likely to result in much more serious action by both the government and companies in an effort to eliminate these practices. The success of these efforts will be greatly dictated by how vigorously the parties enforce their own regulations.

Source: Stewart Toy et al., "The Defense Scandal," *Business Week,* July 4, 1988, pp. 28–30.

motivation is an intervening variable (that is, an internal psychological process unavailable for direct observation and accessible for judgment only through inference)? If Georgia appears interested in her work, she is motivated; if she looks uninterested, she is unmotivated, even though this appraisal may well be inaccurate. Another common performance measurement dilemma occurs when a firm tries to evaluate a top-level manager—for example, the vice-president of marketing. The further up the organization one goes, the more difficult it is to develop precise, measurable standards. Whatever criteria are selected, they will be vague. Management has found that as work becomes less technical, standards become more difficult to develop; appraisals are exceedingly hard to make. For this reason, a trend has developed in recent years toward evaluating workers almost exclusively on objective bases. If a standard is not measurable, it is not employed. This approach, the flaws of which are obvious, still has the major asset of greatly reducing subjective, biased evaluations. It also provides direction for subordinates, who know the bases on which their performance will be judged.

Correcting Deviations

The correction of deviations should begin with an investigation of why the errors occurred. Sometimes a planning premise may have been wrong. Sales may have been lower than anticipated because of an overly optimistic forecast. Or a strike in the plant may have caused unexpected delays in production. The cause of the deviation will help determine the appropriate action. But a key point to be noted here is that some problems are no one's fault. From time to time even the best market forecasts will be wrong. For example, a few years ago a large distiller marketed a dry white whiskey that, despite an extensive market research program, failed to achieve widespread acceptance. And in the case of a union strike, the walkout may be more a function of union demands than of management offers. The company may be able to give a maximum offer of 12 percent in salary and 7.2 percent in fringe benefits over a 2-year period. If the union refuses to settle for less than 20 percent and 12.8 percent respectively, a strike may occur. In short, not all deviations are directly attributable to any single individual or group, and if management tries to assess blame for every error, employee attitudes toward work may suffer, in which case the short-term success in appraisal could lead to a long-term productivity decline.

After the cause is identified, problem-solving measures can be enacted.

Of course, there are times when a manager will make an error in judgment or a worker will handle an order improperly. When this happens, if the errors are grave or habitual, corrective action may require the replacement of the individual or the assignment of additional training. However, the action can be determined only after the specific causes of the deviation have been evaluated.

Establishing Effective Feedback

An ideal control system provides timely feedback that can be used to monitor and correct deviations.[3] A basic illustration is provided by the human body. If

---

[3]See for example, John J. Keller, et al., "AT&T: The Making of a Comeback," *Business Week*, January 18, 1988, pp. 56–62.

something happens that causes the body to leave its "normal" state, basic control mechanisms will attempt to reestablish the status quo. This self-regulating, or control, property is known as homeostasis. For example, if a man cuts his finger, his body will begin working to coagulate the blood and close the wound. The feedback mechanism in the human system can perform phenomenal feats if conditions are somehow bearable: Some people who suffer massive heart attacks or are in major car accidents do survive.

The same basic concept of feedback is present in the thermostat system of a house. The desired temperature is programmed when the resident sets an indicator that communicates the setting to the system that controls the furnace. If a family desires 68°F, the heating unit will maintain the temperature at this level, turning on and off as necessary.

An organization also requires a feedback system. With the information provided by such a system, the company can monitor activities, identifying those that are not in accord with plans and taking the necessary corrective action. Figure 7-1 depicts the establishment of such a system.

Organizations must develop effective feedback control systems.

It should be noted, however, that organizational control systems differ from those found in the human body and the home thermostat: The body and the thermostat are essentially automatic and employ, at least in the short-run, only data from within the system. Organizational control, on the other hand, is seldom automatic. Usually, by the time feedback results are evaluated, other errors have occurred, and the organization is in a "catch-up" situation. In addition, organizational control employs data from outside the system. This occurs in the corrective process when the manager decides how to handle deviations, thereby introducing new decisions or inputs into the process. For this reason, mechanical control systems are often known as *closed-loop* systems, whereas organizational control systems are often called *open-loop* systems. Naturally, the latter must be viewed on a spectrum. If most organizational decisions are handled via established policies or procedures, the system is more nearly automatic than one requiring managers to formulate their own action. Nevertheless, even with feedback, organizational control presents a challenge to the manager.

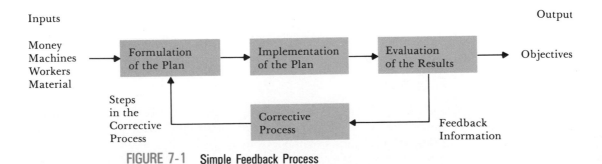

FIGURE 7-1   Simple Feedback Process

REQUIREMENTS FOR AN EFFECTIVE CONTROL SYSTEM

The process of control is not automatic. If the organization wants an effective control system, it has to tailor one to its own specifications. In addition to the two previously mentioned requirements—that controls be objective and that the manager employ the exception—the five following characteristics are common to many effective control systems.

Providing Useful, Understandable Information

Control systems will differ from organization to organization and from manager to manager. Information that is valuable to one individual may be useless to another. The key question each must ask is, what information do I need to control the activities within my jurisdiction? This approach is valuable for two reasons. First, it forces individual managers to decide what they need to know and in what form. This definition and selection process is known as information design and results in useful, understandable data; it will be discussed in more detail later in the chapter. Second, the approach provides a basis for screening out irrelevant reports and information that the individual may be receiving.

Timeliness

Controls should quickly report deviations. In addition, a well-designed system should be capable of identifying potential problem areas before they manifest themselves. For example, forecasting a cash flow for the next ninety days based on optimistic, most likely, and pessimistic conditions can provide management with a short-run financial picture. If it appears likely that the company will run out of cash—that is, only under the most optimistic conditions will it remain in the black—there may still be time to negotiate a loan with a local bank. In this way, controls become lead rather than lag factors.

Flexibility

Most plans will deviate from expectations, and some will be outright failures. Unless a control system is flexible, it will be unable to maintain control of operations during such events. The value of flexible control can be readily seen in the use of flexible budgets, which increase or contract on the basis of the volume of business. Flexibility helps management control operations regardless of economic conditions.

Economy

A control system must be worth the expense. However, it is often difficult to determine when the marginal costs associated with the system equal the marginal revenues obtained from it. Naturally, a small company cannot afford to install the expensive systems employed by a large corporation, but often it must consider a minor control expenditure, such as a time clock. The company will want to know whether the clock will reduce tardiness and whether it will cause work output to increase. Perhaps the clock will reduce tardiness. But perhaps the output will decrease. (The reverse outcomes might also occur.) Even assuming that tardiness is reduced, it is still possible that people will not do more work. They must just sit around waiting to clock out at 5:00 P.M. On the other hand, productivity may rise, and although a large firm may be able to absorb low productivity, a small one may not; so the system could prove useful to the latter. In either event, if a firm decides to put in a time clock, it must be willing to compare productivity (and the related issue of morale) both before and after the installation. Only in this way can it be sure that the control mechanism has been economical. This guideline also applies to revenues and expenses associated with control systems that are much more difficult to evaluate. For example, what is the cost-benefit ratio attached to a new monthly progress report that must be submitted by all unit managers? This kind of question will be difficult to answer in many cases, as it requires a highly subjective estimate. Nevertheless, some attempt must be made to do so.

Leading to Corrective Action

An effective control system must lead to corrective action; merely uncovering deviations from plans is not enough. The system must also disclose where the problem areas are and who or what is responsible for them. From here management can evaluate the situation and decide upon the appropriate action.

TRADITIONAL CONTROL TECHNIQUES

Management can employ its choice from among a large number of control techniques. Some of the more traditional ones include budgeting, break-even analysis, and personal observation.

Budgeting

In the Chapter 5 discussion of budgets, it was noted that organizations often use them to harmonize functional plans. Used in this way, the budget is a type of plan, specifying anticipated results in numerical terms. However, the *budget* is also a control device that provides a basis for feedback, evaluation, and follow-up.

Comprehensive Budgeting

A "from-the-bottom-up" approach is used.

Many organizations use *comprehensive budgeting* when all phases of operations are covered by budgets. This often begins with the submission of budget proposals by subordinate managers. After the proposals are discussed with the superiors to whatever extent is necessary, they are next forwarded to higher management. The result is a bottom-up approach, which ensures consideration of the needs and desires of, and participation by, lower management in the budgeting process. However, the process does not stop here. At the top of the organization there is often a budget committee whose purpose is to review the entire program. In a manufacturing firm, for example, this committee may consist of the president and the vice-presidents of finance, marketing, and production, who have line authority to make whatever final budget revisions are necessary. In other cases, the committee may be staffed by lower ranking personnel who have advisory authority only. In either case, the result is an integration of the individual budgets into a comprehensive one and the paring away of excessive requests. Thus, although everyone has an input into the budget, top management maintains the authority to make necessary adjustments. This power is very important, for some departments will request 130 percent of what they need and hope to be cut back no more than 20 percent. Of course, the challenge is in knowing where to cut. An overall 30 percent reduction in budget requests is harmful to those units that are not padding their estimates and helpful to those that are. For this reason, top management must impress on its employees the importance of submitting reasonable budgets and must also try to ensure that they do.

Zero-base Budgeting

At the present time *zero-base budgeting* (ZBB) is being used by a half-dozen states, a score of cities, and several hundred companies, including Texas Instruments, Southern California Edison, Union Carbide, Westinghouse, and Playboy Enterprises.[4] The concept of ZBB, which is often applied to support services, is rather simple:

> Managers, starting at the lowest "cost centers" of an organization, must justify everything they do as if they were building their operation from scratch. Every manager isolates basic services and overhead items he controls—a typing pool, a computer, or a mailroom, for example—and then writes a brief outline of why each exists and how much it costs. This outline—or "decision package" in ZBB jargon—usually identifies a minimum expenditure level below the current outlay, plus an expanded service level if more money were available. It also examines alternative ways of performing a task, such as hiring temporary help or outside contractors. Finally, managers rank all their decision packages by priority and pass them on to their superiors, who go through the same exercise at a higher plane.[5]

---

[4]Burton V. Dean and Scott S. Cowen, "Zero-Base Budgeting in the Private Sector," *Business Horizons*, August 1979, p. 78.

[5]"What it Means to Build a Budget from Zero," *Business Week*, April 18, 1977, p. 160.

When it comes to actual production areas such as product lines, however, ZBB is applied somewhat differently. In these cases the company decides how much profit it wants to make on its investment. Then each unit or division submits a budget requesting a given amount of money and stating the amount of profit that can be expected from this investment. By carefully reviewing each budget proposal and the expected return, the top management can prune the marginal lines and put its money behind the most promising winners.

Proponents of ZBB cite many advantages, some of which follow:

1. ZBB focuses the budgeting process; it directs the firm toward a comprehensive analysis of its needs and goals.

2. ZBB is efficient, as it combines planning and budgeting into one process instead of the two somewhat related functions they have been under traditional systems.

3. ZBB ensures that all managers, whatever their level in the firm, evaluate in detail the cost-effectiveness of their units' activities.

4. ZBB, because it involves every manager, gives firms the benefit of much expanded management participation in planning and budgeting at all organizational levels.

Opponents of ZBB, meanwhile, note that it requires a great deal more time, work, people, and money than more standard approaches to budgeting. Many business firms that have used ZBB, however, think that it saves more money than it costs. For example, Southern California Edison claims savings of over $300,000 annually thanks to ZBB; Westinghouse Electric saved $2.4 million in overhead costs in just one year with ZBB; and Ford Motor once said that its savings ran into "the millions."[6] In fact, ZBB is catching on so fast around the country that consulting companies now hold ZBB seminars for business firms, and the major accounting firms advise their clients on zero-based budgeting.[7]

Avoiding Inflexibility in Budgeting

Budgets are useful planning and control tools, but they can prove cumbersome in the event of overbudgeting. It is not sound practice to spell out all expenses in such detail as to deprive the manager of freedom of action. Some managers become so committed to carved-in-stone dollar amounts that they assign higher priorities to the budget than to organizational objectives. This is counterproductive management that can even cause a firm a profit loss,

---

[6]Ibid.

[7]For more on this topic, see Mark W. Dirsmith and Stephen F. Jablonsky, "Zero-Base Budgeting as a Management Technique and Political Strategy," *Academy of Management Review*, October 1979, pp. 555–65; and James D. Suver and Ray L. Brown, "Where Does Zero-Base Budgeting Work?" *Harvard Business Review*, November–December 1977, pp. 76–84.

though the penny-wise manager certainly does not want or expect that to happen. But such a manager does make it possible.

Problems caused by such inflexibility have led to alternative budgeting forms, and one which has received a great deal of attention is the *variable expense budget*. This budget is used to complement different levels of activity. When a budget period ends, calculations are made as to what the expenses for each unit should, by projections, have been. If activity was as expected, departments almost certainly will be within their budgets. However, if volume was much higher than expected, many departments will have overspent. With the variable expense budget, the firm in such a position can at this point, computing from a predetermined formula, adjust departmental budgets according to current reality. But it is necessary to recall that the variable budget is not a substitute for a comprehensive budgetary program. Rather, it is a supplement to it.

Various forms of flexible budgets are being used.

Some companies use a *supplemental monthly budget*, a variation of the variable budget. Under this plan, the firm determines a minimum operational budget. Just prior to the beginning of each month, a supplemental budget that provides the units with additional funds is drawn up. This approach differs from the variable budget in that adjustments are made before the period begins rather than when it is over.

The *alternative budget* is another version of the flexible budget. Under this approach, the company establishes budgets for high, medium, and low levels of operations. Then, at the beginning of the particular period, managers are told under which budget they will be operating.

All these approaches indicate the need for flexibility in the budgeting process. As sources of information feedback, they can perform a useful function for the manager. However, a manager must not become too reliant on them. It is essential that a manager regard budgets only as tools for attaining organizational control.

Break-even Point

Break-even analysis is another common control technique. At the end of any given period of operation, an organization hopes to make a profit. In order for this to happen, total revenue must exceed total costs. For purposes of analysis, costs can be divided into two categories: fixed and variable. *Fixed costs* are those that will remain constant (at least in the short-run) regardless of operations. Some examples are property insurance, property taxes, depreciation, and administrative salaries. *Variable costs* are those that will change in relation to output. Labor salaries and cost of materials are examples.

The break-even point occurs when fixed and variable expenses are covered.

In computing the *break-even point* (BEP), the manager uses three cost-revenue components: total fixed cost, selling price per unit, and variable cost per unit. By subtracting the variable cost associated with the unit from its selling point, a margin-above-cost is obtained. This margin can then be applied to the total fixed cost, with the BEP occurring when the total of these margins equals total fixed cost. In simplified mathematical terms:

$$BEP = \frac{TFC}{P - VC}$$

where BEP = Break-even point in units
TFC = Total fixed cost
P   = Price per unit
VC = Variable cost per unit.

Consider the following example. Company A has conducted market research on a new product and has determined that it can sell 25,000 units at $10 each. The firm's total fixed costs are $120,000, and its variable cost per unit is $4. Given this information, will the venture be profitable? The answer is going to depend on the BEP. Applying the relevant data to the formula results in the following:

$$BEP = \frac{\$120,000}{\$10 - \$4}$$
$$= \frac{\$120,000}{\$6}$$
$$= 20,000 \text{ units.}$$

The firm's BEP is 20,000 units. Figure 7-2 illustrates this solution graphically. Sales are projected at 25,000 units; therefore, the venture should prove profitable. However, if market research showed a demand of anything under 20,000 units, the company could not break even on the project.

BEP analysis is a useful control device because of its emphasis on the marginal concept. In addition, it helps establish initial guidelines for control. In the example of Company A, fixed costs should remain at $120,000, variable cost per unit should be $4, and profits should occur after 20,000 units are sold. If costs or expected sales change, management has a basis for evaluating the impact and taking any necessary corrective action.

Personal Observation

Personal observation is another common control technique. Although it is employed in virtually every organization, it is especially common in small and medium-sized firms. Nonprofit organizations that are under little pressure to show results on a time-cost basis also make wide use of it.

A firsthand view can be useful.

Although personal observation alone is an incomplete form of control, it is an excellent supplement to budgets and break-even analysis. Despite all the information reported to modern managers, they still find that they can learn some things only by such means as a walk through the firm. There is no substitute for a firsthand view of operations, and personal observation provides just this.

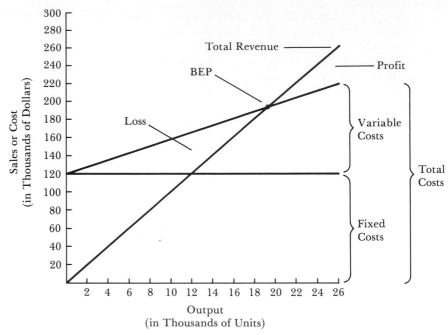

FIGURE 7-2   Break-even Point Computation

Personnel Performance

*Performance evalua-
tion process defined.*

Managers need to control more than things; they also have to monitor the personnel performance. This is done through *performance evaluation,* a process in which individual performance is evaluated and decisions made regarding salary increases, promotions, additional training, transfers and/or separation.

There are a number of ways in which performance evaluations are conducted. One of the most common is the *graphic rating scale* (see Figure 7-3) in which each employee's performance in a number of different areas is evaluated. The form is filled out by merely placing an "X" in the appropriate box.

Another popular approach is the *paired comparison.* In this process each worker in a unit is compared to every other worker. The final result is a listing of the personnel from the best to the poorest. Using Figure 7-3 as a guide, the manager would give a "1" to the worker with the greatest job knowledge, a "2" to the one with the second greatest amount of job knowledge, and so on. The manager would follow the same approach in handling each of the other job factors. When finished, each person's total score would be computed; the one with the lowest total would be judged the best worker followed by varying levels of performance on down to the one with the highest score who would be judged the poorest worker. If there are any ties, these are broken by identifying the factor that is judged most important, for example, results on

	Excellent	Good	Satisfactory	Average	Poor
Job Knowledge					
Work Quantity					
Work Quality					
Judgment					
Cooperation					

FIGURE 7-3   Graphic Rating Scales (Partial Form)

assigned work, and selecting the one who had the best score on this factor. In contrast to the graphic rating scale, paired comparison prevents the manager from evaluating everyone as equally good (or bad).

A third common approach is *management by objectives* (MBO). In this process the superior and subordinate jointly decide those objectives the latter will pursue. At the end of an agreed upon time, usually six months to a year, performance is evaluated and objectives for the next period are then set. In contrast to the graphic rating scale and paired comparison which are most often used at the lower levels of the hierarchy, MBO can be used throughout the structure.

Evaluations must be job related.

The biggest problem with many evaluations is that they are not tied closely enough to job-related behavior. They do not adequately measure how well the individual is performing. A second problem is that the managers are not trained in how to evaluate, so that what one person calls an excellent performance is rated average by another manager. At present, there is a great deal of time and attention being given to making evaluations more job-related and, where possible, quantifying or fully explaining what each level of performance requires. Table 7-1 provides an illustration of how this can be done.

SPECIALIZED CONTROL TECHNIQUES

In addition to traditional control techniques, management has developed many specialized tools to improve the quality of control. Space does not allow discussion of all of them, but two will be examined: information design and time-event analyses.

TABLE 7-1
Level of Performance by Performance-based Criteria

Criteria	Performance Level		
	Outstanding	Superior	Competent
Production as a percentage of budget ("Quantity of Work")	120% or more	110%–120%	100%–110%
Quality control reject percentage ("Quality of Work")	0.5% or less Anticipates problems and takes preventive action.	.05%–1% Recognizes source of all problems and can take corrective action.	1%–2% Recognizes source of most problems and is able to correct using standard procedures.
Percentage of jobs shipped on time (Supervision)	100% Subordinates are well trained and motivated; team effort evident; no wasted effort.	98% Subordinates are trained and motivated individually but not working as a team; occasional duplication of effort.	95% Subordinates are trained but not working together as a team; occasional duplication of effort.

Source: Reprinted by permission of the publisher from "Performance Appraisal: Match the Tool to the Task," by John D. McMillan and Hoyt W. Doyel, *Personnel*, July–August 1980, p. 16. Copyright © 1980 American Management Association, New York. All rights reserved.

Information Design

Information design is critical to an organization, especially since the advent of modern computers that can provide a wealth of data on virtually any area the manager would like to examine. Without some system for filtering out relevant from irrelevant information, managers can find themselves swamped with reports and numbers, most of which are meaningless to them.

The result has been the development of specialized organizational systems and procedures designed to provide useful information to the operating manager; the data can be presented in whatever form is needed for control purposes. In some large corporations, managers simply have to determine what they need, when they need it, and the format in which they would like it. Often, managers ask for the automatic transmission of periodic reports. A spin-off of this concept is seen in corporations whose service departments keep executives informed by forwarding copies of articles and reports appearing in newspapers and journals on topics that the managers have indicated are of interest to them. In this way, individual managers can keep up on their specialized areas without personally having to spend a lot of time searching journals for useful information.

Time–Event Analyses

Some of the most successful approaches to control have been attained through *time–event analysis,* which is a number of techniques that permit the manager to see how all the segments of the project interrelate, evaluate overall progress, and identify and take early corrective action on problem areas. One of the earliest techniques, still in use, is the chart developed by Henry Gantt. The principles contained in this chart have served as the basis for both Program Evaluation and Review Technique (PERT) and milestone scheduling.

Gantt Chart

The Gantt chart is a control technique that is easy to read and understand.

The *Gantt chart* has proved to be a useful planning and control technique. The basic concept involves the graphic depiction of work progress over a period of time. Figure 7-4 provides an illustration.

An examination of the figure reveals that three orders are being filled, each requiring the performance of certain operations. For the week illustrated in the chart, Order 1 is scheduled for manufacturing on Monday and Tuesday, assembling on Wednesday, painting on Thursday, and testing on Friday. Order 2 is scheduled for manufacturing on Monday, Tuesday, and Wednes-

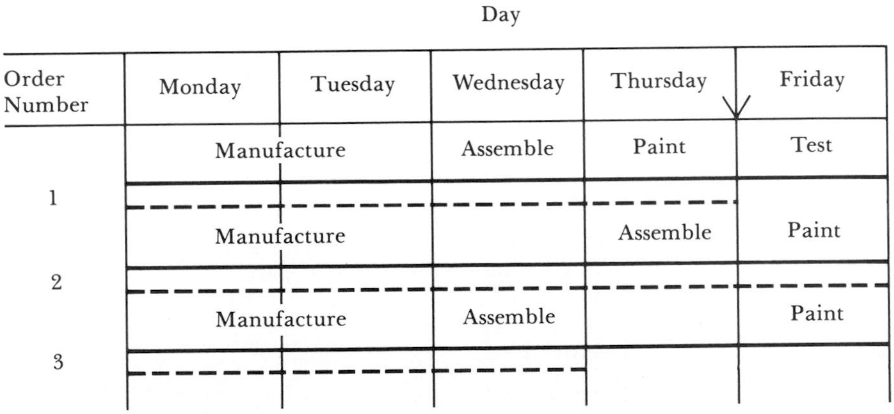

Day

Order Number	Monday	Tuesday	Wednesday	Thursday	Friday
	Manufacture		Assemble	Paint	Test
1					
	Manufacture			Assemble	Paint
2					
	Manufacture		Assemble		Paint
3					

FIGURE 7-4   Simplified Gantt Chart

day, assembling on Thursday, and painting on Friday. Order 3 is scheduled for manufacturing on Monday and Tuesday, assembling on Wednesday and Thursday, and painting on Friday. The solid vertical lines in the figure indicate the time required for each operation; the dotted horizontal lines denote progress. The "V" after Thursday indicates that the chart reflects the situation as of the close of business on that day. Based on this information, it is evident that Order 1 is on time, Order 2 is a day ahead of schedule, and Order 3 is a day behind. With this information, the manager is in a position to control the situation—for example, by transferring those working on Order 2 to Order 3 and making up the lost day. This concept of identifying the work to be done and plotting it on a time axis has provided the foundation for PERT.

Program Evaluation and Review Technique

The manager receives only pertinent data.

PERT was developed by the Special Projects Office of the United States Navy and applied to the planning and control of the Polaris Weapon System in 1958. The technique has proved very useful in managing complex projects. It is too elaborate for sensible use in lesser projects.

Relationships among the events are determined.

PERT employs what is called a time-event network. In building the network, events and activities are first identified. An *event* is a point in time when an activity is begun or finished; it is generally represented in the network by a circle. An *activity* is an operation required to accomplish a particular goal; it is represented in the network by an arrow. Figure 7-5 illustrates a simple PERT network that might be used for such a project as building a house. Although an actual PERT network would normally be far

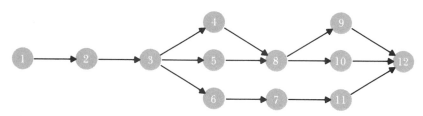

1. Begin House
2. Install Basement
3. Erect Frame
4. Put in Floors
5. Put on Roof
6. Put Brick around Bottom of House
7. Finish Upper Outside Part of House
8. Wire Inside
9. Install Electric Heating Unit
10. Install Electric Kitchen Appliances
11. Put in Doors and Cabinets
12. Complete House

FIGURE 7-5   Simple PERT Network

too complex and unwieldy for such a small project, this figure provides an example of the network. The events are numbered for purposes of identification. The network not only identifies all events but also establishes a relationship among them. For example, Event 3 in Figure 7-5 cannot be completed before Event 2; and Event 8 must be finished before Event 10 can be started.

Expected time can be calculated.

Once the PERT network is constructed, attention is focused on time estimates. Quite often the people responsible for each activity assist in determining optimistic, most likely, and pessimistic time estimates for accomplishing their respective activities. These estimates are then used to compute the *expected time* for each activity. The equation for this is:

$$t_E = \frac{t_o + 4t_m + t_p}{6}$$

where t_E = Expected time
t_o = Optimistic time
t_m = Most likely time
t_p = Pessimistic time.

Figure 7-6 illustrates a PERT network with the three estimates for each activity and the expected time (expressed in weeks, directly below each activity estimate in parentheses). For example, the expected time between Events 1 and 2 is:

$$t_E = \frac{8 + 4(10) + 12}{6}$$

$$t_E = 10 \text{ weeks.}$$

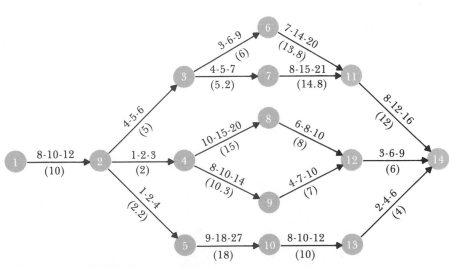

FIGURE 7-6   PERT Network with Time

The critical path is the longest path.

For control purposes, it is now possible to determine the *critical path*, which is the sequence of activities and events that is longer than any other. In Figure 7-6, only five possible paths through the network exist. Along with their expected times, they are:

Path	Expected Times	Total
1–2–3–6–11–14	10.0 + 5.0 + 6.0 + 13.8 + 12.0	46.8
1–2–3–7–11–14	10.0 + 5.0 + 5.2 + 14.8 + 12.0	47.0
1–2–4–8–12–14	10.0 + 2.0 + 15.0 + 8.0 + 6.0	41.0
1–2–4–9–12–14	10.0 + 2.0 + 10.3 + 7.0 + 6.0	35.3
1–2–5–10–13–14	10.0 + 2.2 + 18.0 + 10.0 + 4.0	44.2

Path 1–2–3–7–11–14 is the critical path, since it is longer than any other.

The final component that must be considered is *slack*, the time difference between scheduled completion and each of the paths. If, for example, the project in Figure 7-6 had to be completed within fifty-two weeks, all the paths would have slack. On the other hand, if the completion date were forty weeks, four of the paths would have negative slack and would have to be shortened if the schedule were to be met. There are a number of ways of doing this. Richard J. Hopeman lists these as follows:

1. The expected time for particular activities may be reduced, if possible.
2. Men, machines, materials, and money can be transferred from slack paths to the critical path or near-critical paths.
3. Some activities may be eliminated from the project.
4. Additional men, machines, materials, and money may be allocated to the critical path or near-critical paths.
5. Some of the activities which are normally sequential may be done in parallel.[8]

Perhaps the major advantage of PERT is that it forces managers to plan. In addition, because of the times assigned to each activity, it provides a basis for identifying critical areas and correcting or monitoring them. PERT's disadvantages are also clear: PERT is practical only for nonrecurring undertakings, and it must be possible to assign times to the events despite the fact that the entire project is new to the company. In addition, some managers criticize PERT's emphasis on time without consideration to cost. As a result, in recent years there has been the development of PERT/COST, in which costs are applied to activities in the network.

---

[8]Richard J. Hopeman, *Production: Concepts, Analysis, Control*, 3rd ed. (Columbus, OH: Charles E. Merrill Publishing, 1976), p. 343.

Milestone Scheduling

Although PERT is useful for sophisticated projects, it is often abandoned as the undertaking comes to a close and complexity declines. Since PERT can help integrate and simultaneously analyze thousands of activities, it is not surprising that less complex control techniques can be more economically employed as a project winds down. One of these is milestone scheduling, an approach used by the National Aeronautics and Space Administration (NASA) in the management of the Apollo Program.[9]

Milestone scheduling, a schedule and control procedure, employs bar charts to monitor progress. In this way, the manager can determine which segments of the undertaking are ahead of schedule, on time, or behind schedule. The technique is very similar to that of the Gantt chart, but the Gantt chart is used exclusively for production activities. Milestone scheduling, on the other hand, can be employed for virtually any undertaking.

Figure 7-7 shows three milestones. The first was begun in January, is scheduled for completion at the end of August, and is on time. The second was begun in March, is scheduled for completion in October, and is currently a month ahead of expectations. The third was begun in April, is scheduled for completion in December, and is currently running a month behind expectations. Milestone scheduling allows the manager to see a program in its simpler parts, thereby providing more effective control than sophisticated techniques.

Milestone scheduling is a useful technique for less complex projects.

CONTROLLING OVERALL PERFORMANCE

Most of the techniques discussed thus far are useful in controlling specific activities, but they do not measure overall performance. Several tools are used for evaluating total accomplishments. Among them are profit and loss, return on investment, key area control, and auditing.

---

[9]*Program Scheduling and Review Handbook,* NHB2330.1 (Washington, D.C.: National Aeronautics and Space Administration, October 1965).

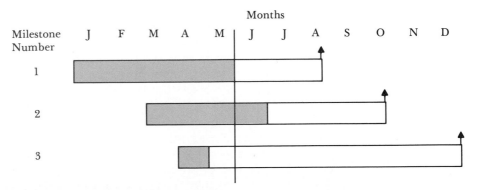

FIGURE 7-7   Simplified Milestone Schedule

REAL-LIFE MANAGERS:

INTERVIEW WITH KAROL KING

Karol King is a team leader for program planning and control at one of Boeing's Texas operations. Karol is responsible for program level scheduling and reporting, the flow-down of schedules, identification and reporting of problems areas associated with meeting contract deadlines, and product transition scheduling.

Q. *What can be done to ensure good control? For example, how do you know that things are being done within the assigned time, cost, and quality parameters?*

A. There are a number of ways that good control can be ensured. One is through the standards that our industrial engineers have assigned to the various manufacturing processes. We know how long it should take to build various components, and the experience curves. Also, we track rejected and reworked parts. The computerized manufacturing system we use keeps track of hours worked, so we can track actuals against budget. We keep an eye to all these factors and watch variances throughout our reporting systems.

Q. *Do you use PERT networks to control these projects?*

A. I expect to use it down the road, but not right now. Networking is a great planning tool, and I am constantly aware of the "constraint" concept in working a project, but no one likes reading a network, so we use bar charts for everything, because of ease in interpretation.

Profit and Loss

Perhaps the most commonly employed overall control is the income statement, which shows all revenues and expenses for the particular period of operation and provides a basis for comparing actual and expected results. Primary concern naturally goes to the basic question of whether or not the firm finished in the black, but it is also possible to ascertain whether and where the firm went wrong during the period, thereby establishing a basis for corrective action. In particular, the company can analyze the income statement in detail, noting how much each unit's operating expense has increased over the last year and determining whether the expenditures of each were justified or are in need of control during the next fiscal period. Similarly, it is possible to compare the profits (and losses) of operating divisions to see which was the most successful and why.

Q.   *What specific types of control action do you take when someone is late with their part of a project?*

A.   That depends on whether the problem is a one-time-only or a repetitive problem which calls for examination of the system we are using. Everyone has to work together, and in our team environment, problems usually surface at meetings, and separate meetings are arranged to address specific problems with the right players. For example, if a vendor is late or the product does not meet spec, several departments will work the issue, and if not suitably resolved, we would seek another vendor. If it is an in-house problem, we have team meetings to brainstorm the options, if the resolution is not obvious; workarounds are developed.

Q.   *How important are interpersonal skills in the control process?*

A.   They are extremely important. In fact, if you divide the control process into technical and human-relations considerations, it's impossible to monitor the technical side of operations without using human-relations skills. A great deal of the control process comes from gleaning accurate and timely information and persuading personnel of the problems and best solutions. Negotiations, reciprocal favors, and give-and-take on both sides are what accounts for success. Many people view the control process as simply monitoring progress towards objectives. They fail to realize that if the process were just mechanistic in nature, it wouldn't be difficult to carry out. However, effective control involves education, communication, and change. Therefore, human relations and technical considerations are irrevocably intertwined.

Return on Investment

ROI measures a firm's ability to manage its assets.

Another widely used control technique is that of *return on investment* (ROI), which measures how well a firm is performing with the assets at its command. The method for computing ROI is presented in Figure 7-8.

The ROI technique is favorably viewed by many companies because it answers a basic question: How well are we doing with what we have? After all, a firm with $4 million in profits is far ahead of one with $10,000 in profits. However, if the former company has a total investment of $10 billion but the latter has one of only $10,000, the smaller firm is doing far better than the larger in terms of overall performance. According to the ROI approach, profits are relative and efficiency is of major importance.

The ROI concept need not be restricted to overall company results. It can be brought down to the divisional product level by way of measuring how

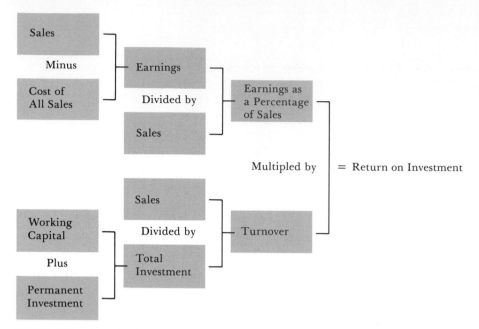

FIGURE 7-8   Computation of Return on Investment

well each division is doing. By comparing results with expectations, problem areas can be pinpointed for control purposes. The important thing to remember about ROI is that a good return will vary by industry. Therefore, results should be judged only in comparison with the competition. Also, exclusive reliance on this technique can lead to preoccupation with financial factors.[10] For this reason, it is advantageous to supplement profit and/or ROI with other overall control techniques, such as key area control.

Key Area Control

General Electric provides a good illustration of a firm employing *key area control.* For more than twenty years, this company has measured results in eight areas: profitability, market position, productivity, product leadership, personnel development, employee attitudes, public responsibility, and integration of short- and long-range goals. GE has not been able to develop the desired measurements for all of these areas, but by concentrating attention on them it has been able to obtain an appraisal of overall performance (see also Social Responsibility in Action: Dealing with Apartheid).

---

[10]For example, for years Du Pont would not approve a new product program yielding less than a 20 percent ROI. As a result, Du Pont passed up xerography and the Land (Polaroid) camera. See "Lighting a Fire under the Sleeping Giant," *Business Week,* September 12, 1970, pp. 40–41.

SOCIAL
RESPONSIBILITY
IN
ACTION:
Dealing
with
Apartheid

One of the most difficult social responsibility issues to confront management over the last decade has been the matter of apartheid in South Africa. What should American firms do about this policy? American multinationals have chosen one of two strategies: Leave South Africa and show the government that the company will not do business in a country that promotes apartheid or stay in South Africa and keep pressure on the government to change its policies.

Those who support leaving South Africa believe that this strategy will eventually break the back of the country's economic system and force it to abandon apartheid policies. Most anti-apartheid spokespeople have supported this approach and a large number of U. S. firms have sold their holdings and left the country.

On the other hand, there are many American firms including Mobil Oil, Goodyear Tire & Rubber, RJR Nabisco, Johnson & Johnson, and United Technologies that continue to do business in South Africa. These firms argue that leaving the country is not helpful in fighting apartheid and that by staying they can help prepare blacks for the post-apartheid era and South Africa's future.

Which approach is correct? The answer appears to be that neither, in and of itself, has proven very effective. Recent research shows that South Africa has not been severely weakened by economic sanctions, and many American firms that have sold out to local black business people have found that employment in their companies has now been reduced. The new owners claim that they need to cut expenses in order to earn a fair return on the purchase price. In short, blacks are not prospering as a result of American firms leaving the country. At the same time, the government views the presence of foreign firms as tacit support for their apartheid policies.

What then is the answer to dealing with this social issue? Two researchers who investigated the situation carefully recommend that firms adopt strategies that attack apartheid both internally and externally by staying in the country and becoming socially responsible. Examples of how this new strategy is being implemented include: (1) the 3M Company pays full wages of any workers who are detained or imprisoned for anti-apartheid activities; (2) Hewlett-Packard has purchased or leased homes in exclusively "white only" areas for black managers; and (3) American film companies have put pressure on their South African distributors who, in turn, have shut down movie theatres in major cities until the local governments allowed all races into the theatres. These types of action, claim the researchers, will be much more effective getting rid of apartheid because it forces change from the inside.

Sources: Marshall Loeb, "What the U. S. Must Do in South Africa," *Fortune,* July 18, 1988, pp. 88–90; Neal Templin, "They're Getting Out of S. Africa," *USA Today,* June 14, 1988, p. 7B; and David Beaty and Oren Harari, "Divestment and Disinvestment from South Africa: A Reappraisal," *California Management Review,* Summer 1987, pp. 31–50.

It is interesting to note that GE prefers to use profitability rather than ROI. In recent years, some financial experts have supported this approach, arguing that the final criterion of success is always profit, whatever the firm's efficiency. It is certainly true that only one of General Electric's eight key areas relates directly to profit. The remainder are related to environmental factors (political, economic, and social) vital to overall control, as the following descriptions illustrate:

General Electric uses these key control areas.

Profitability. Total profits after all expenses, including cost of capital, are deducted.

Market Position. Share of the market is one of the key criteria here. In addition, the company attempts to measure customer satisfaction and to discover what the consumer wants but is not getting.

Productivity. Goods and services produced and sold are compared with the inputs necessary to arrive at some measure of productivity.

Product Leadership. Includes market position, innovation, and the ability to take advantage of new ideas in producing successful new products.[11]

Personnel Development. The key criterion employed here is whether or not people are available when needed. Is there an adequate supply of manpower for meeting new and complex assignments in addition to filling vacancies?

Employee Attitudes. Absenteeism, labor turnover, and safety records are some of the criteria employed to evaluate attitudes. Another is the use of employee surveys.

Public Responsibility. Attention in this area is focused on many groups, including employees, customers, and the local community. In each case, indices have been developed to evaluate how well the company is doing.

Integration of Short- and Long-Range Goals. By encouraging formulation of long-range planning, the company ensures that short-run goals reflect these long-range objectives.

The GE approach is only one of many that can be employed for key area control. However, it emphasizes the importance of determining major criteria and monitoring performance in accord with the results obtained. No organization can maintain control of every aspect of operation. Instead, it must identify those that provide a basic picture of how well things are going and abide by the feedback obtained. Some organizations rely upon various forms of auditing to help perform this function.

---

[11]For more on this topic see John A. Quelch, Paul W. Farris, and James M. Olver, "The Product Management Audit," *Harvard Business Review*, March–April 1987, pp. 30–33.

Auditing

Hearing the word *audit,* an individual may immediately think of a public accounting firm. However, three basic types of audits are useful for overall control: external audits, internal audits, and management audits (see Management in Action: Intelligence Gathering).

External Audit

External audits are conducted by outside accounting people.

An *external audit* is conducted by accountants from outside the firm. It entails the examination and evaluation of the firm's financial transactions and accounts. This audit is generally performed by a certified public accounting firm, which expresses its opinion of the hiring company's financial statements in the areas of fairness, consistency, and conformity with the accepted principles of accounting. Usually this audit entails a detailed verification of all important balance sheet items with a view toward ascertaining whether the major assets, liabilities, and capital accounts are being accurately reported. The CPA firm does not delve into such nonfinancial areas as evaluating plans, policies, and procedures. However, when one realizes that the auditors will only certify accounts that are in order, it is evident that they provide an indirect control over all operations.

Internal Audit

Internal audits are conducted by company personnel.

An *internal audit* is conducted by the organization's own staff specialists. In essence, the auditing team examines and evaluates the firm's operations, determining where things have gone well and where corrective action is needed. Generally, much of the auditors' work is restricted to the financial area, but this need not be the case. They can also be useful in evaluating nonquantitative areas. In this kind of review, the internal audit goes further than its external counterpart and approaches what is commonly known as the management audit. Many firms have found in recent years that these staff specialists often can be quicker, cheaper, and more effective than external auditors.[12]

Management Audit

Some management audits are carried out by the firm itself.

A *management audit* picks up where a financial audit leaves off. Sometimes the audit is conducted by the firm itself, in which case it is known as a *self-audit,* an approach first advocated back in the 1930s.[13]

The purpose of the self-audit is to examine the company's position on a periodic basis, often every two, three, or five years. By studying the market

---

[12]Robert E. Kelley, "Should You Have an Internal Consultant?" *Harvard Business Review,* November–December 1977, pp. 110–20.

[13]Billy E. Goetz, *Management Planning and Control* (New York: McGraw-Hill, 1949), p. 167.

trends, technological changes, and political and social factors affecting the industry, the company can construct a forecast of the external environment.

Next, the audit turns to the firm itself. How well has it maintained its industry position? What is the competitive outlook? How do the customers feel about the firm's products? Answers to these questions help relate the company to its industry.

On the basis of the results, the firm can examine overall objectives and policies; and future and continuing programs, procedures, personnel, management, and financial positions can be put into clearer focus. If the self-audit is continued, the auditor's attention moves from the macro- to the micro-level; eventually all segments and activities of the company are analyzed. But this concept of continuation points toward the biggest problem of the self-audit: Many firms simply do not or cannot find time to conduct one. Furthermore, those who do have found very real dangers associated with using their own employees, from whatever level or levels. Bias, lack of competence to judge, inability to gain information from noncooperating individuals, intrafirm politics that lead to contradictory information, and stresses extended on the auditors are among the common hazards self-auditors experience.

Others are conducted by outside organizations.

One way of overcoming this problem is to employ an external management audit such as that conducted by the American Institute of Management (AIM). Founded a number of years ago by Jackson Martindell, the institute uses a list of 301 questions to rate companies in the areas of fiscal policies, health of earnings, fairness to stockholders, research and development, sales vigor, economic function, directors, corporate structure, executive ability, and production efficiency.[14] Each of the ten areas is assigned a point value, with 3,500 of the 10,000 possible points allotted to managerial elements. To obtain a rating of "excellent," a company must receive 7,500 points.

The AIM audit is only one technique for conducting a management audit. Many others are available, from the approach recommended by W. T. Greenwood[15] for evaluating the overall firm to the one employed by the United States Department of Defense in evaluating companies bidding on major defense contracts. It appears that the future will see even greater interest in this area, for management consulting and accounting audit firms have found management audits to be an attractive area for expansion for a number of years now.[16] This is not surprising, though it is a rather new phenomenon. But these consulting firms are taking what is actually a small

---

[14]Jackson Martindell, *The Scientific Appraisal of Management* (New York: Harper & Bros., 1950), and *The Appraisal of Management* (New York: Harper & Bros., 1962); see also Theodore D. Weinshall, "Help for Chief Executives," *California Management Review*, Summer 1982, pp. 47–58.

[15]W. T. Greenwood, *A Management Audit System*, rev. ed. (Carbondale, IL: School of Business, Southern Illinois University, 1967).

[16]See "Should CPAs Be Management Consultants?" *Business Week*, April 18, 1977, pp. 70, 73.

step from their current activities to management auditing. Perhaps the future will see the development of a certified management audit analogous to the current independent certified accounting audit.

■ SUMMARY

In this chapter the controlling process has been examined. The three basic steps in this process are the establishment of standards, the comparison of performance with these standards, and the correction of deviations. The key to the entire process rests on effective feedback.

In attaining feedback, the manager can use various control techniques. Some of the more traditional include budgeting, break-even analysis, personal observation, and personnel performance evaluation. Some of the more specialized entail information design and time-event analyses, such as PERT and milestone scheduling. Since these analytic techniques are not designed to control overall performance, the manager needing overall performance control can simply turn to such other techniques as profit and loss, return on investment, key area control, and auditing.

■ REVIEW AND STUDY QUESTIONS

1. What are the three basic steps in the controlling process? Describe each.
2. Why is feedback so important for effective control?
3. What are the requirements for an effective control system? List and explain some of them in your own words.
4. Of what value is budgeting in the controlling process? Does budgeting lead to inflexibility? Explain.
5. How can the break-even point assist the manager in controlling operations? Explain, incorporating the following terms into your discussion: unit price, total fixed cost, and variable cost per unit.
6. How can personnel performance be evaluated? Cite and describe two approaches.
7. What is information design? How is it of value to the manager?
8. Why is PERT a useful control technique? As you explain, incorporate the following terms into your discussion: events, activities, expected time, and critical path.
9. Why is return on investment so widely used as an overall control technique? Is it better than a profit and loss approach? Explain.
10. What is key area control? What are some of the areas used by General Electric in controlling its operations? Explain the importance of each as you would expect it to be used by GE.

11.   How useful are external audits in the control process? Internal audits? Management audits? Which do you think is best? Why?

■ SELECTED REFERENCES

Andrews, Nina. "Buying Lollipops for $65 Million." *New York Times*, August 25, 1988, pp. 25, 27.

Axline, Larry L. "Hiring a Consultant? First Do Your Homework." *Personnel*, November–December 1981, pp. 39–43.

Beaty, David, and Oren Harari. "Divestment and Disinvestment from South Africa: A Reappraisal." *California Management Review*, Summer 1987, pp. 31–50.

Brinkerhoff, Derick W., and Rosabeth Moss Kanter. "Appraising the Performance of Performance Appraisal." *Sloan Management Review*, Spring 1980, pp. 3–16.

Buchele, R. B. "How to Evaluate a Firm." *California Management Review*, Fall 1962, pp. 5–17.

"Consultants Move to the Executive Suite." *Business Week*, November 7, 1977, pp. 76, 79.

Dean, B. V., and S. S. Cowen. "Zero-Base Budgeting in the Private Sector." *Business Horizons*, August 1979, pp. 73–83.

Dirsmith, M. W., and S. F. Jablonsky. "Zero-Base Budgeting as a Management Technique and Political Strategy." *Academy of Management Journal*, October 1979, pp. 555–65.

Drucker, Peter F. *Management: Tasks, Responsibilities, Practices.* New York: Harper & Row, 1974, chap. 39.

Edward, Mark R., Michael Wolfe, and J. Ruth Sproull. "Improving Comparability in Performance Appraisal." *Business Horizons*, September–October 1983, pp. 75–83.

Friedman, Barry A., and Robert W. Mann. "Employee Assessment Methods Assessed." *Personnel*, November–December 1981, p. 69–74.

Giglioni, G. B., and Arthur G. Bedeian. "A Conspectus of Management Control Theory: 1900–1972." *Academy of Management Journal*, June 1974, pp. 292–305.

Harper, Stephen C. "A Developmental Approach to Performance Appraisal." *Business Horizons*, September–October 1983, pp. 68–74.

Kearney, William J. "Improving Work Performance through Appraisal." *Human Resource Management*, Summer 1978, pp. 15–23.

Keller, John J. et al. "AT&T: The Making of a Comeback." *Business Week*, January 18, 1988, pp. 56–62.

Kelley, R. E. "Should You Have an Internal Consultant?" *Harvard Business Review*, November–December 1978, pp. 110–20.

Kirkland, Richard I. Jr. "Entering a New Age of Boundless Competition." *Fortune*, March 14, 1988, pp. 40–48.

Labaton, Stephen. "New Group to Sue to Aid Copyrights." *New York Times*, July 25, 1988, p. 26.

Martindell, Jackson. *The Appraisal of Management.* New York: Harper & Row, 1962.

McMillan, John D., and Hoyt W. Doyel. "Performance Appraisal: Match the Tool to the Task." *Personnel*, July–August 1980, pp. 12–20.

Quelch, John A., Paul W. Farris, and James M. Olver. "The Product Management Audit." *Harvard Business Review*, March–April 1987, pp. 30–33.

Schreyogg, Georg, and Horst Steinmann. "Strategic Control: A New Perspective." *Academy of Management Review*, January 1987, pp. 91–103.

Sherwood, John J. "Hiring a Consultant? Establish a Collaborative Approach." *Personnel*, November–December 1981, pp. 44–49.

Smith, Howard L., Myron D. Fottler, and Borje O. Saxberg. "Cost Containment in Health Care: A Model for Management Research." *Academy of Management Review*, July 1981, pp. 397–407.

Smith, Lee. "The World According to AARP." *Fortune*, February 29, 1988, pp. 96–98.

■ CASE: Safety Margins

Anne Marie Mosolini has been with the Widget Works Company for only a couple of months, but already she could tell that the job was to her liking. One of the things she enjoyed most was the rapid responsibility increases that came her way. For example, she had been told to make up a departmental budget for the next fiscal year. After poring over past budgeting requests and talking to her subordinates, Mosolini submitted her proposal. The next step in the process was to meet with her superior and defend the requests. Then her proposal would be sent up the line. Her staff had told Mosolini that top management seldom cut back any requests. The key hurdle was getting one's superior to approve a recommended budget.

As a result, Mosolini spent most of the morning preparing herself for this meeting. She felt that everything in her request was essential, and she wanted to be able to defend each item. The meeting, however, did not go according to her expectations. Her superior, Blake Cotton, began:

> "Anne Marie, I've examined your budget request and would like to talk to you about a few items. For example, you estimate $77,612 under administrative expenses."
>
> "Yes sir. I can show you the worksheet I used, if you'd like."
>
> "Oh, that's not necessary. The only reason the figure caught my eye was that it was such an odd amount. Look, let's round it off to $80,000."
>
> "Okay."
>
> "And there are a few other budget estimates I see here that are also in need of rounding, so I'll just change them also."

"How much of an estimate does that make it?"

"Exactly $240,000."

"Well, that's a little bit higher than what I need. Are you sure it's okay?"

"Sure, don't worry about it. You can never tell when something is going to cost a little bit more than you initially thought."

"Okay, Blake. It's all right with me if it's all right with you."

"Fine. And, oh, by the way, how did you arrive at these other estimates?"

"Well, I worked back from what I thought my department would be doing this fiscal year to how much it would cost to get this work done. There's a manual that was sent around to me, and I took my basic format from it."

"That certainly is one way to get a handle on it. But I'd suggest that you be sure to add some safety margins to each of your requests."

"Safety margins?"

"Sure, you know. A little something extra just in case things go wrong. Besides, you never know when management is going to cut around here, and it always pays to have asked for a little more than you need when that happens. Do you know what I mean?"

"I think so."

"Fine. Here's your budget back. Besides the figure rounding, add in 10 percent across the board, and return it to me. I'll forward it from here."

Questions

1. Is Cotton right or wrong in suggesting that Mosolini change her budget requests? Explain.

2. How common do you think this kind of action is? Be specific.

4. Why do you think this conversation occurred? Explain.

■ CASE: Efficiency versus Profitability

Samuel Frenz was a product division manager at Darby Inc., a midwestern manufacturing firm. In the late 1970s, the Darby management decided to abandon its profitability control guideline and begin evaluating product divisions on the basis of return on investment. Management hoped to measure overall efficiency in this way.

The idea was fine with Frenz, and for the next decade his division's ROI rose from 12.3 percent to 15.7 percent. However, during the late 1980s the division began to encounter vigorous competition, and although the market for its product increased, Frenz had to spend more and more money on advertising and personal selling to maintain market share. The result was an eventual decline in his division's ROI, which had fallen to 13.7 percent by 1989. This in turn prompted comments from the top management, and Frenz was called into his boss's office:

"Sam, the board of directors has been reviewing product division ROI's, and yours is the only one that has declined. Quite frankly, the board is concerned."

"Well, I am too, but if that board thinks you can improve ROI in such a competitive industry, it is sitting up nights waiting for the tooth fairy. We have had to spend a lot of money on advertising and personal selling. I'd like to know one company with a better ROI than ours. Or one competitive division that can match mine."

"I understand. But the question is, what are you going to do to improve your division's ROI?"

"I'd like to pose a different question. Why is the board evaluating my ROI? Don't those people know that when you get as large as we are, in as competitive an industry as this, ROI slips? Why don't they evaluate me on profitability? My profits are up over last year, but I can't hold my ROI performance at an all-time high."

"Do you want to write the board a letter outlining your proposal?"

"Well, I'm not in a position to tell you what to do. I'm the one on the carpet. What do you think would help me and the board get together on how we look at things?"

Questions

1. What are the advantages of using ROI as an overall control technique? What are the disadvantages?

2. Should the board switch back from ROI to profits? Give your reasoning.

3. How would you answer Frenz's last question? Explain, indicating why you would recommend switching to profitability or sticking with ROI.

■ CASE: The Dean's Dilemma

Things had certainly changed at State University. When Dean Williams had first come to the College of Business, life seemed much simpler. However, as inflation spiraled upward, the taxpayers of the state gave every indication that they wanted to stop pouring money into the university. As a result, the university administration announced a general tightening up. Departmental lines would be cut and hiring determined on a need basis. As if this were not enough, legislators began raising the question of faculty evaluations. How do we know we are getting our money's worth, they asked, if there is no evaluation process?

In response to the question, the university administration announced that it was going to look into the matter. Thereupon, all deans were asked to poll their colleges for the purpose of deciding what form of evaluation they felt was fair for judging performance. Two camps sprang up in the College of Business. The first wanted to evaluate teaching as the first criterion, with community affairs and research secondary. The other group wanted research as the primary judgment criterion and teaching and community affairs as secondary criteria. The positions could be summarized as follows:

Teaching as Primary

Position for: The university has been established by the people of this state to perform a specific service, namely the dissemination of knowledge to the students. This is the primary basis on which teachers should be evaluated. The evaluation process should take two paths: evaluations by the students in the classroom and evaluation by the department chairpersons on the basis of classroom observation.

Position against: Teaching is certainly important, but there is no way to judge truly effective performance. The students are going to be biased in their opinion, those receiving the highest grades being more positive in their comments about the instructors than those receiving the lowest grades. Thus the system encourages an easy grading policy. In addition, the chairpersons are incapable of judging all the people because they are not experts in all areas. For example, how can a management chairperson with an emphasis in organizational behavior judge a colleague teaching mathematical decision making? Teaching is valuable, but because it cannot be quantified, it should be discarded as a basis for evaluation.

Research as Primary

Position for: The only objective criterion available for judging teaching ability is research. A professor who conducts research is going to be better prepared than one who does not. In addition, the instructor has a responsibility to not only teach but enhance the reputation of the university, and this can be done most effectively through research. In short, "publish or perish" is the only way to improve the quality of education, and it should be the basis for all evaluations.

Position against: To engage in a policy of "publish or perish" is to get into the numbers game. In addition, how is one to evaluate the contribution of each article? And in the case of books, is not remuneration in the form of royalties sufficient? Why should people be promoted or receive high evaluation when all they are doing is enhancing their own financial positions? Research is important, but it must not be allowed to occupy a primary position.

Questions

1. How should faculty performance be evaluated? Explain.
2. In light of your answer to the above question, what kinds of measuring tools should a dean employ to ensure that a faculty is doing a good job? Explain in detail.

■ CASE: Correcting the Situation

Motorola used to be the world's largest producer of semiconductors. However, by the late 1980s the firm had fallen into fourth place, and its other electronics product lines from cellular phones to modems were under strong attack from foreign competitors. Product quality and delivery time were also major problems. In an effort to control the situation and turn things around, the company has made a number of important decisions.

One major decision was to send its people back to school. The company decided that 1.5 percent of each manager's payroll should be devoted to training, and, since 1984, managers have spent more than 3.2 million hours in class. This training has been used to help them study technical subjects ranging from design-for-assembly and just-in-time inventory to risk-taking and the management of change. The company has also gone back to the basics with some of its employees by teaching them to read and to understand basic mathematics. These courses are fundamental to an understanding of such key topics as statistical control processes.

How well have these courses paid off? Today factory defects are down 400 percent over three years ago. Additionally, workers are better able to adjust to new technology and work productivity in areas such as cellular phone assembly is up 1,000 percent over the last 36 months.

The company is also establishing tougher goals and giving bigger rewards to those who achieve them. There are now incentive bonuses designed to encourage higher productivity from the work force.

The firm is also working to achieve teamwork between employees in different departments. By training personnel from throughout the firm—marketing, quality control, engineering—in the same class group, Motorola is finding that interdepartmental rivalry is beginning to decline. The groups are starting to work together outside of the classroom. One researcher summed up the current situation by noting, "Motorola may never again be number one in chips, but other key products, including cellular, two-way mobile radios, pagers, and modems, remain leaders that are gaining unit share in markets worldwide. The company is chalking up some notable victories in quality, cost-cutting, and customer relations."

Questions

1. Does Motorola make use of the basic controlling process? Explain.

2. What key areas of control does the company use in measuring how well it is doing? Identify and describe three.

3. What role has education played in the control process? Explain.

Source: Lois Therrien, "Motorola Sends Its Work Force Back to School," *Business Week*, June 6, 1988, pp. 80–81.

■ SELF-FEEDBACK EXERCISE: Objectives for Control Purposes

The following is a list of 14 objectives that, in part or in whole, are pursued by many firms. Look over the list and place a "14" next to the one that you believe is most important for a successful enterprise. Continue this process on down to the last objective which receives a ranking of "1." Then enter your answers in the space provided and read the interpretation of the exercise.

_____   1.   Profits should be as high as possible.

_____   2.   The company's growth rate should be faster than that of the competition.

_____   3.   The firm should produce its goods and services as efficiently as possible.

_____   4.   Absenteeism and turnover should be low.

_____   5.   The company should provide equal opportunity to all of its employees.

_____   6.   The company must continue to develop new goods and services.

_____   7.   Personnel training should be provided to all employees on an ongoing basis.

_____   8.   Profit as a percentage of invested capital should be greater than the interest rate being charged on bank lines of credit.

_____   9.   The company's share of the industry should be maintained and, if possible, increased.

_____   10. Steps should be taken to keep production costs as low as possible.

_____   11. Worker tardiness should be reduced and, if possible, eliminated.

_____   12. The firm should be an active member of the local civic community.

_____   13. Innovation and new product development should be primary areas of consideration.

_____   14. The development of the organization's human resources should be of paramount importance to management.

Answers

1. _____   5. _____   9. _____   12. _____
2. _____   6. _____   10. _____   13. _____
3. _____   7. _____   11. _____   14. _____
4. _____   8. _____

Interpretation

Take your answers and total them across by adding together the following seven sets of numbers: 1 and 8; 2 and 9; 3 and 10; 4 and 11; 5 and 12; 6 and 13; and 7 and 14 and entering your totals after the set of numbers and before the category they represent. Your answers indicate how important each of the seven different categories is.

Numbers	Total	Category
1 and 8	_____	Profit
2 and 9	_____	Market position
3 and 10	_____	Productivity
4 and 11	_____	Employee attitudes
5 and 12	_____	Public responsibility
6 and 13	_____	Product leadership
7 and 14	_____	Personnel development

Although all seven categories are important, some are more viewed as more important than others. Most executives who have taken this self-feedback exercise place profit, market position, productivity, and product leadership in the four highest category and, in most cases, in this exact order.

■ COMPREHENSIVE CASE: The New Product Proposal

Background

Ian McDever took over the reins of his father's small manufacturing firm, McDever, Inc., in 1964. The company had been founded in 1939 by Ian's father, Robert. The latter was a close personal friend of a businessman who had been awarded a large government contract for machine parts. The contract required the businessman to subcontract some of the work. The man urged Robert to quit his job at the local manufacturing firm and open his own shop. Robert did and when the contract was completed in 1941, there were more jobs to follow. During World War II, McDever's annual sales rose to $350,000, and by 1954 the firm was grossing $1.2 million a year. Most of the work was done under subcontracting arrangements, although the company also bid successfully on a number of jobs for which it was the prime contractor.

When Ian returned from engineering college in 1950, he joined the business. His father needed his help in two areas: design and sales. The two men had decided that the best way to make the firm grow rapidly was to develop their own product lines and sell them directly. Most of the company's work had been in manufacturing parts for use in industrial machinery. Many of these parts could be improved through more effective engineering design. This is where Ian came in. From 1950 to 1964, he and his 'father spent countless hours studying industrial machinery and building a secondary market (often called aftermarket) business. The two would discuss what was needed. Then Ian would begin designing and building the parts; they would be tested and, if all went well, become part of the company's line.

In the beginning Ian spent most of his time designing and overseeing the manufacturing of replacement equipment and parts, and his father would directly contact businesses that he knew could profit from buying them. After five years, however, the product line was so big and the number of business representatives coming by every day was so great that the two owners decided to develop their own sales force to visit the factories and market the product line. This plan went extremely well, and when Robert retired in 1964 annual sales had reached $44 million.

In the more than twenty-five years since Robert's retirement, Ian has built the company into a household word in the equipment replacement market. Sales in 1988 were $206 million and rose to $228 million the next year. Recently Ian has been thinking about moving into another field: portable computers. The market is very competitive but Ian believes that his company could do extremely well there.

Environment

The computer field is dominated by a handful of firms that offer a variety of different machines. During the 1980s, the fastest growth has been in microcomputers. These are the desk top models and portable computers that can be seen just about anywhere else that computers are sold.

Thanks to major breakthroughs in "chip technology," today's microcomputers have the same power that the giant mainframe computers of the 1960s had. These machines are not only powerful; they are versatile. As a result, many firms are buying microcomputers to assist their executives both in obtaining information on current operations and in making decisions based on these data.

Perhaps the biggest problem for those competing in the market is the share versus profit dilemma. From 1980 to 1988 prices in the industry dropped by approximately 50 percent. State-of-the-art technology coupled with efficient production allowed manufacturers to provide better machines at a lower price. On the negative side, as prices tumbled so did profit margins; firms such as IBM and Apple, who were trying very hard to maintain a high market share (25 percent or higher), were finding that these low-priced microcomputers required a great deal of time and effort for the profit that was earned. Larger profits were available from larger machines, such as the minicomputers (the next step up from microcomputers) and the mainframe computers. Yet a large firm could not solely focus its attention on minicomputers and mainframe computers because the biggest growth was in microcomputers.

The large manufacturers were keeping competitors on their toes by introducing new models approximately three times a year. It was obvious to many industry observers that IBM, in particular, intended to maintain a sizable market share. Most of its new microcomputer offerings were intended to compete directly with current products from the competition. Every time IBM engaged in direct competition, competitors were forced to lower their prices because on a head-to-head basis, none of them could successfully meet IBM's competition.

Most of the firms in the industry, including the largest ones, did not manufacture their own computer parts. They focused most of their attention on developing new technology for the machines and marketing the end products either directly, as in the case of IBM Product Centers, or through retail stores.

By 1988 one microcomputer that was beginning to attract a lot of attention was the portable personal computer, popularly known as the laptop. Different version of the machine were available, but they all had a two common features: light weight and compactness. Additionally, some offered hard-disk drives and had backlit screens, which made it easier to read the liquid-crystal display. Some of the most popular models were these:

Brand	Model	Weight with Battery	Features	Price
Datavue	Sparc EL	9.0 lb.	Backlit screen, dual floppies	$1,200–1,300
NEC	Multispeed/EL	11.5	Same	1,400–1,500
	Multispeed HD	14.3	Same, plus 20MB hard disk	2,300–2,400
Sharp	PC-4502	10.6	Backlit screen, dual floppies	1,200–1,300
	PC-4521	12.4	Same, plus 20MB hard disk	2,200–2,300
Tandy	1400LT	13.5	Backlit screen, two floppies, 768K memory standard	1,599
Toshiba	T1000	6.4	Sidekick software	700–800
	T1200FF	9.9	Backlit screen, two floppies	1,600–1,700
Zenith	Supersport2	13.35	Same	1,500–1,700
	Supersport 286/20	14.56	Same, plus 80286 processor, 20MB hard disk	3,500

Source: Reprinted from August 8, 1988 issue of *Business Week* by special permission, copyright © 1988 by McGraw-Hill, Inc.

Strategy

Ian was well aware of the above information and had been giving serious thought to manufacturing a portable computer. The dimensions that he had in mind were similar to those of the Zenith. The machine would weigh six pounds and be small enough to fit into a briefcase. There would be a liquid-crystal screen that would display eighteen lines of material with eight columns per line. There would also be a 20 MB (megabyte) hard-disk and a backlit screen.

Because he traveled so much, Ian knew that he, personally, would use a portable personal computer (PC) if the machine were compatible with his IBM machines back at the office. It would save him a lot of time if he could work in his hotel room rather than simply making notes and getting everything taken care of when he returned to the plant. Many of the people he visited every month told him that they also could profit from the use of a truly portable PC.

With his knowledge of manufacturing, Ian had made a rough estimate of how much it would cost his firm to produce its own portable PC. The profit margin per machine depended on how many were produced, since cost per unit declines with increases in output. Ian estimated that to produce 4,000 units it would cost approximately $100 each for assembly and $900 for parts. The spread between the $2,000 selling price and the $1,000 cost associated with manufacturing and assembling the machine was accounted for by: (a) profit margin to the dealer who was selling the machine, (b) marketing/administrative overhead in the company, and (c) profit to the firm.

Ian believed that he and his staff could design the basic parts of a portable PC and get 4,000 of them built by a subcontractor for approximately $1,000 per machine. There would be no fixed expense on the part of his company, since this would all be taken care of by the subcontractor. The biggest difficulty in selling them would be reputation; no one had ever associated Ian's firm with computers. However, if he started off selling them to the companies with which he had been doing business for the last twenty-five years, and provided a one-year guarantee against defects, he might be able to get all 4,000 sold at a retail price of around $2,000.

Marketing

Ian knows a great deal about manufacturing; marketing is his weak suit. Last week he brought in the head of his marketing department and discussed his portable PC ideas with the individual. The marketing manager agreed that the basic plan had merit; however, he pointed out a couple of flaws in Ian's thinking. The biggest was that most firms will not buy a computer from a company that they believe is going to be out of the business in a couple of years. The purchaser is looking for ongoing service and the assurance of future availability for purchase of more machines that are compatible with the current one.

Another point the marketing manager made was that if the 4,000 units could not be sold within one year, the cost of carrying the inventory could be quite high. The alternative would be to make an arrangement with a retailer such as Sears to handle the machines. This would provide the opportunity for greater sales. On the other hand, it would also mean that Ian's firm would have to put money into advertising the line. Additionally, firms such as IBM give retailers a 15 to 20 percent discount off list price. Assuming a 20 percent discount, the $2,000 selling price would now drop to $1,600, leaving a margin of $600 after manufacture and assembly. Allowing another $300 per machine for transportation, advertising, and sundry expenses would result in a net profit of $300 per machine.

Ian listened quietly to the marketing manager. There was only one flaw he could see in the manager's logic; if the machines were sold through retailers, it is likely that more than 4,000 could be sold the first year.

During the same meeting, Ian and the marketing manager discussed key factors for success in the industry. In the latter's view, there were three that were vital to success: reputation, product quality, and price. The last two are within the company's grasp. The marketing manager believed, however, that unless a firm has its product in the market place for at least five years, customers would be reluctant to buy it. In backing up this argument, he noted the recent case of a chief executive officer who told the head of manufacturing, "You can buy any computer system you want. But if it's not IBM and there's a problem with it, your job will be on the line." This, he felt, is the type of image that the company must surmount if it hopes to succeed in this market.

Future

Ian is convinced that he can succeed in marketing a portable PC. Last year his firm's net profit was $17 million. As owner of 80 percent of the stock, he can essentially do as he pleases, and with such strong profits over the last ten years, there is little likelihood that this venture will threaten the survival of the firm. In fact, at $1,000 per computer the total cost for the entire 4,000 units will be only $4 million and some of these will be used in-house by Ian's own staff.

Overall, Ian believes the upside gains justify the downside losses. If all 4,000 units are sold at a net price of $1,600, there will be a profit of $300 per machine. Since he would spread out the delivery of the machines to 333 per month, he estimates that at any one time he would have no more than 1,000 units on hand. This means an average investment of $1 million ($1,000 per machine $\times$ 1,000 units in inventory). Thus his return on investment, computed by dividing profit/investment would be:

$$\frac{4,000 \text{ units} \times \$300 \text{ profit}}{\$1,000,000 \text{ (average inventory)}} = \frac{\$1.2 \text{ million}}{\$1 \text{ million}} = 120 \text{ percent}$$

In Ian's mind the entire idea is a good one.

Questions

1. In your own words, what is the nature of the industry? Describe it and then using Figure 4-3 describe the portable PC market.

2. What will Ian's strategic plan have to contain? Sketch it out in general terms. Then show the organization structure that will support this plan. What will the latter look like? Draw it.

3. Overall, is Ian making a wise decision in deciding to move forward? Using the ideas in the control chapter, does his decision justify itself? Explain your answer.

PART 3

THE QUANTITATIVE SCHOOL OF MANAGEMENT

Chapter 8 examines the fundamentals of decision making. In this chapter consideration is given to the steps in the decision-making process and the techniques commonly used in carrying out these steps. This includes the assignment of probabilities and the use of such approaches as marginal analysis, financial analysis, the Delphi technique, brainstorming, the Gordon technique, and whole-brain thinking. Attention is also focused on the three basic conditions under which decisions are made: certainty, risk, and uncertainty.

In Chapter 9 modern quantitative decision-making tools and processes are reviewed. There are many quantitative approaches that can be used to improve the effectiveness of decision making. Illustrations include inventory control techniques, game theory, queuing theory, the Monte Carlo method, decision trees, and heuristic programming. Chapter 9 examines each of these and relates their relevance and value to decision making.

Chapter 10 is devoted to information systems and decision making. The chapter begins by explaining how an information system can be of value to a manager in decision making. Then a brief description is provided regarding the way in which an information system is designed. The heart of the chapter addresses computers in modern organizations and the ways in which these machines help to carry information and improve the manager's decision-making ability. Attention is also focused on the behavioral impact that information systems can have on the personnel.

The last chapter in this part addresses operations management. This chapter brings together much of what has been discussed in Chapters 8–10 and shows how it can be used on the job. The initial part of the chapter discusses the productivity issue and relates some of the latest technological developments that are occurring on the factory floor. Then some of the major functions of operations management are examined, including product design, production planning, purchasing, inventory control, and quality control.

The overall purpose of this part of the book is to provide a general framework for understanding the quantitative school of management. While the major areas bear some relationship to those in the previously discussed school, management process, their focus is much more quantitative and "hands on." The engineering emphasis of the early quantitative school proponents such as Frederick Taylor and his lieutenants is still obvious.

CHAPTER 8

Fundamentals of Decision Making

GOALS OF THE CHAPTER

The goal of this chapter is to examine the fundamentals of decision making. A review of the steps in the process will be followed first by an analysis of the impact of personal values on the decision-making process. Next, the types of decisions and the conditions under which they are made—that is, certainty, risk, and uncertainty—will be scrutinized. Then, three of the more common decision-making techniques—marginal analysis, financial analysis, and the Delphi technique—will be reviewed in detail. Finally, creativity and decision making will be explored.

When you have finished this chapter, you should be able to:

1. Define the steps in the decision-making process.
2. Discuss what is meant by the term *rationality* and relate its importance in understanding the decision-making process.
3. Explain how values affect decision making.
4. Outline a classification system for examining all decisions, including organizational and personal decisions, basic and routine decisions, and programmed and nonprogrammed decisions.
5. Relate the three basic conditions under which decisions are made.
6. Discuss the role of objective and subjective probability in decision making.
7. Describe the benefit of marginal analysis.

8.   Explain the importance of financial analysis in decision making.

9.   Describe how the Delphi technique works.

10.   Relate the steps in the creative thinking process and the ways in which brainstorming and the Gordon technique promote creative thought.

11.   Explain what is meant by whole-brain thinking and discuss its value in decision making.

DECISION-MAKING PROCESS

Decision making involves choosing from among alternatives.

Decision making is the process of choosing from among alternatives. Regardless of the specific steps employed by the manager, some formal diagnosis must be conducted, alternative solutions formulated and analyzed, and a decision made regarding the approach to take. This is as true in the development of strategic, intermediate, and operational plans as it is in solving simple job problems.

One of the primary characteristics of this entire process is the dynamism, the steps being implemented within a time framework. The past is the time dimension in which the problem is identified and diagnosed. The present is the point at which the alternatives are formulated and a choice made regarding the plan of action. The future is the time period during which the decision will be implemented and an evaluation made regarding the outcome.

RATIONALITY AND THE MEANS—END HIERARCHY

There are degrees of rationality in decision making.

Not all decisions made by workers are rational. Some are nonrational; others are irrational. The same is true of managers. In addition, degrees of rationality exist. A man lost in the desert may wander in circles. His solution may be wrong, but is it not rational? Virtually everyone in this situation walks around in circles. This raises the question of precisely what is meant by the term *rational*. Some people assign the term to actions that attain a given end. In this case, the man in the desert is not acting rationally because his actions are not leading him out of his dilemma. Other individuals feel that *rational* refers to a choice of the best alternative of those available. In this case, the man is probably acting rationally because of the alternatives facing him. He may conclude that no one knows he is lost, so he cannot rely on a search party's finding him. His only salvation rests in saving himself by, for example, finding the nearest oasis. The only way to do this is to start walking and hope to locate one before too long.

It is difficult to separate means from ends.

Some decision theorists believe that rational decisions are forthcoming if appropriate means for reaching desired goals are chosen. However, it is often difficult to separate means from ends, for every end is really just a means to another end. This is what is known as the *means–end hierarchy*. When the man in the desert finds the oasis, he will remain there, using it as his base of operations (means) until he can establish contact with the outside world and have help sent to him (end). The plane that takes him out (means) will allow him to return to his old way of life (end).

Rationality, within the decision-making framework, is a relative term— dependent upon the situation and the individuals involved. An objectively rational *organizational* decision designed to ensure the company a profitable year may be welcomed by the employees until they learn that it calls for the elimination of all Christmas bonuses; then it is seen as a nonrational or irrational decision. Likewise, *personally* rational decisions such as the establishment of thirty-minute coffee breaks to eliminate excessive fatigue may be favorably viewed by the workers but seen by the management as disastrous to overall company efficiency. One reason for the imprecision in decision making is the personal values of the people involved.

PERSONAL VALUES AND DECISION MAKING

All managers bring a certain set of values to the workplace. These values can be broken down and applied to managers on an individual basis. Edward Spranger identified six such values: theoretical, economic, aesthetic, social, political, and religious. The description of each is presented in Table 8-1. When William D. Guth and Renato Tagiuri employed this classification scheme with high-level United States executives attending the Advanced Management Program of the Harvard Business School Seminar, they obtained the following average profile:[1]

Value	Score
Economic	45
Theoretical	44
Political	44
Religious	39
Aesthetic	35
Social	33
	240

The scores represent the importance of the values as seen by the average manager in the study.

Managers' personal values influence their decision making.

The economic, theoretical, and political scores seem justifiably high, for the top manager must be interested in efficiency and profit (economic), possess conceptual skills required for endeavors such as long-range planning (theoretical), and be able to get along with people and convince them to work

---

[1] William D. Guth and Renato Tagiuri, "Personal Values and Corporate Strategy," *Harvard Business Review*, September–October 1965, p. 126. The questionnaire was designed to yield 240 points distributed over the six values.

TABLE 8-1
Spranger's Value
Orientations

1. The *theoretical* man is primarily interested in the discovery of truth, in the systematic ordering of his knowledge. In pursuing this goal he typically takes a ''cognitive'' approach, looking for identities and differences, with relative disregard for the beauty or utility of objects, seeking only to observe and to reason. His interests are empirical, critical, and rational. He is an intellectual. Scientists or philosophers are often of this type (but they are not the only ones).

2. The *economic* man is primarily oriented toward what is useful. He is interested in the practical affairs of the business world; in the production, marketing, and consumption of goods; in the use of economic resources; and in the accumulation of tangible wealth. He is thoroughly ''practical'' and fits well the stereotype of the American businessman.

3. The *aesthetic* man finds his chief interest in the artistic aspects of life, although he need not be a creative artist. He values form and harmony. He views experience in terms of grace, symmetry, or harmony. Each single event is savored for its own sake.

4. The essential value for the *social* man is love of people—the altruistic or philanthropic aspect of love. The social man values people as ends, and tends to be kind, sympathetic, unselfish. He finds those who have strong theoretical, economic, and aesthetic orientations rather cold. Unlike the political type, the social man regards love as the most important component of human relationships. In its purest form the social orientation is selfless and approaches the religious attitude.

5. The *political* man is characteristically oriented toward power, not necessarily in politics, but in whatever area he functions. Most leaders have a high power orientation. Competition plays a large role in all life, and many writers have regarded power as the most universal motive. For some men, this motive is uppermost, driving them to seek personal power, influence, and recognition.

6. The *religious* man is one ''whose mental structure is permanently directed to the creation of the highest and absolutely satisfying value experience.'' The dominant value for him is unity. He seeks to relate himself to the universe in a meaningful way and has a mystical orientation.

together as a team (political). However, the researchers also found that the profiles varied considerably in regard to religious, aesthetic, and social values, indicating that one must not be too hasty in trying to construct a stereotype of the typical executive.

The personal values of each manager can have a significant effect on the decision-making process. This is one reason that social action programs, for example, internally generated and heavily funded by the company itself, have been undertaken by many business firms in recent years.[2] Managers are

[2]See, for example, Fred Luthans, Richard M. Hodgetts, and Kenneth R. Thompson, *Social Issues in Business*, 5th ed. (New York: Macmillan, 1987).

much more oriented toward social responsibility than they were a decade ago although managerial values in general remain unchanged[3] (see Social Responsibility in Action: Management's Changing Values).

TYPES OF DECISIONS

Managers make many decisions, and in order to obtain a clear understanding of the decision-making process, a classification system is useful. Three such systems are available, each based on different types of decisions. They are organizational and personal decisions, basic and routine decisions, and programmed and nonprogrammed decisions.

Organizational and Personal Decisions

Organizational decisions can be delegated to others.

Organizational decisions are those made by executives in their official managerial roles. The adoption of strategies, the setting of objectives, and the approval of plans are a few examples. The implementation of such decisions is often delegated to others; thus, the decisions require the support of many people throughout the organization if they are to be properly implemented.

Personal decisions are not delegated.

Personal decisions relate to the manager as an individual, not as a member of the organization. Such decisions are not delegated to others because their implementation does not require the support of organizational personnel. Deciding to retire, taking a job offer from a competitive firm, or slipping out and spending the afternoon on the golf course are all personal decisions.

Although it is possible to distinguish between organizational and personal decisions according to definition, in practice it is not. For example, when a company president who believes in social activism decides to make a concerted effort to hire the hardcore unemployed, a personal decision is translated into an organizational one. Many decisions made by managers have both organizational and personal elements in them.

Basic and Routine Decisions

Basic decisions can have major organizational effects.

A second approach is to classify decisions into basic and routine categories. *Basic decisions* can be viewed as much more important then routine ones. They involve long-range commitments, large expenditures of funds, and such a degree of importance that a serious mistake might well jeopardize the well-being of the company. Selection of a product line, the choice of a new plant site, or a decision to integrate vertically by purchasing sources of raw materials to complement the current production facilities are all basic decisions.

Routine decisions are often repetitive in nature, having only a minor impact on the firm. For this reason, most organizations have formulated a host of

---

[3]James A. Lee, "Changes in Managerial Values: 1965–1986," *Business Horizons,* July–August 1988, pp. 29–37.

SOCIAL
RESPONSIBILITY
IN
ACTION:
Management's
Changing
Values

Every decade begins with someone making a pronouncement about the changes that can be expected in management's values. "This decade," a prognosticator will report, "will see a dramatic change in management values typified by a more participative management approach, the demise of organizational bureaucracies, and a decline in the work ethic among young people." By the end of the decade researchers will quietly be admitting that many of their forecasts were inaccurate. However, these same forecasts, or many similar to them, will again be made for the upcoming decade.

What do we know about managerial values for the 1990s? The answer is that they are likely to be similar to those of the 1980s. This certainly is true if the past is any indicator of the future. So while management may not move social responsibility to the top of its agenda, social-action programs will not fall to the bottom either. In fact, if there are any changes in management social responsibility values it is likely to be an increase. This has been made particularly clear by research conducted among managers at the Aeronautical Equipment Division of Sperry Rand. The first survey was run in 1965 and the most recent was conducted in 1986. Although the individuals participating in the two surveys were different, the basic rankings of the characteristics of ideal managers had not changed very much. They were the following:

1965	1986
Decision making	Future planning
Develop new methods	Decision making
Future planning	Develop new methods
Belief in subordinates	Sensitive to feelings
Capacity for loyalty	Belief in subordinates
Sensitive to feelings	Capacity for loyalty
Quantifiable variables	Quantifiable variables
Respect for authority	Religious/ethical values
Hard work	Family obligations
Religious/ethical values	Respect for authority
Risk taking	Risk taking
Family obligations	Hard work
Status differences	Support of government
Support of government	Personal friendships
Personal friendships	Status differences

The data show that the characteristics of ideal managers have not changed much over the last two decades. However, there have been some minor changes including increases in the need to be socially responsible. For example, notice that "Sensitive to feelings," "Belief in subordinates," "Capacity for loyalty," "Religious/ethical values," and "Family obligations" have all increased slightly. Overall, managers of the 1990s will be as socially responsible of those of the 1980s.

Source: James A. Lee, "Changes in Managerial Values: 1965–1986," *Business Horizons,* July–August 1988, pp. 29–37.

Routine decisions have only minor impact on the firm.

procedures to guide the manager in handling them. Some individuals in the organization, who spend most of their time making routine decisions, find these guidelines very useful.

At this point it may be helpful to define procedures and policies. *Procedures* are guides to action. Often referred to as types of plans, they relate the chronological steps entailed in attaining some objective. Sometimes procedures are drawn up for use in a particular department. In a retail store, for example, five steps may be involved in the return of faulty merchandise; the first would involve making sure that the goods were not damaged by the buyer, and the last would be the department manager's approval. Other procedures, such as a discrepancy in a paycheck, are organizational. The employee must tell the payroll department to have the pay recalculated and, if there has been an error, must return the incorrect check for a revised one. Procedures are useful in helping with routine decisions because they break processes down into steps.

Procedures are guides to action and usually consist of a list of chronological steps toward some goal.

Policies are guides to thinking and action.

Policies, often confused with procedures, are also types of plans, but they are guides to thinking as well as to action. As a result, they do not tell a manager how to do something; they merely channel the decision making along a particular line by delimiting the span of consideration. For example, a department may have a policy of hiring only those with a college education. However, how does one define a college education? If the manager is willing to accept one year of job experience and three years of formal college as the equivalent of a four-year diploma, more than mere action is involved; the manager has had to think to determine the equivalency line. The manager knows no one without a college degree or its equivalent (action) is acceptable and can confine all energies to evaluating the latter cases (thinking). In this case, a policy is helpful to the manager because it limits the number of people eligible for a job in the department. Policies are also useful at the organizational level. For example, a firm may have a policy of setting up new plants in cities with a population of at least 100,000. This is a guide to action because it limits the number of eligible cities. It is also a guide to thinking because now the executive must decide in which particular city to build the new plant. Policies play an important role in handling basic decisions.

Programmed and Nonprogrammed Decisions

Programmed decisions are routine; unprogrammed decisions are novel and structured.

Herbert Simon, borrowing from computer technology, has proposed the classification of decisions into the areas of programmed and nonprogrammed. These two types can be viewed on a continuum, programmed being at one end and nonprogrammed at the other. *Programmed decisions* correspond roughly to the routine decisions, with procedures playing a key role. *Nonprogrammed decisions* are similar to the category of basic decisions, being highly novel, important, and unstructured in nature. Policies play an important role in making these decisions. The value of viewing decision making in this manner is that it permits a clearer understanding of the methods that accompany each type.

DECISION-MAKING CONDITIONS

There are three possible conditions under which decisions can be made; certainty, risk, and uncertainty.

Certainty

Certainty is present when the manager knows exactly what will happen. Although *certainty decisions* constitute only a small percentage of managerial decisions, they do occur. For example, $10,000 invested in a government note for one year at 6 percent will return $600 in interest. Although it can be argued that there is a degree of risk in everything, including government notes, for all practical purposes this investment can be labeled as a sure thing.

Certainty is present when the manager knows the outcome of each alternative.

Likewise, the allocation of resources to various product lines often constitutes decision making under conditions of certainty. The manager knows what physical resources are on hand and the amount of time it will take to process them into finished goods. If there are two or three processes available, the manager can conduct a cost-contribution study to determine which is most profitable (if profit is the decision guideline) or which will produce the good most quickly (if speed is of the essence). In dealing with fixed quantities such as raw materials and machines, the manager is often making decisions under certainty, the prime goal being that of determining the desired objective. Once this is accomplished, the manager can simply evaluate the alternatives and choose the best one.

Risk

Risk is present if the manager has only partial information for evaluating the outcome of each alternative.

Most of the manager's decisions are *risk decisions*; that is, some information is available but it is insufficient to answer all questions about the outcome. One method often used to assist the decision maker is that of probability estimates.[4]

Probability Estimates

Although the manager may not know with a high degree of certainty the outcome of each decision, it may still be possible to estimate some level of probability for each of the alternatives. Such estimates are often based on experience. The manager draws on past occurrences in determining the likelihood of particular events. Naturally, no situation is ever identical to a previous one, but it may be sufficiently similar to justify using experience as a guide. Probability assignments permit a determination of the expected values of all events. For example, consider the case of the firm with four available strategies: A, B, C, and D. Each has a *conditional value*, which is the profit that

---

[4]For more on risk-taking behavior see Avi Fiegenbaum and Howard Thomas, "Attitudes Toward Risk-Return Paradox: Prospect Theory Explanations," *Academy of Management Journal*, March 1988, pp. 85–106.

Available Strategies	Conditional Value	×	Success Probability	=	Expected Value
A	$1,000,000		0.05		$ 50,000
B	800,000		0.10		80,000
C	750,000		0.20		150,000
D	400,000		0.65		260,000

TABLE 8-2
Expected Values for Strategies A–D

will be returned to the firm if it is implemented and proves successful; a *probability*, which is a likelihood of success; and an *expected value*, which is the result of the conditional value multiplied by the probability. These data can be arranged as in Table 8-2.

Table 8-2 illustrates that the manager should opt for Strategy D because it promises the greatest expected value. Although it has the lowest conditional value of all four, the probability of success is far higher, resulting in the large expected value.

Objective and Subjective Probabilities

Objective probability can be assigned on the basis of past experience.

If a probability can be determined on the basis of past experience, it is known as an objective probability. What is the probability of obtaining a head in the toss of a fair coin? It is 0.5. Over the long run, there will be just as many heads as tails. Likewise, many companies are able, on the basis of past experience, to assign objective probabilities to events such as predicting success on a particular psychological test. Persons whose test scores are in the top 20 percent may have an 0.8 probability of success as a manager. This would indicate that eight out of every ten in this category have done well as managers.

Subjective probability is often assigned on the basis of gut feel.

Sometimes, however, it is not possible to determine a suitable objective probability estimate. The manager may not feel there is sufficient information to determine whether the success probability is 0.5 or 0.8. In this case, the individual must make a subjective estimate, employing what is commonly called gut feel.

Although not as precise as an objective probability, subjective probability is nevertheless better than completely ignoring the probabilities of occurrence associated with the various alternatives. It also provides a basis for sharpening one's judgment since subjective probability assignments will occur again.

Risk Preference

The assignment of probabilities is never as simple as it might appear. The decision maker who finalizes the assignment is the ultimate arbiter, and different managers will assign varying estimates to identical alternatives for various reasons.

Some managers take risks; others avert risk.

For example, most managers are greater risk takers when investing or spending company funds than when they have their own money at stake. Furthermore, in making a decision on plant and equipment, some will demand a higher success probability than if the same amount were being invested in advertising, while others will do just the opposite. In short, attitudes toward risk vary. Why? Part of the answer is found in the fact that some people have a high dislike for risk while others have a low dislike for it. Another part of the answer is found in the fact that managers who are risk averters in some situations are gamblers in others.

Regardless of the reason, managers' risk preferences will play a key role in determining their probability assignments. Figure 8-1 presents the preference curves of high, average, and low risk-takers. The S-curve illustrates the risk preferences of people in their personal lives. When the stakes are low, most individuals tend to be more willing to gamble than when they are high. For example, the author has asked businessmen if they would be willing to accept an outright gift of $5 or would prefer to take a chance on winning $15 or nothing against the correct call of the flip of a coin. Most have taken the latter alternative, being willing to gamble for $15 or nothing. Conversely, when the stakes are raised to $50,000 and $150,000 respectively, most managers choose the certain $50,000 sum. Objectively speaking, they are unwise, for the expected value of the $150,000 is $75,000 ($150,000 × 0.5), since the odds are fifty-fifty that they will call the flip of the coin correctly. However, the managers prefer the guaranteed $50,000.

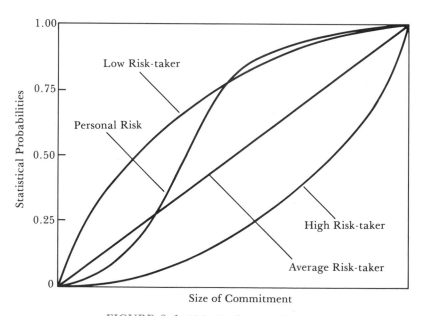

FIGURE 8–1 Risk–Preference Curves

Uncertainty

Uncertainty decisions are those for which managers feel they cannot develop probability estimates because they have no way of gauging the likelihood of the various alternatives. It is very difficult to say precisely when this occurs. Many individuals contend that experience and the ability to generalize from similar situations make uncertainty impossible; the manager can always assign some probability estimates to a decision matter.[5] Yet there are times when executives feel they are indeed dealing with uncertainty. Nevertheless, *Probability estimates should be developed even if the manager must make a decision under uncertainty.* research shows that they are wise to construct conditional values for each alternative under each state of nature. For example, an airplane manufacturer is considering the production of a giant helicopter for the military, and three basic design versions are under serious consideration: A, B, and C. The first is the most sophisticated and expensive of the three, while the last is the least sophisticated and expensive. The two basic states of nature are seen as being either a generation of peace or continual fighting of brushfire wars. Furthermore, the manufacturer has assigned conditional values to the respective strategies and states of nature, as shown in Table 8-3. Additionally, if peace prevails, the military will buy the least expensive helicopter, but if brushfire wars continue, it will purchase the most expensive.

What decision should the manager make? If there is no reason for believing that one event is more likely to occur than any other, the manager *Equal probability can be applied to all events.* can employ what is called the *Laplace criterion,* which applies equal probabilities to all states of nature. If this approach is followed, the firm should manufacture Helicopter C, because it offers an expected value of $2,500,000 ($4,500,000 × 0.5 + $500,000 × 0.5), which is greater than the value from either of the other strategies, as Table 8-4 shows. Helicopter A has an expected value of $2,375,000 (− $250,000 × 0.5 + $5,000,000 × 0.5); Helicopter B has an expected value of $1,000,000 ($1,000,000 × 0.5 + $1,000,000 × 0.5).

A second approach is the use of the *maximin,* or pessimism, *criterion,* which holds that the manager should ascertain the worst conditions for each

---

[5]Tom Post, "Managing the Unknown," *Success,* July–August 1988, p. 20.

TABLE 8-3
Conditional Values Associated with Manufacturing Giant Helicopter

| | States of Nature | |
Strategies	Generation of Peace	Continual Brushfire Wars
Helicopter A	−$ 250,000	$5,000,000
Helicopter B	1,000,000	1,000,000
Helicopter C	4,500,000	500,000

TABLE 8-4
Expected Values for Manufacturing Giant Helicopter Using Laplace Criterion (Equal Probability)

| | States of Nature | |
Strategies	Generation of Peace	Continual Brushfire Wars
Helicopter A	−$ 125,000	$2,500,000
Helicopter B	500,000	500,000
Helicopter C	2,250,000	250,000

A pessimistic approach can be used.

strategy. As Table 8-4 shows, the figures in this case are − $250,000 for A, $1,000,000 for B, and $500,000 for C. The strategy that offers the best payoff under these conditions should be implemented; in this case Helicopter B should be manufactured. By using this approach, the manager maximizes the minimum gain; hence the term *maximin*.

An optimistic approach can be taken.

A third approach is the use of the criterion of optimism, commonly called the *maximax criterion*. Since the manager is unsure of the outcome, it is just as rational to be optimistic as pessimistic. The manager can logically look on the bright side and assign a probability of, for example, 0.8 to the likelihood of the most favorable outcomes of each strategy and 0.2 to the least favorable outcomes of each. Then the best and worst conditional values associated with these three strategies can be multiplied by their respective probabilities to obtain weighted values, as seen in Table 8-5. Finally, these values can be added. In this instance, Helicopter A is the best choice.

Dealing with decisions under uncertainty is no easy task. In the three approaches used here, a different strategy emerged as the most favorable each time. The assumptions the manager makes regarding conditional values and probability estimates and the methods employed in evaluating the alternatives will all influence the outcome.

DECISION-MAKING TECHNIQUES

Attention has thus far been focused mainly on the environment in which the manager makes decisions—certainty, risk, and uncertainty. However, it is also useful to examine some of the specific techniques that have proved valuable in the decision-making process. Three of these techniques are marginal analysis, financial analysis, and the Delphi technique.

Marginal Analysis

Marginal analysis has been of interest to economists for years. In its essence, *marginal analysis* is concerned with the extra output that can be attained by adding an extra unit of input. For example, if one more machine is added to the assembly line and 200 more widgets are produced each day, the daily marginal product from that machine is 200. If a new air-conditioning system

TABLE 8-5

Application of Optimism Criteria to Conditional Values for Helicopter Manufacture (0.8 Optimism and 0.2 Pessimism)

	Conditional Values		Weighted Values		
Strategy	Best Condition	Worst Condition	Best Condition	Worst Condition	Sum of Weighted Values
Helicopter A	$5,000,000	−$ 250,000	$4,000,000	−$ 50,000	$3,950,000
Helicopter B	1,000,000	1,000,000	800,000	200,000	1,000,000
Helicopter C	4,500,000	500,000	3,600,000	100,000	3,700,000

is installed, making the environment more pleasant, and if 500 more widgets are subsequently produced each week, the weekly marginal product from the air conditioner is 500.

The manager can use the concept of the margin to answer such questions as how much more output will result if one more worker is hired. The answer, often called *marginal physical product*, provides a basis for determining whether or not one new worker will bring about profitable additional output.

Marginal Physical Product

Consider the case of the new shipping manager who has five workers loading five trucks. After pondering the matter, the manager hires five new workers; two people are now loading each truck. The result, as seen in Table 8-6, is that the total number of boxes loaded each day rises from 800 to 2,000. Two employees working as a team are able to do more than they could if working independently. With a third team worker, the daily total rises to 2,900.

Output may be increased if one worker is added.

As the table shows, the total mounts to 4,000 and then drops off to 3,700 when the number of workers per truck reaches seven. Why? Various causes can be cited. On the physical side, there may simply be too many people; they may be getting in each other's way. A behaviorist might wonder whether the

TABLE 8-6

Units of Marginal Physical Product

Number of Workers per Truck	Total Boxes Loaded	Marginal Physical Product
0	0	0
1	800	800
2	2,000	1,200
3	2,900	900
4	3,500	600
5	3,900	400
6	4,000	100
7	3,700	(300)

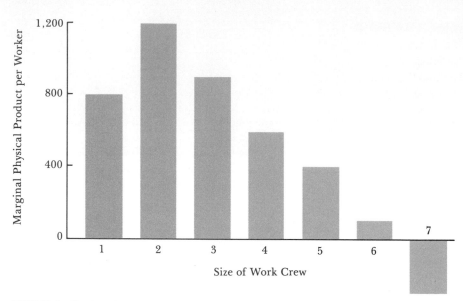

FIGURE 8–2   Bar Graph of Physical Product

seven are horsing around more or whether they may have an informal agreement to hold down output. In either event, seven workers per truck are too many.

If this manager's decision must rest solely on output, six is the ideal team size. However, there is a diminishing marginal physical product after the second worker is hired. The contributions from the third through the sixth increase the total but reduce the average from 1,000 boxes when there are two workers to 967, 875, 780, and 667 respectively as the next four workers are added. This rise in the total output with the accompanying decline in the marginal physical product is seen in Figures 8-2 and 8-3 respectively.

Profit Consideration

However, profit is of more importance than mere physical output.

The decline in marginal output will limit the size of the work crew. More realistically, however, the manager will refine the decision further with a consideration of profit. How much money will the company make at each work crew size? Table 8-7 shows total profits under the premise that there is a ten-cent profit for every box loaded if all costs except work crew wages are considered. It is evident from the data that the company stands to make $240 a day if there are five people on the work crew. Any other size will result in less profit. In making such decisions, managers must consider profit as well as productivity.

Most decisions do not require the manager to maximize profit or output. In some cases, however, this is the objective. For example, consider the case of the aerospace firm that is pondering the acceptance of a subcontract to build communication satellite subsystems. The major contractor wants eight of

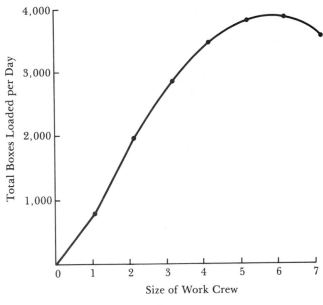

FIGURE 8–3 **Total Output**

them built and would like to know whether the company is willing to undertake the contract. The purchase price of each subsystem will be $18,000. In order to determine the profitability of the venture, the firm must first construct its cost and revenue data, as seen in Table 8-8. The information reveals that if the company manufactures all eight subsystems, it will lose $26,000. The ideal production is six, for at this point the firm will net $32,000. This is also seen in Figure 8-4, where the data are presented graphically. The profit point at which the distance between total revenue and total cost is greatest is that corresponding to six units. The company should therefore refuse the contract.

TABLE 8-7 **Profit per Truck**	Number of Workers	Salary Cost per Day	Profit per Box before Loading Salaries	Boxes Loaded	Total Profit before Loading Salaries	Total Profit
	1	$ 30	$.10	800	$ 80	$ 50
	2	60	.10	2,000	200	140
	3	90	.10	2,900	290	200
	4	120	.10	3,500	350	230
	5	150	.10	3,900	390	240
	6	180	.10	4,000	400	220
	7	210	.10	3,700	370	160

	Number Manufactured	Total Revenue	Total Cost	Total Profit	Marginal Revenue	Marginal Cost
TABLE 8-8 Costs and Revenues Associated with Manufacture of Communications Subsystems	1	$ 18,000	$ 30,000	($12,000)	$18,000	$30,000
	2	36,000	35,000	1,000	18,000	5,000
	3	54,000	40,000	14,000	18,000	5,000
	4	72,000	50,000	22,000	18,000	10,000
	5	90,000	60,000	30,000	18,000	10,000
	6	108,000	76,000	32,000	18,000	16,000
	7	126,000	110,000	16,000	18,000	34,000
	8	144,000	170,000	(26,000)	18,000	60,000

Marginal revenue and marginal cost must be computed.

The solution can be verified further if the *marginal revenue* and *marginal cost* data in Table 8-8 are examined. For every unit manufactured, the company obtains marginal revenue of $18,000. However, it also has an accompanying marginal cost associated with the production. A scrutiny of this marginal revenue (MR) and marginal cost (MC) data shows that for the sixth unit the firm will increase overall profit by $2,000 ($18,000 − $16,000). At seven units, overall profits will decline by $16,000; this is so because the marginal

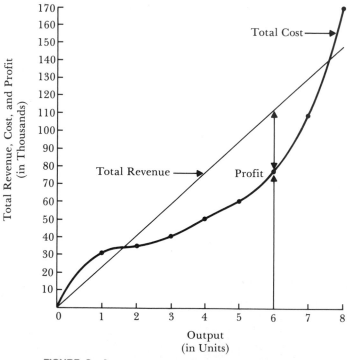

FIGURE 8–4   Maximum Profit Determination

revenue is still only $18,000, but the marginal cost now associated with this unit is $34,000. Obviously, the company should agree to manufacture no more than six units. The profit maximization rule is to manufacture to the point where MC equals MR or, if they do not equalize, to the last point where MR is larger than MC (as in this case). Such an analysis can prove a useful decision-making technique for the manager. It not only helps identify the maximum profit point; it also prevents the undertaking of unprofitable ventures.

Financial Analysis

Although marginal analysis is useful to the manager, it is nonetheless a specialized technique that considers situations only one at a time. It is therefore not a particularly helpful long-range guide to action. To provide a dynamic view of the future, many managers have turned to financial analytical techniques, which can be used for such functions as estimating the profitability of an investment, calculating the payback period, and/or analyzing discounted cash inflows and outflows.

After-tax profitability is one guideline.

Consider the situation of the manager who is evaluating the purchase of two machines, A and B, solely on the basis of after-tax profitability. Which machine will provide more net profit for the firm? Machine A costs $150,000 and has an estimated useful life of five years. Machine B costs $200,000 and also has a five-year useful life. As seen in Table 8-9, when depreciation and taxes are deducted, Machine A will return $55,000 in net income, whereas Machine B will net the firm $60,000. Therefore, on the basis of after-tax profitability, Machine B will be the manager's choice.

It should be noted, however, that although the B alternative is more profitable, it also entails an added investment of $50,000. This raises the question of whether the manager has made a wise choice by allowing net profit to be the sole guide? After all, should the company not expect to obtain more profit from the larger investment? Sometimes a manager is on sound ground when opting for the alternative returning the greatest net profit; other times, however, one may forego the consideration of profit and concentrate on the *payback period*, which is the length of time it will take the company to recover its investment. Table 8-10 presents the cumulative cash recovery period. Estimating weekly recovery as 1/52 of the annual total, it will require approximately 3 years, and 33 weeks to recover the $150,000 invested for Machine A, and 3 years, and 37 weeks to recover the $200,000 invested for Machine B. On the basis of the payback period, the manager would opt for Machine A.

Payback period is another guideline.

Net present value is a third guideline.

A third approach, even more useful than the previous two, is that of *net present value.* With this method the manager evaluates the expected return from each investment, using a discounted dollar analysis of cash inflows. Such an analysis presents future cash inflows in terms of current dollars. The longer the manager has to wait for the inflows, the less they are worth in current dollars. For purposes of illustration, assume that the manager

TABLE 8-9
Evaluating an
Investment on the
Basis of Net Profit

Machine A

Year	Added Income before Taxes	Depreciation	Taxable Income	After-tax Income (Assuming 50 Percent Tax Rate)
1	$ 30,000	$30,000	$ 0	$ 0
2	50,000	30,000	20,000	10,000
3	60,000	30,000	30,000	15,000
4	80,000	30,000	50,000	25,000
5	40,000	30,000	10,000	5,000
			$110,000	$55,000

Machine B

Year	Added Income before Taxes	Depreciation	Taxable Income	After-tax Income (Assuming 50 Percent Tax Rate)
1	$ 40,000	$40,000	$ 0	$ 0
2	60,000	40,000	20,000	10,000
3	80,000	40,000	40,000	20,000
4	100,000	40,000	60,000	30,000
5	40,000	40,000	0	0
			$120,000	$60,000

Notes: Investment for Machine A is $150,000; Machine B, $200,000. Both machines have an estimated life of five years. Depreciation is on a straight-line basis.

TABLE 8-10
Evaluating an
Investment on the
Basis of Payback
Period

Machine A

Year	After-tax Income	Depreciation	Annual Cash Recovery	Cumulative Cash Recovery
1	$ 0	$30,000	$30,000	$ 30,000
2	10,000	30,000	40,000	70,000
3	15,000	30,000	45,000	115,000
4	25,000	30,000	55,000	170,000
5	5,000	30,000	35,000	205,000

Machine B

Year	After-tax Income	Depreciation	Annual Cash Recovery	Cumulative Cash Recovery
1	$ 0	$40,000	$40,000	$ 40,000
2	10,000	40,000	50,000	90,000
3	20,000	40,000	60,000	150,000
4	30,000	40,000	70,000	220,000
5	0	40,000	40,000	260,000

TABLE 8-11
Discounted Cash Flows
for Machines A and B

	Machine A			
Year	Outflows of Cash	Inflows of Cash	Discount Factor	Discounted Dollars
0	$150,000	$ 0	1.000	$150,000
1	0	30,000	0.909	27,270
2	0	40,000	0.826	33,040
3	0	45,000	0.751	33,795
4	0	55,000	0.683	37,565
5	0	35,000	0.621	21,735
Scrap value (20%)		30,000	0.621	18,630
				$172,035

	Machine B			
0	$200,000	$ 0	1.000	$200,000
1	0	40,000	0.909	36,360
2	0	50,000	0.826	41,300
3	0	60,000	0.751	45,060
4	0	70,000	0.683	47,810
5	0	40,000	0.621	24,840
Scrap value (20%)		40,000	0.621	24,840
				$220,210

chooses to discount the future inflows of funds by 10 percent. In this case the annual cash flow recovery in Table 8-11 has to be multiplied by the appropriate discount factor. For example, a dollar returned a year from today is worth 90.9 cents using a 10 percent discount, while a dollar returned two years from today is worth 82.6 cents in current dollars. By multiplying the cash inflows by their respective discount factors, as seen in Table 8-11, discounted dollars can be calculated for the five-year investment. Then, to obtain the net present value, the manager must merely subtract the initial investment from the discounted dollar total and opt for that alternative which returns the greatest amount. Machine A will return $22,035 ($172,035 − $150,000), whereas Machine B will return $20,210 ($220,210 − $200,000). The manager should, therefore, choose alternative A.

The Delphi Technique

The *delphi technique* uses a combination quantitative and qualitative approach to decision making, and it has become very popular for technological forecasting. Developed by the Rand Corporation, the Delphi at present is used by fifty to one-hundred major corporations. In essence, the approach pools the opinions of experts and calls for:

1.   An anonymous prediction of important events in the area in question, from each expert in a group, in the form of brief statements.

2.   A clarification of these statements by the investigator.

3.   The successive, individual requestioning of each of the experts, combined with feedback supplied from the other experts through the investigator.[6]

In the first round of questioning, the experts might be asked individually to list, for example, the developments they believe will occur in their fields within the next twenty years that will have a significant effect on the company. Each may also be asked to comment on the desirability, feasibility, and timing of these developments. Figure 8-5 provides an illustration of the format that might be used.

Delphi allows the participants to revise their estimates.

Then, in a second round, the investigator gives each expert a composite of the predictions made by the others and the opportunity to modify his or her original estimates. This process is usually followed by still further rounds, often a total of five. The result is generally a consensus among the participants regarding the most significant events that will affect the company (Events A, E, H, and I), the likelihood of their eventual development (90 percent, 70 percent, 60 percent, and 40 percent), and the time period in which they can be expected to occur (1990, 1995, 2000, 2005).

Despite its apparent lack of scientific rigor, Delphi has proved very successful. In fact, the Rand Corporation has validated the technique through controlled experimentation. Its use has not been confined exclusively to technological forecasting. It has also been successfully employed, for example, to help participants formulate responses to questions whose answers are already known—for example, how many votes were cast for Lincoln in 1860, or how many Texas oil wells were there in 1960? In most cases, after a few

---

[6]"The Basic Delphi Method," *Harvard Business Review*, May–June 1969, p. 81.

Desirability			Feasibility			Timing (Year by Which Probable Event Will Have Occurred)		
High	Average	Low	High	Likely	Unlikely	10 Percent Probability	50 Percent Probability	90 Percent Probability

FIGURE 8–5   Delphi Technique, Round One

rounds of questioning, the consensus has moved close to the actual answer, and it is thus easy to see why Delphi is so popular.[7]

Technical and Nontechnical Factors

Technical factors such as chance occurrence can undermine a forecast.

The major problem confronting many forecasters is that of evaluating technical and nontechnical factors. In the technical area, for example, a pharmaceutical company might estimate that total chemical control of hereditary defects will be made practicable through molecular engineering by 1999. However, what if by chance occurrence someone stumbles onto a discovery and makes a major breakthrough in this field in 1994? How can such developments be forecast?

Nontechnical factors such as lack of public acceptance can also undermine a forecast.

Meanwhile, on the nontechnical side, there is the problem of lack of public acceptance. The American supersonic transport (SST) is an illustration. In 1963, when the United States learned that the British and French were going to combine their efforts to build the Concorde, an SST, President Kennedy urged the Congress to allocate funds for a feasibility study. By 1970, the plane was already in the mock-up stage, but by this time the entire project had become a political issue. The Nixon administration stood squarely behind the development and production of the craft, but the public apparently did not; and this was reflected in the vote of the Congress. One reason was undoubtedly studies—for example, one at Columbia University, which showed that the government and the contractors stood to lose large sums of money if the plane was built. People were just not going to pay the extra money to get, for example, from New York to London a few hours earlier. Nontechnical factors (lack of demand for the aircraft, lack of profit for all parties involved) proved to be more important than the technical ones.[8]

A Strategic Criteria Approach

In recent years some firms have developed a strategic criteria approach to use in determining whether a potentially radical technological innovation will be successful.[9]

First, inventive merit is examined.

The approach is rather simple. First, the organization examines whether the technological innovation has "inventive merit." George R. White and Margaret B. W. Graham have described the process of determining whether an inventive concept really has such merit:

---

[7]For an in-depth review of this area, see Richard M. Hodgetts, *The Business Enterprise: Social Challenge Social Response* (Philadelphia: W. B. Saunders, 1977), pp. 295–318.

[8]For more on the application of the Delphi technique, see Richard J. Tersine and Walter E. Riggs, "The Delphi Technique: A Long-Range Planning Tool," *Business Horizons*, April 1976, pp. 51–56; and Richard M. Hodgetts, "Applying the Delphi Technique to Management Gaming," *Simulation*, July 1977, pp. 209–212.

[9]The information in this section is based on George R. White and Margaret B. W. Graham, "How to Spot a Technological Winner," *Harvard Business Review*, March–April 1978, pp. 146–52.

A truly significant inventive concept will use its new combination of scientific principles to relieve or avoid major constraints inherent in the previous art. In the case of the transistor, elimination of the heated cathode of a vacuum tube allowed portable radio size and weight to be reduced while offering longer battery life and greater reliability. Similarly, for the jet transport case, the Pratt & Whitney J57 engine used the key invention of twin spool geometry to overmatch all existing jets in power and fuel economy as well as to surpass all piston and turboprop engines in power and speed.[10]

Next, embodiment merit is determined.

Second, the firm examines the innovation's "embodiment merit." How much information and technology is currently available and how many new breakthroughs must take place in order to make the innovation a reality?

Then operational merit is evaluated.

Third is "operational merit." Can the innovation be handled by the company's current organization structure and business practices, or will operations have to be drastically changed? For example, a firm that is already manufacturing and retailing stereo equipment may have no trouble handling new stereo innovation. It has the basic manufacturing know-how and the outlets for selling it. On the other hand, if the company developed a radically new product but had no sales or marketing organization, it would be at a disadvantage. A new type of hearing aid is an example. Competitors with a less efficient hearing aid will probably have the right structure and business practices already in operation; for this reason, they are likely to continue to dominate the market.

Market merit is then determined.

Fourth, "market merit" must be considered. In so doing, the manager must give attention to two factors: (1) Is there a sufficient demand for the product? (2) Can total revenue be increased by reducing price and/or increasing the attractiveness of the product?

The inventive merit and embodiment merit combine to give potency to technology. The operational merit and market merit help the organization identify its business advantage. In turn, technology potency and business advantage bring about innovation success. Table 8-12 provides an example of how these four kinds of merit can be used in assessing various types of products. In the case of the American SST it is the market value that defeats the project's prospects.

CREATIVITY AND DECISION MAKING

Not all decisions are quantitative in nature; some are the result of creative thinking. Effective advertising is an example. The best ads tend to be different or unique in some way. They help people differentiate between the company's message and those of the competition, resulting in an increased market share for the firm. At the heart of this success is the creative-thinking process.

---

[10]Ibid., p. 147.

TABLE 8-12
Assessing
Technological Winners

Product: Computerized Cars	
Inventive merit	A digital microprocessor control of engines will decrease pollution and improve fuel consumption.
Embodiment merit	Sensors and actuator components, not computer chips, will be required.
Operational merit	The expansion of car manufacturers and their suppliers into onboard computerized activities will result in major new design, manufacturing, and marketing opportunities.
Market merit	This innovation will help the manufacturer maintain old market share.

Product: American SST	
Inventive merit	The plane will reduce air travel time but cause sonic boom and require high fuel consumption.
Embodiment merit	Major advances will be required in engines, controls, structures, and pollution analysis.
Operational merit	The U.S. transcontinental market will be unable to support the SST fleet.
Market merit	The value of customer time saved is, at best, unclear.

Creative-thinking Process

There are four steps in the creative-thinking process: preparation, incubation, illumination, and verification. During the *preparation* stage the manager becomes mentally prepared to make the decision. This phase is characterized by information gathering. Sometimes information comes in the form of reports and other types of data; at other times it is a result of direct experience.

There are four steps in the creative think-ing process.

The second stage is *incubation.* After gathering the necessary data, the manager will often sit back and let the subconscious mind work on the problem. Quite often the result will be a better decision than one that is forced or made in a hurry. On the other hand, if the manager is unable to come up with an effective approach after, say, three to five days, the individual will go back to stage one and start the process anew by gathering additional data or reviewing what is there.

The third stage is *illumination.* This phase is characterized by the manager realizing the best decision to make. Sometimes the decision will suddenly hit the individual; at other times it will slowly dawn on the person. In any event, the manager now knows what to do.

The final stage is *verification.* This stage is reached when the manager modifies or makes final changes in the solution. Quite often the decision will need some fine tuning because of minor problems. After the problems have been resolved, the decision can be fully implemented.

INTERVIEW WITH KAREN BRINKMAN

Karen Brinkman is an executive vice-president and chief information officer at a major southeast bank. Karen received her undergraduate degree (magna cum laude) from the University of Miami and her MBA from Harvard University. In her top management position, Karen is responsible for providing the chairman of the board and the other senior executives with information that will facilitate their decision making in matters ranging from the development of new financial structures for lenders to the most effective strategy to employ in merger and acquisition activities to the effective structuring of the bank's asset–liability portfolio.

Q.   *What types of decisions do you most commonly make?*

A.   Most of my decisions relate to providing recommendations on the financial management of the bank. After examining relevant data, I'll make recommendations related to such things as mergers, acquisitions, profitability issues, asset–liability management, how we can respond most effectively to new government regulations, what changes are taking place in the environment with which we'll have to deal, etc.

Q.   *What types of decision making techniques do you use in formulating these recommendations?*

A.   We rely heavily on computer modeling. What I often do is provide "what if" scenarios. For example, if we acquire a certain piece of equipment, here are the likely benefits and drawbacks that will be associated with the decision. In this way, the executive who will be making the final decision will have the relevant financial facts that will help him or her decide what to do. Similarly, if we are thinking about acquiring a financial institution, we want to know how this

Creative-thinking Techniques

Brainstorming is a popular technique.

It is difficult, if not impossible, for the average manager to be creative on the spur of the moment. However, there are techniques that can help stimulate creative thinking. Many of these are group participation approaches. The most popular is *brainstorming*, which was developed as a method of encouraging creative thinking in an advertising agency. Since its development, the technique has been applied in many situations where it is desirable to obtain a large number of ideas for solving a problem.

The typical brainstorming session begins with the group leader, often the manager, telling the participants the problem under analysis and urging acquisition will affect our profitability and our market share. My job is to provide relevant data to the senior-level group that will make this decision. My information doesn't tell them what to do, but it does give them the data they need for making the decision.

Q.   *Are the decisions you make mostly routine or nonprogrammed?*

A.   That depends on the nature of the decision. We have a great many computer programs we've developed for simulating situations or providing a framework for financial decisions. In these cases, all we have to do is modify the program. However, there are some situations that are unique and it requires us to go back to square one and develop a whole new series of data and interrelationships for evaluating the decision. A good example is mergers and acquisitions (M&A). You seldom can rely on something you did in the past to guide you in making M&A decisions. The situation is always unique.

Q.   *Do you ever use creative decision-making techniques?*

A.   Oh, absolutely. I don't want you to think that this is simply computer modeling and quantitative analysis. When you're in the financial arena you have to be able to develop products and services that the competition either doesn't have or won't develop. You have to create a niche for yourself. We are continually brainstorming about new customer-service delivery approaches that will differentiate us from the competition, as well as ways in which we can manage the results of these approaches. Let me give you a simple example. In the home mortgage market we've been able to develop a viable product by providing at-home service, very competitive rates, and rapid processing of loans. Customers like this and the word gets around. We're now a major player in this market with a significant share of the business because we analyzed the environment and then made the right decisions in getting in. A lot of what I do as the chief information officer helps provide us not only an immediate competitive advantage over the other financial institutions but a sustainable advantage and this means we'll make money both short-term and long-term.

them to be as creative and imaginative as they can in formulating their thoughts (see Table 8-13). Initial emphasis is placed on generating as many ideas as possible without too much consideration of their realism. As people suggest ideas, the others are encouraged to build on them or use them as a basis for developing their own ideas. The final result is often a solution that is creative and superior to anything that would have resulted from individual decision making.

The Gordon technique is used for technical problems.

Another common brainstorming approach is the *Gordon technique.* This is most commonly used for handling technical problems. Unlike brainstorming, however, the participants are not told about the total problem under consideration. They are merely given a hint or stimulus in the form of a word

TABLE 8-13
Popular Creative-thinking Techniques

Osborn Brainstorming
Rules:
1. Judicial thinking or evaluation is ruled out.
2. Freewheeling is welcomed.
3. Quantity is wanted.
4. Combinations and improvements are sought.

Suggestions for the Osborn technique:
1. Length: forty minutes to one hour, sessions of ten to fifteen minutes can be effective if time is short.
2. Do not reveal the problem before the session. An information sheet or suggested reference material on a related subject should be used if prior knowledge of the general field is needed.
3. Problem should be clearly stated and not too broad.
4. Use a small conference table which allows people to communicate with each other easily.
5. If a product is being discussed, samples may be useful as a point of reference.

Gordon Technique
Rules:
1. Only the group leader knows the problem.
2. Free association is used.
3. Subject for discussion must be carefully chosen.

Suggestions for the Gordon technique:
1. Length of session: two to three hours are necessary.
2. Group leader must be exceptionally gifted and thoroughly trained in the use of the technique.

General Suggestions That Apply to Both Techniques:
1. Selection of personnel: a group from diverse backgrounds helps. Try to get a balance of highly active and quiet members.
2. Mixed groups of men and women are often more effective, especially for consumer problems.
3. Although physical atmosphere is not too important, a relaxed pleasant atmosphere is desirable.
4. Group size: groups of from four to twelve can be effective. We recommend six to nine.
5. Newcomers may be introduced without disturbing the group, but they must be properly briefed in the theory of creative thinking and the use of the particular technique.
6. A secretary or recording machine should be used to record the ideas produced. Otherwise, they may not be remembered later. Gordon always uses a blackboard so that ideas can be visualized.
7. Hold sessions in the morning if people are going to continue to work on the same problem after the session has ended; otherwise, hold them in the late afternoon. (The excitement of a session continues for several hours after it is completed and can affect an employee's routine tasks.)
8. Usually it is advisable not to have people from widely differing ranks within the organization in the same session.

Source: Charles F. Whiting, "Operational Techniques of Creative Thinking," *Advanced Management,* October 1955, p. 28.

or phrase and asked to give their ideas. For example, if the research and development manager wanted to know how to develop a more fuel-efficient engine, the individual might start off with the phrase "fuel efficiency." From here the engineers would brainstorm by suggesting ideas on ways to develop an engine that was more fuel efficient than the current offerings. More specifics on this approach are contained in Table 8-13.

Left-brain—Right-brain Dominance

In recent years attention has also been focused on creativity and brain function.[11] Most people are either left-brain dominated or right-brain dominated. The left brain controls the right side of the body and the right brain controls the left side of the body. This dominance also dictates the way people do things. For example, left-brain people tend to be very logical, rational, detailed, active, and objectives oriented. Right-brain people are more spontaneous, emotional, holistic, nonverbal, and visual in their approach to things.

Whole-brain thinking is now being developed.

Left-brain people make decisions differently from right-brain people.[12] They tend to be less creative and imaginative. Most managers fit into this category. In an effort to get them to use both sides of their brain, some companies are now giving their people "whole-brain" training in which the participants learn how to use each side of their brain (see Intrapreneurship in Action: Developing Executive Brain Skills). The focus is on making highly rational thinkers more creative and inducing highly intuitive persons to supplement their approach with greater emphasis on detail, logic, and procedure. Some of the exercises used include (a) internal brainstorming—freeing one's imagination and then evaluating the ideas; (b) cinematics—envisioning situations in one's mind; (c) inside-outs—turning facts upside down in an effort to find fresh solutions; (d) suspenders—overstimulating the left side of the brain in order to free the creative right side; (e) hearings—learning how to move into either brain side at will; and (f) uprights—learning how to shift left when the situation demands it.[13] The approach is proving to be an excellent supplement to standard creative thinking techniques such as those described above.[14]

■ SUMMARY

This chapter has examined the fundamentals of decision making. The decision-making process consists of: (1) identifying the problem, (2) diagnosing the situation, (3) collecting and analyzing data relevant to the issue, (4) ascertaining solutions that may be used in solving the problem, (5) analyzing these alternative solutions, (6) selecting the one that appears most likely to solve the problem, and (7) implementing it. Yet the decision-making process

---

[11]Weston H. Agor, "Nurturing Executive Intrapreneurship with a Brain-Skill Management Program," *Business Horizons*, May–June 1988, pp. 12–15.

[12]Daniel Robey and William Taggart, "Measuring Manager's Minds: The Assessment of Style in Human Information Processing," *Academy of Management Review*, July 1981, pp. 375–83.

[13]Jacquelyn Wonder and Priscilla Donovan, *Whole-Brain Thinking* (New York: William Morrow and Company, Inc., 1984), p. 11.

[14]For more on this area see Tim Smithin, "Maps of the Mind: New Pathways to Decision-Making," *Business Horizons*, December 1980, pp. 24–28.

INTRAPRENEURSHIP IN ACTION: Developing Executive Brain Skills

One way to increase organizational productivity is by developing intrapreneurship, and many organizations are finding that brain-skills management programs can help in this process. Research shows that intrapreneurial managers tend to be right-brain thinkers. They are more intuitive than they are analytical. How can these skills be identified, nurtured, and used? One way is through the use of what are called brain-skill management (BSM) programs.

A BSM program has three major parts: diagnostic testing, custom placement based on the situation or problem, and training in brain-skill development. The diagnostic testing is used to identify which managers are right-brain and which are left-brain. This gives the organization a basis for determining the assignments at which each manager can excel.

Based on the results, managers are then assigned to various projects or problems. For example, a manager who is a right-brain thinker will be teamed up with other similarly intuitive individuals and assigned situations or problems that require creative solutions. Similarly, those who are left-brain thinkers will be grouped and assigned problems that require analysis, logical thought, and detailed coordination. Each group will work in those areas where it excels.

Finally, managers are given brain-skills training so that they can further develop their abilities. For example, right-brain thinkers are taught how to strengthen their intuitive skills by learning such techniques as self-hypnosis, guided imagery, and lateral styles of thinking. This, in turn, will increase their intrapreneurial skills.

Does this form of training really pay off? Research shows that it does. In one case the Department of Defense put fifteen super-grade executives through a brain-skills management training course in order to strengthen their intrapreneurial abilities. The agency found that by the end of the program the executives had been able to develop a series of proposals designed to increase productivity, stimulate motivation, and improve operations. One of the major challenges facing organizations today is that of finding new and more effective methods of increasing productivity. BSM programs are one of the latest developments in this area, and they appear to be a very effective way of teaching and nurturing intrapreneurial skills which are so important to organizational productivity.

Source: Weston H. Agor, "Nurturing Executive Intrapreneurship with a Brain-Skill Management Program," *Business Horizons*, May–June 1988, pp. 12–15.

is much more than simply following a list of steps; a great deal of subjective as well as objective evaluation must take place. For example, the personal values of the top manager will play a significant role in the assignment of risk and uncertainty probabilities. In many cases even modern managerial decision making may well be 75 percent subjective, 25 percent objective.

Nevertheless, the manager must be as rational as possible, drawing upon all available techniques and guidelines in choosing among the various alternatives. Some of the techniques that are most useful in this process include the Laplace criterion, the maximin criterion, the maximax criterion, marginal analysis, financial analysis, and the Delphi technique. And these represent only a few of the techniques available to the modern manager. Modern decision making is notable for the great variety of decision-making aids it has discovered.

The last part of the chapter examined creativity and decision making. Creative thinking has four stages: preparation, incubation, illumination, and verification. There are a number of techniques that can be used to help stimulate creative thinking. Two of the most popular are brainstorming and the Gordon technique. Recent interest has also been generated in the area of whole-brain thinking: teaching managers to use both sides of their brain. Left-brain thinkers are being taught to be more creative; right-brain thinkers are being shown how to approach problem solving more logically and sequentially. This latter area is extremely important in decision making and is the focus of attention in the next chapter.

■ REVIEW AND STUDY QUESTIONS

1. What is meant by the term *decision making?*
2. What are the steps in the decision-making process? Explain each.
3. What is meant by the term *rationality?* Are all decisions rational ones? Defend your answer.
4. How does value orientation affect the decision-making process? Give an illustration.
5. What are organizational decisions and personal decisions? Basic and routine decisions? Programmed and nonprogrammed decisions? Give an illustration of each.
6. How does a procedure differ from a policy?
7. What are the three basic conditions under which decisions are made? Explain each.
8. What roles do objective and subjective probability play in the decision-making process?
9. How does risk preference affect the decision-making process?
10. Of what benefit is marginal analysis to the manager in the decision-making process? Give an illustration.
11. Of what value is financial analysis to the manager in the decision-making process? Give an illustration.
12. How can a manager use the Delphi technique in making a technological forecast? Explain by discussing the steps in the process.

13. How can a strategic criteria approach help a business forecast the success of a technological innovation? Explain.

14. How does the creative thinking process work? Be sure to include in your answer a discussion of the four stages of the process.

15. How does brainstorming differ from the Gordon technique? Explain.

16. How does a left-brain thinker differ from a right-brain thinker? Compare and contrast the two.

17. Of what value is whole-brain thinking to effective decision making? Explain your answer.

■ SELECTED REFERENCES

Agor, Weston H. "Nurturing Executive Intrapreneurship with a Brain-Skill Management Program." *Business Horizons*, May–June 1988, pp. 12–15.

Anderson, Paul A. "Decision Making by Objection and the Cuban Missile Crisis." *Administrative Science Quarterly*, June 1983, pp. 201–22.

Drucker, Peter F. *Management: Tasks, Responsibilities, Practices*. New York: Harper & Row, 1974, chap. 37.

Einhorn, Hillel J., and Robin M. Hogarth. "Decision Making: Going Forward in Reverse," *Harvard Business Review*," January–February 1987, pp. 66–70.

Fiegenbaum, Avi, and Howard Thomas. "Attitudes Toward Risk-Return Paradox: Prospect Theory Explanations." *Academy of Management Journal*, March 1988, pp. 85–106.

Guth, William D., and Renato Tagiuri. "Personal Values and Corporate Strategy." *Harvard Business Review*, September–October 1965, pp. 123–32.

Hodgetts, Richard M. "Applying the Delphi Technique to Management Gaming." *Simulation*, July 1977, pp. 209–12.

Ives, B. D. "Decisions Theory and the Practicing Manager." *Business Horizons*, June 1973, pp. 38–40.

Lee, James A. "Changes in Managerial Values: 1965–1986." *Business Horizons*, July–August 1988, pp. 29–37.

McGann, Joseph E., and Thomas N. Gilmore. "Diagnosing Organizational Decision Making through Responsibility Charting." *Sloan Management Review*, Winter 1983, pp. 3–15.

Neumann, S., and E. Segev. "Human Resources and Corporate Risk Management." *Personnel Journal*, February 1978, pp. 76–79.

Post, Tom. "Managing the Unknown," *Success*, July–August 1988, p. 20.

Robey, Daniel, and William Taggart. "Measuring Managers' Minds: The Assessment of Style in Human Information Processing." *Academy of Management Review*, July 1981, pp. 375–83.

Roman, D. D. "Technological Forecasting in the Decision Process." *Academy of Management Journal*, June 1970, pp. 127–38.

Rowe, Alan J., Warren Bennis, and James D. Boulgarides. "Desexing Decision Styles." *Personnel*, January–February 1984, pp. 43–52.

Sihler, W. W. "Framework for Financial Decisions." *Harvard Business Review*, March–April 1971, pp. 123–35.

Simon, Herbert I. *The New Science of Management Decision*. New York: Harper & Bros., 1960.

Smithin, Tim. "Maps of the Mind: New Pathways to Decision Making." *Business Horizons*, December 1980, pp. 24–28.

Stanley, John D. "Dissent in Organizations." *Academy of Management Review*, January 1981, pp. 13–19.

Wonder, Jacquelyn, and Priscilla Donovan. *Whole-Brain Thinking*. New York: William Morrow and Company, Inc., 1984.

■ CASE: Making Imagination Pay Off

One of the major activities carried out by many business firms is the creation of new goods and services. In fact, among large consumer goods firms like Johnson & Johnson and 3M, more than 25 percent of the product line consists of products that have come to market in the last five years. Some of the latest products to reach the market are designed to meet the needs of small market niches. For example, Abbott Laboratories has developed an AIDS antibody test and Merck has discovered a cholesterol-lowering drug. Other products are much more widely used.

Many of these new goods are a result of emerging markets. For example, in the early 1970s Corning Glass tried to sell General Motors a new line of safety windshields. The big automaker was not interested, but the company did express an urgent need for an antipollution device that would help it produce a car that would meet the new air emission controls that Congress was about to enact. After checking and ensuring that a market did exist for the product, Corning scientists went to work on the problem. They created a ceramic device that was porous enough to do the job and then developed a new process that turned out precision-made units. Today, as a result, the company sells over $150 million annually of these ceramic antipollution devices.

In the early 1980s Procter & Gamble's share of the baby diaper market declined dramatically. The firm decided to fight back by developing a product that would be more absorbent than any on the market. In the process, the company's research and development people turned out a diaper that was both highly absorbent and much thinner than previous models. Mothers were impressed with the new product's characteristics and the firm's share of the market has now increased to over 50 percent.

New product development decisions are the future lifeblood of many firms. Despite the large investments and the high risks that are often involved, this activity will continue to be a major one for many companies throughout the current decade.

Questions

1. Of the values set forth by Edward Spranger, which two are most reflected by the firms in this case? Explain.

2. Were the decisions to proceed with new product developments examples of decision making under risk or uncertainty? Defend your answer.

3. Are R&D scientists left-brain or right-brain people? Explain your answer.

Source: Kenneth Labich, "The Innovators," *Fortune*, June 6, 1988, pp. 49–64.

■ CASE: One, Two, or Three

Lawrence Sims had fought the proposed increase in plant facilities. "It's a poor idea," he told the board of directors, "because there just isn't enough demand to sustain this increased supply. Four major firms have entered our industry in the last year, and three more are knocking on the door; they know a profitable venture when they see one. The days of high prices and high profits are over. We are in for at least a decade of severe competition. Instead of increasing our capacity, we ought to be considering a new industry to invest funds in, one that might make us a 15 percent return on investment. Right now we have all our eggs in one basket, and we are jeopardizing them by increasing our commitment with a 25 percent increase in plant. We may even be endangering the basket. This is irresponsible!"

The board listened attentively but outvoted the president. Plant expansion was ordered for completion within eighteen months. Sims decided that the only way to salvage the company was to find some way of increasing demand for the product. After ten months of investigation and research, the president and his top executives agreed that three basic strategies were available. First, they could increase the amount of advertising from $300,000 to $400,000. This would result in total sales of $30 million. Second, they could lower the price of the product by 20 percent. Market research data indicated that this would lead to sales of $60,000,000. Finally, they could opt for a strong research and development program. If the firm invested $1 million in R&D, sales for the upcoming year would be $25 million. In terms of success probability, the executives estimated that the first of these strategies had a 60 percent chance of succeeding, the second had a 20 percent chance, and the third had a 70 percent success probability. In addition, the tax rates associated with the three were 48, 50, and 46 percent respectively.

Questions

1. Is this a case of decision making under certainty, risk, or uncertainty? Explain.

2. What are the expected values associated with each of the three strategies? Show all your calculations. In light of your work, which of the three strategies should the management choose?

3. Will the net profit margin before taxes associated with each of the three strategies have any bearing on the final decision? Explain why or why not.

CASE: The Car Dealer's Dilemma

A local car dealer has been making an estimate of the number of cars his agency will sell with three strategies—low price, increased advertising, and improved service—under two states of nature—average or dynamic growth of the gross national product (GNP). His data are shown in the table:

Strategies	States of Nature	
	Average Growth of GNP	Dynamic Growth of GNP
Low price	1,300 cars	1,400 cars
Increased advertising	1,200 cars	1,600 cars
Improved service	1,250 cars	1,500 cars

Questions

1. Using the Laplace criterion, which applies equal probability to all states of nature, which of the above three strategies should the dealer implement? Give your reasoning.

2. If the dealer uses the maximin approach, which of the above three strategies should he implement? Explain.

3. If the dealer employs a maximax criterion and assigns a 0.8 probability to dynamic growth and a 0.2 probability to average growth, which of the above alternatives should he implement? Explain.

CASE: The Advertising Campaign

A large southeast metropolis has just finished constructing an elevated train system. Known as Metro Rail, the system has thirty-five train stations spread throughout the city. There currently are plans to extend the system to the suburbs, but this expansion will not get under way for at least another year.

The city commission believes that with this new transportation system, traffic congestion during morning and evening rush hours will be greatly reduced. Additionally, given the fact that there are many retired people who live in this metropolis, the commission is convinced that these residents will be able to move about the city in a more leisurely way by taking the train than by riding the bus. In particular, each train station has a large indoor area where riders can wait in comfort for the train, and posted time schedules for the trains are proving to be very reliable.

The Metro Rail complex cost $1.5 billion. Much of this cost was paid by the federal government. In order to secure federal funding for expansion of the system and to meet the arguments of local critics who say that the entire project was a waste of money, the city is going to have to prove that the complex is being heavily used and is a benefit to the metropolis. Unfortunately, statistics do not bear out this assumption. Average daily ridership during the first three months has been under 7,000. (There are over 1.5 million people in the metropolis.) The commission believes that the major problem is one of changing living habits. Most working people are accustomed to driving to their jobs, and retired citizens are used to taking the bus. These habits will have to be changed if the city is to get full use from its new train system.

Four months after the Metro Rail opened, the city commission decided to bring in an advertising agency for the purpose of acquainting the public with the advantages of riding the train and, it was hoped, change their current transportation habits. Jane Whitney is president of this ad firm. Yesterday she had the first meeting with her people regarding the type of campaign they would run. She put a strong emphasis on the need for creativity and original thinking. The group is scheduled to meet again tomorrow and every day next week. Jane has three weeks to present the commission with a fully developed advertising campaign. Once it is approved, the ads will then be released to the radio, TV, and print media.

Questions

1. What is the exact nature of the problem confronting Jane? In what way will an understanding of the decision making process help her identify and refine her job? Be complete in your answer.

2. Given the nature of the problem, what creative thinking technique(s) would you recommend that Jane employ? Explain your answer.

3. If the people on the commission are all engineers by training, will this make her job of selling them on her recommended campaign any harder? Why or why not?

■ SELF-FEEDBACK EXERCISE: Risk-taking and You

How much of a risk-taker are you? Read each of the following scenarios and place a checkmark next to your choice. The scoring procedures and interpretation are provided at the end of the exercise.

1. You are a college football coach and are ranked number two in the polls. You are playing the number-one-ranked team for the national title and are three points behind with five seconds to go. You have two choices. One is a very short field goal that will earn you a tie. The other is a trick play that will give you a touchdown if it works. Following are the probabilities or odds that the risky play will succeed. Check the lowest probability that you would consider acceptable for the risky play to be attempted.

   _____ The chances are 1 in 10 that the play will work.
   _____ The chances are 3 in 10 that the play will work.
   _____ The chances are 5 in 10 that the play will work.
   _____ The chances are 7 in 10 that the play will work.
   _____ The chances are 9 in 10 that the play will work.
   _____ You would not try the play regardless of the probability of success.

2. You have inherited $25,000 and intend to invest it in the stock market for a period of one year. You have decided on one of two stocks. Stock A is a blue chip and will provide you a return of between 6 to 9 percent. Stock B is a speculative issue that, if things go well for the firm, will double in value over the next year. If things do not go well, however, it is likely that you will lose your entire investment. What is the lowest probability that you would consider acceptable before investing in Stock B?

   _____ The probability of the firm's doing well is 1 in 10.
   _____ The probability of the firm's doing well is 3 in 10.
   _____ The probability of the firm's doing well is 5 in 10.
   _____ The probability of the firm's doing well is 7 in 10.
   _____ The probability of the firm's doing well is 9 in 10.
   _____ You would not invest in the issue regardless of the probability of success.

3. You own your own small research and development firm. You want to hire a research scientist and two have applied. Ms. A is very intelligent and will fit in well, although she is unlikely to generate any significant research and development discoveries. Mr. B is brilliant and has a large number of patents to his name. However, he is very difficult to work with and is regarded by colleagues as something of a screwball. What is the lowest probability of his working out with your firm that you would consider acceptable before hiring him?

   _____ A probability of 1 in 10.
   _____ A probability of 3 in 10.
   _____ A probability of 5 in 10.
   _____ A probability of 7 in 10.
   _____ A probability of 9 in 10.
   _____ You would not hire him regardless of the probability of his working out well.

4. Your company is going to expand operations and the final choice is up to you. One location is Phoenix where the expected return on investment is 15 percent. The other is a South American country where the expected return is 22 percent. However, there is a chance that after the general elections next year, the overseas operations might be nationalized and your firm would lose all of its investment. What is the lowest probability of nationalization not occurring that you would consider acceptable before setting up operations in this country.

_____ The chances are 1 in 10 that nationalization will not occur.
_____ The chances are 3 in 10 that nationalization will not occur.
_____ The chances are 5 in 10 that nationalization will not occur.
_____ The chances are 7 in 10 that nationalization will not occur.
_____ The chances are 9 in 10 that nationalization will not occur.
_____ You will not recommend expansion into this country regardless of the likelihood of nationalization.

5. You are at the Kentucky Derby and have your eye on two horses: the favorite who is going off at even money and a long shot who is going off at 25 to 1. You intend to bet $100. What is the lowest probability you would accept before betting on the long shot?

_____ 1 chance in 10.
_____ 3 chances in 10.
_____ 5 chances in 10.
_____ 7 chances in 10.
_____ 9 chances in 10.
_____ You would not bet the long shot regardless of its probability of winning.

6. If you stay in your current headquarters location, you can expect average raises for the rest of your time with the firm. If you take an offer to head up the company office in Buffalo, you will eventually be called back to headquarters and may be promoted into the upper ranks of management. Your promotion status will depend on how well you perform in Buffalo. Check the lowest probability that you would consider acceptable before agreeing to head up the Buffalo office.

_____ 1 chance in 10 of doing well in Buffalo.
_____ 3 chances in 10 of doing well in Buffalo.
_____ 5 chances in 10 of doing well in Buffalo.
_____ 7 chances in 10 of doing well in Buffalo.
_____ 9 chances in 10 of doing well in Buffalo.
_____ You would not take the Buffalo assignment regardless of the probability of later promotion.

7. Your college baseball team is two runs behind with men on first and second in the bottom of the ninth. There is one out and the opposition

has just brought in its star relief pitcher. Your team is sending up its best batter. The individual is hitting .455 and leading the nation in home runs and runs batted in. The three men to follow have batting averages of .244, .310, and .271, respectively. Your friend believes that your team will lose and is willing to bet you $100 that he is right. What is the lowest probability of your team's winning that you would accept before taking the bet?

_____ 1 chance in 10.
_____ 3 chances in 10.
_____ 5 chances in 10.
_____ 7 chances in 10.
_____ 9 chances in 10.
_____ You would not accept the bet regardless of the odds.

8. You are having trouble with your car. If you take it to the dealer it will cost you $450, but the work will be guaranteed for a period of 60 days. If you have the car fixed at the local service station, it will cost you $125 but the work will not be guaranteed. What is the lowest probability that you would accept before taking the car to the service station to have the work done?

_____ 1 chance in 10 that the work is done right.
_____ 3 chances in 10 that the work is done right.
_____ 5 chances in 10 that the work is done right.
_____ 7 chances in 10 that the work is done right.
_____ 9 chances in 10 that the work is done right.
_____ You would not take the car to the service station regardless of the probability of success.

9. You have two one-year job offers. The first is a guaranteed $20,000. The second is for $5,000 plus 5 percent of all sales you make. What is the lowest probability of your making over $20,000 that you would consider acceptable before taking the second offer?

_____ 1 chance in 10.
_____ 3 chances in 10.
_____ 5 chances in 10.
_____ 7 chances in 10.
_____ 9 chances in 10.
_____ You would not accept the second offer regardless of the probability of making over $20,000.

10. You are going to be entering the College of Business and have narrowed your selection of majors to marketing and accounting. You would be happy majoring in either. The marketing department has a very low flunkout rate but the salaries being paid to marketing graduates is much less than that paid to accountants. On the other hand, the accounting

department is notorious for its high flunkout rate. What is the lowest probability you would accept of your successfully completing the accounting program?

_____   1 chance in 10.
_____   3 chances in 10.
_____   5 chances in 10.
_____   7 chances in 10.
_____   9 chances in 10.
_____   You would not major in accounting regardless of the probability of getting through the program.

Scoring

Go back to each of your answers and note the probability that you checked. If you checked 1 in 10, your score on the situation is 1; if you checked 5 chances in 10, your score on that situation is 5, and so on. If you said that you would not take the chance, your score for that situation is 10. Notice that the lower your risk-taking willingness in a particular situation, the higher your score. Now enter your 10 scores below and total them.

1.   ____
2.   ____
3.   ____
4.   ____
5.   ____
6.   ____
7.   ____
8.   ____
9.   ____
10.   ____
Total   ____

Interpretation

Are you a high risk-taker? Are you basically a risk-avoider? The answer will depend on how low (or high) your score is. Based on all of those who have taken this exercise, the following provides a general picture of willingness to take risk:

10–40   High risk-takers
41–70   Moderate risk-takers
71–100   Low risk-takers

Modern Quantitative Decision-Making Tools and Processes

Mathematical decision making has been given increased emphasis in recent years. The goal of this chapter is to examine some of the mathematical tools and processes currently being employed by managers, especially those in the area of operations management. However, the quantitative approach has both advantages and disadvantages. On the positive side, for example, quantitative techniques make it possible to screen out many of the subjective processes that often cause a decision to go awry. Also, quantitative processes sometimes allow faster and more accurate solutions to complex problems. On the other hand, quantitative tools cannot guarantee effective decision making; they have numerous limitations. For example, if the mathematical expression or model does not properly represent reality, the answer will be wrong. If, say, a manager estimates that Decision A will produce either $1 million or nothing and that it has a success probability of 10 percent, whereas Decision B will produce either $200,000 or nothing and it has a success probability of 90 percent, it will be wiser to choose Decision B. The former has an expected payoff of only $100,000 [($1,000,000)(0.10) + ($0)(0.90)], but the latter has an expected payoff of $180,000 [($200,000)(0.90) + ($0)(0.10)].

But what if the manager is wrong in these estimates? What if Decision A's probability for success is really 0.90 and Decision B's is only 0.10? Then, because of erroneous probability assignments, the manager has made a serious mistake. Decision A's expected payoff of $900,000 [($1,000,000)(0.90) + ($0)(0.10)] will be much larger than Decision B's payoff of $20,000 [($200,000)(0.10) + ($0)(0.90)].

It must also be remembered that sometimes the costs associated with a quantitative solution do not justify the returns: A mathematical approach may be much more expensive than a nonmathematical one. Additionally, it is often difficult to quantify all the necessary variables associated with a problem, and in such cases it may not be possible to use a quantitative approach.

Nevertheless, many managers find mathematical tools and techniques very helpful in the decision-making process. In this chapter some of the most useful tools will be examined. In certain cases in the chapter, a mathematical explanation will be given, whereas in others, because of time and space limitations, only a qualitative description is offered.

When you have finished this chapter, you should be able to:

1. Define the term *operations research*.

2. Discuss the value of linear programming in the decision-making process.

3. State the importance of the economic order quantity formula in solving inventory control problems.

4. Solve simple game theory problems.

5. Explain how both queuing theory and the Monte Carlo method can help the manager in decision making.

6. Describe a decision tree and state its value in handling both short- and long-run problems.

7. Provide some illustrations of the kinds of problems managers often solve with heuristic programming.

OPERATIONS RESEARCH

The application of quantitative methods to decision making began in earnest during World War II. The approach has been termed *operations research*, or management science. Herbert A. Simon tersely summed up its history when he wrote:

Operations research is a movement that, emerging out of the military needs of World War II, has brought the decision-making problems of management within the range of interests of large numbers of natural scientists and, particularly, of mathematicians and statisticians. The operations researchers soon joined forces with mathematical economists who had come into the same area—to the mutual benefit of both groups. And by now there has been widespread fraternization between these exponents of the "new" scientific management and . . . industrial engineering. No meaningful line can be drawn any more to demarcate operations research from scientific management or scientific management from management science.[1]

Since it is so difficult to specify the domain of operations research, there has been considerable confusion over the use of the term. Some attach it to any new mathematical approach to decision making. Others (for example, mathematicians, physicists, and engineers) claim that an interdisciplinary approach must be involved. Still others contend that the process or technique must be sophisticated before it falls under the heading of OR. In an attempt to make the area understandable, Harold Koontz, Cyril O'Donnell, and Heinz Weihrich have identified the essential OR decision-making methods as follows:

Here are the essential methods of OR.

1. An emphasis on models that symbolize the relationship among the variables that are involved.
2. An emphasis on goals and the development of techniques for measuring effectiveness.
3. The incorporation of at least the most important variables into the model.
4. The design of a mathematical model.
5. The quantification of all variables to the greatest degree possible.
6. The supplementation of quantifiable data with the use of probability.[2]

Using these essentials, operations research has developed a number of problem-solving tools and techniques, including linear programming, inventory control, game theory, queuing theory, and Monte Carlo simulation. Before examining these, however, keep in mind that these tools help decision makers but are no substitute for experience and judgment.

LINEAR PROGRAMMING

What is linear programming?

One of the most widely used techniques of operations research is that of *linear programming*. Robert O. Ferguson and Lauren F. Sargent have described it as:

A technique for specifying how to use limited resources or capacities of a business to obtain a particular objective, such as least cost, highest margin, or least time, when those resources have alternative uses. It is a

---

[1]Herbert A. Simon, *The New Science of Management Decision* (New York: Harper & Bros., 1960), p. 15.

[2]Adapted from Harold Koontz, Cyril O'Donnell, and Heinz Weihrich, *Management*, 8th ed. (New York: McGraw-Hill, 1984), p. 224.

technique that systematizes for certain conditions the process of selecting the most desirable course of action from a number of available courses of action, thereby giving management information for making a more effective decision about the resources under its control.[3]

Characteristics of linear programming problems.

All linear programming problems must have two basic characteristics. First, two or more activities must be competing for limited resources. Second, all relationships in the problem must be linear. If these two conditions exist, the technique can be employed. One of the best ways to grasp the fundamentals of the approach is to use it to solve a particular problem. Following is a simple illustration of an allocation problem, using one of the most common linear programming approaches, the graphic method.

The Graphic Method

Company A wishes to maximize its profit by manufacturing two products: Model A and Model B. A wholesaler has signed a contract promising to take off the company's hands at a predetermined price all the goods it can manufacture over the next thirty days. The basic question, therefore, is how many units of each to manufacture. Analysis reveals the data in Table 9-1.

Here is a mathematical expression of the constraints.

Taking into account the information in the table, how many Model A and Model B units should be manufactured? Merely looking at the data will not provide an answer. However, the analyst can draw certain conclusions in regard to the constraints. For example, no more than 21,000 hours of manufacturing time are available to produce the two models. The constraint can be written in this way:

$$15A + 10B \leq 1,200 \text{ hours.}$$

Likewise, the other three constraints (painting, assembly, and test) can be expressed as follows:

$$1A + 1B \leq 1,200 \text{ hours}$$
$$3A + 2B \leq 3,000 \text{ hours}$$
$$3A \leq 2,400 \text{ hours.}$$

In addition, maximization of the profit objective can be expressed by the statement:

$$\text{Profit maximization} = \$400A + \$300B,$$

subject, of course, to the initial four constraints and to the fact that A and B cannot be negative. Since there is no such thing as negative production, $A \geq 0$ and $B \geq 0$.

Having identified the constraints and the profit maximization function, the maximum number of units that can be manufactured can now be determined.

---

[3]Robert O. Ferguson and Lauren F. Sargent, *Linear Programming* (New York: McGraw-Hill, 1958), p. 3.

TABLE 9-1
Company A's
Resources

| Product | Hours Required per Unit | | | | Profit per Unit |
	Manufacture	Paint	Assembly	Test	
Model A	15.0	1.0	3.0	3.0	$400
Model B	10.0	1.0	2.0	—	300
Hours available during next 30 days	21,000	1,200	3,000	2,400	

That is:

$$15A + 10V \leq 21{,}000 \text{ hours.}$$

If

$$B = 0,$$

then

$$15A \leq 21{,}000$$
$$A \leq 1{,}400.$$

Conversely, if

$$A = 0,$$

then

$$10B \leq 21{,}000$$
$$B \leq 2{,}100.$$

Thus, if only one model is produced, the greatest number of Model A and Model B units that can be manufactured is 1,400 and 2,100 respectively. This can be graphed as in Figure 9-1.

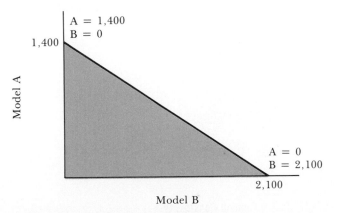

FIGURE 9-1   Manufacturing Constraints

The maximum number of units of A and B respectively that can be painted is:

$$1A + 1B \leq 1{,}200 \text{ hours.}$$

If

$$B = 0,$$

then

$$1A \leq 1{,}200$$
$$A \leq 1{,}200.$$

Conversely, if

$$A = 0,$$

then

$$1B \leq 1{,}200$$
$$B \leq 1{,}200.$$

This can be graphed as in Figure 9-2.

In terms of the assembly constraint, the number of Model A and Model B units that it is possible to assemble can be determined as follows:

$$3A + 2B \leq 3{,}000.$$

If

$$B = 0,$$

then

$$3A = 3{,}000$$
$$A \leq 1{,}000.$$

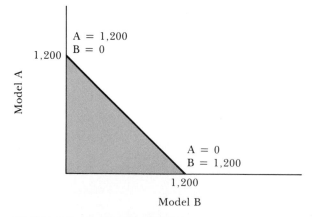

FIGURE 9-2   Painting Constraints

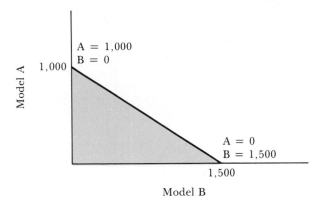

FIGURE 9-3   Assembly Constraints

Conversely, if

$$A = 0,$$

then

$$2B \leq 3,000$$
$$B \leq 1,500.$$

This can be graphed as in Figure 9-3.

Finally, although Model B requires no testing, the number of Model A units that it is possible to test can be determined as follows:

$$3A \leq 2,400$$
$$A \leq 800.$$

This can be graphed as in Figure 9-4.

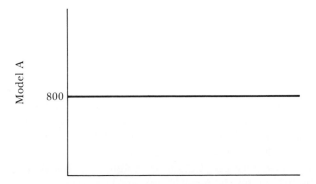

FIGURE 9-4   Testing Constraints

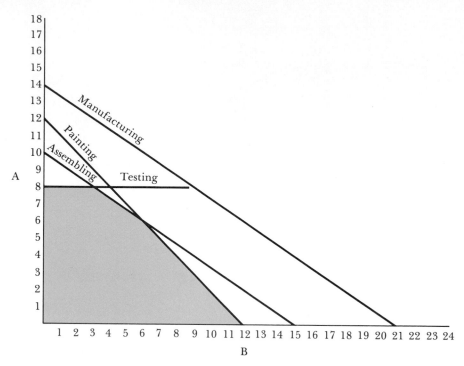

FIGURE 9-5   Feasibility Area (in hundreds of units)

The feasibility area represents all possible production combinations.

All four graphs can then be consolidated; what emerges is Figure 9-5. The area that is shaded is the feasibility area; that is, any combination of Model A and Model B can be produced as long as it falls within this area. Everything outside the area is infeasible because those particular combinations will require more manufacturing, painting, assembling, and/or testing hours than are available.

The next question is, what combination of those that are feasible should be manufactured? It has already been ascertained that:

$$\text{Profit Maximization} = \$400A + \$300B.$$

The computation of the isoprofit line is explained.

Therefore, for every three units of A or four units of B sold, the profit will be identical: $1,200. The ratio of A to B will be 3 to 4. If this ratio is maintained, starting as close to the origin as possible and gradually working outward, all combinations of feasible production can eventually be analyzed. Figure 9-6 shows this, the isoprofit line, for $1,200. If this line is continued out to its furthest point from the origin, it will either come to rest on one of the lines forming the feasibility boundary area, or it will nick one of the four points labeled A, B, C, and D respectively in the figure. The slope of the isoprofit line shows that it will probably touch one of the four points before continuing out into the infeasible area, and this is precisely what happens.

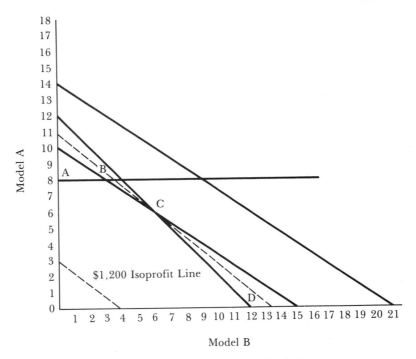

FIGURE 9-6 $1,200 Isoprofit Line (in hundreds of units)

The isoprofit line will touch Point C, and it is here that profit is maximized at 600 units of Model A and 600 units of Model B. This can be verified by examining all four points—A, B, C, and D.

Point A: $400 (800) + $300 (0)   = $320,000.
Point B: $400 (800) + $300 (300)   = $410,000.
Point C: $400 (600) + $300 (600)   = $420,000.
Point D: $400 (0)   + $300 (1,200) = $360,000.

No other combination will result in as much profit as that obtained at Point C. This statement can be tested. The verifier simply has to remember the constraints that are present—for example, that one unit of A cannot be traded for one unit of B because it takes more time to manufacture a unit of A than to manufacture a unit of B.

These are the limita-
tions of linear pro-
gramming.
Linear programming can be used in the solution of many kinds of allocation decision problems, but its application is certainly limited. The first limitation is that the decision problem must be formulated in quantitative terms for linear programming to be employed effectively. In many instances, the costs associated with gathering these data outweigh the savings obtained from the use of the technique. Likewise, many allocation problems do not lend themselves to this approach because the relationship between the variables is not linear. Approximate solutions are sometimes possible in such

cases. Finally, unless all variables are known with certainty, in which case the model is deterministic, it is sometimes impossible to use the technique. Nevertheless, the approach has many advantages, and its application in the area of business decision making is increasing.

INVENTORY CONTROL

Another common problem faced by some managers is that of maintaining adequate inventories. No one wants to have too many units available because there are costs associated with carrying these goods. On the other hand, a store that runs out of inventory risks losing a customer's future business (see International Business in Action: Cheaper by the Dozen). To resolve this dilemma, the manager must analyze costs and formulate some assumptions about supply and demand.

Two types of costs merit the manager's consideration. The first are *clerical and administrative costs*, expenses associated with ordering inventory. Every time an order for more goods is placed, time and effort are expended. Naturally, if a firm wished to reduce these particular costs to their lowest possible level, it could place one order covering all the goods that would be needed for the entire year. However, that is a very unrealistic solution in view of the second type of costs, popularly known as carrying costs. *Carrying costs* are the amount of money invested in the inventory and other sundry expenses covering storage space, taxes, and obsolescence. The greater the inventory the firm carries, the greater its carrying costs will be.

Solving the Problem

Three assumptions are often made in determining optimal inventory size.

One way for the manager to solve the inventory problem is to make certain assumptions regarding future demand and then attempt a solution. Three of the most common assumptions made in determining optimal inventory size are that: (1) demand is known with certainty; (2) the lead time necessary for reordering goods is also known with certainty; and (3) the inventory will be depleted at a constant rate. These assumptions can be diagrammed as in Figure 9-7.

These three assumptions are obviously not realistic at all times, but they do provide a basis from which the manager can make a decision. Now the manager has to decide whether to use what can be labeled a trial-and-error approach or an OR tool known as the *economic order quantity* (EOQ) formula.

The EOQ formula is important. To show how this is so, one can solve a problem using two methods: trial and error and EOQ. Assume that Guy Smith is the manager of an appliance department for a large eastern discount store. He has estimated annual demand for blenders for the upcoming year to be 5,000. Further, he has calculated the order costs (clerical and administrative) as $100 per order and has broken down carrying costs into component parts as follows: (1) the value of a blender is $20; (2) insurance, taxes, storage, and other expenses are 5 percent per year; and (3) average inventory carried

INTERNATIONAL
BUSINESS
IN
ACTION:
Cheaper
by
the
Dozen

Over the last ten years a number of quantitative management techniques have been used by business firms in their efforts to reduce overhead and balance inventory. One of the most successful approaches has been that of Alan Sugar, a British entrepreneur. His strategy is "pile 'em high and sell 'em cheap." Rather than employing sophisticated quantitative analysis, Sugar relies heavily on high discounting and volume purchasing.

In 1980 Sugar's company, Amstrad, was a $19-million-a-year firm that was supplying stereos and videocassette recorders. Sugar then began branching out into the microcomputer business. In 1985 the firm introduced its first word processing computer. Industry analysts estimated annual demand at 50,000 units. Sugar priced his machine at $570 and was soon selling 50,000 units a month. Within a year his company was the first European firm to introduce an inexpensive IBM PC clone which sold for under $600. It took less than 12 months for Amstrad to double the British PC market, and he then pushed into France and Spain.

How does Sugar do it? By farming out the manufacturing to a network of Asian subcontractors that produce the machines at rock-bottom prices. If prices get too high or profit margins too slim, Sugar abandons the market. For example, in 1984 he left the VCR market. However, he was back 18 months later with a televideo—a unit that combines TV and VCR.

Recently Amstrad has been setting up wholly-owned subsidiaries in both Europe and the United States. The firm has also introduced a series of new products including a laptop computer, two low-price CD players, a four-channel music-mixing system for home use, and a low-price camcorder. The company has also struck a deal with IBM that gives it worldwide access to IBM patents. As a result, analysts believe that revenues and pretax margins should grow at an annual rate of 20 percent. Quite obviously Alan Sugar's philosophy of volume selling at discount prices is proving to be a highly successful quantitative decision-making approach.

Source: Richard L. Kirkland, Jr., "Pile 'Em High and Sell 'Em Cheap," *Fortune,* August 29, 1988, pp. 91–92.

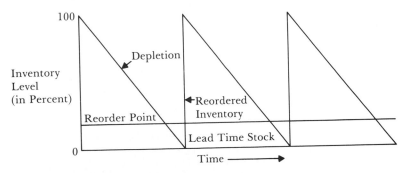

FIGURE 9-7   Constant Depletion Rate

at any one time is equal to total inventory divided by two.[4] It should be noted that carrying costs consist of the value of the inventory tied up at any one time and the costs associated with these particular goods.

In the first instance, Smith can take these data and construct the total costs associated with each of a number of reorder levels. Table 9-2 shows the results of this trial-and-error process.

The Table 9-2 data indicate that Smith would be best off by placing 6 orders of 833 blenders each throughout the year. However, two points should be noted. First, Smith does not know that 6 is the ideal number of times to reorder. He merely knows that of the Table 9-2 alternatives, it is the best. But what about the other reorder possibilities: 4, 5, 7, 8, 9, and 11 to 19? A second difficulty is that many inventory problems are much too sophisticated to be solved by such a simple approach. For this reason, the EOQ formula is often employed:

The economic order quantity is stated.

$$EOQ = \sqrt{\frac{2DA}{vr}},$$

where   D = Expected annual demand
A = Administrative costs per order
v = Value per item
r = Estimate for taxes, insurance, and other expenses.

When the data are placed in the formula, it appears as follows:

$$EOQ = \sqrt{\frac{2(5,000)\,(\$100)}{(\$20) \times (0.05)}}$$

$$= \sqrt{\frac{\$1,000,000}{\$1}}$$

$$= \sqrt{1,000,000}$$

$$= 1,000.$$

The manager's best decision will therefore be to reorder in quantities of 1,000. This will require the placement of 5 orders throughout the year, an alternative Smith has not yet pursued. The answer can be further verified through hand calculation. Five orders will result in total order costs of $500. The carrying costs will equal $1,000 \div 2 \times (\$20 \times 0.05)$, or $500 more. Thus,

---

[4]This is so because average inventory is always going to be equal to half of total inventory, given a constant depletion rate. For example, if a firm orders 1,000 widgets and sells them at the rate of 20 a day for 50 days, no widgets will be left at the end of 10 weeks. However, the amount on hand at the midpoint of each week will be as follows: 950, 850, 750, 650, 550, 450, 350, 250, 150, 50. Adding these figures and dividing the total by 10 produces 500. Thus in the EOQ formula the average inventory is determined to be

$$\frac{\text{Total inventory}}{2}$$

	Number of Orders Placed	Size of Each Order	Order Cost	Carrying Cost Inventory/2 × $20 × 0.05	Total Cost
TABLE 9-2 **Trial-and-Error** **Approach**	1	5,000	$ 100	$2,500.00	$2,600.00
	2	2,500	200	1,250.00	1,450.00
	3	1,667	300	833.50	1,133.50
	6	833	600	416.50	1,016.50
	10	500	1,000	250.00	1,250.00
	20	250	2,000	125.00	2,125.00

by ordering 5 rather than 6 times a year, Smith can improve his total cost by $16.50 ($1,016.50 − $1,000). Figure 9-8 provides a graphic illustration of this solution.

The EOQ is only one of the many mathematical techniques that have been developed to help the manager make decisions.[5] Another is game theory.

GAME THEORY

Game theory has not been widely used in solving business problems, but it has provided important insights into the elements of competition. The manager's job is to choose the best strategy available, taking into account his or her own actions and those of the competition. Thus, an understanding and appreciation of strategy can prove very useful.

[5]Henry Ekstein, "Your Business Cardiogram," *Success*, July–August 1988, pp. 24, 27.

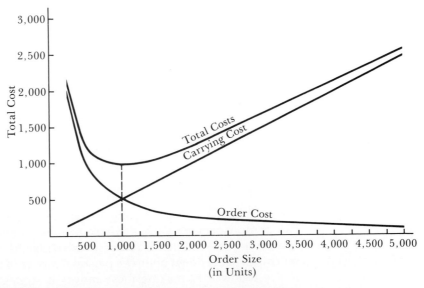

FIGURE 9-8   Order, Carrying, and Total Cost Relationships

INTERVIEW WITH KARL SOMMERS

Karl Sommers is lead quality engineer for microwave modules at the Westinghouse Defense and Space Center. Karl has a master's degree in management science and a Ph.D. in general management. Karl is also a certified manufacturing engineer and is responsible for ensuring that the microwave modules provided to the company by both in-house and outside vendors are produced in a timely manner and meet cost and quality specifications.

Q.   *What types of quantitative decision making do you use in your work?*

A.   There are a number of different tools that are employed. Before describing two of the most important, however, keep in mind that I am responsible for seeing that we receive high-quality, high-reliability circuit cards and microwave modules that are used in weapons systems, both in aircraft and naval vessels. One of the most important quantitative techniques is sampling. We have to have the highest quality output from our suppliers and this requires that we continually sample the shipments to ensure that they meet our specifications. A second quantitative tool is a version of allocation theory. We have facilities all over the world that are capable of building the cards and modules that we need. So we have to decide whether it is most cost effective to have these facilities produce the output or whether we should have it farmed out to external vendors. This is a cost-related decision. If we find that it is cheaper to produce it in-house, the next question is: Who should make it? Which factory should be given the order and by when do we need to have delivery?

Game theory involves conflict of interest situations.

   Game theory involves what are termed conflict of interest situations. One individual or organization has goals that conflict with those of other individuals or organizations. In addition, in game theory two or more alternative courses of action are always available, even though the manager never has full control over any of them. Commenting on the aspect of conflict, John McDonald, in his book *Strategy in Poker, Business and War*, has written:

> The strategical situation in game theory lies in the interaction between two or more persons, each of whose actions is based on an expectation concerning the actions of others over whom he has no control. The outcome is dependent upon the personal moves of the participants. The policy followed in making these moves is strategy. Both the military strategist and the business man act continuously in this state of

Q.   *Why not just run your worldwide factories round the clock? Wouldn't this reduce your cost per unit and result in your having all of the output you need?*

A.   Sure, but it would also be very expensive to do it this way. Not only would we have high carrying costs but the materials might be too old. Our units can't be more than 120 days old or they have to be reinspected and pass a solderability test. This is all part of new military specifications that are designed to provide high-quality, high-reliability parts. So rather than storing parts long-term, we work on a "hand to mouth" basis. Moreover, we use a first-in, first-out approach so that nothing sits around too long.

Q.   *Do you use any other quantitative decision-making tools?*

A.   We use various control procedures for keeping track of production performance and ensuring the goods are provided to us as needed. We also work hard to monitor quality and to ensure that the units we are getting from our vendors meet specifications. We have materials being provided to us from Texas, Puerto Rico, Mexico, Barbados, and Europe. If something does not measure up to specifications, we have to be able to identify the problem quickly and then move to take the needed corrective action. As I said before, the piece parts that make up the assemblies cannot be more than 120 days old. So if we receive some shipments of defective material, we have to scurry to replace them because we don't have large quantities sitting in the warehouse as backup. However, the thing to remember about quantitative techniques that are used for decision making is that they have practical applications. We don't use any technique that doesn't have a bottom-line result. For us, quantitative decision making is not a theoretical idea but a practical application; a proactive tool for facilitating or ensuring on-time delivery of quality products within cost.

suspended animation. And regardless of the amount of information given them—short of the ideal of perfect information—they generally act in the final analysis on hunch; that is, they gamble without being able to calculate the risk.[6]

Saddle Point Zero-sum Games

In a zero-sum game, one competitor's loss is the other's gain.

Most analysis conducted in the area of game theory has involved two-party zero-sum games. In these games are two competitors, one of whose gain is always the other's loss. This concept can be seen more clearly through the construction of a payoff matrix that shows what each competitor stands to

---

[6]John McDonald, *Strategy in Poker, Business and War* (New York: W. W. Norton, 1950), p. 16.

win or lose. Before the matrix is drawn, however, it should be noted that a basic assumption of game theory is that neither side is any smarter than the other; both sides, therefore, know the payoffs in the matrix. The question, in light of these payoffs, is what each side should do.

Consider, for example, two companies (Y and Z) with the following four alternative strategies:

Company Y
A = Lower price.
B = Improve product quality.

Company Z
C = Increase advertising.
D = Hire more people in sales.

The payoff matrix for these respective strategies, in terms of gains and losses for Company Y, is seen in Figure 9-9.

In light of this, which strategy is most desirable to Company Y? The answer would appear to be Strategy A, for the company stands to gain $3 million, regardless. Conversely, Strategy C seems most desirable to Company Z, which stands to lose no more than $3 million and which might gain $4 million. Thus the best strategy appears to be A, C.

The logic can be verified by employing two of the most useful ideas developed in decision theory, the concepts of minimax and maximin. Minimax involves minimizing the maximum loss, and maximin involves maximizing the minimum gain. Both concepts can be applied to the payoff matrix in Figure 9-10 to determine whether there is a *saddle point*, or ideal strategy. One determines the existence of a saddle point first by identifying the largest number in each row (Row Minima) and then ascertaining the smallest number in each column (Column Maxima). If the largest number in Row Minima equals the smallest number in Column Maxima, a saddle point exists.

Using the minimax and maximin concepts allows the saddle point (ideal strategy) to be determined.

		Company Z Strategies	
		C	D
Company Y Strategies	A	$3 Million	$3 Million
	B	− $4 Million	$5 Million

A 2 × 2 matrix illustration

FIGURE 9-9   **Company Y Payoff Matrix**

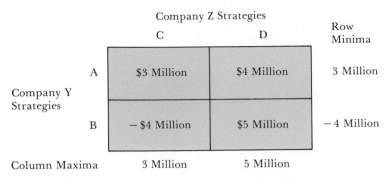

Company Z Strategies

	C	D	Row Minima
A	$3 Million	$4 Million	3 Million
B	− $4 Million	$5 Million	− 4 Million
Column Maxima	3 Million	5 Million	

Company Y Strategies

FIGURE 9-10   Determining Whether a Saddle Point Exists

The saddle point is found.

Since the largest number in Row Minima is indeed equal to the smallest number in Column Maxima, there is a saddle point or ideal strategy. This occurs at Point A, C. Thus it has been possible to identify the ideal strategy by means of a visual analysis.

The basic concept of game theory can be expanded into even larger matrixes. For example, consider the effect of the following six strategies:

Company Y
A = Lower price.
B = Improve product quality.
C = Increase advertising.

Company Z
D = Open more distribution centers.
E = Provide easier credit terms.
F = Hire more people in sales.

When these six strategies are placed in a matrix, the payoffs, from the standpoint of Company Y, are shown in Figure 9-11.

A visual analysis of Figure 9-11 shows that Strategy B is most favorable to Company Y. The least the firm will gain with this strategy is $8 million, and it can possibly gain $14 million. Conversely, Strategy E appears most favorable to Company Z, since the most it can lose is $8 million; this is in contrast to Strategies D and F, by which it can lose $14 million and $10 million respectively. However, because this matrix is a little more difficult to analyze than the previous one, it is desirable first to ascertain whether or not there is a saddle point. Figure 9-12 shows how this can be done.

Here the saddle point is calculated.

There is a saddle point in the figure, the ideal strategy being B, E. Thus Company Y should initiate Strategy B, and Company Z should opt for Strategy E. It is important to remember that it pays neither side to opt for any other strategy if there is a saddle point. For example, according to the Figure 9-12 matrix, if Company Y maintains Strategy B, Company Z stands to lose

Company Z Strategies

	D	E	F	
A	$2 Million	$6 Million	$12 Million	
Company Y Strategies B	$14 Million	$8 Million	$10 Million	A 3 × 3 matrix illustration
C	− $4 Million	$4 Million	− $6 Million	

FIGURE 9-11   Company Y Payoff Matrix

much more than $8 million if it switches to either of the other strategies, whether D or F. Likewise, if Company Y changes to Strategy A or Strategy C while Company Z stays with Strategy E, Company Y will not gain as much as before.

Nonzero-sum Mixed Strategy Games

Most situations are nonzero-sum in nature.

The game theory illustrations to this point have all been examples of zero-sum games, but in realistic business settings zero-sum conditions rarely occur. Assume, for example, that profit per unit is $1, demand is 1,000 units, and total profit in the market is $1,000. Firms A and B both wish to obtain profits of $750 but, based on current information, they know this to be impossible; the combined profits of the two cannot exceed $1,000. Thus, only the firm capturing 75 percent of the market will succeed. On the other hand,

Company Z Strategies

	D	E	F	Row Minima
A	$2 Million	$6 Million	$12 Million	2 Million
Company Y Strategies B	$14 Million	$8 Million	$10 Million	8 Million
C	− $4 Million	$4 Million	− $6 Million	− 6 Million
Column Maxima	14 Million	8 Million	12 Million	

FIGURE 9-12   Saddle Point Calculation

if the demand were to increase from 1,000 to 2,000 units, both companies could capture equal shares of the market and more than attain their respective goals. Because there are increases in demand, most businesses face conditions characteristic of nonzero-sum games when dealing with sales volume because most decisions are not made at the direct expense of the competition. They are thus nonzero-sum in nature.

Likewise, most strategy situations do not have saddle points. For example, consider the matrix in Figure 9-13, which is a slight adaptation of Figure 9-12, with its accompanying Row Minima and Column Maxima calculations.

There is no saddle point in the figure, for the maximum of Row Minima is $6 million, whereas the minimum of Column Maxima is $8 million. When there is no saddle point, it becomes necessary to design a mixed strategy. For example, if Company Y chose Strategy B, Company Z would go to Strategy E, choosing to lose $6 million. However, if Y knew what Z was going to do, it would opt for Strategy C, thereby increasing its payoff from $6 million to $16 million. In turn, if Company Z knew this, it would choose Strategy F, thereby gaining $6 million. And so it goes, with each company second-guessing the other. The only possible way to take advantage of the situation is to determine some combination or mixed strategy. The method of calculating this will not be discussed here, but it should be noted that this mixed approach is far more realistic than the ideal, or saddle-point, strategy. If one firm found itself in an unfavorable saddle-point situation, it would alter its strategies drastically, thereby upsetting the old payoff matrix and establishing one more favorable to itself. Another way in which this discussion has been somewhat unrealistic is that the examination of game theory has dealt with only two competitive sides. In a business setting, however, a firm is generally competing against many companies. Nevertheless, the concept of game theory has proved very useful in providing an understanding of the elements of competition. Its basic ideas have been experimentally expanded into

In most strategy situations there is no saddle point.

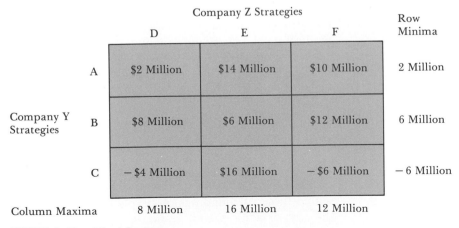

		Company Z Strategies			Row Minima
		D	E	F	
	A	$2 Million	$14 Million	$10 Million	2 Million
Company Y Strategies	B	$8 Million	$6 Million	$12 Million	6 Million
	C	−$4 Million	$16 Million	−$6 Million	−6 Million
Column Maxima		8 Million	16 Million	12 Million	

FIGURE 9-13   **Mixed Strategy**

bargaining and negotiating interactions and, for about twenty years now, have been employed in general management simulation games to train managers in strategy formulation and implementation.

QUEUING THEORY

Queuing theory helps the manager balance waiting lines and service.

Another OR technique is that of *queuing theory,* often called waiting-line theory, which employs a mathematical technique for balancing waiting lines and service. These lines occur whenever there is an irregular demand, and the manager must decide how to handle the situation. If the lines become too long and the waiting time proves excessive, customers will go elsewhere with their business. Conversely, if there is too much service, customers will be very happy but the costs will outrun the revenues. If, for example, one goes grocery shopping on Saturday morning, every cash register may have an attendant and an average waiting time of fifteen minutes. Since these conditions exist all over town, the manager must be concerned only with keeping the registers open. However, what should be done during slack periods, such as Tuesday morning? If the manager assigns only two people to the registers, there may be a sudden influx of customers, who suddenly create long lines. On the other hand, if the manager keeps all the registers going and only a few customers show up, most of the clerks will just be standing around drawing their paychecks.

The supermarket manager presents a very simple illustration because it takes little thought or effort to move people from the stockroom to the cash register and back. As long as a sufficient number of employees are on hand, they can be transferred around the store; and waiting lines are simply not an insurmountable problem. However, the concept can be applied to a business firm faced, for example, with a problem of plant layout. How many loading docks and fork trucks will be needed to keep the company delivery trucks' waiting time at an acceptable level? If there are too many docks and fork trucks, there will be no waiting time for loading and unloading, but the expense of building the facilities will be great. Conversely, too few docks and fork trucks entail a great deal of expensive waiting time. By means of mathematical equations, queuing theory can provide an answer to this particular problem. Sometimes, however, when arrival and service rates are not controllable, it becomes difficult to evaluate alternatives by means of equations alone. When this occurs, a Monte Carlo approach can often prove useful.

MONTE CARLO TECHNIQUE

The *Monte Carlo technique* uses a simulation approach for the purpose of creating an artificial environment and then evaluating the effect of decisions within these surroundings. A simple illustration of a simulation is found in the case of aerodynamic testing conducted on model airplanes in a wind tunnel. By simulating the effect of air currents and gale winds on the craft, engineers can evaluate the proposed design and construction.

The Monte Carlo technique allows the manager to simulate various conditions and determine the best answer from the results.

Monte Carlo is another type of simulation that attempts, via a random number generator or table, to simulate a particular environment and the effect of various decisions made within this artificial setting. For example, if a plant manager wants to determine the optimum number of trucks for the firm's delivery fleet, the problem is basically one of discrimination: If there are too many, capital investment in the trucks, coupled with excessive idle time, will prove too high. The optimum number can be determined by using the Monte Carlo technique. First, the number of shipments arriving at the loading dock must be determined; next, the time it takes to make deliveries must be ascertained. Then the expenses of owning and operating the fleet have to be computed. Finally, the costs associated with being unable to make all deliveries on time must be calculated. Employing this basic information plus some other supplemental data and some random numbers, it is possible to simulate results based on different fleet sizes. The process can be continued until the manager finds the optimum number of trucks. However, the technique is not restricted merely to determining fleet sizes. It has been successfully used in many diverse activities, from simulating machine breakdowns to determining arrivals and departures at airports.

DECISION TREES

Another OR tool is the decision tree. Many managers weigh alternatives on the basis of their immediate or short-run results, but a decision-free format permits a more dynamic approach because it makes explicit some elements that are generally only implicit in other analyses. A *decision tree* is a graphic method that a manager can use in identifying the various courses of action that can be taken in solving a problem, assigning probability estimates to events associated with these alternatives, and calculating the payoffs corresponding to each act-event combination.

For example, consider the case of a firm that has expansion funds and must decide what to do with them. After careful analysis, the firm identifies three alternatives: (1) use the money to buy a new company, (2) expand the facilities of the current firm, or (3) put the money in a savings account. In deciding which alternative is best, the company has gathered all the available information and constructed the decision tree that is Figure 9-14.

This figure has four important components, common to all decision trees. First is the decision point, which is represented by a square that indicates where the decision maker must choose a course of action. Second is a chance point, represented by a circle, which indicates where a chance event, over which the firm has no control, is expected; some examples of chance events are solid economic growth, stagnation, and high inflation. Third is a branch, which is represented by a line that flows from the chance points to indicate events and their likelihood—for example, 0.5 for solid growth, 0.3 for stagnation, or 0.2 for high inflation. Finally, at the far right, a payoff is associated with each branch. The payoffs are called conditional payoffs since their occurrence depends on certain conditions. For example, in Figure 9-14

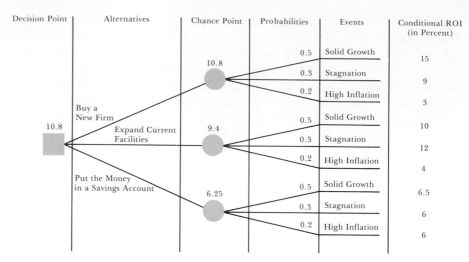

Decision Point	Alternatives	Chance Point	Probabilities	Events	Conditional ROI (in Percent)
		10.8	0.5	Solid Growth	15
			0.3	Stagnation	9
			0.2	High Inflation	3
10.8	Buy a New Firm	9.4	0.5	Solid Growth	10
	Expand Current Facilities		0.3	Stagnation	12
			0.2	High Inflation	4
	Put the Money in a Savings Account	6.25	0.5	Solid Growth	6.5
			0.3	Stagnation	6
			0.2	High Inflation	6

FIGURE 9-14   Decision Tree for Investing Expansion Funds

the conditional return on investment (ROI) associated with buying a new firm and having solid economic growth is 15 percent, but this return depends on both of the two preceding factors—buying the firm and having solid growth.

In building a decision tree, the company starts by identifying the various alternatives, the probabilities and events associated with each, and the amount of return that can be expected from each. Having then constructed the tree, the firm rolls it back; proceeding from right to left, the analyst begins the decision-tree interpretation.

This analysis begins when the analyst multiplies the conditional ROIs at the far right of the tree by the probability of their occurrence. For example, if the company buys a new firm and there is solid growth in the economy, as in Figure 9-14, it will obtain a 15 percent ROI. However, the probability of such an occurrence is 0.5. Likewise, the probabilities associated with stagnant growth, where the return will be 9 percent, and high inflation, where the return will be 3 percent, are 0.3 and 0.2 respectively. To determine the expected return associated with buying a new firm, the analyst multiplies each of the conditional ROIs by its respective probability and then totals the products. For the first alternative, buying the firm, the calculation is:

Conditional ROI	Probability	Expected Return
15.0	0.5	7.5
9.0	0.3	2.7
3.0	0.2	0.6
		10.8

For the second alternative, expanding current facilities, the calculation is:

Conditional ROI	Probability	Expected Return
10.0	0.5	5.0
12.0	0.3	3.6
4.0	0.2	0.8
		9.4

For the third alternative, investing the money, the calculation is:

Conditional ROI	Probability	Expected Return
6.5	0.5	3.25
6.0	0.3	1.80
6.0	0.2	1.20
		6.25

These expected returns are often placed over the chance points on the decision tree. But they can be determined only after the tree has been drawn and the analysis of the branches has been conducted.

As can be seen in the figure, the first alternative is the best because it offers the greatest expected return. Decision trees help the manager evaluate alternatives because they identify both what can happen and the likelihood of the events' occurrences. To be able to do both, the decision tree builder moves from left to right, but the decision tree analyst moves from right to left.

In recent years many companies have frequently used decision trees to handle situations that span two or more years. For example, consider the case of a company that must decide whether to buy a new machine or use overtime in handling current demand. The new machine will cost $30,000, whereas the overtime will cost $5,000. Whichever decision is made, the company will stay with it for one year and then make a follow-up decision. If it has installed a new machine in the first year, it may install a second machine, institute overtime, or use the existing facilities to the fullest. If it has opted for overtime in the first year, it may then install a new machine, install the machine and use overtime as well, or simply institute overtime. Figure 9-15 illustrates the decision tree for this two-year period. The conditional profit is, of course, shown on the right side of the decision tree.

In order to determine the best initial decision—buying a new machine or using overtime—it is necessary to start by rolling the tree back from the right. First, the conditional profits must be multiplied by their probabilities. For example, starting at the top of the tree, to determine the expected values of installing the second machine, the calculation is $120,000 × 0.2 + 90,000

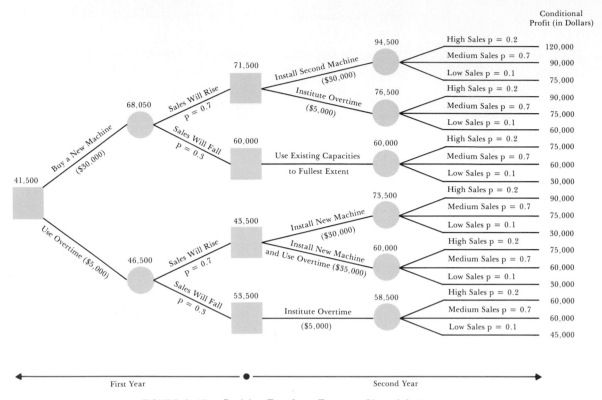

FIGURE 9-15   Decision Tree for a Two-year Plan of Action

× 0.7 + 75,000 × 0.1 = $94,500. The same calculations for each of the other branches give expected values of $76,500, $60,000, $73,500, $60,000, and $58,500, respectively. These numbers have all been entered in the figure over their respective chance points.

Next, again starting at the top of the tree, the cost of installing a second machine must be compared with the cost of instituting overtime. When the costs of each are subtracted from their expected values of $94,500 and $76,500, the results are $64,500 and $71,500, respectively. Since the latter is greater, the firm will choose it.

The next alternative down the tree calls for using existing facilities to the fullest extent. Since this alternative has no additional costs associated with it, the $60,000 is carried back intact. Next is the cost of installing a new machine ($73,500 − $30,000 = $43,500) versus installing the machine and using overtime ($60,000 − $35,000 = $25,000). Since the former is less expensive, it is chosen. Then, on the lowest branch, there is the $58,500 expected value minus the $5,000 overtime, resulting in a new expected value of $53,500.

At this point, the analysis has run through the second year decisions; it is necessary to roll the branches back only one more year. Again starting at the top, a 0.7 probability is associated with the $71,500 expected value and a 0.3 probability is associated with the $60,000 expected value. From the sum of these answers $30,000, the cost of buying a new machine, is subtracted. The calculation follows:

$$\begin{array}{rcl}
\$71,500 \times 0.7 & = & \$50,050 \\
\$60,000 \times 0.3 & = & \underline{18,000} \\
& & \$68,050 \\
& & \underline{-30,000} \quad \text{(new machine cost)} \\
& & \$38,050
\end{array}$$

This is the expected value of buying the new machine immediately. The expected value of using overtime in the first year is:

$$\begin{array}{rcl}
\$43,500 \times 0.7 & = & \$30,450 \\
\$53,500 \times 0.3 & = & \underline{16,050} \\
& & \$46,500 \\
& & \underline{-5,000} \quad \text{(use of overtime)} \\
& & \$41,500
\end{array}$$

Since the latter expected value, $41,500, is greater than the former, $38,050, the company should first opt for overtime rather than a new machine. If sales rise, it should install a new machine the second year. Close examination of Figure 9-14 shows that if sales rise in the first year, the company is better off just installing a new machine rather than installing the machine *and* using overtime ($73,500 versus $60,000). Finally, if sales fall in the first year, the company should continue to use overtime.

The decision tree does not provide definitive answers. However, it does allow the manager to weigh benefits against costs by assigning probabilities to specific events and ascertaining the respective payoffs. As Efraim Turban and Jack R. Meredith note:

> The unique feature of decision trees is that they allow management to view the logical order of a sequence of decisions. They show a clear graphical presentation of the various alternative courses of action and their possible consequences. Using the decision tree, management can also examine the impact of a series of decisions (multiperiod decisions) on the objectives of the organization. The graphical presentation helps in understanding the interactions among alternative courses of action, uncertain events, and future consequences.[7]

[7]Efraim Turban and Jack R. Meredith, *Fundamentals of Management Science*, 2nd ed. (Dallas, TX: Business Publications, 1981), p. 94.

HEURISTIC PROGRAMMING

Not all operations research approaches rely upon sophisticated mathematics. *Heuristic programming,* generally called heuristic problem-solving, is on the opposite end of the spectrum from the rigorous methodology used in some of the already examined OR techniques. Some problems are too large or too complex to be solved by a computer. Others are too unstructured; they leave a quantitative approach out of the question. In cases such as these, heuristic programming is often employed (see Communication in Action: Learning to Communicate Differently).

Heuristic means "serving to discover." Such an approach to problem solving is subjective as well as objective in nature, relying upon experience, judgment, intuition, and advice. Two of the most common heuristic approaches to problem solving are rules of thumb and trial and error.

Heuristic program-ming employs rules of thumb and trial and error.

Problems are often nothing more than brain twisters that force the manager to think. Consider the following example. An epidemic has broken out in a city. All twelve local hospitals have called a nearby pharmaceutical manufacturer and asked to have a particular serum delivered immediately. It generally takes three weeks to manufacture this serum, but the pharmaceutical company just happens to have a quantity of it on hand. Accordingly, the serum is placed in vials, wrapped in twelve individual packages, and rushed to the shipping dock. By this time, the crisis in the city has become so great that if each hospital does not have its allotted serum within the hour, patients will begin dying. Just as the manager of the pharmaceuticals shipping dock rushes the packages to the waiting delivery truck, a call comes: The worker who wrapped the packages reports that one of them is missing a five-ounce vial of serum. The vial is being sent down immediately, and in the two minutes the delivery will take, the manager's job is to ascertain which hospital has been shorted on its serum. The only available tool for the shipping dock manager is a balance scale. The problem, then, is how to isolate the package that is missing the vial of serum.

There are a number of ways to solve the problem. One is to place six packages on each side of the scale. The side with the light package will not go down so far as the side with the fully-packed allotments. By making this measurement, the manager reduces the number of possibilities to six. Then, by placing three on each side of the scale, it is possible to reduce the possibilities by half again. Three packages are left. There is time for only one more weighing. How should it be done? The answer is simpler than it seems. If the manager puts one package on each side of the scale the answer is clear: Either the light package will not be able to balance the heavier or the two packages will balance, thus showing that the short package is the one left off the scales.[8]

---

[8]Adapted from Paul J. Gordon, "Heuristic Problem Solving: You Can Do It," *Business Horizons,* Spring 1962, pp. 43–53.

COMMUNICATION
IN
ACTION:
Learning
to
Communicate
Differently

Many managers report that they have trouble thinking creatively. This is not difficult to understand. Creativity is usually not part of their jobs. They are paid to deal with facts and get things done "realistically"; these demands often do not require a creative approach to decision making.

Recently, however, managers have come to realize that creative thinking can enhance their ability to make decisions. How can they be more creative? What can they do to stimulate the formation of "new" ideas in their minds? One of the most effective methods is known as inside-out thinking. It involves having the individual do something that is totally out of character. The following are examples.

Think of the exact opposite of what you want to do. For example, one company that manufacturers locks has its designers and engineers first focus on how to pick the lock. Then realizing what they don't want thieves to do, they work on overcoming the problem by making it more difficult for the lock to be opened.

Assume that all of your information is wrong. By doing this the manager is forced to check the facts and rethink the problem-solving approach. This is particularly helpful in generating "new" ideas as well as finding commonly overlooked problems with the "old" way of doing things.

Look at the environment in which the decision must be made. Instead of concentrating on the narrow parameters of the decision, examine the "space" in which the choice must be made. For example, rather than focusing on why people are not doing as much work as they should, look at the environment in which they work. Perhaps the answer lies out there instead of with the personnel themselves. Possibly the work environment is not conducive to maximum efficiency.

Be someone else. For example, if there is a problem in getting materials delivered on time, put yourself in the supplier's position. Look at things from his standpoint. Why is the individual late with deliveries? What are the reasons? Is there some way the individual can improve things? If so, offer these suggestions. If not, then get another supplier. Before deciding what to do, however, engage in some creative thinking.

Reverse the physical characteristics of the problem. For example, if there is not enough space to store all of the firm's materials, picture some of them as being suspended from the ceiling. If there is too much room taken up with reports and files, imagine them on microfiche or computer stored. Are these possibilities for solving the space shortage problems? If so, pursue them.

These approaches all have one thing in common. They help managers look at problems from a different angle by means of inside-out thinking.

Source: Jacquelyn Wonder and Priscilla Donovan, *Whole-Brain Thinking* (New York: Morrow and Company, Inc., 1984).

From Job \ To Job	1	2	3	4
Empty	30	40	50	60
1	0	35	15	25
2	45	0	40	35
3	10	20	0	10
4	25	40	30	0

FIGURE 9-16   Setup Time (in minutes)

As another illustration, consider the following case. A supervisor is in the process of assigning work to a machinist. On this particular day, the machinist must do four jobs, and the supervisor wants to keep setup time to a minimum. The individual's machine is currently empty and needs to be set up for the first of the four jobs. The setup times from job to job are stated in Figure 9-16.

With the machine empty, as shown in the figure, it will take thirty minutes to set up Job 1, forty to set up Job 2, fifty to set up Job 3, and sixty to set up Job 4. Once the first job is complete, the machinist can go on to the second. In order to read Figure 9-16, assume that the supervisor chooses to have Job 3 done first; it will take fifty minutes to set up. From the figure, reading across from Job 3 on the left, it is known that the setup times for moving from Job 3 to Jobs 1, 2, and 4 are ten, twenty, and ten minutes respectively. If the supervisor should choose Job 2 second, the setup will take twenty minutes. Continuing on, suppose that the supervisor selects Job 4 for the third one: setting it up will take thirty-five minutes. Finally, reading down Figure 9-16 to Job 4 and across to Job 1, one can determine that the last job setup will take twenty-five minutes. Recapitulating the order and the times of the jobs gives the following summary:

Jobs	Setup Time (in minutes)
3	50
2	20
4	35
1	25
	130

	Sequence Job Numbers	Setup Times	Total Minutes
TABLE 9-3 **Enumeration Results**	1–2–3–4	30 + 35 + 40 + 10	115
	1–2–4–3	30 + 35 + 35 + 30	130
	1–3–2–4	30 + 15 + 20 + 35	100
	1–3–4–2	30 + 15 + 10 + 40	95 Minimum
	1–4–2–3	30 + 25 + 40 + 40	135
	1–4–3–2	30 + 25 + 30 + 20	105
	2–1–3–4	40 + 45 + 15 + 10	110
	2–1–4–3	40 + 45 + 25 + 30	140
	2–3–1–2	40 + 40 + 10 + 35	125
	2–3–2–1	40 + 40 + 20 + 45	145
	2–4–2–3	40 + 35 + 40 + 40	155
	2–4–3–2	40 + 35 + 30 + 20	125
	3–1–2–4	50 + 10 + 35 + 35	130
	3–1–4–2	50 + 10 + 25 + 40	125
	3–2–1–4	50 + 20 + 45 + 25	140
	3–2–4–1	50 + 20 + 35 + 25	130
	3–4–1–2	50 + 10 + 25 + 35	120
	3–4–2–1	50 + 10 + 40 + 45	145
	4–1–2–3	60 + 25 + 35 + 40	160
	4–1–3–2	60 + 25 + 15 + 20	120
	4–2–1–3	60 + 40 + 45 + 15	160
	4–2–3–1	60 + 40 + 40 + 10	150
	4–3–2–1	60 + 30 + 20 + 45	155
	4–3–1–2	60 + 30 + 10 + 35	135

The four jobs will take 130 minutes of setup time. Was the 3–2–4–1 sequence the one with the lowest setup time?

Table 9-3 presents the twenty-four different sequences for the four jobs. Note that the lowest time sequence is 1–3–4–2. Was this the sequence you chose? Most people do choose this one by following a simple rule. In moving from empty to the first job, they opt for the one with the lowest setup time and employ this same rule in moving from the first to the second job, second to the third, and third to the fourth. Depending on the setup times, such a heuristic rule can provide the best answer. A heuristic approach will not always give the best answer, but heuristics can often help the manager arrive at good answers to work problems. For example, this supervisor's solution was better than twelve of the other sequences. However, a more careful analysis of the information in Table 9-3 would have led to another thirty-five minutes of reduced setup time.

These kinds of problems do not warrant sophisticated techniques, and they are far more common than those requiring linear programming and Monte Carlo simulation. Resource allocation, inventory control, plant layout, and job shop scheduling are all problems that can sometimes be solved through heuristic programming.[9]

■ SUMMARY

This chapter introduced operations research (OR) and some of its distinguishing characteristics. It then presented five of the main areas of concern for operations management personnel. The chapter next examined some of the modern quantitative decision-making tools and processes, most of them falling under the heading of operations research. These varied in complexity and mathematical rigor, but all are of value to managers in the decision-making process.

Linear programming assists the manager in determining price-volume relationships for effective utilization of the organization's resources. The example used in this chapter illustrated how the technique could be employed to allocate scarce resources while simultaneously maximizing profit. The second technique discussed, the economic order quantity formula, helps the decision maker determine at what point and in what quantities inventory should be replenished. The third technique discussed, game theory, is useful in providing the manager with important insights into the elements of competition. Sometimes this competition is best represented as a zero-sum game with a saddle point, but more often it is typified by a nonzero-sum game without a saddle point, in which case it is necessary to use a mixed strategy in solving the problem. A fourth quantitative technique is queuing (waiting line) theory, which employs mathematical equations in balancing waiting lines and service. When it becomes difficult to evaluate alternatives by means of equations alone, many managers turn to the Monte Carlo technique, which uses a simulation approach and provides the decision maker with an opportunity to evaluate the effect of numerous decisions within the simulated environment. On the basis of simulation results, the manager is in a position to make the decision that best attains the objective.

Still another OR tool, and one that has been receiving increased attention in recent years, is the decision tree. This technique, which is less mathematical than those already mentioned, helps the manager weigh alternatives based on immediate and long-run results by encouraging the individual to: (1) identify the available courses of action; (2) assign probability estimates to the events associated with these alternatives; and (3) calculate the payoffs corresponding to each act-event combination. Heuristic programming, which was examined last, is the least mathematical of all OR techniques. Yet it is used far more often by the manager in everyday decision making (through rules of thumb and the use of trial and error) than any of the other OR tools.

---

[9]See also Hillel J. Einhorn and Robin M. Hogarth, "Decision Making: Going Forward in Reverse," *Harvard Business Review*, January–February 1987, pp. 66–70.

■ REVIEW AND STUDY QUESTIONS

1. What are the distinguishing characteristics of operations management? What are some of the primary areas of concern for operations management personnel? Explain.

2. What is meant by the term *operations research?*

3. In your own words, define linear programming. What are its advantages to the manager in the decision-making process? What are its drawbacks?

4. What is the graphic technique?

5. Of what value is game theory to the manager?

6. What are the variables involved in the economic order quantity formula? Of what value is the formula to the manager? Explain.

7. In game theory, what is meant by the term zero-sum game? Nonzero-sum game? Saddle point?

8. Explain this statement: Most decisions made by the manager are nonzero-sum in nature.

9. What is meant by a mixed strategy?

10. What is meant by queuing theory?

11. Of what decision-making value is the Monte Carlo method to the manager? Explain.

12. How do decision trees help the manager in making long-run decisions? Short-run decisions?

13. What is heuristic programming?

14. Explain this statement: Many of the daily problems faced by managers are solved by means of heuristic programming.

■ SELECTED REFERENCES

Agor, Weston H. "Nurturing Executive Intrapreneurship with a Brain-Skill Management Program." *Business Horizons,* May–June 1988, pp. 12–15.

Brown, R. V. "Do Managers Find Decision Theory Useful?" *Harvard Business Review,* May–June 1970, pp. 78–79.

Chase, R. B., and J. J. Aquilano. *Production and Operations Management: A Life Cycle Approach,* 3rd ed. Homewood, IL: Richard D. Irwin, 1981.

Churchman, C. W., R. L. Ackoff, and E. L. Arnoff. *Introduction to Operations Research.* New York: Wiley, 1957.

Cook, R. M., and R. A. Russell. *Contemporary Operations Management: Text and Cases.* Englewood Cliffs, NJ: Prentice-Hall, 1980.

Einhorn, Hillel J., and Robin M. Hogarth. "Decision Making: Going Forward in Reverse." *Harvard Business Review,* January–February 1987, pp. 66–70.

Ekstein, Henry. "Your Business Cardiogram." *Success,* July–August 1988, pp. 24, 27.

Fiegenbaum, Avi, and Howard Thomas. "Attitudes Toward Risk and the Risk-Return Paradox: Prospect Theory Explanation." *Academy of Management Journal,* March 1988, pp. 85–106.

Kirkland, Richard L., Jr. "Pile 'Em High and Sell 'Em Cheap." *Fortune,* August 29, 1988, pp. 91–92.

Magee, J. F. "Decision Trees for Decision Making." *Harvard Business Review,* July–August 1964, pp. 126–38.

Markland, Robert E. *Topics in Management Science,* 2nd ed. New York: John Wiley & Sons, 1983.

Moore, Franklin, and Thomas Hendrick. *Production Operations Management.* Homewood, IL: Richard D. Irwin, 1980.

Paranka, S. "Competitive Bidding Strategy." *Business Horizons,* June 1971, pp. 39–43.

Post, Tom. "Managing the Unknown." *Success,* July–August 1988, p. 20.

Robey, Daniel, and William Taggart. "Measuring Managers' Minds: The Assessment of Style in Human Information Processing." *Academy of Management Review,* July 1981, pp. 375–83.

Simon, Herbert A. *The New Science of Management Decision.* New York: Harper & Bros., 1960.

Smithin, Tim. "Maps of the Mind: New Pathways to Decision Making." *Business Horizons,* December 1980, pp. 24–28.

Trueman, Richard E. *Quantitative Methods for Business Decision Making.* Hinsdale, IL: Dryden Press, 1981.

Vandell, R. F. "Management Evolution in the Quantitative World." *Harvard Business Review,* January–February 1970, pp. 83–92.

Wonder, Jacquelyn, and Priscilla Donovan. *Whole Brain Thinking.* New York: William Morrow and Company, Inc., 1984.

■ CASE: A Little of This and a Little of That

The Willowby Company had lost quite a bit of money in the previous year. As a result, its president, Norma Thurber, was determined to maximize profits as quickly as possible and show good first-quarter results. In attempting to carry out this objective, James Rogers, production manager at Willowby, found himself confronted with a resource allocation problem. The company was manufacturing two kinds of industrial machines, Type A and Type B. After examining the resources available to him, Rogers determined that he could solve the problem by means of the graphic method of linear programming. An analysis of the situation revealed that the following combinations and constraints for the two products were present:

Constraints	Type A	Type B
Assembly time	120 machines	240 machines
Available paint	150 machines	150 machines
Special casing for Type A	100 machines	—
Special casing for Type B	—	120 machines
Engines	180 machines	180 machines

After plotting these constraints on a graph, Rogers determined that there were five points within the feasibility area, permitting the following combinations of Type A and Type B to be manufactured:

1. 100 A and   0 B
2. 100 A and   40 B
3.   90 A and   60 B
4.   30 A and 120 B
5.   0 A and 120 B

In addition, each unit of A would result in a $300 profit to the firm and each unit of B would bring in $200 in profit.

Questions

1. Verify the accuracy of the above five points by drawing a graphic representation of the constraints.
2. Which of the above five alternatives is most profitable to Willowby? Show your work.
3. What other types of problems could Rogers solve by means of the graphic method? Give an illustration.

■ CASE: A Penny Saved Is a Penny Earned

Many firms that are short of working capital turn to Henry Ekstein to help them line up investors. In some cases Ekstein is able to get them the money they need without having to turn to outside sources. Where are these funds? They are in the company's inventory. Ekstein reports that far too many firms fail to adequately control their inventory, and as a result they are continually short of cash.

There are a number of simple techniques that Ekstein uses to help drive home his point. One is to create a graph that shows the firm's inventory depletion and replacement. In many cases these graphs illustrate the businesses order inventory well before they run out. As a result, the companies end up maintaining too big a safety stock. Their inventory investment is always much higher than it should be. Some companies get themselves into this bind without realizing what they are doing. For example, at a refrigerator factory firm he visited, Ekstein found that during lulls in the daily production the company had the workers cutting up extra coils of sheet metal for future use. This kept everyone busy during the day. The problem was that these coils had to be stored and more sheet metal ordered with no sales to show for this investment. The company would have been better off letting the workers sit idle rather than building up additional inventory.

How can companies better control their inventories? Ekstein recommends a number of useful steps. First, identify the ten items supplied by outside vendors that absorb the biggest share of the firm's purchasing dollar and work to control this inventory. Second, carefully determine how long it will take to reorder inventory for suppliers, and set the safety stock levels and reorder quantities with this information in mind. Third, look for additional sources of supply in case a current supplier cannot or will not meet the need for fast reorders. Fourth, get everyone in the firm associated with the production function to accept the fact that inventory reordering is one of their responsibilities. Every penny that is saved goes to the bottom line. Every penny that is wasted comes right off the bottom line.

Questions

1. In what way were the workers making coils actually working to the detriment of the company?

2. What was meant by the case statement, "carefully determine how long it will take to reorder inventory for suppliers, and set the safety stock levels and reorder quantities with this information in mind." Explain.

3. How useful is Ekstein's advice? Give your reasoning.

Source: Henry Ekstein, "Your Business Cardiogram," *Success,* July–August 1988, pp. 24, 27.

■ CASE: An Economic Approach

Ed Sharp, local manager of a radio and television retail store, used to reorder merchandise on the basis of gut feel. As he explained to one of his friends, "I don't know *exactly* when to reorder merchandise; I just use my best judgment." However, one day Robin Steele, his niece and a student in the Business College at State University, dropped by the store for a visit. When Steele learned of her uncle's unscientific approach to reordering inventory, she was shocked. "You should take a more refined approach to things, Uncle Ed," she said. "There are lots of decision-making tools and techniques you could use. For example, there's the economic order quantity formula. It can pinpoint exactly how many units you should order at any one time."

Sharp was impressed and decided to try his niece's suggestion. Together the two chose one of the most popular items in the store, a small AM-FM radio. After examining past sales records, they were able to obtain the following information: (a) the expected annual demand for the radio was 750 units; (b) the administrative costs associated with placing an order were $20; (c) the value of each radio was $30; and (d) the estimate for taxes, insurance, and other expenses was 10 percent.

Questions

1. Using a trial-and-error approach, construct a table showing the size of each order, the order cost associated with this size, the carrying cost, and the total cost if Sharp reorders inventory 1, 2, 3, 4, 5, 10, and 20 times per year.

2. Using the EOQ formula in this chapter, determine the most economic reorder quantity.

3. How much money has Steele saved her uncle's store if Sharp uses the EOQ formula rather than trial and error, assuming that he now reorders five times a year? Explain.

■ CASE: The Big Payoff

Gloria Adler, science editor of a large publishing house, is about ready to release a new basic biology textbook. She intends to obtain a large share of the basic biology text market. Although there are many competitors, one in particular is also coming out with a new biology book. Therefore, Adler must formulate her strategy very carefully. For this reason, instead of just designing her own plan of action, she has decided to ask herself what the opposition is going to do. She has come up with six basic strategies. Adler intends to use the first three; the second three are those that she has heard will be employed by the competition. Adler's strategy is:

1. Price the book lower than any other on the market.
2. Provide 10,000 complimentary copies to university professors.
3. Hire more salespeople to call on university professors and explain the strong points of the text.

The opposition's strategy is:

1. Give large quantity discounts to the bookstores.
2. Substantially increase the advertising budget.
3. Print the text on extremely high quality paper so as to enhance its aesthetic value.

After giving the matter a great deal of thought, Adler has concluded that the following payoff matrix represents the outcomes in thousands of textbooks that will occur under each of the above strategies:

Questions

1. After determining the numbers in Row Minima and Column Maxima, can you find a saddle point? If so, what strategic advice would you give Adler? If not, of what value is the above information to Adler?

2. If the competition is aware of the above payoff matrix and concludes it is an accurate representation of reality, what will the other company do? Explain, bringing the concept of mixed strategy into your discussion.

■ SELF-FEEDBACK EXERCISE: Are You a Left-Brain or Right-Brain Thinker?

Heuristic problem solvers are right-brain people. Are you? Answer each of the following questions and enter your responses in the place provided. An interpretation of your answers is provided at the end of the exercise.

1. With which of the following statements do you most agree?
   _____ a. Daydreaming is a waste of time.
   _____ b. Daydreaming is an important way of planning things out.

2. Which of the following best describes you.
   _____ a. You frequently have strong hunches and you follow them.
   _____ b. You do not rely on hunches when making important decisions.

3. Which of the following is most typical of you:
   _____ a. In getting things done throughout the day, you simply let things happen.
   _____ b. You make a list of those things you need to do.

4. Are you well organized?
   _____ a. Yes.
   _____ b. No.

5. Do you like to change the decor of your room or office?
   _____ a. Yes.
   _____ b. No.

6. How do you like to learn a new dance?
   _____ a. By finding out the steps and then repeating them mentally.
   _____ b. By imitating someone who knows the steps.

7. Do you express yourself well verbally?
   _____ a. No.
   _____ b. Yes.

8. Are you goal-oriented?
   _____ a. Yes.
   _____ b. No.

9. When you want to remember directions, a name, or a news item, how do you do it?
   _____ a. Write notes.
   _____ b. Visualize the information.

10. Do you remember faces easily?
    _____ a. No.
    _____ b. Yes.

11. When speaking, do you:
    _____ a. Choose exact, precise words.
    _____ b. Make up words.

12. In a communication setting, which are you most comfortable being:
    _____ a. The listener.
    _____ b. The talker.

13. Can you tell fairly accurately how much time has passed without looking at your watch?
    _____ a. No.
    _____ b. Yes.

14. What type of social situation do you prefer:
    _____ a. Spontaneous.
    _____ b. Planned in advance.

15. In preparing yourself for a new or difficult task, which do you prefer to do:
    _____ a. Mentally picture yourself succeeding.
    _____ b. Obtain extensive data regarding the task.

16. Do you prefer to work alone or in a group?
    _____ a. Alone.
    _____ b. In a group.

17. Which of these subjects did you like the best:
    _____ a. Geometry.
    _____ b. Algebra.

18. In notetaking, do you print?
    _____ a. Never.
    _____ b. Frequently.

19. Do you have frequent mood changes?
    _____ a. No.
    _____ b. Yes.

20. Are you good at interpreting body language:
    _____ a. Yes.
    _____ b. No.

Scoring

Indicate your answers to all 20 questions by circling the answer to each in the appropriate column.

	Column I	Column II
1.	a	b
2.	b	a
3.	b	a
4.	a	b
5.	b	a
6.	a	b
7.	b	a
8.	a	b
9.	a	b
10.	b	a
11.	a	b
12.	b	a
13.	a	b
14.	b	a
15.	b	a
16.	a	b
17.	b	a
18.	a	b
19.	a	b
20.	b	a

Interpretation

Column I represents left-brain thinking; Column II represents right-brain thinking. If you circled more answers in Column I than II, you see yourself as someone who is logical, analytical, and rational in his or her approach to things. If you circled more answers in Column II, you see yourself as creative, imaginative, and spontaneous in your approach to things. If you had 8 to 12 answers per column, you perceive yourself as a whole-brain thinker.

Information Systems and Decision Making

In addition to helping identify and evaluate alternative courses of action, quantitative school advocates are concerned with getting this information to those who need it. When this activity is added to those described in Chapters 8 and 9, it becomes obvious that, just like the process school, the quantitative school can be viewed as a closed loop of interrelated activities. Figure 3-2 showed that the process school consists of planning, organizing, and controlling. Figure 10-1 shows how the quantitative school can be diagrammed. The part of the figure that has not yet been examined is the "convey the results" section. This transmittal of results is done through the use of information systems, which are studied in this chapter. The first goal of the chapter is to examine such systems. The second goal is to explore the role of computers in them. The third goal is to study links connecting the quantitative school to the process and behavioral schools.

When you have finished this chapter, you should be able to:

1. Explain how an information system can help improve a manager's decision-making ability.
2. Describe how an information system is designed.
3. State some of the major uses of computers in modern organizations.

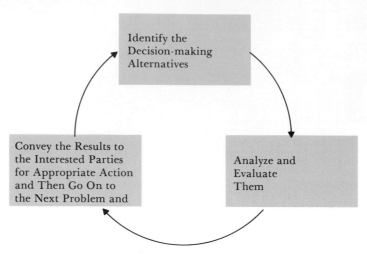

FIGURE 10-1   Quantitative School Functions

4. Discuss some of the shortcomings of computers.

5. Illustrate some of the behavioral impacts that information systems can have on organizational personnel.

6. Discuss the links that exist between the quantitative and process schools and the quantitative and behavioral schools.

INFORMATION SYSTEMS DESIGN

Managers have many functions. They are strategists who formulate objectives, disseminators of information who communicate these goals to other organizational members, and company spokespersons who provide information to outsiders. Managers can, therefore, be thought of as nerve centers, responsible for obtaining external and internal information and passing it on to various groups. This managerial information processing system can be depicted as in Figure 10-2.

Perhaps the major problem faced by modern managers is that of receiving more information than they really need. In recent years many firms have dealt with this problem by developing their own information systems. An *information system* is:

> an organizational method of providing past, present, and projection information relating to internal operations and external intelligence. It supports the planning, control, and operational functions of an organization by furnishing uniform information in the proper time frame to assist the decision-making process.[1]

[1]Walter J. Kennevan, "MIS Universe," *Data Management*, September 1970, p. 63.

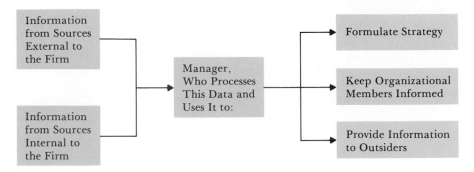

FIGURE 10-2   The Manager as an Information Processor

Designing an Information System

Information systems have one primary goal: providing managers with the data necessary for making intelligent decisions. Since there are three basic levels in the managerial organization (upper, middle, and lower management), each with different interests and viewpoints, it is evident that much of this decision-making information will have to be tailor-made to meet the needs of the respective levels. The way to do this becomes clear with the recognition that two basic inputs are necessary in any effective information system. The first can be called major determinants, factors that play a role in structuring the type of information that management will be receiving. According to William M. Zani, an information systems expert, they consist of opportunities and risks, company strategy, company structure, management and decision-making processes, available technology, and available information sources.[2] The roles of these determinants will become more evident in the next section, where an information system blueprint is examined.

There are major determinants in information system design.

The second input consists of key success variables, the factors and tasks that determine success or failure. They will differ, of course, from company to company and from industry to industry:

> For a consumer goods company manufacturing nondifferentiated products, the key success areas might be product promotion and understanding customer responses to product, marketing, and competitive changes. . . . For a manufacturer of commodity products, manufacturing and distribution cost control and efficiency might be the major determinants of success.[3]

These critical success factors will then be translated into primary measures which are monitored to ensure that everything goes well. For example, in the

[2]William M. Zani, "Blueprint for MIS," *Harvard Business Review*, November–December 1970, p. 96.

[3]Ibid., p. 98.

	Critical Success Factor	Primary Measure
TABLE 10-1 Critical Success Factors and Primary Measures in a Microwave Company	Image in financial markets	Price/earnings ratio
	Technological reputation with customers	Orders/bid ratio Customer "perception" results
	Market success	Change in market share for each product Growth rates of the company's markets
	Risk recognition in major bids and contracts	The firm's years of experience with similar products "New" or "old" customers Prior customer relationships
	Profit margin on jobs	The bid profit margin as a ratio of profit on similar jobs in this product line
	Company morale	Absenteeism and turnover Informal feedback
	Performance to budget on major jobs	Job cost budgeted as a percentage of the actual cost

Source: Adapted from John F. Rockart, "Chief Executives Define Their Own Data Needs," *Harvard Business Review*, March–April 1979, p. 89. Copyright © 1979 by the President and Fellows of Harvard College; all rights reserved.

case of one microwave company, the critical success factors and primary measures in Table 10-1 were identified.[4]

The Blueprint Itself

Blueprints bring key success variables together.

The well-designed management information system blueprint brings together the determinants and key success variables, since all these factors are interrelated. For example, the general business environment (opportunities and risks) and the company resources (personnel, money, machines, material, and information) help establish overall strategy. In turn, this strategy serves as a basis for development of the organization structure. All four of these factors are related to the organization's key success variables. This interrelationship is schematically illustrated in Figure 10-3.

As just noted, the organization is structured to include three levels of managers, all of whom need vital information for decision making. Top management is greatly interested in major developments in the external and internal arenas that will have an impact on the organization's strategic plan. Middle-level managers need information that will help them coordinate the activities of upper and lower levels. Individuals at the lower managerial levels require data related to the production of goods and services. In designing the

[4]For more on this, see John F. Rockart, "The Changing Role of the Information Systems Executive: A Critical Success Factors Perspective," *Sloan Management Review*, Fall 1982, pp. 3–13.

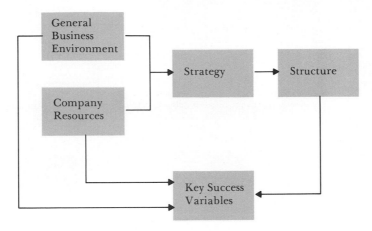

FIGURE 10-3   A Partial Information Systems Blueprint

information-decision system for each level, developers must focus primary attention on the relevance of the data to decision making.

Decision-making information will differ by level.

The information required at the top levels tends to be more encompassing in nature, forming the basis for strategic planning decisions. Setting objectives, designing the organization structure, and choosing new product lines are examples of the types of subjects that would be included. At the intermediate levels the data need to be somewhat more specific and to include information useful for activities such as formulating budgets, planning working capital, and measuring, appraising and improving management performance. At the lower levels the data have to be very specific; they might even be programmed through the use of mathematical models and techniques. Here, the information would include such items as information on production scheduling, inventory control, and the measurement, appraisal, and improvement of worker efficiency.

Working with these information requirements, the organization can develop an overall information system design, which will remain in operation for as long as it is useful. However, with new sources of information constantly developing, with new information requirements and with information technology continually changing, the system will have to be periodically revamped. Nevertheless, employing just the information in this section, the student of management can extend Figure 10-3 and develop a total information system blueprint as seen in Figure 10-4.

The design not only gives primary emphasis to information system determinants and key success variables but is also structured with the needs of management in mind. It follows a from-the-top-down philosophy. This is important, for as Zani notes:

> If the design of management information systems begins on a high conceptual level and on a high managerial level as well, a company can avoid the unfortunate "bottom up" design phenomenon of recent

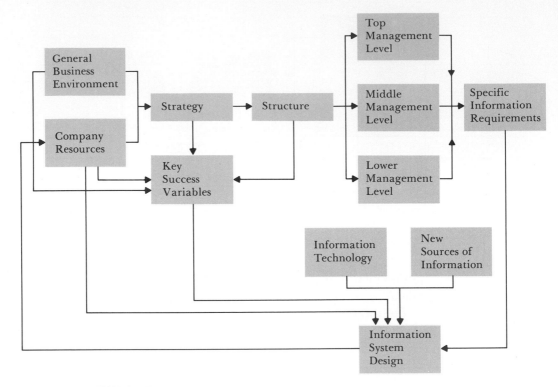

FIGURE 10-4   Total Information System Blueprint

history and begin to develop the real, and very great, potential of MIS as a tool for modern management.[5]

In recent years many firms have instituted and employed management information systems.[6] The benefits these systems offer make them very valuable management tools.

INFORMATION SYSTEMS AND THE QUANTITATIVE SCHOOL

A cursory analysis of information systems might puzzle the uninitiated person, who might well wonder why the quantitative school advocates get involved in designing them. So far, this text has described their interests as resting heavily in the area of mathematical formulas. In the last two decades, however, computers have begun to play a major role in organizational life. The initial interest of the quantitative theorists in the computer was for calculation purposes. Many of the quantitative decision-making tools discussed in the previous chapter are used in conjunction with the computer. By developing prepackaged computer programs for handling EOQ, linear programming, queuing theory, and Monte Carlo simulation problems, the

[5]Zani, p. 100.

[6]Robert J. Mockler, "Computer Information Systems and Strategic Corporate Planning," *Business Horizons*, May–June 1987, pp. 32–37.

quantitative theorists can often save themselves hundreds of hours of work time.

As computers have become more commonplace in industry, individuals who were trained to program these machines and provide management with the output have emerged. In addition to computer programmers, systems analysts also have arrived on the scene. Although their emphasis is not as quantitative as is the mathematicians', these computer people share a number of common characteristics with today's management scientists, including: (1) the application of scientific analysis to managerial problems, (2) the goal of improving the manager's decision-making ability, (3) a high regard for economic effectiveness criteria, (4) a reliance on mathematical models, and (5) the use of electronic computers.

Computer and quanti-
tative people have
much in common.

Of course, the computer-oriented employees are far less quantitative than their mathematical counterparts. In fact, in recent years some of them have contended that they are actually members of a fourth school of management—a systems school. (The validity of this type of claim will be addressed in greater detail in Chapter 16. It is first necessary to see what these systems people do.) It has already been noted that some of them help design information systems. Others work directly with the computer, a work area to be investigated now. A person able to delve into this topic, however, must keep in mind two facts: First, not all information systems are computerized. Second, the computer can do a lot more than merely solve mathematical equations and provide information for management decision making. However, as Boehm has so well noted:

> The uncertainties of these times have forced a shot-gun marriage between the executive decision maker and the systems analyst. This blending of human intuition, broad and nimble, with mathematical precision backed by the power of the computer, has brought the planning and conduct of business to a high plateau of rationality.
>
> Today more than half the companies in the *Fortune* "500" list have access to computer programs that model the national and world economies as integrated systems and that can be manipulated mathematically, thereby relating company policy and performance to many important economic factors. Many other companies, large and small, subscribe to such systems analysis models through their bankers or consultants.[7]

INFORMATION SYSTEMS AND COMPUTERS

The past three decades have seen the entry of automation into business enterprises. Webster defines *automation* as "the technique of making an apparatus (as a calculating machine), a process (as of manufacturing) or a system (as of bookkeeping) operate automatically."[8] In broad terms, there

---

[7]George A. W. Boehm, "Shaping Decisions with Systems Analysis," *Harvard Business Review*, September–October 1976, p. 91.

[8]Webster's *Third New International Dictionary*, vol. 1. s. v. "automation."

have been four main areas of automation development: (1) automatic machinery, (2) integrated materials handling and processing equipment, (3) control mechanisms, and (4) electronic computers and data-processing machines. The fourth category—computers in particular—will be the center of focus here because of the role computers play in the area of information systems.

Modern Computers

Computers are of two types: analog and digital.

Modern computers are of two general types: analog and digital. The *analog computer* is a measuring machine used principally by engineers in solving job-related problems. The *digital computer* is a counting machine which, by electrical impulses, can perform arithmetic calculations at a speed far in excess of human capacity; for this reason it is of great value to business firms.

The basic concept of the digital computer dates back hundreds of years. However, Charles Babbage, the nineteenth-century English mathematician and mechanician, is regarded as the originator of the modern automatic computer. In 1834 Babbage conceived the principle of the analytical engine, which was similar to the modern-day computer in that it would handle a large number of variables that could be fed into the machine on punched cards.

Computer power has increased dramatically.

Today, of course, with the advent of the electronic computer, Babbage's concept has been developed to far greater depth than he ever imagined. Over the last thirty years, four generations of electronic computers have emerged, and a fifth is on the horizon. The first relied on vacuum tubes and magnetic drums, the second on solid state devices and drum or magnetic cores, and the third on solid logic technology and monolithic integrated circuits. Fourth-generation computers, often referred to as "information handlers," rely on silicon chips and are more versatile and powerful than any of their predecessors. In particular, they allow users to access files directly, obtain information needed for decision making, and order the implementation of problem solutions. As more integrated circuits are placed on a chip, computer power will increase while the cost per million instructions will decline.[9] (See Figure 10-5.)

Over the last five years computer systems have also become much more interactive and user-friendly. In addition to *time-sharing*, whereby more than one person can use the computer at the same time, these machines employ *on-line processing*, which means that transactions are fed into the computer as they occur (cash registers that function as remote computer terminals are a good example), and operate on *real time*, which means that files are updated as soon as new information is received. The future promises even greater developments (see Technology in Action: Computers of the Future). As a

---

[9]John Markoff, "The Chip at 30: Potential Still Vast," *New York Times,* September 14, 1988, pp. 32, 40.

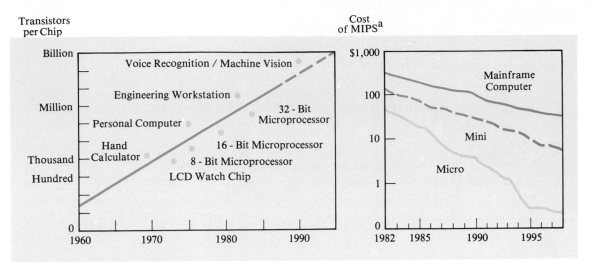

a Millions of instructions per second, a measure of computer speed.

FIGURE 10-5   Computer Performance and Cost

Source: *The New York Times,* September 14, 1988, p. 33. Copyright © 1988 by The New York Times Company. Reprinted by permission.

result, today's computer people are no longer members of the data processing department; rather, they belong to the information management department. Their job is now to provide the systems necessary to ensure that all employees have the information needed to do their jobs well. To the extent that this need can be met through a computerized information system, their role is a key one.[10]

Minis and Micros

One of the major technological advances has been the minicomputer (mini). The machine is medium-sized, in contrast to the large mainframe computer (mainframe), and has not only large memory storage and calculation capability but also is able to interact with the mainframe computer. In the case of a retail chain, for example, the mainframe will hold the central data bank information for all of the company's stores, while each unit will have its own mini for keeping track of transactions, reporting them to the mainframe, and getting information vital to the efficient operation of the store from the central computer. Remote terminals are used in this process for entering and receiving data from the computer. This overall system is known as *distributed data processing,* a term which means that at least some portion of the

Minis are tied to the mainframe.

---

[10]See, for example, Robert L. French, "Making Decisions Faster with Data Base Management Systems," *Business Horizons,* October 1980, pp. 33–36.

Over the past decade computers have proved invaluable to management in increasing productivity and reducing paperwork burdens. The future will see even more reliance on these machines. It is estimated that in 1985 approximately 20 percent of all managers had personal computers (PCs) on their desks. By 1990 this will increase to 33 percent; and during this decade the number of PCs in offices will rise from 20 million to 46 million.

The number of functions that computers will be able to carry out will also increase. On a scale of 1 to 10, here is how ten experts from industry, universities, and government agencies recently ranked the likelihood of the following events:

- Computers will be able to recognize handwriting.   7.9

- There will be combined telephone/computer/TV.   7.8

- There will be instant access to all available information.   7.1

- There will be voice-controlled computers.   6.7

- There will be flat desktop computers.   6.2

Other predictions include shirt-pocket and notebook-like devices that will respond to handwritten and spoken queries and commands, and supercomputers that will be 1,000 times more powerful than today's models.

In addition, computers will be programmed so that all a manager has to do is punch a two-digit number in order to monitor inventories, cash flow, cost of sales, or other critical information. Another important development will be computer software that allows the computer to keep track of inventory, sales, cash flow, financial news, and market reports and to make this information instantly available throughout the organization. Most firms will also make use of electronic mail systems through which they will be able to send and receive intraorganizational memos, letters, and reports. Some experts are even predicting the emergence of an electronic calendar that keeps executives organized and on schedule, tracks management objectives, arranges meetings, sends reminders of deadlines, and warns when a project is falling behind. In short, computer technology is going to make the manager's job easier to perform.

Sources: Gene Bylinsky, "Technology in the Year 2000," *Fortune,* July 18, 1988, pp. 92–100; and Joel Dreyfuss, "Catching the Computer Wave," *Fortune,* September 26, 1988, pp. 78–82.

computing function is carried on outside a centralized location. Figures 10-6 through 10-8 illustrate how minis are typically used for distributed data processing in retail operations.

Notice that in Figure 10-6 the company headquarters uses a mainframe to keep track of all the operations, while each office has a mini that is used for its own operations. Within each store, as shown in Figure 10-7, the mini controls both point-of-sale transactions as well as administrative and billing

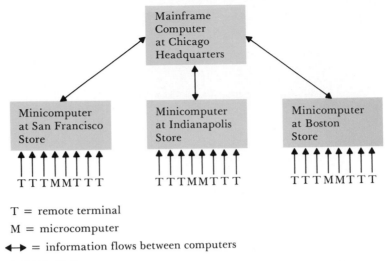

T = remote terminal

M = microcomputer

↔ = information flows between computers

FIGURE 10-6   Distributed Data Processing at the Retail Store Level

functions. If one of these functions, such as point-of-sale, requires more computer power, then it is often handled by a mini which, in turn, is tied into the computer controlling overall store operations. This latter example is illustrated in Figure 10-8.

Micros have created managerial work stations.

Microcomputers (micros) are smaller in size than minicomputers and are particularly useful in helping managers obtain computer-generated information for use in decision making. Two of the most popular of these are the IBM personal computer (IBM/PC) and the Macintosh from Apple, although there are many other models and manufacturers. Micros are small desk-top models that can be used for word processing, electronic mailing, report retrieval, filing, graphic displays, and so on. Thanks to these machines, the average manager now has a means of easily accessing the computer. They have turned the manager's desk into a workstation.

The overall term used to describe computer technology and applications that link the manager and the computer is *decision support systems* (DSSs). The

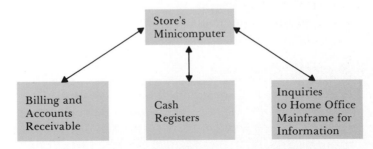

FIGURE 10-7   Minicomputer's Functions at the Retail Store Level

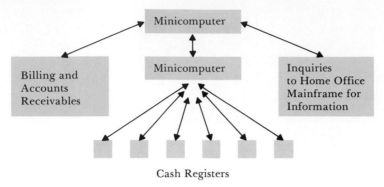

Cash Registers

FIGURE 10-8   Use of More than One Minicomputer at the Retail Store Level

objective of computer designers is to bring together the machine and the people so that each can communicate with the other, the end result being more effective decisions. This is why DSSs are of such great importance to the information system area.[11] Up to 25 percent of the average manager's day is taken up with the inefficient search for information and/or waiting around for the necessary data to be delivered. DSSs are designed to overcome this problem, and it seems likely that in the future more and more remote terminals will be used by managers in their effort to speed along the retrieval and reporting of data. Consider the following example.

> Atlantic Richfield Co. of Los Angeles . . . installed an elaborate $300,000 system of Xerox-designed word processors linked to a central memory bank. The system enables professionals in the corporate systems department to type and send memos among themselves as well as prepare their own reports and even store and retrieve research. Not only has this saved time and effort by file clerks and administrative assistants, but the entire department of 95 now functions smoothly with only five secretaries, a 1-to-19 ratio that compares with a 1-to-5 relationship throughout the rest of the corporate offices.[12]

At the same time, computers are now being linked together so that they can talk to each other. As a result, the manager can now tie into the entire system rather than merely into the data bank of one particular machine.[13] And the future promises more important breakthroughs as more powerful

---

[11]Peter G. W. Keen, "Decision Support Systems: Translating Analytic Techniques into Useful Tools," *Sloan Management Review,* Spring 1980, pp. 33–44.

[12]Christopher Byron, "Fighting the Paper Chase," *Time,* November 23, 1981, p. 66.

[13]"Linking Office Computers: The Market Comes of Age," *Business Week,* May 14, 1984, pp. 140–48.

The fundamental elements of the computer have remained the same.

minis and micros enter the market place.[14] Like it or not, many managers are going to find that the modern computer is an integral part of the equipment they will need in getting their job done.

Yet, despite the development of new computer technology, the fundamental elements of the machine have remained basically the same: input, processing, and output. First the data are fed into the computer. Then the material is processed; that is, the computer coordinates material, makes computations on the data, or works out logical decisions. Finally, the computer translates material into output, which often takes the form of printed paper or a picture displayed on a screen. Since the computer can perform these operations in a fraction of the time it would take to complete them manually, it has become an important management tool. However, a computer will only do what it is programmed to do.

Computer Programming

The *computer program* provides the machine with the step-by-step directions it is to follow. This program is usually fed into the computer on punched cards or, if it is going to be used over and over again, stored on tape or disk and called into action by the operator. Programs are generally written in computer language, and in many cases they can be purchased from computer firms. However, for a problem or assignment that is unique to the firm, a special program has to be written or a current one modified.

When a program is bought, it is often useful to first construct a flow chart of the operation to ensure that the program will be executed properly. This chart can then be translated into computer language. Figure 10-9 illustrates the flow diagram used by an investor who is pondering the purchase of a new stock. The individual has certain prerequisites which all new stocks must meet. First, they must be listed on the New York Stock Exchange. Second, their price/earnings ratio must be under ten. Third, their current prices must not be within 80 percent of their annual highs. If these three conditions are met and if sufficient funds are available in the bank or brokerage accounts, the investor will buy the stock. If not, the individual will evaluate the wisdom of taking a bank loan to buy the stock. Otherwise, the investor will compare the new stock with those in his or her present portfolio. If it appears to be a better buy than any of those currently there, the individual will sell the less profitable issues and purchase as many shares of the new stock as the proceeds make possible.

A flow diagram helps the programmer see the logic of the instructions. Anyone who has ever done any programming can attest to the fact that the

---

[14]"AT&T Takes Its First Giant Steps into Commercial Computers," *Business Week*, April 9, 1984, pp. 100–102.

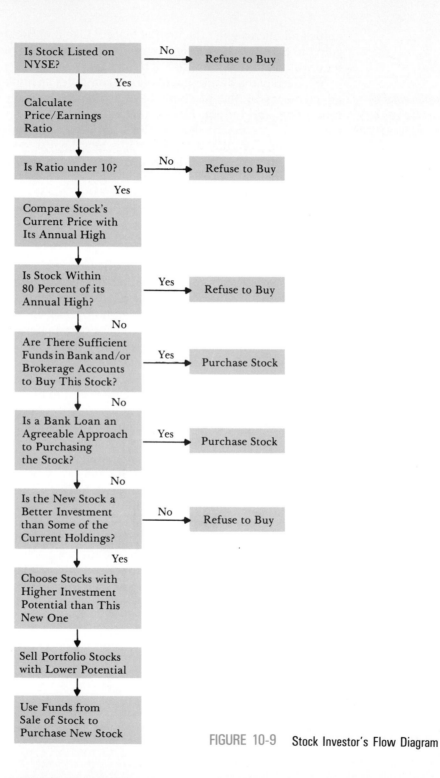

FIGURE 10-9   Stock Investor's Flow Diagram

machine operates with no brain of its own. The programmer should expect to take almost nothing for granted (although the latest computers have some flexibility along these lines). The computer will reject a program that lacks explicit instructions, or it will produce a result that is meaningless or totally wrong.

Computer program-ming teaches logic.

On the positive side, however, computer programming teaches logic. Since the computer has no mind of its own, the programmer must proceed slowly and accurately. When the machine rejects a program as illogical, the programmer, despite all the work put into the program, knows that the flow diagram is erroneous; something has been omitted or one part of the diagram is nonsensical.

Computer Uses

The computer has many uses, from handling routine paperwork to providing information for top-level decision making. The most common uses are the routine ones. Most companies employ the computer to perform arithmetic and bookkeeping functions, such as processing the payroll, computing customer account balances, or processing stockholder lists.

Inventory Control

One computer use is inventory control.

One of the widest uses of the computer is for inventory control. In retail stores, for example, it is common to find small coded tickets attached to all merchandise. When the items are sold, the tickets are torn off and sent to a central locale where the data are either placed on punched cards or read directly into the computer. In this way, the number of units on hand can be determined on a day-to-day basis, and more inventory can be ordered at the appropriate time. In recent years, large retail firms have automated their operations even further and, via machines on the sales floor, can report transactions directly to the computer. These point-of-sale systems are making it easier to control inventory.

Airline Reservations

Airlines reservations processing is another computer use.

Another major application of the computer is in airline reservations which also provides an illustration of real time. When an airline clerk requests a seat on a particular flight, the computer in turn scans its memory, reports whether seats are available on the desired flight, and automatically sends back a confirmation while simultaneously reducing the number of available seats.

Data Bank

Data banks are a third computer use.

The data bank is another approach that is gaining in popularity. Information on a subject is fed into the computer memory, thereby creating a bank of data from which individuals with questions on this subject can obtain ready answers. Airlines use this concept in regard to scheduled flights and departure times. For example, a man in San Francisco has business in

Chicago on Friday. He then wants to go on to New York. What is the earliest flight he can catch after 6:00 P.M. on Friday that will take him to Kennedy International? The agent in San Francisco will probably not know, since the person seldom handles Chicago to New York requests; but the airline will have stored this standard information in the computer so that the agent can readily get it for the passenger. Some insurance companies deposit all insurance policies in the data bank.[15] Agents seeking answers to policyholder questions can obtain, through telecommunications, up-to-date responses. Other firms feed personnel information into the data bank, including statistics such as salaries, work experience, educational background, and performance appraisals. In this way, they can obtain an immediate profile of an individual being considered for promotion or a list of personnel with a particular skill or training. In the case of IBM, managers can obtain information on business activities in their own particular regions:

> A marketing manager, for example, addresses the computer with a code number that identifies him and his responsibilities. When he inquires about the state of his business, the system displays on a screen a preanalyzed report on marketing activities in his particular region. Thus the user gets the information he needs but nothing more.[16]

Automatic Bank Teller

Automatic bank tellers are another computer use.

Another computer application is the automatic bank teller. In most parts of the country today, an individual can obtain money from a bank-teller machine after hours or on weekends by means of a special credit card. By placing this card in the machine, which is hooked up to a computer, and entering through a keyboard a personal identification code number and the amount to be withdrawn, the customer will automatically receive a packet of money and a coded receipt.[17] Furthermore, if the supply of funds allocated to the automatic teller begins to run low because of excessive withdrawals, the computer will alert a bank manager, who can come down and make more money available. In addition, the computer-run machine is capable of receiving deposits, transferring funds from checking to savings (and vice versa), and accepting time-credit loan payments.

Electronic Office

The electronic office is still another.

Another recent development has been the electronic office. Thanks to computers, it is now possible to handle typing functions faster than ever. Virtually every large organization now has word-processing capability. Many

---

[15]William J. Bruns, Jr. and F. Warren McFarlan, "Information Technology Puts Power in Control Systems," *Harvard Business Review*, September–October 1987, p. 90.

[16]Boehm, "Shaping Decisions with Systems Analysis," p. 96.

[17]Currently, in most places, withdrawals are limited to $200 a day.

secretaries no longer use electric typewriters to produce letters and memo-randums. They type them on word-processing machines or personal comput-ers that perform word-processing chores; in this way deletions, additions, and rearranging can be done before the final copy is ever printed. This development has helped to increase both the output and the accuracy of written communications. Some organizations also have developed electronic mail systems. One of the characteristics of these systems is the ability to convey the same memorandum to a number of different people and, at the same time, to store the original document in a computer file, thereby eliminating the need for physical filing of the memorandum. These develop-ments are reducing the time and costs associated with internal communiques while helping to increase the overall efficiency of the enterprise.[18]

Simulation

In recent years, computer *simulation* has also been employed to handle "what if" questions. By simulating a situation, the manager can plug in different decisions and evaluate the outcome of each:

> If, say, the manager enters the price, the expected volume, and certain budgetary decisions, the computer will provide a pro forma profit and loss statement for that item. The judgment of the manager is used to suggest alternatives for consideration. The power of the computer is used to carry out the manager's understanding of the quantitative relationships between inputs and outputs—e.g., prices, volumes, and annual profits. The judgment of the manager is . . . called on to determine if the answer is acceptable or if further trials should be made to secure data or judgments which may produce a more acceptable output.[19]

Computer simulations must be accurate.

The key to the successful use of the computer in this instance is determined by how well the company has been able to simulate actual conditions. If the model is accurate, the information being fed back to the manager is reliable; if not, the data upon which the individual is basing the decision is worthless.

A number of firms have recently moved toward the use of computer simulation in helping their managers make decisions. In addition to the effect of price on quantity, other typical "what if" questions include:

> If a proposed new item of equipment is purchased or leased, what will be the effects on profits and cash flow of alternative financing methods?

[18]For more on this subject, see Louis H. Mertes, "Doing Your Office Over—Electronically," *Harvard Business Review*, March–April 1981, pp. 127–35.

[19]Curtis H. Jones, "At Last: Real Computer Power for Decision Makers," *Harvard Business Review*, September–October 1970, p. 79.

If a wage increase is granted, what will be the effect on production rates, use of overtime, risk of seasonal inventory, and so on, for a production program?[20]

The questions, along with the assumptions made by the simulation designer and/or manager, are fed into the computer and evaluated according to the probability of their occurrence. The answer is then printed out in whatever form is desired; rate of return, cost analysis, balance sheet, and income statement are all possible examples. Figure 10-10 provides a general illustration.

In addition, some firms have developed models that help them make decisions when some particular problem develops. Consider the following:

At 9:32 A.M. a blowout! A blast furnace breaks down in the steel plant. Cold iron will have to be heated to produce the molten iron normally supplied to the refining process from this furnace. Processing time will be almost doubled, reducing the shop's production capacity by 60%. The cost per ton of steel will certainly rise sharply as a result of the increased processing time. But how much will it rise?

Using a remote time-shared computer terminal in his office, a manager at Island Steel Company defines the new conditions resulting from the equipment failure and enters them in a set of models which simulate the steelmaking process and the costs involved. At 11:26

---

[20]James B. Boulden and Elwood S. Buffa, "Corporate Models: On-Line, Real-time Systems," *Harvard Business Review*, July–August 1970, p. 67.

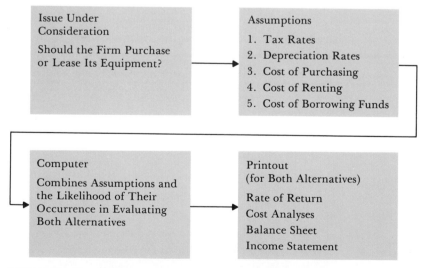

FIGURE 10-10   Simulation of a Purchase versus Lease Strategy

A.M.—less than two hours later, the same morning—he estimates the new cost figures and prepares a revised corporate profit projection . . . the computer has vastly enhanced his decision-making capability.[21]

Thus, the computer has proved to be a valuable tool for management decision making. However, there are some very important drawbacks which also merit consideration.

Drawbacks to Computers

The most common argument raised against computers is that they are expensive investments which are never fully utilized. However, many managers, determined to have the latest, most sophisticated equipment, allow themselves to be sold more hardware (that is, computer machine) than they really need. As *Business Week* has noted: "Perhaps only members of the Flat Earth Society would deny that data-processing technology has revolutionized almost every aspect of the operation of a business. Yet even the strongest proponents of that revolution concede that the computer equipment in place at most companies has grown in sophistication much faster than the managerial capability for directing its use.[22]

Some companies buy expensive toys instead of the hardware they really need.

A second problem is that managers have a habit of overrating computer results, failing to remember that the output is only as valid as the input. Researchers Fred Luthans and Robert Koester, for example, conducted an experiment in which they determined that individuals with no computer training are more willing to abide by information presented in computer printout form than in noncomputer printout form. In short, people who lack a computer background are often awed by computer results and assign to them a validity and reliability that is not actually justified.[23]

Computer information can be overrated.

A third major problem is information overload. Computers can generate enormous quantities of data, but can the manager effectively use all of this information? Based on his research, O'Reilly reports that while perceived information overload brings about high satisfaction it also lowers the performance of decision makers.[24] So more is not necessarily better; in fact it can be detrimental to the overall decision-making process.

Managers also tend to overrate the capabilities of the computer, creating a third kind of problem. In reality the limitations of the machines are severe, but many decision makers see the machines as characterized by HAL, the on-board computer in *2001: A Space Odyssey*.[25] Highly sophisticated, HAL was

Computer capability can be overrated too.

[21]Ibid., p. 65.

[22]"Solving a Computer Mismatch in Management," *Business Week*, April 2, 1979, p. 73.

[23]Fred Luthans and Robert Koester, "The Impact of Computer Generated Information on the Choice Activities of Decision Makers," *Academy of Management Journal*, June 1976, pp. 328–32.

[24]Charles A. O'Reilly III, "Individuals and Information Overload in Organizations: Is More Necessarily Better?" *Academy of Management Journal*, December 1980, pp. 684–96.

[25]Arthur C. Clarke, *2001: A Space Odyssey* (New York: New American Library, 1968).

capable of phenomenal feats. In fact, he could virtually think like a human. Unfortunately, there was an error in his program. But, being humanlike, he fought for survival and killed most of the crew before he was finally deprogrammed and rendered harmless. In reality, HAL is still very much a concept. While there are computer programs for playing chess and other interactive games, there is still a long way to go before computers will be able to handle many of the decision-making chores facing operating managers. Simply put, artificial intelligence in the form of "smart" computers is not as far advanced as many people believe. These machines are often able to make decisions only in narrow fields of expertise and, if a problem falls outside this area, the computer is unable to respond appropriately.[26]

In fact, many of the promises made about the computer, outside the sphere of computational work, have simply not materialized. Over a decade ago Curtis H. Jones reported that, with the possible exception of logistics, the trend is actually away from computerized management decision making.[27] Since then things have not changed a great deal. Companies such as Western Electric, Hughes Aircraft, and Fairfield Manufacturing have all, to varying degrees, followed this retrenchment approach, shifting all or part of the decision-making functions from the computer to staff members. Of course, other companies are moving in the opposite direction, but the point is that the computer is only a management tool. It is not a replacement for the human decision maker. Along these lines, Steven L. Alter has observed:

> My findings show what other researchers have reported: applications are being developed and used to *support* the manager responsible for making and implementing decisions, rather than to *replace* him. In other words, people in a growing number of organizations are using what are often called decision support systems to improve their managerial effectiveness.[28]

As long as managers are aware of what the computer cannot do, they are in a good position to evaluate and maximize its usefulness in the decision-making process.

INFORMATION SYSTEMS AND PEOPLE

A well-designed information system can provide the manager with all the information necessary to make effective decisions. However, since this decision process takes place at every level of the organization, it is inevitable that information systems will have an impact on the people who work within it. Before discussing the effects of such systems on organization members, it

---

[26]Beau Sheil, "Thinking about Artificial Intelligence," *Harvard Business Review,* July–August 1987, pp. 91–97.

[27]Jones, p. 78.

[28]Steven L. Alter, "How Effective Managers Use Information Systems," *Harvard Business Review,* November–December 1976, p. 97.

is important to note how the quantitative school overlaps that of the management process and behavioral areas. The quantitative people provide information useful in planning and controlling operations, two areas of key importance to the process school. However, the quantitative people do sometimes create behavioral problems in the organization's employees, who often feel threatened by new information systems and the introduction of computer facilities.[29] This section examines the link between the quantitative and behavioral schools by studying the impact of change brought on by information systems.

How is the introduction of a new information system received by organization personnel? Whenever change is introduced into an organization, there is a chance that it will result in some dysfunctional behavior. Quite simply, change tends to frighten people; and the greater the change, the more likely it is that people will resist it or react to it by way of defense mechanisms of one form or another.

Change in information systems is often viewed by employees simply as a more efficient information tool; in such cases it is welcomed. However, change brings uncertainty and is therefore sometimes viewed by employees as a threat; in such cases it can result in the development of frustration or anxiety. The response, of course, will depend on the situation and the individuals affected. What must be realized is that, like all other changes introduced into the system, information systems can cause behavioral problems.

Factors Causing Dysfunctional Behavior

New information systems can cause dysfunctional behavior.

Research indicates that when an information system is introduced into the organization, five major factors can cause dysfunctional behavior.[30]

First, the new system often necessitates redefinition of departmental boundaries. Some people are transferred to other departments; others stay in their present unit but are given new or expanded duties. In either case these changes, even though they may bring about greater organizational operating efficiency, can cause employee resistance because they upset the status quo in the formal organization structure.

Second, there may be an accompanying effect on the informal structure: "An organization tends to develop a system of values, ethical codes, taboos, special working relations. . . . The impact of a new system on the informal structure can be as serious in terms of creating behavioral disturbances as the impact on the formal structure."[31]

---

[29]Carol A. Beatty and John R. M. Gordon, "Barriers to the Implementation of CAD/CAD Systems," *Sloan Management Review*, Summer 1988, pp. 25–33.

[30]G. W. Dickson and John K. Simmons, "The Behavioral Side of MIS," *Business Horizons*, August 1970, pp. 59–71.

[31]Ibid., p. 61.

INTERVIEW WITH JOSIE LEBAR

Josie Lebar is the treasurer for Silver Lining Systems, a rapidly growing, successful computer networking and communications company. The firm specializes in installing PC networks, as well as teaching businesses how to use the computer. Silver Lining also sells and installs computer hardware and software accounting and communication systems to the market at large, trains personnel to use these systems, and provides the necessary support help to the client. In addition to her job as comptroller, Josie is actively involved in providing support assistance to these clients, who range from small accounting firms to Fortune 500 corporations.

Q. *What new changes in computers can we expect that will have an effect on the way business is conducted during the 1990s?*

A. The major one will be that people are going to rely much more heavily on the computer for communication purposes. For example, electronic mail will become more popular and written communiques in the form of inter- and intradepartmental memos that are physically sent to each individual will decline. If someone wants to communicate with you, the person will send you an electronic mail memo. All you will have to do is periodically check your electronic mailbox and pick up your messages. This development will expand communication lines and make it easier both to send information to others and get it from them. The system will be particularly useful for personnel in companies that have more than one work shift. You'll be able to leave a computer message and know that someone hasn't failed to deliver it or the other person forgot to go to his or her mail tray to check for messages. It's all on the computer and everyone is trained to check for messages on a periodic basis.

Third, some people, especially older ones with many years of company service, often see the development as threatening. They believe the new system will replace them.

Fourth, in many organizations change is introduced without proper consideration of the opinions, fears, or anxieties of the employees. When this error occurs, the management information system faces trouble from the very start.

Fifth, and closely related to the above factor, is the method of introducing change. Douglas McGregor, the noted behaviorist, has written: "A fair

Another change will be increased computer power. This will allow even the smallest firms to cut some of their operating costs. Small offices, for example, will be able to automate significant parts of their operation. Word processing is a good example since typing and filing is often a big expense in many small operations. Firms will now be able to reduce their labor costs and become more market competitive. This computer development will also free up personnel to do less busy work and more think work. For example, even small CPA firms will find themselves able to conduct "what if" financial projections and provide more substantive investment and tax advice than ever before. Their job will become more than just one of helping a client maintain financial records.

A third change will be computer voice recognition. By the end of the 1990s computers will be able to identify voice commands and respond appropriately. This development will not only greatly reduce (if not totally eliminate) the need for dictating equipment, but it will cut the time needed to produce written communiques such as memos, letters, and reports.

Q. *Many people seem to be afraid of computerization. Given the fact that there seem to be so many advantages associated with the use of these machines, why do computers scare people?*

A. This fear is becoming less common, although it certainly exists. Mainly it's because the machines test the person's learning skills, and many people are insecure about learning a new skill which they think they will be monitored and tested. They are convinced that if they can't master the computer or quickly learn to use it to help them do their job, they are going to look dumb. They believe the machine will identify them as incompetent and management will then fire them. However, these fears are usually short-lived. The latest machines are extremely user-friendly, and once people learn how to use them the fear of unemployment tends to dissipate. At this point I hear many people say, "Wow, I can't believe we used to operate around here without computers. How did we ever do it?" In short, computers are going to become an integral part of every organization's information system and decision-making process.

amount of research has pointed up the fact that resistance to change is a reaction primarily to certain methods of instituting change rather than an inherent human characteristic."[32] Of course, these are not the only factors that may lead to dysfunctional behavior. They are, however, the most common and can result in a host of frustration reactions.

[32]Douglas McGregor, "The Scanlon Plan through a Psychologist's Eyes," in *Technology, Industry and Man,* ed. C. A. Walker (New York: McGraw-Hill, 1968), p. 124.

Frustration Reactions

Common frustration reactions include aggression, projection, and avoidance.

When one or more of the above factors is present, organizational personnel may encounter frustration. This frustration can manifest itself in many ways. The three general patterns most often associated with the introduction of a new information system are aggression, projection, and avoidance. To bring all of this together, consider the case of a company that installs a new system and, in the process, redefines departmental boundaries and breaks up an informal organization. How do the members of the informal group respond to the situation? Using a needs-satisfaction approach, Figure 10-11 provides an illustration.

Aggression is an attack (physical or nonphysical) against the object believed to be causing the problem. Sometimes this takes the form of sabotage. More commonly it occurs when people try to beat the system, as in the following example:

> The setting was an information system in a complex organization designed to collect man-hours in different work stations on a daily basis. Workers were frequently rotating from one workstation to another during the day, and were supposed to clock in and out each time they moved from one station to another. During the course of an interview, one worker indicated that there had been some "ganging up" on an unpopular foreman. Workers would not punch out of a particular area when leaving for another workstation or would punch in at the unpopular foreman's area and then work in a different area.[33]

Projection occurs when people blame something (or someone) for their own shortcomings. For example, if incompetent managers claim that the new

---

[33]Dickson and Simmons, p. 62.

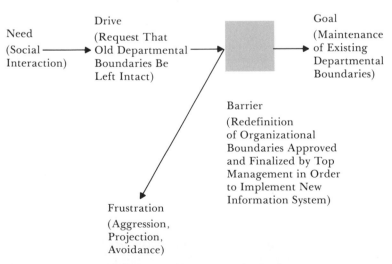

FIGURE 10-11   Frustration Created by a New Information System

information systems are feeding them insufficient information for making effective decisions, they are projecting blame for their own shortcomings onto a setup victim.

Avoidance takes place when people withdraw from a situation because it is too frustrating for them. With an information system this can occur, for example, if managers find they can receive the same information in less time from a different source and so react by ignoring the system's output. Richard L. Daft and Norman B. MacIntosh made this particularly clear when they noted that many information systems are simply too sophisticated and costly for the firms using them. The result is that people do not use them; instead they find ways to circumvent them. The best rule of the road is: When in doubt, use a simple system. Daft and MacIntosh have said it this way:

> Organizations should simply try to avoid the big, costly information system errors: don't waste time and money imposing an elaborate information system upon craft activities; don't expect technical professional tasks to struggle along without adequate information system support; don't use precise, voluminous information in a basic research setting; and don't provide massive reports and information to people engaged in routine work.[34]

The Organization and Information Systems

Thus far the negative effects of information systems on the organization have been examined in general terms. In order to make a more specific analysis, it is necessary to consider the impact of such systems on those who will be using them. The orientations of the developers, often computer specialists and systems designers, and the users, typically managers and operating personnel, are often quite different. Table 10-2 provides a comparison.

The users do not always see things the way the systems designers do. The latter typically view the information system as helpful to the organization because better and more useful data will be provided for decision making. The former often see a new information system as personally threatening. This situation becomes clearer through a close look at the four distinct subgroups in the organizational hierarchy: operating personnel, operating management, technical staff, and top management.[35] Each will respond differently.

Organization subgroups respond differently.

Operating personnel consist of two basic groups, nonclerical and clerical. The nonclerical people perform such functions as filling out forms or entering prepunched cards in a source recorder. When an organization computerizes or puts in a new information system, these people often feel threatened. Although some turn to minor sabotage, such as "forgetting" to do certain

---

[34]Richard L. Daft and Norman B. MacIntosh, "A New Approach to Design and Use of Management Information," *California Management Review,* Fall 1978, p. 91.
[35]Ibid., pp. 63–67.

TABLE 10-2
Computer Designers and Computer Users: A Comparison

Orientation	Computer Designers	Computer Users
Goal orientation	Are interested in the latest computer technology	Want easy-to-understand solutions
	Like to solve problems in elegant ways	Focus on solving problems in the most practical way
	Are agents of change	Tend to resist change
Time orientation	Long-term projects	Short-term projects
	Can wait for feedback	Like immediate feedback
Interpersonal orientation	Are problem oriented	Are people oriented
	Are technical in thinking	Are human-conceptual in orientation
	Like to analyze and evaluate things	Like to make decisions
Formality of the structure	Like freedom of action	Work through the formal hierarchy
	Have a few formal rules	Have many formal rules
	Are project oriented	Pursue varied goals
	Often bypass the chain of command	Follow the chain of command very closely

things or making deliberate mistakes, most employ projection, blaming the system for everything that goes wrong in the office.

Clerical workers mainly process input and convert it into output, and they are considered part of the information system itself. Changes in their work patterns may entail moving them from a manual to an *electronic data processing (EDP) system*, for example. Although some clerical people may be displaced, most are maintained in greatly upgraded jobs which require more education and formal training. Even so, these workers tend to have negative initial reactions because they believe they are going to be replaced. Like their nonclerical counterparts, they adopt projection behaviors and start blaming the new system for any mistakes that occur.

Operating managers are all management personnel from first-line supervisors up to and including middle management. These individuals receive much of the output from information systems (see Management in Action: Information Systems by Committee). However, the systems also tend to centralize decision making and increase the control of higher-level managers over their subordinates. As a result, when operating managers fight the system, they do so by providing inadequate support to it and by failing to use the decision-making information provided by it. In so doing, they employ aggression, avoidance, and projection.

The technical staff, which consists of programmers and systems designers, is most involved with the information system. For this reason, it exhibits none

One of the biggest problems with committees is that they are a waste of time and money. Their work could easily be assigned to individual managers who could handle things faster and more economically. There is one area, however, where committees are proving to be worth their salt: managing information systems. There are two forces bringing about the creation of these committees: decentralization and strategy choice.

As computers, especially micros, have become commonplace in business, managers no longer have to wait around for computer printouts and other data from the major mainframe. They are able to use their micros to get whatever data they need for decision making. As a result, the centralized computer information system of the 1970s has now given way to a decentralized one in which managers have increased authority over their own operations.

At the same time businesses are finding themselves spending three or four times as much on information systems technology as they did a decade ago. This is resulting in the formation of information systems committees to monitor what and how information technology is managed in the firm. These committees are being charged with linking corporate strategy with information technology strategy. In doing so, four areas are being given priority.

Direction setting. This function links corporate strategy and computer strategy. It consists of setting objectives for the use of computers, formulating strategy to focus on these goals, devising policies that are consistent with these objectives, and reviewing and approving long-range computer plans for ensuring that they are in harmony with priorities and goals.

Structuring. The focus here is on making certain that organization design is appropriate to ensure effective use of computers. Particular attention is given to the centralization versus decentralization issue.

Staffing. This function is concerned with selecting the right managers for essential computer-related positions.

Advising and auditing. The purpose of these functions is to ensure that computer activity is kept on the right track. The advising responsibility involves helping top computer managers with problem solving. The auditing function calls for an evaluation of the company's performance in using computers.

Is the information systems committee just a passing fad or will it endure as an organizational form? Richard Nolan, after surveying 109 companies that had functioning corporate-wide executive steering committees, reports that there has been a dramatic increase over the past eight years in the number of firms using such committees. This growing use has led him to conclude that, "Though the committee structure has always been cumbersome . . . it is proving to be the most effective way to deal with the forces of computer decentralization without dissipating the company's investments in building a computer capability. It has also proved to be the most effective vehicle for making strategic choices among computer-based technologies and for deciding how fast the company should move toward their adoption."*

*Richard L. Nolan, "Managing Information Systems by Committee," *Harvard Business Review*, July–August 1982, p. 79.

of the common dysfunctional behavior patterns. On the other hand, the technical staff does not get along well with the operating managers. There seems to be a natural clash between the system designers (technical staff) and the system users (operating managers).

Top management is little affected by new information systems. Research shows that many top executives just do not get involved in designing the corporate information system. Some may attend short computer courses in order to obtain background information in the area, and many pay lip service to the value of such systems in effective decision making. Most executives, however, are unconcerned with the area.[36] The reasons for resistance are explained in greater depth in Table 10-3.

This section has examined the behavioral effects of information systems, with primary emphasis on some of the dysfunctional aspects. Although the

---

[36]For more on how modern organizations can go about managing this problem, see Fred R. McFadden and James D. Suver, "Costs and Benefits of a Data Base System," *Harvard Business Review*, January–February 1978, pp. 131–39; and Richard L. Nolan, "Managing the Crises in Data Processing," *Harvard Business Review*, March–April 1979, pp. 115–26.

TABLE 10-3

Causes for Resistance to Information Systems (by Working Groups)

	Operating (Nonclerical)	Operating (Clerical)	Operating Management	Top Management
Threats to economic security		X	X	
Threats to status or power		X	X*	
Increased job complexity	X		X	X
Uncertainty or unfamiliarity	X	X	X	X
Changed interpersonal relations or work patterns		X*	X	
Changed superior-subordinate relationships		X*	X	
Increased rigidity or time pressure	X	X	X	
Role ambiguity		X	X*	X
Feelings of insecurity		X	X*	X*

X = The reason is possibly the cause of resistance to information system development.
X* = The reason has a strong possibility of being the cause of resistance.

Source: G. W. Dickson and John K. Simmons, "The Behavioral Side of the MIS," *Business Horizons,* August 1970, p. 68. Copyright 1970 by the Foundation for the School of Business at Indiana University. Reprinted with permission.

problems described are common, not every change leads to them. The situation does not have to be this way. Many frustration reactions can be prevented if management: (1) works closely with the affected units, training them to understand and accept the new system by pointing out the benefits to the company while ensuring that any displaced employees are given jobs elsewhere in the organization; (2) designs the system with cogent inputs from all affected groups so that information from the system is both timely and useful; and (3) attains top management support from the very beginning. There are many advantages to be gained from a management information system, and a firm can obtain them if it is aware of the potential problems and pitfalls associated with the establishment of such a system. As Archie Carroll, a frequent contributor to the literature has noted, "Developing a successful computer-based information system requires more than just technical knowledge. An awareness of human needs and behavior is as important a component as specialized knowledge.[37]

■ SUMMARY

This chapter has examined two topics: information systems and the computer. Many information systems are computerized, but this is not universal. Nevertheless, the two areas have one common characteristic: They help relate the departments and units of the organization into a harmonious system.

The primary goal of any information system is to provide decision-making information to the manager. For this reason, a well-designed system must be planned with the needs of management in mind and must follow a from-the-top-down philosophy. In addition, the system must discriminate by organization level, providing the right kinds of information to each. For example, top management will need general information from which to formulate strategic plans. Middle management will need more specific data for drawing up budgets and measuring and appraising managerial performance. Lower-level management will need very specific data for use in areas such as production scheduling and inventory control.

The modern computer is often employed as part of an information system, providing necessary information to managers throughout the hierarchy. In addition to performing bookkeeping and arithmetic functions, it is also being used for such functions as inventory control and airline reservations processing. Another one of its latest applications is answering "what if" questions through simulation.

Despite their great value, computers have some important drawbacks, of which management must be aware. First, many companies tend to buy more

---

[37]Archie B. Carroll, "Behavioral Aspects of Developing Computer-Based Information Systems," *Business Horizons*, January–February 1982, p. 42.

complex computers than they need. Second, many managers place too much faith in computer printout results. Third, many managers tend to overrate the capabilities of the computer. There are a large number of things people still do much better than any machine and qualitative decision making is one of them.

The introduction of an information system into an organization can bring about dysfunctional behavior such as aggression, projection, and avoidance. In order to overcome these problems, management must be willing to adopt a participative decision-making approach that introduces the new system, relates its advantages to the personnel, and assures that any persons replaced because of it will have employment secured for them elsewhere.

This chapter has also noted how management information and computer systems help managers do better planning and controlling, thereby establishing the fact that there is a link between the quantitative and process schools. Likewise, it has been noted that information systems can bring about dysfunctional behavior, thus illustrating that any advocate of the quantitative school must also be aware of the behavioral side of enterprise; there is thus a link between the quantitative and behavioral schools. Another area where many of these decision-making ideas are put into action is that of operations research. This will be the focus of our attention in the next chapter.

■ REVIEW AND STUDY QUESTIONS

1. What is a management information system? Explain.

2. What is the primary objective in the design of an effective information system?

3. What role should information system determinants and key success variables play in an information system design?

4. How does the modern computer differ from its early counterpart? What technological changes have occurred? What new ones can be expected in the next decade?

5. How are mini- and microcomputers being used by business? Explain.

6. Why are computer programs so important to the processing of computerized data?

7. What are four common uses of the computer? Explain.

8. How is the computer being employed in answering "what if" questions? Give an illustration.

9. What are the basic drawbacks to the use of computers?

10. What are the three common dysfunctional forms of behavior often associated with the introduction of a new management information system? Explain each.

11. According to recent research, how do operating personnel tend to oppose the introduction of an information system? Operating management? Technical staff? Top management?

12. In what ways do information systems provide a bridge between the quantitative school and the process school? The quantitative school and the behavioral school?

■ SELECTED REFERENCES

Alber, Antone F. "Get Ready for Electronic Publishing." *Business Horizons,* January–February 1983, pp. 51–55.

Alter, Steven L. "How Effective Managers Use Information Systems." *Harvard Business Review,* November–December 1976, pp. 97–104.

"AT&T Takes Its First Giant Steps into Commercial Computers." *Business Week,* April 9, 1984, pp. 100–105.

Beatty, Carol, and John R. M. Gordon. "Barriers to the Implementation of CAD/CAM Systems." *Sloan Management Review,* Summer 1988, pp. 25–33.

Boehm, George A. W. "Shaping Decisions with Systems Analysis." *Harvard Business Review,* September–October 1976, pp. 91–99.

Bruns, William J., Jr., and F. Warren McFarlan. "Information Technology Puts Power in Control Systems." *Harvard Business Review,* September–October 1987, pp. 89–94.

Buss, Martin D. J. "Penny-Wise Approach to Data Processing." *Harvard Business Review,* July–August 1981, pp. 111–17.

Bylinsky, Gene. "Technology in the Year 2000." *Fortune,* July 18, 1988, pp. 92–98.

Carroll, Archie B. "Behaviorial Aspects of Developing Computer-Based Information Systems." *Business Horizons,* January–February 1982, pp. 42–51.

Dery, David. "Putting Information Technology to Work." *California Management Review,* Spring 1980, pp. 68–76.

Dickson, G. W., and John K. Simmons. "The Behavioral Side of MIS." *Business Horizons,* August 1970, pp. 59–71.

Dreyfuss, Joel. "Catching the Computer Wave." *Fortune,* September 26, 1988, pp. 78–82.

French, Robert L. "Making Decisions Faster with Data Based Management Systems." *Business Horizons,* October 1980, pp. 33–36.

Hutsell, William R., and Steven L. Quisenberry. "The Computer as Tool: Forecasting Salary Costs." *Personnel Journal,* June 1981, pp. 461–63.

Keen, Peter G. W. "Decision Support Systems: Translating Analytic Techniques into Useful Tools." *Sloan Management Review,* Spring 1980, pp. 33–44.

"Linking Office Computers: The Market Comes of Age." *Business Week,* May 14, 1984, pp. 140–48.

Mansour, Ali H. "The Determinants of Computer Based Information System Performance." *Academy of Management Journal,* September 1983, pp. 521–33.

Markoff, John. "The Chip at 30: Potential Still Vast." *New York Times,* September 14, 1988, pp. 32, 40.

Mertes, Louis H. "Doing Your Office Over—Electronically." *Harvard Business Review,* March–April 1981, pp. 127–35.

Mockler, Robert J. "Computer Information Systems and Strategic Corporate Planning." *Business Horizons,* May–June 1987, pp. 32–37.

O'Reilly III, Charles A. "Individuals and Information Overload in Organizations: Is More Necessarily Better?" *Academy of Management Journal,* December 1980, pp. 684–96.

"Publishers Go Electronic." *Business Week,* June 11, 1984, pp. 84–97.

Rockart, John F. "The Changing Role of the Information Systems Executive: A Critical Success Factors Perspective." *Sloan Management Review,* Fall 1982, pp. 3–13.

Sheil, Beau. "Thinking about Artificial Intelligence." *Harvard Business Review,* July–August 1987, pp. 91–97.

■ CASE: Somebody Goofed

Computers often help organizations by processing information quickly—but, unfortunately, not always efficiently. Sometimes the computer is programmed incorrectly; sometimes it is not given the latest information. The result can be frustrating, as seen by the following incidents:

> The Social Security Administration notified a woman that because her husband had died, his monthly benefits were cut off. It took the man four months to get the local benefits office to recognize that he was still alive and that it was all a computer error.
>
> A woman received a credit card bill for $00.00. Ignoring it, she soon began to receive weekly notices regarding her "unpaid balance." Finally, she sent the firm a check for $00.00 and the notices stopped—but she then received a charge for late payment of the bill.
>
> A large hotel sent its past customers a letter thanking them for their patronage and telling them of the hotel's new modernization plan. Unfortunately, the computer programmer requested the wrong mailing list, and the hotel was deluged with phone calls from husbands demanding an explanation for their wives, who were themselves demanding explanations, some threatening divorce.

In an effort to prevent such computer goofs, Shell Oil has set up a toll-free telephone line for customers who call about their computerized bills.

Corning Glass Works has installed a computer to deal with complaints about the quality and durability of its products. The computer types an individualized letter in response to a consumer's gripe and, if necessary, triggers an order to a warehouse for a replacement part. In view of the tremendous computerization of business and considering how computers are being relied on to respond to computer-related errors, most Americans admit that they never expect to return to an era when most business dealings are on a person-to-person basis. Rather, they believe they will have to live with computer-generated problems.

Questions

1. What are some of the advantages of using computers? Do they outweigh the disadvantages? Explain.

2. What does this case suggest about the fallibility of computers and computer programmers?

3. Since computers are apparently here to stay, what steps can managers take to prevent incidents such as those described in this case?

■ CASE: The Old Ways Are Best

When the Savonarola Corporation brought in an outside management consulting firm, it asked the firm to examine company operations from top to bottom. Return on investment had not risen above 6 percent in three years, and top management felt something had to be done. The company was relying on the consultants to tell it what this should be.

Six weeks later, the consultants submitted their list of recommendations. One called for the design of a new management information system. "Savonarola managers at the present time are relying too heavily on an outdated and ineffective reporting system," read part of the report. "This system should be scrapped and a new one designed from the top down, with major emphasis given to providing up-to-date, relevant data useful for decision making."

The idea sounded fine to the top-level staff, who ordered the DP (data processing) departments to design a new information system. After talking to people at all levels of the hierarchy and evaluating the current reporting system, the DP people submitted their proposal. The plan looked fine on paper, and the corporate president ordered it implemented.

Over the next twelve months, however, the company's return on investment failed to reflect any great changes in efficiency. As before, ROI stood below 6 percent. When top management decided to find out why, one of the areas it examined was the new information system. In essence, the executives discovered that managers at all levels of the organization were still relying on their old reporting systems. Virtually no one was using any of the data provided by the new system. When one of the managers was asked why he was not utilizing the new system, he replied, "Why should I? I have my own reporting system, and it tells me all I need to know. If you ask me, this whole new information system design was just a waste of money, and I could have told you that a long time ago."

Questions

1. What kinds of information should a manager receive from a well-designed information system? Explain, incorporating the term *key success variables* into your answer.
2. What error did Savonarola make in this case?
3. What recommendations are now in order? Explain your answer.

■ CASE: Simulation Programs

Ed Stoner, president of a medium-size firm, has come to realize that in the manufacturing business one always has to expect the unexpected. For example, two months ago one of the large machines in his company's Plant 3 went down, and it took almost two days to repair it. A few weeks later Stoner learned that the company had lost 14 percent of its total weekly output because of the machine's downtime. This cost the firm $87,000 in sales and $12,500 in profit before taxes. These data were determined by the accounting department and were based on previous cost and revenue figures.

Yesterday Stoner had a visit from a software computer salesperson who wanted to develop a "what if" software package for Stoner's firm. The package would be designed to help Stoner and his managers determine the overall effects of machine downtime, work stoppages, increases in the cost of goods sold, and a host of other key operational factors.

The computer firm would begin by analyzing Stoner's business operations, determining the relationships between critical operating factors and financial results. It would then write a computer simulation that could be used in determining the overall effect of a host of production problems. Additionally, the simulation would be useful later for anticipating problems and making early decisions, thereby reducing the overall negative effect should one or more problems occur. The salesperson explained it this way:

> By feeding a potential problem into the simulation we will develop for you, your managers can determine the overall effect of that problem on their operations. An income statement for the next three, six, and twelve months can also be determined after allowing for the problem. Finally, working backward, your people can devote their energies to preventing the most serious problems from occurring. For example, if a delay in the

delivery of vital raw materials has the greatest effect on your firm's income, a second supplier can be found and used as a backup whenever the first one cannot deliver the needed materials on time.

Of course, this is only one way the simulation can help. However, it illustrates how potential problems can be resolved through decision making today. And if something unanticipated does happen, the program will provide your people with assistance in analyzing the overall effects on operations and profitability, and it will help you pinpoint key decision areas that have to be addressed.

Stoner liked the basic idea of a "what if" program, although he felt overwhelmed by its many ramifications. He was also concerned that by relying on a computer program, he might be taking too much decision-making power out of the hands of his own people. "And," he worried aloud, "what if something goes wrong with the computer? What if the program is incorrect or fails to address some major problem? What will I do then?" Stoner told the salesperson to come back in a month. He planned in the interim to discuss the matter with his top managers.

Questions

1. How valuable can these "what if" simulation programs be in providing information for managerial decision making?
2. What are the drawbacks to using them? Explain.
3. What should Stoner do? Why?

■ CASE: Controlling Operations More Efficiently

Companies use their computers to perform many different functions. One of the major ones is controlling operations by providing critical information for decision making. This use of "information technology" is proving very profitable in helping firms implement their strategies more efficiently. It is also beneficial in gaining and maintaining market share.

One interesting case is provided by a national insurance firm that decided to reorganize its computer files by customer name rather than by policy number. This new arrangement was more effective because it allowed an agent to call up an insured's file quickly and review the individual's coverage. With this information at hand, the agent was then in a position to suggest replacement of outmoded insurance or to recommend a supplement to current coverage. This new approach was much more "market-driven" than the old one and proved extremely effective in helping the company hold on to its customers. In an industry like insurance, where a large percentage of current revenue is generated by new customer sales rather than additional sales from old customers, this strategy helped the company gain an edge on the competition.

In another case a passenger elevator firm decided to centralize all service calls and then assign the work to the various field offices. Under the old arrangement, the field office personnel had serviced passenger elevators within their geographic area. With the centralized information system, the firm was able to pinpoint those customers who needed the most service and those problems that most often recurred. Armed with this information, the company was able to improve the quality of its service, allocate service calls more efficiently to the field offices, schedule preventive maintenance regularly for customers, and adjust staff levels and retrain service representative as needed. The ultimate result was that the firm was able to cut service costs and increase its market share.

Questions

1. In what way did the insurance company link its information systems and computer operations?

2. How did the change in strategy help the passenger elevator company become more "market responsive?" Explain.

3. In what way did the new strategies of both firms help them provide higher quality service? Be complete in your answer.

Source: William J. Bruns, Jr. and F. Warren McFarlan, "Information Technology Puts Power in Control Systems," *Harvard Business Review,* September–October 1987, pp. 89–94.

■ SELF-FEEDBACK EXERCISE: Forecasting the Future of Computers

What is the likely future of computers? What types of breakthroughs can we expect both in computer technology and in the functions performed by these machines? Read each of the following 20 statements and determine the likelihood of the occurrence by the year 2000. If you believe the possibility is 50 percent or greater, answer true; if you believe the possibility is less than 50 percent, answer false.

T F 1. Voice-controlled computers will be commercially available.

T F 2. Sophisticated computers will be able to beat master chess players.

T F 3. Computer-aided design and computer-aided manufacturing systems will replace many architects and engineers.

T F 4. There will be a dramatic increase in the use of computer-friendliness.

T F 5. Computer-run telephones will be able to provide instantaneous translation of foreign messages into English.

T F 6. Computers will be able to serve as full-fledged electronic wind tunnels for testing new aircraft design.

T F 7. Mathematical modeling of complex phenomena that are influenced by a large number of variables will become possible.

T F 8. A one-billion byte chip will be invented.

T F 9. The computer will result in organization structures becoming taller.

T F 10. Computers will be able to convert hand-written notes into typewritten material.

T F 11. There will be the emergence of highly sophisticated software that will tap the full potential of supercomputers.

T F 12. Computers will make complete medical diagnoses and leave the doctor free to prescribe treatment.

T F 13. Thanks to medical computer technology, the AIDS virus will be totally defeated.

T F 14. Medical computer technology will play a major role in the defeat of lung cancer.

T F 15. Thanks to medical computer technology, leukemia will be eliminated.

T F 16. There will be an elimination of most telephones since people will communicate via computers.

T F 17. Thanks to medical computer technology, heart disease will be more effectively diagnosed and treated.

T F 18. Laptop models will become more compact and more powerful.

T F 19. While the computer will play an important role in helping analyze and evaluate medical data, it will not result in the defeat of either Alzheimer's or Parkinson's disease.

T F 20. Computers will bring about massive unemployment in many industries.

Answers

1. True.	6. True.	11. False.	16. False.
2. False.	7. True.	12. False.	17. True.
3. False.	8. True.	13. False.	18. True.
4. True.	9. False.	14. False.	19. True.
5. False.	10. True.	15. False.	20. False.

Interpretation

If you had 15 more right, you have a pretty good idea of likely computer developments during the 1990s. If you had less than 15 right, review your answers. You may seriously be overrating (or underrating) the effectiveness or scope of computer technology.

Operations
Management

The goals of this chapter are to examine the area of operations management, explain the importance of productivity and technology to this area, and discuss the functions of operations management. The first part of the chapter introduces the operations management process and describes the three basic phases of this process. This section is followed by a discussion of the modern factory and the two areas receiving the most attention: productivity and technology. Finally, four of the major functions of operations management are described in detail.

When you have finished studying all of the material in this chapter, you should be able to:

1. Describe the operations management process.

2. Explain how productivity is measured and why this area is of major importance to operations management.

3. Relate some of the latest technological developments that are occurring on the factory floor.

4. Discuss what happens in the product design stage.

5. Explain how production planning helps mesh demand forecasts with scheduled resource outputs.

6. Relate some of the most effective procedures for ensuring effective purchasing and inventory control.

7. Describe the current quality control challenge facing management and the role being played by quality control circles in meeting this challenge.

NATURE OF OPERATIONS MANAGEMENT

Operations management is the process of designing, operating, and controlling a production system that takes physical resources and transforms them into goods and services. The field of operations management is often referred to as "ops management" or "P/OM," which stands for production and operations management. Many people think of factory management when they hear these terms, but there is a lot more to the field that just this. On the other hand, it is true that ops management is heavily concerned with productivity in the workplace, and much of the work done in this area relates to technology and the improved quality of production output.

Operations management defined.

Operations Management Process

Operations management can be described in terms of three basic phases: input, transformation process, and output. Inputs are the raw materials used in the process. The transformation process is the equipment, machinery, tools, and technology that convert these inputs into outputs. The outputs are the completed goods and services that are sold to the customer. In producing a finished good for sale to the final consumer, the operations management process may be repeated a number of times because the outputs of some producers will serve as inputs for other producers. For example, a steel plant will take iron ore (input) and turn it into steel (output). This will then be sold to a car manufacturer who will take the steel (input) and turn it into an automobile (output). Figure 11-1 illustrates the process.

Inputs

Raw materials and human talent are common inputs.

The most common inputs are physical raw materials and human talent. Using the example of the automobile, the inputs are aluminum, steel, glass, rubber, and so forth. The human talents are the skills of the assembly line workers and the abilities of the management. Analogous situations exist in nonmanufacturing environments. For example, in a restaurant the inputs are raw vegetables, poultry, meat, and other foods, as well as the skills of the chef, the

FIGURE 11-1   **The Operations Management Process**

serving help, and the management. In a university, the inputs are the classrooms, libraries, and other facilities coupled with the abilities and skills of the professors and administrative staff and personnel.

Transformation Process

The transformation process turns inputs into outputs.

The transformation process consists of those activities used in turning the inputs into the desired outputs. In the automobile plant it is the actual assembly of the car. In the restaurant it is the preparation of the menu, the cooking and serving of the food, and the creation of the "right" environment. At the university it is the lectures, assignments, tests, and professor-student interaction.

Outputs

Outputs are the result of transformation.

The outputs are the final result of the transformation process. In the case of the auto manufacturer, it is a ready-to-drive car. In the restaurant it is a sated, satisfied customer. At the university it is an educated graduate.

The basic concepts of ops management were of major interest to Frederick Taylor and the scientific managers. They helped build America into a major industrial nation. Over the last decade, however, this leadership has undergone a noticeable decline. In particular, the Japanese have shown that they can build many things smaller, cheaper, and with more reliability than can the Americans. This has resulted in a renewed U. S. interest in the area of operations management. It has also brought about a "rediscovery" of the factory floor as the area where greater technology and operations management skills must be concentrated if American firms are to regain their competitive edge.

THE MODERN FACTORY

There are two major operations management areas that businesses are now looking at very closely. The first is productivity; the second is technology. The two are interlinked and serve as focal points in carrying out ops management functions.

Productivity

Productivity is measured by the equation: output/input.

Productivity is measured by the equation: output/input. If a company can increase its output without changing the input, productivity increases. Yet, this is not the only way to raise productivity. If output can be kept the same while inputs are reduced, productivity gains are also obtained. Similarly, if output goes up faster than input or declines at a slower rate than input, productivity increases. Most firms focus either on increasing output while leaving input the same or on increasing output at a faster rate than input.

The biggest concern about U. S. productivity is that since 1973 many industrial countries, including Japan, France, and Germany, have been outpacing the United States.[1] (The Japanese, in particular, have made major gains although they, too, are beginning to have their problems. See International Management in Action: The Changing Work Ethic on page 386.) Many reasons for this development has been cited. One of the most common is declining investment in research and development (R&D). However, this assumption is simply not true. From 1965 to 1975 the United States invested approximately $60 billion annually in R&D, and over the next decade this annual expenditure rose to $100 billion. By 1988 the yearly R&D expenditure stood at $123 billion.[2] Another argument is that government regulation, tax disincentives, poor labor relations, and a loss of the work ethic are causing the productivity problem. Industry analysts and consultants have found these arguments also are wrong. The real answer is management ineffectiveness. Arnold Judson, head of a major consulting firm, states that "management ineffectiveness is by far the single greatest cause of declining productivity in the United States."[3] Richard Mackin, another industry consultant, gathered data from 109 chief executive officers in manufacturing, transportation, clerical/service, and public utilities, and found that they all supported the belief that poor productivity was a result of poor management.[4] The problem is management ineffectiveness. What has happened is that management has employed a piecemeal approach to its productivity efforts, provided inadequate coordination among the various departments, and allocated insufficient investment in management and supervisory training and development. (For more on this subject see Table 11-1.) The result is that the Japanese, and others, have made major inroads at the expense of the United States.

What does management need to do? There are many answers to this question.[5] The major one is to realize that causal variables such as effective leadership, well-designed plants, and highly motivated personnel can all help raise productivity.[6]

Steps for improving productivity.

There are many ways in which organizations are attempting to do this. Some of the most important steps include: (1) a long-term commitment by management to personally becoming a part of the productivity effort; (2) communicating to the employees the need for greater attention to productivity; (3) working with the employees in setting realistic and useful productivity

[1]Karen Pennar, "The Productivity Paradox," *Business Week*, June 6, 1988, pp. 100–102; and Norman Jonas, "Can America Compete?" *Business Week*, April 20, 1987, pp. 45–47.

[2]Stuart Gannes, "The Goods News about U. S. R&D," *Fortune*, February 1, 1988, pp. 48–56.

[3]Arnold S. Judson, "The Awkward Truth about Productivity," *Harvard Business Reviews*, September–October 1982, p. 93.

[4]Richard F. Mackin, "An Analysis and Comparison of Factors Influencing Productivity in Four Industry Groups," Ph.D. diss., Nova University, Fort Lauderdale, FL, 1984.

[5]Robert E. McGarrah, "The Decline of U. S. Manufacturers: Causes and Remedies," *Business Horizons*, November–December 1987, pp. 59–67.

[6]Jon English and Anthony R. Marchione, "Productivity: A New Perspective," *California Management Review*, January 1983, p. 64.

TABLE 11-1	Reasons for Success	Percentage	Reasons for Disappointment	Percentage
Causes of Success or Disappointment in Improving Productivity	Capital investment in plant, equipment, and process	72	A piecemeal, unplanned approach to improving productivity	66
	Top management commitment and involvement	61	Inadequate coordination among departments or functional areas (excessive functional or departmental autonomy)	42
	Good financial controls and information systems	45	Insufficient investment in management and supervisory training and development	41
	Good employee relations	38	Lukewarm commitment and involvement by top management	40
	Good communications	35	Insufficient awareness by engineering of the manufacturing implications of product and process designs	39
	Competent middle managers in all departments	34	Weaknesses in industrial and manufacturing engineering	39
	Effective industrial and manufacturing engineering staff	29	Weak first-line supervision	35

goals; (4) establishing a climate that is conducive to a strong productivity effort; (5) designing methods for measuring productivity progress; (6) rewarding those who contribute to this progress; and (7) being continually on the lookout for new techniques for improving productivity.[7] The latter, in particular, is resulting in new technology on the factory floor.

Technology

Another major development taking place in the modern factory is the introduction of new technology. Many factories are old and unable to

---

[7]For more see Jack Meredith, "The Strategic Advantages of the Factory of the Future," *California Management Review*, Spring 1987, pp. 27–41; and Stephen S. Cohen and John Zysman, "Why Manufacturing Matters: The Myth of the Post-Industrial Economy," *California Management Review*, Spring 1987, pp. 9–26.

	Reasons for Success	Percentage	Reasons for Disappointment	Percentage
TABLE 11-1 *continued*	Coordination and cooperation among organizational functions and departments	27	Poor communication	32
	Training and development of supervisors and managers	23	Insufficient investment in work-force training	32
	Engineering sensitivity to manufacturing implications of product and process designs	22	Poor financial controls or information systems	24
	A comprehensive, systematic company-wide approach to productivity improvements	22	Weak middle managers	21
	Training of work force	20	Decline of work ethic	20
	A loyal, skilled work force	18	Lack of incentives or appropriate rewards (or disincentives)	20
	Incentives and rewards	14	Insufficient capital for improved plant and equipment	17
	Cooperative union leadership	6	Poor employee relations	9
			Poor relationship with union leaders	8

Source: Reprinted by permission of the *Harvard Business Review.* Exhibit from "The Awkward Truth about Productivity," Arnold S. Judson, September–October 1982, p. 94. Copyright © by the President and Fellows of Harvard College; all rights reserved.

Note: A survey regarding productivity performance was conducted using a sample of 236 top-level executives from a cross section of 195 U. S. industrial companies; the table lists the reasons they gave for success or disappointment in improving productivity.

produce as efficiently as the competition. It is not necessary to close their doors, however; what is needed is better equipment and machinery. One of the most significant developments has been that of robots.

Robots

Robots can increase productivity

Robots are programmable machines that can perform numerous factory tasks, including lifting, welding, carrying parts, assembling, spray painting, and inspecting. They are also useful in doing jobs that are either difficult or

When it comes to operations management techniques, many people cast their eyes toward the Japanese. This country's success in areas such as automobiles, calculators, computers, photographic equipment, radios, televisions, and watches make it the envy of the world. It seems that the Japanese know how to make things better than their competitors. What accounts for this ability? Some people argue that it is the Japanese work ethic. They are incurable workaholics who enjoy finishing one assignment and racing on to another. They also have a very high regard for their fellow workers, preferring a team approach in contrast to the American style of individualism. It is now evident, however, that the Japanese work ethic, with all of its surrounding mythology, is beginning to undergo some serious changes. Consider some of the following incidents reported by *Fortune* magazine.

1. Workers rarely show up early any more to warm their machines before their shifts start.

2. Workers will screw in a bolt but, if the clock strikes five in the middle of the process, they will stop turning and leave the line.

3. Defying precedent, young management trainees actually take all of the 15 vacation days allotted to them.

4. Young Japanese work very hard during duty hours but are unwilling to go beyond the strict call of duty and turn a good enough performance into a superb one.

5. More and more college graduates are now describing themselves as oriented toward "home" rather than toward "the company."

What is causing these changes? One of the most significant causes is the economy. As things have gotten better many Japanese feel less of an urge to go out and work as hard as before. They prefer to spend more time with their family and friends. When the workday comes to an end, they go home. Will these changes result in a decline in Japanese work output? No one knows for sure. However, it is becoming obvious that the United States is not the only country where the work ethic is being eroded, leading some experts to contend that this ethic is more economically based than culturally determined.

Source: Some of the material in this story can be found in Lee Smith, "Cracks in the Japanese Work Ethic," *Fortune,* May 14, 1984, pp. 162–64.

dangerous. For example, many companies assign robots to the three Ds— dull, dirty, and/or dangerous tasks—or the three Hs—hot, heavy, and/or hazardous jobs. Yet the main function of robots continues to be productivity increase.

At General Electric's Louisville plant, computer-aided engineering and robotic equipment enable the company to produce 20% more dish-washers in 20% less floor space. At the GE locomotive facility in Erie, 68 machine operators formerly took 16 days to produce a locomotive frame. Now with the help of several robots, 8 unskilled workers do the job in 1 day. At some warehouses of Walgreen's, the drug chain, where packers handled 110 less-than-case-load shipments per hour, robots now load 900 per hour.[8]

In recent years robot manufacturers have found that these machines have to be able to do more than one or two things; they must be programmable for multiple functions. These "brainy" robots are now beginning to take over the market.[9]

One of the biggest hurdles in using robots is overcoming the fear of employees that they will be replaced by these machines. A number of ways to reassure employees are in use. One is by introducing the personnel to these robots by means of demonstrations and orientation programs. Westinghouse, for example, uses an elaborate and extensive employee education program including meetings at which (a) management stresses the importance of remaining competitive, and (b) demonstrations of the robots are provided. Sometimes these demonstrations work out better, than expected.

> During the last of the . . . performances *[at Westinghouse]*, which was put on for the union committee, what could have been a public relations disaster turned out to be a blessing. The robot malfunctioned; its heavy arm smashed onto the table, knocking over and breaking all the glass and other props. Everyone laughed. The manufacturing manager's embarrassment gave way to gratification.

"The employees saw that it was only a stupid machine and could make mistakes," he said later. "If I had to do it again, I would run that mistake right into the robot's program."[10]

New Plant Life

New technologies are being used.

In addition to robots, management is making many other changes designed to breathe new life into outmoded plants. For example, supersonic welders are being used to produce consumer goods. In one factory the welder focuses beams of high-frequency sound on the water nozzle of a dishwasher. These vibrations heat the part by jostling its molecules into a frenzy. The temperature is more precisely controlled than with a flame, allowing the nozzle to be mounted more securely to the dishwasher frame. The entire operation is controlled by a computer and when the job is finished, another computer-controlled device attempts to pull the nozzle off. If it succeeds, the weld is

---

[8]Fred K. Foulkes and Jeffrey L. Hirsch, "People Make Robots Work," *Harvard Business Review*, March–April 1984, p. 96.

[9]"Automatix: Gaining an Edge with Brainy Robots," *Business Week*, June 18, 1984, pp. 60, 64; "Sweden's ASEA: Its Robots Reach for the U. S. as a High-tech Drive Begins to Pay Off," *Business Week*, January 16, 1984, pp. 104–105.

[10]Foulkes and Hirsch, p. 99.

bad and the computer notes the flaw for later repair. Later on down the assembly line, a laser eye routes the unit to a repair station.

Another recent development is lower-powered ultra sound that can be used for final inspections. Sound waves from these instruments are passed through finished products and the echoes alert a computer to any hidden flaws or defects.[11]

These technological developments are helping organizations modernize their plants rather than building new ones from the ground up. Many are also reducing the number of product variations that they manufacture. They now realize that by producing just a few sizes or varieties of a product, they can obtain much higher output with far fewer defects. The Japanese and Germans have done this sort of thing for years. Consider Michelin, the tire manufacturer. While American firms were making hundreds of different kinds of tires, Michelin was offering only a radial in few sizes and varieties.

Another important development has been the reduction in the number of people working in factories.[12] The average size of these work forces is slowly going down as management allows attrition (retirements, transfers, resignations) to take its toll. The work is made up by the machines, many of which are not only faster than humans but also more accurate.

OPERATIONS MANAGEMENT FUNCTIONS

There are a number of operations management functions. Four of the most important are product design, production planning, purchasing and inventory control, and quality control. The following discussion examines each of these.

Product Design

Product design is the first stage.

The first stage in producing anything is the product design. If the firm is creating the product from the start, it will be solely responsible for the design. If the product is manufactured under a subcontracting agreement, the design is typically provided by the client.

In those cases in which the product is to be newly created, product design begins with an identification of consumer needs and an analysis of the market (See also Ethics in Action: Don't Copy). This step is then followed by a selection of the product, the formulation of a preliminary design, product testing, and then final design.

Much of this work is done with the use of computers. For example, using computer-aided design (CAD), engineers can now produce blueprints without ever having to lift a pencil. They can draw directly on a cathode ray tube and move the design in any direction they wish—up and down, to the side,

---

[11]For more on these developments see: William J. Broad, "U. S. Factories Reach into the Future," *New York Times*, March 13, 1984, pp. C1, C5.

[12]Roger W. Schmenner, "Every Factory Has a Life Cycle," *Harvard Business Review*, March–April 1983, p. 123.

Product design can take many forms. In some cases, unfortunately, it involves copying materials that belong to others. One of the most obvious examples is the firm that obtains blueprints or contract bids that are being submitted by a competitor and uses this information to gain an unfair advantage. This is clearly illegal. However, there are other behaviors that are more commonplace and, at least in the view of some companies, neither illegal nor unethical. Photocopying is an excellent example. If used for educational purposes, photocopying copyrighted material usually is no problem. However, if a firm wants to copy an article about strategic planning from, say, the *Harvard Business Review* and distribute it to all 500 executives in the firm, can it simply submit the article to its duplicating and processing department and ask for 500 copies? Or does it have to write to the *Harvard Business Review* and either get formal permission or purchase 500 reprinted articles? The answer is that the firm should contact the journal and ask for permission. If the publisher feels that 500 copies are too many and there should be a fee or reprints must be purchased, the company is morally (as well as legally) obligated to comply. In practice, most companies never contact the publisher. They simply copy whatever they want.

This has resulted in recent action to crack down on copyright law infringement. Book publishers, trade journals, scientific periodicals, and the Authors League have formed an organization known as the Copyright Clearing Center. One of the association's primary goals is to sue companies that refuse to pay royalties to holders of copyrights.

To date 50 large companies have signed license agreements with the Center by which they agree to pay a fee for the right to make copies. Many firms, however, are waiting to see if they can be legally compelled to pay fees for photocopying copyrighted materials. In one closely followed case six publishers of scientific and technical journals have brought suit against Texaco, which is charged with regularly photocopying materials from these journals without having obtained proper authorization. The maximum penalty is $50,000 per infringement. Texaco says that it is unaware of any copyright infringement by its personnel.

What has the publishers even more concerned is the fact that new technology is likely to leapfrog photocopying and enable firms to reproduce magazines and books by reading them directly into computer systems. How will they protect themselves against this new development? Quite obviously ethics plays a major role in the copying process, and many firms are simply finding it in their own best interests to look the other way on this issue.

Source: Stephen Labaton, "New Group to Sue to Aid Copyrighters," *New York Times,* July 25, 1988, p. 26.

back and forth—as well as stretch it out, color or shade it, change or add depth, and so forth. Moreover, when they have finished their work, they can produce a printed copy to look at and, if they are not satisfied with the results, go back and make additional modifications. CAD is making design work much easier.

Production Planning

In the production planning process, management brings together the demand forecasts for the goods with the scheduled resource outputs. This procedure is often accomplished through the use of master production schedules that ensure coordination of all activities. In this process management determines how the raw materials, components, machines, and manufacturing operations are to be synchronized. Then, when the entire process is under way, if something should go wrong, management can consult the master schedule to determine how to solve the problem. For example, if a machine were to break down, the company would use the schedule to decide how to reroute the work so as to keep everything on plan. Additionally, manufacturing firms are beginning to plan more strategically. Operational considerations no longer dictate production planning.

A manufacturing decision that might be downright stupid in operational terms alone may look very different when seen from a strategic perspective. Consider a simple example. An appliance maker found that it could extend the life of its product and save $1.75 per unit in warranty costs by substituting a newly designed part. Against expectation, it turned out that the new part would add more than $2 to the cost of each unit—hardly an attractive proposition, operationally speaking. But on strategic grounds the move still made excellent sense. By sparing the end user cost and inconvenience over the product's lifetime, it would strengthen the company's sales message and increase the product's value in the customer's eye. Management's decision to go ahead has since been rewarded by a hefty gain in market share.[13]

Another recent development has been shorter product life cycles. Years ago a company might plan on a five-year cycle for a new good. The first year would be the introductory phase, the next would be growth, the third and fourth would be maturity, and the last would be the decline and phase-out stage. Today this approach is no longer realistic. New products are coming onto the market so rapidly that the average product life has declined dramatically. It is no longer uncommon to find one- and two-year life cycles. As a result, many firms are now coordinating their product design and production planning so that after producing a limited number of one product model, they switch and start manufacturing something else. These short production runs used to result in a much higher cost per unit than did long production runs; however, this is no longer true. Thanks to modern technology, it is possible to turn out 500 units at the same cost per unit as 5,000 units. A large portion of this uniformity is a result of computer-aided manufacturing (CAM) techniques, which allow much greater control over the production process. Using CAM, managers are able to route each part through the proper sequence of machines, to instruct each machine in the

---

[13]Elizabeth H. Haas, "Breakthrough Manufacturing," *Harvard Business Review*, March–April 1987, pp. 75–81.

proper sequence of operations for each part, and to allocate these tasks in such a way as to optimize the working time available from all machines. CAM also eases design and engineering chores. The result is a flexible manufacturing system. The value of such a system has been particularly obvious in foreign plants.

> . . . foreign manufacturers have carried CAM applications much further than their American counterparts. The Fujitsu Fanuc plant in Japan, for example, uses robots to make robots; during the third shift, all lights are turned off because no workers are present. The Japanese are also far along toward completion of a plant that will run with no blue-collar workers at all. The Germans already have a highly automated factory for making airplane wing sections. Of course, small ''islands'' of flexible manufacturing exist within large American plants in the automobile and a few other industries, but even these are rare showpieces.
>
> In the United States, CAM applications are mostly limited to the use of programmable controls on single machines, a practice that subtly reinforces narrow concepts of what CAM can do. One manufacturer applies CAM to the production of exhaust pipes for cars; a computer controls the location and configurations of the several bends required for various automobile models. However, the company regards its venture into CAM as a simple replacement of old machines with new machines, not as a first experience with a new technology of far-reaching potential.[14]

As American firms begin to more fully develop their use of flexible manufacturing systems, they will be able to respond more quickly to changing product demand, altering production to fit the product life cycle. They will also find that these techniques will greatly improve their return on investment.

Purchasing and Inventory Control

Purchasing and inventory control are two of the major areas of operations management because of their importance to bottom-line profit. Some of the largest manufacturers have found that even when they design high-demand products and produce them according to the master plan, they are unable to generate the desired returns on investment. The disappointing returns occur because of poor purchasing and inventory control procedures.

In order to control costs effectively, most firms find that it pays to purchase standard and/or expensive items through a centralized purchasing department, while minor purchases are made by the department that needs them.

---

[14]Bela Gold, ''CAM Sets New Rules for Production,'' *Harvard Business Review*, November–December 1982, p. 91.

Purchasing procedures are developed.

This approach has several important benefits. First, the purchasing department personnel become familiar with the reliability and quality of the various vendors and know whom to call on in the future and whom to avoid. Second, a centralized purchasing approach allows the company to buy in large lots and obtain quantity discounts. Third, the time and effort spent in purchasing activities is reduced because the personnel know where to buy needed materials and are familiar with the procedures to be used in placing orders and following up on deliveries. Fourth, some firms are moving toward full vertical integration because it gives them greater control over their purchasing and inventory situations.[15]

Just-in-time approaches are being used.

Inventory control probably has received more attention than any other operations management function because of the fact that it offers the greatest savings to the company. If the amount of inventory can be reduced by 50 percent, most manufacturing firms would find their return on investment increasing by at least 20 percent. Large inventories have a dampening effect on profitability. This fact has led many firms to reduce their inventories by turning to "just-in-time" approaches. *Just-in-time (JIT) inventory* is the purchase or production of materials just in time for use. Of course, such a hand-to-mouth approach can be dangerous, in that inventory shortages are likely to occur from time to time. By closely tying together purchasing and usage of materials, however, companies are coming to realize that JIT is a very useful concept.[16] The Japanese popularized the idea, but many American firms are now using it to control not only initial inventory but work-in-process as well.[17]

Most firms use MRP.

In pulling together all of the operations management functions, many firms use some form of *material requirements planning* (MRP). This is a systematic, comprehensive manufacturing and controlling technique that increases the efficiency of both purchasing and inventory control.

The concept of material requirements planning (MRP) . . . offers purchasing managers an innovative basis for projecting future inventories in manufacturing operations. MRP can improve the inventory results of a traditional . . . system because it allows the operating manager to plan material requirements to meet the final assembly schedule. Once a firm's final assembly schedule has been determined and the product bills of material have been finalized, it is possible to determine precisely the future material needs for the final assembly schedule. The bill of

---

[15]Ted Kumpe and Piet T. Bolwijn, "Manufacturing: The New Case for Vertical Integration," *Harvard Business Review,* March–April 1988, pp. 75–81.

[16]Richard J. Schonberger, "A Revolutionary Way to Streamline the Factory," *Wall Street Journal,* November 15, 1982, p. 24; Lewis Beman, "A Big Payoff from Inventory Control," *Fortune,* July 27, 1981, pp. 76–80.

[17]See for example: E. Earl Burch and John M. Garris, "Lower Costs through Work-in-Process Inventory Control," *Industrial Management,* May–June 1983, pp. 27–31.

material for a given finished product can be broken down, or "exploded," and extended for all component parts to obtain that product's exact material requirements for each component part. Similarly, the requirements for a given component used in several products can be cumulated for all finished products to be produced.[18]

In handling materials-requirement planning, there are three approaches that can be used. One is the conventional approach which allows plant managers to make such decisions. If the firm has a number of plants, each operates autonomously. The problem with this approach is that some plants will order too much inventory resulting in high carrying costs. Most large firms have done away with the conventional approach, substituting a centralized system in its place. Under this arrangement senior production management people decide how much to order for all plants combined. Working from an overall master schedule for the entire company, these individuals control things from on top. The biggest problem with this approach is that it forces senior-level people to become involved in volumes of detailed variables which they do not have time to digest. On the other hand, if they work only with summaries of the relevant data, they will lack the in-depth information needed for making the most effective decisions. Most recently a hierarchical approach has been suggested by some operations management experts. In this arrangement, known as hierarchical production planning (HPP), corporate management, plant managers, and shop superintendents on the factory floor all participate in the production plan. HPP integrates both JIT inventory and MRP within its domain.

HPP integrates JIT inventory and MRP.

At the corporate level, the managers decide how production will be allocated among the plants. At the plant manager level, total demand per month for groups of items to be purchased and/or produced is determined. At the shop level, the superintendents break the plan down into its short-term components and see that everything is coordinated properly. Figure 11-2 provides an illustration of the process. Commenting on its value to business, Harlan Meal, an operations management expert, writes:

> One of the greatest strengths of the hierarchical approach is its ease of implementation. A system that makes decisions in a sequential fashion facilitates the implementation of support systems sequentially, which is easier and less risky than implementing in a system that deals with all decisions in a single process.
>
> The design of the hierarchical structure should include consideration of implementation. Ideally, the several levels will be sufficiently independent, so that the modification of one level will have minimum

---

[18]W. C. Benton, "Purchase Quantity Discount Procedures and MRP," *Journal of Purchasing and Materials Management*, Spring 1983, p. 30.

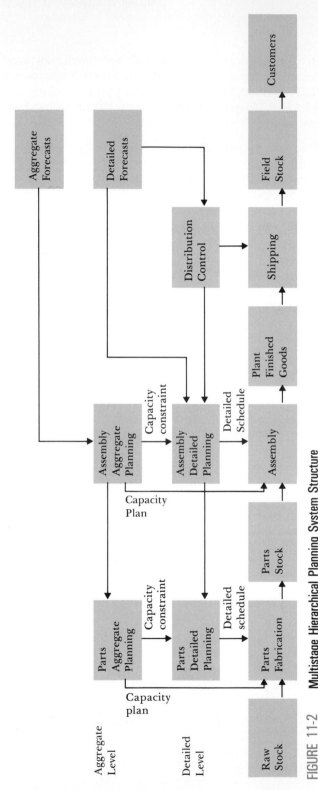

FIGURE 11-2   Multistage Hierarchical Planning System Structure

effect on other levels. In this case, the sequence of implementation in the hierarchy makes little difference. Usually it is best to implement first the decisions that provide the most benefits.

Implementation from the top to the bottom improves the most important decisions first and is often effective, since each time a decision-support system is to be implemented the mechanism that provides the needed constraints is already in place.[19]

Using techniques like JIT inventory, MRP, and HPP, business firms are finding that they are better able to control their inventory. This type of control has allowed them to spend more time focusing on what may well be the major concern of most American manufacturers: quality control.

Quality Control

Quality control is a key area of attention.

In recent years quality control has become a key focal point for operations management. One reason is because many customers think that Japan, in particular, has mastered the challenge of quality control, while the United States lags far behind. In 1980 this may well have been true. More recent statistics, however, show that American firms have greatly closed the gap. Consider the following comments from David A. Garvin, who has made a systematic analysis of quality performance among both Japanese and American firms:

Although the evidence is still fragmented, there are a number of encouraging signs. In 1980, when Hewlett-Packard tested 300,000 semiconductors from three U. S. and three Japanese suppliers, the Japanese chips had a failure rate of one-sixth that of the American chips. When the test was repeated two years later, the U. S. companies had virtually closed the gap. Similar progress is evident in automobiles. Ford's Ranger trucks, built in Louisville, Tennessee, offer an especially dramatic example. In just three years, the number of "concerns" registered by the Louisville plant (the automaker's measure of quality deficiencies as recorded at monthly audits) dropped to less than one-third its previous high. Today, the Ranger's quality is nearly equal that of Toyota's SR5, its chief Japanese rival.[20]

One of the major reasons for this improvement in their quality control is that American firms have come to realize that basic changes were necessary in their philosophy. The old ways were no longer paying off. A change in thinking was required, one that came closer to the Japanese approach in

---

[19]Harlan C. Meal, "Putting Production Decisions Where They Belong," *Harvard Business Review*, March–April 1984, p. 111.

[20]David Garvin, "Quality on the Line," *Harvard Business Review*, September–October 1983, p. 73.

	Old	New
TABLE 11-2 **Quality Control Philosophies: Old versus New**	Poor quality is a result of the declining work ethic.	If properly managed, American workers are as good as, or better than, any in the world.
	Quality is secondary to profit.	Quality is one of the best ways to ensure profit.
	Higher quality means higher costs.	Higher quality means lower costs.
	Quality problems will always exist; management's job is to minimize them.	Quality problems are not inevitable; management should plan for "zero quality defects."
	Quality control problems should be caught and remedied.	Quality control problems should be eliminated by better operations management techniques.
	Quality control is a problem for the people in that department.	Quality control is everyone's job.
	Suppliers are adversaries and should be regarded with suspicion.	Suppliers are part of the organization's team.
	Suppliers should be chosen on the basis of low bid.	Suppliers should be chosen on the basis of quality and reliability.
	Most quality problems are a result of poor employee workmanship.	Most quality problems are a result of poor management systems.

which every worker is responsible for quality control as opposed to a situation in which responsibility is held only by the Quality Control Department. These old and new approaches are contrasted in Table 11-2. Firms are also coming to realize that there are many aspects to quality including performance, reliability, durability, serviceability, aesthetics, and perceived quality. These are now being addressed seriously.[21] At the same time, many firms have begun to using quality control circles to help them attain a more decentralized, hands-on approach to the problem.

Quality Control Circles

Quality circles have become popular.

In recent years the quality *control circle* has become a popular approach for realizing both productivity and quality goals,[22] and at the present time approximately 500 firms are using them.[23] The concept, which makes use of participative management, is quite simple in design:

---

[21]David A. Garvin, "Competing on the Eight Dimensions of Quality," *Harvard Business Review*, November–December 1987, pp. 101–109.

[22]See for example: Richard M. Hodgetts and Wendell V. Fountain, "The Defense Department Evaluates a Quality Circle Program," *Training and Development Journal*, November 1983, pp. 98–100; and Robert Wood, Frank Hull, and Koya Azumi, "Evaluating Quality Circles: The American Application," *California Management Review*, Fall 1983, pp. 37–53.

[23]Ricky W. Griffin, "Consequences of Quality Circles in an Industrial Setting: A Longitudinal Assessment," *Academy of Management Journal*, June 1988, p. 339.

A circle consists of a small group of people (three to fifteen; ideally about eight) within a company who do similar kinds of work. The group volunteers to meet on a regular basis, usually an hour a week, to identify, analyze, and solve problems in its members' work areas. Their training consists of learning techniques of problem solving, data gathering, and problem analysis. Within circle meetings, members begin by brainstorming a list of problems they might want to solve, then narrow the list to a few problems that seem most desirable and practical to attack. When they have come up with a solution to the problem they have currently chosen to work on, circle members present their recommendations to management in a formal presentation. If these recommendations are approved, the circle then implements the solution.[24]

Quite often a facilitator from outside the department is used to monitor the meetings, while the group leader, often a first-line supervisor of the work group from which the members are drawn, guides the circle's efforts. In choosing a leader, certain characteristics are desirable, including enthusiasm, the ability to organize and work with others, and use of a participative management style.

Circle members do similar work.

The members of a circle are drawn from those doing similar work and their focus is on solving problems related to their work area. This process usually begins with a training of the group members[25] followed by a listing of those problems the group would like to solve. From the list, one problem is selected for attention. Its cause is examined and a plan of action is then developed. The latter includes the formulation of objectives for the program (see Table 11-3) and agreement on data collection and problem-solving techniques. Once the solution is determined, it is presented to management for approval and is then implemented.

There are many benefits from quality circles (QCs). Some of the major ones[26] include:

1. Cost savings due to members' analysis of problems and implementation of recommended solutions.

2. Significantly improved attitudes, especially those concerning the level of trust in the organization, communication, perceived quality of supervision, perceived human orientation of the organization, and the degree of involvement in decision making by employees.

---

[24]William L. Mohr and Harriet Mohr, *Quality Circles* (Reading, MA: Addison-Wesley, 1983), p. 23.

[25]Larry R. Smeltzer and Ben L. Kedia, "Training Needs of Quality Circles," *Personnel*, August 1987, pp. 51–55.

[26]Newton Margulies and Stewart Black, "Perspective on the Implementation of Participative Approaches," *Human Resource Management*, Fall 1987, p. 406.

TABLE 11-3
**Typical Ways of
Measuring a Quality
Circle's Progress**

Quantitative	Qualitative
Increases in output	Improved attitudes
Reduction in amount of tardiness	Increased personal growth of the circle members
Reduction in overall absenteeism	Enthusiasm of circle members for the group's objectives
Increased overall productivity of the group	Improved working relationships among the circle members
Cost savings	Support of top management for circle objectives
Increased quality of output	Decrease in interpersonal conflicts among the personnel
Reduction in customer complaints	Request by circle members for more training
Reduction in rework costs	Support of middle management for circle objectives
Decline in the number of accidents among group members	Formal recognition of the circle by the organization
Increased return on investment	Improvement in problem solving by group members
Increased profit	Perpetuation of the circle's existence
Reduction in employee grievances	Increased motivation and morale of circle members

3. Increased abilities of employees and managers alike in work-related problem identification and analysis and resolution.

4. Increased management awareness of the use of participation in improving the communication channels between employees and supervisors.

5. Increased abilities in the conduct of meetings, interpersonal processes, and the resolution of conflicts.

6. Increased awareness throughout the organization of issues influencing the performance of the organization management strategy to shop floor issues.

There are many quality circle pitfalls.

On the other hand, there are many potential pitfalls that can result in problems, and managers must be aware of these. One of the most important is measuring the quality circle in terms of cost savings only. Many circles do not produce great cost savings, but they do generate high morale and teamwork and for this reason are well worth the effort. A second common error is the assignment of people to these circles. This effort should be voluntary, and coercion or pressure to join them should be avoided at all times. A third pitfall is the failure to realize that members must be adequately trained for their roles in the circle. Unless the individuals understand how to identify and analyze job-related problems and then gather data related to resolving the situation, the circle can prove to be a complete waste of time. A fourth common problem is choosing issues that are too large in scope to be dealt with efficiently. Unless the problems are manageable by the circle members, a lot of time is spent uselessly. A fifth major shortcoming is the failure of the circle to get proper management support.

While these five are only a handful of the problems and pitfalls that face quality circles, they are representative of the kinds of issues that the group must face as it begins to tackle its job.[27] After these types of problems have been surmounted, the circle is usually able to perform quite well, especially for the first year or so. Now, however, many organizations are finding that after a while the novelty of the quality circle wears off and many of the groups begin to stagnate. At this point management must work on reviving the enthusiasm and rebuilding the morale of the group. Some of the most helpful approaches include: (1) giving the members more advanced training so that they can attack still more job-related problems; (2) recognizing the circle's achievement through an in-house newspaper or some other method of showing management's appreciation for all the circle has done; (3) inviting upper management to attend circle meetings, ask questions, and generate support for the group's continued efforts; and (4) having members help get a new quality circle started. In short, a QC program is not a quick fix approach to job-related problems; it is a long-term investment. The benefits it offers to the area of operations management must not be underrated; nor should the challenges. As Mohr and Mohr have noted:

> Because we are part of a highly competitive worldwide economy . . . we must return to an era of steadily increasing productivity and improving quality while satisfying the needs of a more educated, sophisticated work force. Quality circles can be a method for achieving these objectives. Learning how to sustain the current level of enthusiasm and momentum for growth of quality circles is an important next step to ensure that they are here to stay.[28]

■ SUMMARY

Operations management is the process of designing, operating, and controlling a production system that takes physical resources and transforms them into goods and services. This system has three basic phases: input, transformation process, and output.

---

[27]For other shortcomings see Murray R. Barrick and Ralph A. Alexander, "A Review of Quality Circle Efficacy and the Existence of Positive-Findings Bias," *Personnel Psychology,* Autumn 1987, pp. 579–91; Thomas Li-Ping Tang, Peggy Smith Tollison, and Harold D. Whiteside, "The Effect of Quality Circle Initiation on Motivation to Attend Quality Circle Meetings and on Task Performance," *Personnel Psychology,* Winter 1987, pp. 799–814; and Griffin, pp. 338–58.

[28]Mohr and Mohr, p. 253.

INTERVIEW WITH RICHARD SCHONBERGER

Richard J. Schonberger is one of the best known experts in the area of manufacturing management. After receiving his Ph.D. in management, he joined the faculty at the University of Nebraska in Lincoln. Soon after writing *Japanese Manufacturing Techniques: Nine Hidden Lessons in Simplicity,* he began getting calls from industry for consulting and speaking engagements, which he now does full-time as president of Schonberger and Associates, Inc. He also lectures on the worldwide circuit, and continues writing articles and books, including *World Class Manufacturing: The Lessons of Simplicity Applied,* which a number of major companies have made required reading for their manufacturing managers.

Q. *What is the current state of technology in manufacturing businesses? What is going on and what can we expect in the future?*

A. The frontiers for the 1990s and for the first decade of the twenty-first century will be applying technology and automation in the workplace. At the present time there is quite a bit of turmoil. Many top companies have decided to go for simplicity first and hold off costly automation until later. For example, all the major automakers and electronics companies are using new concepts to design products that are simple to produce. One place where automation is paying off right now is computer-aided design. Another is the use of programmable machines such as robot welders used in auto production and computer numerical controlled machines used by metal fabricators. The best strategy is to do the

At the present time there are two major operations management areas that are getting a great deal of attention: productivity and technology. Productivity is measured by the equation: output/input. The major reason that American productivity has declined vis-a-vis other nations is management ineffectiveness. Too often companies have used a piecemeal approach to their productivity efforts, provided inadequate coordination among the various departments, and allocated insufficient investment in management and supervisory training and development. Today, efforts are under way to correct these mistakes. Meanwhile, in the area of technology, business firms are now turning to robots and other state-of-the-art inventions, including supersonic welders and lower-powered ultra sound.

easy quality-improving, waste-reducing things first. That way you don't automate the waste.

Q. *How widespread are inventory control practices? Do small firms use them as well as large ones?*

A. All good firms today have already revolutionized their inventory control practices. There are a number of ways they have done this. One is by eliminating stockrooms and putting the work-in-process in small amounts right next to the machines. This form of "hand-to-mouth" inventory control is extremely effective in cutting delay and exposing quality and other problems soon after they occur. A supplemental approach is to have suppliers provide daily delivery of materials, and in some cases two or three times a day. Working closely with their suppliers, firms are able even to eliminate the need for quality inspection since this function is carried out by the suppliers.

Q. *What is the current status of quality circles? Are they as popular as ever?*

A. Quality circles faded in popularity a few years ago, but they are being renewed in different forms. In the past, many of them were organized around existing functional organizations and these didn't work out very well. The successful teams are organized after work cells are formed based on work flow. This helps increase the team's effectiveness. In the case of companies that must respond quickly to their customer, these newly designed work teams (the term quality circle isn't used so much any more) greatly increase customer-responsiveness. So quality circles are not going to be a thing of the past, but we see them emerging as teams formed of chains of makers and users.

There are a number of important operations management functions. One is product design, which consists of planning products to meet customer demand. A second is production planning, which ties together demand forecasts with scheduled resource outputs. A third is purchasing and inventory control, in which management is now making wide use of just-in-time inventory, material requirements planning, and hierarchical production planning. A fourth is quality control, which many firms are pursuing by the use of quality circles. Taken together these four major areas of operations research are helping management meet the challenge for low cost, high quality output that is being demanded by today's more informed customers.

■ REVIEW AND STUDY QUESTIONS

1. What is meant by the term operations management? Put it in your own words.

2. The operations management process consists of three basic phases. What is meant by this statement? In your answer be sure to describe each of the phases.

3. How is productivity measured? How well are American firms doing in this area in contrast to Japanese firms? Explain.

4. Why has productivity in many American firms not gone up as rapidly as it has in many other countries? What accounts for this development? How can it be overcome?

5. In what way is technology invading the factory floor? Give some examples and discuss their importance to increased productivity.

6. What takes place in the product design stage? What role can be played here by computer-aided design? Explain.

7. How does production planning help mesh demand forecasts with scheduled resources? Cite an example in your answer.

8. Do well-run companies use a centralized or decentralized approach to purchasing? Why? Explain your answer.

9. What is materials requirement planning all about? How does hierarchical production planning help refine this process? Explain.

10. In what way has management's philosophy of quality control changed? Describe at least five differences.

11. How does a quality circle work? Of what value are these circles? Have they ever been used successfully? Cite three examples.

12. What are some of the pitfalls or problems that accompany the use of quality circles? Describe three.

■ SELECTED REFERENCES

Agor, Weston H. "Manage Brain Skills to Increase Productivity," *Personnel*. August 1986, pp. 42–46.

Anderson, John C., and Robert G. Schroeder. "Getting Results from Your MRP System." *Business Horizons*, May–June 1984, pp. 57–64.

Argote, Linda, Paul S. Goodman, and David Schkade. "The Human Side of Robotics: How Workers React to a Robot." *Sloan Management Review*, Spring 1983, pp. 31–41.

"Automatix: Gaining an Edge with Brainy Robots." *Business Week*, June 18, 1984, pp. 60, 64.

Barrick, Murray R., and Ralph A. Alexander. "A Review of Quality Circle Efficacy and the Existence of Positive-Findings Bias." *Personnel Psychology,* Autumn 1987, pp. 579–92.

Batdorf, Leland, and Jay A. Vora. "Use of Analytical Techniques in Purchasing." *Journal of Purchasing and Materials Management,* Spring 1983, pp. 25–29.

Benton, W. C. "Purchase Quantity Discount Procedures and MRP." *Journal of Purchasing and Materials Management,* Spring 1983, pp. 30–34.

Blair, John D., and Carlton J. Whitehead, "Can Quality Circles Survive in the United States?" *Business Horizons,* September–October 1984, pp. 17–23.

Broad, William J. "U. S. Factories Reach into the Future." *New York Times,* March 13, 1984, Section C, pp. 1, 5.

Burch, Earl E., and John M. Garris. "Lower Costs through Work-in-Process Inventory Control." *Industrial Management,* May–June, 1983, pp. 27–31.

Cohen, Stephen S., and John Zysman. "Why Manufacturing Matters: The Myth of the Post-Industrial Economy." *California Management Review,* Spring 1987, pp. 9–26.

Cox, James F., Robert W. Zmud, and Steven J. Clark. "Auditing an MRP System." *Academy of Management Journal,* June 1981, pp. 386–402.

Dillon, Linda S. "Adopting Japanese Management: Some Cultural Stumbling Blocks." *Personnel,* July–August 1983, pp. 72–77.

English, Jon, and Anthony R. Marchione. "Productivity: A New Perspective." *California Management Review,* January 1983, pp. 57–66.

Foulkes, Fred K., and Jeffrey L. Hirsch. "People Make Robots Work." *Harvard Business Review,* January–February 1984, pp. 94–102.

Garvin, David A. "Quality on the Line." *Harvard Business Review,* September–October 1983, pp. 65–75.

Garvin, David A. "Competing on the Eight Dimensions of Quality." *Harvard Business Review,* November–December 1987, pp. 101–109.

Gitlow, Howard S., and Paul T. Hertz. "Product Defects and Productivity." *Harvard Business Review,* September–October 1983, pp. 131–41.

Gold, Bela. "CAM Sets New Rules for Production." *Harvard Business Review,* November–December 1982, pp. 88–94.

Griffin, Ricky W. "Consequences of Quality Circles in an Industrial Setting: A Longitudinal Assessment." *Academy of Management Journal,* June 1988, pp. 338–58.

Haas, Elizabeth H. "Breakthrough Manufacturing." *Harvard Business Review,* March–April 1987, pp. 75–81.

Hodgetts, Richard M., and Wendell V. Fountain. "The Defense Department Evaluates a Quality Circle Program." *Training and Development Journal,* November 1983, pp. 98–100.

Jonas, Norman. "Can America Compete?" *Business Week,* April 20, 1987, pp. 45–47.

Lewis, Paul. "Europe's 'Factories in Space,'" *New York Times,* May 14, 1984, Section D, p. 10.

Li-Ping Tang, Thomas, Peggy Smith Tollison, and Harold D. Whiteside, "The Effect of Quality Circle Initiation on Motivation to Attend Quality Circle Meetings and on Task Performance." *Personnel Psychology*, Winter 1987, pp. 799–814.

McNamara, Carlton P. "Productivity Is Management's Problem." *Business Horizons*, March–April 1983, pp. 55–61.

Meal, Harlan C. "Putting Production Decisions Where They Belong." *Harvard Business Review*, March–April 1984, pp. 102–111.

Meredith, Jack. "The Strategic Advantages of the Factory of the Future." *California Management Review*, Spring 1987, pp. 27–41.

Pennar, Karen. "The Productivity Paradox." *Business Week,* June 6, 1988, pp. 100–102.

Pollack, Andrew. "High Tech: Japan's Approach." *New York Times*, June 12, 1984, pp. 31–32.

Reddy, Jack, and Abe Berger. "Three Essentials of Product Quality." *Harvard Business Review*, July–August 1983, pp. 153–59.

"The Revival of Productivity." *Business Week,* February 13, 1984, pp. 92–100.

Seymour, Sally. "The Case of the Willful Whistle-Blower." *Harvard Business Review,"* January–February 1988, pp. 103–109.

Shetty, Y. K. "Key Elements of Productivity Improvement Programs." *Business Horizons*, March–April 1982, pp. 15–22.

Smeltzer, Larry R., and Ben L. Kedia. "Training Needs of Quality Circles." *Personnel*, August 1987, pp. 51–55.

"Sweden's ASEA: Its Robots Reach for the U. S. as a High-tech Drive Begins to Pay Off." *Business Week*, January 16, 1984, pp. 104–105.

Takeuchi, Hirotaka, and John A. Quelch. "Quality is More than Making a Good Product." *Harvard Business Review*, July–August 1983, pp. 139–45.

Weick, Karl E. "Misconceptions about Managerial Productivity." *Business Week*, July–August 1983, pp. 47–52.

Wood, Robert, Frank Hull, and Koya Azumi. "Evaluating Quality Circles: The American Application." *California Management Review*, Fall 1983, pp. 37–53.

■ CASE: Harvey's Plan

Over the last three years productivity at the Josephone Corporation has declined by 11 percent. As a result the firm has had to raise its prices to customers and the overall effect is beginning to tell on the company's bottom line. Three years ago, return on investment was 18 percent. Since then it has dropped each year to its current level of 8.7 percent.

The head of manufacturing, Harvey Hedrick, admits that he is having a difficult time understanding why productivity is down. The firm has installed new equipment during each of the last three years, helping it keep pace with similar decisions by its competitors. Given the fact, however, that the latter have not raised their prices more than 2 percent annually, while Josephone's prices have gone up an average of 5.4 percent a year, it is obvious to management that its costs must be rising faster than those of the competitors.

At the senior-level management meeting six months ago, Harvey was asked what he was doing to deal with the productivity problems. In his response, he noted in particular that each area of the factory was being examined by the supervisors, who were there for the purpose of determining where productivity improvements might be introduced. "If we find some area where we believe changes in equipment or work flow would lead to increased productivity, we are going to make those changes immediately." Harvey went on to explain that he believed the most effective approach to productivity was a decentralized one. "The people who know best where productivity changes should be made are the individuals down on the floor. I believe that if we turn this function over to the supervisors and the other operating personnel, they will help us solve this problem in a much more economic manner than if we made these decisions from the top. We have to be careful not to centralize the productivity problem and take it away from those who are best equipped to deal with it. If we let them know that we are counting on them and then stand back and let them get to the tasks, we will get the best results."

Some of the members of the top management team believe Harvey is approaching the problem in the wrong way. They contend that productivity needs strong support from the top coupled with an overall planned approach that will take all segments of the factory into account. They argue that Harvey is promoting a piecemeal, unplanned approach to the problem. Harvey admits that his approach is piecemeal, but he argues that it certainly is not unplanned. "You're confusing decentralization with lack of planning," he told them. "Just wait and see. Within six months we're going to have productivity right back where it was three years ago."

The results of Harvey's six-month effort were reported yesterday. Productivity is down another 3 percent. Based on these data, top management has decided to try a different approach to dealing with the productivity problem.

Questions

1. What is productivity all about? Put it in your own words. In what way has the loss of productivity hurt the company? Explain.

2. Why did Harvey's plan not work? What was wrong with it?

3. Is the top management right in its approach? Should things be more centralized and planned from the top? Are their ideas better than those of Harvey? Defend your answer.

■ CASE: A Hand-to-Mouth Recommendation

Things at Urwaldt Manufacturing have not been going well lately. The most recent financial statements show that return on investment has declined sharply. The accounting people, responding to a request from top management, have made an audit of all operational areas and found that the biggest cause of the declining return on investment has been sharply increasing inventory. Two years ago Urwaldt carried $300,000 of inventory. Today that figure stands at $1,450,000.

The accounting people have suggested that the Production Department sharply cut its inventory. They recommend a more hand-to-mouth approach. According to the accounting analysis submitted to top management last week, if production reduced its inventories by 60 percent and began ordering smaller quantities from the suppliers on a weekly, as opposed to monthly, basis, carrying costs and warehousing costs would shrink dramatically. These recommendations have been forwarded to the Production Department for its consideration but the latter do not think that these proposals are good ones.

The biggest argument by the Production Department is that smaller purchases will eventually lead to inventory shortages and the need to slow down, if not halt, production. As sales have increased, argues the Production Department, the need for larger inventories has gone up. They contend that there is no way to reduce inventory levels. The head of the department concluded his comments on this subject by noting, "I know that return on investment is important. However, the reduction of inventory levels is not the answer. We will have to look elsewhere to solve this problem."

Questions

1. Are there any firms that use hand-to-mouth inventory or is this suggestion a totally new one? Explain your answer.

2. How does hand-to-mouth inventory work? What are its advantages? What are its drawbacks? Identify and describe at least three of each.

3. Is the head of production right or are the accounting people right? Defend your position.

■ CASE: It's a Quality Problem

Over the past ten years productivity has become a major concern for American business firms. One of the major reasons for this development has been the onslaught of foreign competition. Overseas firms are finding America to be a land of opportunity. Foreign products often last longer, have fewer defects, are cheaper, and command more market attention in the states than do domestically produced goods.

What does the future promise? Regrettably, for many firms it will be more of the same. In the last four years American productivity growth has begun to slip and annual growth in manufacturing productivity ranks far behind that of France, Britain, and Japan. Additionally, most areas of the world are spending more on automation than is the United States.

What do American firms need to do? One of the major steps is to improve quality. This can take a number of different forms depending on the particular good or service that is being sold. For automotive and other hard goods, there are eight forms of quality that are now being given attention. They are these:

1. Performance—goods must work as intended. For example, cars must have rapid acceleration, good handling, and a comfortable ride.

2. Reliability—goods must function without problems for an extended period of time.

3. Durability—goods must last a long time, for example, TV sets and refrigerators should last at least ten years; properly maintained cars should last twelve.

4. Serviceability—goods should be able to be serviced quickly and easily.

5. Aesthetics—goods should have the look, feel, taste, or smell that reflects personal preferences.

6. Conformance—goods should be manufactured within design and standards.

7. Features—goods should have the necessary "bells and whistles" that supplement the basic product and make it more appealing, such as automatic tuners on TVs and permanent-press cycles on washing machines.

8. Perceived quality—goods should be seen by the consumer as having the requisite quality.

If American firms can create their goods and services with these eight characteristics in mind, they stand a good chance of recapturing market share and becoming a more dominant force in the world market.

Questions

1. Of the eight characteristics of quality described in this case, which one is most important for auto producers? Why?

2. Which of these eight characteristics would be most important in the production of TV sets? Which would be second most important? Third most important? Explain.

3. The service sector of the U. S. economy has lower productivity than the goods-producing sector. Which of the eight characteristics do you think would be of most value in running an effective restaurant? Identify and describe three.

Sources: Karen Pennar, "The Productivity Paradox," *Business Week,* June 6, 1988, pp. 100–102; and David A. Garvin, "Competing on the Eight Dimensions of Quality," *Harvard Business Review,* November–December 1987, pp. 101–109.

▪ CASE: Sometimes It Takes a Little Bit Longer

One of the Big Three automakers has recently been having a problem with its union. It seems that some of the workers on the line are unable to get their jobs done in the assigned time. One of these groups is putting on the stabilizer bars. According to management, it was possible to install the bar in approximately 50 seconds. Since 60 seconds were allocated for this chore, the firm felt that this was more than enough time in which to do the work. The assemblers complained to the union, however, that they could not complete this phase of the job in 60 seconds because the bars were built incorrectly. They were slightly too large, and instead of snapping into place they had to be worked in. As a result it took approximately 75 seconds to put in each one.

Last week the company and the union agreed to have an outside expert examine the job. When the man was finished, he told management that the average stabilizer bar was indeed too long. For some reason the bar was one-eighth of an inch longer than it should have been and this made it difficult to install. Management went back and looked at all of the blueprints for the car. According to these specifications, the bar should have fit in exactly right. "I don't know what the problem is," one of the engineers remarked, "but there's something wrong. It just doesn't fit the way it's supposed to. Maybe the auto frame is off by an eighth of an inch. I just don't know.

In any event, management has decided to straighten out the problem by giving the workers 80 seconds in which to install each bar. At the same time the company has announced that it is going to change the production specifications of the bar to shave off the eighth of an inch. When the workers heard about the decision, they were elated. One of them predicted, however, that the basic problem would recur. "There are so many parts to a car that it is practically impossible to manufacture all of them to specification and, even when you do, there is likely to be a mistake in the blueprints. What we really need around here is a quality circle to prevent further occurrences of the type we have just had with the stabilizer bar." The union representative agreed with the man but when the matter was broached to the company supervisor, the latter told them to forget the entire thing. "We're not interested in quality circles. We can get by without them. If everyone pitches in and does his job right the first time, quality circles won't be necessary."

Questions

1. What is a quality circle? How do they work? Who is usually a member of the group?

2. What types of problems do quality control circles address? Cite at least three examples in your answer.

3. Based on the case data, would the company be wise to use quality circles? How could they help? What should the firm have to know about them before going ahead with their implementation? Explain.

■ SELF-FEEDBACK EXERCISE: Productivity's Challenge to America

What do you know about productivity, operations management, and the United States's ability to compete effectively in the business arena? To find out, answer each of the following questions. The correct response and accompanying explanation are provided at the end of the exercise.

T F **1.** The standard of living in the United States is beginning to decline.

T F **2.** The quality of U. S.–produced goods is falling.

T F **3.** Productivity in our services industry is increasing faster than in any other sector of the economy.

T F **4.** The inventory on hand at most U. S. firms is higher, on average, than that on hand in Japanese firms.

T F **5.** American firms invest slightly more money per worker in new machinery and equipment than do their Japanese counterparts.

T F **6.** About 1 percent of all goods produced in the U. S. electronics industry have quality defects and need reworking.

T F **7.** Italy's productivity growth rate from 1979 to 1986 was lower than that of the United States.

T F **8.** West Germany's productivity growth rate from 1979 to 1986 was greater than that of the United States.

T F **9.** Sweden's productivity growth rate from 1979 to 1986 was greater than that of the United States.

T F **10.** Great Britain's productivity growth rate from 1979 to 1986 was lower than that of the United States.

T F **11.** Overall, Japan's manufacturing equipment is newer than that of the United States.

T F **12.** Annual productivity in the United States increased between 1980 to 1987.

T F **13.** Annual productivity in the United States increased between 1983 to 1987.

T F **14.** The average annual spending growth for factory automation is slightly greater among American firms than among Asian firms (including Japan).

T F **15.** The average annual spending growth for factory automation is slightly greater among American firms than among European firms.

T F **16.** Many American firms have been increasing their productivity by reducing the size of their operations.

T F **17.** The primary reason why American firms are losing the productivity race is that competitors have new equipment.

T F **18.** The primary reason why American firms are losing the productivity race is that competitors have better technology.

T F **19.** Research shows that improved productivity quality can help a company regain lost market share.

T F **20.** Most American firms are now abandoning quality circles because they are not cost-effective.

Answers and Explanations

1. True. It is increasing at a decreasing rate.
2. False. Quality is increasing.
3. False. Productivity in the service industry is increasing more slowly than in the manufacturing area.
4. True. American firms have higher inventory levels.
5. False. They invest less.
6. False. It ranges between 8 to 10 percent.
7. False. It is higher than that of the U. S.
8. True.
9. True.
10. False. It is higher than that of the U. S.
11. True.
12. True.
13. False. It declined between 1983 to 1987.
14. False. It is higher for Asian firms.
15. False. It is higher for European firms.
16. True.
17. False. They have better management.
18. False. The Americans also have excellent technology, but the competitors are using more effective management practices.
19. True.
20. False. They are still using them.

■ COMPREHENSIVE CASE: Jackson's Dilemma

In the office machine business, service is everything—it is all important. When a computer, a typewriter, or a photocopying machine breaks down, the customer wants immediate service. Every hour that the machine is down can mean hundreds of dollars of lost revenues.

The firms that dominate this industry are large: IBM, Digital Equipment, Hewlett-Packard, Xerox. Their prices are high, and the cost of maintenance or service agreements often run from 10 to 20 percent of the machine's purchase price. These high prices have encouraged competition, and over the last decade the overall share of the market held by these giants has slipped.

The biggest problem for small firms is that of finding a protected market niche. If they get too big, one of the majors will attack them. For example, in recent years IBM has offered portable computers for the purpose of attacking Compaq's niche and preventing it from dominating this segment of the market. IBM has also gotten into the photocopying business, an area that was once regarded as Xerox's domain.

With the majors picking off the growing smaller firms and attacking each other, no company in the industry is totally free from competition. Those that have chosen their niche well, however, have been able to effectively resist most competition.

Small firms have found their strongest weapon to be price. The major firms cannot afford to offer their products at such low prices because their strategic plans call for growth rates of 12 to 18 percent annually, and this level cannot be achieved by getting into price wars. The majors pick off the largest and most lucrative segments of the industry and allow everyone else to fight for the rest. If a particular niche is much larger than a major thought it was, however, the firm will then move into this overlooked niche. A good example was seen in IBM's decision to enter the personal computer market. For a while it had allowed Apple to dominate this segment of the industry, but once it became obvious that there was a large market there, IBM moved in.

The biggest problem for the large firms is that of marketing to small clients. They are accustomed to selling to large accounts that buy on the basis of machine capability. Price is a secondary consideration, since these accounts can save millions of dollars annually through the effective use of business machines. Smaller clients, however, are more skeptical of the value of these machines and are much more price sensitive. The client wants to see exactly how much money the machine is going to save his or her small business. In the computer area, stores like Sears, which sell the IBM personal computer, have been much more successful in selling IBM products than has this firm's own retail outlets. The same is true for other types of office machinery, including photocopiers.

The Firm

Jackson Carpenter owns a small business machine store in the heart of a major metropolis. Located in the downtown business area, he has a lot of walk-in customers and is able to charge premium prices for his equipment. Given his location, however, he is also subjected to a great deal of competition from the major manufacturers whose sales forces comb the area. For this reason, Jackson has expanded his market to other areas throughout the city. His most lucrative deal has been the library contract he obtained last year.

This contract gives Jackson the exclusive right to install photocopying machines in all city libraries. These machines are used by the public for making copies of materials that they want to take home with them. The typical cost per page is 10 cents, although Jackson has some very high-quality machines in the larger libraries and charges fifteen cents a copy on these machines. The fifteen-cent copies are better for books and periodicals that have dark backgrounds or material that is faded and requires a machine that can register everything on the page.

The number and types of machines that are installed are determined by each library. Small ones prefer a copier that produces reasonable facsimiles. Larger ones like to have at least three copiers, with one that can provide good-quality reproduction. In all there are seventy libraries serviced by Jackson. The average library has two copiers, one that provides ten-cent copies and another that offers fifteen-cent copies.

The arrangement with the libraries is a very simple one. Jackson buys, installs, and maintains the machines. Each library is responsible for seeing that its copier has paper, for removing the money every evening, and for keeping a daily record of the receipts. At the end of each month, revenues are divided between the libraries and Jackson on a fifty/fifty basis. Without taking maintenance into account, the contract is a very lucrative one for Jackson. The average machine costs him $2,000, can be fully depreciated over three years, qualifies for a 10 percent income tax credit, and can be sold at the end of three years for 20 percent of its original price. During its three-year life the machine will generate an average income of $20 per day, 330 days a year. These data result in the following computation of return on investment over the three-year life.

Revenues ($20 per day × 330 day × 3 years/2 since Jackson must split the revenues with the library)	$9,900
Depreciation of machine	2,000
Taxable income	7,900
Tax (46 percent rate)	3,634
Net income	4,266
Depreciation savings	2,000
Tax credit (10 percent of cost)	200
Total income from investment	$6,466
Annual return on investment:	$6,466/2,000 = 3.233/3
	= 107.8 percent

Jackson can gross a return of 107.8 percent a year on each machine. Additionally, when the copier is sold at the end of its useful life, the tax on the $400 received from its sale is 46 percent of 40 percent, resulting in an additional inflow of $326.40. This amount raises the average return on investment to 113.2 percent annually.

This is the good news. The bad news is that if these machines break down very often, the return on investment falls rapidly. There are a number of expenses not accounted for in the above figures. These include the service truck, the equipment, and the maintenance person who fixes the machines. In the photocopying business, it is important to have malfunctioning machines working as soon as possible. While Jackson grosses only ten dollars per machine per day, if five or six machines are down this is sixty dollars of lost revenue, most of which comes out of net income. Additionally, while the average machine generates twenty dollars a day, those in the inner city at the largest public library often gross eighty dollars a day, and during final exam week at local schools, they can reach $200 daily. In contrast, some of the outlying libraries produce only twenty to thirty dollars a week, and when their machines break down it can take the maintenance truck an hour to reach their location. Each of the service calls to one of these libraries takes almost half a day. Yet there is nothing Jackson can do to cut these expenses. His contract calls for him to provide service within twenty-four hours, and this requirement sometimes forces him to hire other repair people on a per-job basis.

The Problem

The biggest problem that Jackson faces with this contract is the cost of maintaining the parts for the machines. He currently is stocking hundreds of different parts. In this way he is certain that any machine that goes down can be repaired quickly.

Jackson buys all of his replacement parts from the major manufacturer of the machine that he installs. He does not allow his maintenance repairman to use parts manufactured by any other company, although it is common in the industry to use such compatible components. They are less expensive and, in some cases, more reliable than the original equipment manufacturer's parts.

Another problem he faces is keeping track of inventory. At the present time Jackson uses a log book in which all deliveries are entered and, as parts are removed from the warehouse and put into the maintenance truck, the number on hand is reduced appropriately. A physical inventory conducted last week revealed that Jackson had 19 percent fewer parts on hand than the log book showed. His accountant has suggested that for control purposes, Jackson switch to a computerized inventory system. "It'll be easier to keep track of what is going on around here and there'll be less chance of your running out of inventory." Jackson, however, does not want to incur the costs of computerization. He feels that it is cheaper to stock more inventory than he will need than it is to work on a hand-to-mouth basis and rely on the computer to keep him abreast of those items he should order.

Jackson's accountant has also suggested that he look into turning the servicing of the machines over to someone else. "Subcontract this part of the work. You'll be dollars ahead and won't have all of the headaches associated with maintaining the machines. Make it someone else's problem. Your return on investment is still going to be very high and you can spend more of your time looking for other lucrative contracts. Also keep in mind that if you get rid of the maintenance end of the contract, you'll be able to free the money you have tied up in inventory. I figure that your return on investment, after you work out the maintenance end of the deal, is about 17 percent. You can subcontract this and still end up with a net of 27 percent."

Jackson believes that the accountant's computations are accurate; however, he is not sure that giving up 10 percent is a good idea. It seems to him that if he streamlined his operations he could reduce the cost of maintenance and end up with more than 27 percent.

The Future

In the mail yesterday Jackson received a letter from the city. The City Commission has decided to allow the installation of pay photocopiers on the ground floor of all city buildings. The city is asking for bids from ten reputable firms. Jackson's is one of these.

There are to be 125 machines installed throughout the city. The contract will be in effect for three years and, if things go smoothly, the commission is empowered to continue it for another three years. Otherwise, new bids will be requested.

Jackson is giving serious consideration to bidding on this contract; however, he is also aware of the problems he is having with maintaining the current machines. He does not want to undertake more than he can handle, but he would certainly like to increase his profits. Given his experience in the area, Jackson believes that he knows where to cut costs and improve service without losing any money from net income. He feels that he has learned a lot about the business over the last year and this will give him an advantage over the competition. Bids are due within ten days.

Questions

1. What are the major problems facing Jackson? Identify and describe the three most important.

2. How can the material in this section of the book be of value to him in solving these problems? Be sure to tie together each problem with the text material that can be useful in resolving it.

3. Should Jackson bid on the new contract? Why or why not? Be complete in your answer, being sure to defend it fully.

PART
4
THE
BEHAVIORAL
SCHOOL
OF
MANAGEMENT

Chapter 12 examines interpersonal and organizational communication processes. Major attention is focused on the barriers to effective communication and the ways in which these can be overcome. Particular consideration is given to perception, inference, status, and resistance to change. Communication channels, both formal and informal, are also reviewed. The last part of the chapter addresses techniques for improving communication effectiveness, including the development of sensitivity, the improvement of face-to-face relationships, the use of understandable, repetitive language, the protection of credibility, and the use of effective listening habits.

Motivation theory is the focus of attention in Chapter 13. After explaining the relationship between needs and behavior, some of the most popular theories of motivation are examined. These include Maslow's need hierarchy, McGregor's Theory X and Theory Y, Herzberg's two-factor theory, and some of the new process theories of motivation that help explain how to specifically motivate individuals.

Chapter 14 addresses the topic of leadership effectiveness. Trait and situational theory are discussed and behavioral theory is examined. Consideration is then given to distinguishing the different types of leadership approaches. The chapter also looks at various contingency theories and examines their value for practicing managers. The last part of the chapter addresses new dimensions of inquiry, including leadership matching and corporate culture.

The final chapter in this part looks at human resource development. It is not enough to communicate well, motivate properly, and lead effectively. There must also be a concern for the overall well-being of the personnel. This involves attention to recruiting, selecting, orienting, training, and developing of the workers. It also includes the well thought out introduction of change, and the use of such techniques as job enrichment, job redesign, sensitivity training, transactional analysis, and human resource accounting, all directed toward developing the full potential of the personnel.

The overall purpose of this part of the book is to examine the basic philosophy and concerns of those who subscribe to the behavioral school of management. There are many such advocates in industry today, and without them organizations would be much poorer places to work.

CHAPTER 12

Interpersonal and Organizational Communication

GOALS OF THE CHAPTER

If management is the process of getting things done through people, communication is the essence of it, for without effective communication no one would know what anyone was supposed to be doing. Nor would there be any basis for answering questions, solving problems, obtaining feedback, or measuring results. The goals of this chapter are to examine interpersonal and organizational communication.

When you have finished this chapter, you should be able to:

1. Describe the steps in the communication process.
2. Note some of the major barriers to effective communication.
3. Discuss the reason that perception is considered to be the overriding cause of poor communication.
4. Identify the two basic types of communication channels available to the manager.
5. Relate the role of the grapevine in informal organizational communication.
6. Discuss the advantages and limitations of both written and oral communication.
7. Explain how managers can improve face-to-face communications and protect their credibility through the use of balance theory.

417

8. Note some of the major bad listening habits and the ways to become a more active listener.

9. Illustrate how the ten commandments of good communication can result in more effective management practices.

INTERPERSONAL COMMUNICATION

One of the most important forms of communication is interpersonal communication, which entails the transmission of meaning from one person to another.

Communication Process

In the *communication process,* the sender constructs a message and passes it to the receiver. This individual interprets the message and takes action in a manner satisfactory to the sender.

Many models have been developed to explain the communication process. One of these, formulated by communication theorist Raymond Ross and presented in Figure 12-1, illustrates the process in complete yet understandable terms. The basic ideas contained in the figure will be developed throughout this chapter.

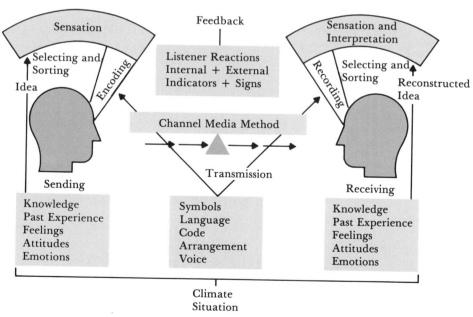

FIGURE 12-1   **The Communication Process**

Source: Raymond S. Ross, *Speech Communication Fundamentals and Practice,* 7th ed., p. 13. Copyright © 1986. Reprinted by permission of Prentice-Hall, Inc., Englewood Cliffs, NJ

Steps in the Communication Process

The important thing to note is that effective communication requires both information and understanding. Unfortunately, too many managers overlook the importance of understanding and subscribe to what is known as the conveyor theory of communication. They see communication as a conveyor that carries messages from one person to another. No real consideration is given to whether the receiver understands or accepts the communiqué. This one-way type of communication is ineffective. Effective communication consists of four steps: attention, understanding, acceptance, and action.

Attention entails getting the receiver to listen to what is being communicated. Quite often this requires overcoming message competition, which occurs when the receiver has other things on his or her mind. For example, assume that the listener, Daniel Jones, has three pressing problems out on the assembly line. In this case, the manager, Harriett Smith, who is trying to communicate with him, faces message competition because she must get Jones to put aside his problems and listen to her for the moment. If the sender does not secure the attention of the receiver, the communication process can go no further.

Understanding means that the receiver grasps the essentials of the message.[1] Many managers find that their attempts to communicate break down at this stage because the receiver does not really know what is expected after the manager's statement. Some executives try to surmount this problem by asking the subordinates whether they understand the message. Such attempts are generally useless because the pressure is entirely on the subordinates, who feel they should say yes. Instead, the manager should ask subordinates to say what they understand. It becomes clear when the individuals repeat the message whether accurate understanding has been achieved. Technology also plays a role in helping people understand (See Technology in Action: Getting the Message Across).

Acceptance implies a willingness on the part of the receiver to comply with the message. As noted earlier, in the discussion of the acceptance theory of authority, feelings and attitudes of subordinates often dictate whether something will get done. In this phase of the process it is sometimes necessary for the manager to sell the subordinate on the idea. For example, employees in a particular company may have a habit of taking turns clocking in their fellow workers. Management, upon learning of this, may order the supervisors to halt the practice. However, the lower-level managers may be opposed to enforcing the directive, believing it will lead to a confrontation with their own subordinates. The department manager may have to point out

Many managers use the conveyor theory of communication.

Attention involves getting the receiver to listen.

Understanding means that the receiver comprehends the message.

Acceptance requires a willingness to comply.

---

[1] Amy Saltzman, "The Personality Factor," *Success*, June 1988, p. 14; John S. Fielden, "Meaning Is Shaped by Audience and Situation," *Personnel Journal*, May 1988, pp. 107–10; Lanny Blake, "Communicate with Clarity: Manage Meaning," *Personnel Journal*, May 1987, pp. 43–50; and Anne Donnellon, Barbara Gray, and Michel G. Bougon, "Communication: Meaning, and Organized Action," *Administrative Science Quarterly*, March 1986, pp. 43–55.

TECHNOLOGY
IN
ACTION:
Getting
the
Message
Across

Technology is changing the way many people communicate. This is true not only in the organization but outside as well. One of the most recent areas in which technology is having a visible impact is in helping organizational personnel go to school in their spare time. Many people have jobs that either hinder their attendance because the work is extremely time-consuming or demanding. Police work is a good example. Many officers find that after a long day on the beat, they are unable to go to class and sit through a 50-minute lecture. Others find that it is difficult to return to school as a 35-year-old adult when everyone else in the class is a teenager.

What can these people do to resolve their dilemma? One answer is to take courses via computers or videocassette lecture. Today there are a number of "electronic universities" that offer courses. The Public Broadcast System is the leader in electronic education. It broadcasts courses from 370 stations to over 200,000 students. Most of these courses are lower-level offerings, but they open the door to freshmen and sophomores who want to get started. At the rate these courses are increasing in number, it may not be too long before people can attend college and get a degree without ever having set foot on campus. *Business Week* reports that:

> Chicago has 10,000 believers. They attend City-Wide Community College, which operates the largest electronic university in the U. S. The school beams 126 hours of lessons ranging from woodworking to physics and economics each week from its own TV station. . . . It also distributes taped copies at local libraries. The courses are so popular that the school outdraws 5 of the 14 local TV stations. "By offering solid, credited courses, we've destroyed the stigma of the TV course," says David A. Milberg, who was hired from CBS to run the station.
>
> Business firms also sponsor courses in areas they find beneficial for their personnel. For example, IBM and AT&T support televideo instruction related to subjects such as computer architecture, artificial intelligence, and management. Students can get these courses via live televideo or tape them on their VCR and view them later. As a result of these latest technological developments, some industry experts are predicting that in the future many students will spend a great deal of their time at home listening to TV lectures or taking computer-generated courses.

Source: Mark Ivey, "Long-Distance Learning Gets an 'A' at Last," *Business Week,* May 9, 1988, pp. 108–10.

that the practice is in violation of company rules. In addition, some of the workers may be arriving late because they know they are being clocked in on time. Once the supervisors realize that management is asking for no more than an equitable solution, they may prove willing to go along with the directive.

*Action entails imple-
mentation of the
communiqué.*

The *action* phase entails implementation of the communication. The challenge facing the manager in this stage is seeing that things are done in the agreed upon manner. Sometimes unforeseen delays will occur; other times expediency will require a change in the initial agreement. Unless the manager puts aside time to check on the progress, communication may falter at this point. For example, Joe Brown calls on his expediter and asks him to check on a particular order and see that it is sent out by the end of the day. The expediter traces the order, finds it, has it filled, packaged, stamped, and sent down to the mail room by 4:00 P.M. However, unless the manager checks, it may occur to no one that the last daily mail pickup is at 3:30 P.M., and the order will sit in the mail room until the next day. By making themselves available for assistance and ensuring that proper action is taken on directives, managers can help their own communication to reach this fourth and final phase.

One of the most effective ways of ensuring that the fourth stage is reached is to communicate to the subordinates the relationship between organization goals and employee needs. Robert Benford reports that at his organization, "we found that most supervisors apparently did see the relationship between the organization's goals and their work units' outputs. However, the more successful supervisors were able to get their subordinates to see this relationship also. Thus objectives were based on meaningful, work-related criteria, and employees were able to calculate the effectiveness of their own work performance."[2] Figure 12-2 illustrates how the communication process can be used in bringing about higher productivity and job satisfaction.

Unfortunately, things do not always work out as planned. Communications do break down and the desired action stage is not attained. Some of the primary reasons for these breakdowns are explained in the next section.

COMMON BARRIERS TO EFFECTIVE COMMUNICATION

Numerous barriers to effective communication exist.[3] Some managers may be inadequate; some subordinates may be unreceptive. More commonly, however, both groups are competent in their jobs and are trying to communicate with each other. Why, then, does communication break down? One barrier has already been examined, namely, message competition. Some of the others include perception, language, status, and resistance to change.

Perception

The overriding cause of most communication problems is *perception*, which can be defined as a person's view of reality. Since no two people have had the

[2]Robert J. Benford, "Found: The Key to Excellent Performance," *Personnel*, May–June 1981, p. 69.

[3]Jerie McArthur and D. W. McArthur, "The Pitfalls (and Pratfalls) of Corporate Communications," *Management Solutions*, December 1987, pp. 15–20.

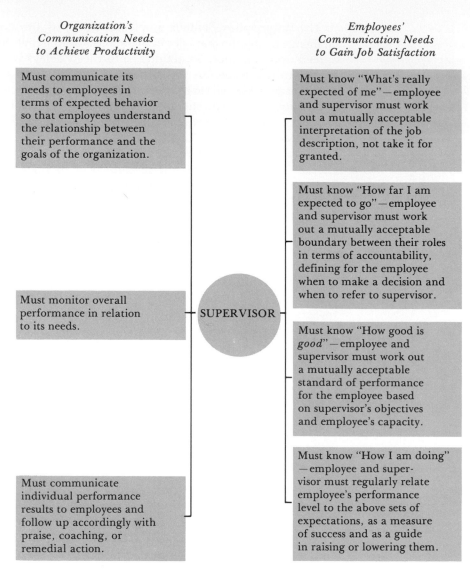

FIGURE 12-2   Factors Affecting Productivity and Job Satisfaction

Source: Robert J. Benford, "Found: The Key to Excellent Performance," *Personnel,* May–June 1981, p. 70. Copyright © 1981 by American Management Association, New York. Reprinted by permission of the publisher. All rights reserved.

Perception can be defined as a person's view of reality.

same training and experiences in life, no two see things exactly alike. The sender's meaning and the receiver's interpretation are not always identical, but it is not necessary that they be so; it is sufficient if the receiver understands the essence of what is being transmitted. In short, from the sender's point of view, the receiver's comprehension must be satisfactory. To some managers this means that subordinates should be "in the ball park," while to others it means "doing it the way I would have done it."

Sensory and Normative Reality

The differences in perception can be attributed to the differences in one's conception of reality. *Sensory reality* is physical reality. A chair, a horse, and a car all represent physical reality. When managers and subordinates communicate about physical reality, there are few communication problems. Both individuals know what is meant by a chair, a horse, and a car. However, there are times when meanings are not so clear-cut, and the receiver of the message may interpret the communiqué differently from its sender. This is known as *normative reality*; it is sometimes also called interpretive reality. Whenever two individuals discuss matters of personal opinion, for example, the chance of communication breakdown is high.

Sensory reality is physical reality.

Normative reality is interpretive reality.

Sensory and normative reality can be placed on a continuum such as this:

Sensory Reality ————————————————— Normative Reality

As one moves from sensory to normative reality, interpretations become increasingly relative. There is no longer any single right answer; instead there are a lot of right answers. Figures 12-3, 12-4, 12-5, 12-6, and 12-7 illustrate this idea. Before reading on, look at the five figures and answer the question accompanying each.

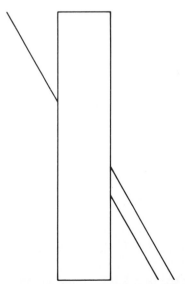

FIGURE 12-3   Using just your eyes, if the line at the bottom of this diagram were drawn through it and emerged at the top, which of these answers would be correct? (a) It would run right into the shorter, lower line at the top; (b) it would run right between the two lines; (c) it would run right into the longer, upper line at the top.

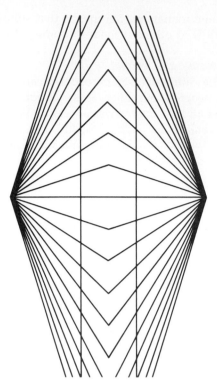

FIGURE 12-4   Do the two vertical lines bend in or bend out at the ends?

Figures 12-3, 12-4, and 12-5 have one right answer. In the first, alternative (a) is correct. It can be verified by placing a piece of paper along the lower line. In the next two, none of the lines running across the diagrams bend in or out; all the lines are parallel. However, the background design makes it appear as if the lines in the first are bending out (Figure 12-4) and the lines in the second are bending in (Figure 12-5).

Figure 12-6 receives three common answers. Most people see a bird or a duck with a big beak; they think the fowl is looking to the left. The second most common response is that a body of water is surrounded by land with an island in the middle. The "spots" north and south of the island are clouds in this interpretation. The third most frequent response is that it is a picture of a rabbit looking to the right; in this view, the bird's beak becomes the rabbit's ears. The author has found that most people fifty years old or more opt for the lake and the island interpretation. People from twenty to fifty years old see a bird or a duck. Grammar and high school students tend to agree that it is a rabbit. Naturally, any of these three could be right because the picture is intentionally designed to allow more than one interpretation.

The final figure (Figure 12-7) receives many different interpretations. Some people see a mask; others believe it is an elephant; still others claim it is

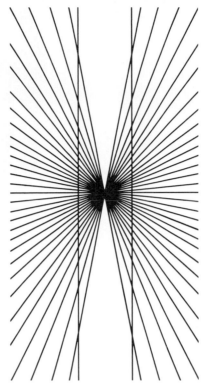

FIGURE 12-5   Do the two vertical lines bend in or bend out at the ends?

burned toast. Another common answer is that it is part of a dock, the ruffles in the upper part representing the rope used in tying up a boat. Still another interpretation is a silhouette of a woman with her hands over her head. Once

FIGURE 12-6   What do you see here?

FIGURE 12-7   **What do you see here?**

again, there is no single right answer. Whatever the person sees is what is there. The point to be extracted from this is that some of the messages sent by managers to subordinates are similar to these last two figures. What the managers believe they said and what the subordinates interpret may be two different things. Too often superiors think their messages fall within the realm of sensory reality, that they are crystal clear, when the messages are actually interpretive and fall within the realm of normative reality. Figure 12-8 illustrates the different interpretations that are possible from one supposedly crystal clear message.

Marketing Requested It . . .

As Sales Ordered It . . .

As Engineering Designed It . . .

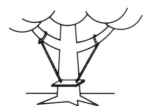

As We Manufactured It . . .

As Plant Installed It . . .

What the Customer Wanted

FIGURE 12-8   **A Perception Problem**

Language, Logic, and Abstraction

Here are basic Aristotelian laws of logic.

Managers use language as the method of representing their ideas. Language is the basis for most communications. Of course, astute managers gear their communiqués to the level of their audience through careful word selection and sentence construction. In addition, they employ certain laws of logic, such as those advocated by Aristotle. First is the law of identity—a house is a house. Second is the law of the excluded middle—the object is either a house, or it is not a house. Third is the law of noncontradiction—something cannot be a house and not a house at the same time. These apparently simple laws of logic relate to communication because they help managers construct and convey messages in an understandable manner. Laws of logic reduce confusion.

Although these laws are helpful, managers still face the problem of abstraction. Abstraction occurs any time something is left out of the message. Yet if managers allowed for no abstraction, they would spend all their time obsessively and expensively spelling out their communiqués. This, of course, is impossible. Managers must assume that if they take care in formulating their messages, subordinates will interpret them the way they were intended. Yet this is not always the case, as the subject of inference shows.

Inference

An inference is an assumption made by a listener or reader.

An *inference* is an assumption made by the listener that may or may not be accurate. Any time a message requires interpretation of the facts, inference enters the picture. The speaker implies and the listener infers. For example, many restaurants have a policy of establishing waiting lists when all their tables are filled. Yet, unknown to many customers, sometimes preferred clientele are moved to the front of the list and seated almost immediately. Professional people, such as clergymen and doctors, often qualify. Whenever faced with such a waiting list, a colleague of the author makes it a habit not only to use the title "Dr." in front of his name but also to ask that he be paged immediately should he receive a call from either neurosurgery or the cardiovascular unit at the nearby hospital. Then he writes his name and car license number on a piece of paper so the parking lot attendant can bring his car around in a hurry should a call come for him. Because of inferences drawn by the headwaiter, this gimmick serves to drastically reduce the "doctor's" waiting time. It should be noted that although the professor makes several implications, he never states that he is an M.D. or that he will receive a call from the hospital. As a Ph.D., he is entitled to be called "Dr.," and there is always a chance that the nearby hospital will call him, no matter how remote the possibility. The communication problem rests with the headwaiter, who reads facts into the message. In this case, of course, inference proves helpful to the professor because the receiver responds the way the sender wishes him to.

However, inferences are often stumbling blocks to effective communication because the receiver misinterprets the message, even one which, unlike the misuse of ambiguity above, is intended to be facilitative or straightforward. For example, a company is having problems in getting its product out and management begins stressing production efficiency. Things go well for the first couple of weeks. Then, suddenly, the production line again starts to have some problems. The general manager calls in one of the company's troubleshooters, explains the situation, and tells him to go down to the line, find out what is causing the trouble, and get rid of it. The man goes down, finds the automatic control unit is causing the problems, pulls it off, and replaces it. In turn, the general manager calls him in and chews him out for stopping the line to put in a new unit. "You don't pull out perfectly good equipment," the manager tells the troubleshooter. "You fix it." What really caused the communication problem? It was inference. In going down to the line the troubleshooter followed the manager's instructions to the letter. He found the trouble, and he got rid of it. Unfortunately, the manager said more than he had in mind. By "get rid of it," the manager meant to convey an order to fix the present unit and only pull it out if absolutely necessary. The manager was operating under the conveyor theory of communication, and it got him into trouble. He thought his message was clear, and it was—to him. As communication theorists like to say, "What's clear to you is clear—to you."

Status

A person's status affects the way messages are received.

Status is "the totality of attributes that rank and relate individuals in an organization."[4] It affects communication because listeners tend to judge the sender as well as the message. Union representatives may feel directives from management are deliberately designed to undermine or weaken their relationship with the work force, and they regard such communiqués as troublesome. On the other hand, complaints from the workers are seen by these people as accurate descriptions of problems and firm bases from which to file charges against management. The union representatives and the membership may have high regard for each other but hold the management in low esteem.

The reverse, of course, is also possible. Management often discounts complaints made against its people as "union rhetoric." However, very few managers regard communiqués from higher echelons as anything but authoritative. Furthermore, the higher in the hierarchy the message originates, the more likely it is to be accepted by managers, because such executives have a great deal of status among the lower-level managers. In

---

[4]Henry H. Albers, *Principles of Management: A Modern Approach,* 4th ed. (New York: Wiley, 1974), p. 172.

short, a person who has status with the listener is regarded as accurate or credible. The messages of lower-status people are discounted accordingly.

Resistance to Change

Basically, people resist change. And the greater the proposed change, the stronger the resistance. For this reason, one of the principles of communication is that the greater the change, the farther in advance must notice be given. A company planning to change work procedures may find it necessary to announce the upcoming changes four weeks prior to their enactment. The same firm planning to move the company plant from Brooklyn to Staten Island may find it necessary to announce the move eighteen months beforehand.

People cope with change in various ways, including avoidance, rejection, and distortion.

Since change and resistance are inevitable, various techniques for coping with change have been developed (see, for example, Communication in Action: Successful Managers Do). For example, consider the case of the company that announces its intentions of hiring the hardcore unemployed. How do people already working there cope with this policy change? One way is avoidance, in which they pretend no policy changes have been announced; they simply ignore the directive. A second common approach is rejection. "Oh, I know what they said, but that's just talk to improve our community image." The third, and most common, is distortion, in which the receiver interprets the message through personal judgment. Those opposing the policy might say the company will bring in one or two token employees, but that is all. Those favoring the policy might claim that virtually all new hiring will be of the hardcore unemployed.

The manager's job is to overcome resistance to change.[5] One way of accomplishing this is to explain how new ideas can be beneficial to subordinates as well as to management. The difficulty of the task is clearly shown in Table 12-1. Research shows that although superiors believe they communicate information about impending changes, subordinates do not agree. Furthermore, careful scrutinization of the table indicates that this communication breakdown increases as the observer moves down the hierarchy. The problem is severe between the top staff and first-line supervisors, but it is even more severe between the supervisors and the workers.

COMMUNICATION CHANNELS

Two types of communication channels are available to the manager: formal and informal. Each can be useful in carrying information to and receiving feedback from other parts of the hierarchy.

---

[5]Richard C. Huseman, Elmore R. Alexander III, Charles L. Henry, Jr., and Fred A. Denson, "Managing Change through Communication," *Personnel Journal,* January 1978, pp. 20–25.

COMMUNICATION
IN
ACTION:
What
Effective
and
Successful
Managers
Do

How important is communication to effective management? Recent research shows that it is one of their most important functions.

Based on a detailed, comprehensive study of what managers really do, researchers have found that four activities are primary: (1) routine communications—exchanging information and handling paperwork; (2) networking—interacting with outsiders, politicking, and socializing; (3) traditional management activities—planning, decision making, and controlling; and (4) human resource management—training, developing, motivating, and disciplining personnel. The two most important of these are communications-related. Managers who were found to be highly effective in terms of quality and quantity of performance, subordinate satisfaction, and organizational commitment of personnel spent a large percentage of their time engaged in routine communications. Managers who received rapid promotions (and who the researchers labelled successful managers) spent a lot of their time in networking activities. Managers who were neither effective nor successful were more likely to balance their time among all four management activities. Here is a percentage breakdown of how the three groups—effective managers, successful managers, and managers in general—spent their time.

	Routine Communications	Networking	Traditional Management Activities	Human Resource Management Activities
Effective managers	44%	11%	19%	26%
Successful managers	28	48	13	11
Managers in general	29	19	32	20

Managers need to be good communicators and, as seen above, for both effective and successful managers, communication and networking accounted for more than 50 percent of what they did. Quite obviously, communication is a key function in the management process.

Source: Fred Luthans, Richard M. Hodgetts, and Stuart A. Rosenkranz, *Real Managers* (New York: Ballinger, 1988).

Formal Channels

Formal channels are those established by the organization's structure. An organization chart, such as the one in Figure 12-9, provides a simple illustration of what is meant by the expression "going through channels."

TABLE 12-1		Top Staff Say about Themselves	Supervisors Say about Top Staff	Supervisors Say about Themselves	Line Workers Say about Supervisors
Do Superiors Tell Subordinates in Advance about Change?	Always	70%	27%	40%	22%
	Nearly always	30	36	52	25
	More often than not		18	2	13
	Occasionally		15	5	28
	Seldom		4	1	12

Source: Adapted from Rensis Likert, *New Patterns of Management* (New York: McGraw-Hill, 1961), p. 52.

This is true whether the communication is going down the chain or coming up. The following discussion examines these channels, with major attention devoted to downward and upward communication and the problems associated with each.

Downward Communication

Downward communication is used to convey directives from superior to subordinate. The classical theorists placed prime attention on this form of communication, and many organizations today continue to do so. Daniel Katz and Robert L. Kahn have identified the five basic purposes of such

Downward communication has five basic purposes.

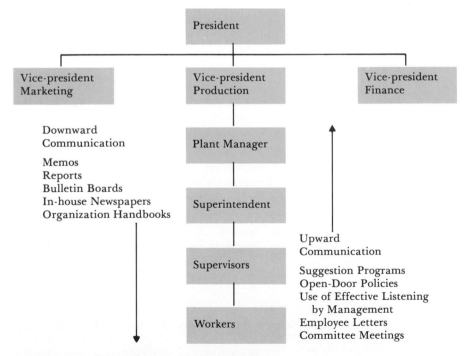

FIGURE 12-9   Formal Channels of Communication

communication as being: to give specific job instructions; to bring about understanding of the work and its relationship to other organizational tasks; to provide information about procedures and practices; to provide subordinates with feedback on their performance; and to provide a sense of mission by indoctrinating the workers as to organizational goals.[6] A downward orientation also helps link the levels of the hierarchy by coordinating activities among them.

There are, however, drawbacks associated with such an orientation. First, it tends to promote an authoritative atmosphere, which can be detrimental to morale. Second, it places a heavy burden on subordinates because much of the information coming down the organizational hierarchy will be expanded, affecting an increasing number of organizational personnel. Third, because of distortion, misinterpretation, or ignorance, information is often lost as it comes down the line. For example, Ralph G. Nichols, studying communication efficiency in 100 business and industrial firms, recorded the following loss of information among six hierarchical levels:

Certain drawbacks are associated with downward communication.

Level	Percentage of Information Received[7]
Board	100%
Vice-presidents	63
General supervisors	56
Plant managers	40
General foremen	30
Workers	20

This communication problem is brought on by the number of links in the chain. The greater the number of people involved, the more likely it is that information loss will occur. One way of overcoming these problems is to supplement downward orientation with an upward emphasis.

Upward Communication

Upward communication provides subordinates with a route for conveying information to their superiors. Research indicates that it does not receive adequate attention from management; therefore, this channel is somewhat damaged by neglect. For example, Rensis Likert has reported that when he and his colleagues at the Institute for Social Research asked managers to think of the most important and difficult communication problem they had

Upward communication channels carry information from subordinates to superiors.

---

[6]Daniel Katz and Robert L. Kahn, *The Social Psychology of Organizations*, 2nd ed. (New York: Wiley, 1978), p. 440.
[7]Ralph G. Nichols, "Listening Is Good Business," *Management of Personnel Quarterly*, Winter 1962, p. 4.

TABLE 12-2	Top Staff Say about Supervisors	Supervisors Say about Themselves	Supervisors Say about the Workers	Workers Say about Themselves
Very free	90%	67%	85%	51%
Fairly free	10	23	15	29
Not very free		10		14
Not free at all				6

TABLE 12-2
How Free Do Subordinates Feel to Discuss Important Job Matters with Their Superior?

Source: Adapted from Rensis Likert, *New Patterns of Management* (New York: McGraw-Hill, 1961), p. 47.

faced during the previous six months, approximately 80 percent said it dealt with downward communication. Only 10 percent indicated that it had involved upward communication.[8]

In achieving accurate feedback from their subordinates, many managers rely upon techniques such as suggestion boxes and the so-called open door policies. However, as seen in Table 12-2, research data shows that these approaches are often ineffective.

Upward communication is poor in many firms.

Subordinates do not feel as free to discuss their views as their superiors believe. Furthermore, upward communication is so poor in many firms that studies have consistently revealed managers as incapable of placing themselves in their subordinates' shoes and accurately responding objectively and realistically to the question, what do the workers want from their jobs? At present, Figure 12-10 seems to represent accurately the frequency and intensity of superior-subordinate communication.

Lateral and Diagonal Communication

Lateral communica-tion occurs among people on the same level of the hierarchy.

Lateral communication, also called horizontal, takes place among departments or people on the same level of the hierarchy. Such an interchange of information often serves to coordinate activities. For example, at the upper levels of a manufacturing firm the vice-presidents of marketing, production, and finance will coordinate their efforts in arriving at an integrated master plan. Lateral communication also occurs between line and staff departments

---

[8]Rensis Likert, *New Patterns of Management* (New York: McGraw-Hill, 1961), p. 46.

FIGURE 12-10   Frequency and Intensity of Upward and Downward Communication

for the purpose of transmitting technical information necessary to carry out some particular function. As seen earlier, Henri Fayol recommended the use of lateral communication in his famous gangplank theory.

Diagonal communication involves the flow of information among departments or individuals on different levels of the hierarchy. This often occurs in the case of line and staff departments, in which the staff has functional authority. It is also common to find diagonal communication among line departments, again in which one of them has functional authority.

Diagonal communication occurs among people not on the same hierarchical level.

Informal Channels

Since formal communication channels represent only a portion of those channels that exist within the structure, much of the communication taking place is informal in nature; it is not planned by superiors. The term most often used to identify these informal channels is the grapevine.

The Grapevine

The *grapevine* can be a source of factual data, although the term carries the connotation of inaccurate information. One reason for this is that anyone can start a rumor or a half-truth circulating through the organization. Since the channel is informal in nature, it is virtually impossible to determine its precise source in order to authenticate or refute its validity. Nevertheless, the grapevine is very useful in supplementing formal channels. Often it is not only a source of factual information; it provides people with an outlet for their imaginations and apprehensions as well. For example, a male supervisor, realizing that he may be beaten out for the upcoming promotion by his female counterpart who has a better production record, may start a rumor that management is putting emphasis on female promotions. This story can benefit the man for two reasons. First, it may cause management to bend over backward to give him the promotion; some firms are still under the apprehension that they must protect themselves from unfair and observably invalid claims of promoting women on the basis of sex alone. Second, if he does not get the promotion, the man can claim blatant discrimination and possibly save face among his peers. It is therefore easy to see the importance of informal communication channels to organizational members, although it should be noted that the manager must not allow the grapevine to serve as a substitute for formal channels.[9]

The expression "the grapevine" carries the connotation of inaccurate information.

Cluster Chains

Everyone in an organization participates in the grapevine. Some people initiate or pass on information given to them by others; other people stimulate talk by their own silences. For this reason, the channel is very

---

[9]Alan Azremba, "Working with the Organizational Grapevine," *Personnel Journal*, July 1988, pp. 38–42.

similar to its formal counterpart, carrying messages in four directions: up, down, horizontally, and diagonally. However, since this channel is strictly verbal in nature, it can be formed and disbanded very quickly. Its spontaneity prevents it from having permanent membership.

The cluster chain is characterized by selective communication.

Nevertheless, there is a logical pattern to informal channels of communication. There are certain individuals to whom messages will be deliberately passed and others who will be deliberately bypassed. This is often known as the *cluster chain channel;* it is characterized by selective communication. For example, Morgan Bay, vice-president of finance, has just been called into the president's office, where he was informed that the "old man" has decided to announce his retirement at the upcoming Christmas party. Several individuals, including Bay, have been in the running for some time. The president has determined that Bay will get the job, but he intends that this remain a secret until the Christmas party in four weeks. When Bay leaves the office, he is elated. He wants to tell someone the news, but on whom can he rely? Finally, he thinks of his best friend, Tom Land. Bay tells Land, who does indeed keep the secret. Bay has been highly selective in his informal communication.

There are also times when individuals want to get news around quickly while maintaining the appearance of its being a secret. For example, Frances Power has decided to quit her job if she cannot get a 15 percent raise, even though she knows the average for the firm is going to be 9 percent. Rather than call her boss directly, she decides to go through the informal chain, telling the boss's secretary "in secret." It is not long before Power's superior comes by to visit with her about her upcoming raise.

Other informal communication channels exist.

The cluster chain is not the only type of chain used in informal communications. Keith Davis, famous for his writings in the behavioral area, has noted that there are three others, as seen in Figure 12-11. There is the *single strand,* in which information is passed through a long line of recipients, for example, from A to Z. There is the *gossip chain,* in which one person tells everyone else, thereby serving as the prime source of information. Finally, there is the *probability chain,* in which information is passed on randomly. The cluster chain, however, is predominant, indicating that people are selective in choosing their informal communication channel links.

The Manager and Informal Channels

It was noted in Chapter 5 that the manager must attempt to use the informal organization to help attain organizational objectives. The same is true of informal channels of communication. One of the greatest advantages of the grapevine is the rapidity with which it can disseminate information. Another is its potential for supplementing formal channels. A third is the predictable pattern of informal communication, which Davis has noted in this way:

1. People talk most when the news is recent.
2. People talk about things that affect their work.

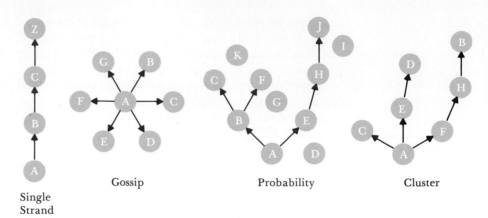

Single
Strand   Gossip   Probability   Cluster

FIGURE 12-11   Types of Informal Communication

3. People talk about people they know.

4. People working near each other are likely to be on the same grapevine.

5. People who contact each other in the chain of procedure tend to be on the same grapevine.[10]

Although the informal organization is not controlled by the manager, it can certainly be employed in helping communicate management's point of view. Of course, success will depend to a great degree on the compatibility of the formal with the informal organization. Still, management must recognize that informal communication networks are an inevitable part of the organization and should endeavor to use them in attaining formal objectives.

COMMUNICATION MEDIA

Media transmission can take the form of words, pictures, or actions. Words are the most commonly used, as evidenced by both oral and written communication. It is therefore essential for the manager to employ them effectively. Pictures are useful aids. The fact that businesses employ them in posters, charts, and blueprints is clear evidence of their value. Action is an important communication medium, as noted by the adage that actions speak louder than words. A grimace, a handshake, a wink, and even silence, have meaning; people will attach significance to them.

Written Communication

Written communica-tion has advantages.

Written communication takes a myriad of forms. Some of the more common ones in business are memos, reports, posters, bulletin-board items, in-house newspapers, and organization handbooks. There are a number of advantages

---

[10]Keith Davis, "Communication within Management," *Personnel*, November 1954, p. 217.

to be gleaned from written communications. One of these is the relative permanence of the communiqué, which provides a record of what was transmitted. Another is the fact that an unclear message can be reread and studied. Moreover, written messages are often more carefully constructed than oral ones because the page gives less opportunity for explanation. Another asset of writing is that a message that must go through many people is protected against continuous reinterpretation. In fact, written communications are often used when a directive contains detailed instructions that are too lengthy to be trusted to oral communication. Still another reason for favoring written messages is that they carry a degree of formality that their verbal counterparts simply do not have.

Written communication also has drawbacks.

On the other hand, written communication has its drawbacks. One is that it is difficult to keep some forms of written communication up-to-date—for example, job descriptions and policy manuals. Things change so fast that these are often in need of revision. In addition, some written communiqués are so lengthy that superiors refuse to read them. An example is seen in the case of reports coming up the line. It is not uncommon for a subordinate to submit a long report and then spend ten minutes briefing the superior on the content. The superior does not have time to wade through the paper, so the oral report by the subordinate becomes necessary.

Oral Communication

Most executives regard oral communication as superior to written. Not only does it save time. It also provides a basis for achieving better understanding. Some of the more common forms are face-to-face verbal orders, telephones, public address systems, speeches, and meetings.

Face-to-face communication is the most effective.

Of these, face-to-face communication is the most effective mode. As with other forms of oral communication, it gives each party an opportunity to respond directly to the other. Disagreement, dissension, fear, tension, and anger can often be eliminated by solving the problem on the spot. This give-and-take gives the participants a basis for clarifying their own position and getting a firsthand view of that held by others. In addition, face-to-face communication provides the sender with an opportunity to note body language, such as gestures and facial responses; the sender can thereby obtain more complete feedback than is available with any other form of oral communication. How a person says something is often as important as what is said.

Large groups impose limitations on communication.

Unfortunately, effective face-to-face communication cannot occur in large groups. With them the manager must rely on such modes of communication as meetings, speeches, and public addresses. A good understanding can often be achieved with these methods, but there is little opportunity for immediate feedback. If some people do not understand the logic behind a particular statement, they must wait until later. Most managers, if they are able to see the group, can recapitulate or reword part of the message if it becomes evident they are not conveying their ideas properly. They will usually do this only if they feel that much of the audience is confused. If it seems that almost everyone understands, the managers may well continue, leaving the one or two confused listeners to work out the meaning for themselves. There is also the case in which managers speak from a company-prepared text, a combination of written and oral communication. Many firms require that managers stay with the text, thereby limiting their freedom and preventing them from clarifying points they feel are not clear to the audience.

Since there are advantages and disadvantages to both written and oral communication, managers must be aware of the problems and pitfalls that prevent a message from being properly interpreted by receivers. Then, by carefully planning their own communications, they can surmount or sidestep these problems.

TOWARD EFFECTIVE COMMUNICATION

Communication presents the manager with a significant challenge. One of the major reasons is that the individual has to determine the best approach to use with each person. Commenting on the mix of employees with which one must cope, an AT&T executive has offered this profile:

> Fifteen million are the "me generation." They expect to be talked with, not to. They expect work rules to be rational and flexible. They want a voice in the company, and they want feedback from their supervisors. You cannot tell them: "That's the way it is."
>
> There are another ten million who are the "pure me generation." They work to live, not live to work. They want a nonstructured, noninvolving job to support their lifestyles. Accordingly, they have no special pride in the organization itself.
>
> About eight million are the "gratefuls." They have had a hard go of it, and they are thankful to have work—but not necessarily thankful to the company providing it.
>
> Finally, we have seven million who are the apples of the supervisor's eye; they are decent and hard working. They believe anything you tell them. . . .[11]

Fortunately, there are numerous techniques available to the manager for improving communication.[12] Some of these help managers convey their message; others are designed to provide them with feedback. Yet all are important because managers need to know whether the receiver understands, accepts, and is willing to take the required action. Managers must

---

[11]Reported in John F. Budd, Jr., "SMR Forum: Is the Focus of Communication on Target?" *Sloan Management Review*, Fall 1982, pp. 52–53.

[12]N. Patricia Freston and Judy E. Lease, "Communication Skills Training for Selected Supervisors," *Training and Development Journal*, July 1987, pp. 67–70.

also know how successful the receiver is in carrying out the directive. Following are some of the most useful techniques for achieving effective communication.

Developing Sensitivity

The foremost way for a manager to improve communication is to be sensitive to the needs and feelings of the subordinates. Although most superiors think they are sensitive, research shows they are neither as perceptive nor as sensitive as they believe. The data in Tables 12-1 and 12-2 have illustrated this. If managers were made aware of and, more difficult, made to seriously consider these findings, it would be a start toward sensitizing them. So would the development of an awareness of nonverbal communication cues. These cues can take many forms. A listener who begins staring out the window may be telling the manager that he is either bored or unwilling to continue listening. A manager who frowns or shakes his head no is telling the speaker that he disagrees. Yet it is not necessary to confine oneself to such obvious nonverbal cues. Consider the manager who pulls a chair around the desk and sits close to a subordinate while discussing a major memo that has just been sent down from top management. This physical closeness indicates that the manager trusts the subordinate, wants the person's input on how to deal with the situation, and is going to communicate openly and freely. This is in direct contrast to the superior who stands up and leans across the desk to reprimand a nervously cringing subordinate whose only wish is to sink through the chair.

All the above are examples of nonverbal communication, and there are many more. In fact, we learn something about people by the ways they walk, stand, move their eyes, or gesture. A manager who is to develop sensitivity must learn to pick up these nonverbal cues and interpret them properly.

Two-way communication is important.

A second useful approach is that of *two-way communication.* By allowing subordinates to speak openly and freely, managers can assure themselves of a more accurate upward flow of information.[13] However, since most do not like to hear unfavorable reports, subordinates tend to screen their comments. Some executives will try to overcome such resistance by telling their staff that they want accurate reporting: Bad news as well as good is to be communicated. If managers really mean this and are able to make people believe it, upward communication can become a reality. However, if they become flustered and angry on hearing bad news, subordinates will again begin paring their reports and removing all unfavorable information.

---

[13]For an interesting discussion on the value of not being totally open see Eric M. Eisenberg and Marsha G. Witten, "Reconsidering Openness in Organizational Communication," *Academy of Management Review*, July 1987, pp. 418–26.

Improving Face-to-Face Relationships

Many managers feel that for them face-to-face communication is the most effective. This form of communication is direct, provides a basis for immediate feedback, and is particularly helpful in building and/or mending organizational relationships. Edgar Schein, the noted organizational psychologist, has recommended the nine following steps for building, maintaining, improving, or repairing these relationships.

Ways to improve face-to-face relationships.

1. Develop self-insight, the ability to see oneself accurately and to evaluate oneself fairly, through feedback from others and systematic self-study. Self-insight is the foundation for effective face-to-face relationships.

2. Develop cross-cultural sensitivity by recognizing and appreciating the values of others. Unskilled workers often have different values and aspirations than do skilled workers; middle managers often have different motives from top managers; finance people typically see things differently from marketing people.

3. Develop cultural/moral humility. This is done by viewing one's own values as not necessarily better or worse than another person's values.

4. Take a pro-active problem-solving orientation. This requires a development of the conviction that interpersonal and cross-cultural problems can be solved.

5. Be personally flexible. Adopt different responses and approaches as dictated by the situation.

6. Develop negotiation skills. Learn how to explore differences creatively, find common ground, and solve the problem.

7. Develop interpersonal tact. Learn how to solve problems without insulting people, demeaning them, or causing them to lose face.

8. Learn repair strategies and skills. Develop the ability to revitalize or rebuild damaged or broken face-to-face relationships.

9. Be patient. Remember that the improvements of face-to-face relationships take time.[14]

Employing Understandable, Repetitive Language

Technical terminology and multisyllabic words may be impressive, but they can also be troublesome to the listener. The manager should try to use understandable language. A supervisor talking to production-line workers must communicate appropriately; so too, of course, must the executive making a report to the board of directors. Effective communication will differ according to the receiver, but it must always be understandable. One way of accomplishing this is to use repetitive language. Sometimes a message will

Understandable, repetitive language will improve communication.

---

[14]Edgar H. Schein, "SMR Forum: Improving Face-to-Face Relationships," *Sloan Management Review*, Winter 1981, pp. 43–52.

not be fully grasped the first time, and a rephrasing or recapitulation is in order. Another guideline is to convey information gradually, building the essence of the message as one goes along. This is especially helpful in conveying technical or sophisticated data.

Using Media Selection Properly

Each media form offers certain advantages.

There are many forms of communication media. Some are better at accomplishing certain objectives than are others. For example, memorandums are very useful in providing information to a mass audience in an inexpensive, fast, convenient, and uniform manner; they also provide a permanent record for both the sender and the receiver. Personal letters are a very good way to convey praise, express appreciation, or appeal to mutual interests. Bulletins are important when conveying urgent or emergency announcements or informing employees of upcoming events. Official reports help keep employees abreast of developments while conveying the information in an official format. Employee handbooks are very useful in (1) acquainting personnel with guidelines for operations, (2) communicating company philosophy, goals, policies, and procedures, and (3) promoting employer-employee understanding. The right medium for the message can improve the chances of gaining the desired response from the receiver. The best medium, however, will depend on such variables as the sender's goals, the content of the message, the values and attitudes of the receiver, and the climate in which the message is sent. As a result, there is no best medium for all messages. Yet, as Walter St. John has noted, there are some truisms that managers should keep in mind for in-house communications:

1. Sharing messages both verbally and in writing is best for important information.
2. Communicating face-to-face is usually best.
3. Relying too heavily on the written word can be disastrous, as can be the requirement "put it in writing."
4. Providing for feedback is essential, regardless of the medium used.
5. Using a variety of media to appeal to the different senses is advantageous.
6. Customizing a medium helps meet unique communications purposes and situations.
7. Understanding and following up on a message should be the goals of good communications. If these are not achieved, the medium has failed.
8. Employing the most expensive medium is sometimes best. Low cost cannot be the ultimate criterion.[15]

---

[15]Walter St. John, "In-House Communications Guidelines," *Personnel Journal*, November 1981, p. 872.

Protecting Credibility

One criterion for managerial effectiveness is credibility, the quality of seeming believable. When Barbara Anderson, the manager, communicates with her subordinates, they listen to and obey her because she has demonstrated through her competence, drive, character, and past performance that she is worthy of their trust. However, the astute manager knows that credibility must not be merely sought; once gained, it must be protected. Every time a manager communicates an order or issues a directive, there is a chance for credibility to be damaged. One way of illustrating the problem and a method for successfully coping with it is through the use of what is called *balance theory.*

Three relationships are significant in balance theory.

Consider the following situation. A manager, Kathleen Fairlane, just told her subordinate that the company has decided to introduce new work procedures. In this instance there are three relevant relationships: (1) the attitude of the receiver toward the sender, (2) the attitude of the receiver toward the new changes, and (3) the receiver's perception of the sender's own attitude toward the changes. Based on the receiver's perception, either a balanced or an unbalanced triad will result. If the receiver has a positive attitude toward both the changes and the sender and, further, believes the latter also favors the new work procedures, there is a balanced triad, as in Figure 12-12. However, if the situation is unbalanced, say because the receiver does not like the new procedures, the situation becomes what is shown in Figure 12-13.

Once the triad is unbalanced, how can balance be restored? There are a number of ways, but the important thing to realize is that the triad must be all pluses or two minuses and a plus. Otherwise, it cannot be balanced.

Ways of establishing balance and protecting credibility vary in quality.

Thus the manager has three options, as illustrated in Figure 12-14: tell the subordinate that she also opposes the new procedures (Triad A); allow the subordinate to develop a negative attitude toward her (Triad B); or persuade the subordinate to accept the new changes (Triad C).

Since the manager's job is to communicate and support directives coming down the line, it is vital that she choose alternative C. This will not only establish balance and protect the manager's credibility with her own

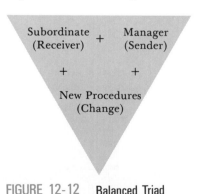

FIGURE 12-12   Balanced Triad

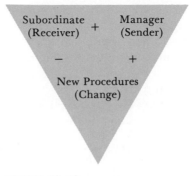

FIGURE 12-13   Unbalanced Triad

subordinates, but it will also prevent alternative A from occurring. One way an effective manager can do this is by emphathizing with the subordinate and demonstrating belief in and positive orientation toward many of the same values and ideals held by the subordinate—for example, good working conditions, a challenging job, a chance for advancement, and recognition. In this way, the manager can personally ensure the subordinate's continuing reliance and trust. Then, credibility protected, the manager can direct attention toward showing the subordinate how the new work procedures will be beneficial in attaining these values and ideals. This will lead in turn to a time for the subordinate to alter the initial, troublesome perception and view the work positively. The result is a balanced triad. By employing balance theory, the effective manager is able to assess communication situations, determine when credibility is threatened, and take the necessary steps to protect it.

Avoiding Bad Listening Habits

The manager spends approximately 70 percent of the day communicating. Ralph Nichols, in breaking down the subfunctions of managers' communication, has estimated that 9 percent is spent in writing, 16 percent in reading,

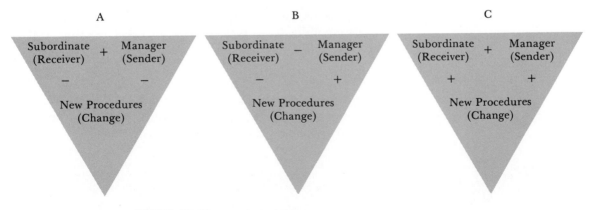

FIGURE 12-14   Balanced Triads

30 percent in speaking, and 45 percent in listening.[16] Yet research shows that managers are not good listeners. Nichols has estimated that when people listen to a ten-minute talk, they operate at only 25 percent efficiency. This is unfortunate because listening to the individual employees is one of the most important methods a manager can use in learning about or evaluating the people in the firm.

Becoming a more effective listener requires an understanding of the ten most common bad habits of listening, which Nichols has defined as follows:

These are the ten most common bad habits of listening.

1. **Calling the subject uninteresting.** Instead of tuning in first and seeing if the speaker has something worthwhile to say, the listener assumes from the start that the topic will be boring.

2. **Tuning the speaker out because of his delivery.** The listener allows delivery to take precedence over content.

3. **Getting overstimulated.** The minute the listener hears something with which he or she disagrees the person stops listening and starts fuming, thereby missing the rest of the message.

4. **Concentrating only on facts, to the exclusion of principles or generalizations.** Facts do not always present the whole picture. Principles and generalizations are often necessary to put everything in its proper perspective.

5. **Trying to outline everything.** Some speakers are less organized then others, and until the individual gets into the presentation, it can be difficult to follow him or her via an outline. Good listeners are flexible in their note taking.

6. **Faking attentiveness.**

7. **Allowing distractions to creep in.**

8. **Tuning out difficult or technical presentations.** This often occurs when managers are listening to financial or quantitatively-oriented reports.

9. **Letting emotional words disrupt the listening process.** Any time a word evokes emotion, there is a good chance that listening will be interrupted.

10. **Wasting thought power.** Most people speak at the rate of 125 words per minute. However, the brain is capable of handling almost five times that number. If the speaker goes on for more than a few minutes, it presents a temptation to the listener to wander, mentally, returning only periodically to check in and see where the speaker is.[17]

---

[16]Ralph G. Nichols, ''Listening: What Price Inefficiency?'' *Office Executive*, April 1959, pp. 15–22.
[17]Adapted from Nichols.

Managers who make a concerted effort to avoid these common pitfalls find that they can improve their level of efficiency far above the 25 percent average.

Becoming an Active Listener

Active listening is a recent topic in the communication field.[18] The term "active listening" means more than just paying attention. It also involves active, empathetic, and supportive behaviors that tell the speaker, "I understand. Please go on." In explaining how an active listener behaves, it is important to describe all five types of listeners: directing, judgmental, probing, smoothing, and active.

There are five types of listeners.

The *directing listener* leads the speaker by establishing the limits and direction of the conversation. The *judgmental listener* introduces value judgments into the conversation. The *probing listener* asks a lot of questions. The *smoothing listener* tries to make light of the problem. The *active listener* attempts to create an environment in which the speaker can express and solve the problem, by feeding back to the speaker neutral summaries of what is being said and then allowing the individual to continue. The responses of all five listeners can be illustrated by showing how each might respond to the same situation. The following is an example:

> *Employee:* "I'm sorry I'm late again. I really got delayed in traffic."
>
> *Directing listener:* "If you'd leave for work earlier, you wouldn't have to worry about traffic jams."
>
> *Judgmental listener:* "Coming in late again really looks bad for you. You better find a way to get here on time."
>
> *Probing listener:* "How come you were late again?"
>
> *Smoothing listener:* "No matter how hard we try, all of us are late from time to time."
>
> *Active listener:* "You sound upset that you were late this morning."

Notice that the active listener encourages the speaker to continue. This type of encouragement is one of the primary characteristics of active listening. Other guidelines, offered by Robert Bolton, are the following:[19]

1. **Do not fake understanding.** If you lose track of what the speaker is saying, ask him or her to explain further.

---

[18]Jane Gibson and Richard M. Hodgetts, *Organizational Communication: A Management Perspective* (New York: Academic Press, 1986), Chapter 3.

[19]Robert Bolton, *People Skills* (Englewood Cliffs, NJ: Prentice-Hall, Inc., 1979), pp. 90–99.

REAL-LIFE MANAGERS:

INTERVIEW WITH JOHN HOOVER

John Hoover is a senior-level manager at the San Francisco branch of the Federal Reserve. John manages five different departments, which are responsible for a wide array of activities ranging from customer relations to check processing to government securities to accounting. He is also responsible for selling financial services to clients and for seeing that these services are properly installed. In his multifaceted role, John spends a large portion of his time communicating with in-house personnel as well as with the public in general and outside clients in particular.

Q.   *What is the biggest communication problem facing most personnel?*

A.   The biggest problem is that they don't listen well. Even in college, when they teach people to communicate more effectively, the focus is almost always on written and verbal communication. Examples include: composition, business letter and report writing, and speech making. However, no one is given a course in effective listening. As a result, many people don't know how to listen effectively. In fact, they don't spend enough time learning to listen. They tend to hear words, but they don't listen to the content. They focus on what *they* want to say, and not on what the *other* person is saying.

Q.   *Are there any other major communication problems you find among organizational personnel?*

A.   Another is poor speaking skills. People don't take time organize their thoughts and the impact of what they are going to say on the other person. If you are going

---

Ways to build active listening skills.

2.   **Do not tell the speaker you know how he or she feels.** This is often seen as patronizing and phony.

3.   **Vary your responses.** There is no single "right" response to every situation. Depending on the environment, paraphrase, remain silent, or given an encouraging word to let the speaker know you are paying attention.

4.   **Focus on feelings.** Do not ignore the emotional content of the message; be aware of the speaker's attitudes, values, and opinions.

5.   **Choose the most accurate feeling word.** Degrees of the word "sad," for example, can be expressed as "very sad," "distraught," "despairing," and "heartbroken."

to verbally communicate a message, you have to tailor it to the audience. What is likely to persuade this other person to your way of thinking? Should you use mostly facts? Or should you appeal to the individual's emotions as well? What information should you communicate first? How should you conclude your comments? What do you want to happen as a result of what you've said? If people took the time to plan their verbal communiques by first answering these types of questions, they would be more effective speakers. Quite often, I find, individuals are more concerned with what they want to say than with ensuring that there has been adequate preparation for conveying the message.

Q.   *Can people become better communicators or is effective communication an innate skill?*

A.   Oh, it's something that you can develop. I don't know anyone who was born a great communicator. You learn the skills and rules as you go along. However, some people are more effective at identifying these basics and developing them more quickly than others. Conversely, some people never seem to get any better at communicating. It's as if they refuse to learn from experience. What they are unable, or unwilling, to grasp is the fact that communication skills can be improved through practice. If you want to learn how to make an effective presentation to the board of directors, you have to plan your presentation, practice it, and, after you have given the talk, evaluate your performance and determine how you can do better the next time. Feedback and self-improvement are critical to the development of effective communication skills. Many people feel that formal communication is just like talking to your next door neighbor. Actually, a good business communicator is more formal and better structured in his or her approach. Good communication is more than "doing what comes naturally." Effective communication involves planning and effort. If you want to be good at it, you have to have the desire and be willing to put in the time to hone these skills.

6.   **Develop a vocal empathy.** If your voice is cold and clinical, the speaker will not feel comfortable. Have your tone of voice and its rate, rhythm, and volume reflect the speaker's emotional state.

7.   **Strive for concreteness and relevance.** Help the speaker come to the point by making your responses specific and, if necessary, asking clarifying questions such as "How did you feel when that happened?"

8.   **Provide nondogmatic but firm responses.** State these responses in such a way that the speaker feels comfortable in disagreeing with your paraphrasing.

9.   **Reflect the speaker's resources.** Often, the speaker will become so involved with his or her problem that the individual focuses on negative

points and neglects strengths. Highlight these strengths when you hear them and thus provide a bit of encouragement to the speaker.

10. **Reflect the feelings that are implicit in questions.** When a speaker asks you directly what you would do, it becomes difficult not to give advice. A truly skilled active listener, however, can reflect the feeling of the direct question back at the speaker.

11. **Accept the fact that many interactions will be inconclusive.** Few listening incidents will come to closure. The active listener often must settle for the knowledge that he or she has left the speaker with a sounder basis for further thought.[20]

Employing the Commandments of Good Communication

Although many guidelines have been put forth to improve communication, one of the most extensive compilations is that constructed by the American Management Association. Often known as the ten commandments of good communication, they are the following:

The American Management Association has provided ten commandments of good communication.

1. **Clarify ideas before communicating.** By systematically thinking through the message and considering who will be receiving and/or affected by it, the manager overcomes one of the basic pitfalls of communication—failure to properly plan the communiqué. The more systematically a message is analyzed, the more clearly it can be communicated.

2. **Examine the true purpose of communication.** The manager has to determine what he or she *really* wants to accomplish with the message. Once this objective is identified, the communiqué can be properly designed.

3. **Take the entire environment, physical and human, into consideration.** Questions, such as what is said, to whom, and when, will all affect the success of the communication. The physical setting, the social climate, and past communication practices should be examined in adapting the message to the environment.

4. **When valuable, obtain advice from others in planning communiqués.** Consulting with others can be a useful method of obtaining additional insights regarding how to handle the communication. In addition, those who help formulate it usually give it active support.

5. **Be aware of the overtones as well as the basic content of the message.** The listener will be affected by not only what is said but how it is said. Voice tone, facial expression, and choice of language all influence the listener's reaction to the communiqué.

---

[20]See also: Cynthia Hamilton, "Steps to Better Listening," *Personnel Journal*, February 1987, pp. 20–21.

6. **When possible, convey useful information.** People remember things that are beneficial to them. If the manager wants subordinates to retain the message, he or she should phrase it so that it takes into consideration *their* interests and needs as well as the company's.

7. **Follow up on communication.** The manager must solicit feedback in ascertaining whether the subordinate understands the communiqué, is willing to comply with it, and then takes the appropriate action.

8. **Communicate with the future, as well as the present, in mind.** Most communications are designed to meet the demands of the current situation. However, they should be in accord with the long-range goals as well. For example, communiqués designed to improve performance or morale are valuable in handling present problems. Yet they also serve a useful future purpose by promoting long-run organizational efficiency.

9. **Support words with deeds.** When managers contradict themselves by saying one thing and doing another, they undermine their own directives. For example, the executive who issues a notice reminding everyone to be in the building by 8:30 A.M. while he or she continues to show up at 9:15 A.M. should not expect anyone to take the notice seriously. Subordinates are always cognizant of such managerial behavior and quickly discount such directives.

10. **Be a good listener.** By concentrating on the speaker's explicit and implicit meanings, the manager can obtain a much better understanding of what is being said.[21]

■ SUMMARY

This chapter has examined interpersonal and organizational communication. It noted that the communication process entails four steps: attention, understanding, acceptance, and action and that implementation of the process occurs in two basic channels: the formal and the informal. The astute manager uses both to advantage, keeping in mind that there tends to be an overemphasis on downward communication and an underemphasis on upward. This is unfortunate, for without some form of upward communication the manager suffers from a lack of feedback. Many managers overlook the need for this feedback, tending to follow the old conveyor theory of communication. They send their subordinates a message and expect them to act accordingly. However, communication does not work that way. People do

---

[21]Adapted from American Management Association, "Ten Commandments of Good Communication," as reported in Max D. Richards and William A. Nielander, eds., *Readings in Management* (Cincinnati, OH: South-Western Publishing, 1958), pp. 141–43.

not always interpret messages in the same way. There are many reasons for this, and all constitute barriers to effective communication. Some of the more important are perception, language, abstraction, inference, status, and resistance to change. In order to overcome these barriers, the manager must take steps to establish lines of feedback. Some of the more effective techniques are sensitivity; understandable, repetitive language; credibility; the avoidance of bad listening habits; and a general adherence to the commandments of good communication. Although many people may think these ideas appear obvious, it is really quite difficult to practice an adherence to them.

■ REVIEW AND STUDY QUESTIONS

1. How does the communication process work? Explain.

2. What is the conveyor theory of communication? How does it work? Is it an accurate description of how communication actually takes place? Explain.

3. What are the four steps for implementing effective communication? Identify and describe each.

4. What are some of the common barriers to effective communication? Identify and describe three of them.

5. How does perception affect communication? Give an example.

6. How can inference bring about communication breakdown? Give an illustration.

7. Why do people resist change? Is change really inevitable? Is resistance? Explain.

8. What is meant by the expression *going through channels?* Put it in your own words.

9. What are informal communication channels? Identify and describe three of the most common.

10. What are the advantages of using written communication? Verbal communication? Identify and describe two of each.

11. How can a manager promote sensitivity? Be complete in your answer.

12. How is balance theory useful to managers who need to protect their credibility? Explain.

13. What are some of the most common bad listening habits? Identify and describe five of them.

14. How can a manager become a more effective listener? Offer some concrete advice.

15. How can a manager obtain feedback for effective communication? Be complete in your answer.

■ SELECTED REFERENCES

Athanassiades, J. C. "The Distortion of Upward Communication in Hierarchical Organizations." *Academy of Management Journal*, June 1973, pp. 207–26.

Budd, John F. Jr., "SMR Forum: Is the Focus of Communication on Target?" *Sloan Management Review*, Fall 1982, pp. 51–53.

Cohen, Lynn Renee. "Nonverbal (Mis)Communication between Managerial Men and Women." *Business Horizons*, January–February 1983, pp. 13–17.

DiGaetani, John L. "The Business of Listening." *Business Horizons*, October 1980, pp. 40–46.

Drake, Bruce H., and Dennis J. Moberg. "Communicating Influence Attempts in Dyads: Linguistic Sedatives and Palliatives." *Academy of Management Review*, July 1986, pp. 567–84.

Giacalone, Robert A., and Stephen B. Knouse. "Reducing the Need for Defensive Communication." *Management Solutions*, September 1987, pp. 21–25.

Greenbaum, H. H. "The Audit of Organizational Communication." *Academy of Management Journal*, December 1974, pp. 739–54.

Hall, J. "Communication Revisited." *California Management Review*, Spring 1973, pp. 56–67.

Hersey, P., and J. W. Kleity. "One-on-One OD Communication Skills." *Training and Development Journal*, April 1980, pp. 56–60.

Kirkham, Roger L. "Communicating to Influence Others More Effectively." *Personnel*, December 1987, pp. 52–55.

McCaskey, M. B., and C. A. O'Reilley III. "The Hidden Messages Managers Send." *Harvard Business Review*, November–December 1979, pp. 135–48.

Nichols, Ralph G. "Listening Is Good Business." *Management of Personnel Quarterly*, Winter 1962, pp. 2–9.

Roberts, K. H., and C. A. O'Reilley III. "Some Correlations of Communications Roles in Organizations." *Academy of Management Journal*, March 1979, pp. 42–57.

Robey, Daniel, and William Taggart. "Measuring Manager's Minds: The Assessment of Style in Human Information Processing." *Academy of Management Review*, July 1981, pp. 375–83.

Rozema, Hazel J., and John W. Gray. "How Wide Is Your Communication Gender Gap." *Personnel Journal*, July 1987, pp. 98–105.

St. John, Walter. "In-House Communication Guidelines." *Personnel Journal*, November 1981, pp. 872–78.

Schein, Edgar H. "SMR Forum: Improving Face-to-Face Relationships." *Sloan Management Review*, Winter 1981, pp. 43–52.

Wycoff, Edgar B. "Canons of Communication." *Personnel Journal*, March 1981, pp. 208–12.

Zelko, Harold P. "Rate Your Communication Skills." *Personnel Journal*, November 1987, p. 133.

■ CASE: Good Work Is Expected

An eastern pharmaceutical company hired an outside management consulting firm to analyze its operations. After five weeks, the consultants made their report to management. One of the areas they had investigated was communication between superiors and subordinates. To its dismay, management learned that there were numerous discrepancies between what superiors said they did and what their subordinates said their superiors did. For example, the consultants conducted a confidential questionnaire survey of 20 percent of the managers and workers; the responses to the question, "Do you tell your subordinates when they do a good job?" are tabulated in Table 12-3.

Management was quite distraught with the findings. As a result, at its next board of directors meeting the chairperson proposed that the firm bring back the consultants to advise and counsel them on how they could deal with this problem. The resolution was passed unanimously.

When the middle and lower-level managers learned of the action, they expressed surprise. One of them said, "Just because the data indicate poor communication is no need to get excited. After all, the workers say lots of things that aren't accurate." A colleague explained, "Look, I expect subordinates to do a good job. I only tell them when they are doing a poor one. If I praised them every time they did something right, they'd all have swelled heads. My approach is to say nothing."

Questions

1. What do the data in Table 12-3 show? Explain your findings.
2. What do you think of the comments from the two managers? Do the two hold valid points of view on the practice of feedback?
3. What types of recommendations would you expect from the consultants? Explain.

TABLE 12-3
Do You Tell Your Subordinates When They Do a Good Job?

	Top Management Says of Itself	Middle Management Says of Top Management	Middle Management Says of Itself	Lower-level Management Says of Middle Management	Lower-level Management Says of Itself	Workers Say of Lower-level Management
Always	93%	82%	95%	63%	98%	39%
Often	7	14	5	15	2	23
Sometimes		4		12		18
Seldom				6		11
Never				4		9

■ CASE: What Do They Want?

What do workers really want from their jobs? This question has long puzzled managers. A recent survey of 1,000 industrial employees and 100 supervisors sought to answer this question. The respondents were provided with a list of 10 items and asked to rank the importance of each to the employees. As seen below, the responses of the supervisors were not the same as those of the workers.

	Supervisors	Employees
Interesting work	5	1
Full appreciation of work done	8	2
Feeling of being in on things	10	3
Job security	2	4
Good wages	1	5
Promotion and growth in the organization	3	6
Good working conditions	4	7
Personal loyalty to employees	7	8
Tactful discipline	9	9
Sympathetic help with personal problems	6	10

Additionally, the responses of the workers varied based on such factors as sex, age, income level, job type, and organizational level. Here is how the 1,000 workers ranked the ten factors.

	Sex		Age				Income Level				Job Type				Organization Level		
	Men	Women	Under 30	31–40	41–50	Over 50	Under $12,000	$12,001–$18,000	$18,001–$25,000	Over $25,000	Blue-Collar Unskilled	Blue-Collar Skilled	White-Collar Unskilled	White-Collar Skilled	Lower Nonsupervisory	Middle Nonsupervisory	Higher Nonsupervisory
Interesting work	1	2	4	2	3	1	5	2	1	1	2	1	1	2	3	1	1
Full appreciation of work done	3	1	5	3	2	2	4	3	3	2	1	6	3	1	4	2	2
Feeling of being in on things	2	3	6	4	1	3	6	1	2	4	5	2	5	4	5	3	3
Job security	5	4	2	1	4	7	2	4	4	3	4	3	7	5	2	4	6

continued

continued

	Sex		Age				Income Level				Job Type				Organization Level		
	Men	Women	Under 30	31–40	41–50	Over 50	Under $12,000	$12,001–$18,000	$18,001–$25,000	Over $25,000	Blue-Collar Unskilled	Blue-Collar Skilled	White-Collar Unskilled	White-Collar Skilled	Lower Nonsupervisory	Middle Nonsupervisory	Higher Nonsupervisory
Good wages	4	5	1	5	5	8	1	5	6	8	3	4	6	6	1	6	8
Promotion and growth in organization	6	6	3	6	8	9	3	6	5	7	6	5	4	3	6	5	5
Good working conditions	7	7	7	7	7	4	8	7	7	6	9	7	2	7	7	7	4
Personal loyalty to employees	8	8	9	9	6	5	7	8	8	5	8	9	9	8	8	8	7
Tactful discipline	9	9	8	10	9	10	10	9	9	10	7	10	10	9	9	9	10
Sympathetic help with personal problems	10	10	10	8	10	6	9	10	10	9	10	8	8	10	10	10	9

Questions

1. What do the responses of the supervisors relate regarding upward communication? Explain.

2. In what way does perception help account for the differences between the supervisory and worker lists? Explain.

3. If management were aware of the findings reported in this case, how could the information be used to help the organization be more efficient? Be complete in your answer.

Source: Reprinted from "What Motivates Employees? Workers and Supervisors Give Different Answers," by Kenneth A. Kovach, *Business Horizons,* September–October 1987, pp. 58–65. Copyright © 1987 by the Foundation for the School of Business at Indiana University. Used with permission.

■ ## CASE: A Two-way Experiment

To emphasize the importance of communication, Maria Fontana, director of in-house training of a large western retail chain, decided to conduct an experiment during an upcoming session with a group of middle managers. When they were all settled in the room, she began by asking the value of two-way communication. All agreed it was of prime importance for effective management. Fontana then asked them how they went about obtaining feedback from subordinates. Although some of the managers contributed ideas, it was evident that the group was unsettled by the question. Finally one of the managers, Milford Graves, spoke up. "Ms. Fontana, two-way communication is great if you have a problem, but most of us really believe we can achieve our goals with successful downward communication. We really don't have trouble getting our meanings across to the workers."

By the hum in the room, Fontana realized that the rest of the managers basically agreed. "Do you mean to tell me that you are all such good communicators that your subordinates know exactly what you are talking about? They never have to ask a question?"

"Well, I'm not saying we're perfect," said Graves, "but speaking personally, I can make myself understood if I really have to. When I make a concerted effort, there is no real need for questions. And I'm not kidding or bragging. I've worked at it a long time, and I'm just that good."

With that Fontana asked Graves to come to the front of the room and read a piece of paper on the podium. While he was thus occupied, she said to the group, "Mr. Graves is looking at the piece of paper I have on the podium. I would like the rest of you to get ready to draw. Mr. Graves is going to describe some diagrams to you, and he is going to tell you how to draw these diagrams. You are to do exactly what he tells you. You are not to ask any questions, make any noise, or provide him with any kind of feedback indicating whether or not you are able to follow the logic of his directives."

Figure 12-15 shows the diagrams Graves was asked to describe to the group. The instructions that accompanied the diagrams told Graves to use no geometric terms. Instead, he was to get the other people in the room to draw these figures by merely using lines, dots, and geographic directions. In addition, he was to keep his head down throughout the experiment so that he could not see the group.

Graves began. By the time he finished it was evident to Fontana that many of the group members were failing to follow some of the directions. "All right, show and tell," she said. "How many of you feel you got all four

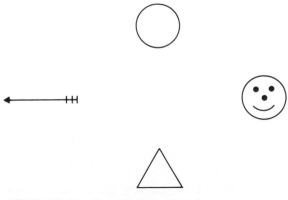

FIGURE 12-15   The First Set of Drawings

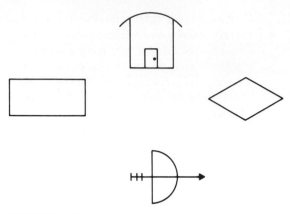

FIGURE 12-16   The Second Set of Drawings

diagrams right?'' Four of the twenty-four raised their hands. Then Fontana held up the diagrams for all to see. It turned out that everyone had at least one of them right, but no one had all four correct. Only seven had three of the four right.

Fontana then ran the experiment again, using the diagrams in Figure 12-16. This time she told Graves to look at the group and answer any questions they had. In addition, if he felt that he had lost the group at any point, he could go back and repeat the directions. At the end of this experiment everyone in the room had at least two of the diagrams right, and twelve had all four correct. ''Well, Mr. Graves,'' said Fontana with a smiling nod, ''you seem to have improved markedly over your first performance.''

''I know,'' he replied, ''but I never really realized how much can be lost if you don't allow people to ask questions. What surprised me even more was how much feedback I was getting just by looking at their faces and their body movements. I guess your point is that there is a tremendous increase in understanding between one- and two-way communication. Right?''

Questions

1. Can this experiment and two-way communication on the job be correlated? Explain.
2. What are some of the most effective ways to promote two-way communication? Explain.

■ CASE: Speed and Comprehension

One of the greatest communication problems is that of getting people to increase their reading speed and comprehension. Take out a clean piece of paper before continuing with this case. Then read the following assignment. Each of the twenty-four items asks you to execute a prescribed activity.

The items vary in complexity, but you should be able to cope easily with them all. This is not an intelligence test. The exercise is designed to measure only how well you read and carry out instructions with accuracy. You have three minutes to complete the exercise. So be sure to time yourself and remain within the constraint. Enter all your answers on the piece of paper.

Read everything before doing anything.

1. Write your name in the upper right corner of the piece of paper.
2. Multiply 23 by 68 and place the result under your name.
3. Draw a square on the reverse side of the paper.
4. Draw a circle inside the square.
5. Draw a diamond inside the circle.
6. Write the month and date in the upper left corner.
7. Multiply the square root of 9 by the square of 16.
8. Subtract 1,462 from 2,221 and place the result in the lower left corner.
9. Underline your answer to Question 2.
10. If a farmer has 17 pigs, and all but 12 die, how many pigs are left alive?
11. Add 14,421 to 27,969 and place the result in the lower right corner.
12. Now subtract 14,421 from 27,969 and place the answer under the result for Question 11.
13. Square the number seven and put your answer immediately below.
14. Compute the square root of 169 and add this to the answer you worked out in Question 13.
15. Write down the name of the sixteenth President of the U. S.
16. Write Ronald Reagan's middle name on the bottom of the page.
17. If Dr. Joyce Brothers married comedian Dickie Smothers, what would her new name be?
18. Which space project was the one that got America to the moon: Gemini, Apollo, or Mercury?
19. Who won the last National League Pennant?
20. Who won the last American League Pennant?
21. Who won the first Super Bowl?
22. Take a number from 1 to 10. Add 10. Subtract 5. Multiply by 7. Square the number. What is your answer?
23. Write down the year you graduated from grammar school as a four digit number—for example, 1983. Add to this your present age. Then write down how long you have been out of grammar school. Finally, write down the year you were born. Add all four numbers together.

24. Carry out the instructions in Question 1 only and ignore all the rest.

Questions

1. What is the purpose of this exercise? What does it relate about communication problems?
2. How can these problems be overcome? Explain.

■ SELF-FEEDBACK EXERCISE: Identifying Inferences

One of the major causes of communication breakdown is inference. The following story is followed by a set of twelve questions. Carefully read the story and then answer the questions by indicating whether each is true (T), false (F), or an inference (I). Answers and explanations are provided at the end of the exercise.

> Jack Fuller is the vice-president of sales for a large national firm. Jack believes that one of the most promising people in his department is Frances O'Hearne who works in sales analysis. Her job consists of identifying where sales are being made and why, and then reporting this information to the sales force. This job is extremely important because it helps the salespeople understand where and why customers are buying the company's products.
>
> Jack knows that every individual who has been promoted to the senior ranks of the firm has had field experience. Frances has not and Jack would like her to take a transfer to the field next month. This transfer would require her to be away from the home office for twelve months. Frances understands Jack's reasoning, but she is reluctant to make the move. Frances is not only happy in her current job, but feels that her contribution to the firm is greater as a sales analyst than it would be as a salesperson. She is also concerned that if she goes into the field, she will never get back to the home office.
>
> Jack has an opening in the field that must be filled by next month. The next opening is not likely to occur for another six months, and Jack feels that Frances's career would be negatively affected by waiting this long. Although she has not turned down the assignment, Frances is delaying her response. Frances's new husband feels that the final decision should be made by her. "You want to make the company a career, so I think you should decide whether or not this is the right move for you," he told her. "The money is good and you certainly would gain important experience. However, if this is not the type of job you want, turn it down. It's not going to be the end of the world for you."

Now answer the following questions without looking back at the story.

T	F	I	1.	Jack Fuller is in the sales area.
T	F	I	2.	Frances O'Hearne works directly for Jack Fuller.
T	F	I	3.	In order to be promoted into the senior ranks an individual has to have field experience.
T	F	I	4.	Frances currently works at the home office.
T	F	I	5.	Frances does not like selling.
T	F	I	6.	Frances knows that Jack is right about the need for sales field experience.
T	F	I	7.	Frances does not like her current job.
T	F	I	8.	Frances has to make a decision soon.
T	F	I	9.	From what can be gleaned from the case, Frances is a new, young bride.
T	F	I	10.	The sales position pays more money than the current position.
T	F	I	11.	Frances would eventually like to get Jack's job.
T	F	I	12.	Frances's husband really does not want her to take a transfer to the field.

Answers and Interpretation

1. True. Jack is the vice-president of sales.
2. Inference. Frances works in Jack's department, but we do not know that she reports directly to Jack.
3. Inference. This has happened in the past, but there is no proof that it will continue to be true.
4. True. The story relates this fact.
5. Inference. We do not know how she feels about selling.
6. Inference. Frances understands his reasoning, but may not agree with it.
7. False. The story says that she likes her job.
8. True. There is only one month left in which to fill the position.
9. Inference. We do not know how old she is.
10. Inference. The story says that the salary is good, but we do not know if it pays more than Frances now earns.
11. Inference. Frances wants to make a career with the firm, but we do not know if she wants Jack's job.
12. Inference. He may or may not. The story is unclear on this point.

CHAPTER
13

Modern
Motivation
Theory

One of the greatest challenges the manager faces is that of motivating the workers. It is a challenge that many supervisors feel they need to learn more about. For example, a recent survey among managers found that of all the areas in which they felt training could be helpful to them, motivation headed the list.[1]

This chapter will examine modern motivation theory. Much of the chapter will deal with what are called content theories. These are concerned with what it is within the individual or environment that stimulates or sustains behavior—that is, what specific things motivate people. The last part of the chapter examines three process theories, which are concerned with explaining how behavior is initiated, directed, sustained, and halted. The goals of this chapter are to acquaint the reader with modern motivation theory and to indicate its relevance to management.

When you have finished this chapter, you should be able to:

1. Relate why motivation is a management challenge.

2. Explain the relationship between needs and behavior.

3. Identify and describe the five basic needs in Maslow's needs hierarchy.

4. Compare and contrast the tenets of management theories X and Y.

5. Discuss the value of money, status, working conditions, increased responsibility, and challenging work in motivating people.

---

[1]Katherine Culbertson and Mark Thompson, "An Analysis of Supervisory Training Needs," *Training and Development Journal,* February 1980, pp. 58–62.

6. Describe some of the new process theories of motivation that emphasize individual stimulation, rather than mass motivation.

UNDERSTANDING THE CHALLENGE

Motivation, the process of inducing people to act in a given way, is one of the most important topics of consideration in American industry today. More and more managers are being heard to remark that "You just can't get good help any more." Undoubtedly this is an overstatement; however, one thing is true. The way in which management motivated our fathers and grandfathers will no longer work today. Numerous reasons can be cited to support this statement. Philip Grant has offered the following explanations:

1. There is a great instability and diversity of values among the work force. People of all ages find it difficult to decide what is really worthwhile in life.

Some reasons for declining worker motivation in America.

2. There are more guaranteed rewards than ever before. As a result, people are finding that they do not have to strive hard to get much of what they want.

3. Rewards are unable to satisfy many emerging needs. Most Americans are able to afford what they want so money and other payoffs that help people obtain food, clothing and shelter now have diminished importance.

4. The work ethic has foundered and stumbled. Fewer individuals today believe that hard work is the sign of a righteous person.

5. There is a reduced cost of failure. Few people are penalized for failure to perform, so there is less effort toward succeeding.

6. Progressive taxation rates eat away much of what one can earn through hard work. So, for many, the payoffs associated with doing the best possible job are not sufficient to entice them to put forth their best efforts.

7. There is more group production and problem solving than ever before. Rugged individualism is no longer in demand and many people are turned off by their inability to succeed through their own individual effort.

8. There is decreased employee loyalty to organizations. Many people have little affiliation or pride in their organization so they do not work very hard for their company.

9. Supervisory authority has eroded over the years. Lacking control over rewards and penalties, these individuals are actually becoming helpless when it comes to motivating their people.

10. People today are interested in short-term payoffs. If they have to work hard for five years to get a promotion, they are not interested; they want

promotions quickly or they will not put out the necessary effort. They live in a world of "here and now."[2]

The Values Issue

In large degree, changing values help explain the manager's need to understand motivation. People today are motivated by things other than money. For example, when Ed Schwarzkopf and Edwin L. Miller asked executives who were considered to be "fast track" managers what the important factors were that they would consider when making a career move, the respondents gave the following five answers:

1. Opportunity for knowledge, experience, and future assignments in this company.
2. Opportunity for greater responsibility.
3. Opportunity for increased pay.
4. Opportunity to improve career mobility.
5. Increased promotion potential.[3]

Notice that except for the third response, all of the others were concerned with personal and career growth. Money was not as important as opportunity and growth. Psychological rewards had greater value to them than did physical rewards. In getting a better fix on the importance of financial goals to these executives, the researchers then asked them to rank six items ranging from very important to very unimportant. Their responses were as follows:

Very important	Educate children
	Improve standard of living
Somewhat important	Travel and enjoyment of recreational activity
	Build a substantial estate
Somewhat unimportant	Save enough for early retirement
Very unimportant	Improve social standing in the community[4]

Workforce values are changing.

Responses such as these indicate that the often cited "blind ambition" theory of executive motivation is simply not true. There are many things of more value to successful managers than simply getting ahead in the

---

[2]Philip C. Grant, "Why Employee Motivation Has Declined in America," *Personnel Journal*, December 1982, pp. 905–909.

[3]Ed A. Schwarzkopf and Edwin L. Miller, "Exploring the Male Mobility Myth," *Business Horizons*, June 1980, p. 39.

[4]Ibid., p. 40.

organization. The same holds true when it comes to employees farther down the line. For example, based on their research, Lauren Jackson and Mark Mindell note that "The most important changes affecting motivation . . . are those in the values of the work force. Whereas pay was traditionally a basic motivator, for instance, other values such as self-worth, leisure time, and more communication from management have recently become primary concerns among employees."[5] An additional comparison of traditional and contemporary values is present in Table 13-1. Findings such as these indicate that motivation is a very complex subject. Many of the intuitive conclusions that managers hold regarding the factors that motivate their people are simply not correct. A sound understanding of motivation must have its foundation in research-based motivation theory. We begin our investigation of this area by considering the subject of needs and behaviors.

TABLE 13-1 Traditional and Contemporary Values of Employees	Traditional	Contemporary
	Strong loyalty to the company	Low loyalty or commitment to the organization
	Strong desire for money and status	A need for rewards to be geared to accomplishments
	Strong desire for promotion up the management hierarchy	A need for organizational recognition of contributions
	Critical concerns about job security and stability	Decreasing concern for job security and stability
	Strong employee identification with work roles rather than personal roles	A need to perform work that is challenging and worthwhile
		A need to participate in decisions that ultimately affect oneself
		Stronger employee identification with one's personal role than one's work role
		A need for communication from management regarding what is going on in the company
		A need to rise above the routine and approach tasks creatively
		A need for personal growth opportunities on the job

Source: Adapted from Lauren Hite Jackson and Mark G. Mindell, "Motivating the New Breed," *Personnel,* March–April 1980, pp. 54–55.

[5]Lauren Hite Jackson and Mark G. Mindell, "Motivating the New Breed," *Personnel,* March–April 1980, p. 53.

NEEDS AND BEHAVIORS

Motivation is an internal, psychological process.

One way of examining motivation is through a need-satisfaction approach.

If managers are to be successful in getting workers to attain organizational objectives, they must understand the fundamentals of motivation. This is not an easy job, for motivation is an intervening variable—an internal, psychological process that the manager cannot see. Rather, the manager can only assume its presence (or absence) based on observance of worker behavior. If the workers are busy at their tasks, the manager may well infer that they are motivated. If they are standing around talking, the manager may conclude that they are not motivated to work.

However, this superficial approach fails to answer a key question: Why do people behave as they do? Although there are various answers, one approach is a need-satisfaction explanation. It is assumed that everyone has needs that require satisfaction. In turn, these needs cause the person to undertake some form of goal-oriented behavior, which is intended to satisfy the need. For example, hunger pangs may lead a person to go into a nearby cafe and eat. Using just this information, it is possible to design a simple diagram of motivation, shown as Figure 13-1. Every individual, of course, has many needs, but it is the need with the greatest strength that tends to dictate current behavior.

Once the need has been satisfied, it declines in importance and another need becomes dominant. The need theory of motivation has been formulated and explained in detail by Abraham Maslow, a psychologist.

MASLOW'S NEED HIERARCHY

According to Maslow, each of us is a wanting being; there is always some need to satisfy. Once one need satisfaction is accomplished, that particular need no longer motivates the person, who is free then to turn to another need, again seeking satisfaction. Maslow has represented the needs in hierarchical form, with those at the lower levels requiring basic satisfaction before the individual can move on to the next level. Figure 13-2 illustrates Maslow's *need hierarchy* of physiological, safety, social, esteem, and self-actualization needs. However, before discussion begins, it should be noted that Maslow never contended that a need must be 100 percent satisfied before the next level becomes important. As he has explained:

> In actual fact, most members of our society who are normal are partially satisfied in all their basic needs and partially unsatisfied in all their basic needs at the same time. A more realistic description of the hierarchy would be in terms of decreasing percentages of satisfaction as we go up

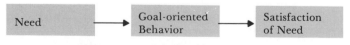

FIGURE 13-1   Simple Motivation Process

FIGURE 13-2   Maslow's Hierarchy of Needs

the hierarchy of prepotency. For instance, if I may assign arbitrary figures . . . it is as if the average citizen is satisfied perhaps 85 per cent in his physiological needs, 70 per cent in his safety needs, 50 per cent in his love needs, 40 per cent in his self-esteem needs, and 10 per cent in his self-actualization needs.[6]

Physiological Needs

The most basic needs are physiological.

At the base of the hierarchy are *physiological needs*, those necessary to sustain life. They include food, water, clothing, and shelter. An individual who lacks the basic necessities in life will probably be motivated primarily by physiological needs. As Maslow put it, "A person who is lacking food, safety, love, and esteem would most probably hunger for food more strongly than for anything else.[7] When this is so, Figure 13-3 accurately depicts the need hierarchy.

Research indicates that satisfaction of physiological needs is usually associated with money—not the money itself in this case, but what it can buy. Although one could look at Figure 13-2 and argue that other needs could also be satisfied with money, it seems clear that the value of this factor diminishes as one goes up the hierarchy. Self-respect, for example, cannot be bought (See also Ethics in Action: Money and Motivation).

Safety Needs

When physiological needs are basically fulfilled, safety needs begin to manifest themselves. One of the most common is protection from physical

---

[6]Abraham H. Maslow, "A Theory of Human Motivation," *Psychological Review*, July 1943, pp. 388–89.

[7]Abraham H. Maslow, *Motivation and Personality*, 2nd ed. (New York: Harper & Row, 1954), p. 37.

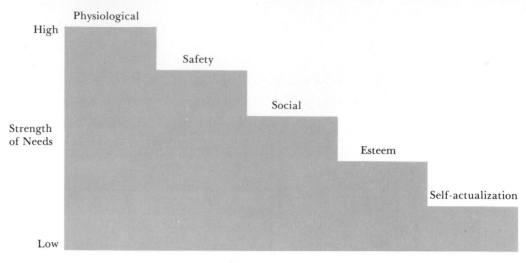

FIGURE 13-3   Need Hierarchy Showing Physiological Needs Dominant

Then come safety needs, which take many forms.

dangers, such as fire or accident. In an industrial setting, signs such as "No Smoking in This Area" and "Beyond This Point Safety Glasses Must Be Worn" provide illustrations of how management attempts to satisfy this need.

A second safety need is economic security. On the job, fringe benefits such as accident, health, and life insurance programs help fulfill this need.

A third common safety need is the desire for an orderly, predictable environment. If this is difficult to understand, one must realize that people often feel threatened by work changes; similarly, they are afraid to voice their opinions on some matters for fear of losing their jobs. In cases like these, safety needs are clearly significant.

Research indicates that some individuals place great emphasis on the safety need—for example those whose parents were heavily security-minded. The parents, often having suffered economic crises, regard themselves as past and potential victims of the environment and pass this strong lack of security on to their children. The offspring, in turn, seek secure, nonthreatening positions in, for example, major corporations or federal bureaucracies, where they can carve out a stable, protected niche for themselves.

Another common source of the security-minded employee is overprotective parents. Continually sheltering their child from disappointment, they paint an unrealistic view of the world. A young person from this kind of family, once out and suffering one of the world's setbacks, is thrown for a loss and is unable to cope with the accompanying frustration, tension, and anxiety. Subconscious security motives developed through interaction with

Are some top managers paid too much money? Many critics of senior management salaries have raised this issue and point to the large salary and bonus packages of top executives. For example, here is a list of the top 20 highest-paid executives, their firms, and the amount each person made in one recent year.

Name	Company	Compensation ($ thousands)		
		1987 Salary and Bonus	Long-term Compensation	Total Pay
Jim Manzi	Lotus	$ 941	$25,356	$26,297
Lee Iacocca	Chrysler	1,740	16,156	17,896
Paul Fireman	Reebok International	15,424	—	15,424
Philip Rooney	Waste Mgt.	950	13,326	14,276
Richard Furlaud	Squibb	1,405	12,480	13,885
Donald Flynn	Waste Mgt.	640	12,577	13,217
John Welch, Jr.	General Electric	2,057	10,574	12,631
Harold Poling	Ford Motor	2,809	7,746	10,555
Jack Clarke	Exxon	787	8,887	9,674
Eugene White	Amdahl	683	8,163	8,846
J. Richard Munro	Time	1,288	6,902	8,190
August Busch III	Anheuser-Busch	1,455	6,525	7,980
Albert Bowers	Syntex	988	6,776	7,764
A. William Reynolds	GenCorp	807	6,890	7,697
David Mitchell	Seagate Tech	1,355	5,800	7,155
Douglas Mahon	Seagate Tech	1,274	5,813	7,087
William Cook	Union Pacific	1,238	5,652	6,890
Michael Eisner	Walt Disney	6,730	—	6,730
Gerald Greenwald	Chrysler	1,316	5,281	6,597
Robert Anderson	Rockwell International	1,460	4,645	6,105

Are these executives worth this much money, or are they overpaid thanks to lucrative salary and bonus plans? While this is a judgment call, one thing is certain: Stockholders are beginning to pay closer attention to executive compensation and to question whether annual million-dollar packages are in the best interests of the firm.

Source: The salary data were reported in "Who Made the Most—And Why," *Business Week,* May 2, 1988, p. 51.

the parents have not prepared the person for this new experience. Safety needs become important to the individual, who is likely to seek a noncompetitive, sheltered environment.

Social Needs

Individuals need to feel needed.

When physiological and safety needs are basically satisfied, *social needs* become important motivators. The individual wants to receive and give acceptance, friendship, and affection. People need to feel needed. Medical research has proved that a child who is not held, cuddled, and stroked can actually die. This is not, of course, a certain event. Many unloved babies survive and grow. But the discovery is important, and it is relevant to the currently popular concept of "stroking." People seek strokes—loving and admiring physical and psychological gestures—from others and, in turn, wish to reciprocate. An example of a psychological stroke is a situation in which George says to his mother, "You look so pretty in that wedding picture," and the mother responds, "George, I've had a miserable day and I haven't even looked at that picture for weeks. You always do know how to make people feel good." The people here give one another a nice little touch, though no physical gestures may have accompanied their statements.

People need this interaction. When it is withdrawn, they suffer. This perhaps accounts for the use by prisons of solitary confinement, which deprives prisoners of the fulfillment of their social needs. The psychological punishment of isolation is perhaps the severest mode of inflicting hurt. The person who is excluded from normal human contact is certainly prevented from either giving or receiving strokes. Some people would say that isolation, even more importantly, is a means of removing people from their own humanness.

The concept of stroking explains why Stanley Schachter has found that people with similar beliefs tend to group together.[8] They share a common bond and can reinforce each other's feelings and convictions through stroking. This is especially true when things are not going well, for misery does love company.

Esteem Needs

Feelings of self-esteem and self-confidence are important.

When physiological, safety, and social needs are essentially satisfied, *esteem needs* become dominant. These needs are twofold: The person must feel important and must also receive recognition from others, as that recognition supports the feelings of personal worth. Recognition is invaluable; without it, many people would conclude that they are greatly overrating themselves. When those around them, however, make it clear that they are indeed important, feelings of self-esteem, self-confidence, prestige, and power are produced. Full satisfaction of these needs, however, must finally rest with the

---

[8]Stanley Schachter, *The Psychology of Affiliation* (Stanford, CA: Stanford University Press, 1959).

individual. For instance, some people believe that they are overrated, that the world would be shocked to learn of their basic inadequacies. No external force can entirely remove that belief. The individual must somehow gain self-confidence in order to value the respect and support of those who offer it.

Research indicates that as the United States moves toward becoming a middle-class society, esteem-related needs such as prestige assume increased importance. People want to keep up with the Joneses and be viewed as important. Vance Packard's sociological book, *The Status Seekers*, portrays this kind of urge.[9] Joining the right country club, obtaining a reputation as a hard worker, and earning advanced degrees are some ways of securing prestige. Some teachers who hold doctoral degrees like to be called "Doctor," feeling that it conveys more of a sense of advancement and importance than "Professor," which is, in fact, the academically superior of the two titles.

Power is another esteem-related need. The power drive begins in early life, when babies realize that their own crying influences their parents' behavior. The famed psychiatrist Alfred Adler contended that this ability to manipulate others is inherently pleasurable to the child.[10] Of course, during the early years, the infant must have this power, being helpless without adults and in need of some method for ensuring their assistance. Later in life, when people can fend for themselves, this physical motive for power changes to one of winning respect and recognition from others. When esteem needs are basically satisfied, self-actualization needs become important.

Self-actualization Need

The realization of one's full potential is also important.

Maslow defined the *self-actualization need* as the "desire to become more and more what one idiosyncratically is, to become everything that one is capable of becoming."[11] At this level of the hierarchy, an individual attempts to realize full personal potential. The person is interested in self-fulfillment, self-development, and creativity in the broadest sense of the word.

Of all five of the needs Maslow identified, the least is known about self-actualization. People satisfy the need in so many different ways that it is difficult to pin down and identify. However, as Paul Hersey and Kenneth H. Blanchard note, competence and achievement are closely related motives, and extensive research has been conducted on them.[12]

Robert W. White has concluded that human beings desire competence because it gives them a form of control over their environment.[13] As they

---

[9]Vance Packard, *The Status Seekers* (New York: David McKay, 1959).

[10]Alfred Adler, *Social Interest* (London: Faber & Faber, 1938).

[11]Maslow, *Motivation and Personality*, p. 46.

[12]Paul Hersey and Kenneth H. Blanchard, *Management of Organizational Behavior: Utilizing Human Resources*, 8th ed. (Englewood Cliffs, NJ: Prentice-Hall, 1988), pp. 43–47.

[13]Robert W. White, "Motivation Reconsidered: The Concept of Competence," *Psychological Review*, September 1959, pp. 297–333.

Competence provides people with a form of control over their environment.

mature, people learn their limitations and capabilities from experience, and they work within these confines. For example, it is rare to find intelligent adults seriously overrating their abilities. They basically know what they can do and will remain within these parameters, choosing an objective that is attainable, such as job mastery. People pit themselves against their work as a goal that is challenging but not beyond attainment. This competence desire is related to the self-actualization need identified by Maslow.

Some individuals have a high need to achieve.

Another such related need is achievement. Some individuals will accomplish more than others because their need to achieve is greater. The noted psychologist, David C. McClelland, and his associates at Harvard have been studying this need for many years.[14] McClelland's highly regarded studies have found that high achievers are neither low nor high risk-takers. Rather, they set moderately difficult but potentially achievable goals for themselves. They like a challenge, but they want some influence over the outcome. They are aggressive realists. In addition, they are motivated more by the accomplishment of a particular objective than by the rewards associated with it. They use money, for example, merely as a means of measuring or assessing progress. High achievers also have a strong desire for feedback on how well they are doing. They want to know the score.

The Individual and the Hierarchy

Hierarchical levels are not clear-cut.

Maslow's theory has general application for the manager, but several points merit specific attention. First, the hierarchy must not be viewed as a rigid structure. Levels are not clear-cut; they tend to overlap. When the intensity of one need is on the decline, the next one may be on the rise, as seen in Figure 13-4. For instance, when the safety need passes the peak of the physiological need, it assumes the dominant role and holds it until the social need rises above it.

Some people may remain at certain levels of the hierarchy.

Second, some individuals remain primarily at the lower levels of the hierarchy, continually concerned with physiological and safety needs. This often occurs among people in underdeveloped areas. Conversely, others may spend a great deal of their time at the upper levels of the hierarchy. If middle-class parents have the best chance of producing high achievers and if the United States is a middle-class society, it follows that Americans probably spend a good deal of their time trying to satisfy social, esteem, and self-actualization needs.

Third, the specific order of needs suggested by Maslow may not apply to everyone; there is certainly no empirical support that it does. For example, for some people esteem needs may be more basic than safety needs.

---

[14]David C. McClelland, J. W. Atkinson, R. A. Cook, and E. L. Lawler, *The Achievement Motive* (New York: Appleton-Century-Crofts, 1953); David C. McClelland, *The Achieving Society* (Princeton, NJ: Van Nostrand, 1961); and David C. McClelland and David H. Burnham, ''Power Is the Great Motivator,'' *Harvard Business Review*, March–April 1976, pp. 100–110.

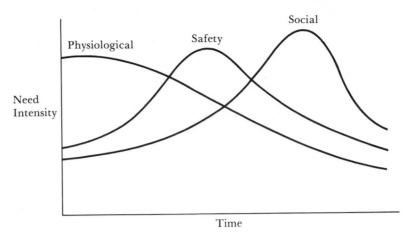

FIGURE 13-4   **Changing Needs**

Maslow's hierarchy lacks empirical evidence.
People respond differently to identical needs.

Fourth, the same type of behavior from two different people does not necessarily represent the same need. One person may speak in a cocky manner because of feeling certain of the subject and more qualified to speak on it than anyone else, while another person may use the exact same approach to hide feelings of insecurity. The former may be fulfilling either esteem or self-actualization needs while the latter is fulfilling the safety need.

Maslow's concept is useful for indicating that individuals have needs. However, in order to motivate workers, the manager must know which needs require satisfaction at which times. Whatever approach the manager takes, it will be based on assumptions about individual workers and their need satisfactions.

McGREGOR'S ASSUMPTIONS

Douglas McGregor provided some important insights into the area of managerial assumptions in his book *The Human Side of Enterprise*.[15] It was McGregor's thesis that "the theoretical assumptions management holds about controlling its human resources determine the whole character of the enterprise. They determine also the quality of its successive generations of management."[16] McGregor's point here was that every management has a philosophy or set of assumptions it uses in handling its workers. In essence, McGregor divided these assumptions into two groups: Theory X assumptions and Theory Y assumptions. Theory X assumptions may be placed on one end of a continuum and Theory Y assumptions on the other.

---

[15]Douglas McGregor, *The Human Side of Enterprise* (New York: McGraw-Hill, 1960).

[16]Ibid., pp. vi–vii.

Theory X

McGregor found Theory X assumptions implicit in much of the literature about organization and in many of the current management practices. The assumptions that underlie *Theory X* are:

1. Management is responsible for organizing the elements of productive enterprise—money, materials, equipment, people—in the interest of economic ends.

2. With respect to people, management is a process of directing their efforts, motivating them, controlling their actions, and modifying their behavior to fit the needs of the organization.

Theory X assumptions.

3. Without this active intervention by management, people would be passive about—or even resistant to—organizational needs. They must, therefore, be persuaded, rewarded, punished, controlled—their activities must be directed. This is management's task—in managing subordinate managers or workers. We often sum it up by saying that management consists of getting things done through other people.

Behind this conventional theory there are several additional beliefs—less explicit, but widespread.

4. The average person is by nature indolent and works as little as possible.

5. The individual lacks ambition, dislikes responsibility, prefers to be led.

6. The average person is inherently self-centered, indifferent to organizational needs.

7. The average person is by nature resistant to change.

8. The average person is gullible, not very bright, the ready dupe of the charlatan and the demagogue.[17]

It might appear at first glance that McGregor was constructing a straw man. But he vehemently disagreed with that notion, observing that Theory X assumptions are actually subscribed to by many managers in United States industry. Furthermore, he noted, "the principles of organization which comprise the bulk of the literature of management *could only have been derived from assumptions such as those of Theory X*. Other beliefs about human nature would have led inevitably to quite different organizational principles."[18]

Prime emphasis is placed on satisfying low-level needs.

The result of Theory X assumptions, according to McGregor, is that many managers give prime consideration to the satisfactions of physiological and safety needs. However, it is quite easy to see that these needs cannot be satisfied while one is on the job. Money, for example, which can purchase food, clothing, and shelter, can only be spent when the worker has left the

---

[17]Adapted from McGregor, pp. 33–34.
[18]Ibid., p. 35.

workplace. Likewise, safety needs, as reflected in fringe benefits such as vacations, profit-sharing plans, and health and medical coverage, yield satisfaction only outside one's place of work. Nevertheless, many managers seem to feel that low-level physiological need satisfaction is of major importance. Why? In the case of money, one answer is found in the simple fact that it is an easy variable to manipulate; managers rely upon it as a motivational tool, giving or withholding financial rewards in an effort to stimulate production. Another reason is the attitude of many managers:

> Most . . . are highly achievement-oriented; in the psychologist's terms, they are "high in *n* Ach." We know that such men attach special significance to money rewards. They are strong believers in steeply increasing financial rewards for greater accomplishment. Because they themselves are particularly interested in some concrete measure that will sensitively reflect how well they have done, it is easy and natural for them to mistake this idea for a related one—namely, that the more money you offer someone the harder he will work.[19]

However, as noted earlier, once the employee's physiological and safety needs are taken care of, attention is focused on higher-level needs, and this is where the problem begins. Management has made no provisions for satisfying these needs, so it offers workers more physiological and safety rewards. If the workers balk at this, management brings out the threat of punishment, which is in accord with the third-listed Theory X tenet. The use of punishment seems to be a logical method of solving the issue; either the workers do the job or management will get tough. However, the problem rests with the fact that management mistakes causes for effects, the result being a self-fulfilling prophecy. Believing punishment is a necessary tool for effective management, the company introduces it the minute the workers start offering resistance, with mental notes: "See, it's just like we said. You have to get tough with these people if you want any performance." Yet it is very often management's fault that the workers are discontent in the first place.

Why do managers have trouble motivating their workers? The answer is that they hold erroneous assumptions about human nature. Management believes it should treat people like children, providing low-level need-satisfaction rewards if work is done well and withholding these benefits if it is done poorly. This carrot-and-stick theory may be useful in getting a donkey to pull a cart, but it seldom works effectively in motivating human beings. A more realistic set of assumptions is contained in Theory Y.

A carrot-and-stick approach is used.

[19]David C. McClelland, "Money as a Motivator: Some Research Insights," in *Organizational Behavior and the Practice of Management*, ed. David R. Hampton, Charles E. Summer, and Ross A. Webber (Glenview, IL: Scott, Foresman, 1973), p. 641.

An Age-old Phenomenon

Before examining Theory Y, however, it should be realized that the basic assumptions of Theory X have existed for years. The philosophy of the early business managers was very similar to that of modern Theory X advocates. Henry P. Knowles and Borje O. Saxburg have identified the assumptions employed by these early managers in this way:

1. The employee is a "constant" in the production equation. The implication here is that man has a fixed nature.

2. The employee is an inert adjunct of the machine, prone to inefficiency and waste unless properly programmed.

3. The employee is by nature lazy; only managers honor the "hard work" creed of the Protestant Ethic.

4. The employee's main concern is self-interest. At work, this is always expressed in economic values.

5. Given appropriate expression, these values will make man fiercely competitive among his peers as an accumulator of financial rewards.

6. Man (at least the working man) must therefore be tightly controlled and externally motivated in order to overcome his natural desire to avoid work unless the material gains available to him are worth his effort.[20]

Theory X, then, is certainly not a new phenomenon; it has been in existence for years. The only notable change is that management has been able to reduce economic hardship and improve working conditions among the employees since the time of Frederick Taylor and his associates. This has all been done, however, without any change in their fundamental theory of management.

Theory Y

Human behavior research has provided the basis for a new theory of management, which McGregor called *Theory Y*. Its assumptions follow:

1. Management is responsible for organizing the elements of productive enterprise—money, materials, equipment, people—in the interest of economic ends.

2. People are not by nature passive or resistant to organizational needs. They have become so as a result of experience in organizations.

3. The motivation, the potential for development, the capacity for assuming responsibility, and the readiness to direct behavior toward organizational goals are all present in people. Management does not put them there.

---

[20]Henry P. Knowles and Borje O. Saxburg, "Human Relations and the Nature of Man," *Harvard Business Review*, March–April 1967, p. 32.

It is a responsibility of management to make it possible for people to recognize and develop these human characteristics for themselves.

4. The essential task of management is to arrange organizational conditions and methods of operation so that people can achieve their own goals best by directing their own efforts toward organizational objectives.[21]

In contrast to Theory X, Theory Y presents a dynamic view of man. The individual is seen as having growth and development capacities, and the problem of motivation is now placed directly in the lap of management. Since the worker has potential, management must decide how to tap it. No longer can management hide behind old Theory X assumptions. Management must re-evaluate its thinking and begin focusing attention on ways of allowing the workers to attain their upper-level needs.

Theory Y Criticism

Theory Y may be overly idealistic.

Many individuals think of Theory X as an outmoded set of ideas, believing Theory Y is a modern, superior view of the worker; but Theory Y also has its critics. Some point out that Theory Y is unreasonably idealistic. Not everyone is self-directed and self-controlled; many workers seem to like security and shun responsibility. As the popular psychoanalyst Erich Fromm has noted, people want freedom, but only within defined limits.[22] George Strauss, the well-known industrial relationist, supports this finding, pointing out that individuals who accept complete freedom in certain areas will demand restrictions in many others.[23] Maslow also echoed the sentiment, stating that gratification of basic needs is important but that it was also the case that unrestricted indulgence could lead to irresponsibility, psychopathology, and inability to bear stress.[24]

Need satisfaction may not occur on the job.

A second criticism of Theory Y is that its advocates tend to believe that the primary place of need satisfaction is on the job. However, many workers satisfy their needs off the job. This is particularly apparent in light of the trend toward a shorter work week; people are seeking satisfaction during their leisure time. Theory Y may thus overemphasize the importance of satisfying higher-level needs in the workplace.

The individual and the organization are not always in conflict.

A third common criticism involves the issue of whether a personality-organization conflict does exist as a characteristic of large-scale mass-production industries. Critics contend that Theory Y assumes that such concepts as work simplification and standardization have reduced job

---

[21]Adapted from McGregor, pp. 47–48.

[22]Erich Fromm, *The Sane Society* (New York: Holt, Rinehart and Winston, 1955), p. 318.

[23]George Strauss, "Some Notes on Power-Equalization," in *The Social Science of Organizations*, ed. Harold J. Leavitt (Englewood Cliffs, NJ: Prentice-Hall, 1963), p. 50.

[24]Abraham H. Maslow, *Toward a Psychology of Being* (Princeton, NJ: Van Nostrand, 1962), pp. 153–54.

satisfaction, though this may be only one cause of organization conflict and may be exaggerated by advocates of Theory Y.

Fourth, many managers can demonstrate good results with a Theory X philosophy. For example, research on management styles among NFL coaches reveals that most of them subscribe to a basic Theory X philosophy as represented by these beliefs:

1. The threat of being cut, benched, or traded will cause a player to perform better.
2. For the most part, players are incapable of motivating themselves.
3. Players should not have much input into the establishment of rules and policies that govern them off the field.[25]

Which of the two theories is correct? The answer depends on the situation and almost always represents some combination of the two. One thing appears certain, however. Most managers tend to underrate the workers, subscribing more heavily to Theory X than to Theory Y. This has been made very clear by Chris Argyris.

ARGYRIS'S IMMATURITY– MATURITY THEORY

Argyris lists seven stages of maturity development.

Chris Argyris, while on the Yale faculty, studied industrial organizations to determine the effect of management practices on individual behavior and personal growth within the organization.[26] According to him, as an individual moves from infancy (immaturity) to adulthood (maturity) seven changes take place. First, the passive state of the infant gives way to the increasingly active state of the child and adult. Second, the maturing child becomes relatively independent. Third, an infant is capable of behaving in only a few ways, whereas an adult has learned to behave in many ways. Fourth, a child tends to have casual, short-term interests; an adult sometimes develops deep, strong interests. Fifth, a child's time perspective is very short. An adult's is longer, encompassing the past, present, and future. Sixth, an infant is subordinate to everyone, whereas an adult is equal or superior to others. Seventh, children lack an awareness of "self," whereas adults are aware of and able to control "self." These seven stages can be viewed as stages in a continuum:

Immaturity ———————————————————————————— Maturity

Argyris contends that most organizations keep their employees in a state of immaturity. Position descriptions, work assignments, and task specialization lead to routine, unchallenging jobs. They also minimize the amount of

---

[25]Kelly Kerin and Charles N. Waldo, "NFL Coaches and Motivation Theory," *MSU Business Topics,* Autumn 1978, pp. 15–18.

[26]Chris Argyris, *Personality and Organization* (New York: Harper & Bros., 1957); *Interpersonal Competence and Organizational Effectiveness* (Homewood, IL: Dorsey Press, 1962); and *Integrating the Individual and the Organization* (New York: Wiley, 1964).

He believes that organizations are structured to keep employees in an immature state.

control workers have over their environment. This, in turn, encourages them to be passive, dependent, and submissive. Argyris would say that keeping people in this state is one of the formal organization's goals. Management likes to control everything and views workers as small cogs in a big machine. This type of thinking is obviously incompatible with the development of a mature personality. The result is incongruity between the mature individual and the formal organization, with its paternalistic interests. Argyris's findings echo McGregor's Theory X assumptions, indicating that management's view of the worker may be the major stumbling block in the motivation process. Unaware of what really motivates nonmanagerial people, management is unable to come up with a viable theory of motivation. One individual who has attempted to shed light on this problem by extending Maslow's hierarchical concept and applying it to the job is Frederick Herzberg.

HERZBERG'S TWO-FACTOR THEORY OF MOTIVATION

In the late 1950s, Frederick Herzberg and his associates at the Psychological Service of Pittsburgh conducted extensive interviews with two hundred engineers and accountants from eleven industries in the Pittsburgh area.[27]

The interview subjects were asked to identify the elements of their job that made them happy or unhappy. Analysis of the findings revealed that when people were dissatisfied, their negative feelings were generally associated with the environment in which they were working. When people felt good about their jobs, they generally associated their feeling with the work itself. Herzberg labeled the factors that prevent dissatisfaction as hygiene factors and those that bring about satisfaction as motivators.

Hygiene Factors

Herzberg called the factors that prevent dissatisfaction *hygiene factors* because their effect on the worker resembles that of physical hygiene on the body. Consider, for example, the case of Art Barney, who slips on an icy path and suffers superficial hand cuts. At home Barney washes his hand and puts iodine on the wound. Two weeks later the hand is back to its normal state. The iodine did not make the hand any better than it was previous to the injury, but it prevented further deterioration, such as gangrene, and helped the hand return to its original state.

This is the function of hygiene. It takes a negative condition (cut hand) and brings it back to its original position (uncut hand). Conversely, if hygienic intervention is withheld, things can go from bad to worse. For example, Nancy Blair, who is in excellent health, will not become any healthier by eating food. But if she does not eat, Blair will eventually become sick and die. Likewise, breathing will not make her any healthier but total inability to breathe will kill her. Hygiene will not improve health beyond one's original

[27]Frederick Herzberg, Bernard Mausner, and Barbara Bloch Snyderman, *The Motivation to Work*, 2nd ed. (New York: Wiley, 1959).

	Hygiene Factors (Environment)	Motivators (Work itself)
TABLE 13-2 **Hygiene and Motivators**	Money Supervision Status Security Working conditions Policies and administration Interpersonal relations	Work itself Recognition Advancement Possibility of growth Responsibility Achievement

state, but it prevents deterioration by returning the person to an original state, which can be called condition zero.

Herzberg found that the workplace contains many hygiene factors. These include money, supervision, status, security, working conditions, policies and administration, and interpersonal relations (see Table 13-2). These factors do not motivate people; they merely prevent dissatisfaction. They produce no growth in worker output, but they prevent loss in performance caused by work restriction. They maintain motivation at zero-level, preventing a negative type of motivation from occurring. This is why they are often referred to as maintenance factors.

Hygiene factors prevent dissatisfaction.

Motivators

Motivators have a positive effect on job satisfaction.

Herzberg found that factors relating to the job itself can have a positive effect on job satisfaction and result in increased output. He called these *motivational factors*, or satisfiers, and identified them as the work itself, recognition, advancement, the possibility of growth, responsibility, and achievement.

Motivation–Hygiene under Attack

Criticism of Herzberg's theory.

Herzberg's two-factor theory presents some interesting ideas, but so do its critics. First, the original population studied consisted only of accountants and engineers. The study is therefore considered unrepresentative of the work force in general. Second, although Herzberg has cited replication of the results of his study among groups such as manufacturing supervisors, hospital maintenance personnel, nurses, military officers, and professional women,[28] other researchers have uncovered different results.[29] In some cases, hygiene or maintenance factors, such as wages or job security, were found to be viewed as motivators among blue-collar workers. In addition, what one

[28]Frederick Herzberg, *Work and the Nature of Man* (Cleveland, OH: World Publishing, 1966); Valerie M. Bockman, "The Herzberg Controversy," *Personnel Psychology,* Summer 1971, pp. 155–89; and Benedict S. Grigaliunas and Frederick Herzberg, "Relevancy in the Test of Motivation-Hygiene Theory," *Journal of Applied Psychology,* February 1971, pp. 73–79.

[29]See Alan C. Filley, Robert J. House, and Steven Kerr, *Managerial Process and Organizational Behavior,* 2nd ed. (Glenview, IL: Scott, Foresman, 1976), pp. 197–200.

person might call a motivator, another person in the same department might term a hygiene factor. In one study conducted among both managerial and professional workers, Donald P. Schwab, H. William DeVitt, and Larry L. Cummings found that Herzberg's hygiene factors were as useful in motivating employees as were his motivators.[30] Third, Victor H. Vroom contends that Herzberg's findings are debatable because his two-factor conclusion was only one of many that could have been drawn from the research.[31] Vroom argues that people are more likely to assign satisfaction to their own achievements and attribute dissatisfaction to company policies. Thus, the Herzberg findings are interpretive at best.

The criticism indicates that the two-factor theory is certainly not universally accepted and that more research is needed before definitive conclusions about it can be drawn. Nevertheless, Herzberg's theory of job satisfaction has helped extend and apply Maslow's need hierarchy to work motivation.

The Need Hierarchy and Motivation–Hygiene

Herzberg's framework is compatible with Maslow's need hierarchy. Maslow's lower-level needs are analogous to Herzberg's hygiene factors, and his upper-level needs correspond to Herzberg's motivators. The comparison between the two is shown in Figure 13-5. As the figure indicates, Herzberg's

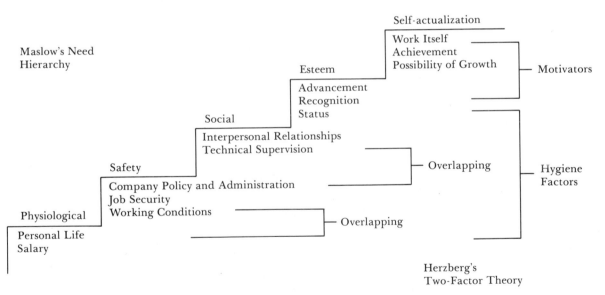

FIGURE 13-5   Comparison of Maslow and Herzberg Models

---

[30]Donald P. Schwab, H. William DeVitt, and Larry L. Cummings, "A Test of the Adequacy of the Two-factor Theory as a Predictor of Self-report Performance Effects," *Personnel Psychology*, Summer 1971, pp. 293–303.

[31]Victor H. Vroom, *Work and Motivation* (New York: Wiley, 1964), pp. 128–29.

REAL-LIFE MANAGERS:

INTERVIEW WITH BILL FIELDS

Bill Fields is the executive vice-president of merchandising and sales for the Wal-Mart Corporation. Wal-Mart has over 1,100 stores nationwide with annual sales of over $21 billion. The firm is the fastest growing major retailer in the country. Bill deals with all of the buying and marketing activities for Wal-Mart and its newly established hypermarts. A veteran of 17 years with the firm, one of his major areas of expertise is an understanding of how to motivate people.

Q.   *What really motivates people?*

A.   That's a broad question because there are so many elements in the process. However, I've found that the most important thing is to get people involved in the decision-making process and give them the opportunity to be creative. People want to use their abilities and talents. If you provide them with the environment to do these things, they'll be motivated. They're also motivated to the extent that they have pride in their jobs and their company and feel that they are part of a winning team.

Q.   *Is money a motivator?*

A.   Oh, sure. However, it's not number one on most people's list. It usually ranks down around third, after the psychological motivators have been addressed.

hygiene factors encompass Maslow's physiological, safety, social, and, to some degree, esteem needs. The reason for placing status in the hygiene category and advancement and recognition in the motivator group is that status is not always a reflection of personal achievement or earned recognition. For example, an individual could achieve status through family ties such as inheritance or marriage. Conversely, advancement and recognition are more often reflections of personal achievement, and thus are more influential as motivators.

However, it must be realized that Maslow and Herzberg both tend to oversimplify the motivational process. Although Herzberg makes an interesting extension of Maslow's theory, neither of their models provides an adequate link between individual need satisfaction and the achievement of organizational objectives. Nor does either of their theories really handle the problem of individual differences in motivation. For this one must turn to process or mechanical theories.

Also keep in mind that I'm generalizing my comments. Everyone has different needs and for some people money is at the top of the list. However, this individual is the exception to the rule.

Q. *In comparison to twenty years ago, it is more difficult to motivate today's young people?*

A. I find that it's actually easier to motivate young people today. I think young people are more interested in the long-run and understand business better than people did twenty years ago. They've grown up in more of a business world than their parents did, so it's easier to communicate with them and get them to see the long-run picture. If you put them into the right environment, you'd be amazed how well today's young people do.

Q. *You mentioned seeing the long-run picture. What do you mean by that?*

A. I mean that there are two ways to try to motivate someone: short-run considerations and long-run considerations. If you're a short-run person, you look at the salary and benefits package that is being offered. If you're a long-run person, you examine the overall environment and opportunities that are being offered by the company and put everything into perspective. A lot of people sacrifice long-run potential for short-run gains. At Wal-Mart we try to develop our people for the long-run. Sure, we offer good salaries and bonus plans but we're also interested in their long-run development, too. We want them to stay with us for their careers. And the best way of accomplishing this goal is to provide them with a motivating environment.

Before doing this, however, two key concepts of modern motivation theory will be examined: expectancy theory and learned behavior.

EXPECTANCY THEORY AND LEARNED BEHAVIOR

Some of the most important modern process theories rely on what is called *expectancy theory*. This concept relates to motivation as follows:

Expectancy theory predicts that an individual will generally be a high performer when he: (1) sees a high probability that his efforts will lead to high performance, (2) sees a high probability that high performance will lead to outcomes, and (3) views these outcomes to be, on balance, positively attractive to himself.[32]

---

[32]L. L. Cummings and Donald P. Schwab, *Performance in Organizations: Determinants and Appraisal* (Glenview, IL: Scott, Foresman, 1973), p. 31.

Need-deprivation and expectancy theory approach are related.

In comparing Maslow's concept of needs with this idea of expectancy, it becomes evident that there are two ways of studying motivational intensity. One can examine need deficiencies, as in Maslow's hierarchy, which promote a particular form of behavior; or one can examine the goals the individual has chosen, in which case motivation is seen as a force pulling the person toward the desired objective. Furthermore, in the case of need deprivation, the emphasis is on internal deficiencies; in the case of expectancy, the focus is on external goals that help alleviate these deficiencies. In essence, although the two ideas are different, they are related. However, motivation researchers today tend to favor the expectancy theory approach. Two of the leading researchers in this field, Lyman Porter and Edward Lawler, cite the following reasons for choosing this approach:

> Basically, the terminology and concepts involved seem to us to be more applicable to consideration of the complexities of human motivation and behavior, and, therefore, more applicable to understanding the attitudes and performance of managers in organizations. The emphasis in expectancy theory on rationality and expectations seems to us to describe best the kinds of conditions that influence managerial performance. . . .
>
> Expectancy theory also greatly facilitates the incorporation of motives like status, achievement, and power into a theory of attitudes and performance. There is a considerable amount of evidence that the central motives for most managers are those for *achievement, self-actualization, power and status, and income and advancement.*[33]

In addition, studies employing expectancy theory have been conducted in both private and public organizations, among employees ranging from production-line operators to managerial personnel. These studies have proved very successful in providing insights into this area of motivation.

If individuals are indeed motivated by expectations, they must have established some relationship between present action and future reward. For example, a person might think, "If I work hard, I will be promoted." This causal relationship is formulated through *learned behavior.* Through either direct or indirect experience, individuals learn to establish cause-effect relationships, which predict how people will respond in a given situation.

Reinforcement is one of the key factors in learned behavior.

One of the key factors in learned behavior is reinforcement. If an individual does something right and the manager wants to reinforce this behavior, the manager must respond in a way which the subordinate finds satisfying—for example, by giving the person a pat on the back or a raise. This response, which is positive reinforcement, will increase the chances that the individual will repeat the behavior in the future. Conversely, if the

---

[33]Lyman W. Porter and Edward E. Lawler III, *Managerial Attitudes and Performance* (Homewood, IL: Dorsey Press, 1968), pp. 12–13.

manager wants to extinguish a given behavior, punishment or negative reinforcement, such as a reprimand or a demotion, will be effective.[34]

When the concept of expectancy theory is combined with that of learned behavior, one has the basis for understanding some of the most important modern motivation theories. One of these is Victor Vroom's expectancy-valence theory.

VROOM'S THEORY

Victor Vroom's motivation theory is complex, but nonetheless it is viewed with great favor. His basic concept can be expressed in the following equation:

$$\text{Motivation} = \Sigma \text{ valence} \times \text{expectancy.}^{35}$$

Motivation is equal to the summation of valence times expectancy. To understand Vroom's theory, three concepts must be grasped: instrumentality, valence, and expectancy.

An individual's motivation is a result of the actual or perceived rewards available upon the accomplishment of some goal. For example, the company wants a man to be productive. But what is in it for him? This will, of course, depend upon the worker's perception of available rewards. Suppose for a moment that the man believes there is a direct correlation between productivity and promotion—that is, that promotion depends on productivity. Then, given this assumption, there are two outcomes to consider. There is the *first-level outcome*, which in this case is productivity, and there is the *second-level outcome*, which, again in this case, is promotion. This introduces the first of Vroom's three concepts, namely, instrumentality. *Instrumentality* is the relationship perceived by an individual between a first-level outcome and a second-level outcome.

Next, one has to consider the man's *valence*, or preference for the first-level outcome (productivity). To make it more meaningful, three variations of productivity will be used: high, average, and low. What is this man's valence for high productivity? This will depend on his desire for promotion. If it is very high, his valence will be positive. If he is indifferent to promotion, it will be zero. If he does not want a promotion, it will be negative. The same logic can be used in determining his valence for average and low productivity. Thus, valence and instrumentality can be brought together in the following way:

Instrumentality is the relationship an individual perceives between a first- and a second-level outcome.

Valence is a person's preference for a particular outcome.

[34]See, for example, Fred Luthans and Robert Kreitner, ''The Role of Punishment in Organizational Behavior Modification (O.B. Mod.),'' *Public Personnel Management*, May–June 1973, pp. 156–61; and Fred Luthans and Robert Kreitner, *Organizational Behavior Modification* (Glenview, IL: Scott, Foresman, 1975).

[35]Vroom, chap. 2.

Valence or preference ——————→ Instrumentality ——————→ Second-level
for first-level   *(Perceived relationships*   outcome
outcome   *between first- and second-*   *(Promotion)*
(Productivity)   *level outcomes)*

In grasping Vroom's theory, one must work backward from instrumentality to valence. An individual's preference for a first-level outcome is dictated
by the extent to which he or she believes this will lead to the attainment of a
second-level outcome.

Vroom's third concept, *expectancy*, is the probability that a specification
will be followed by a particular first-level outcome. For example, what is the
probability that if the man works hard he can attain high productivity? This
objective probability will range from zero (no chance) to one (certainty). If the
worker is convinced that with hard work he can attain high productivity, his
expectancy will be equal to one. These three concepts, instrumentality,
valence, and expectancy, are incorporated in Figure 13-6.

Motivation is thus in Vroom's *expectancy-valence theory* equal to the
algebraic sum of the products of the valences of all first-level outcomes (the
person's preference for each of the first-level outcomes) times the strength of

*Expectancy is the
probability that a
specific action will
yield a particular
first-level outcome.*

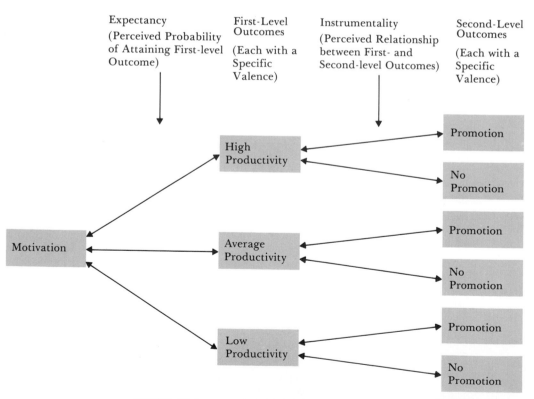

FIGURE 13-6   **An Example of Vroom's Expectancy–Valence Model**

the expectancy that the action will be followed by the attainment of these outcomes (the probability of attaining the respective first-level outcome). This formula helps the manager understand what motivates the individual worker.

It cannot be denied that Vroom's theory is difficult to comprehend. Because of the complexity of his motivation formula, this text does not apply it to a specific situation; an understanding of the basic ideas is sufficient. But it should be kept in mind that current researchers have higher regard for Vroom's theory than for most of the other motivation theories. As J. G. Hunt and J. W. Hill note:

> More work must be done before we can make any statements concerning the overall validity of Vroom's model. But the rigor of his formulation, the relative ease of making the concepts operational, and the model's emphasis on individual differences show considerable promise. We are also encouraged by the results of relatively sophisticated studies testing the theory. We believe it is time for those interested in organizational behavior to take a more thoroughly scientific look at this very complex subject of industrial motivation, and Vroom's model seems a big step in that direction.[36]

At the present time research in this direction is continuing.[37]

PORTER AND LAWLER'S MODEL

Another modern process theory is that proposed by Lyman Porter and Edward Lawler.[38] Porter and Lawler's model, also based on the expectancy theory of motivation, implies that individuals are motivated by future expectations based on previous experiences. In essence, their model contains a number of key variables, including effort, performance, reward, and satisfaction. Figure 13-7 illustrates the relationship among these variables.

It is important to note that Porter and Lawler use a semi-wavy line between performance and intrinsic rewards to indicate that a direct relationship exists if the job has been designed in such a way that a person who has performed well can be rewarded with an internally generated payoff, such as a feeling of accomplishment. The wavy line between performance and extrinsic rewards in the figure shows such rewards are often not directly related to performance—for example, an externally generated payoff such as a pay increase. The arrow between performance and perceived equitable

---

[36]J. G. Hunt and J. W. Hill, "The New Look in Motivation Theory for Organizational Research," *Human Organization*, Summer 1969, p. 108.

[37]Lynn E. Miller and Joseph E. Grush, "Improving Predictions in Expectancy Theory Research: Effects of Personality, Expectancies, and Norms," *Academy of Management Journal*, March 1988, pp. 107–22.

[38]Porter and Lawler.

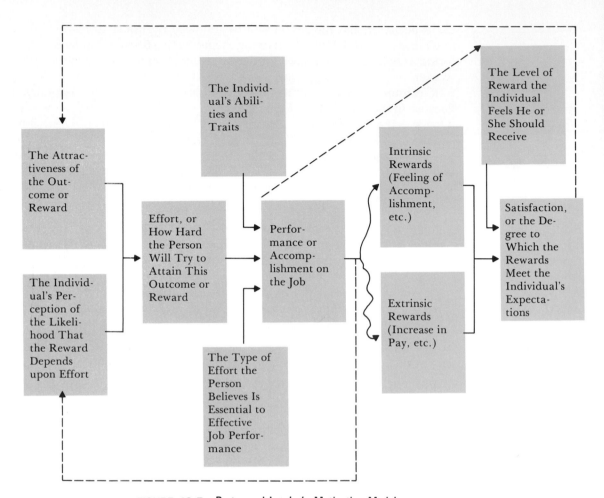

FIGURE 13-7   Porter and Lawler's Motivation Model

Source: Adapted from Lyman W. Porter and Edward E. Lawler III, *Managerial Attitudes and Performance* (Homewood, IL: Richard D. Irwin, 1968), p. 165.

rewards depicts the fact that people's performance influences their perception of what they should receive. To put it experientially, if a woman does not get the level of rewards she believes she should, satisfaction will be negatively affected.

Lawler has made several refinements of his own, presented in the model in Figure 13-7. In particular, he believes that there are two types of expectancies: E→P (effort leads to performance) and P→O (performance leads to a specific outcome).

A person's effort or motivation is influenced by his or her perception of the relationship between effort and performance (if I work hard, will I obtain the desired performance?) and the perception of the relationship between performance and a specific outcome (if I have high performance, will I get a promotion?). Finally, the person's valence for the promotion must be considered. Some people have suggested a simple way of integrating all three ideas into a formula for determining an effort or motivation index, which is stated this way:

$$\frac{E \rightarrow P}{(0 \text{ to } 1.0)} \times \frac{P \rightarrow O}{(0 \text{ to } 1.0)} \times \frac{\text{Valence}}{(-1.0 \text{ to } 1.0)} = \frac{\text{Effort}}{\text{Index}}$$

Employing this formula, consider the case of Steven Acres, who believes that effort is directly related to performance (1.0); that high performance is very likely to bring about the desired outcome of promotion (0.8); and he has a high valence for the promotion (0.9). In this case, Steven's effort or motivation index is: $1.0 \times 0.8 \times 0.9 = 0.72$.

In contrast, consider the case of Ruth Schule, who believes effort is directly related to performance (1.0); but high performance is not likely to bring about a promotion (0.4), although she does have a high valence for the promotion (0.9). In this case Ruth's effort or motivation index is: $1.0 \times 0.4 \times 0.9 = 0.36$. Note that if one of the three factors in the effort index is low, motivation suffers greatly.[39]

Returning to the Vroom model and comparing it with the one in Figure 13-7, it is evident that the latter is more comprehensive. It also proposes the relationship between rewards and performance, concluding that an individual's satisfaction is a function of the rewards received. In turn, these rewards are brought about by performance. Thus:

$$\text{Performance} \xrightarrow[\text{to}]{\text{leads}} \text{Rewards} \xrightarrow[\text{bring about}]{\text{which}} \text{Satisfaction}$$

This is a rather interesting finding since many managers feel that a happy worker is a productive worker—in other words, that satisfaction leads to performance. However, Porter and Lawler report just the opposite; performance causes satisfaction.

The performance-satisfaction controversy still rages.

Today the performance-satisfaction controversy continues. Which is the cause? Which is the effect? To further confuse the issue, it should be noted that there are some individuals who contend that both performance and satisfaction are caused by the reward system.[40]

---

[39]For more on this subject see Richard M. Steers and Lyman W. Porter, *Motivation and Work Behavior* (New York: McGraw-Hill, 1975), chap. 6.

[40]Charles N. Greene, "The Satisfaction-Performance Controversy," *Business Horizons*, October 1972, pp. 31–41; John M. Ivancevich, "The Performance to Satisfaction Relationship: A Causal Analysis of Stimulating and Nonstimulating Jobs," *Organizational Behavior and Human Performance*, December 1979, pp. 350–65; Robert H. Garin and John F. Cooper, "The Morale–Productivity Relationship: How Close?" *Personnel*, January–February 1982, pp. 57–62; Rabi S. Bhagat, "Conditions under Which Stronger Job Performance–Job Satisfaction Relationships May Be Observed: A Closer Look at Two Situational Contingencies," *Academy of Management Journal*, December 1982, pp. 772–89.

SOCIAL

RESPONSIBILITY

IN

ACTION:

Focusing

on

the

Workers

What can management do to meet its social responsibility obligation of making the work as meaningful and enjoyable as possible? What can it do to provide personnel with an environment that is motivational? Six of the most useful steps are the following:

1. **Match the people and the work.** Everyone has certain strengths. Some people are good at detail work; others do a better job if they work at more broadly based tasks. Some perform best when left alone; others like a great deal of guidance. To the extent that the manager can match the personalities of the workers with the demands of the task, the people will be motivated to do a good job.

2. **Make the task clear.** Surprising as it is to the average manager, there are many personnel who do not fully understand what they are supposed to be doing or how to actually get the job done. The workers give it their best effort, but they are unsure of whether their work is being properly directed.

3. **Give positive feedback.** Let people know when they have done a good job. Don't keep it a secret; share it. Spoken acknowledgments usually take only a few minutes and if the person did good work, a memorandum for the individual's personnel file is not out of order.

4. **Let people know the rewards.** Most subordinates try to do a good job, but they would work even harder if they were sure of the rewards they could attain. By making clear the relationship between performance and different types of rewards, the manager can "hook" the subordinate on doing a good job.

5. **Personalize the nonmonetary reward system.** Not everyone is motivated by the same thing. By individualizing the rewards so that people are better able to achieve the things they want, the manager ensures a higher motivated work force. This point is particularly valid in the case of nonmonetary rewards. For example, some people work better if they are given praise; others prefer to be left alone; still others like the manager to drop by and talk with them on occasion. Managers should strive to accommodate the subordinates.

6. **Remove the roadblocks.** Effective managers understand that their personnel will occasionally have trouble getting things done because of supervisory or organizational roadblocks. Sometimes the manager, personally, will make a mistake, such as criticizing a subordinate for something that was not the individual's fault. At other times the manager will find that there are not sufficient resources to get a particular job done and will find it necessary to fight for more funds. These efforts result in a removal of roadblocks, leading both to higher work output and to employee motivation.

Although research is still being conducted in an attempt to resolve the issue, one fact is indisputable. Rewards are important in the motivation process and the level of these rewards must be commensurate with what the individual believes they should be. This concept is known as equity theory, and although it was treated in Porter and Lawler's model, it will be considered separately now (see Social Responsibility in Action: Focusing on the Workers).

EQUITY OR SOCIAL COMPARISON THEORY

People compare their rewards with those received by others.

Equity theory, also called *social comparison theory,* is an extension of Chester Barnard's concept about the worker's weighing what he or she is getting from the company against what he or she is giving to the company. However, equity theory goes further, contending that the individual evaluates not only his or her personal position, but that of others as well. People are motivated not only by what they get but also by what they see, or believe, others are getting. They make a social comparison of inputs (education, effort, time spent on the job) and rewards (money, working conditions, recognition) for themselves and others in the organization. For example, Rogers feels that he is entitled to a raise of $1,000 for the upcoming year. His superior calls him and tells him he is going to get $1,750. Rogers is elated. However, later in the day he discovers that Linz, his archrival, has received $2,300. Now Rogers is angry because he feels he is giving as much to the company as Linz, but he is receiving less. Initially, he was happy with the "extra" $750 but now he is not, because social comparison has shown that Linz is getting a bigger reward than he. Figure 13-8 shows how this social comparison works.

When people feel they are not being properly treated, tension results. This tension can bring about absenteeism and turnover. In fact, some research studies have found that an employee's perception of equitable treatment is a stronger prediction of absence and turnover than are variables related to job satisfaction.[41]

A number of alternatives are available to relieve this tension. For example, Rogers may quit his job. Or he may go to his boss and demand more money, thereby establishing equality with Linz. Or he may stop comparing himself with his rival because he cannot hope to keep up. If he feels the need, he can find a different rival. Or he can do less work. However, the most likely

---

[41]John E. Dittrich and Michael R. Carrell, "Organizational Equity Perceptions, Employee Job Satisfaction, and Departmental Absence and Turnover Rates," *Organizational Behavior and Human Performance,* August 1979, pp. 29–40.

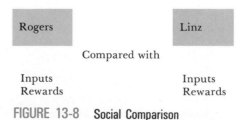

FIGURE 13-8   Social Comparison

alternative is that he will change his perception of Linz's input-reward ratio. For example, "Linz has three kids and I only have one, so my $1,750 will go a lot further than his $2,300."

It is also interesting to note that some research shows that people who feel overpaid, at least initially, tend to do more work. In this way the individuals justify the higher salaries. However, in time people usually reevaluate their skills and position and conclude that they are indeed worth their pay. At this time, their output drops back to its former level. This accounts for the belief of some researchers that money is a short-run motivator at best, and only one tool among many that the manager can use in the motivation process. As McClelland has pointed out:

> [Money] is a treacherous tool because it is deceptively concrete, tempting many managers to neglect variables in the work situation and climate that really affect productivity. In the near future, there will be less and less excuse for neglecting these variables, as the behavioral sciences begin to define them and explain to management how they can be manipulated just as one might change a financial compensation plan.[42]

Perhaps the greatest shortcoming of equity theory is that not enough empirical research has yet been conducted. The theory is intuitively appealing and it can certainly be tied in to the Porter-Lawler model. However, too much of the research to date has been conducted in laboratory rather than real-world settings. The researchers must go out into the world of work. Summing up their review of the literature in this area, Michael R. Carrell and John E. Dittrich come to this conclusion:

> Equity field research can be directed at the expectancy–performance or reward–satisfaction–valence linkages in the Porter-Lawler expectancy motivation model. This model and the general proposition derived from it offer several potential areas of field research. But there is a primary need for further development, measurement, and testing of employees' internal dimensions of perceived equity. The relationship of perceived equity to other criterion variables such as grievance rates, absence, turnover and safety performance also should be examined in the field.
>
> Finally, further field research is needed to determine if the laboratory based relationships between equity perceptions and demographic characteristics, reward allocation, and quality of performance also exist in actual organizations.[43]

---

[42]McClelland, "Money as a Motivator," p. 649.

[43]Michael R. Carrell and John E. Dittrich, "Equity Theory: The Recent Literature, Methodological Considerations, and New Directions," *Academy of Management Review*, April 1978, p. 208. For more on this theory see: Richard A. Cosier and Dan R. Dalton, "Equity Theory and Time: A Reformulation," *Academy of Management Review*, April 1983, pp. 311–19.

NEW DIRECTIONS: THEORY, RESEARCH, AND PRACTICE

Over the last decade, the theory and research of motivation has switched from consideration of needs-based approaches to expectancy theory and equity theory. This is not to say that need-based theories have not provided important insights regarding motivation; however, there are some problems with implementing them. One is that there is a whole set of organizational factors that make it difficult to individualize the rewards and emphasize upper-level intrinsic needs. The more heterogeneous and larger the particular work force, the more difficult it becomes to do so. Additionally, the influence of social norms and expectations on individual behavior still requires additional work by content theorists.[44] Expectancy theories, equity theory, and operant conditioning address some important aspects of motivation not considered by content theory, including the assumptions that:

1. Rewards should be closely tied to behavior.
2. Rewards should be frequent and consistent.
3. People are motivated by expected outcomes.
4. Employees are motivated by a desire for fairness.

A contingency theory is needed.

Pulling these ideas together, it becomes obvious that motivation theory is a combination of content and process approaches. What is needed is the development of a contingency theory of motivation. The question is not whether expectancy theory ideas or equity theory concepts offer a better theory of motivation, but rather under what conditions or circumstances each works best. Additionally, as Mitchell points out, there is a third issue which complements the other two.

Because many jobs are, in fact, interdependent, social, and subject to change, more theory and research needs to be generated on how group processes affect motivation. Strategies, such as team building or other interventions designed to increase commitment and motivation need to be studied as motivational models. An understanding is needed of the effects of such interventions on motivated behaviors and how these behaviors contribute to performance. It is hoped that more attention to the above issues will result in a more comprehensive understanding of not only the causes of motivation, but how and when and where different strategies should be used.[45]

Mitchell recommends that questions such as those presented in Table 13-3 be used when examining the motivation process. These queries are designed to

---

[44]Terence R. Mitchell, "Motivation: New Directions for Theory, Research and Practice," *Academy of Management Review*, January 1982, pp. 84–85.

[45]Ibid., p. 86.

TABLE 13-3
A Flow Diagram of Questions about Motivation

1. Can performance be defined in individual, behavioral terms? If not, develop a separate measure of motivation.

2. Is motivation important for performance, or are abilities and situational factors more important? If motivation is important, but not the same as performance, develop a separate measure of motivation.

If one cannot meet the requirements of questions 1 and 2, it may not be worth it to proceed further. If, however, motivation is important for performance and performance is a good reflection of motivation or a good measure that motivation exists, then proceed with the analysis.

3. Is the reward system rigid and inflexible? In other words, are people and tasks grouped into large categories for reward purposes?

4. Is it difficult to observe what people are actually doing on the job?

5. Is an individual's behavior dependent heavily on the actions of others?

6. Are there lots of changes in people, jobs, or expected behavior?

7. Are social pressures the major determinants of what people are doing on the job?

If questions 3 through 7 are answered with a no, then some system combining a needs analysis with goal setting, expectancy, and equity ideas should be effective.

Source: Tence R. Mitchell, "Motivation: New Directions for Theory, Research and Practice," *Academy of Management Review*, January 1982, pp. 84–85. Reprinted with permission.

help the manager consider both content and process theory questions. Yet even if this goal is accomplished, there is a great deal more that needs to be done. Mitchell explains it this way:

> The obvious implication for the practitioner is that the cost of implementing one of the more traditional motivation systems (MBO, behavior modification) might outweigh the benefit under these latter conditions. Until there are better answers to the question of how to influence motivation when these conditions exist, it will be difficult to develop any sort of comprehensive strategy for enhancing motivation. Thus, although the focus of current research is coming to recognize the importance of social processes, changes in jobs or people . . . and problems in flexibility and ability to give feedback . . . few remedies for these problems have been developed. Until this is done, a substantial inadequacy will remain in the ability to understand and influence motivation on the job.[46]

The quest continues.   For all intents and purposes, motivation is a subject of great interest to theorists and practitioners alike; however, it is still proving to be an elusive quarry. There are so many interdependent elements, that to date no significant contingency theory of motivation has been forthcoming. For the present, the subject remains one that is both critical and elusive. Nevertheless, the quest goes on.

[46]Ibid., p. 87.

■ SUMMARY

This chapter has examined modern motivation theory. The first part of the chapter reviewed some of the reasons for declining worker motivation in America. Then the relationship between needs and behavior was shown through the use of Maslow's hierarchy. These ideas were then refined and applied to the workplace through Herzberg's model. Both theories provide important general insights into workers' behavior, because they stress the importance of examining the causes of human activity and partly answer the question of what specific things motivate people.

Managers must also be concerned with explaining how behavior is initiated, directed, sustained, or halted. To do this they must understand process theories. This chapter examined three of these theories: Vroom's expectancy-valence theory, Porter and Lawler's motivation model, and equity or social comparison theory. All three place great emphasis on individual motivation.

In the past few years, increased attention has been given to these process theories because of their value in applying general motivation theory to specific situations. Currently there is interest in the formulation of a contingency theory of motivation that would integrate content and process ideas. Yet whatever approach managers use, one question must remain foremost—what will motivate the workers to attain organizational objectives? When this question is answered, managers are enabled to examine the area of leadership. When people who manage know what will motivate the people they manage, they can focus attention on leading them. This subject is the topic of the next chapter.

■ REVIEW AND STUDY QUESTIONS

1. What are some reasons for declining worker motivation in America? Identify and describe five.
2. How do contemporary employee values differ from traditional values? Compare and contrast the two.
3. Is there any relationship between needs and behavior? Explain.
4. What are the five needs in Maslow's hierarchy? What relevance do they have to the study of motivation?
5. How do the assumptions of Theory X differ from those of Theory Y?
6. What is Argyris's immaturity–maturity theory? Do you agree or disagree with his findings?
7. What does Herzberg mean by hygiene factors? Identify some of them.
8. What does Herzberg mean by motivators? Identify some of them.
9. What relationship do Herzberg's and Maslow's theories bear to one another in general and specifically to motivation? Explain.

10. In your own words, explain what Vroom means by instrumentality? Valence? Expectancy? Explain each.

11. Of what value is Vroom's theory to the practicing manager?

12. How does Porter and Lawler's model expand the ideas presented by Vroom?

13. Of what value is the Porter–Lawler model to the practicing manager?

14. What is meant by equity or social comparison theory? Give an illustration. What is its relevance to motivation theory?

15. Of what value would a contingency theory of motivation be? Explain.

■ **SELECTED REFERENCES**

Baird, Lloyd. "Managing Dissatisfaction." *Personnel*, May–June 1981, pp. 12–21.

Bhagat, Rabi S. "Conditions under Which Stronger Job Performance–Job Satisfaction Relationships May Be Observed: A Closer Look at Two Situational Contingencies." *Academy of Management Journal*, December 1982, pp. 772–89.

Bronstein, Richard J. "The Equity Component of the Executive Compensation Package." *California Management Review*, Fall 1980, pp. 64–70.

Brown, Martha A. "The Relationship of Values and Job Satisfaction: Do Birds of a Feather Work Well Together?" *Personnel*, November–December 1980, pp. 66–73.

Carrell, Michael R., and John E. Dittrich. "Equity Theory: The Recent Literature, Methodological Considerations, and New Directions." *Academy of Management Review*, April 1978, pp. 202–10.

Cook, C. W. "Guidelines for Managing Motivation." *Business Horizons*, April 1980, pp. 61–69.

Cosier, Richard A., and Dan R. Dalton. "Equity Theory and Time: Reformulation." *Academy of Management Review*, April 1983, pp. 311–19.

Dittrich, John E., and Michael R. Carrell. "Organizational Equity Perceptions, Employee Job Satisfaction, and Departmental Absence and Turnover Rates." *Organizational Behavior and Human Performance*, August 1979, pp. 29–40.

Garin, Robert H., and John F. Cooper. "The Morale–Productivity Relationship: How Close?" *Personnel*, January–February 1981, pp. 57–62.

Grant, Philip C. "Why Employee Motivation Has Declined in America." *Personnel Journal*, December 1982, pp. 905–909.

Greene, Charles N. "The Satisfaction–Performance Controversy." *Business Horizons*, October 1972, pp. 31–41.

Herzberg, Frederick, Bernard Mausner, and Barbara Bloch Snyderman. *The Motivation to Work*. New York: Wiley, 1959.

Inbar, Dan, and Mike M. Milstein. "The ABCs of Organizational Behavior." *Personnel*, June 1987, pp. 51–56.

Ivancevich, John M. "The Performance to Satisfaction Relationship: A Causal Analysis of Stimulating and Nonstimulating Jobs." *Organizational Behavior and Human Performance*, December 1978, pp. 350–65.

Jackson, Lauren Hite, and Mark G. Mindell. "Motivating the New Breed." *Personnel*, March–April 1980, pp. 53–61.

Lindsay, C. A., E. Marks, and L. Gorlow. "The Herzberg Theory: A Critique and Reformulation." *Journal of Applied Psychology*, August 1967, pp. 330–39.

Locke, Edwin A., Gary P. Latham, and Miriam Erez. "The Determinants of Goal Commitment." *Academy of Management Review*, January 1988, pp. 23–39.

McClelland, David, J. W. Atkinson, R. A. Cook, and E. L. Lawler. *The Achievement Motive*. New York: Appleton-Century-Crofts, 1953.

McGregor, Douglas. *The Human Side of Enterprise*. New York: McGraw-Hill, 1960.

Maslow, Abraham H. *Motivation and Personality*. New York: Harper & Bros., 1954.

Meyers, Kenneth A. "Why Companies Lose Their Best People—And What to Do about It." *Business Horizons*, March–April 1981, pp. 42–45.

Miller, Lynn E., and Joseph E. Grush. "Improving Predictions in Expectancy Theory Research: Effects of Personality, Expectancies, and Norms." *Academy of Management Journal*, March 1988, pp. 107–22.

Miller, William. "Motivation Techniques: Does One Work Best?" *Management Review*, February 1981, pp. 47–52.

Mitchell, Terence R. "Motivation: New Directions for Theory, Research, and Practice." *Academy of Management Review*, January 1983, pp. 80–88.

Perry, James L., and Lyman W. Porter. "Factors Affecting the Context for Motivation in Public Organizations." *Academy of Management Review*, January 1982, pp. 89–98.

Piamonte, John S. "An Employee Motivational System That Leads to Excellent Performance." *Personnel*, September–October 1980, pp. 55–66.

Porter, Lyman W., and Edward E. Lawler III. *Managerial Attitudes and Performance*. Homewood, IL: Richard D. Irwin, 1968.

Rappaport, Alfred. "How to Design Value-Contributing Executive Incentives." *Journal of Business Strategy*, Fall 1983, pp. 49–59.

Scanlan, Burt K. "Creating a Climate for Achievement." *Business Horizons*, March–April 1981, pp. 5–9.

Schwarzkopf, Ed A., and Edwin L. Miller. "Exploring the Male Mobility Myth." *Business Horizons*, June 1980, pp. 38–44.

Sullivan, Jeremiah J. "The Three Roles of Language in Motivation Theory." *Academy of Management Review*, January 1988, pp. 104–15.

Vroom, Victor H. *Work and Motivation*, New York: Wiley, 1964.

Walker, Lawrence R., and Kenneth W. Thomas. "Beyond Expectancy Theory:

An Integrative Motivational Model from Health Care." *Academy of Management Review*, April 1982, pp. 187–94.

Zemke, Ron. "So Long Skinner . . . Hello, Cog Sci?" *Training*, July 1988, pp. 63–67.

■ CASE: **Money and Motivation**

Is money a motivator? Some people say it always is; others believe that it depends on the situation. For example, someone earning $10,000 a year will probably be more motivated by a raise of $1,000 than someone earning $100,000 a year. Still other people believe that every raise must be separated into two parts: that which is given for cost of living (no motivation potential) and that which is given for merit (high motivation potential). Certainly that is the feeling of the union at the Waderford Corporation.

Last month the union went on strike after being unable to obtain a "cost of living plus 3 percent" contract from the management. The latter was willing to give cost of living but no more. The union refused. "Why," asked the president of the union, "should we settle for a mere cost of living? This leaves us no better off than we were last year. We want to start getting ahead of inflation. The management staff certainly does not settle for just the cost of living. Why should we?"

An arbitrator has been called in to help resolve the dispute. However, it appears as if the strike will be a long one. The union has built up a rather large strike fund and seems unwilling to settle for anything less than an "above cost of living" contract. Management, for its part, has expressed its refusal to go any higher than the cost of living. As one of the managers put it, "Now we both know the other guy's position, so it will now boil down to who's going to give in first."

Questions

1. How important is money as a motivator? Explain your answer.

2. In addition to money, what else motivates people to work hard? Cite some illustrations.

3. When is money likely to be one of the most important motivators (if not *the* most important), and when is it likely to finish way down the list? Based on your answer, what conclusions can be drawn regarding the use of money as a motivator?

■ CASE: **Keeping Them Motivated**

Many of the employees at Steelcase, Inc., the office-furniture company in Grand Rapids Michigan, earn 35 to 50 percent more than their base rate thanks to a piecework incentive program. This system is so motivational that employees have been known to skip coffee breaks and to keep lunch hours short, so that they can devote more time to assembling furniture. In addition, the firm has a profit-sharing plan. This plan has served to bolster average salaries by as much as 70 percent.

Yet these are not the only reasons why the company's turnover is so low and morale is so high. The firm also offers its personnel a system of "flextime" so that those individuals with children or other outside responsibilities can vary their work hours to meet their other demands.

For example, Denise Francis, a payroll administrator on flextime, works a 9 A.M. to 3 P.M. shift. She is allowed to take time out if she needs it and is otherwise free to set her own schedule, so long as she puts in 40 hours a week. "It makes my life easier," says Francis, who is divorced and cares for two daughters, 11 and 14 years old. "If one of my kids is sick and the doctor says, 'Bring her in,' I can just go."

Another motivational feature is a "cafeteria style" benefit plan that allows the workers to choose from a wide selection of options. For example, there are eight medical plans, three dental plans, and a variety of disability and insurance offerings. Each employee can tailor a health plan to meet his or her specific needs. Additionally, if an individual does not use all of the money available for these benefit programs, the remaining funds can be put into a retirement program or taken in the form of cash.

How successful has the company's pay and benefit package been in motivating the employees? Turnover is a mere 3 percent, profits are extremely high, and the work force remains nonunionized. Some industry experts predict that many other firms are likely to follow Steelcase's lead.

Questions

1. Does money motivate the Steelcase employee? Explain.

2. What types of psychological rewards motivate these employees? Give an example.

3. What conclusions about motivation can you draw as a result of the data in this case? Cite two.

Source: Bob Cohn, "A Glimpse of the 'Flex' Future," *Newsweek*, August 1, 1988, pp. 38–39.

■ CASE: A New Philosophy

When Andrew Anderson was laid off from his production job at a textile mill, he immediately found work at another firm in a nearby town. This new job pays $100 less a week. Yet, when he was recalled to the mill last month, Anderson chose to stay at this new job. Why? Because he finds that the new firm is much less regimented than the old one.

In particular, what Anderson likes is his new company's philosophy of labor-management relations. Blue-collar workers are treated basically the same as white-collar employees. They get weekly salaries instead of hourly wages, participate in the company pension program, and get paid for absences caused by illness. In addition, the supervisors use loose, as opposed to close, control. The result, Anderson feels, is a more meaningful work environment.

In fact, one of the things that Anderson noticed as soon as he took his new job was that the supervisor did not recite a long list of disciplinary rules. Instead, the manager simply said that the company relied on the workers to do things properly. There was no formal system of rules and penalties that would be applied when a mistake was made. Anderson liked this and felt it motivated him to do a better job.

Apparently he is not alone. Company officials reported last week that this approach to motivating employees is working extremely well. Product output in the plant is 35 percent higher than that of other plants in the industry. Also, absenteeism is running at a 3 percent level, as compared to 6 percent for the competition, and turnover as a result of voluntary resignations is only 4 percent. This compares to an average of 16 percent in the industry.

Questions

1. What particular needs in Maslow's hierarchy does this new philosophy help Anderson satisfy?

2. Are these new conditions an illustration of hygiene factors or motivators?

3. Using Porter and Lawler's model of motivation, how can you explain the increases in output in this plant, where this philosophy has been adopted, as compared to plants of the competitors?

■ CASE: Looking for Practical Value

Sally Brendshaw is a new department manager in a bank. She is also pursuing a master's degree in business. Last Tuesday, in her organizational behavior class, she learned about expectancy theory. She finds the theory interesting, although she wonders how it can be of practical value to her.

At her bank everyone has a semiannual review, at which time raises are given out. Typically, an individual can expect to receive 3 to 5 percent each time. In rare cases a manager will recommend more than 5 percent, but Brendshaw knows of no instance where a person received less than 3 percent. This review schedule, in her opinion, is a good one because just as the motivational effect of the first semiannual raise is wearing off, the person is given a second one. However, she does realize that the difference between average performers (6 percent annually) and high achievers (10 percent annually) is only 4 percent and feels that this does not greatly motivate the latter.

The other motivational tool is promotion. Brendshaw has averaged a promotion every two years during her six-year tenure with the bank. However, she is painfully aware that this pace cannot last. Most managers are getting promotions once every five years, and some of those above her in the hierarchy have not been promoted since Brendshaw has worked at the bank. Therefore, it is clear to her that promotions from within are not very motivational because they come too infrequently. To really move up, one has to jump to another bank.

In addition to money and recommendations for promotion, Brendshaw feels she can motivate her people by praising them and keeping them informed about what is going on. However, all of this is really part of content theory, while expectancy theory is part of process theory. It seems to Brendshaw that she really knows all she has to know about motivation; she also cannot believe that expectancy theory is of any practical value to her.

Questions

1. What is the difference between content theory and process theory? Compare and contrast the two.

2. Could expectancy theory have any practical use for Brendshaw? Explain how she could use it.

3. In addition to the above answer, what other recommendations would you make to help Brendshaw motivate her subordinates? Be specific.

■ SELF-FEEDBACK EXERCISE: What Motivates You?

Read each of the following 20 potential motivators and place a "20" after the one that would most motivate you. Continue this process on down to the one which you would find least motivational and give it a ranking of "1." Then transfer your responses to the answer sheet and read the interpretation.

_____	a.	Increased salary
_____	b.	Opportunity to head a new product development group
_____	c.	Low-cost company loan
_____	d.	Promotion (even though no raise is given)
_____	e.	Increased authority
_____	f.	Larger office
_____	g.	Improved working conditions
_____	h.	Chance to implement your own ideas
_____	i.	Better retirement package
_____	j.	Autonomy in carrying out your job
_____	k.	Larger desk.
_____	l.	Opportunity to learn new skills
_____	m.	Recognition for a job well done
_____	n.	Bigger expense account
_____	o.	Opportunity to use your personal initiative

———— p.   Increased fringe benefits
———— q.   Private company office
———— r.   Chance to use your creative skills
———— s.   Office with a window
———— t.   Challenging work

Answer sheet

Enter below the number you gave to each of the motivators and then total the two columns.

	Column I		Column II
————	a.	————	b.
————	c.	————	d.
————	e.	————	f.
————	g.	————	h.
————	i.	————	j.
————	k.	————	l.
————	m.	————	n.
————	o.	————	p.
————	q.	————	r.
————	s.	————	t.
Total ======		======	

Interpretation

Your responses in Column I indicate the motivational value of physical rewards. Your responses in Column II indicate the motivational value of psychological rewards. If your totals are within 10 points of each other, you are equally motivated by physical and psychological rewards.

CHAPTER 14

Leadership
Effectiveness

GOALS OF THE CHAPTER

What makes the effective leader different from the ineffective leader? Perhaps the answer rests in the very definition of management, namely, getting things done through people. In any event, there are some managers who are successful at their jobs and others who are not. The goals of this chapter are to investigate the nature of leadership and to examine some of the current theories of leadership. The central theme will be leadership *effectiveness*.

When you have finished this chapter, you should be able to:

1. Define the term *leadership*.
2. Discuss the relevance of trait theory to the study of leadership.
3. Explain what is meant by situational theory and why it is so highly regarded today.
4. Relate the value of continuum models to the understanding of leadership.
5. Describe the importance of two-dimensional models in the study of leadership.
6. Relate the value of contingency leadership theory to the modern manager, with particular attention to Fred Fiedler's contingency model and Robert House's path–goal theory.
7. Discuss new dimensions of leadership inquiry, including corporate culture.

THE NATURE OF LEADERSHIP

Management theorists have defined *leadership* in many different ways. For example, Martin Gannon says it is ''the directing of the activities of

501

immediate subordinates."[1] Richard Daft calls it "the ability to influence other people toward the attainment of goals."[2] David Van Fleet defines it as, "an influence process directed at shaping the behavior of others."[3] Arthur Bedeian sees it as "the process of influencing individual or group activities toward achievement of enterprise objectives."[4] Synthesizing current views, one can accurately say that most writers in the field of management feel leadership is a process of influencing people to direct their efforts toward the achievement of some particular goal or goals. As such, leadership is a part of management. Of course, managers must do more than merely lead, but if they fail to influence people to accomplish assigned goals, they fail as managers.

Every organization needs leaders, but what is it that distinguishes these individuals from others? For years, many people have sought to answer this question; in the course of the study, people have tried many methods, some sheer quackery. The analysis of handwriting (graphology), the study of skull shapes (phrenology), and the investigation of the position of the stars and other celestial elements upon human affairs (astrology) have all been employed. The two most scientific approaches that have been used are trait theory and situational theory.

Trait Theory

Clear-cut findings have not been obtained.

Trait theory examines successful leadership from the standpoint of the individual's personal characteristics; that is, what is it about this particular person that indicates a good leader? In 1940, Charles Byrd examined twenty lists of traits that were attributed to leaders in various surveys but discovered that not even one item appeared on all lists.[5] Later in the decade, William O. Jenkins, after reviewing a wide spectrum of studies encompassing such diverse groups as children, and business, professional, and military personnel, categorically stated that, "No single trait or group of characteristics has been isolated which sets off the leader from the members of his group."[6] This undoubtedly accounts for the decline in the importance of trait theory. Clear-cut results have just not been forthcoming, the reason being that the method fails to consider the entire leadership environment. Traits are important, but they are only one part of the leadership picture. The members of the work group and the situation itself (task, technology, goals, structure)

---

[1]Martin J. Gannon, *Management* (Boston: Allyn and Bacon, 1988), p. 272.

[2]Richard L. Daft, *Management* (Hinsdale, IL: Dryden Press, 1988), p. 368.

[3]David Van Fleet, *Contemporary Management* (Boston: Houghton Mifflin, 1988), p. 352.

[4]Arthur G. Bedeian, *Management*, 2nd ed. (Hinsdale, IL: Dryden Press, 1988), p. 424.

[5]Charles Byrd, *Social Psychology* (New York: Appleton-Century-Crofts, 1940), p. 378.

[6]William O. Jenkins, "A Review of Leadership Studies with Particular Reference to Military Problems," *Psychological Bulletin*, January 1947, pp. 74–75.

are also major variables, for leadership is a function of the leader, the follower, and the situation; that is, $L = F(l, f, s)$.

Yet, despite its failures, one must not discard trait theory too hastily, for it has made some contributions toward clarifying the nature of leadership. For example, some of the commonly listed traits of effective leaders include intelligence, understanding, perception, high motivation, and a possession of human relations attitudes.[7] On the other hand, trait theory tends to be more descriptive than analytical; therefore its value in predicting success has been, at best, limited. As a result, trait theory has been replaced to a large degree by situational theory.

Some commonly listed leader traits.

Situational Theory

Situational theory, which has been more empirical and exhaustive in defining leadership characteristics, is now more commonly accepted than trait theory. According to this theory, a finite number of situational factors or dimensions that vary according to the leader's personality, the requirements of the task, the expectations, needs, and attitudes of the followers, and the environment in which all are operating have to do with the definition of the leader. For example, management researchers Alan C. Filley, Robert J. House, and Steven Kerr, after conducting a review of the literature, found that the following factors tend to have an impact on leadership effectiveness:

These factors influence leadership effectiveness.

1. History of the organization.
2. Age of the previous incumbent in the leader's position.
3. Age of the leader and his or her previous experience.
4. Community in which the organization operates.
5. Particular work requirements of the group.
6. Psychological climate of the group being led.
7. Kind of job the leader holds.
8. Size of the group led.
9. Degree to which group-member cooperation is required.
10. Cultural expectations of subordinates.
11. Group-member personalities.
12. Time required and allowed for decision making.[8]

---

[7]For more on trait theory, see Steven Altman, Enzo Valenzi, and Richard M. Hodgetts, *Organizational Behavior: Theory and Practice* (Orlando, FL: Academic Press, 1985), chap. 8.

[8]Alan C. Filley, Robert J. House, and Steven Kerr, *Managerial Process and Organizational Behavior,* 2nd ed. (Glenview, IL: Scott, Foresman, 1976), pp. 241–42. See also Fred E. Fiedler and Martin M. Chemers, *Leadership and Effective Management* (Glenview, IL: Scott, Foresman, 1974), pp. 28–31.

The situational studies all tend, unfortunately, to focus on widely differing variables. Although they are not contradictory, neither do they support one another. What they do illustrate is that certain types of leadership behavior are effective in certain kinds of situations.

LEADERSHIP BEHAVIOR

Since the nature of leadership has been discussed, attention will now be focused on the various types of leadership behavior—that is, how leaders act with their groups.

A Leadership Continuum

The most common approach is to view leadership behavior on a continuum, such as the one illustrated in Figure 14-1. Moving from the left to the right in the figure, the reader sees the manager exercising less authority and the subordinates receiving greater freedom.

Leadership character-istics vary.

The manager who stays on the left side of the continuum operates with an *authoritarian leadership style.* This person tends to determine all policy, maintain close control of the subordinates, and tell people only what they need to know to get the work done. Conversely, the manager on the right side of the continuum is known as a democratic leader. This person allows employees to have a say in what goes on, uses less control, and encourages feedback from subordinates. The behavior continuum illustrates that various options are available to the manager. Figure 14-1 also indicates that there are two general types of leadership style. One emphasizes the work to be done (boss-centered leader) and the other gives attention to the people who are doing this work (employee-centered leader).

This model has been criticized as too descriptive and not sufficiently helpful to the practicing manager. However, in recent years Robert Tannenbaum and Warren H. Schmidt have updated a well-known article they wrote in 1958, pointing out the importance of the external environment and the interdependence between the organization and its people.[9] Today, these researchers' approach is more sophisticated and encompassing than it was earlier.

Likert's Management Systems

Another approach, similar to the leadership continuum, has been developed by Rensis Likert and his associates at the Institute for Social Research of the University of Michigan. After conducting leadership research in hundreds of organizations, Likert discovered four basic *management systems,* which can be

---

[9]Robert Tannenbaum and Warren H. Schmidt, "How to Choose a Leadership Pattern," *Harvard Business Review,* May–June 1973, pp. 162–75, 178–80.

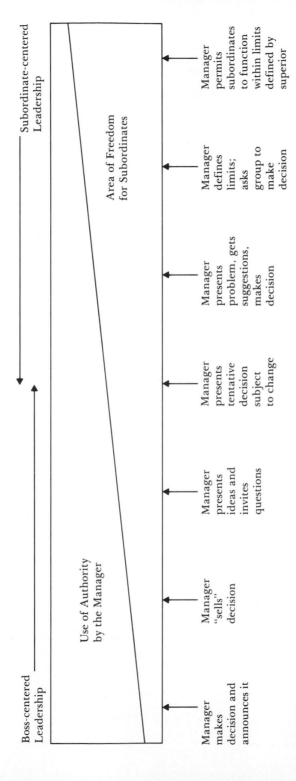

FIGURE 14-1 Continuum of Leadership Behavior

Source: Reprinted by permission of the *Harvard Business Review.* Exhibit from "How to Choose a Leadership Pattern" by Robert Tannenbaum and Warren H. Schmidt, May–June 1973, p. 96. Copyright © 1973 by the President and Fellows of Harvard College. All rights reserved.

SYSTEM 1	SYSTEM 2	SYSTEM 3	SYSTEM 4
Exploitative- *Authoritative*	*Benevolent-* *Authoritative*	*Consultative-* *Democratic*	*Participative-* *Democratic*

FIGURE 14-2   Likert's System

depicted on a System 1 to System 4 continuum, shown in Figure 14-2. These systems can be discussed very much as he did in his 1967 book, *The Human Organization:*

System 1. Management has little confidence in the subordinates as seen by the fact that they are seldom involved in the decision-making process. Management makes most decisions and passes them down the line, employing threats and coercion when necessary to get things done. Superiors and subordinates deal with each other in an atmosphere of distrust. If an informal organization develops, it generally opposes the goals of the formal organization. (*Exploitive–authoritative.*)

Likert discovered these four basic systems of leadership.

System 2. Management acts in a condescending manner toward the subordinates. Although there is some decision making at the lower levels, it occurs within a prescribed framework. Rewards and some actual punishment are used to motivate the workers. In superior–subordinate interaction, the management acts condescendingly and the subordinates appear cautious and fearful. Although an informal organization usually develops, it does not always oppose the goals of the formal organization. (*Benevolent–authoritative.*)

System 3. Management has quite a bit of confidence and trust in the subordinates. Although major important decisions are made at the top, subordinates make specific decisions at the lower levels. Two-way communication is in evidence, and there is some confidence and trust between superiors and subordinates. If an informal organization develops, it will either support or offer only a slight resistance to the goals of the formal organization. (*Consultative–democratic.*)

System 4. Management has complete confidence and trust in the subordinates. Decision making is highly decentralized. Communication not only flows up and down the organization but among peers as well. Superior-subordinate interaction takes place in a friendly environment and is characterized by mutual confidence and trust. The formal and informal organizations are often one and the same. (*Participative–democratic.*)[10]

---

[10]Adapted from Rensis Likert, *The Human Organization* (New York: McGraw-Hill, 1967), pp. 4–10.

Systems 1 and 4 approximate the Theory X and Theory Y assumptions which were discussed in Chapter 13. System 1 managers are highly job-centered and authoritarian; System 4 managers are highly employee-centered and democratic.

In evaluating an organization's leadership style, Likert's group has developed a measuring instrument, a sample of which is illustrated in Figure 14-3. The instrument uses fifty-one items to encompass variables related to leadership, motivation, communication, interaction-influence, decision making, goal setting, control, and performance goals. By evaluating a manager in each of these areas, the manager or analyst can compile a profile. For example, an individual may be basically a System 2 manager, essentially a benevolent-authoritative leader (see Figure 14-2). The same type of profile can be constructed for the organization as a whole as well as for individuals.

Research Results and Management Systems

Likert reports that most managers feel high-producing departments are on the right of the continuum (System 4), whereas low-producing ones are on the left (System 1). Some research results seem to support this pattern. For example, Figure 14-4 shows the results of a study of clerical supervisors. Those section heads who were closely supervised tended to have lower-producing units than those who were under general supervision.

A study of railroad maintenance-of-way crews provided the results in Figure 14-5. Supervisors who ignored mistakes or tried to use them as educational experiences in showing their crews how to do the job correctly had higher-producing sections than their critical-punitive counterparts.

When workers in a service operation were asked how free they felt to set their own pace, the general pattern of responses was similar to that of the previous two studies, as Figure 14-6 shows.

Likert has found that "supervisors with the best records of performance focus their primary attention on the human aspects of their subordinates' problems and on endeavoring to build effective work groups with high performance goals."[11] In short, they are the employee-centered managers.

There is a problem, of course, with this approach to leadership. Simply put, it seems to argue that a System 4 style is always superior. In recent years, however, it has become evident that these management systems are less useful for telling people the style to employ than they are in identifying the style a manager is using currently. With both sets of information, a comparison can be made between present style and current performance in judging the effectiveness of the manager's approach. Therefore, Likert's systems are now employed more for evaluation purposes than anything else.[12]

---

[11]Rensis Likert, *New Patterns of Management* (New York: McGraw-Hill, 1961), p. 7.

[12]This concept will be discussed in greater detail in Chapter 15.

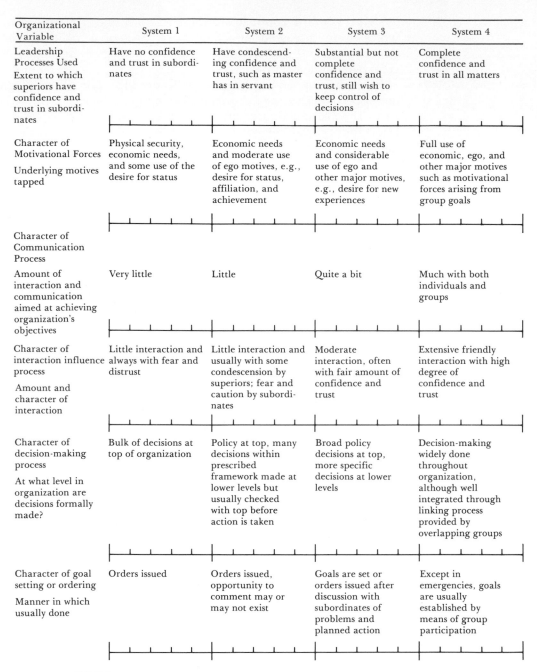

Organizational Variable	System 1	System 2	System 3	System 4
Leadership Processes Used Extent to which superiors have confidence and trust in subordinates	Have no confidence and trust in subordinates	Have condescending confidence and trust, such as master has in servant	Substantial but not complete confidence and trust, still wish to keep control of decisions	Complete confidence and trust in all matters
Character of Motivational Forces Underlying motives tapped	Physical security, economic needs, and some use of the desire for status	Economic needs and moderate use of ego motives, e.g., desire for status, affiliation, and achievement	Economic needs and considerable use of ego and other major motives, e.g., desire for new experiences	Full use of economic, ego, and other major motives such as motivational forces arising from group goals
Character of Communication Process Amount of interaction and communication aimed at achieving organization's objectives	Very little	Little	Quite a bit	Much with both individuals and groups
Character of interaction influence process Amount and character of interaction	Little interaction and always with fear and distrust	Little interaction and usually with some condescension by superiors; fear and caution by subordinates	Moderate interaction, often with fair amount of confidence and trust	Extensive friendly interaction with high degree of confidence and trust
Character of decision-making process At what level in organization are decisions formally made?	Bulk of decisions at top of organization	Policy at top, many decisions within prescribed framework made at lower levels but usually checked with top before action is taken	Broad policy decisions at top, more specific decisions at lower levels	Decision-making widely done throughout organization, although well integrated through linking process provided by overlapping groups
Character of goal setting or ordering Manner in which usually done	Orders issued	Orders issued, opportunity to comment may or may not exist	Goals are set or orders issued after discussion with subordinates of problems and planned action	Except in emergencies, goals are usually established by means of group participation

FIGURE 14-3 Likert's Instrument for Measuring Management Systems

Source: Adapted from Rensis Likert, *The Human Organization* (New York: McGraw-Hill, 1967).

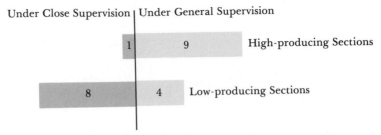

Number of Supervisors:

Under Close Supervision | Under General Supervision

1 | 9 | High-producing Sections

8 | 4 | Low-producing Sections

FIGURE 14-4   Supervision and Production

Source: Reported in Rensis Likert, *New Patterns of Management* (New York: McGraw-Hill, 1961), p. 9.

Two-dimensional Leadership

An extension of Likert's leadership continuum is found in two-dimensional leadership models, as reflected in the work of the Ohio State University researchers and Robert Blake and Jane Mouton's managerial grid.

Ohio State Leadership Research

In 1945, researchers in the Bureau of Business Research at Ohio State University began an extensive inquiry into the area of leadership. Eventually, they narrowed down leader behavior into two dimensions: initiating structure and consideration. *Initiating structure* referred to "the leader's behavior in delineating the relationship between himself and members of the workgroup and endeavoring to establish well-defined patterns of organization, channels of communication, and methods of procedure," and *consideration*

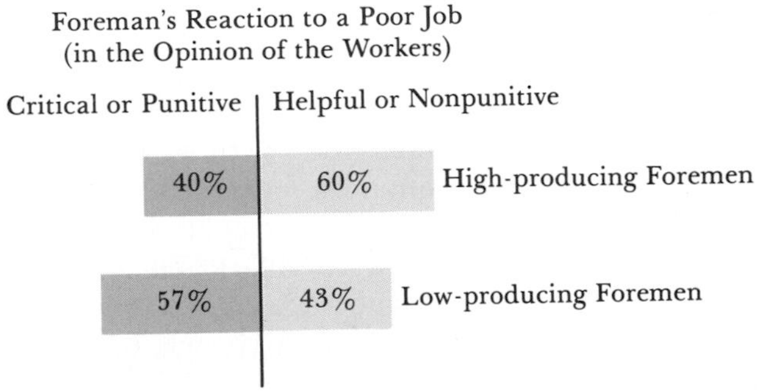

Foreman's Reaction to a Poor Job
(in the Opinion of the Workers)

Critical or Punitive | Helpful or Nonpunitive

40% | 60% | High-producing Foremen

57% | 43% | Low-producing Foremen

FIGURE 14-5   Foreman's Reaction to a Poor Job (In the Opinion of the Workers)

Source: Reported in Rensis Likert, *New Patterns of Management* (New York: McGraw-Hill, 1961), p. 11.

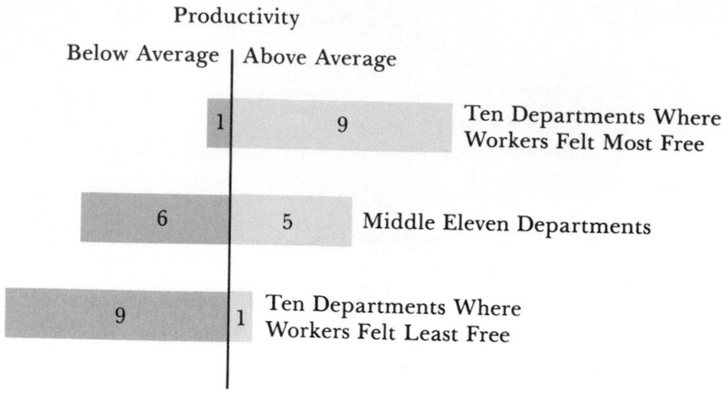

Productivity

Below Average | Above Average

FIGURE 14-6   Relationship between Freedom to Set Own Pace and Department Productivity

Source: Reported in Rensis Likert, *New Patterns of Management* (New York: McGraw-Hill, 1961), p. 8.

referred to "behavior indicative of friendship, mutual trust, respect, and warmth in the relationship between the leader and the members of his staff."[13]

In gathering information about the behavior of leaders, the Ohio State researchers developed the now-famous *Leader Behavior Description Questionnaire (LBDQ)*. The LBDQ contains items relating to both initiating structure and consideration and is designed to describe how a leader carries out activities. Items related to initiating structure encompass such areas as the rules and regulations the leader asks people to follow, the degree to which the leader tells the followers what is expected of them, and the assignment of members to particular tasks. Items relating to consideration deal with such topics as the amount of time the leader finds to listen to group members, the leader's willingness to undertake changes, and the degree to which the leader is friendly and approachable.

Initiating structure and consideration are separate dimensions.

From their work, the researchers found that initiating structure and consideration were separate and distinct dimensions. A person could rank high on one dimension without ranking low on the other. Thus, instead of being on a continuum, such as the one shown in Figure 14-7, the leader could prove to be a combination of both dimensions. On the basis of these findings, the researchers were able to develop the leadership quadrants shown in Figure 14-8. This figure can be used in describing leadership styles, regardless of hierarchical position, age, or sex.[14]

[13]Andrew W. Halpin, *The Leadership Behavior of School Superintendents* (Chicago: Midwest Administration Center, University of Chicago, 1959), p. 4.

[14]Gregory H. Dobbins and Stephanie J. Platz, "Sex Differences in Leadership: How Real Are They?" *Academy of Management Review*, January 1986, pp. 118–27.

Initiating ——————————————————————————————— Consideration
Structure

FIGURE 14-7   An Initiating Structure-Consideration Continuum

A leader who is high on structure but low on consideration is greatly interested in the work the job involves, such as planning the activities and communicating information necessary to get the tasks done on time. Conversely, a leader who is high on consideration but low on structure tends to encourage superior-subordinate cooperation and works within an atmosphere of mutual respect and trust. The leader who is high on both dimensions is interested in both the work and the people that the job entails. The leader who is low on both dimensions tends to stand back and let the workers do their jobs without interference or interaction; there is very little overt leading from this person. Which of the four is best? The answer is going to vary. In some situations the individual who is high on structure is superior; in other cases the manager who is high on consideration is most effective; other times the leader who is high on both dimensions does the best job; still other times the leader who is low on both dimensions is most desirable.

The quadrant approach to examining leadership behavior is more realistic than a continuum because it permits simultaneous consideration of two factors. This undoubtedly accounts for the fact that those who used to view leadership on a continuum are now modifying their views.

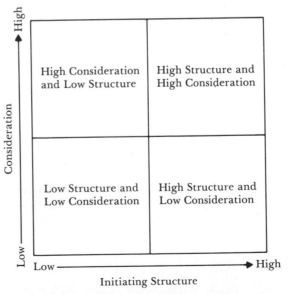

FIGURE 14-8   Ohio State Leadership Quadrants

Managerial Grid

Another two-dimensional approach is the *managerial grid* developed by Blake and Mouton. After undertaking research of their own, they rejected the Ohio · State four-quadrant paradigm and developed their own now-famous Grid®.[15] Along the vertical axis they placed the term "Concern for People" and along the horizontal axis, the term "Concern for Production." In addition, they placed a scale, ranging from 1 to 9, on each axis; its purpose was to measure degree of concern.

Blake and Mouton identified five basic leadership styles.

As Figure 14-9 shows, Blake and Mouton identified five basic leadership styles. The person who is a 1,1 manager has little concern for either people or production. The 1,9 manager has great concern for people but little concern for production. The 9,1 manager has a great concern for production but little concern for people. The 5,5 manager balances the concern for people and production although neither is maximum concern. The 9,9 manager demonstrates maximum interest for both people and production.

Unlike much of the research done on leadership, Blake and Mouton's managerial grid has proved to be a useful tool for developing effective managers. Many companies have found such training helpful to their people in terms of redirecting their orientation, for example, getting a 1,9 manager more interested in the production side of the job or a 9,1 manager more interested in the personal aspect.

Six-Phase Program

Blake and Mouton propose a six-phase program to attain these objectives. The two initial phases involve management development and the last four help the manager work toward more complex goals of organizational development. Briefly outlined, these are:

They also proposed an implementation program.

Phase 1: Laboratory-Seminar Training. Conducted by line managers who have already taken the seminar, the purpose of this phase is to introduce the managerial grid concept. During this period managers analyze and assess their own leadership style.

Phase 2: Team Development. The concepts from Phase 1 are transferred to the job situation, and each work group or department decides its own 9,9 ground rules and relationships.

Phase 3: Intergroup Development. Focus is placed on building 9,9 ground rules and norms between groups in the work unit. Tensions between the groups are identified and examined in way of eliminating them.

---

[15]Robert R. Blake, Jane S. Mouton, and Benjamin Fruchter, "A Factor Analysis of Training Group Behavior," *Journal of Social Psychology*, October 1962, pp. 121–30.

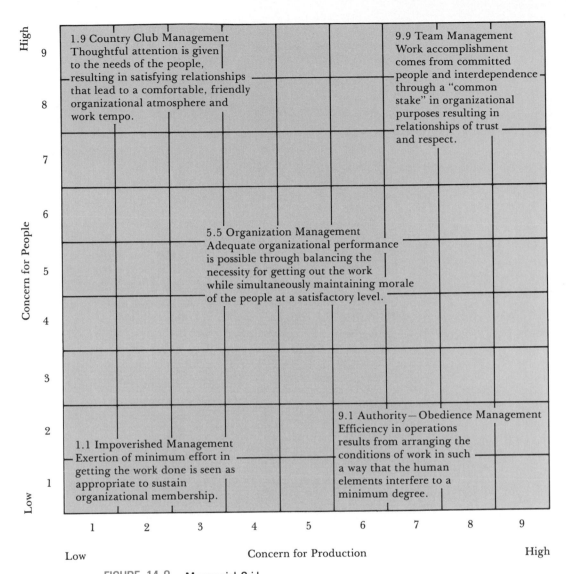

FIGURE 14-9 Managerial Grid

Phase 4: Organizational Goal Setting. Attention is now focused on overall organizational goals. In addition, the identification of broad problems, for example, cost control, overall profit improvement, and union-management relations, requiring commitments from all levels, is undertaken.

Phase 5: Goal Attainment. The goals and problems identified in Phase 4 are studied in greater depth and appropriate actions formulated and implemented.

Phase 6: Stabilization. Changes brought about during the first five phases are evaluated and reinforced to prevent any pressure toward "slipping back."[16]

Which of the managerial grid styles is best? Based on their seminars, Blake and Mouton report that 99.5 percent of the participants say that a 9,9 style is the soundest way to manage.[17] Furthermore, after taking a reading two to three years after the Grid® has been used in a company, they have found many managers still holding to their 9,9 position. More importantly, Blake and Mouton themselves believe that the 9,9 style is best and argue that empirical research supports their position. They state part of their argument against a situational or contingency approach in this way:

> Contingency theorists reject the concept of one best style of leadership on at least four points. These are related to insufficient time, lack of subordinates' competence to participate, wastefulness of involving others, and the mistaken notion that a 9,9 orientation is a static as contrasted with a dynamic approach to supervision. We know that each of these is subject to management and is therefore no basic justification for shifting behavior to make it "fit" the status quo.
>
> Shifting from an "it all depends" to a "one best way" concept of leadership is what supervisory effectiveness training is—or should be—about.[18]

Contingency theorists, who argue that a leadership style that depends on the situation is superior to a universal 9,9 style, have probably made the most significant attack against this position. Fred Fiedler's is perhaps the most widely known contingency approach.

Fiedler's Contingency Model

After years of empirical research, Fiedler has developed what is commonly called a *contingency model of leadership effectiveness.*[19]

The essence of Fiedler's research is that any leadership style can be effective, depending on the situation. The manager must therefore be an adaptive individual. Employing Blake and Mouton's terminology, sometimes

---

[16]Robert R. Blake, Jane S. Mouton, Louis B. Barnes, and Larry E. Greiner, "Breakthrough in Organization Development," *Harvard Business Review*, November–December 1964, pp. 137–38.

[17]For more on the value of the managerial grid to performance, see: Robert R. Blake and Jane S. Mouton, "Increasing Productivity through Behavioral Science," *Personnel*, May–June 1981, pp. 59–67.

[18]Robert R. Blake and Jane S. Mouton, "What's New with the Grid?" *Training and Development Journal*, May 1978, p. 7.

[19]Fred E. Fiedler, *A Theory of Leadership Effectiveness* (New York: McGraw-Hill, 1967).

the leader should be a 9,9 manager, other times a 5,5, and still other times a 1,1 manager. According to Fiedler, three major situational variables determine the leader's effectiveness:

Fiedler deals with three major situational variables.

1. **Leader–member relations**—how well the leader is accepted by subordinates.
2. **Task structure**—the degree to which subordinates' jobs are routine and spelled out in contrast to being vague and undefined.
3. **Position power**—the formal authority provided for in the position the leader occupies.

Figure 14-10 shows that it is possible to derive eight combinations or conditions through these three dimensions.

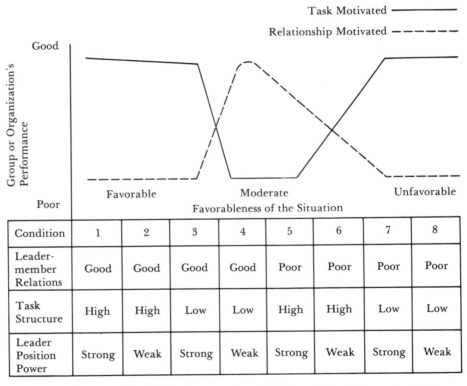

Condition	1	2	3	4	5	6	7	8
Leader-member Relations	Good	Good	Good	Good	Poor	Poor	Poor	Poor
Task Structure	High	High	Low	Low	High	High	Low	Low
Leader Position Power	Strong	Weak	Strong	Weak	Strong	Weak	Strong	Weak

FIGURE 14-10   Leadership Performance in Different Situational Favorableness Conditions

Source: Reprinted by permission of the publisher, from "The Leadership Game: Matching the Man to the Situation," by Fred E. Fiedler, *Organizational Dynamics*, Winter 1976, p. 11. Copyright © 1976 by American Management Association. All rights reserved.

Note that above the eight conditions in the figure there is a schematic representation of the performance of relationship- and task-motivated leaders in different situational conditions. The vertical axis in the figure shows the group's or organization's performance. The horizontal axis indicates the favorableness of the situation—that is, the degree to which the situation provides the leader with control and influence. The dotted line illustrates the performance of relationship-motivated leaders. It is best when their relations with the subordinates are good but task structure and position power are low. They also perform well when subordinate relations are poor but task structure and position power are high. Both of these are situations of moderate favorableness.

Task-motivated leaders perform best when all three of the factors defining control and influence are either high or low. Thus task-motivated leaders do best in either highly favorable or highly unfavorable situations. Commenting on the data in the figure, Fiedler has noted:

> We can improve group performance either by changing the leader's motivational structure—that is, the basic goals he pursues in life—or else by modifying his leadership situation. While it is possible, of course, to change personality and the motivational structure that is a part of personality, this is clearly a difficult and uncertain process. It is, however, relatively easy to modify the leadership situation. We can select a person for certain kinds of jobs and not others, we can assign him certain tasks, give him more or less responsibility, or we can give him leadership training in order to increase his power and influence. . . .
>
> We will be better served by training our leaders in how to change their leadership situations than in how to change their personalities. Our recent studies of contingency model training show that leaders can recognize the situations in which they tend to be most successful and they can modify their situations so that they perform more effectively. We have reason to believe that this approach holds considerable promise for the future of leadership training.[20]

Fiedler's model is important.

Fiedler's model is important for three reasons. First, it places prime emphasis on effectiveness. Second, it illustrates that no one leadership style is best; the manager must adapt to the situation. Third, it encourages management to match the leader and the situation.[21] If the situation is very favorable or very unfavorable, appoint a task-oriented manager; otherwise,

[20]Fred E. Fiedler, "The Leadership Game: Matching the Man to the Situation," *Organizational Dynamics*, Winter 1976, pp. 12, 15–16.

[21]For another view of this idea see Lars-Erik Wiberg, "Should You Change Your Leadership Style?" *Management Solutions*, January 1988, pp. 5–12.

use an employee-centered manager. In fact, Fiedler has developed a self-paced workbook, called *Leader Match*, that helps leaders learn to diagnose their situations, identify their style, and modify the situational variables so as to improve their own performance.[22]

One of the major arguments made against Fiedler is that he has not identified all of the major situational variables. For example, Steven Kerr, Chester A. Schriesheim, Charles J. Murphy, and Ralph M. Stogdill have identified other such variables, including the ability of the leader to influence the subordinate and the role of subordinate expectations on leader behavior.[23]

Another criticism is that Fiedler's model does not explain how situational favorableness affects the relationship between leader behavior and subordinate performance. But Fiedler is continuing his research and will undoubtedly address these shortcomings and try to strengthen the applicability of the theory.[24]

Path–Goal Theory of Leadership

The leader should reduce roadblocks and increase the chances for personal satisfaction.

Another contingency theory of leadership, proposed by Robert J. House and advanced by House and Terence R. Mitchell, is the *path–goal theory*.[25] This theory is rather simple, holding that the leader's job is: (a) to help the subordinates by increasing their personal satisfactions in work-goal attainment, and (b) to make the path to these satisfactions easier to obtain. Leaders achieve this by clarifying the nature of the work, reducing the road blocks from successful task completion, and increasing the opportunities for the subordinates to obtain personal satisfactions. Subordinate motivation will increase to the degree that the leader succeeds. The specific leadership style that will work best is determined by two situational variables: the characteristics of the subordinates and the task itself.

If the subordinates are working on highly unstructured jobs and their tasks are unclear, they will welcome leader direction. If they receive it, ambiguity will be reduced and individual job satisfaction will increase. Conversely, if

[22]Fred E. Fiedler and Linda Mahar, "A Field Experiment Validating Contingency Model Leadership Training," *Journal of Applied Psychology*, June 1979, pp. 247–54.

[23]Steven Kerr, Chester A. Schriesheim, Charles J. Murphy, and Ralph M. Stogdill, "Toward a Contingency Theory of Leadership Based upon the Consideration and Initiating Structure Literature," *Organizational Behavior and Human Performance*, August 1974, pp. 62–82.

[24]Fred E. Fiedler and Linda Mahar, "The Effectiveness of Contingency Model Training: A Review of the Validation of Leader Match," *Personnel Psychology*, Spring 1979, pp. 45–62.

[25]Robert J. House, "A Path–Goal Theory of Leader Effectiveness," *Administrative Science Quarterly*, September 1971, pp. 321–38; and Robert J. House and Terence R. Mitchell, "Path–Goal Theory of Leadership," *Journal of Contemporary Business*, Autumn 1974, pp. 81–97.

INTERVIEW WITH MODESTO MAIDIQUE

Modesto "Mitch" Maidique is the president of Florida International University (FIU), the state university in Miami. Mitch has a Ph.D. in electrical engineering from the Massachusetts Institute of Technology. He has been on the faculties of both the Harvard Business School and Stanford University, co-founded Analog Devices, Inc., Semiconductor Division, now a $300 million manufacturer of intergrated-circuit equipment, and was a leading international venture capitalist before being chosen as FIU's fourth president. The university today has almost 20,000 students in 171 programs offered by 10 colleges.

Q. *How would you describe an effective leader?*

A. There are many things that an effective leader has to be, but the most important is that the individual have integrity. Management teams are often complex groups of people who are striving to attain multiple goals, and the leader has to rely heavily on the team members to carry out their tasks without operating under conditions of close control. This can only be done if the individuals have high integrity and honesty.

A second important characteristic of the successful leader is a high level of energy and stamina. Good leaders have a willingness to work hard. Sometimes they are called on to put in a 15- or 20-hour day. Anyone without a high level of energy and stamina will be unable to stay the course.

A third key characteristic is the willingness to take risks and to admit when you are wrong. It is impossible to be highly effective without making some decisions that are wrong. However, when these mistakes are uncovered, the

the individuals are working on structured tasks and they know what they should be doing, the leader should use less directiveness if he or she wants highly satisfied subordinates. Gary A. Dessler, who has helped House refine the theory, explains these points:

> ambiguous, uncertain situations have the potential for being frustrating; in such situations the structure provided by the leader will be viewed as legitimate and satisfactory by subordinates. On the other hand, in routine situations, such as might be encountered on assembly-line tasks, the additional structure provided by a task-leader might be

individual has to have the courage to accept the responsibility and move on from there.

Q. *In terms of leadership, is there much of a difference between being president of a major university and being president of your own company?*

A. Having served in both capacities, I can tell you that there is. The major difference is the interests of the personnel. In a private business people are interested in increased efficiency and profits. In a university setting the primary interest of the personnel is the acquisition and dissemination of knowledge. This makes the university an interesting place to lead because an effective president has a dual agenda: On the one hand, I am responsible for running the university as efficiently as possible; on the other hand, I have to help the faculty secure the resources needed to conduct research and to teach students. I have to be a combination business person and academic.

Q. *Does this dual-type agenda concern you? After all, isn't it possible that over time one of these focuses will become more important and the other will lose importance, and the university will suffer as a result?*

A. If that were to happen, the university certainly would suffer. However, this will not occur because both agendas, efficiency and knowledge, will remain major areas of consideration. Of course, there is a natural friction between these two goals. Individuals who are primarily interested in running the university efficiently will give research and teaching secondary consideration and vice versa. The best-led universities, however, balance a concern for these two goals because they realize that both are critical areas. The university is something of a hybrid organization because its successful operation requires the pursuit of diverse, and sometimes conflicting, objectives. An effective university president knows how to balance these demands in a way that results in the optimum attainment of both sets of goals.

viewed as illegitimate and redundant by the subordinates, who might therefore become dissatisfied.[26]

The path–goal theory is actually based on Victor Vroom's theory of motivation, which was examined in Chapter 13. Although such terms as instrumentality, valence, and expectancy are not used directly, their meanings are readily evident in the theory.

---

[26]Gary A. Dessler, *Organization and Management,* 2nd ed. (Reston, VA: Reston Publishing Co., 1982), p. 347.

Currently, many leadership researchers have high regard for the path–goal theory. One reason is that the model does not indicate the "one best way" to lead but suggests instead that a leader select the style that is most appropriate to the particular situation. Of course, its full value will not be known before more research is conducted, but it does hold promise in helping explain leadership effectiveness, and it is the subject of rigorous and plentiful study.[27]

The student should keep in mind, however, that the theory has some problems. For example, research does not fully support the data in Figure 14–11. It has been found that high leader direction on unclear tasks does not always bring about high satisfaction. Also, the theory has its greatest value at the supervisory levels of management; it has not been equally effective at the upper levels.[28]

NEW DIMENSIONS OF LEADERSHIP INQUIRY

Up to this point, primary attention has been given to leadership theories designed to increase the manager's ability to influence subordinates. Over the last several years, new dimensions of leadership inquiry have begun to develop. Three of the most interesting relate to the desire of young managers to lead, the ways in which leaders can be matched with organizational strategy, and the role of corporate culture in effective leadership. The following examines each of these three.

Who Wants to Lead?

One of the biggest challenges facing organizations today is that of finding people who are willing to lead. This has been made particularly clear from research conducted at AT&T.

In the late 1970s the American Telephone and Telegraph Company began its second major longitudinal study of managers, eager to see if new college graduates entering the management work force of the Bell System's twenty-three operating companies were comparable to a similar group of twenty years before. . . . When it came to measures of

---

[27]Andrew D. Szilagyi and Henry P. Sims, Jr., "An Exploration of Path–Goal Theory of Leadership in a Health Care Environment," *Academy of Management Journal*, December 1974, pp. 622–34; H. Kirk Downey, John E. Sheridan, and John W. Slocum, Jr., "Analysis of Relationships among Leader Behavior, Subordinate Job Performance and Satisfaction: A Path–Goal Approach," *Academy of Management Journal*, June 1975, pp. 242–52; Thomas C. Mawhinney and Jeffrey D. Ford, "The Path–Goal Theory of Leader Effectiveness: An Operant Interpretation," *Academy of Management Review*, July 1977, pp. 398–411; and Chester Schriesheim and Mary Von Glinow, "The Path–Goal Theory of Leadership: A Theoretical and Empirical Analysis," *Academy of Management Journal*, September 1977, pp. 398–405.

[28]Altman, Valenzi, and Hodgetts.

	High Leader Direction	Low Leader Directon
Clear Task	Low Satisfaction	High Satisfaction
Unclear Task	High Satisfaction	Low Satisfaction

FIGURE 14-11   The Path–Goal Theory of Leadership

motivation, the research data delivered a formidable shock. By and large the new recruits were inclined neither to push their way up the organization nor to lead others. In short, the new managers weren't motivated to act like managers.[29]

Young managers have different values.

These findings were uncovered through tests that examined a series of important leadership-related areas. For example, when desire for upward mobility or motivation toward powerful, high status, and well-paying positions were examined, young managers scored significantly lower on all advancement items, as well as on half of the general and money-related items. These scores led researchers Ann Howard and James Wilson to note that, "Although the new recruits seemed to be motivated internally toward task accomplishment, if the challenge they seek in their work is not readily available, it is unlikely that money or advancement opportunities will inspire their work efforts.[30]

Additionally, when both groups were asked to speculate five years ahead and indicate what they foresaw, the older managers were much more positive regarding the likelihood that they would hold challenging jobs with the opportunity to learn and accomplish new things, that the company would make a strong effort to furnish all of the resources they needed to do a good job, and that they would be able to build deep friendships with at least two or

---

[29]Ann Howard and James A. Wilson, "Leadership in a Declining Work Ethic," *California Management Review*, Summer 1982, p. 33.

[30]Ibid., p. 35.

They are also less willing to take command.

three work associates. There was also a big difference in the "dominance" scale on the Edwards Personal Preference Schedule, which measures preferences for leading and directing others. The older managers were much more willing to take command. These managers also held a much higher need for superior approval; their young counterparts did not have as strong a need for such approval.

On the other hand, when asked about assisting others who were less fortunate than they, treating others with kindness or sympathy, or being generous with others, the young managers scored significantly higher than the older ones. The former want to give as well as receive emotional support.

Findings such as these are not restricted to AT&T. They are common in organizations all around the country. Daniel Yankelovich, the noted authority on work values, relates the phenomenon to the emergence of a new breed of worker.[31] Research by him and his associates:

> . . . points to a declining work ethic in which loyalty to the organization has been replaced by loyalty to the self, where concern for work has been superseded by concern for leisure, and identification with a work role has developed to preoccupation with individual needs and pleasures. Respect for authority and a belief in the importance of rules, once taken for granted in the corporate setting, are increasingly drowned in a pool of skepticism and cynicism.[32]

These findings indicate that the theories presented in this chapter will be effective only if those charged with leading are willing to accept the responsibility of their position.[33] Current research points to the fact that the challenge of leadership will continue to be a major issue for organizations for the foreseeable future.[34]

Matching the Leader and the Strategy

Another area currently gaining attention is that of matching the leader to the strategy (see Intrapreneurship in Action: Leadership Matching). The idea is similar to that proposed by Fiedler, although, as will be seen, there are some very major differences in terms of both management level and task. Individuals interested in the area have begun investigating three important aspects of leader-strategy match: (1) the organization's stage of growth, (2) current management style, and (3) manager prototype. Milton Leontiades

---

[31]Daniel Yankelovich, *New Rules: Searching for Self-Fulfillment in a World Turned Upside Down* (New York: Random House, 1981).

[32]Ibid., p. 39.

[33]Sharon Geltner, "How to Be a Great Boss," *Nation's Business*, August 1988, pp. 24–25.

[34]Alex Mironoff, "Teaching Johnny to Manage," *Training*, March 1988, pp. 49–53.

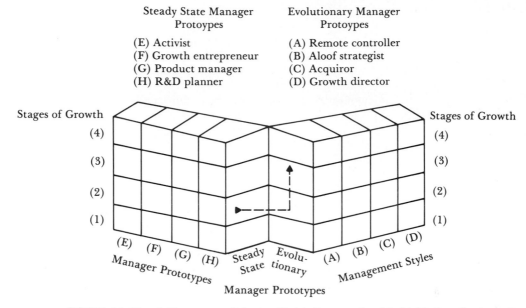

Steady State Manager
Protoypes

(E) Activist
(F) Growth entrepreneur
(G) Product manager
(H) R&D planner

Evolutionary Manager
Protoypes

(A) Remote controller
(B) Aloof strategist
(C) Acquiror
(D) Growth director

FIGURE 14-12   A Management Selection Model: Corporate Level (with Manager Prototypes)

has provided a state-of-the-art model to explain how current researchers are attempting to bring all three together.[35] Figure 14-12 depicts his management selection model.

There are four stages of growth illustrated in Figure 14-12. A *stage one firm* is an enterprise that operates within a single industry and offers but a single product line. A *stage two firm* has an enlarged scale of operations and is dominant within its industry, often having diversified into a number of product lines within that industry. A *stage three firm* is typified by diversification into industries out of, but related to, the company's original business. A *stage four firm* is one that has diversified into industries and products that are unrelated to its core business (see Intrapreneurship in Action: Leadership Matching).

The second dimension of the model, management styles, can be described in terms of two basically different philosophies of management: *steady state* and *evolutionary.* Steady-state-managed firms confine their strategy to competition within their respective industry. Evolutionary-managed firms follow

---

[35]Milton Leontiades, "Choosing the Right Manager to Fit the Strategy," *Journal of Business Strategy,* Fall 1982, pp. 58–69.

Over twenty years ago Fred Fiedler recommended matching the leader to the situation. More recently, consultants and practicing managers have begun following this advice. One of the most interesting approaches has been set forth by two consultants who have pointed out that every business goes through a number of different phases or situations. Each situation requires a different type of approach by the executive. In choosing the best person, it is necessary to match the situation, the major job thrusts, and the specific characteristics of the ideal managers. Here are some examples that tie together intrapreneurship and leadership characteristics.

Intrapreneurship Challenge	Major Job Thrusts	Specific Characteristics of the Ideal
1. Startup	Creating a vision of the business Building a management team Establishing necessary expertise	Hands-on orientation In-depth knowledge of critical technical areas High energy level Personal magnetism Knowledge of key management functions
2. Turnaround	Rapid problem diagnosis Accuracy	Take charge person Risk-taker Excellent strategist
3. Dynamic growth	Increase market share Market Manage rapid change Have clear vision of the future	Ability to balance priorities Moderate risk-taker Crisis management skills

Manager selection should follow strategy.

a broader approach, including the divestiture of existing business and industry change through acquisition.

The third dimension of the model is the managerial prototypes. Leontiades offers four that can be found in steady state management style and four with evolutionary management styles. These are described in Table 14-1. A firm that moves to a different stage of growth may require a different managerial prototype. Likewise, a company that changes strategy from a steady state to an evolutionary state will certainly need a different managerial prototype. Figure 14-12 is designed to help illustrate the need to have manager selection *follow* strategy. For example, if a firm that operates in growth stage one decides to move to growth stage four, can the same chief executive officer be as successful as previously or do the demands of the

continued

Intrapreneurship Challenge	Major Job Thrusts	Specific Characteristics of the Ideal
4. Redeployment of efforts in existing business	Manage change Establish effectiveness in limited market areas	Highly persuasive Moderate risk-taker Sensitive to people Good organizer
5. Liquidation/ divestiture of poorly performing businesses	Cut losses Make tough decisions Make best deals	Tough-minded Highly analytical Risk-taker Not concerned with being liked
6. New acquisitions	Integration Establishing sources of information and control	Analytical ability Interpersonal influence Good communication skills Personal magnetism

Many managers like this approach because it shows how leadership theory can be put into practice. Of course, much more work must be done before a complete model or series of recommendations can be drawn up regarding the specific characteristics of ideal executive candidates; however, the above is a very good point of departure.

Source: This material was extracted from Marc Gerstein and Heather Reisman, "Strategic Selection: Matching Executives to Business Conditions," *Sloan Management Review,* Winter 1983, p. 37.

situation dictate the need for another leader? If a stage two firm, with an R&D planner in charge, decides to become a stage three firm where a remote controller will function best, should the current leader step aside for a different one?

At the present time, models such as that presented in Figure 14-12 are being used more to generate discussion and analysis than they are to provide definitive direction. They are important, however, because they offer a means of blending leadership theory with leadership practice through a contingency-based approach. Additionally, they provide an excellent basis for combining strategic implementation considerations with those of top management staffing decisions. They can also be used in choosing business-level managers to head the organization's SBUs, and they offer assistance in

TABLE 14-1 Chief Executive Officer Characteristics		**Four Prototypes Considered to Be Steady State Managers**
	Activist	Small companies; modest growth expectations; achieve growth internally within present markets; little time on strategic planning; concentrate on restricted areas of business.
	Growth entrepreneur	Small companies; aim for very rapid sales growth; internal growth most important; CEO involved in all decision making.
	Product manager	Large or small companies; conservative growth expectations; count on internally developed products in new and present markets; expenditures on new products high; CEO heavily involved in strategic planning—creating a climate.
	R&D planner	Medium to large companies; CEO vitally involved in strategic planning of new product ventures; CEOs view companies as pioneers or market leaders.
		Four Prototypes Considered to Be Evolutionary Managers
	Remote controller	Large companies; view roles in financial terms; new products and acquisitions are important; almost half consider companies to be conglomerates; low involvement in internal growth activities.
	Aloof strategist	Large companies; aspire to fast growth; new products and acquisitions equal in growth plans; head multidivisional companies; leave operating details to staffs; see acquisitions as critical; CEO sees role as strategic planner for growth
	Acquirer	Large and small companies; fairly rapid growth; mainly from acquisitions; project lower internal growth than other groups; very low expenditures for product development; about 40 percent class companies as conglomerates; CEO sets strategic guidelines for divisions
	Growth directors	Large companies; rapid growth within traditional markets—from existing products, new products and acquisitions; expenditures on new products are low; delegation of day-to-day work to subordinates; CEOs have direct responsibility for acquisitions

performing portfolio analysis similar to that discussed in Chapter 5.[36] Commenting on his own work in this area, Leontiades writes:

> The quality of strategy can only be decided by future events, but managers are required to make decisions from among an almost unlimited set of current strategy alternatives. Just as in the past, the future will prove some managers right and some managers wrong. To improve the odds, the type of manager should be suited to the firm's type of strategy. . . . Without such a linkage, a company risks sacrificing a well-laid strategy to a manager ill-suited to implement it, or hiring a key manager but without a clear strategy for that particular choice.[37]

The Role of Corporate Culture

Another leadership area that has been getting a great deal of recent attention is corporate culture. *Corporate culture* refers to the behaviors, actions, attitudes, and expectations of the organizational personnel. Every enterprise has its own culture or way of doing things. At the heart of this culture are the values of the organization. After conducting a detailed investigation of corporate cultures, Terrence Deal and Allan Kennedy report that successful firms place a great deal of emphasis on values. The companies also share three important characteristics.

Characteristics of cultures.

- They stand for something—that is, they have a clear and explicit philosophy about how they aim to conduct their business.
- Management pays a great deal of attention to the economic and business environment of the company and to communicating them to the organization.
- These values are known and shared by all the people who work for the company—from the lowlist production worker right through to the ranks of senior management.[38]

These core values are often reflected in the fundamental character of the organization. Quite often they are identifiable from the company's sloganline theme. For example, at Sears, Roebuck the theme is "quality at a good price"; at Du Pont it is "better things for better living through chemistry"; and at Caterpillar it is "24-hours parts service anywhere in the world." These values are important because they flow down the line and influence the way everyone works.

In addition to values, Deal and Kennedy report that successful firms also make use of heroes, rites and rituals, and communications to foster the

---

[36]See Leontiades, pp. 64–69.

[37]Ibid., p. 69.

[38]Terrence E. Deal and Allan A. Kennedy, *Corporate Cultures: The Rites and Rituals of Corporate Life* (Reading, MA: Addison-Wesley, 1982), p. 22.

Heroes set the examples.

culture and ensure that everyone is working in the same direction. Heroes are individuals who do things right, allowing the company to point to them and say, "See how that person did it. Let him (or her) be an example to you." Sometimes heroes are founders of the firm, as in the case of Sam Walton of Wal-Mart; at other times they are individuals who came later and led the organization to greatness, such as Thomas Watson of IBM; at still other times they are current employees, such as Lee Iacocca of Chrysler, or some other individual who has done a good job for the last twenty-five years and whom management wants to use as a role model.

Rites and rituals reinforce effort.

Rites and rituals consist of ceremonies and awards that serve to reinforce effort and accomplishment. At IBM there is an annual award to all who make their sales quota. At Intel when someone does something well, the manager gives the person a handful of M&M candies (a ritual started years ago by the founder of the firm). At Mary Kay Cosmetics, sales awards evenings rival the Academy Awards for pageantry and entertainment. Each organization has its own way of using rites and rituals to reinforce behaviors.

Communication keeps the culture alive.

Communications are employed in carrying cultural beliefs throughout the organization. This cultural network keeps the beliefs and values alive and shared across levels, divisions, and people.

After examining a large number of successful firms, Deal and Kennedy were able to classify them into four different cultural groups based on such factors as the amount of risk that the leader takes, how quickly feedback can be obtained regarding the success or failure of decisions, and who the heroes and/or survivors are in the organization. Table 14-2 provides a brief description of these four cultures.

What makes the analysis of corporate culture important to the study of effective leadership? The answer is best stated by Deal and Kennedy.

> Today, everyone seems to complain about the decline in American productivity. The examples of industries in trouble are numerous and depressing. Books proclaim that Japanese management practices are the solution to America's industrial malaise. But we disagree. We don't think the answer is to mimic the Japanese. Nor do we think the solution lies with the tools of "scientific" management: MBA's analyses, portfolio theories, cost curves, or econometric models. Instead we think the answer is as American as apple pie. American business needs to return to the original concepts and ideas that made institutions like NCR, General Electric, International Business Machines (IBM), Procter & Gamble, 3M, and others great. We need to remember that people make businesses work. And we need to relearn old lessons about how culture ties people together and give meaning to their day-to-day lives.[39]

---

[39]Ibid., pp. 4–5.

			Organizations	
TABLE 14-2	Name		Feedback	Commonly	How Heroes
Organizational Culture	of the	Risks	from	Using This	and/or
Profiles	Culture	Assumed	Decisions	Type of Culture	Survivors Behave
	Tough-Guy, Macho	High	Fast	Construction, TV, radio, management consultants	Have a tough attitude Are individualistic Can tolerate high risks
	Work Hard/ Play Hard	Low	Fast	Real estate, computer firms, door-to-door salespeople	Are super salespeople Are very friendly Use a team approach to solving problems
	Bet Your Company	High	Slow	Oil, aerospace, capital goods manufacturers, military	Can endure long-term ambiguity Always double check their decisions Are technically competent Have a strong respect for authority
	Process	Low	Slow	Banks, insurance companies, utilities, governmental bureaucracies	Are very cautious in their approach to things Are orderly and punctual Are good at attending to detail Always follow procedures

Source: Adapted from Terrence E. Deal and Allan A. Kennedy, *Corporate Cultures: The Rites and Rituals of Corporate Life* © 1988, Addison-Wesley Publishing Co., Inc. Reading, MA. Adapted from Chapter 6, pages 107–127. Reprinted with permission.

Using Culture as a Leadership Tool

An understanding of corporate culture is important to effective leadership for three reasons. First, culture helps the manager (especially a new one) "read" the organization. By noticing what the company says about itself, what its history is, the kinds of people who work there, the way people act, and the career paths that are used to get to the top, managers can learn a great deal about how the organization actually works. This is extremely important for the individual who wants to accomplish things and to advance.

Culture helps leaders manage change.

Second, culture helps leaders both introduce and manage change. By knowing how people in the organization think and act, the manager is in a good position to decide how to bring about change. For example, if the environment is one in which the tough-guy, macho culture exists (see Table 14-2), then a change that promises high risk and fast feedback is more likely to be accepted than any other. Conversely, if the leader is working in a large bureaucracy (a process culture), the change should entail low risk and slow feedback; the people who work here are not accustomed to dealing with rapid change.

Culture reinforces core beliefs.

Third, culture is important because it provides the glue that holds the organization together. This statement is particularly true for enterprises that have operations throughout the country and/or world. By developing a particular type of culture, top management ensures that everyone in the enterprise is functioning as a member of the overall team. All successful organizations have been able to do this. Consider McDonald's, the fast-food franchise. Despite the fact that it operates all over the world, there are certain core beliefs that hold the organization together: quality, service, convenience, and value. These beliefs are repeated over and over to the personnel. Perspective franchise holders, who are required to attend the company's Hamburger University where they learn how to operate a franchise, also become familiar with the McDonald's culture. In the field, this culture is reinforced by inspectors who check to see that McDonald's standards are being followed. Then there are contests and ceremonies to honor the most successful franchiseholders, and regional associations among the franchiseholders to keep them aware of the parent company's values.

This pattern of culture reinforcement exists in all successful organizations, regardless of their field of endeavor. The Roman Catholic Church is an excellent example.

> . . . how has the Roman Catholic church maintained its sway for so many centuries? Not by strategic planning systems. Not by layers upon layers of middle managers. But through one of the strongest and most durable cultures ever created. It is a culture rich in rituals and ceremonies of all kinds: white smoke from the chimney in the Sistine Chapel; a pope's blessing from the small balcony; masses and other religious rituals that govern the behavior of millions around the world. It is a culture that is rich with heroes, stories, and mythologies; martyrs; missionaries; saints; a Polish freedom-fighting pope; heroes for people to identify with day-to-day. And finally, whether you agree with it or not, it is a culture founded on the bedrock of a set of meaningful (to its followers) beliefs and values.[40]

In fact, upon close analysis all successful organizations capture something of a religious tone in their particular cultures.[41] At IBM good service is sacrosanct; at McDonald's quality is a guiding light; at Procter & Gamble "doing what is right" is virtually a sacrament. During the 1990s the role and

---

[40]Ibid., p. 195.

[41]Jon P. Alston, *The American Sumarai: Blending American and Japanese Managerial Practices* (Berlin: de Gruyter, 1986); and Karl E. Weick, "Organizational Culture as a Source of High Reliability," *California Management Review,* Winter 1987, pp. 112–27.

When an organization decides to change its culture, the result can be a more competitive and profitable enterprise. However, if the decision to change is not carefully implemented there can be ethical and legal problems. This has been made particularly clear in the case of those organizations that have been trimming their ranks in an effort to downsize and become more efficient. In the process, many managers who have been with the firm for a long time have been released. Is this fair? Or is the effort to change the culture and make the enterprise more successful resulting in unethical decisions?

Some management analysts believe that culture changes can be disruptive and can have an undesired negative impact. For example, if an individual has been getting good evaluations for a number of years, can the organization suddenly terminate the person? The enterprise can, if the planned cultural change requires the elimination of these jobs. However, this may not be an equitable way of treating the personnel. Similarly, an organization may encourage employees to be honest and to report unethical or illegal behavior. On the other hand, if these individuals who do blow the whistle are forced out of the organization or encounter problems because of their behavior, the enterprise is saying one thing but doing another. How can organizations ensure that their new cultures do not result in ethical or legal problems? Four of the most helpful suggestions are these:

1. Set realistic goals and do not promise more than can be delivered. For example, do not convey the message "we dismiss people only after they have been rated as unsatisfactory and have not improved their performance" unless this policy is to be followed. Individuals who are rated as satisfactory and are then terminated because of a company-wide cutback will view this decision as unethical.

2. Be sure that the organization's goals and values reflect the needs of the personnel as well as the enterprise. One way of doing this is to get employee involvement in goal-setting.

3. Do not automatically opt for a "strong" culture that requires conformity and team commitment. Be sure that there is room for diversity and dissent, and allow for grievance or complaint mechanisms and other internal review procedures.

4. Provide training programs for managers and supervisors who are adopting and implementing corporate values. These programs should explain the underlying ethical values and principles and present the practical aspects of carrying out procedural guidelines.

Source: Bruce H. Drake and Eileen Drake, "Ethical and Legal Aspects of Managing Corporate Cultures," *California Management Review*, Winter 1988, pp. 107–23.

importance of organizational culture promises to be one of the most interesting new areas of attention in the study of leadership (see Ethics in Action: Changing a Corporate Culture).

■ SUMMARY

This chapter has defined leadership as the process of influencing people to direct their efforts toward the attainment of some particular goal or goals. What makes an individual an effective leader? Some people feel the answer rests with personal traits and, to some degree, they are right. However, situational theory is more commonly accepted today—that is, some leadership styles are more effective than others; "best" depends on the situation.

One way of studying leadership is by placing the elements of leadership on a continuum. Rensis Likert's research, for example, shows that an employee-centered manager is more effective than a job-centered manager. But in recent years scholars and practitioners alike have found a two-dimensional model more realistic, since it sidesteps an either-or-approach and allows consideration of two factors. The Ohio State leadership research and the Blake-Mouton grid are both illustrations of the two-dimensional approach.

The most widely accepted approach now is probably Fred Fiedler's contingency model, which places prime emphasis on three major situational variables: leader-member relations, task structure, and position power. Fiedler's model is important because it stresses effectiveness, illustrates that no one leadership style is best, and encourages management to match the leader with the situation. More recently, Robert House has postulated the path–goal theory. Both of these theories emphasize the importance of the adaptive leader who can rise to the demands of the situation.

The last part of the chapter examined new dimensions in leadership inquiry. Particular attention was given to the declining work ethic, the importance of matching the leader and the strategy, and the role of corporate culture. All three are of importance in the study of leadership effectiveness. A related area is that of human resource development, a topic that will be the focus of attention in the next chapter.

■ REVIEW AND STUDY QUESTIONS

1. How is trait theory related to the study of leadership?
2. Why is situational theory so well accepted today? Explain, incorporating the word *adaptive* into your discussion.
3. What does Rensis Likert mean by Systems 1, 2, 3, and 4? Which is the best? Why?
4. How do two-dimensional leadership models differ from leader continuum theories? Which is more accurate? Why?
5. What is the managerial grid? What leadership dimensions does it measure?

6. According to managerial grid advocates, what leadership style is most effective? Is this right or wrong? Explain.

7. What is the theme of Fred Fiedler's contingency model of leadership effectiveness?

8. What are the three major situational variables in Fiedler's contingency model? Explain, giving some illustrations of practical applications of the model.

9. In your view, how valuable is the path-goal theory to the modern manager?

10. What did the AT&T study uncover regarding the willingness of the young manager to lead? What significance does this have for modern organizations?

11. How can organizations go about matching the leader to the strategy? Offer five realistic guidelines that can be of value.

12. What is meant by the term *corporate culture?* What are the major characteristics of corporate culture? Explain.

13. How do the following cultures differ: tough-guy macho, work hard/play hard, bet your company, process? Compare and contrast them.

14. In what way is culture an important leadership tool? Explain.

■ SELECTED REFERENCES

Allcom, Seth. "Leadership Styles: The Psychological Picture." *Personnel,* April 1988, pp. 46–54.

Bailey, Ronald. "Not Power but Empower." *Forbes,* May 30, 1988, pp. 120–23.

Bellman, Geoffrey M. "The Staff Manager as Leader." *Training,* February 1988, pp. 39–45.

Blake, Robert R., and Jane S. Mouton. "Increasing Productivity through Behavioral Science." *Personnel,* May–June 1981, pp. 59–67.

Brache, Alan. "Seven Prevailing Myths about Leadership." *Training and Development Journal,* June 1983, pp. 120–26.

Conger, Jay A., and Rabindra N. Kanungo. "Toward a Behavioral Theory of Charismatic Leadership in Organizational Settings." *Academy of Management Review,* October 1987, pp. 637–47.

Davidson, William L. "CEO Management Style in the Closely Held Company." *Business Horizons,* February 1980, pp. 60–63.

Davis, T. R. V., and Fred Luthans. "Leadership Reexamined: A Behavioral Approach." *Academy of Management Review,* April 1979, pp. 237–48.

Deal, Terrence E., and Allan A. Kennedy. *Corporate Cultures: The Rights and Rituals of Corporate Life.* Reading, MA: Addison-Wesley, 1982.

Fiedler, Fred E., "The Leadership Game: Matching the Man to the Situation." *Organizational Dynamics,* Winter 1976, pp. 6–16.

Flowers, V. S., and C. L. Hughes. "Choosing a Leadership Style." *Personnel,* January–February 1978, pp. 48–59.

Hinkin, Timothy R., and Chester A. Schriesheim. "Power and Influence: The View from Below." *Personnel,* May 1988, pp. 47–50.

Hosmer, La Rue Tone. "The Importance of Strategic Leadership." *Journal of Business Strategy,* Fall 1982, pp. 47–57.

Howard, Ann, and James A. Wilson. "Leadership in a Declining Work Ethic." *California Management Review,* Summer 1982, pp. 33–46.

Jelinek, Mariann, Linda Smircich, and Paul Hirsch. "Introduction: A Code of Many Colors." *Administrative Science Quarterly,* September 1983, pp. 331–38.

Kerin, Roger A. "Where They Come from: CEOs in 1952 and 1980." *Business Horizons,* November–December 1981, pp. 66–69.

Kurtz, David L., and Louis E. Boone. "A Profile of Business Leadership." *Business Horizons,* September–October 1981, pp. 28–32.

Leontiades, Milton. "Choosing the Right Manager to Fit the Strategy." *Journal of Business Strategy,* Fall 1982, pp. 58–69.

Lester, Richard I. "Leadership: Some Principles and Concepts." *Personnel Journal,* November 1981, pp. 868–70.

Likert, Rensis. *New Patterns of Management.* New York: McGraw-Hill, 1961.

Likert, Rensis. *The Human Organization.* New York: McGraw-Hill, 1967.

McClelland, David C., and D. H. Burnham. "Power Is the Great Motivator." *Harvard Business Review,* March–April 1976, pp. 100–110.

Manz, Charles C. "Self-Leadership: Toward an Expanded Theory of Self-Influence Processes in Organizations." *Academy of Management Review,* October 1986, pp. 585–600.

Manz, Charles, and Henry P. Sims, Jr. "Self-Management as a Substitute for Leadership: A Social Learning Theory Perspective." *Academy of Management Review,* July 1980, pp. 361–87.

Seltzer, Joseph, and Rita E. Numerof. "Supervisory Leadership and Subordinate Burnout." *Academy of Management Journal,* June 1988, pp. 439–46.

Sinetar, Marsh. "Developing Leadership Potential." *Personnel Journal,* March 1981, pp. 193–96.

Smircich, Linda. "Concepts of Culture and Organizational Analysis." *Administrative Science Quarterly,* September 1983, pp. 339–50.

Tannenbaum, Robert, and Warren H. Schmidt. "How to Choose a Leadership Pattern." *Harvard Business Review,* May–June 1973, pp. 162–75, 178–80.

Toomey, Edmund L., and Joan M. Connor. "Employee Sabbaticals: Who Benefits and Why." *Personnel,* April 1988, pp. 81–84.

Wallach, Ellen J. "Individuals and Organizations: The Cultural Match." *Training and Development Journal,* February 1983, pp. 29–34.

Wilkins, Alan L., and William G. Ouchi. "Efficient Cultures: Exploring the Relationship Between Culture and Organizational Performance." *Administrative Science Quarterly,* September 1983, pp. 468–81.

CASE: **Old Habits**

Joe Chila was known around the company as a tough cookie, definitely a System 1 man. However, he was also a good manager. He seemed to get his work out on time, his subordinates appeared to respect him, and he showed promise as a manager. Chila's superior, Frank Dunbar, decided to send him to a week-long training program entitled "Developing an Effective Leadership Style." Dunbar believed the training would help improve Chila's style.

During the program, Chila was introduced to many different concepts, from Rensis Likert's four systems to the Blake-Mouton grid to Fred Fiedler's contingency model. When it was all over, Chila returned to work and began to practice much of what he had learned. "If employee-centered managers are often more effective than job-centered managers, maybe I should try to change my style," he reasoned. Following up, Chila took two steps. First, he called a meeting of his staff to discuss work assignments and get their opinions. Second, he told them that from that point on there was going to be less checking on their work. He was going to employ loose control and rely on them to do their jobs correctly.

For the next three months things went along smoothly. At first the workers were puzzled by Chila's sudden change in style. However, after they realized that he really intended to be more employee-oriented than before, they increased their output and began to establish lines of communication with him. Chila liked the new approach, and so did the employees he supervised. However, as the end of the year approached, the usual push for increased productivity began to be felt. First, a memo came down from top management to all supervisors urging greater output. Then Dunbar called Chila in to tell him to keep things going at as fast a clip as possible. The pressure began to build up. Overtime work was assigned to the production crews, and the company went to Saturday and Sunday shifts. Chila found himself working a twelve-hour day and a six-day week.

With the increased pressure, he started making more and more decisions without consulting his crew. He assigned jobs as he saw fit and spent more time than usual out on the line checking up on things. By the middle of October, he had reverted to his old style. This continued until the beginning of the year when things got back to normal. During the first week of January Chila called the men together:

"Listen, Mr. Dunbar has just talked to me and he says we did a real good job during that end-of-the-year rush. Now that we're back on an even keel, let's start talking about job assignments and how we're going to handle things for the next three months. I'd like to show you what Mr. Dunbar wants us to do and perhaps some of you have ideas on how we can handle these things."

One of the workers spoke up: "Hey, Joe, before we get into that, let me ask you a question. Why didn't you ask us to help you draw up some work plans during that big end-of-the-year push?"

"Well, I don't know. I guess I was just too busy getting things done to think about it. You know how it is when you get pushed. You find yourself going back to your old way of doing things. Listen, you guys, if you find me doing that again, let me know."

The workers promised to do so.

Questions

1. According to his new style, in which would you place Chila: System 1, 2, 3, or 4? Explain.

2. Why were his subordinates skeptical when Chila switched from being a work-oriented manager to an employee-oriented manager?

3. Suggest some methods that managers might use to avoid slipping back to old, undesirable leadership styles, and explain how they should work.

■ CASE: The Fast Gun

Hank Sidney has been president of his company for seven years, and initially things had gone very well. Sales increased an average of 17 percent a year, and return on investment during Sidney's term had never been lower than 15.3 percent. However, a problem developed as other firms gradually began to realize the kind of profits that could be attained in the industry and started moving in. As they did, competition increased and Sidney's big profit margins began to shrink. Prices dropped as each company tried to capture and retain large market shares. Within a few years, Sidney's firm was barely able to keep its head above water. It was then that the board of directors decided that he had to go.

This was not an easy choice for the directors to make. Everyone liked Sidney. He was a pleasant, easygoing, friendly individual. The management respected him, and the workers seemed to hold him in the highest regard. Nevertheless, the board felt that the president was unable to turn the company around, and the members would have to get someone who could.

The eventual choice was Fred Hightower, a general manager who worked for one of the company's competitors. Hightower told the board that he would take the job only if he were allowed to do things his way. In turn, he promised results. The board agreed.

Within six months of his appointment, the new president had fired over half of the old management team and one-third of the workers. In addition, he refused to hire any new personnel. If someone quit or was fired, those who were left had to pick up that additional work. When asked about this procedure, Hightower gave the following explanation:

When I came in here, the company was going broke. There were too many people in management positions who were doing nothing. I got rid of them. The workers were having a field day with an average guy putting in only a five-hour day. Well, I changed all that by tightening things up. Now everyone around here has to pull his or her own weight. There's no room for fat when a company is in trouble. So I got rid of it.

It was difficult to argue with Hightower since his leadership style seemed to get results. For example, in the first eighteen months of his tenure, the company had as large a share of the market as ever; and return on investment had risen to over 16 percent.

Some of the directors, however, felt that his style was too rough. They believed that the company was going to get in trouble if it thought a System 1, task-oriented manager could continue to achieve such results in the long run. These directors acknowledged the fact that Hightower had been very successful, but they wondered if there would not be a backlash. "Doesn't the task-centered manager run the risk of driving off his best workers and irreparably damaging morale?" they asked. One of the directors compared Hightower with a fast gun in the Old West. "You know," he said, "a fast gun would be brought in to save the town. But once he had done his job, the mayor would have to get rid of him because he was bad for the town's reputation. I think Hightower falls into this category." The chairman of the board disagreed. "We were elected by the stockholders to protect their interests. When we brought Hightower in, we told him he could do things his way. Besides, we have to evaluate a man's leadership style by how effective it is. And he sure has been effective." On this point no one had any disagreement. But few of the directors felt entirely comfortable with the discussion.

Questions

1. Why was Sidney ineffective in turning the company around?
2. How do you account for such results? An employee-centered leader is supposed to be superior to a task-centered leader. What happened?
3. Do you think Hightower should be replaced or retained? Explain.

■ CASE: A Changing Culture

Most business firms function in a competitive ever-changing environment. As a result, it is not uncommon to find them changing product lines, dropping losers, pushing winners, and doing everything they can to maintain and build market share. In the process, many of them are finding that their corporate culture is changing. R. J. Reynolds is a good example.

Mention the firm's name and many people immediately think of tobacco products, specifically cigarettes; however, Reynolds is a lot more than just tobacco. It also is in the restaurant business, frozen foods, fast foods, and, until recently, energy and shipping. Reynold's acquisitions and divestitures in recent years have resulted in a very different company from the one that existed twenty years ago. Consider some of its major acquisitions since 1969: Sea-Land Industries (transportation), Aminoil International (energy), Burman Oil's U. S. properties (energy), Del Monte (food), Heublein (including Kentucky Fried Chicken, beverage, and food), Bear Creek (mail order), Canada Dry (beverage), and Nabisco (food). Add to these its tobacco lines (Camels, Winston, Salem, etc.), its development company (real estate), and its Skolniks Bagel Bakery restaurants, and the result is a more than $15-billion business. Of course, Reynolds has sold some of these businesses in recent years, most notably Sea-Land Industries, and is currently contemplating the sale of Aminoil and Burman. These divestitures mean more money to buy still other things, thereby helping the company fashion a strategy that will take them through the rest of the decade.

Specifically, Reynolds intends to put its money into cigarettes, food, and beverages and get rid of the rest. The big question is whether the company can accomplish these aims without greatly changing its corporate culture and the ingredients that have helped it be successful. Tobacco, for example, accounts for almost 50 percent of the firm's business, but this market is likely to shrink as fewer and fewer people smoke. Food and beverages seem to be an even more competitive area, with many competitive giants prepared to battle Reynolds for increased retail space for their products. Thus the product lines that the firm is keeping do not guarantee an easy time for the company; nevertheless, it appears determined to realign its strategy and pursue its niche in the consumer markets.

Questions

1. Using Table 14-2, in what type of culture do consumer goods firms operate? Defend your answer.

2. Using Table 14-2, in what way is Reynolds' culture likely to change as it continues to shed its noncigarette, nonfood, and nondrink lines? Explain.

3. What types of problems are the leadership of the firm likely to encounter as it attempts to pursue its search for growth in consumer markets? Be complete in your answer.

■ CASE: Improving the Leadership

In an effort to improve its leadership, General Motors is currently having many of its top managers attend a course called "Leadership Now." The program is designed to rejuvenate the leadership abilities of the firm's 2,500 managers, all the way up to the chairman and chief executive.

One of the primary reasons for this new program is GM's desire to teach its people to respond more quickly to problems. As one General Motors training manager put it, "The automobile market is very unpredictable today; people need to respond much more quickly, much more nimbly, and that requires a different type of leadership." In particular, GM is looking for leadership that will create vision and energy to take the company into the 1990s.

General Motors has come to realize that its old, neat organization chart with its quasi-military discipline was ineffective in helping the enterprise keep pace in a fast-moving, competitive market. For too long the company gave primary attention to the process of leadership, rather than its substance. The firm believes that its new leadership training program will change all of this. In particular, the program is designed to open up lines of communication, and to encourage leaders to delegate more authority.

One of the activities in "Leadership Now" is to have subordinates rate their boss, and to use this feedback to help the latter improve his or her performance. This information is used to show the leader how the subordinates see him or her. If this subordinate profile is not in line with the leader's own perception of his or her profile, the training program helps the leader understand the reasons for the differences and to work towards making the necessary changes. For example, if the subordinates say that the leader does not keep them informed about what is going on in the unit and the leader reports that he does, there is a basis for comparison. Why does this perceptual gap exist? What can be done about it?

The program is also designed to help leaders become more participative in their approach to managing people. The success of the Japanese auto manufacturers with their participative management programs has convinced GM that it must follow suit.

A third objective of the training program is to get participants to realize that they are all in the same boat and it is necessary to communicate with each other and work as a team. One of the trainers put it this way:

> Everyone opens up and realizes they're in the same boat. It's highly emotional. The trainer or facilitator is there to make sure everyone is open and honest with one another and to encourage people that there's nothing to fear by saying what's on your mind and in your heart.

Questions

1. In terms of Likert's systems, which system of leadership is GM encouraging its managers to use? Explain.
2. Which of the five leadership styles in Figure 14-9 is the company trying to encourage among its managers? Defend your answer.

3. Is GM's new training program in line with its culture or is this an effort to change the culture? What does your answer relate about the problems that might be encountered in implementing these training ideas back on the job?

Source: Doron P. Levin, "G.M. Bid to Rejuvenate Leadership," *New York Times,* September 3, 1988, pp. 17, 18.

■ SELF-FEEDBACK EXERCISE: What Is Your Leadership Style?

What type of leader are you? Assume that you are a manager (the specific position you hold is irrelevant). Read and rank the five statements that follow each of the activities in this exercise. Place a "1" next to the most typical behavior, a "2" next to the second most common behavior, on down to a "5" next to the least typical behavior. There can be no ties. When you have finished all five activities, transfer your answers to the answer sheet. Then total the five columns of numbers.

1. Planning.
    a. _____ I plan work for each subordinate after discussing targets and schedules with the person. I make individual assignments and ensure that each person knows to check back with me whenever further assistance is needed.

    b. _____ I plan for the subordinates, set quotas where needed, and assign the steps to be followed. I also establish checkpoints for measuring their performance.

    c. _____ I jointly review the whole picture, and get reactions, ideas, and commitments from subordinates who may have relevant facts. Goals, schedules, responsibilities, and checkpoints are then developed.

    d. _____ I let my subordinates have planning responsibilities for their jobs.

    e. _____ I suggest the steps to be followed and offer my assistance to subordinates in arranging their activities.

2. Decisions that affect subordinates.
    a. _____ I get the picture of what my subordinates want and use this as the basis for decisions that affect them.

    b. _____ I discuss decisions with those who will be affected, giving them facts from my viewpoint and getting facts as perceived by them. After evaluating the alternatives, decisions are made on the basis of mutual understanding.

    c. _____ I make decisions and, once made, I stick to them.

d. _____ I meet with each person who is going to be affected by one of my decisions and listen to this person's point of view. Then I make the decision, giving those who are affected by it the reasons behind my choice.

e. _____ My decision tends to follow the thinking of my boss.

3. New ideas from subordinates.

a. _____ I evaluate the idea. If it is sound, I implement it; if it is not, I reject it.

b. _____ I review the idea to be sure that it has not been presented before. If the idea looks workable, I then recommend that the individual develop it further.

c. _____ I compliment the individual who came up with the idea and encourage the person to develop it in more depth.

d. _____ I neither accept nor reject the idea; I simply make note of it. Then I either pass it up the line for action by others or table it indefinitely.

e. _____ I stimulate new ideas by analyzing their usefulness with those who propose them. If the idea is implemented, the originator gets credit for them; if not, an understanding is reached as to why the idea cannot be used.

4. Time budgeting.

a. _____ I schedule my activities within the framework of long-term objectives. In this way, I can shift to handle emergencies without crisis.

b. _____ I do not need to schedule my activities. Day-to-day demands keep me occupied.

c. _____ My schedule is flexible so that I can be at the disposal of the boss and my subordinates when they need me.

d. _____ I schedule my activities to reach a satisfactory level of performance without pushing too hard. I ease pressure on myself through an orderly routine.

e. _____ I plan a schedule of activities in advance. By being organized, I can use my time to maximum advantage. I do not allow too much disruption of my schedule.

5. Managerial work.

a. _____ I rarely lead but I do extend help.

b. _____ I exert vigorous effort and others join in.

c. _____ I drive myself and others.

d. _____ I put out enough effort to get by.

e. _____ I try to maintain a good steady pace.

Answer Sheet

Transfer your answers to the sheet below by matching up the letter and number. For example, if you gave a "5" to the "a" choice in number one, place a "5" next to the "a" in Row 1. When you are finished, total each of the five columns.

	I		II		III		IV		V	
1.	_____	a.	_____	d.	_____	b.	_____	c.	_____	e.
2.	_____	d.	_____	e.	_____	c.	_____	b.	_____	a.
3.	_____	b.	_____	d.	_____	a.	_____	e.	_____	c.
4.	_____	d.	_____	b.	_____	e.	_____	a.	_____	c.
5.	_____	e.	_____	d.	_____	c.	_____	b.	_____	a.
Totals	_____		_____		_____		_____		_____	= 75

Interpretation

Columns I through V represent the 5,5, 1,1, 9,1, 9,9, and 1,9 leadership styles respectively. For most people, the lowest number is in Column IV and the highest is in Column II. They tend to use the 9,9 leadership style more than any other. Your five numbers in ascending order indicate your first, second, third, etc. leadership style preferences. The most common profile is 9,9, 5,5, 1,9, 9,1 and 1,1. The second most common profile is 9,9, 5,5, 9,1, 1,9 and 1,1. Of course, the "best" profile is determined by the situation.

CHAPTER 15

Human
Resource
Development

Adherents of the behavioral school believe strongly in the importance of communication, motivation, and leadership. They also realize that, at times, communication will break down, motivation will be poor, and leadership will be less than effective. They believe that the way to prevent or minimize the negative impact of such factors is to develop the organization's human resources through the use of the latest behavioral techniques.

Human resource development serves as a control loop that feeds back into the original behavioral effort. For example, using just three behavioral areas—communication, motivation, and leadership—one can tie them together by noting that the manager must first communicate with the subordinates, for this is the basis of effective motivation and leadership. Second, the individual must try to motivate the people toward attaining organizational objectives. Finally, the manager has to adapt the leadership style that will be most effective in each particular situation. In carrying out each of these three functions (communicating, motivating, and leading), the manager must constantly be aware of the fact that the people in the organization are its most important assets and must be treated accordingly. One way of ensuring that they are is through a human resource development philosophy, which is usually implemented through human resource programs. It is thus possible to develop the initial conceptual framework for the behavioral school that Figure 15-1 shows.

This human resource effort actually begins when a person is first hired and continues throughout the employee's tenure with the organization. The goal

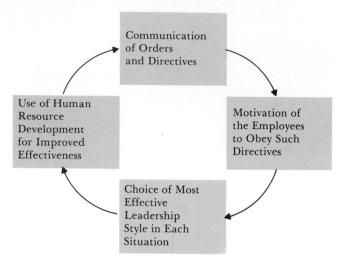

FIGURE 15-1   Behavioral School Functions

of this chapter is to examine some of the tools and techniques that modern organizations are using for developing and improving human resource effectiveness.

When you have finished this chapter, you should be able to:

1. Describe the staffing function.
2. Describe what job enrichment is and explain the major arguments both for and against this human resource development tool.
3. Tell how the job characteristics model can be of value to the modern manager.
4. Explain the value to modern managers of management by objectives and of sensitivity training.
5. State the benefits of transactional analysis in understanding and communicating with subordinates.
6. Describe human resources accounting and how organizations can make periodic evaluations of these assets.

STAFFING

Managerial concern for an individual employee's human resource development begins when the individual is hired and does not end until the person's employment is terminated. Many organizations point to the attention they give to training and developing people's human resource potential; but in fact this effort really starts with the staffing function. *Staffing* involves the recruiting, selecting, training, and developing of individuals for organizational purposes.

Human Resource Forecasting

The first step in the staffing process is that of human resource forecasting.[1] The organization must determine how many people it will need to manage operations over the next six to twelve months, how many it has currently, and how any gap will be handled. If more people must be hired, the firm must recruit and select. If some people must be dismissed, layoffs and firings must be addressed.

It is becoming more and more common to find human resources planning tied directly into the organization's strategic plan. As Julia Galosy has noted, "Interest in meshing human resources planning with strategic business planning is widespread. Doing so makes eminently good sense . . . because even the best strategic plan has little hope of success if the right people are not in place at the right time to implement it."[2] Figure 15-2 illustrates how the overall human resources strategy can be integrated into the overall plan. The staffing process per se begins with recruiting and selecting.

Recruiting and Selecting

Recruiting is naturally connected to human resources planning. Once an organization realizes that it needs more employees, it has to identify sources for locating and recruiting them. One of the most common sources is the internal pool of candidates. Is anyone currently working for the organization who could fill one or more of the vacancies? In answering this question, some firms have developed manager replacement charts, an example of which is provided in Figure 15-3.

If internal sources do not produce enough acceptable candidates for the job openings, external sources can be tapped. Some of the most common are high schools, junior colleges, four-year colleges and universities, employment agencies, and temporary help suppliers. Firms commonly use newspapers and other media in seeking job applicants from external sources.

Trade and competitive sources are a third source of job applicants. Trade associations often have newsletters or magazines that contain job ads. An organization will often pick up an applicant after learning through unofficial sources that some individual is unhappy with a current employer.

Having obtained a group of potential employees, the organization must choose those it wishes to hire. The selection process is sometimes quite

---

[1]Richard B. Frantzreb, "Human Resource Planning: Forecasting Manpower Needs," *Personnel Journal*, November 1981, pp. 850–55.

[2]Julia Reid Galosy, "Meshing Human Resources Planning with Strategic Business Planning: One Company's Experience," *Personnel*, September–October 1983, p. 26. For more on this topic see Laurence J. Stybel, "Linking Strategic Planning and Management Manpower Planning," *California Management Review*, Fall 1982, pp. 48–56, and Lloyd Baird and Ilan Meshoulam, "Managing Two Fits of Strategic Human Resource Management," *Academy of Management Review*, January 1988, pp. 116–28.

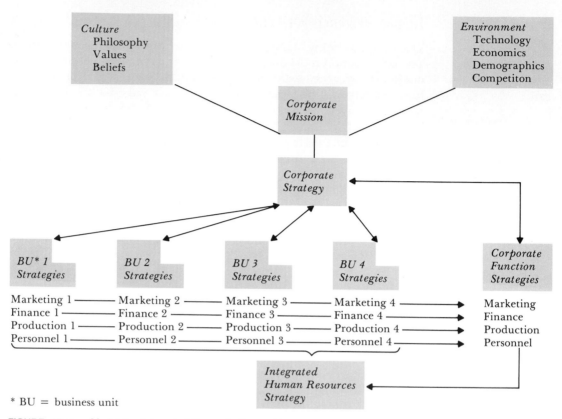

FIGURE 15-2   Model for Integrated Strategic Human Resources Management

Source: Reprinted by permission of the publisher from "Meshing Human Resources Planning with Strategic Business Planning: A Model Approach," by Lloyd Baird, Ilan Meshoulam, and Ghislaine DeGive, *Personnel,* September–October 1983, p. 21. Copyright © 1983 by American Management Association, New York. All rights reserved.

Then a selection decision is made.

simple, while in other cases it is very involved. The larger the organization, the more likely that the process will contain a series of formal, detailed steps. Regardless of firm size, some of the common steps in the selection process are: (1) a preliminary application screening in which the individual fills out an application blank; (2) a preliminary interview to screen out the obviously unsuitable or uninterested applicant; (3) employment tests designed to find out how well an individual can do a job; (4) a checking of reference sources; (5) a physical exam to ensure that the individual is in good health; and (6) a decision to hire. The primary objective of these steps is to ensure a proper job match between the new employees and the work.[3]

---

[3]For more on this, see Ann Coll, "Job Matching Brings Out the Best in Employees," *Personnel Journal,* January 1984, pp. 54–60.

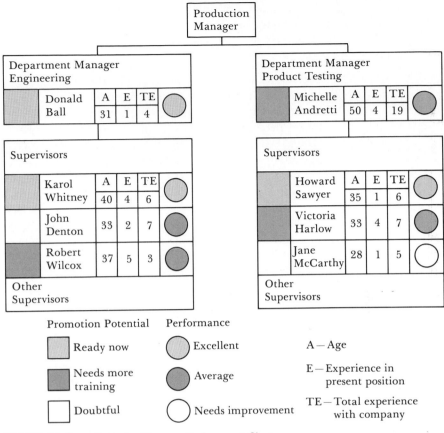

FIGURE 15-3   Part of a Manager Replacement Chart

Orienting

The next staffing phase is that of orientation. Many firms find that proper orientation helps them keep their new recruits. A good example is provided by Corning Glass Works. One of their senior managers summed up this problem by noting:

> Our new people were getting the red-carpet treatment while being recruited, but once they started work, it was often a different story—a letdown. Many times we threw them right into the fray, before they learned the ropes. Often their first day was disorganized and confusing, and sometimes this continued for weeks. One new person told us: "You're planting the seeds of turnover right at the beginning."
>
> It became clear that we needed a better way to help our people make the transition to their new company and community. We needed a way to help them get off on the right foot—to learn the how-tos, the wheres, the whys; to learn about our culture, our philosophies, our total

company. And we had to ensure the same support for a newly hired secretary in a district office, a sales representative working out of his/her home, or an engineer in a plant.[4]

The firm met this challenge by putting together an orientation program that did more than help new recruits through the first two weeks. It provided orientation over a fifteen-month period. The results were well worth the effort. During the implementation phase of the program, turnover declined by 69 percent. This led one of the company's vice-presidents to note that, "Solid orientation of new people is no longer looked at as a luxury, or an option, at Corning. It's a cornerstone of our overall productivity strategy."[5] Many other firms are also finding that a strong orientation program pays off. Transamerica Occidental Life Insurance, for example, makes its new personnel part of the company team from the very first day by having the individual's manager accompany the person to the first orientation session and introduce the individual to the group.[6] Another common approach is to have the first-line supervisor[7] or immediate boss continue the orientation back on the job site.

Effective orientation can reduce turnover.

Training and Development

After it has hired a person, an organization must determine the training and development deficiencies the individual has and the types of training that may be indicated. Among lower-level employees, the most common is on-the-job training, in which the supervisor or another co-worker shows the individual how to do the job. Another is off-the-job training, in which case the individual is sent to a vocational school or institute where training is provided (See Social Responsibility in Action: Getting Them Ready for Work). Finally, coaching and counseling by the new employee's immediate manager are often useful. The purpose of these types of training is to familiarize the individual with the new job and in turn, to encourage maximum efficiency in the new employee's performance.[8]

Workers are given practical training.

Training and development for managers is often more involved. Some of the common approaches are: (1) rotating the individual from one job to another to broaden the person's managerial experience; (2) having the new

Managers are given practical and theoretical training.

---

[4]Edmund J. McCarrell, Jr., "An Orientation System That Builds Productivity," *Personnel*, November–December 1983, p. 33.

[5]Ibid., p. 41.

[6]Joan P. Klubnik, "Orienting New Employees," *Training and Development Journal*, April 1987, pp. 46–49.

[7]Dave Day, "A New Look at Orientation," *Training and Development Journal*, January 1988, pp. 18–20.

[8]Jack J. Phillips, "Training Programs: A Results-Oriented Model for Managing the Development of Human Resources," *Personnel*, May–June 1983, pp. 11–18.

INTERVIEW WITH CONNIE BUTLER

Connie Butler is an employee development specialist for Dade County, Florida. Connie is responsible for developing and coordinating programs for the 24,000 employees in the county. This responsibility covers a wide gamut of programs including orientation, communication, motivation, and leadership. In a typical year Connie will orient and/or train up to 3,000 people in helping ensure that the human potential of these individuals is more fully utilized.

Q. *How important is orientation in the development of effective personnel?*

A. It's critical. The new employee has to learn the organizational culture and the most effective way of beginning this process is through the orientation program. Second, it's important for people to see the "big picture" in terms of what the organization looks like, the goods and services it provides, and where they will fit into the overall scheme of things. Third, orientation provides an opportunity to share technical information with new employees and get them prepared for their jobs. Fourth, everyone starting a new job wants to know about their benefits and pay package. Orientation provides this information.

Q. *You've worked in both the private and the public sector. Are training needs any different between the two?*

A. Not really. The basic needs and training programs are similar. A lot of people argue that in the public sector we don't have to train people to be bottom-line oriented because we are not a for-profit organization. However, this thinking is inaccurate. The director of the Metro Zoo, the manager of the Metro Rail, the chief of police, and all other senior-level managers are responsible for their areas of operation and must answer to the county manager. They must operate within their budgets and be able to show that these funds are being spent efficiently and effectively.

Q. *What is the biggest human relations challenge in the personnel/human relations area?*

A. I think it's that of carefully choosing incoming personnel. We have thousands of job applications every year, and many of these people are highly trained and experienced. It can be a difficult chore deciding which one(s) to choose.

Q. *Are there that many people who want to work in the public sector? Most people believe that the turnover rate is extremely high and it's difficult to keep personnel.*

A. That may be true in some municipalities, but certainly not in ours. For every 100 people we hire, 83 stay with us for their career. Of course, we're continually expanding operations and a 17 percent turnover creates plenty of new jobs. However, our benefit package and overall working conditions are very good, and many people enjoy making a career with us. We know how to create the "right" human resource management environment.

manager do role playing in a classroom setting, with problems or situations that are commonly encountered on the job designed into the exercises; and (3) coaching and counseling by the superior. Unlike lower-level training and development, managerial training is oriented toward both theory and practice.

On-the-Job Follow-Up

In large organizations the staffing functions, except for coaching and counseling, are often performed by the personnel department. However, once this department has finished, further training and development are the responsibility of the manager; this is why the manager must understand what human resource development (HRD) is and how it works.

JOB ENRICHMENT

In 1973 a government report entitled *Work in America* revealed the accuracy of a suspicion many people had long held.[9] Most workers were dissatisfied with their jobs:

> The principle sources of worker discontent . . . are to be found in the confines of the individual workplace itself. The central villains of the piece are (1) the process of work breakdown and specialization associated with the pernicious influence of Frederick W. Taylor and his industrial engineer disciples, and (2) the diminished opportunities for work autonomy, resulting from the shift in focus of jobs from self-employment or small scale enterprise to large interpersonal corporate and government bureaucracies.[10]

While these trends have been recognized for many decades, the 1973 report found a revolutionary change in attitudes and values among many members of the work force, including youth, minority members, and women. With higher expectations generated by increased educational achievement, these groups—and the majority of workers in general—are placing greater emphasis on the intrinsic aspects of work and less on the strictly material rewards. As an attempt to overcome these problems and increase employee motivation, many firms today are adopting an approach known as job enrichment.

---

[9]W. E. Upjohn Institute for Employment Research, *Work in America: Report to the Secretary of Health, Education, and Welfare* (Cambridge, MA: M.I.T. Press, 1973).

[10]Harold Wool, "What's Wrong with Work in America? A Review Essay," *Monthly Labor Review,* March 1973, p. 38.

SOCIAL
RESPONSIBILITY
IN
ACTION:
Getting
Them
Ready
for
Work

The United States is currently facing a major challenge. Many of those who are entering the job market lack the skills needed to perform the work. A number of reasons account for this development. One is that technology is upgrading the work required in most jobs. Second, job growth is proving to be fastest in the high-skill occupations, and these jobs require individuals who are well-educated. Third, many jobs are being reorganized, and the types of skills needed to perform them are changing.

At the present time, over 75 percent of those entering the work force have limited verbal and writing skills. They have a reading vocabulary of no more than 6,000 words, and they have a reading rate of not more than 215 words per minute. This will equip them to handle only low-level jobs, and the latest statistics from the Labor Department reveal that only 40 percent of new jobs will require these low-level skills. The remainder of the jobs that will become available by the turn of the century will require much greater reading, writing, and technical skills. As a result, business is now beginning to get involved in massive retraining and reeducation programs designed to get personnel up to speed.

These programs take a number of different forms. One is job retraining that teaches workers those skills they should have learned in school or that upgrades their training so that they can handle work-related assignments. For example, the New York Telephone Company has technology centers where telephone employee repairers are taught how to splice fiber optics and to operate hand-held computers that are used to keep track of orders. Xerox has begun a program to train its suppliers how to use Japanese-style quality control. Blue Cross and Blue Shield has a remedial education program that is designed to help its employees complete their high school education. These programs are proving to be very important in retraining workers and equipping them with the skills they will need for handling the demanding jobs that are now beginning to emerge.

Source: Aaron Bernstein, "Where the Jobs Are Is Where the Skills Aren't," *Business Week*, September 19, 1988, pp. 104–108.

Meaningful Work

Job enrichment is an extension of job enlargement.

Job enrichment is an extension of job enlargement. But where *job enlargement* just gives the person more work, job enrichment provides the opportunity for increased recognition, advancement, growth, and responsibility. The technique is a direct extension of Herzberg's two-factor theory of motivation and has been highly popularized by M. Scott Myers, formerly of Texas Instruments (TI), and Robert N. Ford of the American Telephone and Telegraph Company (AT&T).

Enrichment can take many forms. Myers has encouraged making "every employee a manager"; employees help plan their own work and control the pace and quality of output.[11] Within this framework, individual workers know the deadlines they must meet and the standards they must maintain. In some cases they are even given the authority to check the quality of the output. In short, management relies on workers to get the job done right. No one looks over their shoulders; they are on their own. Myers has described one of these situations as follows:

> Assemblers on a radar assembly line are given information on customer contract commitments in terms of price, quality specifications, delivery schedules, and company data on material and personnel costs, break-even performance, and potential profit margins. Assemblers and engineers work together in methods and design improvements. Assemblers inspect, adjust and repair their own work, help test completed units, and receive copies of customer inspection reports.[12]

Positive results have been obtained.

At AT&T, Ford has reported that after job enrichment was initiated in the shareholder relations department, there was a 27 percent reduction in the termination rate and, over a twelve-month period, an estimated cost saving of $558,000.[13] Other firms have introduced the approach on their assembly lines. For example, Motorola has workers who put together and test an entire unit by themselves.[14] Cadillac has abandoned some of its small assembly lines in favor of each worker building one complete part.[15]

Nor is job enrichment working only in the United States. Volvo, the Swedish automaker, has found that work teams can be more effective than assembly lines. Its Kalmar factory in southern Sweden is completely different from the factories of U. S. automakers:

> The design for Kalmar incorporated pleasant, quiet surroundings, arranged for group working, with each group having its own individual rest and meeting areas. The work itself is organized so that each group is responsible for a particular, identifiable portion of the car—electrical systems, interiors, doors, and so on. Individual cars are built up on self-propelling "carriers" that run around the factory following a movable conductive tape on the floor. Computers normally direct the

---

[11]M. Scott Myers, *Every Employee a Manager: More Meaningful Work through Job Enrichment* (New York: McGraw-Hill, 1970).

[12]M. Scott Myers, "Every Employee a Manager," *California Management Review*, Spring 1968, p. 10.

[13]Robert Janson, "Job Enrichment: Challenge of the 70's," *Training and Development Journal*, June 1970, p. 7.

[14]"Motorola Creates a More Demanding Job," *Business Week*, September 4, 1971, p. 32.

[15]"G.M.: The Price of Being 'Responsible,'" *Fortune*, January 1972, p. 172.

carriers, but manual controls can override the taped route. If someone notices a scratch in the paint on the car, he or she can immediately turn the carrier back to the painting station. Under computer control again, the car will return later to the production process wherever it left off.[16]

Each work group at the Kalmar plant has its own areas for incoming and outgoing carriers and can pace itself as it wishes, organizing work inside its own areas, with the members working individually or in subgroups to suit themselves. Additionally, to gain a sense of identification with the work, each team does its own inspecting.

The Volvo management admits that it costs a little bit more money to build a nontraditional plant. However, the plant has begun to show increased productivity over its traditional assembly plants. More important, perhaps, is the fact that a recent union survey of Kalmar employees revealed that almost all of them were in favor of the new work arrangements. This has led Volvo to increase its focus on working groups at other plants.[17] It has also resulted in greater attention being focused on Scandinavian management techniques.[18]

Job enrichment research in the United States also reveals that it can be a useful technique in overcoming several previously mentioned causes of worker alienation, because it shifts the emphasis from the traditional management style to a more modern one. Table 15-1 illustrates this finding. The key, of course, rests with structuring the job correctly.[19] As Robert Ford points out, "When the work is right, employee attitudes are right. That is the job enrichment strategy—get the work right."[20]

Recent research shows that one place in which a restructuring of the work and an increase in autonomy and quality of work life, sometimes referred to as QWL, has helped is at the General Motors plant in Tarrytown, New York. Commenting on the results to date, Robert H. Guest, who has been writing on the quality of work life for more than twenty-five years, has reported:

By May 1979 the Tarrytown plant, with the production of a radically new line of cars, had come through one of the most difficult times in its history. Considering all the complex technical difficulties, the change-over was successful. Production was up to projected line speed. The

---

[16]Pehr G. Gyllenhammar, "How Volvo Adapts Work to People," *Harvard Business Review*, July–August 1977, p. 107.

[17]Ibid., p. 108.

[18]Ron Zemke, "Scandinavian Management—A Look at Our Future," *Management Review*, July 1988, pp. 44–47.

[19]Richard C. Grote, "Implementing Job Enrichment," *California Management Review*, Fall 1972, pp. 16–21.

[20]Robert N. Ford, "Job Enrichment Lessons from AT&T," *Harvard Business Review*, January–February 1973, p. 106.

TABLE 15-1	Traditional Style	Modern Style
Characteristics of Traditional and Modern Management Styles	1. Management dictates the goals and standards to the subordinates.	1. Management and the subordinates participate in setting goals and standards.
	2. The manager checks worker performance and evaluates it as either an achievement or a failure.	2. The manager encourages the subordinates to check their own performance and counsels them on how to capitalize on their mistakes.
	3. The manager works out all the shortcuts and does all the innovating.	3. The manager encourages the subordinates to develop their own new methods and induces them to innovate.
	4. The manager is basically a Theory X individual.	4. The manager is basically a Theory Y individual.

Source: Reprinted by permission of the *Harvard Business Review.* Exhibit adapted from "Motivating People with Meaningful Work" by William J. Roche and Neil L. MacKinnon, May–June 1970, p. 100. Copyright © 1970 by the President and Fellows of Harvard College; all rights reserved.

relationship among management, union, and the workers remained positive in spite of unusual stress conditions generated by such change.

As the production manager puts it, "Under these conditions, we used to fight the union, the worker, and the car itself. Now we've all joined together to fight the car." Not only were the hourly employees substantially involved in working out thousands of "bugs" in the operations, but plans were already underway to start up QWL orientation sessions with more than 400 new workers hired to meet increased production requirements.

Tarrytown, in short, has proved to itself at least that QWL works.[21]

Other firms have also reported great success with QWL efforts such as participative management. Rohm & Haas Bayport Inc. has reduced the number of levels in its hierarchy and increased personnel participation in decision making.[22] General Foods uses interfunctional work teams that allow the personnel to employ their talents to the fullest.[23] Other firms are turning

[21]Robert H. Guest, "Quality of Work Life—Learning from Tarrytown," *Harvard Business Review,* July–August 1979, p. 85.

[22]Don Nichols, "Taking Participative Management to the Limit," *Management Review,* August 1987, pp. 28–32.

[23]Marc Bassin, "Teamwork at General Foods: New & Improved," *Personnel Journal,* May 1988, pp. 62–68.

to self-managed work teams,[24] and some unions are even finding it beneficial to become involved in QWL efforts.[25] The primary reason for these developments is the positive effect they produce in the organization including:

1. Cost savings dues to members' analysis of problems and implementation of recommended solutions.

2. Significantly improved attitudes, especially those concerning the level of trust in the organization, communication, perceived quality of supervision, perceived human orientation of the organization, and the degree of involvement in decision making by employees.

3. Increased abilities of employees and managers alike in work related problem identification and analysis and resolution.

4. Increased management awareness of the utility of participation in improving the communication channels between employees and supervisors.

5. Increased abilities in the conduct of meetings, interpersonal processes, and the resolution of conflicts.

6. Increased awareness throughout the organization of issues influencing the performance of the organization (from management strategy to shop-floor issues).[26]

Job Enrichment under Attack

Despite such successes, not everyone has found that job enrichment pays off. Although individuals such as Herzberg, Myers, and Ford[27] sing its praises, others have raised doubts about the technique.[28] M. D. Kilbridge, for example, discovered that assembly-line workers in a television plant did not

---

[24]Charles C. Manz and Henry P. Sims, Jr., "Leading Workers to Lead Themselves: The External Leadership of Self-Managing Work Teams," *Administrative Science Quarterly*, March 1987, pp. 106–29.

[25]James W. Thacker and Mitchell W. Fields, "Union Involvement in Quality-of-Worklife Efforts: A Longitudinal Investigation," *Personnel Psychology*, Spring 1987, pp. 97–111.

[26]Newton Margulies and Stewart Black, "Perspectives on the Implementation of Participative Approaches," *Human Resource Management*, Fall 1987, p. 406.

[27]William J. Paul, Jr., Keith B. Robertson, and Frederick Herzberg, "Job Enrichment Pays Off," *Harvard Business Review*, March–April 1969, pp. 61–78; M. Scott Myers, "Overcoming Union Opposition to Job Enrichment," *Harvard Business Review*, May–June 1971, pp. 37–49; and Robert N. Ford, *Motivation through the Work Itself* (New York: American Management Association, 1969).

[28]For an excellent summary of these criticisms, see William E. Reif and Fred Luthans, "Does Job Enrichment Really Pay Off?" *California Management Review*, Fall 1972, pp. 30–37; and Fred Luthans and William E. Reif, "Job Enrichment: Long on Theory, Short on Practice," *Organizational Dynamics*, Winter 1974, pp. 30–49.

necessarily regard the repetitive work as either frustrating or dissatisfying.[29] In another study, William E. Reif and Peter P. Schoderbek found that some workers actually liked routine jobs because the daily routine gave them time to daydream or socialize without impairing their productivity.[30]

It is not necessary to seek out new companies using the technique if one wishes to uncover shortcomings of job enrichment. Findings at Texas Instruments and AT&T illustrate that many of the early promises just have not materialized. Mitchell Fein, for example, has assessed TI's program as follows:

> Texas Instruments' management was probably more dedicated to job enrichment than any other company in the world. They earnestly backed their managing philosophies with millions of dollars of efforts. After 15 years of unrelenting diligence, management announced in its 1968 report to the stockholders its program for "increasing human effectiveness," with the objective: "Our goal is to have approximately 10,000 TI men and women involved in team improvement efforts by the end of 1968 or 1969." Since TI employed 60,000, the program envisioned involving only 16 percent of its work force. The total involved was actually closer to 10 percent.[31]

Job enrichment has shortcomings.

In the case of AT&T, Robert Ford himself has reported that "of the nineteen studies, nine were rated 'outstandingly successful,' one was a complete 'flop,' and the remaining nine were 'moderately successful.'"[32] One reason for such cases may well be, as found by a recent study, that firms using job enrichment "seem to have a limited understanding of the concept, are unsure of how or where to apply it, and have only a vague notion of what to expect from it or how to evaluate it."[33]

In short, job enrichment has not been an overwhelming success. Why not? Reif and Luthans have proposed three reasons: Some workers do not find satisfaction in the work place, so job enrichment has no value for them; some workers prefer boring or unpleasant jobs with good social interaction to enriched jobs that reduce the opportunity for such interaction; and some workers react to the technique with feelings of inadequacy and fears of failure.[34] Additionally, Reif, this time working with David N. Ferrazzi and

---

[29]M. D. Kilbridge, "Do Workers Prefer Larger Jobs?" *Personnel*, September–October 1960, pp. 45–48.

[30]William E. Reif and Peter P. Schoderbek, "Job Enlargement: Antidote to Apathy," *Management of Personnel Quarterly*, Spring 1966, pp. 16–23.

[31]Mitchell Fein, "Approaches to Motivation," unpublished paper, 1970, p. 20.

[32]Ford, p. 188.

[33]Luthans and Reif, p. 33.

[34]Reif and Luthans, p. 36.

Robert J. Evans, Jr., found that some workers have great difficulty adjusting to enriched jobs;[35] and Jan Muczyk and Bernard Reimann have noted that without effective leadership the effort can prove ineffective.[36] This is not to say that job enrichment is worthless; many benefits can be gained from it. But it must not be viewed as an organizational panacea for managing human assets. It has benefits and drawbacks, and management must be aware of both.[37]

JOB REDESIGN

Despite the arguments against job enrichment, behavioral scientists continue to study ways of building motivational potential into work. One of the outcomes has been the *job characteristics model*, which is presented in Figure 15-4. The model consists of three parts: core job dimensions, critical psychological states, and personal and work outcomes. In studying the model, it is easiest to move from the work outcomes back to the core job dimensions.[38]

---

[35]William E. Reif, David N. Ferrazzi, and Robert J. Evans, Jr., "Job Enrichment: Who Uses It and Why?" *Business Horizons*, February 1974, p. 76.

[36]Jan P. Muczyk and Bernard C. Reiman, "Has Participative Management Been Oversold," *Personnel*, May 1987, pp. 52–56.

[37]Steven D. Norton, Douglas Massengill, and Harold L. Schneider, "Is Job Enrichment a Success or a Failure?" *Human Resource Management*, Winter 1979, pp. 28–37; and Antone F. Alber, "The Real Cost of Job Enrichment," *Business Horizons*, February 1979, pp. 60–72.

[38]For more on this, see J. Richard Hackman, Greg Oldham, Robert Janson, and Kenneth Purdy, "A New Strategy for Job Enrichment," *California Management Review*, Summer 1975, pp. 57–71.

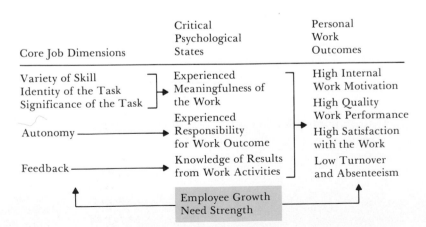

FIGURE 15-4   Job Characteristics Model

Core Job Dimensions

Personal and work outcomes are the end results the organization can achieve when work is designed properly. These outcomes are a result of the critical psychological states that Figure 15-4 identifies. If these psychological states are created, the outcomes will occur. At the heart of the model are the core job dimensions. If the organization can design these five dimensions into the job, there is a good chance that the personal and work outcomes identified will be attained. Definitions of the core job dimensions follow:

> **Variety of skill.** The degree to which the job calls for activities involving different talents and skills.
>
> **Identity of the task.** The degree to which the job allows for completion of a whole and identifiable piece of work.
>
> **Significance of the task.** The degree to which the job has an impact on the lives or work of other people.
>
> **Autonomy.** The degree of control the worker has over the job.
>
> **Feedback.** The amount of information the worker receives in regard to how well the work is being performed.

These are the core job dimensions.

Research shows that if a job has autonomy, feedback, and at least one of the other three core job dimensions, chances of motivating the worker are good. But it should also be kept in mind that the employee must have a need for such a job. If the person's growth need strength is low, redesigning the work will not increase motivation.

At the present time, research is continuing into the ways of redesigning jobs[39] so that they contain higher degrees of these core job dimensions. Research attention is also going toward the determination of the conditions under which greatest motivation can be achieved.[40]

MANAGEMENT BY OBJECTIVES

Another approach that has gained in popularity is *management by objectives* (MBO). Filley, House, and Kerr report that it is perhaps the most widely employed organizational dynamics effort.[41] Like job enrichment, MBO gives the subordinate a voice in what goes on. Although first advocated by Peter Drucker, in his 1954 book, *The Practice of Management,* MBO has been made famous by George S. Odiorne, who describes it as:

---

[39]Barnard J. Reilly and Joseph A. DiAngelo, Jr., "A Look at Job Redesign," *Personnel,* February 1988, pp. 61–65.

[40]David A. Whitsett and Lyle Yorks, "Looking Back at Topeka: General Foods and the Quality-of-Work-Life Experiment," *California Management Review,* Summer 1983, pp. 93–109.

[41]Alan C. Filley, Robert J. House, and Steven Kerr, *Managerial Process and Organizational Behavior,* 2nd ed. (Glenview, IL: Scott, Foresman, 1976), pp. 489–503.

a process whereby the superior and subordinate managers of an organization jointly identify its common goals, define each individual's major areas of responsibility in terms of the results expected of him, and use these measures as guides for operating the unit and assessing the contribution of each of its members.[42]

The MBO process.

In essence, the MBO process entails a meeting between superior and subordinate for the purpose of setting goals for the latter that are in line with overall company objectives. The two individuals jointly establish: (a) what the subordinate will do, (b) the time in which the work will be done, and (c) the method for performance evaluation. Finally, when the allotted time is over, they meet again to review the results and set further goals. Figure 15-5 provides a view of the MBO process in action.

One of the greatest benefits of MBO is the participation it allows the subordinate in the goal-setting process. A second is the clear statement of what is to be done and how performance will be measured; this clarity appears to reduce ambiguity and employee anxiety. A third benefit is the fact that MBO can be used by virtually any organization, public or private.[43]

---

[42]George S. Odiorne, *Management by Objectives* (New York: Pitman Publishing, 1965), pp. 55–56.

[43]See, for example, Rodney H. Brady, ''MBO Goes to Work in the Public Sector,'' *Harvard Business Review*, March–April 1973, pp. 65–74.

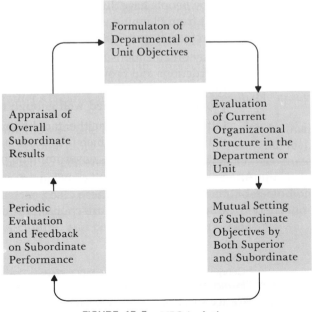

FIGURE 15-5 **MBO in Action**

After attending one of these sessions, the participant is supposed to be more open with subordinates, more willing to communicate with them, and more determined to use a leadership style to which they can favorably and comfortably respond. In many cases this is precisely what happens, and the manager is better off for having participated in the training or, as it is often called, the T-group session. However, not everyone would agree. Sensitivity training also has its opponents who argue that sensitivity training is of little, if any, value. For example, William J. Kearney and Desmond D. Martin sent a mail questionnaire to 300 business firms employing 1,000 or more people throughout the United States.[48] Two hundred twenty-five of the questionnaires were returned and used in describing the responses. Of these, 40.4 percent of the respondents said that their firm believed that sensitivity training had improved the performance of the managers. However, 43.4 percent said it had not. Additionally, while 26.2 percent of the respondents said that they would personally recommend to other firms that they emphasize sensitivity training in their management development programs, 48.9 percent said they would not.

Who is right, then—the supporters or the opponents?[49] This is a difficult question to answer. John B. Miner, for example, reports that a considerable amount of research has been directed to finding out whether the T-group approach really does change people. His answer is that it does. ''Thus, potentially at least it can alter value structures on a broad basis and pave the way for widespread reorganization. Managers appear to become more sensitive, more open in their communication, more flexible, and more understanding of others.''[50] On the other hand, surprisingly, there are many important aspects of sensitivity training on which virtually no research has been conducted. Marvin D. Dunnette and John P. Campbell, for example, after conducting a comprehensive review of the literature, found little research into the effects of sensitivity training on an individual's ability to face up to and resolve personal conflict, analyze information, or implement solutions to organizational problems.[51]

Nevertheless, there is currently such enthusiasm and confidence in this technique that it will undoubtedly continue to be a major organizational development for a long time to come.

Sensitivity training has great potential value.

---

[48]William J. Kearney and Desmond D. Martin, ''Sensitivity Training: An Established Management Development Tool?'' *Academy of Management Journal,* December 1974, pp. 755–60.

[49]For further views of the pros and cons of sensitivity training, see Filley, House, and Kerr, *Managerial Process and Organizational Behavior,* pp. 498–503.

[50]John B. Miner, *The Management Process: Theory, Research, and Practice,* 2nd ed. (New York: Macmillan, 1978), p. 346.

[51]Marvin D. Dunnette and John P. Campbell, ''Laboratory Education: Impact on People and Organizations,'' *Industrial Relations,* October 1968, p. 23.

TRANSACTIONAL ANALYSIS

Transactional analysis (TA) is a technique described by Eric Berne, a California social psychiatrist, in his best seller, *Games People Play.*[52] Although Berne died almost simultaneously with the publication of his book, the TA approach has been further popularized by Thomas A. Harris in his own best seller, *I'm OK—You're OK* (1969), and by Muriel James and Dorothy Jongeward in their two very successful co-authored books, *Born to Win* (1971) and *Winning with People* (1973). The transactional approach has also been used in popular psychology books on a number of subjects of interest to managers, among them alcoholism and inappropriate language use. In essence, TA helps the manager communicate with and understand people through an analysis of both the manager's and the subordinates' behaviors, especially including their communications.

Ego States

At the heart of TA is the concept of ego states. Everyone has three ego states: the parent, the adult, and the child.

The *parent ego state* contains the attitudes and behavior that a child receives, sometimes only through the perceptions and interpretations of childhood, from his or her parents. For better or worse, parents leave an indelible mark on the child by communicating to the latter their beliefs, their prejudices, and their fears. A person acting in a manner uncritically absorbed from the parents is said to be in the parent ego state. Generally this occurs when the individual acts in an officious way or assumes a dominant role. (This is the way it is to be done.)

At the heart of TA is the concept of ego states.

The *adult ego state* is characterized by attention to fact gathering and objective analysis. No matter what prejudices or emotions were communicated by the parents, a person who is in the adult state deals with reality from an objective standpoint and analyzes the situation as dispassionately or realistically as possible. (Let's look at the facts.)

The *child ego state* contains all impulses learned as an infant. A person in this ego state can be described in terms such as curious, impulsive, sensuous, affectionate, or uncensored. The individual is acting just the way a child acts. A common illustration is people at a football game who are rooting and cheering. They are uncensored and impulsive. (We want a touchdown!)

These three ego states are often described by one-word adjectives. The parent state is referred to as *taught*, the adult state as *thought*, and the child state as *felt*. In addition, for purposes of analysis, the three are often diagrammed as in Figure 15-6.

---

[52]Eric Berne, *Games People Play* (New York: Grove Press, 1964). Berne, a medical doctor, had made a formal presentation of the transactional theory in *Transactional Analysis in Psychotherapy* (New York: Grove Press, 1961).

FIGURE 15-6   Simplified Ego State Structure

Types of Transactions

Throughout a normal day, people will move from one ego state to another. The manager's job is one of discerning which ego state the person is in and then responding appropriately. To do so requires that the manager, presumably in an adult state, be aware of the three basic types of transactions: complementary, crossed, and ulterior.

Complementary Transactions

Complementary transactions are appropriate and expected.

Berne defines a *complementary transaction* as one that is "appropriate and expected and follows the natural order of healthy human relationships."[53] Sometimes an employee will ask the manager a simple question (adult ego state) and expect a truthful response (adult ego state). Figure 15-7 illustrates the transaction.

It is not necessary, however, that people remain in the adult state at all times. For example, a worker may feel sick and ask to go home. In this case, the worker's act, although it is appropriate, may be compared to that of a child requesting a favor from a parent (please, Mommy, may I?). In turn, the manager assumes the parent role (you certainly may). Such a transaction is illustrated in Figure 15-8. As long as the manager responds appropriately, there is a complementary transaction, and communication and understanding are achieved.

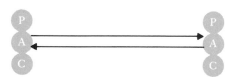

Employee:
Will there be any overtime
work this weekend?

Manager:
To the best of my knowledge
there will be.

FIGURE 15-7   A Complementary Transaction

[53]Ibid., p. 29.

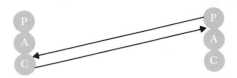

Employee:
Boss, I don't feel good. I'd like
to clock out and go home.

Manager:
Go ahead. You can finish up
that job you're on tomorrow.

FIGURE 15-8   A Complementary Transaction

Crossed Transactions

Crossed transactions
are inappropriate or
unexpected.

Crossed transactions occur when there is *not* an appropriate or expected response. A diagram of the transaction can show this most clearly. Figures 15-9 and 15-10 are two examples, the first being one in which the manager errs, the second being one in which the subordinate creates the problem.

Ulterior Transactions

Ulterior transactions
always involve more
than two ego states.

Ulterior transactions are the most complex because they *always* involve more than two ego states. Usually, the real message is disguised under a socially acceptable transaction. For example, the manager wants one of the subordinates to take a job in a branch office, believing the individual needs this experience in order to succeed with the firm. However, the manager also believes the subordinate is unwilling to make the change. The manager therefore sends the person two messages, which can be seen in Figure 15-11. The verbal one is represented by a solid arrow, the ulterior one by a dotted arrow.

The manager appears to be stating a fact but in reality is appealing to the subordinate's child state by throwing out a challenge and hoping the subordinate will respond appropriately. If the subordinate says, "You're right, I want to stay here at the home office," the manager has failed, for the

Subordinate:
I was on vacation last week and
didn't get a copy of the new policy
changes. Do you happen to have
an extra copy?

Manager:
What do I look like, the printing
office? If you want one, go up
to personnel and get one.

FIGURE 15-9   A Crossed Transaction

Manager:
Barry, according to the master
schedule it's your turn to stay late
tonight and clean up the work place.

Subordinate:
Oh, c'mon. I have a heavy date
tonight. Why don't you get
someone else, huh?

FIGURE 15-10   A Crossed Transaction

individual has answered the overt message only and responded on an
adult-to-adult basis. On the other hand, if the manager injures the subordinate's pride (which is intended in this particular transaction), the worker
might say, "I think I can handle the job; I'd like to try it." In so doing, the
subordinate responds as a child. (I can too do it. Just you watch!) The point to
remember is that when there are disguised messages, the transaction is
ulterior.

TA and the Manager

Transactional analysis has been used by a number of firms, including
American Airlines, to help managers understand and deal with their
subordinates. As long as managers realize that both they and their employees
have ego states and operate within them, they are in a position to analyze
what is being said and how they should respond. One of the things TA
emphasizes is building a strong adult ego state and encouraging others to do
the same. The manager who can do this will deal with subordinates in a
forthright and objective manner. Occasions naturally occur when subordinates are justified in adopting other ego states. For example, an employee
may sulk upon failing to get a promotion (child state); the manager offers
encouraging words (parent state). However, it is important to refrain from

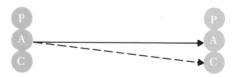

Manager:
Frank, there's been talk about
sending you to the branch office,
but I'm not so sure you're the
right man.

Subordinate:
You're right. I want to stay
here at the home office.

FIGURE 15-11   An Ulterior Transaction

using ulterior transactions or treating subordinates as if they have no place in the decision-making process. If the manager can do this, the workers will respond more effectively. In explaining how TA can help managers communicate change, reduce resistance, and encourage participative decision making, American Airlines offered the following advice:

> What can you do to minimize your own as well as others' resistance to change and to improve efforts to improve? Remember that resistance to change comes from the Parent or the Child. Sometimes resistance can be reduced by providing or obtaining more data about the change. Involving people in some aspect of the decision-making (thereby requiring the use of their Adult) will help to get them unhooked from their Parent or Child reactions.
>
> The method you use in trying to improve something is also extremely important. Telling people they *should* or *must* (Parent initiated "oughtmanship") improve something will probably hook their Child (and therefore generate resistance). For example, telling a group of employees, "You *must* improve your customer service and also reduce costs" will likely generate only anger, anxiety, guilt or fear (Child reaction).
>
> Similarly, telling people that they should worry (thereby hooking their Child) about this same problem will probably not lead to improvement or change. On the other hand, the more relevant data you give employees about service and cost performance problems, the more likely you will engage their Adults in problem-solving.[54]

HUMAN RESOURCES ACCOUNTING

The ultimate objective of all the programs and techniques discussed thus far in the chapter is that of obtaining maximum efficiency. When an organization decides to review its effectiveness, it will usually examine its financial statements, such as the balance sheet, in which physical assets (cash, accounts receivable, inventory, and plant) are recorded. However, nowhere in the financial statements of most firms is there any accounting for either the productive capability of the workers or the goodwill of the customers. In the case of the work force, for example, many variables can make one firm superior to another, including:

1. Level of intelligence and aptitudes.
2. Level of training.
3. Level of performance goals and motivation to achieve organizational success.
4. Quality of leadership.

---

[54]Lyman Randall, *P–A–C at Work* (Dallas, TX: American Airlines, 1971), p. 46.

5. Capacity to use differences for purposes of innovation and improvement, rather than allowing differences to develop into bitter, irreconcilable, interpersonal conflict.

6. Quality of communicating upward, downward, and laterally.

7. Quality of decision making.

8. Capacity to achieve cooperative teamwork versus competitive striving for personal success at the expense of the organization.

9. Quality of the control processes of the organization and the levels of felt responsibility which exist.

10. Capacity to achieve effective coordination.

11. Capacity to use experience and measurements to guide decisions, improve operations, and introduce innovations.[55]

Nowhere on the balance sheet are these factors accounted for. In an attempt to overcome this deficiency, an area known as *human resources accounting* has developed. The method has taken two paths: viewing the acquisition and development of personnel as an investment, and obtaining a regular evaluation of these assets by measuring what are called causal and intervening variables. The following discussion will examine both of these approaches.

Personnel as an Investment

If a company is to be successful, it needs to hire and maintain competent people (see International Management in Action: Losing the Edge). How much are these people worth to the firm? This is a question human resources accounting attempts to answer. As Rensis Likert points out, this term

refers to activity devoted to attaching dollar estimates to the value of a firm's human organization and its customer goodwill. If able, well-trained personnel leave the firm, the human organization is worth less; if they join it, the firm's human assets are increased. If bickering, distrust, and irreconcilable conflict become greater, the human enterprise is worth less; if the capacity to use differences constructively and engage in cooperative teamwork improves, the human organization is a more valuable asset.[56]

One way for the company to decide how much its human assets are worth would be to determine the amount of money it took to hire, train, and retain these people. Offsetting this figure will be such factors as retirement,

---

[55]Rensis Likert, *The Human Organization* (New York: McGraw-Hill, 1967), p. 148.

[56]Ibid., pp. 148–49.

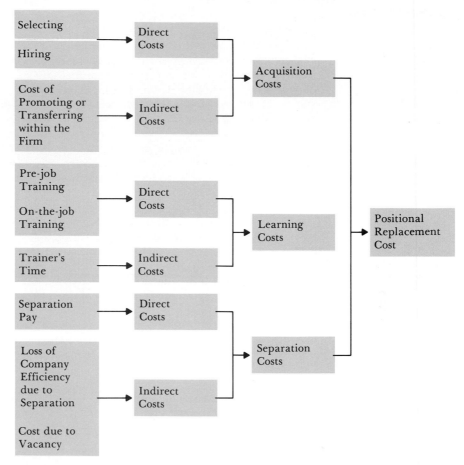

FIGURE 15-12   Determining Human Resource Replacement Costs

Source: Adapted by permission from Eric G. Flamholtz, "Human Resource Accounting: Measuring Positional Replacement Costs," *Human Resource Management,* Spring 1973, p. 11.

transfers, separations, and obsolescence (or failure to keep up) on the part of the employees. Figure 15-12 illustrates this cost analysis. If one wished to include the customer in this analysis, the cost of maintaining goodwill could be written in and loss of customer orders (ill will) deducted.

A dollar-investment approach is used.

Another method has been proposed by Philip H. Mirvis and Barry M. Macy, who developed a model for reflecting member participation in light of attendance at work and performance while on the job. Factors in the former category included absenteeism, turnover, strikes, and tardiness. In the latter were production under standard, quality under standard, grievances, accidents, unscheduled downtime, machine repair, material utilization, and inventory shrinkage. Mirvis and Macy then analyzed a firm and determined

INTERNATIONAL
MANAGEMENT
IN
ACTION:
Losing
the
Edge

Many countries and companies are attempting to emulate Japanese management principles and concepts. However, there is a growing concern that many Japanese firms are failing to properly treat their human resources. More and more Japanese are finding that despite their long working hours and the extra effort they put into their jobs, they are unable to afford the luxuries that an average American family takes for granted.

Consider Akira Chizuka, a member of Japan's middle class. Akira, who has to spend three hours a day commuting to work, earns $33,000 a year. This sounds like a fairly good salary, until one begins examining the cost of living in Japan. Akira and his wife live in a three-bedroom apartment that has a total area of less than 500 square feet. Rent and utilities take $1,615 a month out of the family paycheck. Fortunately, the Chizukas do not have air conditioning, which would easily drive their utility bill up by 30 percent. Most of the remaining salary goes toward taxes, food, clothing, and other necessaries. Akira's wife, Keiko, works at a department store to help pay for clothing and to provide herself with some pocket money. Yet the couple is able to save only $150 a month, and this is not enough to generate the necessary 20 percent needed for a down payment on a house. Will they be able to buy a home in the near future? This is unlikely.

Nor is this the only major difference between Japanese and American lifestyles. The average American's home is approximately 1,600 square feet while the typical Japanese family lives in a house with just over 900 square feet. The average U. S. family has 2.2 cars compared to 0.88 for the Japanese. American families spend approximately 15 percent of their income for food, while Japanese spend around 26 percent.

The bottom line to this economic comparison is that many Japanese are beginning to feel that they are not members of the middle class. They are working hard, but they do not have much to show for it. This is even resulting in companies having difficulty hiring and retaining young people. As *Business Week* reports:

> Impatience with the slow earning curve on Japan's traditional career path is already driving talented young people away from basic industries. "Computer companies such as Fujitsu and Hitachi are no longer attracting the best engineering students," warns Haruhisa Ishida, a professor of computer science at Tokyo University. He also worries that too many top students are being lured into the financial sector. "This could have dire implications for Japan's competitiveness in high technology."

If Japan cannot correct this problem, the 1990s are going to see a major change in the country's economic strength. Personnel are too critical a national resource to be wasted.

Source: Barbara Buell, Neil Gross, and Charles Gaffney, "The Myth of the Japanese Middle Class," *Business Week,* September 12, 1988, pp. 49–52.

how much each of these factors was affecting it. They found that tardiness was costing the firm $56,920 a year, absenteeism was costing $286,330 annually, and losses owing to quality below standard was estimated at $663,589.[57] Human resources are thus reflected in an organization's financial statements. By managing these resources well, the organization can increase productivity and profits. Figure 15-13 shows how human resources investments can be converted into productive job behavior.

Obviously, converting human assets into dollars in the financial statements is a difficult task because the approach is very subjective. After all, how does one really decide the costs associated with the retention or loss of personnel? No definitive answer will be presented here; the entire area is still in the developmental stages. It should be noted, however, that some companies are actually trying to reflect human resources in their financial statements.[58] If human resources accounting continues to grow at its current pace, other firms will undoubtedly be doing the same.

Periodic Evaluation of Human Resources

A second suggested approach is periodic evaluation of the state of the company's human resources. One way of doing this, in the opinion of some human resources accounting people, is to use Likert's four management systems, which were discussed in Chapter 14. By determining whether a company is operating under System 1, 2, 3, or 4, it may be possible to draw conclusions about how the human resources are being managed. The primary thesis of proponents of this theory is that the current state of a company's human resources will be reflected in future performance. If today's workers are operating under a System 3 or System 4 manager, future performance should be high. If they are working under a System 1 or System 2 manager, future performance will be lower.

When Likert's management systems are used to measure the current state of the human resources, questions such as those presented earlier (see Figure 14-3) are employed. Based on the responses, the researchers approximate a profile of the system under which the company is operating. In addition, three types of variables are examined. These are:

1. **Causal (or independent) variables,** which determine the results the company is going to achieve. Management decisions, business strategies, and leadership behavior are all illustrations.

---

[57]Philip H. Mirvis and Barry M. Macy, "Human Resource Accounting: A Measurement Perspective," *Academy of Management Review*, April 1976, pp. 76–83.

[58]William C. Pyle, "Monitoring Human Resources—On Line," *Michigan Business Review*, July 1970, pp. 19–32; D. M. C. Jones, "Accounting for Human Assets," *Management Decision*, Summer 1973, pp. 183–94; and Geoffrey M. N. Baker, "The Feasibility and Utility of Human Resource Accounting," *California Management Review*, Summer 1974, pp. 17–23.

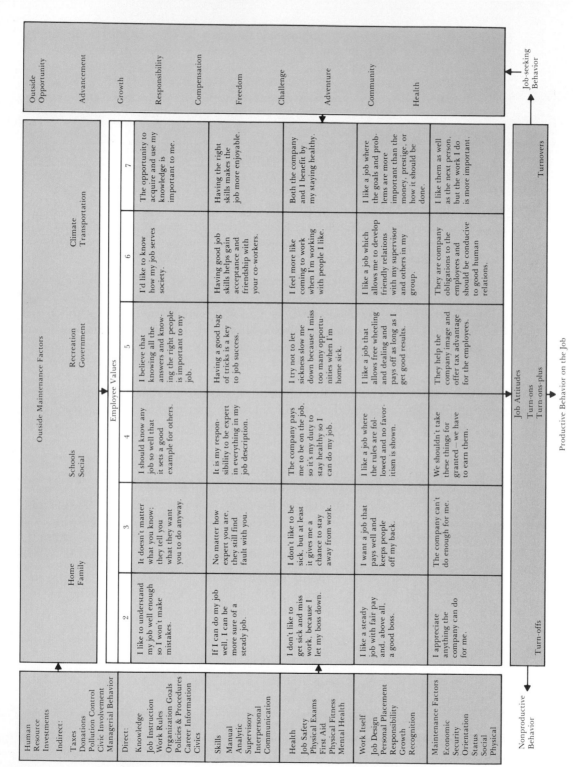

FIGURE 15-13 Conversion of Human Resource Investments into Behavior on the Job

Source: M. Scott Myers and Vincent S. Flowers, "A Framework for Developing Human Assets." Copyright © 1974 by the Regents of the University of California. Reprinted from *California Management Review*, Vol. XVI, no. 4, p. 14, by permission of the Regents.

2. **Intervening variables,** which reflect the internal state of the organization. Loyalty, attitude, and motivation are all illustrations.

3. **End-result (or dependent) variables,** which reflect the organization's achievements. Earnings, productivity, and costs are all illustrations.

Intervening variables are important.

According to human resource experts, a company's earnings, productivity, and costs (end-result variables) are a result of causal variables, such as business strategies and leadership behavior. However, one must do more than merely analyze cause-effect relationships. It is also necessary to examine the transformation process or intervening variables. For example, why does a particular leadership behavior result in higher earnings? The answer may well be found in such factors as loyalty, attitude, and motivation.

This particular concept has important implications for management because it indicates that a change in leadership style (causal variable) will result in a change in factors such as costs or earnings (end-result variables) only if there is change in factors such as loyalty, attitude, motivation, and so on (intervening variables). This particular idea is often used by human resources accounting people to illustrate what they call the *liquidation of human assets.* In essence, human resource accountants believe that a company that wishes to increase its current earnings can do so if it moves toward System 1. Figure 15-14 provides an illustration.

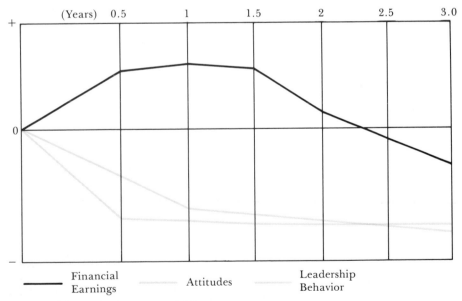

FIGURE 15-14   **Moving toward System 1**

Source: Courtesy of Dr. Tony Hain, General Motors Institute.

Changes in Leadership Style

As seen in Figure 15-14, by changing its strategy and leadership behavior (causal variables) the company can improve its short-run financial position (end-result variable). Of course, this lasts for only a few years and then deteriorates. However, one point to be noted from Figure 15-14 is that as the firm moves toward System 1, leadership behavior declines; managers become increasingly autocratic and start applying pressure in an attempt to improve earnings. This behavior is followed by a decline in employee attitudes and motivation. During this same period, it is also common to find some of the best workers leaving the firm. The company is thus liquidating its human resources. In a manner of speaking, it is analogous to selling machinery and equipment at a discount. On the positive side, however, the financial picture (earnings) improves and, in the above illustration, remains there for two years before finally dropping below the initial level of zero.

The same basic concepts are used by human resources people to explain what happens when a company moves toward System 4, as Figure 15-15 illustrates. First the leadership behavior (causal variable) is changed. This is followed by improvement in attitudes (intervening variable) and then improvement in earnings (end-result variable).

If the management moves toward System 1, it can milk or liquidate its human assets and achieve short-run increases in earnings. However, after a

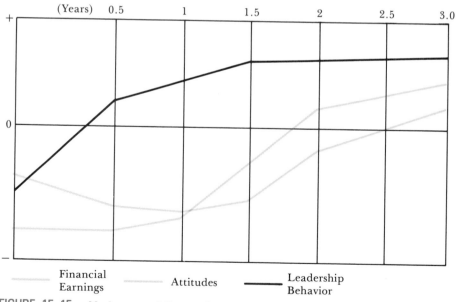

FIGURE 15-15   **Moving toward System 4**

Source: Courtesy of Dr. Tony Hain, General Motors Institute.

given time period the intervening variables will come into play and the earnings will decrease. Thus, in the short run, it may be advisable to change to System 1 when a critical financial situation develops, but this approach cannot be maintained indefinitely.

Conversely, moving toward System 4 may not result in any increases in earnings for quite a while. As Likert points out, *"Changes in the causal variables toward System 4 apparently require an appreciable period of time before the impact of the change is fully manifest in corresponding improvement in the end-result variables."*[59] This entails a good deal of faith on the part of the management, which must be willing to continue moving toward System 4.

William M. Fox echoes Likert, noting:

It has been found, for example, that there is a six-to-twelve month interval between positive changes in top management behavior and positive changes in organization climate and subordinate leadership. In turn there is a seven-to-eighteen month lag between positive changes in subordinate leadership and group performance improvement and reduced absenteeism. Grievance rate reduction takes only about six months and changes in satisfaction take place within a matter of days or weeks.

Reciprocal relationships are in evidence, also. We see that subordinate performance improvement and increased satisfaction help to cause positive changes in leadership behavior with a time lag of approximately one month.[60]

Causal and intervening variables are lead factors.

Human resources researchers thus believe that the firm's current financial position may not reflect the true status of the causal and intervening variables, for these are lead factors. However, changes in these variables will be reflected in future financial statements, and this is why they are so important.

The measurements of the causal and intervening variables should be obtained for the corporation as a whole and for each profit center or unit in the company. . . . By using appropriate statistical procedures, relationships can be computed among the causal, intervening, and such end-result variables as costs and earnings. . . . These estimates of probable subsequent productivity, costs, and earnings will reveal the earning power of the human organization *at the time* the causal and

---

[59]Rensis Likert, *The Human Organization,* pp. 80–81. For more on this subject, see William F. Dowling, "At General Motors: System 4 Builds Performance and Profits," *Organizational Dynamics,* Winter 1975, pp. 23–38.

[60]William M. Fox, "Limits to the Use of Consultative-Participative Management," *California Management Review,* Winter 1977, p. 21.

intervening variables were measured, even though the level of estimated subsequent earnings may not be achieved until much later. These estimates . . . provide the basis for attaching to any profit center, unit, or total corporation a statement of the present value of its human organization.[61]

The future of the firm depends on its ability to manage its human assets today.

One further point must be noted before this discussion ends. Figures 15-14 and 15-15 represent only a general pattern of results as postulated by human resources researchers. As Koontz, O'Donnell, and Weihrich note:

To date, only a few experiments have been undertaken to measure the investment costs and losses in human resources. While it is believed that present "value" of human resources . . . can be reasonably well approached through the use of the Likert measurements, there is still little evidence that this has been done with an acceptable degree of creditability.[62]

On an overall basis, then, judgment on the value of human resources accounting must be withheld until more research has been conducted in the area.

■ SUMMARY

This chapter has examined some of the latest tools and techniques for managing the firm's human assets. The chapter began by describing the staffing process, where human resource development efforts first begin.

The remainder of the chapter was devoted to the study of some of the human resource development programs currently being used in modern organizations. Job enrichment is one that has been getting a great deal of attention. It is currently employed in a number of firms, including TI, AT&T, GM's Cadillac division, and overseas in Volvo plants. In essence, job enrichment places primary emphasis on Herzberg's motivators: advancement, growth, and responsibility. Yet despite wide acceptance, the technique has a number of vociferous critics who claim that it does not always work. Three of the primary reasons cited are that some workers do not find satisfaction in the work place; some people prefer boring, unpleasant jobs with good social interaction to enriched jobs that reduce the opportunity for such interaction; and some workers react to the technique with feelings of inadequacy and fears of failure.

---

[61]Ibid., p. 150.

[62]Harold Koontz, Cyril O'Donnell, and Heinz Weihrich, *Management*, 7th ed. (New York: McGraw-Hill, 1980), p. 797.

One of the primary ways of redesigning jobs is by building core job dimensions into them. It has been found that these dimensions are frequently correlated with such outcomes as high work motivation, high quality performance, high satisfaction, low turnover, and low absenteeism.

Another technique that has also gained a great deal of popularity because of its potential for helping the manager carry out decision-making, communication, and control functions is management by objectives. In essence, MBO entails a meeting of superior and subordinate for deciding: (a) what the subordinate will do, (b) length of time needed, and (c) how performance will be evaluated. In addition to its participative decision-making feature, subordinates like the technique because it tells them what is expected of them, thereby reducing ambiguity and anxiety.

Sensitivity training is designed to make managers more aware of their own actions and their effect on others, in addition to obtaining better insight into what makes subordinates tick. Another approach, which is less emotive but just as valuable to managers who need help communicating with their people, is transactional analysis. A number of companies, including American Airlines, have used this technique to help their managers communicate more effectively with their subordinates.

The last technique examined was human resources accounting. This technique suggests that the company evaluate its personnel and that this evaluation be reflected in the firm's financial statements. Well-trained, well-motivated people are an asset. Another approach is to evaluate personnel on a periodic basis by measuring causal, intervening, and end-result variables. This technique gives management a reading on the kind of performance it can expect from its people in the near future.

■ REVIEW AND STUDY QUESTIONS

1. What is involved in the staffing process? Identify and describe the activities that are carried out.

2. What is the primary goal of job enrichment? Will we see more of it in the rest of the 1980s? Explain your answer.

3. What are some of the arguments against job enrichment?

4. What is job redesign? Incorporate the job characteristics model into your answer.

5. How does management by objectives work? Explain in some detail.

6. What are some problems associated with the use of MBO?

7. In what way can sensitivity training be of value to the manager?

8. How does TA help the manager communicate with and understand the subordinates? Bring into your discussion the three basic types of transactions: complementary, crossed, and ulterior.

9. Why should a company think of its personnel as an investment? Should personnel be accounted for in financial statements?

10. What is a causal variable? An intervening variable? An end-result variable? Of what value is this information to management?

11. In general, can a company improve its short-run earnings by switching from a System 4 to a System 1 management? Explain.

12. Explain why a company moving from a System 1 to a System 4 management does not experience an immediate increase in earnings.

■ SELECTED REFERENCES

"Baby Boomers Push for Power." *Business Week*, July 2, 1984, pp. 52–62.

Baird, Lloyd, and Ilan Meshoulam. "Managing Two Fits of Strategic Human Resource Management." *Academy of Management Review*, January 1988, pp. 116–28.

Baird, Lloyd, Ilan Meshoulam, and Ghislaine De Give. "Meshing Human Resources Planning with Strategic Business Planning: A Model Approach." *Personnel*, September–October 1983, pp. 14–25.

Barton, Richard F. "An MCDM Approach for Resolving Goal Conflict in MBO." *Academy of Management Review*, April 1982, pp. 231–41.

Barton-Dobenin, J., and Richard M. Hodgetts. "Management Training Programs: Who Uses Them and Why?" *Training and Development Journal*, March 1975, pp. 34–40.

Brief, A. P., and R. J. Aldag. "The Job Characteristic Inventory: An Examination." *Academy of Management Journal*, December 1978, pp. 569–670.

Briscoe, Dennis R. "Organizational Design: Dealing with the Human Constraint." *California Management Review*, Fall 1980, pp. 71–80.

Cherrington, D. M., and J. L. England. "The Desire for an Enriched Job as a Moderator of the Enrichment-Satisfaction Relationship." *Organizational Behavior and Human Performance*, February 1980, pp. 139–59.

Coll, Ann. "Job Matching Brings Out the Best in Employees." *Personnel Journal*, January 1984, pp. 54–60.

Crystal, John C., and Richard S. Deems. "Redesigning Jobs." *Training and Development Journal*, February 1983, pp. 44–46.

Frantzreb, Richard B. "Human Resource Planning: Forecasting Manpower Needs." *Personnel Journal*, November 1981, pp. 850–55.

Galosy, Julia Reid. "Meshing Human Resources Planning with Strategic Business Planning: One Company's Experience." *Personnel*, September–October 1983, pp. 26–35.

Gist, Marilyn G. "Self-Efficacy: Implications for Organizational Behavior and Human Resource Management." *Academy of Management Review*, July 1987, pp. 472–85.

Harris, Philip R., and Dorothy L. Harris. "Human Resources Management, Part 1: Charting a New Course in a New Organization, a New Society." *Personnel*, September–October 1982, pp. 11–17.

Harris, Philip R. and Dorothy L. Harris. "Human Resources Management: Charting a New Course in a New Organization, a New Society, Part 2." *Personnel*, November–December 1982, pp. 31–42.

Harvey, James L. "Nine Major Trends in HRM." *Personnel Administrator*, November 1986, pp. 102–109.

Hunsaker, Phillip L. "Strategies for Organizational Change: The Role of the Inside Change Agent." *Personnel*, September–October 1982, pp. 18–28.

Kelly, Charles. "Remedial MBO." *Business Horizons*, September–October 1983, pp. 62–67.

Kesner, Idalene, and Dan R. Dalton. "Turnover Benefits: The Other Side of the Costs' Coin." *Personnel*, September–October 1982, pp. 69–76.

Kiggundu, Moses N. "Task Interdependence and the Theory of Job Design." *Academy of Management Review*, July 1983, pp. 499–508.

Klubnik, Joan P. "Orienting New Employees." *Training and Development Journal*, April 1987, pp. 46–49.

McGarrell, Edmund J., Jr. "An Organizational System That Builds Productivity." *Personnel*, November–December 1983, pp. 32–41.

Mahoney, Francis X. "Targets, Time, and Transfer: Keys to Management Training Impact." *Personnel*, November–December 1980, pp. 25–34.

Marquardt, Michael J., and Howard Schuman. "Getting an HRD Job Abroad." *Training and Development Journal*, February 1988, pp. 25–30.

Mines, Herbert T. "Finding and Using Executive Talent." *Business Horizons*, June 1980, pp. 45–48.

Mossop, Mary Walsh. "Total Teamwork: How to Be a Leader, How to Be a Member." *Management Solutions*, August 1988, pp. 3–9.

Phillips, Jack J. "Training Programs: A Results-Oriented Model for Managing the Development of Human Resources." *Personnel*, May–June 1983, pp. 11–18.

Pierson, David A. "A Technique for Managing Creative People." *Personnel*, January–February 1983, pp. 12–26.

Pringle, Charles D., and Justin G. Longenecker. "The Ethics of MBO." *Academy of Management Review*, April 1982, pp. 305–11.

Quick, James C., Lawrence Schkade, and Mark E. Eakin. "Thinking Styles and Job Stress." *Personnel*, May 1986, pp. 44–48.

Smith, Eddie C. "Strategic Business Planning and Human Resources: Part 1." *Personnel Journal*, August 1982, pp. 606–10.

Smith, Howard R. "The Uphill Struggle for Job Enrichment." *California Management Review*, Summer 1981, pp. 33–38.

Stanislao, Joseph, and Bettie C. Stanislao. "Dealing with Resistance to Change." *Business Horizons*, July–August 1983, pp. 74–78.

Stiner, F., Jr., and Richard M. Hodgetts. "The Social Audit and the Unit of Measurement." *Virginia Accountant*, September 1975, pp. 47–51.

Stybel, Laurence J. "Linking Strategic Planning and Management Manpower Planning." *California Management Review*, Fall 1982, pp. 48–56.

Truskie, Stanley D. "Getting the Most from Management Development Programs." *Personnel Journal*, January 1982, pp. 66–68.

Whitsett, David A., and Lyle Yorks. "Looking Back at Topeka: General Foods and the Quality-of-Work-Life Experiment." *California Management Review*, Spring 1983, pp. 93–109.

■ CASE: Flextime for the Eighties

During the last five years a great deal of interest in the use of flexible work schedules has been generated. The basic idea has a number of different variations. In one the workers are allowed to come in at any time during the early to mid-morning and, depending on when they arrive, leave for home in the late afternoon or early evening. In other arrangements the employees are allowed to work thirty-two hours one week and forty-eight the next. Regardless of the specific conditions, flextime (F-T) can be distinguished by a number of different features, including the following:

Band width   This refers to the number of hours in the interval between the earliest possible starting time and the latest possible finishing time. A firm where the workers can start as early as 5:00 A.M. and finish as late as 8:00 P.M. has a greater band width than one where the hours are 7:00 A.M. and 7:00 P.M. respectively.

Core hours   These are the hours when the individual workers must be at work. In many jobs no person can arrive later than 11:00 A.M. and no one can leave before 3:00 P.M.

Flexible hours   These are the hours within which the individual can make choices about times to start and stop work. For example, the person may be allowed to come to work any time between 5:00 A.M. and 11:00 A.M. and go home after putting in eight hours—that is, any time between 1 P.M. and 7 P.M.

Banking   In some cases employees are allowed to work more than forty hours (or whatever the required number is) per week so that they can bank the surplus and use it later. In the same way people can work less than forty hours at these firms, run a deficit, and pay it back later or out of hours already in surplus.

Do flextime programs really improve worker performance and lead to higher morale and satisfaction? Although not all the studies indicate this, a large number report very positive results. For example, Barron H. Harvey and Fred Luthans studied three groups of workers. One was allowed to determine its work schedule on a daily basis (daily flextime), one was allowed to determine its schedule at the beginning of each month (staggered), and the third continued to remain with the traditional schedule (fixed). The major emphasis of the Harvey-Luthans study was to compare the effect that daily flextime and staggered hours had on employee satisfaction. They concluded that the "results support our contention that giving employees more control over jobs will have a beneficial effect. The group given daily flextime . . . experienced improved satisfaction and seemingly less absenteeism and turnover, and better performance. The staggered hours and fixed hours groups did not experience such beneficial results."[63]

Robert T. Golembiewski and Carl W. Proehl, Jr., echo these remarks. They surveyed the empirical literature on flexible work hours and concluded that:

> despite real limitations in available studies, both behavioral and attitudinal data encourage F-T applications. "Hard" data indicate that F-T is at least low-cost and may indeed imply handsome dividends on several critical organizational measures. "Soft" data strongly reinforce such a bias toward F-T applications, as seen from three organizational perspectives—that of employees, first line supervisors, and managers.[64]

Questions

1. In your own words, explain flextime.

2. In what ways do flextime programs help an organization develop its human resources? Make your answer complete.

3. What variations of flextime would you expect to find being used during the 1990s? Explain.

■ CASE: **A Liquidation of People**

When Iris Johnson became vice-president of manufacturing at the Walters Corporation in 1986, the firm had been in a downward spiral. Profits had declined from $473,000 in 1977 to just over $250,000 in fiscal 1983; return on investment during this period had dropped from 9.3 percent to 4.0 percent.

Within twenty-four months, however, Johnson turned the financial picture completely around. The accountant's report for these eight quarters revealed the following:

---

[63]Barron H. Harvey and Fred Luthans, "Flexitime: An Empirical Analysis of its Real Meaning and Impact," *MSU Business Topics*, Summer 1979, p. 36.

[64]Robert T. Golembiewski and Carl W. Proehl, Jr., "A Survey of the Empirical Literature on Flexible Workhours: Character and Consequences of a Major Innovation," *Academy of Management Review*, October 1978, p. 852.

Year	Quarter	Profit	ROI
1987	1	$ 290, 000	4.3
	2	370,000	4.6
	3	420,000	4.9
	4	550,000	6.1
1988	1	625,000	7.2
	2	750,000	8.1
	3	895,000	9.4
	4	1,050,000	10.7

Then, to the president's dismay, Johnson submitted her resignation. She had been offered a job at twice her current salary, had decided to accept it, and would be leaving by the end of the month.

With only four weeks in which to find a replacement, the company quickly put out feelers to see who might fill the position. All reports seemed to indicate that Paul Robertson, factory manager for a large eastern firm, was the ideal choice. Robertson was invited in to see the facilities and financial reports. Toward the end of his visit he and the Walters president had a chance to sit down and talk.

"Paul, you've been here for three days now. Everyone is immensely impressed with your record and we'd like you to be our new vice-president of manufacturing. What do you say?"

"I appreciate the offer, Mr. Canyon. Quite frankly, though, I've decided not to accept. I just don't want to step in and spend the next two years rebuilding the firm."

"Rebuilding? Why, we have the best books in the industry."

"True, sir. On paper you look great. But what about the fact that half of your skilled work force has quit in the last eighteen months? These people are going to have to be replaced."

"Well, yes, we have lost some people. But Iris Johnson stepped into a tough position. She had to tighten things up. Before she came, we were losing money. She made everyone start to pull their own weight."

"And in the process, she alienated what sound like your best employees. She milked your human assets just about dry. I think you've gotten just about all the earnings you're going to get out of your current work force. The way I see it, you have a major rebuilding program on your hands. The woman you think you're grateful to has actually liquidated your most important asset—your people."

Questions

1. If Robertson is correct in his analysis, how has the vice-president of manufacturing liquidated the firm's human assets? Explain.

2. Why did the firm allow this to happen? Why did the president not take corrective action before this time?

3. What must the company do now? Explain.

■ CASE: The Abrasive Manager

Many HRD programs are designed to help managers lead their people more effectively. Sometimes, however, managers need to realize that their personal style can be most responsible for their problems. One of the most common management style problems is that of the manager with an abrasive personality. Some questions that help managers to determine whether they are abrasive follow:

When you talk to others in the organization, do you try to straighten them out?
Do you need to be in full control?
Do your personal remarks take up a large percentage of time during meetings?
Do you have a need to debate?
Do you like to acquire symbols of power and status?
Are people afraid to discuss things with you?
Do you quickly rise to attacks or challenges?
Are you reluctant to give people the same privileges as you have?
Do people think and speak of you as cold and distant?
Do you see yourself as more competent than your boss and/or your peers—and let them know it by the way you act?

Yes answers to seven or more of these indicate an abrasive personality. Attention toward identifying abrasive people and having their superiors work with them to overcome this problem has increased in recent years. If this proves ineffective, the firm or the individual might seek outside professional help.

Questions

1. How many of the questions in this case did you answer in the affirmative? What does this tell you about yourself?

2. In addition to these questions, what others would you ask in helping identify an abrasive personality?

3. Which of the HRD programs in this chapter could be helpful to a superior who is working to reduce a subordinate manager's abrasiveness? Explain your reasoning.

■ CASE: Making the Work More Meaningful

There are many ways that firms try to achieve peak performance from their people. At General Foods (GF), the company makes wide use of interfunctional work teams. These teams consist of individuals from a variety of different areas including marketing, finance, and production.

Each member of the work team remains a member indefinitely, and is expected to contribute to all aspects of that business. For example, the financial person on the Minute Rice team contributes ideas for advertising, strategy, package design, and product quality, as well as financial areas. This approach tends to be job enriching and stimulates team participation and involvement. Other benefits of the interfunctional work team approach include:

- More sharing and integration of individual skills and resources.
- Untapping and use of unknown member resources.
- More stimulation, energy, and endurance by members working jointly than is usual when individuals work alone.
- More emotional support among team members.
- Better performance, in terms of quantity and quality, more wins, more innovation.
- More ideas for use in problem solving.
- More commitment and ownership by members around the team goals, higher motivation.
- More sustained effort directed at team goals.
- More team member satisfaction, higher motivation, and more fun.
- The sense of being a winner, greater confidence, and the ability to achieve more.

GF has found that team approaches are important vehicles for both building and maintaining member loyalty. The group gives the individuals a focal point for identification. The members feel that what they are doing is important and, the higher group morale creates an environment that is enjoyable, exciting, and rewarding. In ensuring that this happens, GF focuses on five specific areas.

First, group goals are clearly set and agreed upon by the members. Second, the group is comprised of individuals with a diversity of skills and perspectives. Third, the leader has a broad, multifunctional viewpoint. Fourth, rules and norms of behavior are openly discussed and agreed upon, and a climate of trust, mutual respect, and innovation is fostered. Fifth, team members are recognized and rewarded for their contributions.

While a team approach such as that at GF will not work for every company, it can be particularly effective under the right conditions. In particular, it helps create the desired QWL for generating the desired productivity and financial results.

Questions

1. Do the team members feel that this interfunctional approach creates an enriched job? Explain.

2. Which of the core job dimensions has GF used to create the desired work outcomes? Be complete in your answer.

3. How could GF periodically evaluate its human resources in order to determine the ongoing value of interfunctional team approach? Explain.

Source: Marc Bassin, "Teamwork at General Foods: New & Improved," *Personnel Journal,* May 1988, pp. 62–68.

■ SELF-FEEDBACK EXERCISE: Evaluating the Motivating Potential Score of Your Own Job

Answer the questions in this self-feedback quiz based on the job you currently hold. If you are not employed, think of the last job you held. If you have never worked, think of the job you would like to get upon completion of your education. (Be realistic in your choice.)

Part I

Answer each of these statements as objectively as possible. Use the following continuum in choosing your response:

1	2	3	4	5	6	7
Very little		A moderate amount			A great deal	

_____ a. How much autonomy does your job allow you in terms of deciding how to go about doing your work?

_____ b. To what degree does your job involve doing a whole or identifiable piece of work as opposed to a small part of an overall piece of work that is then completed by someone else?

_____ c. To what degree does your job allow you to use a variety of skills and talents as opposed to doing the same routine over and over again?

_____ d. How important or significant is your job in terms of its effect on the lives or well-being of other people?

_____ e. To what degree does your job itself (as opposed to other workers or your boss) provide you with feedback regarding how well you are doing.

Part II

Read each of the statements below and indicate the degree to which each is an accurate or inaccurate description of your job. Use the following scale in making the description.

1	Very inaccurate.	5	Slightly accurate.
2	Mostly inaccurate.	6	Mostly accurate.
3	Slightly inaccurate.	7	Very accurate.
4	Uncertain.		

_____   1. My job requires me to use a number of different complex or high-level skills.

_____   2. My job is set up so that I have the opportunity to do an entire piece of work from beginning to end.

_____   3. The work I do provides me the opportunity to determine how well I am doing.

_____   4. My job is complex and nonrepetitive.

_____   5. My job performance affects a lot of other people.

_____   6. My job allows me the opportunity to use personal initiative and judgment in doing the work.

_____   7. My job provides me the chance to finish the work I begin.

_____   8. My job provides me a large amount of feedback regarding how well I am doing.

_____   9. My job gives me considerable opportunity for both independence and freedom in carrying out the work.

_____   10. My job is very important and/or significant in the broader scheme of things.

Go back and make sure you have answered each question or statement. Then enter your answers below in the appropriate place noting that the letters refer to your answers to Part I and the numbers refer to your answers to Part II.

A. Skill Variety	B. Task Identity	C. Task Significance
c. _____	b. _____	d. _____
1. _____	2. _____	5. _____
4. _____	7. _____	10. _____
Total _____	Total _____	Total _____
D. Autonomy	E. Feedback	
a. _____ ´	e. _____	
6. _____	3. _____	
9. _____	8. _____	
Total _____	Total _____	

Interpretation

The descriptions of each of the above five core job dimensions were provided in the chapter. Should you be unsure of what any of them mean, go back and reread them. Now compute your motivating potential score (MPS) by first averaging the above scores by dividing *each* total by three. The highest total you can now have for each area is seven. Use your five averaged numbers to complete the following MPS formula:

$$\text{MPS} = \left[\frac{\text{Skill Variety} + \text{Task Identity} + \text{Task Significance}}{3} \right] \times (\text{Autonomy}) \times (\text{Feedback})$$

$$\text{MPS} = \left[\frac{\underline{\quad} + \underline{\quad} + \underline{\quad}}{3} \right] \times (\quad\quad) \times (\quad\quad)$$

The national average MPS score for all jobs is approximately 130. How high is yours in relation to this?

Now plot your five core job dimension scores on the following graph. Notice that we have placed the national average for all jobs on the graph, so you have a point of reference in determining how each of your scores compares.

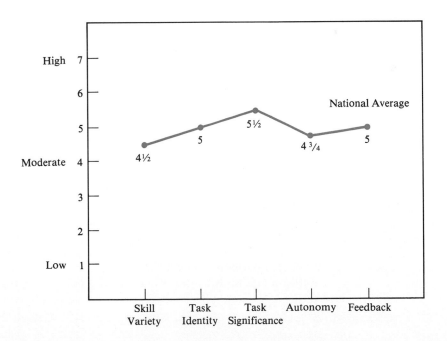

■ COMPREHENSIVE CASE: The New President's Dilemma

The Situation

Things have really been a mess at the Longworth Company. Over the last three years labor turnover has averaged 23 percent annually, and the union has filed five major grievances against the firm. A four-month strike occurred last year, and there is a dissatisfaction in the management ranks. If the present rate of turnover among these people continues, it will exceed 31 percent by year's end.

It was because of developments like this that Bedford Charles was just chosen to take over as president of Longworth. The board of directors looked Charles's record over very carefully. He had been president of a large firm in a different, but closely related, industry. While there, he had taken a firm with similar problems and turned it around and put it in the profit column within twenty-four months of his appointment as CEO. The Longworth board is hoping that he can do the same thing at Longworth.

As part of the agreement, the board agreed to allow Charles to bring his three immediate subordinates with him. "We are part of a management team," he told the board. "I would never agree to come to Longworth without them. I do not feel the company has time for me to get settled in and choose a management team, and without one there is little likelihood that the firm can be saved." The board agreed, three weeks ago, and Charles took over as Longworth's president.

His first step was to interview some of the managers in the organization. In particular, he wanted to find out exactly what the managers thought were the firm's worst problems. Charles also spent some time talking to several groups and the outgoing president. The latter had been fired by the board because his performance had been poor. Charles's logic in wanting to talk to the man was, "This will provide me with some insights regarding how *not* to manage the firm. Also, there may be some areas where he has better insight than I do. Perhaps there are some groups within the firm who are determined to prevent progress at any price. The old president could help me identify these people. Also, he might have tried to implement some ideas that should have produced good results. I would like to get an idea of what he wanted to do but did not get time to do. Likewise, would he be willing to tell me any things he did that went wrong? Whatever he tells me will give me a perspective on the company's problems."

Charles decided to talk also with the union people to get insights into labor-management problems. Why did the four-month strike take place? Charles knows what the management's explanation is, but he would like to know what the union's position is.

Charles made up his mind to talk to the workers in the production plant and to the salespeople because he feels that they, too, can provide him with useful information. The production people are unionized and could be expected to tell him a story similar to that of the union, but they might also provide some new insights as to what the overall problems are and how they can be handled. The salespeople could give him an idea of some of the problems faced by non-union employees who work at the lower levels of the organization.

Charles felt that he would be able to formulate a plan of action for resolving the situation after he had the opportunity to interview all of these people and find out what has been going on. The following is a summary of what he learned from each of the individuals and groups he interviewed in this fact-gathering mission.

Management Team

Charles was able to talk to all top managers in the firm within the first week of his arrival. He also managed to meet and have short discussions with some management team members at the middle and lower levels of the hierarchy. From the top people, he learned that the previous president apparently did not really have a plan of action. The remaining managers basically believed that the organization should be able to run itself. Therefore, instead of working with the top managers as a team, the old president had allowed each department to go off on its own. This meant that the finance department had to try to make order out of the chaos. Twice during the first year of the old president's tenure the company had a cash flow problem. In both cases this was caused by the president's approval of machinery and equipment purchases without prior approval from the finance department.

Although most of the managers felt that the former president lacked leadership ability, they agreed that he jumped in with both feet when something caught his interest. For example, there was a discussion about whether to buy a new computer. While the finance department opposed it on the grounds that it was not cost effective, the head of computer services prevailed on the president to order its purchase. The president personally supervised the acquisition and placement of the machine. Many of the managers disagreed with this leadership style, feeling that the president's job was too important to be taken up with such minor matters as worrying about the delivery of a piece of hardware.

When Charles summarized everything the managers had told him about the past president, he concluded that the individual had just two leadership behaviors. The first was to be a laissez-faire manager who essentially did nothing. This seemed to be his preferred style. Second, though, he did sometimes turn on, and when he decided to take action, he assumed many of the System 1 leader characteristics. He simply pushed his way through and got those things accomplished that he wanted done.

The other major finding that came out of Charles's discussions with the managers was that the overall climate in the organization was poor. This was the result of the ex-president's continual rough manner in union negotiations. This abrasiveness had led to ill will between the two groups. In the minds of many managers, the strike resulted directly from the president's refusal to budge from his initial offer to the union. He had simply refused to come back to the bargaining table; to him, that was a matter of personal freedom. The union eventually made the firm come back to the bargaining table and hammer out an agreement by taking the company to court and getting a court ruling in its favor. In the process, the firm lost four months' productivity that year as well as $3.5 million of gross profit. The president retaliated by announcing that new machinery and equipment was going to be purchased and, therefore, some of the work force would be let go. This decision was in accord with the labor contract, in the president's interpretation, and he proceeded to implement his threat. "It soon became a battle of us versus them," said one manager, "and we were finding that they were not going to let us run all over them. If the board of directors had not stepped in and gotten rid of the president, we would have had another prolonged strike."

Some of the managers felt that the president was really a nice person but one who was unable to put up with disagreement or confrontation. "He wanted the union to go along with his proposed contract, and when they didn't, he became nasty with them. This is pretty surprising when you realize that he had a real good track record up to the time he took over here. In fact, before we hired him, we interviewed a number of candidates and did a background search on all of them. He was known by his associates as a very human relations-oriented guy. It just goes to show. Sometimes you can get fooled."

The Union

The basic problem evidenced in Charles's discussions with the union people was that the company has not lived up to the terms of its contract. They agreed that the new work procedures that had been introduced and the new machinery that had been installed during the past year were not in violation of the contract. However, the contract had a clause which said that no employee would be dismissed "except for just cause." The past president had argued that, with new machinery, there could be a cutback in the work force. In fact, he pointed out that it would be necessary to reduce the work force by fifteen people in order to meet the bank payments for the machines.

The union responded that these people should be found jobs elsewhere in the firm. However, the ex-president simply scorned their arguments and in so doing precipitated the strike. At present, the union is waiting to see what Charles will do. Ten of the fifteen people who had been terminated had been rehired after the strike, but feelings of anger and distrust are still strong among the union workers.

In addition, the union people told Charles that the management is not to be trusted. They disagree with top management's assessment that the president was responsible for all the problems that occurred. They consider top management staff to be responsible also. "They advised the president to do a lot of things he did, and they should be replaced just like him," said one of the union officials. "Unless you begin by cleaning up your own group, you are never going to get on good working terms with the employees."

The Salespeople

The salespeople's discontent could be traced back to one specific source: disagreement over their remuneration. Five years ago all salespeople were on a combination plan of salary plus commission. However, the company decided that it would be better for both parties if the salaries were raised and the commissions dropped.

Initially, this was fine with the salespeople because the salary levels were set so high that most of them could not ever have hoped to earn this amount of money in a normal sales year. However, as inflation began to increase and the purchasing power of the dollar declined, management did not increase sales salaries accordingly. At the end of the first three years, the salespeople began to complain that they were now earning less than they would have been under the old salary-and-commission plan. In fact, while the rest of the workers, who were unionized, received an average annual increase of 8 percent during these three years, salespeople received only 4 percent. The company argued that the salespeople were given very high salaries when the old plan was scrapped and that they therefore should not be upset. The firm, management stated, was now simply allowing the other workers to catch up.

An additional problem in sales was the reorganization, during the past year, of the sales areas. Some salespeople were given much larger territories than they had previously had, while others were brought into the office and given managerial jobs. Neither group was pleased with this decision. Charles determined that only about 10 percent of the sales force planned, when he took over, to remain with the company for the next two years unless some changes were made in the current compensation policy. Also, he decided to have one of his assistants conduct a comparison study to see how well the average salaries of the salespeople compare with those of competitive firms.

The Workers

The workers themselves feel they are well represented by the union and the number of new gripes they raised, in contrast to those Charles heard from the union representatives, was minimal. However, they raised two issues that he had not heard previously.

The first was related to the assembly-line people. Currently, there is an assembly-line operation that has each individual putting together one or two parts of a small hand tool and then passing it on to the next person. The line workers believe that they would be more efficient if they could each assemble the entire hand tool. Time spent in passing the work from one person to the next could be saved, and the workers feel they would like the job a lot more if they could personally finish an entire hand tool by themselves.

The second issue was that of flextime. Many of the workers feel that since they do not work on the assembly-line operations, there is no need for them to be in the plant by 8:00 A.M. "Why not let us show up by 10:00 A.M., put in our eight hours, and then go home?" one of them said. "That way I could drop my kids at school, have a leisurely breakfast, and come in here wide awake and ready to work." Other workers echoed those sentiments.

The Past President

The past president was the last individual Charles talked with. This man had been busy interviewing with other firms for a job and had not had time to meet with him previously. In essence, the former president did not tell Charles much that coincided with what the others had said. The president felt that the workers were basically lazy and in need of constant control. "If you take your eye off them for a minute, they goof off," he told Charles. The ex-president also felt that the union was continually looking for ways to break its contract with the company. It had a large strike fund built up, and the recently fired president believed the union representatives had called for last year's strike in order to spend some of this money as well as convince the workers that they had their best interests in mind. With understandable sarcasm, the jobless executive said, "If you don't call a strike every now and then, the membership begins to think you don't love them. And look at the results. In the recent union election every single member of their team was reelected. How do you like that? They got the workers to spend part of their strike fund and reelect them as well. If you ask me, the workers simply like to be led around like a bunch of sheep. They don't question what the union reps tell them. They simply like to believe that it is an 'us or them' situation, and they are delighted to take it out on us. To listen to the union tell it, management is directly and solely responsible for everything that has gone wrong around here since Day One."

The former president also told Charles that without his get-tough style, the union would have run the company into the ground years before: "Don't trust them for a minute. Also, keep the top management staff I put together. Believe me, those guys can be relied upon when the going gets tough." Charles promised his predecessor that he would think about it.

Making a Decision

Now the time has come for Charles to make some tough decisions. He has to decide what should be done in resolving the conflicts that exist both within and among these various organizational groups. He believes that the situation is not so basically bad that it cannot be saved. However, he also knows that it is going to take a very well-thought-out approach. The last thing Charles wants to do is to make some major decisions that turn out to be wrong. Although he would like more time to study the facts, Charles has decided that he will have a plan of action formulated within a week. With it, he is going to begin the process of trying to put the company back together again.

Questions

1. What behavioral problems have led to the present state of affairs at the Longworth Company? Make your answer complete, and refer to the text as widely as possible.

2. In order of importance, rank the problem areas at Longworth and sketch out recommendations for each. How would you suggest the president deal with each major issue?

3. What other recommendations would you make to the president to ensure that such problems do not recur? Explain.

PART 5

THE FUTURE OF MANAGEMENT THEORY

It is very useful to have schools of management thought as a framework in studying modern management. However, it is necessary for the student of management to understand that some topics do not fit neatly into such a framework. The subjects to be examined here in Part 5 are the current status of management theory (especially as that is related to systems theory), social responsibility, and international business.

Chapter 16 begins with a discussion of the systems school of thought. This is followed by an examination of both general systems theory and applied systems concepts. Next, attention is focused on the general applicability of the systems approach for the practicing manager, with primary consideration given to viewing the organization as an open system. Then the three levels of management in the hierarchy are examined in systems terms. Finally, the chapter reviews the current status and future development given to a contingency theory of management.

Chapter 17 devotes attention to social responsibility. The modern business firm realizes that it must be responsible, not only to the needs of its customers and workers but also to the public at large. This chapter discusses equal opportunity, ecology, and consumerism, with major consideration given to the challenges they present to business.

Chapter 18 focuses on the challenges and opportunities facing those firms that decide to expand their operations into the international arena. Particular attention will be devoted to evaluating the possible advantages and disadvantages associated with going overseas; the various issues in organizing, staffing, and controlling such an undertaking; and the role of the multinational American corporation in the international economic arena.

Chapter 19 examines the future of management. In this chapter consideration is given to reviewing the contributions of early classic management theory, discussing current developments in management theory, and describing some major trends in management including the continued focus of key result areas, the challenge of managing talent in a work force, and the continuing trends of professionalism in management.

CHAPTER 16

Management Theory: Current Status and Future Direction

The current major schools of management thought have now been presented. The question remaining is: Where does management theory go from here? The answer, of course, is that no one knows for sure. However, two major lines of thought currently have the greatest support. The first contends that the three schools—process, quantitative, and behavioral—will merge into a systems school. One group of authors has summarized the position in this way:

> Although the process, behavioral, and quantitative approaches have been widely adopted, a growing group of practitioners and academicians have felt that another approach—the systems approach—would encompass the subsystems emanating from each of the other approaches.[1]

---

[1]Max S. Wortman, Jr., and Fred Luthans, eds., *Emerging Concepts in Management,* 2nd ed. (New York: Macmillan, 1975), p. 319.

597

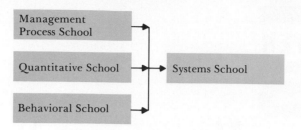

FIGURE 16-1   The Future Direction of Management Theory: One View

If this is true, the development of modern management theory can be represented by Figure 16-1.

There seems to be more support, however, for the second point of view, which holds that a systems school of thought already exists and that the trend is now toward a situational, or contingency, theory of management. This thinking is represented by Figure 16-2.

If one keeps in mind that Figures 16-1 and 16-2 represent only two major points of view and that many scholars and practitioners have their own ideas (see Communication in Action: Theory in Retreat), it should be evident that there is currently much disagreement about the future direction of management theory.

However, one thing does seem clear. Any examination of the current status and future direction of management theory must consider the subject of systems. Such questions as these—What is a system? How is the concept valuable in management theory? Is there a systems school of thought?—all merit consideration. The goal of this chapter is to deal with these questions and, in the process, to offer some general guidance about the direction management theory is likely to take in the next ten years. Attention will first be focused on what some people call the systems school and on the issues of what the basic systems philosophy is and why it has not been discussed

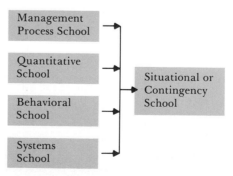

FIGURE 16-2   The Future Direction of Management Theory: A Second View

Management theory seems to be somewhat in disorder, according to some experts in the field. One of these, Joseph McGuire, a well-respected authority in the field, contends that there has not been very much progress in the last twenty-five years. Why not? Numerous reasons can be cited. Professor McGuire has noted three important ones, all directly related to communication.

First, the area of management theory has increasingly become the province of people who have been educated in management schools by management professors. In recent years, practitioners have not made many contributions to the field while professors have. As academics began to dominate the management classrooms, they slowly squeezed out the practitioners. Consider some of the early contributors to management and their background: Taylor, an engineer; Fayol, a mining executive; Munsterberg, an industrial psychologist; Urwick, a management consultant; Barnard, a utility president. Few management professors are also active managers in industry.

Second, there has been a movement toward scientism in management theory and an emphasis on research methodology rather than on theoretical substance or managerial relevance. Many of those who teach management know about it only from what they read or the research they conduct. They lack direct experience and, as a result, present only one side of the picture. When the very popular *Academy of Management Journal* first appeared in 1958, the publication was devoted to vocational and professional values. Today the *Journal* accepts only empirically based articles that require research and analysis. Practicing managers not only do not contribute, they do not read it.

Third, there has been a shift away from economics as the most important discipline underlying management theory and toward the behavioral sciences. The basic, efficiency, profit-oriented, productivity concerns of early management teachers have given way to a more psychologically based, nebulous, nonprofit-oriented focus. Those who helped found business schools in America would be at a loss to explain some of the current trends.

These developments show that management theory has moved from practical considerations to abstract ones. What will the future hold? The answer is: a move in the opposite direction. Theory is fine as far as it goes, but it is no substitute for effective management practices. More and more university professors are now realizing that if what they teach is not applicable or useful in the real world, it is of limited value. The best schools are those which blend management theory with management practice. They communicate with both students and practitioners of management.

Source: Some of these ideas can be found in Joseph W. McGuire, "Management Theory: Retreat to the Academy," *Business Horizons*, July–August 1982, pp. 31–37.

previously. Then the general area of the application of systems to organizations will be examined, followed by a discussion of management theory in the future.

When you have finished this chapter you should be able to:

1. Discuss the systems school of management.
2. Explain why successful organizations have to function like open systems.
3. Explain how adaptive and maintenance mechanisms are important to organizational survival.
4. Describe the three levels of managerial systems and the types of managers who function at each level.
5. Give your opinion of where management theory appears to be heading, incorporating into your answers the concept of a contingency theory of management.

THE SYSTEMS SCHOOL

Some researchers consider that the systems school is a new school of management thought that emerged sometime in the 1960s. Although this is open to question, there are many computer and systems analysts who believe that systems theory has now developed to the stage where the formation of a systems school is justified. Whether or not they are right, it is useful for the student of management to have a general idea of what is meant by the term *systems school*. In essence, two major areas merit consideration. The first, general systems theory, contains the conceptual and philosophical bases of the systems approach.

General Systems Theory

Perhaps the key word in the vocabulary of this school is *system*. Although many definitions are available, one of the most succinct is that put forth by Fremont E. Kast and James E. Rosenzweig: A system is an organized, unitary whole composed of two or more interdependent parts, components, or subsystems and delineated by identifiable boundaries from its environmental suprasystem.[2]

Systems school advocates see all variables in the environment as mutually dependent and interactive. Before the importance of the systems concept to management is examined, some attention should be focused on what is called general systems theory. Systems theorists believe that much of systems management theory originated with general systems theory. In addition, an examination of this topic provides a basis for analyzing other important management related areas, including the movement of individuals into and

Many systems management concepts originated with general systems theory.

---

[2]Fremont E. Kast and James E. Rosenzweig, *Organization and Management,* 3rd ed. (New York: McGraw-Hill, 1979), p. 18.

out of the system; the interaction of individuals with their environment; the interaction of individuals with each other; and the general growth and stability problems of systems.[3]

Systems Levels

Perhaps the most famous article written on systems theory is "General Systems Theory—The Skeleton of Science" by Kenneth Boulding.[4] In this article Boulding put forth a classification of the nine hierarchical levels in the universe. He described them as follows:

1. The first level can be called the level of *frameworks* and represents a static structure. Examples include geography and the anatomy of the universe.

2. The next level could be referred to as the level of *clockworks* and is characterized by a simple, dynamic system with predetermined, necessary motions. The solar system is an illustration.

3. Next is the level of the control mechanism of cybernetic system, nicknamed the *thermostat* level. The homeostasis model, so important in physiology, is an illustration.

4. Then comes the open system of the self-maintaining structure, which can be called the level of the *cell*. At this level, life and reproduction enter the scheme.

Boulding's system classification scheme.

5. The fifth level is the *genetic-societal level.* This is typified by the plant, which dominates the empirical world of the botanist.

6. Next comes the *animal* kingdom. It is characterized by teleological behavior, increased mobility and self-awareness.

7. Then comes the *human* level. In addition to possessing nearly all the characteristics of animal systems, the individual is also capable of employing language and symbols.

8. The eighth level is that of *social organizations.* At this level, concern is given to the content and meaning of messages, the nature and dimensions of value systems, the transcription of images into historical records, the subtle symbolizations of art, music and poetry, and the complex gamut of human emotions.

9. The final level of the structure is *transcendental systems.* These are the ultimates, the absolutes and the inescapable unknowables, which exhibit systematic structure and relationship.[5]

---

[3]Kenneth E. Boulding, "General Systems Theory—The Skeleton of Science," *Management Science,* April 1956, pp. 200–202.
[4]Ibid., pp. 197–208.
[5]Ibid., pp. 202–205.

A cursory review of these levels indicates that the first three are concerned with physical or mechanical systems and that they therefore have basic value for people in the physical sciences, such as astronomy and physics. The next three levels deal with biological systems and are thus of interest to biologists, botanists, and zoologists. The last three are concerned with human and social systems and are of importance to the arts, the humanities, the social sciences, and, in a more specialized way, modern management.

This classification scheme is important in understanding the systems school because it contains the basic theme of the systems approach: all phenomena, whether in the universe at large or in a business organization, are related in some way.

A second contribution of Boulding's article is the emphasis it places on integration. One of his major contentions is that specific disciplines are too narrow in their focus, whereas a general approach lacks substantive content.

> Somewhere however between the specific that has no meaning and the general that has no content there must be . . . an optimum degree of generality. It is the contention of the General Systems Theorists that this optimum degree of generality in theory is not always reached by the particular sciences.[6]

Integration of knowledge from many fields is encouraged.

In order to overcome this deficiency, Boulding recommends an integration of knowledge from many fields. "Because, in a sense, each level incorporates all those below it, much valuable information and [many] insights can be obtained by applying low-level systems to high-level subject matter."[7] The thinking of these systems theorists, however, is not confined to such an esoteric area as general systems theory. They have also put forth some concepts that have practical application.

Applied Systems Concepts

Proponents of a systems school like to point to useful management tools and techniques that apply the systems concept. Some of these ideas, such as operations research, simulation, PERT, and the critical path method, are directly related to management decision models.

Several management decision models came from general systems theory. The systems approach takes the "big picture" view.

Another set of tools and techniques can be placed under the heading of the systems approach. These are tools that help the manager choose a course of action by analyzing objectives and comparing costs, risks, and payoffs associated with the alternative strategies. By employing a big picture, or systems, approach, the manager can evaluate the interrelationships of all factors under consideration. One such approach, discussed in Chapter 6, is

---

[6]Ibid., pp. 197–98.

[7]Ibid., p. 207.

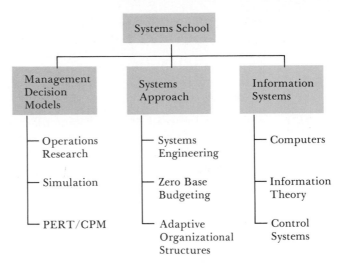

FIGURE 16-3   A Classification of the Systems School

Source: Adapted from Richard Schonberger, "A Taxonomy of Systems Management," *Nebraska Journal of Economics and Business,* Spring 1973.

adaptive organization structures. Another, discussed in Chapter 7, is zero-base budgeting. A third, which will be covered in this chapter, is systems engineering.

Information systems can be valuable.

The third set of systems tools and techniques is in the category of information systems. These are systems designed to provide managers with knowledge and task-specific data useful in carrying out their jobs. Such examples as computers, information theory, and control systems have been discussed in Chapter 10.

These three main types of tools and techniques all provide illustrations of how the systems concept has proved useful to business. They are classified in Figure 16-3.

A School or a Subsystem?

Is there a systems school of management?

The information presented so far indicates that the systems ideas may well be sufficiently different from those of the process, quantitative, and behavioral approaches to justify the naming of a fourth school of management thought. Critics, however, argue that the systems concept is already being used by the three major schools. For example, many of the ideas in Figure 16-3 have already been examined in the preceding eleven chapters. In addition, process advocates argue that management theory consists of planning, organizing, and controlling processes; each is thus an interrelated subsystem of the overall management system. Behavioralists claim that for years they have been viewing the organization as a group of interrelated formal and informal systems. Quantitative school proponents feel that the systems school is really a part of their own; certainly that was how the school was presented in Chapters 3 and 10 of this text. Systems analysts, computer programmers, and so on, were all placed in the quantitative school, and there is a good reason for this. As one researcher has noted:

> Starting in about 1970, the quantitative approach turned away from emphasis on narrow operations research techniques toward a broader perspective of management science. The management science approach incorporates quantitative decision techniques and model building as in the OR approach, but it also incorporates computerized information systems and operations management. This latter emphasis in the quantitative approach marked the return toward a more broadly based management theory.[8]

The systems concept has general value for management.

Is the systems approach, then, sufficiently different to justify a new school; or is it really a subsystem of one or more of the current approaches? For the purposes of this text the systems approach will be considered a part of the quantitative area.

Yet the systems concept itself is too important to be dropped without further elaboration. It contains many useful ideas for the student of management. One of these is the technique of viewing the organization as an open system.

THE ORGANIZATION AS AN OPEN SYSTEM

Open systems constantly interact with their external environments.

When the planning process was discussed in Chapter 4, the areas of environmental analysis and forecasting were examined. Likewise, in Chapter 5, when the organizing process was reviewed, common forms of departmentalization were examined. However, when these processes are analyzed from a systems approach, the organization is seen as operating in an open system, constantly interacting with its external environment. These *open systems* are characterized by flexible equilibrium, as depicted in Figure 16-4. They are continually receiving external inputs, which in turn are being transformed into outputs. Information on the adequacy of the output is fed back into the system for purposes of adjustment and correction; all this is shown in the model in Figure 16-4.

One common open system, familiar to all, is the biological system. In the case of fish, for example, the input could be food, which is transformed into energy and results in healthy and perhaps larger fish. If one wished to go further into the fish system, changes could be made in the environment. For

---

[8]Fred Luthans, ''The Contingency Theory of Management,'' *Business Horizons,* June 1973, p. 68.

FIGURE 16-4   An Open System

example, one might add warm water to the tank and see how the fish adapt to the new surroundings. In both cases, external inputs are introduced into the process and transformed into some kind of outputs.

The same process can be applied to a business organization. For example, a host of economic resources serve as inputs—money, machines, material, and information. In systems theory thinking, these can be combined in some fashion (organization process) for the purpose of attaining certain output, as seen in Figure 16-5.

This basic model can be made more sophisticated by breaking down the organizational process into some preliminary design—for example, marketing, production, and finance departments; such a process is illustrated in Figure 16-6. In this illustration, the relationships between each of the departments and (1) the external environment, (2) the other two departments, and (3) the organization at large become clearer.

Adaptive and Maintenance Mechanisms

Two other important systems concepts useful in analyzing open systems are adaptive and maintenance structures. In an open system, the organization must be able to adapt. At the same time, however, it must maintain a relative state of balance. Two mechanisms are thus in operation. The first, *adaptive mechanisms*, encourage response to the external and internal environments. The second, *maintenance mechanisms*, attempt to stop the system from changing so rapidly that it is thrown out of balance. While the two mechanisms may sometimes be in conflict, both are vital to an organization's

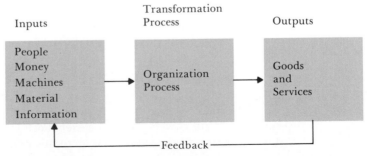

FIGURE 16-5   The Organization as an Open System

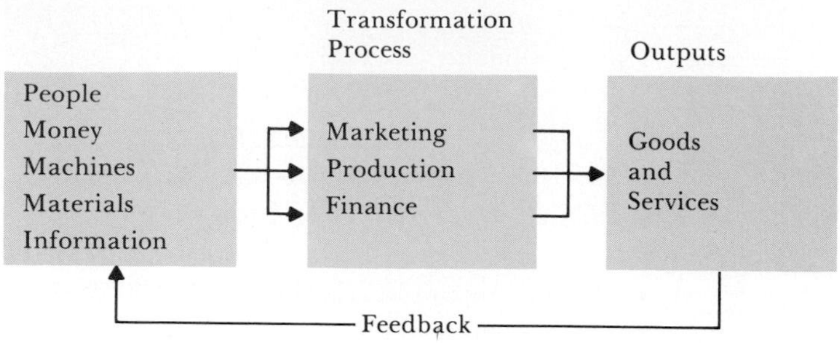

FIGURE 16-6   A More Refined Design of an Open System

survival. However, there are problems which arise in the use of both adaptive and maintenance mechanisms.

Adaptive mechanisms lead to change.

Adaptive forces lead to change and keep the organization viable, but they can also create tension and stress. For example, consider the case of a business firm that wishes to hire a junior accountant. The company needs the person to help handle the increase in accounts that has occurred over the last year. It turns out, however, that the starting salary for such an accountant is higher than that of some lower-level managers who have been with the firm for three years. The company must hire the accountant if it is to keep up, but doing so may create anxiety among the established management personnel. Although this may be a natural reaction, it illustrates the problems associated with adapting to environmental conditions.

Maintenance mechanisms are conservative influences.

Maintenance forces are conservative influences that work to prevent disequilibrium. The problem is that they may stunt an organization's growth by encouraging timidity when boldness is needed. In addition, excessive attention to maintenance factors can result in a breakdown of the open system. In Figure 16-6, this process could begin if the firm decided not to hire the new accountant. By choosing to maintain present conditions, the company would fail to adapt to its external environment. If it continued to ignore developments in the external arena, concentrating all of its attention on maintaining intracompany equilibrium, the firm would become a closed system. When this occurs, the business faces the danger of entropy.

Entropy and Contrived Adaptivity

Closed systems are characterized by entropy.

One of the characteristics of a closed system is entropy. This term originated in thermodynamics, and it refers to the tendency of a closed system to move toward a chaotic, random, or inert state. Webster defines entropy as "the ultimate state reached in the degradation of the matter and energy of the universe."[9] All closed physical systems are subject to this force of entropy. Over a period of time the force increases and, ultimately, the system stops.

---

[9]*Webster's Third New International Dictionary*, s. v. "entropy."

Since a closed network has no external inputs, the system has no real hope for survival. Eventually, entropy will take its toll.

In open biological and social systems, however, entropy can be arrested and may even be transformed, through external inputs, into negative entropy. Biological systems, at least in the short run, provide a good illustration. Drawing upon the resources in their surroundings, organisms are able to survive for a period of time. For most humans, food, clothing, and shelter are the basic resources. As one ages, increased attention is given to medicine. Eventually, however, death occurs, for even biological systems are subject to deterioration.

Social systems are contrived.

Social systems, however, are another matter; they are not mechanical or biological, they are contrived. Human beings establish them for a particular purpose and although the founding individuals may die, others can take their place and keep the system alive. As Daniel Katz and Robert L. Kahn note:

> Social structures are essentially contrived systems. People invent the complex pattern of behavior that we call social structure, and people create social structure by enacting those patterns of behavior. Many properties of social systems derive from these essential facts. As human inventions, social systems are imperfect. They can come apart at the seams overnight, but they can also outlast by centuries the biological organisms that originally created them. The cement which holds them together is essentially psychological rather than biological. Social systems are anchored in the attitudes, perceptions, beliefs, motivations, habits, and expectations of human beings.[10]

In order for the social system to continue, however, there must be the proper balance between maintenance and adaptive forces. Maintenance forces are motivated toward maintaining stability and predictability within the organization. They work to preserve a state of equilibrium. These forces, for example, encourage the organization to make no appreciable shifts in the current pattern of activities. If the company wants to sell more goods and services, it should work toward getting current customers to buy more. In short, maintenance forces urge the organization to maintain the status quo. On the other hand are adaptive forces, which are pushing the organization to respond to external environmental factors such as changes in the market-place. Rather than trying to sell more goods and services to the same customers, these forces encourage an expansion of market activities by offering new products and services in new market niches. Adaptive forces encourage the organization to generate appropriate responses to external conditions.[11]

---

[10]Daniel Katz and Robert L. Kahn, *The Social Psychology of Organizations,* 2nd ed. (New York: Wiley, 1978), p. 37.

[11]Ibid., chap. 4.

These systems concepts—flexible equilibrium, adaptive mechanisms, maintenance mechanisms, entropy, and contrived adaptivity—are all useful in understanding the truly dynamic nature of the modern organization. It is important to realize, however, that an effective organization can also employ these concepts in maintaining a viable, adaptive, ongoing organization system.

TOTALLY ADAPTIVE ORGANIZATION SYSTEMS

Adaptive organizations can survive indefinitely.

Total systems design has great promise.

The organization is a man-made system, capable of indefinite survival if the proper balance between maintenance and adaptive forces can be attained. Figure 16-7 provides an illustration of a totally adaptive business organization system. The figure shows how marketing and production activities can be carried on in the attainment of organizational goals. The finance department and the rest of the enterprise are represented in the boxes entitled "Current State of the Organization," indicating that the decisions made by both marketing and production depend on conditions in the remainder of the organization. A control process is also built into the model which will, in turn, lead to a redesign of the marketing and/or production systems should disequilibrium occur. The model adapts itself to changing conditions by continuously contrasting internal and external environmental conditions and the effect of both on the goals being pursued.

The concept of total systems design is not, of course, restricted to business organizations. It can be applied to such diverse activities as police work and city planning as long as the total system is examined. Any attempt to deal with the organization on a micro-level can have disastrous effects because all input factors are not being considered. For example, in police work the objective is to prevent crime. One of the best ways to do this is to concentrate resources on high-crime areas and thereby discourage potential criminals as well as apprehend those who have committed crimes. This can be done by feeding information about people and living conditions in the city into a computer which can then analyze the data and provide relevant information to the police regarding how to organize their forces.

Various cities have used this basic approach in attempts to identify trouble spots. For example, teams of mathematicians, economists, physicists, political scientists, and sociologists can be employed as "idea people," to construct a mathematical model of a city. Then, after the environment of the metropolis is simulated, a computer can be used to analyze the results and identify those sectors of the city where problems are most likely to occur. Through the use of employment data, living conditions, and other social factors, it has been possible to pinpoint such problems as high crime areas, locales where social services are required, and neighborhoods which are becoming overly crowded and in need of assistance.

Business firms also make wide use of adaptive organization systems. Henry Mintzberg has noted that there are a series of distinct organization

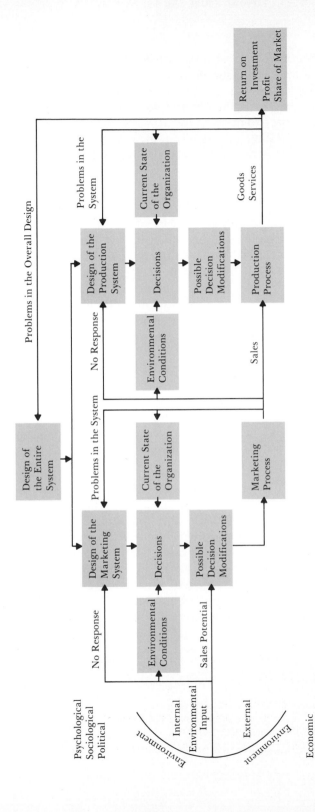

FIGURE 16-7 A Totally Adaptive Organization System

Source: Adapted from Stanley D. Young, "Organization Total System," *Proceedings of the 4th Annual Midwest Management Conference*, Carbondale, IL, 1966.

configurations or structures that are being employed by managers ranging from a basically simple structure in which one or two top managers and a group of people do the basic work to adhocratic structures which are characterized by highly flexible designs.[12]

It is apparent by now that systems concepts are very useful in both understanding an organization and relating it to its environment.[13] The general systems concept can also be applied within the firm in the examination of managerial systems.

MANAGERIAL SYSTEMS

The organization has been viewed as an open, adaptive system. Attention will now be focused on managerial systems. Talcott Parsons has suggested three managerial levels in the hierarchy of complex organizations: technical, organizational, and institutional.[14]

The *technical level* is concerned with the actual production and distribution of products and services. This not only entails turning out physical output but also includes the areas that support this activity—research and development, operations research, and accounting.

The *organizational level* coordinates and integrates work performance at the technical level. It is concerned with obtaining the continued flow of inputs into the system, maintaining the necessary markets for the outputs from the system, determining the nature of technical tasks, ascertaining the scale of operations, and establishing operating policies.

The *institutional level* is concerned with relating the activities of the organization to the environmental system. As Parsons notes, the organization not only has to

> operate in a social environment which imposes the conditions governing the processes of disposal and procurement, it is also part of a wider social system which is the source of the "meaning," legitimation, or higher level support which makes the implementation of the organization's goals possible. Essentially, this means that just as a technical organization (at a sufficiently high level of the division of labor) is controlled and "serviced" by a managerial organization, so, in turn, is the managerial organization controlled by the "institutional" structure and agencies of the community.[15]

---

[12]Henry Mintzberg, "Organization Design: Fashion or Fit?" *Harvard Business Review,* January–February 1981, pp. 103–15.

[13]"How Academia Is Taking a Lesson from Business," *Business Week,* August 27, 1984, pp. 58–60.

[14]The middle level in Talcott Parson's hierarchy will be referred to here as "the organizational level," since there are managers at all three levels. Parsons, though, actually called the second level "the management level."

[15]Talcott Parsons, *Structure and Process in Modern Societies* (New York: Free Press, 1960), pp. 63–64.

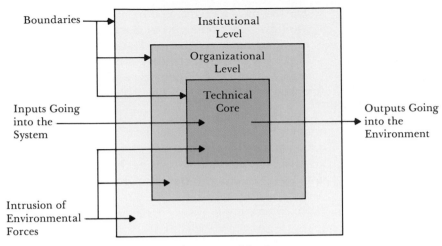

FIGURE 16-8   The Organization as a Composite System

Source: Adapted by permission from Thomas A. Petit, "A Behavioral Theory of Management," *Academy of Management Journal,* December 1967, p. 346.

The managerial system spans all three levels by organizing the people, directing the technical work, and relating the organization to its environment. These three levels are illustrated as a composite system in Figure 16-8.

The technical level, or core, is concerned with turning out a product or service at a profit. In order to do this, it often attempts to set up a boundary between itself and the external environment, thereby forming a closed system. The reasoning is that if the environment is too dynamic, it will never get anything done; the people in it will be continually responding to external influences. Modern technology provides an illustration of the intruding environmental force and its effect at this level. For example, companies often find that the products they are manufacturing are obsolete even before they leave the assembly line. However, at some point the design must be frozen and production begun. The technical core is subject to external influences, but it does attempt to minimize them.

Conversely, the institutional level experiences a great degree of uncertainty over environmental conditions, and the organization is unable to set up major boundaries. As a result, management at this level is by nature a very open system, and primary attention is devoted to innovation or adaptation.

The organizational level operates between these two extremes. It coordinates the technical and institutional levels, tries to straighten out irregularities and disturbances occurring in both, and serves as an all-around mediator. In a manner of speaking, it is a buffer between the maintenance (technical level) and the adaptive (institutional level) mechanisms. Thomas A. Petit has described the three levels in this way:

The technical level is highly oriented to closed systems.

The institutional level is very open-system-oriented.

The organizational level coordinates the other two levels.

The technical level has a boundary that does not seal it off entirely from the firm's environment but does have a high degree of closure. The organizational level has less closure and consequently is more susceptible to the intrusion of external elements. The institutional level has a highly permeable boundary and therefore is strongly affected by uncontrollable and unpredictable elements in the environment.[16]

The three levels are interrelated, constituting subsystems in this overall organizational structure. Each level has individual characteristics, but coordination among them is necessary for effective performance. At the same time, however, it is possible to examine the specific requirements of each organizational level in order to classify the managers who work there.

Types of Managers

In the past, most managers were classified by organizational level (executive, middle manager, first-line supervisor) or function (sales manager, production manager, financial manager). Today, however, managers are being classified according to many criteria, including the work itself, time horizon, and decision-making strategy.

Technical Managers

Technical managers have engineering viewpoints.

Because *technical managers* are concerned with producing goods and services as economically as possible, they tend to have an engineering point of view. They are also pragmatic, quick to adopt what will work for them and discard what will not. They like problems with concrete solutions, such as what criteria to employ when investing in fixed equipment or the optimal relation that should exist between production and inventory levels. They work best when confronted with quantitative (as opposed to qualitative) issues. They also tend to have a very short-run time horizon, being most interested in the operational aspects of the job.

Institutional Managers

Institutional managers have philosophical viewpoints.

Institutional managers face the challenge of coping with uncertainty brought on by uncontrollable and unpredictable environmental elements. For them, major concern rests with ensuring the organization's survival. This is done in two ways. First, institutional managers continually survey the environment, noting both opportunities and threats. Second, based on the findings, they develop cooperative and competitive strategies for dealing with these elements, thereby reducing uncertainty. In order to conduct this surveillance and construct viable strategies, they need to have a long-run time perspective. They tend to be philosophical in viewpoint, capable of translating

---

[16]Thomas A. Petit, "A Behavioral Theory of Management," *Academy of Management Journal,* December 1967, p. 346.

qualitative environmental changes into quantitative estimates of their impact on the organization. This requires wisdom, experience, and good judgment in the formulation of strategy.

Organizational Managers

Organizational managers are mediators.

As already noted, *organizational managers* coordinate the efforts of the technical and institutional levels. In order to do this, the organizational manager needs to be something of a politician, capable of adopting a short- or long-run perspective, depending on the situation, and able to achieve a compromise between the technical and institutional managers. As Petit has noted in his article:

> Organizational managers use the decision-making strategy of compromise. The best interests of the firm are not served by following either the computational [technical manager] or judgmental [institutional manager] strategies exclusively. The organizational managers attempt to influence the balance between the two according to the nature of the problems facing the firm. Since these problems may be either immediate or in the future, organizational managers have both a short-run and a long-run horizon.
>
> The viewpoint of the organizational manager is basically political. He must always be concerned with what is possible rather than ideal in mediating between technical and institutional managers.[17]

Table 16-1 shows the differences among these three types of managers.

THE SYSTEMS POINT OF VIEW

The systems point of view suggests that management continually faces a dynamic environment consisting of forces that are not within its total control. Of course, some organizations have attempted to overcome this problem. The giant trusts of the early 1900s and the major conglomerates of today both represent attempts by powerful organizations to obtain major control over their environment. For the most part, however, the organization and the environment still constitute interacting forces.

The same pattern exists within the organization itself. Managers in all departments and at all levels are interdependent. Job descriptions and work assignments, for example, represent only general guidelines regarding what the managers are supposed to be doing. In actuality, as Leonard Sayles noted in his well-known book, *Managerial Behavior,* the

> systems concept emphasizes that managerial assignments do not have these neat, clearly defined boundaries; rather, the modern manager is placed in a network of mutually dependent relationships. . . . The one

---

[17]Ibid., p. 348.

TABLE 16-1
Characteristics of Managers in the Managerial System

Type of Manager	Task	Point of View	Technique	Time Perspective	Decision-Making Strategy
Technical	Technical rationality	Engineering	Quantitative	Short-run	Computational
Organizational	Coordination	Political	Mediation	Both short- and long-run	Compromise
Institutional	Deal with uncertainty and relate the organization to its environment	Philosophical and conceptual	Environmental survey; strategy formulation	Long-run	Subjective and judgmental

Source: Adapted from Thomas A. Petit, "A Behavioral Theory of Management," *Academy of Management Journal,* December 1967, p. 349.

enduring objective is the effort to build and maintain a predictable, reciprocating system of relationships, the behavioral patterns of which stay within reasonable physical limits. But this is seeking a moving equilibrium, since the parameters of the system (the division of labor and the controls) are evolving and changing. Thus the manager endeavors to introduce regularity in a world that will never allow him to achieve the ideal. . . . Only managers who can deal with uncertainty, with ambiguity, and with battles that are never won but only fought well can hope to succeed.[18]

Organizing is a dynamic process.

This appears to be a very radical change from the organizing process that was discussed in Chapter 5 in very clear, rigid, and easy-to-grasp terms. The process may now seem to have become topsy-turvy. It must be remembered, however, that with this modern systems view the element of dynamism takes on new dimensions; and the heretofore simple concepts of planning, organizing, and controlling are viewed from a much more flexible and realistic perspective.[19]

MANAGEMENT THEORY IN THE FUTURE

At this point no one can definitively state what will happen by the year 2000 in the development of management theory. However, there is a current trend toward at least a partial synthesis of these three schools of thought. This is a welcome sign, given the fact that some researchers, such as Harold Koontz, have found that the number of different groups or schools has actually increased in the last twenty years as a result of their splitting off from current ones. For example, while this text addressed researchers and theorists who have an economic or mathematical orientation as members of the quantitative school, Koontz reports that there are now three subsets of this school: mathematics, decision theory, and economic theory groups.[20] The current status of management theory is therefore more cluttered than ever—if one wants to look only at the bleak side of the picture (see, for example, International Management in Action: The Japanese Management Theory Jungle on pages 618–19). There is also a basis for optimism, for recent research also reveals that certain signs show the various schools beginning now to synthesize somewhat.

[18]Leonard Sayles, *Managerial Behavior* (New York: McGraw-Hill, 1964), pp. 258–59.

[19]For more on this see Richard L. Daft, *Organization Theory and Design*, 2nd ed. (St. Paul: West Publishing, 1986).

[20]Harold Koontz, "The Management Theory Jungle Revisited," *Academy of Management Review*, April 1980, p. 182.

INTERVIEW WITH SHELDON BECHER

Sheldon H. Becher is a CPA and president of Becher, Herzog, Nall & Company, P.A., a well-known regional accounting firm. Sheldon has had a variety of business and accounting experience during his 35-year career. His firm specializes in handling both business and private accounts and provides a variety of services ranging from income tax preparation to mergers, acquisitions, and public issues.

Q.   *In managing your business, what are the key segments that have to be coordinated? Is the business like a system?*

A.   There are two key segments that have to be coordinated: the client and the in-house personnel. The client is looking for various forms of assistance often ranging from help in filing his or her income taxes to planning for the future such as creating and funding a retirement program or determining the size of a credit line that will be needed at the bank. Our in-house personnel are responsible for providing the technical information research that serves as the basis for these decisions. For example, if a business owner wants to start a company retirement program, we can tell the individual how much he or she can afford to put aside to fund the plan. We also can help set up the plan and ensure that all of the associated accounting work is properly completed and the correct tax forms are filed with the government in a timely manner.

The business is like a system because these two groups, the client and the in-house personnel, have to be coordinated very carefully. Each has a critical role to play in our success, and if that role is carried out correctly we are going to do extremely well. If not, there are going to be problems.

Signs of Synthesis

The current convergence of thinking is still in its formative stage, but a number of reported developments indicate a trend toward partial synthesis. Some of the major cited reasons include the following:

1.   There is now a much greater emphasis on the distillation of fundamental management concepts than there has been at any point in the past.

2.   It is now becoming increasingly clear that the systems approach to management is not unique; nor does it represent a better way of managing. Rather, it is part and parcel of the manager's job. Far from being a school of thought, it is now being recognized simply as a means of carrying out managerial tasks.

Q. *So these two groups are systems that interact or depend on each other. Is that right?*

A. That's correct. The needs of the client and the expertise of our people have to blend. The client typically wants services such as tax preparation or business advice, and our people have the expertise to provide these services. However, there's a third group involved here and that's the people like myself who orchestrate the entire melody. I never have my own personnel deal directly with a major client. I remain the primary link. If something needs to be done, I have my people research it. For example, if the client needs a quarterly tax form prepared or a financial statement drawn up for the bank, I will assign someone to provide it based on the information I received directly from the client. However, I continue to be the main link between the client and the staff—and there's good reason for this. Many accountants, especially those who are young and inexperienced, are very good at what they do, but they don't have the experience to see the big picture and know what the ending should be. If they dealt directly with the client, they would be entering the arena unprepared. Most of our clients need someone who listens to what they desire, can identify how their needs can be taken care of, and can then see that the proper steps are taken. My partners and I play the major role in this process. We represent the firm to the outside environment, but seldom get involved in the day-to-day mechanical chores of compiling and entering data into the computer or making entries for cash flow calculations and projections. Our firm is a large system with many smaller systems networked inside of it. Each network has to carry out a particular function. Some of these networks focus on identifying what needs to be done, others work on getting the tasks accomplished. Together, we have been successful but only because each one knows his or her individual job skills and responsibilities and can carry it out like a symphony orchestra.

3. It is also increasingly clear that the contingency approach to management is not new. Managers have been using it for years. However, the fact that contingency research in such areas as organizing, motivating, and leading is now being actively pursued will increase our understanding of these processes and how to carry them out more effectively.

4. It is now being recognized that management theory is not as broad a topic area as is organization theory. The latter refers to almost any type of interpersonal relationship. Today's management scholars are realizing that they should be addressing management theory, a narrower field and one which is easier to research and understand.

5. There is currently more information about motivation than ever before. Of course, this provides a better understanding of how and why people

INTERNATIONAL
MANAGEMENT
IN
ACTION:
The
Japanese
Management
Theory
Jungle

Not only does management theory somewhat resemble a jungle, but attempts to describe parts of it face a junglelike entanglement. For example, consider some of the most common explanations of why Japanese firms are so successful in their efforts to compete with American companies.

Manufacturing Management. According to this line of reasoning, Japanese success can be described in terms of better manufacturing management. This includes such things as the use of just-in-time inventory, effective quality control, clean facilities, and responsible employees.

Quality Circles. The quality circle theory ascribes the effectiveness of Japanese management to an effective application of participation, sharing of decision making, greater employee commitment to the job, and increased work satisfaction.

Statistical Quality Control. Supporters of this approach argue that Japanese success can be traced directly to effective quality control, following the adage of "do it right the first time."

Long-term, Bottom-line Results. This line of reasoning holds that the Japanese do better than their American competitors because they are willing to look at the long run and take the time necessary to develop market niches.

Decision Making. Proponents of this explanation hold that the Japanese use of group decision making, as opposed to individual decision making, provides better overall results.

Some management experts do not try to explain the difference in terms of one factor. They use a more integrated model. Three of the best known are the following:

act as they do. In particular, attention to organizational climate and the way in which it affects motivation is receiving productive attention.

6. A melding of motivation and leadership theory is taking place, since researchers have realized that the two are interdependent and that both are affected by organizational climate.

7. A coalescence is also taking place between studies of individual and group behavior. Researchers interested in studying one are realizing that the other cannot be ignored. In fact, writers in the field of organizational behavior are now beginning to understand that behavioral elements in group operations must be closely integrated with organization design, staffing, planning, and controlling.

8. The impact of technology on organizational structure, behavioral patterns, and the overall management process is now being recognized and better understood.

The Seven S's. This approach argues that Japanese success can be explained in terms of seven variables: strategy, structure, staff, skills, systems, style, and superordinate goals. The interaction of these variables produces the effective results.

Organizational. Others believe that the answer is found in the overall organizational approach used by the Japanese. In contrast to the Americans, for example, they use: lifetime employment, slow evaluation and promotion, nonspecialized career paths, implicit control mechanisms, collective decision making, collective responsibility, and a holistic concern for the employee.

Human Resources. Still others contend that the differences can be explained in terms of human resource development. They hold that the Japanese do a better job of developing an internal labor market, they articulate a company philosophy that stresses cooperation and teamwork, and they use a well-defined socialization process for hiring and integrating new employees into the firm.

Are any of these approaches correct? Each of them partly explains the success of Japanese firms. More importantly, they help relate why the management theory jungle exists. Just as in the above approaches, each individual begins with personal experiences and tries to explain things from that point of view. So far from being a general discussion of reality, the management theory jungle partly explains why it may prove impossible for a generally agreed upon theory of management ever to emerge.

Source: Some of this material can be found in J. Bernard Keys and Thomas R. Miller, "The Japanese Management Theory Jungle," *Academy of Management Review,* April 1984, pp. 342–53.

9. Some management scientists are beginning to see that their emphasis on quantitative tools is insufficient to get things done. The manager's job is more encompassing and complex than this, and there is now a move toward incorporating more nonquantitative emphases into their approaches.

10. Finally, more of an effort is being made toward clarifying management terms and thereby overcoming misapplications of semantics, one of the greatest causes of what Koontz has called the management theory jungle. Many texts in the field, including this one, contain glossaries which define some key terms operatively, as they are used throughout the book.[21]

---

[21]Koontz has written more on this subject in his April 1980 article.

But That Is All

The ten points listed above encapsulate findings from the recent literature. Many are not at all surprising. They already have been clearly enunciated in this text. However, a final warning is in order for those who are optimistic enough to believe that the schools of management thought that were studied in the last twelve chapters will soon fade. It must be remembered that these schools are a partial result of the training, experience, and personal attitudes of the members. It is unlikely that behavioralists will soon abandon their orientation to the study of management at work in order to join ranks with management process people. Nor are the latter likely to change their minds and decide that the quantitative people or the behavioralists have better insights into the study of management than theirs. Each still has personal biases. It is thus unreasonable to expect anything more in the 1990s than a general synthesis of some interrelated areas of concern. Some progress has been made; much more is yet to come:

> Despite some signs of hope, the fact is that the management theory jungle is still with us. Although some slight progress appears to be occurring, in the interest of a far better society through improved managerial practice it is to be hoped that some means can be found to accelerate this progress.[22]

■ SUMMARY

This chapter has examined the so-called systems school of management. Attention was first focused on general systems theory because of the importance assigned to it by systems school advocates. Then the applied concepts of the systems approach, likewise presented from its advocates' point of view, were reviewed. Finally, the question of whether the systems approach is a new school or a subsystem of a current one was examined. Although it is difficult to deny the existence of a systems body of knowledge, it appears that the systems school is actually part of the quantitative school.

Attention was then focused on the general value of understanding the systems concept, beginning with the organization as an open, adaptive system. Since business organizations are contrived systems, they can survive the onset of entropy and, unlike their biological counterparts, exist indefinitely, depending, of course, on how well they are managed. On the one hand, they must be responsive to change (adaptive mechanisms); on the other hand, they must not change so quickly that they are seriously thrown out of equilibrium (maintenance mechanisms). Finding the right balance is one of the keys to indefinite survival.

---

[22]Koontz, p. 186.

The systems concept was next used to examine managerial systems. Three levels exist in the managerial system of a complex organization: technical, organizational, and institutional. The technical level is concerned with producing the goods or services. The organizational level coordinates and integrates the technical and institutional levels. The institutional level relates the activities of the organization to the environmental system. Within this system are three types of managers, one for each of the levels. The technical manager is a nuts-and-bolts individual; the organization manager is more like a political mediator; and the institutional manager is a conceptual-philosophical decision maker. Yet, although there are different levels and interests within the structure, all three must combine their talents and energies in the attainment of overall organizational objectives.

In order to achieve this blending of talent and energy, managers must plan, organize, and control. They must also make decisions and employ the latest quantitative methods where applicable; and they must understand and utilize the abilities of their subordinates through effective communication, motivation, and leadership. In short, the management process, quantitative, and behavioral schools are all still important to modern managers. In fact, managers today draw on the concepts of all three in carrying out their duties. The systems approach encourages this.

The last section of the chapter examined management theory in the future, noting that some synthesis among the schools of management thought appears to be going on. Ten specific reasons were cited. However, it was also noted that this synthesis is unlikely to result in a major change in the three schools of thought explored in this textbook. The management process school, the quantitative school, and the behavioral school of management thought will continue to endure into the indefinite future.

■ REVIEW AND STUDY QUESTIONS

1. Of what value is general systems theory to the systems school of management? Explain.

2. What is an open system?

3. How does a system show the impact of entropy?

4. In what way is a business organization a contrived system?

5. What are maintenance mechanisms? What are adaptive mechanisms? How do they affect the organization structure?

6. What is a totally adaptive organization?

7. Describe each of the three managerial levels in the hierarchy of complex organizations.

8. Explain how the tasks and viewpoints of the managers of these three hierarchical levels differ.

9. Of what value is the systems approach to the practicing manager?
10. Identify and describe five signs of synthesis among the schools of management.

■ SELECTED REFERENCES

Boulding, Kenneth E. "General Systems Theory—The Skeleton of Science." *Management Science*, April 1956, pp. 197–208.

Cleland, David I., and W. R. King. *Management: A Systems Approach.* 2nd ed. New York: McGraw-Hill, 1975.

Daft, Richard L. *Organization Theory and Design.* 2nd ed. St. Paul: West Publishing, 1986.

Dunbar, Robert L. M. "Toward an Applied Administrative Science." *Administrative Science Quarterly*, March 1983, pp. 129–44.

Duncan, W. J. "Transferring Management Theory to Practice." *Academy of Management Journal*, December 1974, pp. 724–38.

Greenwood, W. T. "Future Management Theory: A 'Comparative' Evolution to a General Theory." *Academy of Management Journal*, September 1974, pp. 500–513.

Kast, F. E., and J. E. Rosenzweig. "General Systems Theory: Applications for Organization and Management." *Academy of Management Journal*, December 1972, pp. 447–65.

Keller, John J. et. al. "A Scramble for Global Networks." *Business Week*, March 21, 1988, pp. 140–48.

Keys, J. Bernard, and Thomas R. Miller. "The Japanese Management Theory Jungle." *Academy of Management Review*, April 1984, pp. 342–53.

Koontz, Harold. "The Management Theory Jungle." *Academy of Management Journal*, December 1961, pp. 174–88.

Koontz, Harold. "The Management Theory Jungle Revisited." *Academy of Management Review*, April 1980, pp. 175–87.

Luthans, Fred. "The Contingency Theory of Management." *Business Horizons*, June 1973, pp. 67–72.

Luthans, Fred, and T. Stewart. "A General Contingency Theory of Management." *Academy of Management Review*, April 1977, pp. 181–95.

McGuire, Joseph W. "Management Theory: Retreat to the Academy." *Business Horizons*, July–August 1982, pp. 31–37.

Mintzberg, Henry. "The Manager's Job: Folklore and Fact." *Harvard Business Review*, July–August 1975, pp. 49–61.

Nehrbass, R. G. "Ideology and the Decline of Management Theory." *Academy of Management Review*, July 1979, pp. 427–31.

Petit, Thomas A. "A Behavioral Theory of Management." *Academy of Management Journal*, December 1967, pp. 341–50.

Robbins, S. P. "Reconciling Management Theory with Management Practice." *Business Horizons*, February 1977, pp. 38–47.

Robey, Daniel. *Designing Organizations.* 2nd ed. Homewood, IL: Richard D. Irwin, 1986.

Tosi, Henry L., Jr., and John W. Slocum, Jr. "Contingency Theory: Some Suggested Directions." *Journal of Management,* Spring 1984, pp. 9–26.

Von Bertalanffy, L. "The History and Status of General Systems Theory." *Academy of Management Journal,* December 1972, pp. 407–26.

Wooten, L. M. "The Mixed Blessings of Contingency Management." *Academy of Management Review,* July 1977, pp. 431–41.

■ CASE: A Great Big Secret

Jackson & Jackson, a large West Coast manufacturer, instituted an in-house supervisory training program under its new president, William Hopkinson. During the initial phase, 10 percent of the managers received training related to both the technical and human relations sides of their jobs. Some critics of the program suggested that the training be suspended at this point since it was really of little value to the supervisors. An analysis of the results, however, showed that all managers participating in this initial training phase had been able to attain an increase in their units' output. The training therefore continued.

Over the next twelve months all the remaining supervisors were put through the program. During this period, productivity increased 27 percent over that of the previous year. In commenting on the value of the program, the vice-president of manufacturing said that she had noticed a number of the supervisors entering the plant earlier than usual in the morning and some staying past the closing whistle.

The results led proponents of the program to call it an unqualified success, but its opponents disagreed. Their arguments took two lines of attack. First, they pointed out that not all supervisors had been able to attain productivity increases. If the training was in fact beneficial, they should have been able to accomplish this. Second, they argued that the surge in output would be short-lived. One of them put it this way:

> What we have here is the old "Hawthorne effect." The supervisors are all excited about being part of this new program, but it won't last long. The training is now complete and the novelty is already beginning to wear thin. Everyone will soon be returning to their old way of doing things. That's the problem with training programs. The initial results are fantastic, but they soon drop off.
>
> Besides all that, we've also got another old standby, the cause-effect identification problem. Look at it this way. We have a new input—the training program. We have a new output—27 percent increase in productivity. But what *causes* this increase? Is it really the training program, or is it something else? What takes place in the transformation

process, the black box? We all know that no one knows, so why attribute it to the training program? Maybe these productivity increases would have occurred in any event. Who knows? It's really all a great big secret.

Questions

1. Something is taking place in the transformation process that is causing a 27 percent productivity increase. What is it? Explain your answer, employing the systems concept.

2. Why does the last speaker in this case refer to the productivity increase as a "great big secret"?

■ CASE: Input/Output

The union at MacKelvey Incorporated had been negotiating a new contract with management for more than three months; and with only thirty days of bargaining time left, there still was no agreement. The management was willing to give an 8.4 percent increase in salary and a 6 percent increase in fringe benefits; the union was asking for 10 and 6.9 percent respectively. However, Paul Aherne, MacKelvey's vice-president of industrial relations, who had been heading the negotiations all along, reported to the president, Georgia Neffen, that he felt an agreement might be near.

"Mrs. Neffen, I think the union would settle for a 9.1 percent salary raise and a 6.3 percent increase in fringe benefits. We've done quite a bit of negotiating over the past 10 weeks, and I'm sure I understand them."

Mrs. Neffen looked noncommittal. "Actually, Mr. Aherne, the board of directors had hoped that the 8.4 percent and 6 percent proposals would lead to a contract."

"I see little chance of that, Mrs. Neffen. If we maintain our present position, we'll either have to hope that the union is willing to work without a contract or face the very real possibility of a strike."

"Obviously, neither of those alternatives is going to be viewed very favorably by the board. On the other hand, we certainly don't want to negotiate a contract any higher than we have to."

"Mrs. Neffen, let me be frank. I think we're almost there now. However, if we force the union to work without a contract or, heaven forbid, strike, we're going to damage one of our most important assets—union-management harmony. We have to think of the workers as inputs in the process of management. If we do something to that input, we stand the chance of seriously endangering the output, namely, our products and services. I think we should promote the goodwill that currently exists between us."

Questions

1. If you regard the workers as an input and the goods and services as an output, how would you describe the transformation process in this case?

2. How does this union contract negotiation fit into a discussion of the systems approach to management?

3. Do you think the company would be wise to follow the advice of its vice-president of industrial relations? Explain your opinion.

■ CASE: Modifications, Modifications

John Chilvers was angry. For the past twelve months he had been in charge of designing a new jet fighter for the United States Navy. After countless days of revising the initial design and incorporating extensive changes, his group was prepared to submit its design for approval. However, just as they were about to do this, Chilvers received a call from his boss asking him to come up to the office immediately.

The boss said: "John, I've called you in because before you submit your plan I want you to know that there's a lot of pressure on us to present the most sophisticated design possible. In addition, if there are any major flaws that result in eventual cost overruns, we're really going to be in trouble. Congress is fed up with paying for contractor mistakes."

"Mr. Adkinson, we've designed this craft five times now. I don't think there's a thing we haven't changed for the better at one time or another. I think it will be the finest plane the navy has ever had," Chilvers replied.

"I'm glad to hear that, John, because the president has really sold the big brass on this one."

"Well, believe me, sir, when we submit our design later in the week, they'll be impressed."

"Actually, John, we want you to wait a month before doing that. We still have a little time before the drawings are due, and the president has asked me to have you go over the material once more."

Chilvers bristled. "What for?"

"To see if you can't improve it a little bit. Surely there's something new you can add here and there," Adkinson said.

"Mr. Adkinson, if you gave me a year I could design an aircraft that's twice as good as this one, but I think there's a point beyond which it's not practical to go. We have a contract and a design that more than fulfills its requirements. At some point you have to quit making changes, freeze the plan, and get on with the production. If we keep delaying, we'll never get to the manufacturing stage."

"Oh, John," said a tolerant-looking Adkinson. "I understand that, of course. But the president wants to be sure that the design is as good as possible. So for the next month I want you and your team to review and make any minor modifications on the material which will improve the overall design.''

Questions

1. Would you classify Chilvers as a technical, organizational, or institutional manager? Explain.
2. Is Adkinson a technical, organizational, or institutional manager? Explain. How about the president? Explain.
3. How does Chilvers' viewpoint as a manager differ from that of his superior? Be specific.

■ CASE: Technology in Action

During the 1990s companies are going to be spending billions of dollars developing worldwide communications systems. Some of these systems are already on-line. For example, Merrill Lynch, the giant stock brokerage house, provides instant access to stock prices, market performance, and other forms of research to its brokers around the country thanks to a communications satellite located 23,000 miles up in space and a series of telecommunications dishes located on Staten Island, New York. This satellite system also helps the broker send buy and sell orders from distant locations to organized stock exchanges, where the actual transactions are handled.

Merrill Lynch is only one of many firms using global network systems to help personnel make decisions and communicate messages. Honda Ltd. has a computer system that allows dealers to determine which warehouses have the inventory they need and then to place the order. SeaLand Corporation, a shipping company in Edison, New Jersey, uses satellites to keep track of its ships at sea. Hewlett-Packard has a global network that allows its executives to conduct video conference meetings.

These examples illustrate the growing trend of global networking. Sales of equipment and transmission lines used for private communications networks which was $14 billion in 1987 and $15.1 billion in 1988 should top $50 billion annually by the turn of the century.

In particular, these developments are causing organizations to change their organization structures. For example, when companies begin increasing their marketing efforts and start covering more and more geographic locales, they often turn to a geographic organization structure. Thanks to high technology communication equipment, some businesses are now changing to a product-line organization structure. They no longer feel that geographic distance is a major factor in choice of organization design. Communication technology is bringing people together so efficiently that common geographic problems are now being surmounted. Firms are even finding that global communication networks can help them improve their service.

American President Cos., the worldwide shipper, devised a complex network of satellite and land-based communications links from New York to Kuwait to help it keep on top of cargo movements throughout Asia and North America. A new feature installed in 1987 lets a customer, who wants to know the whereabouts of a shipment, call an APC computer on a toll-free number and a digitized voice-response systems will give the location in 10 seconds. The network "wasn't put in to pay bills," says W. B. Seaton, APC's chairman, but to help make better decisions about how to route APC's ships, trains, and trucks. "Our Bombay office moved from the 17th century to the 20th century."

Questions

1. How is technology making organizations more responsive to their environments? Explain.

2. As technology increases, will managers tend to be more technical, organizational, or institutional in their orientation? Why?

3. Will increased technology result in managers becoming more systems-oriented in their approaches? Why or why not?

Source: John J. Keller et. al., "A Scramble for Global Networks," *Business Week,* March 21, 1988, pp. 140–48.

■ SELF-ASSESSMENT EXERCISE: What Type of Manager Are You?

Read and answer or complete each of the following statements by placing a "3" next to the alternative with which you most agree on down to a "1" next to the alternative with which you least agree. Interpretations are provided at the end of the exercise.

1. Managers need to be more _____ in their focus.
   _____ a. short-run
   _____ b. short- and long-run
   _____ c. long-run

2. How important are the following goals:
   _____ a. large market share
   _____ b. high productivity
   _____ c. high morale

3. How important are the following goals:
   _____ a. return on investment
   _____ b. human resources development
   _____ c. cost control

4. How important are the following goals:
   _____ a. low turnover and absenteeism
   _____ b. production output
   _____ c. sales growth

5. Managers need to be more _____ in their approach.
   _____ a. quantitative
   _____ b. strategic
   _____ c. human relations-oriented

6. Effective managers need to be more _____ in their point of view.
   _____ a. political
   _____ b. philosophical
   _____ c. engineering

7. The most important skill for a manager is:
   _____ a. technical
   _____ b. human
   _____ c. conceptual

8. The most effective decision-making strategy is often:
   _____ a. subjective and judgmental
   _____ b. computational
   _____ c. compromising

9. Product quality is primarily a function of:
   _____ a. good marketing research
   _____ b. high group morale
   _____ c. good engineering

10. Organizations of the 1990s will have to be more _____ driven.
    _____ a. personnel-
    _____ b. technology-
    _____ c. market-

11. Managers of the 1990s will need to be most interested in:
    _____ a. cost-cutting techniques
    _____ b. the impact of international trade
    _____ c. the linkage between technology and people at work

12. Managers of the 1990s will need to be most interested in:
    _____ a. motivation of personnel
    _____ b. forecasting of future developments
    _____ c. computerization of facilities

Answers

Match your answers with the appropriate letters.

Column I		Column II		Column III	
1.	_____ a	_____ b		_____ c	
2.	_____ b	_____ c		_____ a	
3.	_____ c	_____ b		_____ a	
4.	_____ b	_____ a		_____ c	
5.	_____ a	_____ c		_____ b	
6.	_____ c	_____ a		_____ b	
7.	_____ a	_____ b		_____ c	
8.	_____ b	_____ c		_____ a	
9.	_____ c	_____ b		_____ a	
10.	_____ b	_____ a		_____ c	
11.	_____ a	_____ c		_____ b	
12.	_____ c	_____ a		_____ b	
Total	══════	══════		══════	

Interpretation

Your answers to Columns I, II, and III relate whether your philosophy is that of a technical, organizational, or institutional manager. Most people have a combination score, although one of these is usually higher than the others. One way of visualizing your profile is by filling in your three scores on the Figure 16-9 and the connecting the three dots. This makes it easier to view your philosophical approach to management.

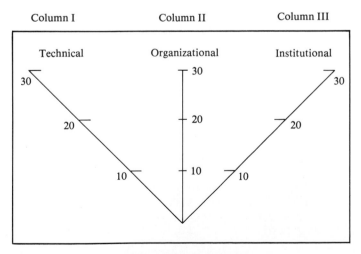

FIGURE 16-9   Assessment of Managerial Style

Social Responsibility:
A Continuing Challenge

GOALS OF THE CHAPTER

Social responsibility has been a continuing challenge to business in the 1980s and the 1990s. The term social responsibility is generally defined as those obligations a firm has to the society in which it operates. More specifically, businesses are realizing that this responsibility encompasses three major areas: equal opportunity, ecology, and consumerism. This chapter examines each of these issues, studying what they are and the types of responses business is making toward them.

When you have finished this chapter, you should be able to:

1. Define what is meant by the doctrine of enlightened self-interest.
2. Describe the major provisions of the Equal Pay Act of 1963, the Civil Rights Act of 1964, and the Age Discrimination Act of 1967.
3. Relate how business is helping ensure equal opportunity for minority workers, minority capitalists, and the physically and mentally handicapped.
4. Explain the current status of women in business and what is being done to ensure equal opportunity for them.
5. Describe the major ecological challenges facing business and what is being done about them, with primary consideration given to air pollution, water pollution, and noise pollution.
6. Describe what consumerism is and how business firms are attempting to meet the problems associated with product safety, including some that appear to have been the result of the Consumer Product Safety Act of 1970.

7. Discuss the future of social responsibility, with specific attention devoted to ethics and personnel assistance.

ENLIGHTENED SELF-INTEREST

By the 1960s, the United States was the most affluent nation that the world had ever known. With this affluence came a social awakening, as many people started questioning conditions in this country and began to call for corrective action in such areas as equal opportunity, ecology, and consumerism. Feeling that the business community had the resources and the know-how to handle problems in these areas, and convinced that many companies had contributed to the problems' existence, the public insisted that business commit part of its efforts to *social responsibility*, the obligations a firm has to the society or community in which it operates and over which it has some economic influence. The public asked businesses to turn toward social activities as well as to its more traditional concerns.

Such action was not in direct accord with many of the traditional objectives of business: profit, survival, and growth. However, it was related by way of the doctrine of *enlightened self-interest*, which holds that business actually serves its own long-run interests when it helps out its own community. For example, since 1935, when the Internal Revenue Code permitted corporations to deduct up to 5 percent of pretax income for charitable contributions, business firms have been extremely active in their support of various charities, even though not everyone has agreed with this action. For example, some stockholders have brought suits against their companies, contending that the contributions are in no way related to the running of the business. The courts, however, have consistently ruled for the firms, holding that such donations do indeed serve the interest of the company even though they provide no direct benefits. In addition, business can contribute to higher education. This issue was settled in 1953 by the New Jersey Superior Court when it ruled that a manufacturing firm could donate funds to Princeton University. The court held that giving financial support was not only a right but a duty, because by helping society the company was actually helping itself. As it was later stated:

By helping society, business serves its own long-run interests.

> By the same logic, expenditures to help improve community educational, health, and cultural facilities can be justified by the corporation's interest in attracting the skilled people it needs who would not move into a substandard community. Similarly, a corporation whose operations must inevitably take place in urban areas may well be justified in investing in the rehabilitation of ghetto housing and contributing to the improvement of ghetto educational, recreational, and other facilities. . . .

Indeed, the corporate interest defined by management can support involvement in helping to solve virtually any social problem, because people who have a good environment, education, and opportunity make better employees, customers and neighbors for business than those who are poor, ignorant, and oppressed.[1]

The doctrine of enlightened self-interest extends further than merely pointing out the benefits of involvement. It is also based on the proposition that failure to assume social responsibility can jeopardize an organization's welfare.[2] If business does not voluntarily do its share, the government will pass legislation and force it to become involved. Nevertheless, not everyone agrees with an active social responsibility stance. A debate still rages between those who believe that business has an obligation to the stockholders only (and therefore should not engage in social responsibility activities) and those who believe that business obligation extends to groups other than shareholders (and therefore should engage in social responsibility activities).[3] For the most part, business people support the prosocial responsibility position. In fact, it is quite common today to see firms assuming a very proactive posture in which they become actively involved in addressing social issues rather than waiting until they are forced to do so. For example, many firms were actively recruiting minorities and women long before equal employment opportunity legislation was enacted. Likewise, instead of waiting for the government to tell them to stop polluting the air, many industrial firms voluntarily replaced their inefficient equipment with low- or pollution-free machinery. Similar social responsibility examples can be cited in which consumer goods firms have pulled their products off the market as soon as a problem appeared. Consider Johnson & Johnson and its swift action in removing all Tylenol capsules after someone tampered with some of the bottles and replaced the contents with cyanide. Procter & Gamble is another example. As soon as Rely brand tampons were linked to toxic shock syndrome, the firm pulled the product off the shelves, thereby removing from the market an item on which $75 million and twenty years of research had been expended. Actions such as these indicate beyond doubt that many firms are taking the issue of social responsibility very seriously. Edward Harness, Chairman of the Board of Procter & Gamble said it best:

Many firms are socially active.

---

[1]Research and Policy Committee of the Committee for Economic Development, *Social Responsibilities of Business Corporations: A Statement on National Policy* (New York: Committee for Economic Development, June 1971), pp. 27–28.

[2]Robert H. Bock, "Modern Values and Corporate Social Responsibility," *MSU Business Topics*, Spring 1980, pp. 5–16.

[3]Thomas M. Jones, "Corporate Social Responsibility Revisited, Redefined," *California Management Review*, Spring 1980, pp. 59–67.

Company management must consistently demonstrate a superior talent for keeping profit and growth objectives as first priorities. However, it also must have enough breadth to recognize that enlightened self-interest requires the company to fill any reasonable expectation placed upon it by the community and the various concerned publics. Keeping priorities straight and maintaining the sense of civic responsibility will achieve important secondary objectives of the firm. Profitability and growth go hand in hand with fair treatment of employees, of direct customers, of consumers, and of the community.[4]

Many explanations have been offered for business's proactive stance. Some say it is a result of newly enacted legislation. Others contend that the business community is merely trying to protect its image. Still others say that business people today are more socially responsible than their predecessors. There is undoubtedly truth in all these statements. Yet, whatever the specific reason, many businesses have been developing programs to cope with the three most important social issues of the day: equal opportunity, ecology, and consumerism.[5]

EQUAL OPPORTUNITY

A number of important areas of equal opportunity action currently provide major challenges to business. In particular, they are legislation, hiring of minorities and the handicapped, support of minority capitalism, and sanctions against discrimination against females.

Legislation

One of the main reasons for the attention business has paid to the area of equal opportunity has been legislation. Three of the most important laws enacted thus far have been the Equal Pay Act of 1963, the Civil Rights Act of 1964, and the Age Discrimination in Employment Act of 1967. Recent guidelines prohibiting sexual harassment have also proven beneficial in ensuring equal opportunity.

The *Equal Pay Act of 1963* was signed on June 10 of that year. Its purpose is to correct "the existence in industries engaged in commerce, or in the

---

[4]"View on Corporate Responsibility," Edward G. Harness, Chairman of the Board, Procter & Gamble, *Corporate Ethics Digest*, September–October 1980, as reported in Elizabeth Gatewood and Archie B. Carroll, "The Anatomy of Corporate Social Response: The Rely, Firestone 500, and Pinto Cases," *Business Horizons*, September–October 1981, p. 9.

[5]Fred Luthans, Richard M. Hodgetts, and Kenneth R. Thompson, *Social Issues in Business*, 5th ed. (New York: Macmillan, 1987), chaps 8–12.

REAL-LIFE MANAGERS:

INTERVIEW WITH ROBIN REITER

Robin Reiter is vice-president of Corporate Community Involvement and Director of the Southeast Banking Corporation Foundation in Miami, Florida. In 1980 Robin was asked to create a new foundation to cover all aspects of corporate giving on behalf of Southeast Bank. In this capacity, she is responsible for formulating policies and procedures, reviewing requests, and initiating activities that will facilitate the needs of Southeast as a leader in corporate community responsibility.

Q.   *To what type of organizations does your foundation give money? For what purposes?*

A.   We don't look at it as giving money away. Rather we think of it as "investing" money in the nonprofit sector, and we did so to the extent of around $1.5 million for 1988. The largest amount goes for health, welfare, and community service, primarily to United Way. These funds go to the Dade Community Foundation, assistance for home-care for the elderly, housing projects, and help in financing many community-based organizations. We sponsor the arts and humanities in the form of grants and technical assistance to art museums, theater groups, and emerging as well as established organizations. Education also gets a big slice of the pie. We also provide scholarships and grants to local universities and colleges, and the bank has a matching gift program whereby bank employees, directors, and board members have an opportunity to individually demonstrate their commitment to education including state-licensed, nonprofit day-care centers.

---

production of goods for commerce, of wage differentials based on sex."[6] Specifically, the act forbids "discrimination on the basis of sex for doing equal work on jobs requiring equal skill, effort and responsibility which are performed under similar working conditions."[7]

The law forbids discrimination in employment.

The *Civil Rights Act of 1964* was signed on July 2. Of its eleven major sections, Title VII is most important to business because it forbids discrimination on the basis of race, color, religion, sex, or national origin. In addition, the act established an Equal Employment Opportunity Commission (EEOC) composed of five members appointed by the president of the United States

---

[6]U. S. Department of Labor, *Information on the Equal Pay Act of 1963* (Washington, D.C.: Government Printing Office, n.d.), p. 1.

[7]Ibid., p. 2.

Q. *Why does the bank invest in the local community and state? What's in it for you?*

A. We don't look on social responsibility in terms of a "something for something" relationship in terms of profit. For example, we gave a grant to a university to sponsor a series on ethics in education because we're hoping that we can be a catalyst for others to consider the depth of opportunities in this community. We want to assist in making this city and state a better place in which to live and work. We want to be a partner with the 21st century. If we do that, then the community is going to thrive and we're going to benefit as a result. However, these are indirect benefits, and that's okay with us. We look on ourselves as a responsible bank that has an obligation to our geographic region of the country. If we can get people to bank with us because they like what we're doing for the local college or community organization or art center, fine. But our foundation has not been set up as a direct marketing tool.

Q. *What does the future hold in terms of your involvement in community affairs? What new programs are on the horizon?*

A. The bank is now making matching contributions to day-care centers and private secondary schools and universities. We are also going to remain very interested in social service delivery systems, as opportunities for the minority communities. These are some of the areas that are getting more of our attention. We are also going to continue to invest in the three main areas that have been our focal points: health, welfare, and community service, the arts and humanities, and education. By the year 2000 Florida is going to be the third largest state in the nation, and this means that there will be both opportunities and responsibilities for those companies that hope to play a major role in the business arena during the 21st century. We intend to be one of those firms.

and approved by the U. S. Senate. The commission's job is to investigate complaints, seek to end violations through conciliation, and ask the U. S. attorney general to bring suit if such conciliation is unsuccessful.

The *Age Discrimination in Employment Act of 1967*, as amended in 1978, protects persons forty through seventy years of age against discrimination in employment. Today, if a thirty-five- and a sixty-five-year-old person both apply for the same job, the employer must make the hiring decision on some factor other than age.[8] This law has done much to prevent the dismissal of people approaching retirement in order to make room for "younger blood."

Another recent development has been the November 1980 guidelines which extend Title VII of the Civil Rights Act and prohibit sexual harassment

---

[8]Paul S. Greenlaw and John P. Kohl, "Age Discrimination in Employment Guidelines," *Personnel Journal*, March 1982, p. 225.

of employees. These guidelines require employers "to take all steps necessary to prevent sexual harassment."[9] One of the most interesting results of the guidelines is that in some cases the courts are now holding employers responsible for the acts of their employees who are guilty of sexual harassment.[10] Consider the case of *Munford v. Barnes and Company* (1977), in which a U. S. District Court judge wrote:

> This Court agrees that an employer may be liable for the discriminatory acts of its agents or supervisory personnel if it fails to investigate complaints of such discrimination. The failure to investigate gives tacit support to discrimination because the absence of sanctions encourages abusive behavior. While the Court declines . . . that an employer is automatically and vicariously liable for all discriminatory acts of its agents and supervisors, the Court does hold that an employer has an affirmative duty to investigate complaints of sexual harassment and deal appropriately with the offending personnel.[11]

These laws and guidelines have been very helpful in providing equal employment, basically because people have not hesitated to use them. For example, in the first eighteen months of its existence, the EEOC received 14,000 complaints. In addition, minority group organizations such as the National Association for the Advancement of Colored People (NAACP) and the Congress on Racial Equality (CORE) have been relatively active in using these laws to bring suit against firms for discriminatory practices. Equal employment, however, has proved to be more than a legal issue. Many firms have voluntarily responded to the challenge by eliminating or reducing their barriers for employment and promotion.

Hiring Minorities and the Handicapped

For years, business firms have made concerted efforts to hire minority group members. Specific programs can be found in literally thousands of companies throughout American industry. These programs range from recruiting and hiring minority employees to training and developing them. Some of the programs are geared more to the hard-core unemployed, such as black or native American ghetto youth; others extend to minorities in general. However, all have one thing in common: They are designed to provide employment opportunities to those who might otherwise have difficulty getting jobs.

---

[9] *EEOC Guidelines on Sexual Harassment*, November 1980, 29 CFR Part 1604.

[10] Terry L. Leap and Edmund R. Gray, "Corporate Responsibility in Cases of Sexual Harassment," *Business Horizons*, October 1980, pp. 58–65.

[11] Ibid., p. 63.

Recently, more and more attention has been focused on hiring the physically and mentally handicapped. The Vocational Rehabilitation Act of 1973 requires such affirmative action in the case of businesses that have contracts or subcontracts with the federal government. A Department of Labor survey of three hundred companies reveal that 91 percent of the firms were in violation of the act.[12] This apparent noncompliance has led to lawsuits by the federal government, resulting in the prediction by two authors that "in the next several years, the employment rights of the handicapped will be a major issue as well as a focus of government attention—following the path in recent years of women's and minorities' work-related rights."[13] How can business firms rectify the situation and get back into compliance? Some of the most effective steps include the following:

The twelve steps for following the Vocational Rehabilitation Act.

1. Adopt a policy of hiring the handicapped.
2. Post equal opportunity posters in conspicuous locations in the workplace.
3. Notify the union of the company's compliance with the act.
4. Include an affirmative action clause or reference in purchase orders or contracts over $2,500.
5. Review medical questionnaires and application forms; remove any language suggesting inappropriate rejection on the basis of the medical examination.
6. Prepare an annual affirmative action program for on-site inspection by compliance officers.
7. Inform management at all levels about the firm's obligations and ask for support from these individuals.
8. Tell employees and applicants that the firm's employment and affirmative action policy statements are available for inspection.
9. Notify recruiters of the employment policy.
10. Invite handicapped employees to identify themselves and relate their status.
11. Review employment qualifications for the purpose of eliminating discrimination against handicapped employees.
12. Review facilities and equipment for reasonable accommodations to the special needs of the handicapped.

---

[12]Gopal C. Pati and John I. Adkins, Jr., "Hire the Handicapped—Compliance Is Good Business," *Harvard Business Review*, January–February 1980, p. 15.

[13]Ibid., p. 14.

Minority Capitalism

Another area where business has been very active is that of promoting minority capitalism. Although some of this activity has been mandated by government, most of it is voluntary.

Meanwhile, many business firms, acting on their own, have designated high-ranking executives to oversee special minority purchasing programs. The National Minority Purchasing Council (NMPC), a trade association, estimates that around 50 percent of *Fortune's* "500" industrial firms currently have established such programs. According to NMPC data, the *Fortune* 500's spending with minority businesses rose from $7 million in 1972 to $1.1 billion in 1977 and is targeted for over $10 billion by the middle of the 1990s. The overall results are promising, as seen by the fact that General Motors, Standard Oil of Indiana, and Borden, Inc., to name but three, have dramatically increased their spending with minority-owned companies. Other examples are:

> A Chicago building maintenance concern owned by a black man is thriving, with a large contract to clean a major corporation's downtown headquarters, bringing in a great deal of revenue.
>
> A twenty-three-year-old catering concern in the black community of another city now does $1.5 million of business annually, with a substantial increase due largely to corporate and federal contracts seeking minorities.
>
> A small black-owned Boston electrical contractor was turned into a multimillion-dollar engineering company when a large construction company seeking to conform to a municipal government set-aside requirement subcontracted more than $5 million of work to it.[14]

Research shows that those firms which are serious about developing minority purchasing programs are setting up formal procedures. A typical five-step approach follows:

1. Holding a meeting of division heads and profit-center managers at which the chief executive officer explains that the company is determined, as a matter of policy, to substantially increase purchases from minority-owned companies.

Five minority purchasing program procedures.

2. Appointing an executive to evaluate and organize the most appropriate minority purchasing program.

3. Drawing up written goals and corporate policy on minority purchases.

---

[14]David E. Gumpert, "Seeking Minority-Owned Businesses as Suppliers," *Harvard Business Review*, January–February 1979, p. 113; for more on this subject, see Larry C. Guinipero, "Developing Effective Minority Purchasing Programs," *Sloan Management Review*, Winter 1981, pp. 33–42.

4. Implementing the program.

5. Making a careful review of the program in terms of both dollars spent and the names of minority businesses which have been involved.[15]

Are such programs helping minority capitalism? Statistics show that they are. Many minority firms are growing by leaps and bounds and some have become multimillion-dollar enterprises. These growth figures are partially accounted for by new developments that encourage minority capitalism.

Discrimination against Women

By the late-1980s, approximately 48 percent of the work force was made up of women, many of whom had begun to enter fields traditionally considered within the male domain. Management is one such area of work. Some of the major reasons for the increased number of women in the workplace are (1) the women's movement and organizations with feminist or egalitarian philosophies and orientations which supported it, (2) recent civil rights legislation promoting affirmative action programs, (3) the changing profile of the U. S. work force, and (4) the increased need for competent business managers. Despite such developments, the eighties also saw discrimination against women in the areas of sexual harassment, salary, and management promotions.

Sexual Harassment

As noted earlier, federal law prohibits sexual harassment of employees. Women, in particular, have found this legislation important in their efforts to secure equal opportunity, as revealed by the fact that the number of sexual harassment charges has risen from 4,272 in 1981 to 7,273 in 1985.[16] In order to obtain assistance under this law, three conditions must be met:

Some women are sexually harassed.

1. A woman must show that the harassment is "gender-specific," which means that women in the organization are being sexually harassed while men are not.

2. The woman must show that she was treated unfairly because she refused to submit to her supervisor's sexual advances.

3. This harassment must have occurred either with the explicit or tacit approval of the employer.[17]

---

[15]Gumpert, p. 114.

[16]David E. Terpstra and Douglas D. Baker, "Outcomes of Sexual Harassment Charges," *Academy of Management Journal*, March 1988, pp. 185.

[17]Leap and Gray, p. 160.

Can women who are sexually harassed get fair treatment if they complain? The answer is a qualified yes. The following example provides a look at the positive side of the picture.

A female sales representative came to the personnel department and complained about the conduct of the male sales department manager. On several occasions he had, in private, questioned the female employee about her sexual habits, method of birth control and social acquaintances. He had also asked her to his home in the evenings but never in the presence of co-workers. The employee turned down his requests and asked for a transfer out of the department. The manager denied her a transfer and gave her a poor performance appraisal.

The personnel department confronted the manager with the employee's allegations. He unequivocally denied ever making any advances or remarks of a sexual nature. However, statements were taken from other females under the manager's purview. Though they never heard him make any remarks or advances to the employee making the complaint, most of the women were themselves recipients of sexual comments that were both inappropriate and unprofessional.

Though the manager denied the allegations, the personnel department had enough evidence to believe that the woman's complaint was valid. The company took immediate and corrective action against the manager in order to limit potential liability.[18]

Examples such as this help to reinforce the fact that many firms refuse to allow sexual discrimination and will take corrective action when they learn about it. One of the most effective ways appears to be in-house training in which managers at all levels of the hierarchy learn what constitutes sexual harassment and how to deal with it. A second common approach is the development and dissemination of a policy statement indicating that the organization opposes sexual harassment and will take action against any individuals found guilty of such practices.[19]

Salary Inequities

Women at all levels of business organizations, according to the latest reports, make less money on the average than do their male counterparts. What

---

[18]George K. Kronenberger and David L. Bourke, "Effective Training and the Elimination of Sexual Harassment," *Personnel Journal*, November 1981, p. 882.

[19]For more on this, see Jacqueline F. Strayer and Sandra E. Rapoport, "Sexual Harassment, 2: Limiting Corporate Liability," *Personnel*, April 1986, pp. 26–33; Jolene Saunders, "Sexual Harassment," *Working Woman*, February 1984, pp. 40, 43; Nancy Davidson, "The Abused Woman: How an Employer Can Help," *Supervisory Management*, April 1984, pp. 16–19; Diane St. James, "Coping with Sexual Harassment," *Supervisory Management*, October 1983, pp. 4–9; Jeanne Bosson Driscoll, "Sexual Attraction and Harassment: Management's New Problems," *Personnel Journal*, January 1981, pp. 33–36; and Mary P. Rowe, "Dealing with Sexual Harassment," *Harvard Business Review*, May–June 1981, pp. 42–46.

Women are not being paid as much as men.

accounts for this difference? The answer is found in the interpretation of the "equal pay for equal work" doctrine of the 1963 Equal Pay Act. Many employers have contended that women do not perform equal work and so cannot receive equal salaries. Working women now file complaints, however, and the U. S. Labor Department has started filing suits. The most important early decision came in 1970, when the U. S. Third Circuit Court upheld a decision against the Wheaton Glass Company of Milville, New Jersey. In its ruling, the court said that the jobs did not have to be identical: If they were "substantially equal," the equal pay law applied. This ruling meant that Wheaton had to pay its female inspector-packers over $900,000 in back pay. Since then numerous firms have also lost equal-pay suits; some of the best known are RCA, American Can, and Pacific Telephone & Telegraph. Despite such legal actions, however, salary discrimination against women continues, and it is optimistic and premature to predict that such inequities will be rectified in the near future.

According to a report released by Congress in late 1982, working women make only about 70 percent as much as working men. Researchers echo these findings. One survey found that 47 percent of women believed there were different salaries in their organization for men and women.[20] When asked to comment on their impressions, two of the typical responses were as follows:

> There's probably reverse discrimination now. Our problem is no longer getting hired. It's what happens to us once we get on the job. The salary thing is so discouraging. I know men with positions similar to mine are doing better financially.
>
> I feel in a real quandary with respect to salary. At the time I started with the company, I simply accepted the fact that as a female I would be paid less. As things have changed I've kept hoping that my salary would be brought up to a level commensurate with the manager to whom I report and he assures me that he's working to change things for me and I have seen some results. But I'm still below level. My more militant friends tell me I should sue but I really don't want to become known as a troublemaker. I've always tried to fit in, be cooperative, and do a good job.[21]

These comments are neither rare nor unrepresentative of working women. Such reactions are especially characteristic of the management level where opportunities for women are still less than they are for men.

On the other hand, changes are being made. One of the major reasons is the increasing number of lawsuits in which women are demanding that wages be tied to the job's worth. They contend that the only way to eliminate the pay bias of sex-segregated jobs is to revalue them on the basis of the skills

---

[20]Corine T. Norgaard, "Problems and Perspectives of Female Managers," *MSU Business Topics,* Winter 1980, p. 24.

[21]Ibid.

and responsibilities they require. In recent years there has been some progress in this direction. For example, within the electrical industry several major manufacturers have in recent years settled sex discrimination charges by agreeing to upgrade jobs held mostly by women. In a case against Westinghouse, the International Union of Electrical Workers used as evidence a 45-year-old company manual setting out of pay scales for different jobs, and stating that women would be paid less because they were women. While none of the electrical industry cases has been fully tried in court, the union has won pay upgrades for women workers in more than a dozen settlements. (In these and other voluntary settlements, women's wages have been raised, while men's wages have not been cut. In cases brought under the civil rights laws, it is illegal to resolve discrimination complaints by reducing the benefits of the favored class.) In another example:

> In 1982, after a study showing widespread underpayment for female-dominated jobs, the state of Minnesota earmarked $22 million to upgrade women's pay. The study found, for example, that clerk stenographers—99.7 percent of them women—had about as hard a job as laborers, all of them men. The clerk stenographers got $1,171 a month while the laborers got $1,521. Some 8,000 state employees, about a third of the state work force, are now receiving adjustments. According to Ann Grune, executive director of the National Committee on Pay Equity, 18 states have undertaken pay equity job evaluation studies.[22]

Management Promotions

Women at the managerial level face problems when they try for promotions. Two main areas of consideration need to be addressed when the topic of management promotions is examined: barriers to promotion and ways of overcoming these barriers.

Women themselves do some things that hold back their career progress.

Barriers.   Three common barriers affect the promotion of women into, and up, the ranks of management. One is the perceptions and personnel approaches of women themselves. Some women are concerned with failure and opt for conservative, low-risk career strategies. Others find it difficult to work with people they do not like. Men, too, at times have these problems, but they have for so long been the primary work-force members that they have had to learn to tolerate people and work situations they may dislike. Still other women, traditionally untrained in the areas, lack an understanding of career planning and development and fail to take steps necessary for promotion or advancement. Finally, some women see luck as a dominant

---

[22]Tamar Lewin, "A New Push to Raise Women's Pay," *New York Times,* January 1, 1984, sec. F, p. 15.

factor in achievement.[23] These kinds of perceptions and personal approaches constitute a major barrier to female management promotions.

Some hiring biases are directed against women.

A second barrier is hiring biases. Research has shown that in some cases, women are substantially more acceptable than men when applying for traditionally female-oriented jobs but considerably less acceptable for traditionally male-oriented jobs.[24] Additionally, there is empirical evidence that individuals applying for jobs commonly held by members of the opposite sex, have to be perceived as more qualified than applicants from the other group in order to get the job:

> The implications of these findings confirm the fact that sex-role stereotyping is very prevalent at the recruiting stage and may be assumed to present a major obstacle in on-the-job conditions to those females placed in non-traditional positions. Moreover, there are indications that on-job decisions and evaluations are less favorable for equally competent women holding managerial positions than males holding those positions.[25]

Organizational barriers may prevent women's rise in management.

A third problem is organizational barriers, which arise from policies, procedures, and systems that determine how the organization will operate. In many cases, businesses function as they have in the past, making the same kinds of promotion decisions. As a result, no woman has ever served at the upper ranks in some organizations. Therefore, when these organizations promote, the odds are against a woman moving up this high—unless, of course, she is seen as overqualified (see Social Responsibility in Action: Women on the Board).

Overcoming the Barriers. How can women overcome these barriers? How can organizations determined to ensure equality in the management ranks help reduce these barriers? There are two basic ways, and they are complementary.

Women should develop social power strategies.

One way is for women to develop specific social power strategies. Women desiring careers in management can use four traditional managerial powers in advancing themselves to and through careers in management, continuing the use of the powers so long as they work. The first of these powers is expert power, through which the woman influences people through her superior skill or business knowledge. The second is informational power, the ability to

---

[23]Christine D. Hay, "Women in Management: The Obstacles and Opportunities They Face," *Personnel Administrator*, April 1980, pp. 31–39; see also "Why Women Aren't Getting to the Top," *Fortune*, April 16, 1984, pp. 40–45.

[24]Ellyn Mirides and Andre Cote, "Women in Management: Strategies for Removing the Barriers," *Personnel Administrator*, April 1980, p. 26.

[25]Ibid.

SOCIAL
RESPONSIBILITY
IN
ACTION:
Women
on the
Board

Over the past decade there has been a small increase in female directors in *Fortune* 500 companies. Research reveals that the larger the company, the more likely it is that there is at least one female director. For example, at the beginning of the 1980s, 66 percent of the largest fifty U. S. industrials had women directors; 24 percent of those who ranked between 201 and 250 had female directors; 14 percent of those who ranked between 451 and 500 had women on the board. Most large firms that do have women on the board have only one.

Why are there not more women? One recent survey obtained responses to this question from 126 of the *Fortune* 500. Here is what they said:

	Number of Companies Choosing This Answer	Percentage of Companies
It is difficult to find educationally qualified candidates.	10	8
It is difficult to find experientially qualified candidates.	44	35
The board is already filled with qualified members.	54	43
We feel it is unnecessary to seek out a(another) female board member at this time.	8	6
We have not yet considered whether to add a(another) female board member.	2	2
We would add a(another) female board member, but we don't know where to look to find one that is qualified.	3	2
We are opposed to constituency representation on boards.	32	25
It is premature for our company.	0	0
It is currently under consideration.	14	11
Other reasons.	36	29

These data reveal that women's progress in the board room is proceeding at about the same rate as it is in the management ranks. Each year sees small gains; there are unlikely to be any significant changes during the 1980s. So while the picture is not very bright, it is not terribly dim either. As one researcher summed it up, "There is a *hint* of optimism."

Because more than one answer to the question was given by the respondents, the total of the column showing numbers of companies is more than 126, and the total for the column showing percentages for each answer is more than 100.

Source: Lloyd D. Elgart, "Women on *Fortune* 500 Boards," *California Management Review*, Summer 1983, pp. 121–27.

provide evaluations to others about why they should believe or behave differently. The third is referent power, by which the woman influences others because they identify with her. Fourth is coercive power, through which the woman can bring negative sanctions (poor performance rating, low recommended raise) against others.[26] Table 17-1 describes some of the ways in which these social power strategies can be employed.

Training programs for women use several common subjects.

A second way of overcoming sexist barriers is through the use of training programs. This approach is being given a great deal of attention today, as managements attempt to identify the specific kinds of programs to offer. Some of the most common subjects in the 1990s will be the functions of a manager, self-awareness, dealing with conflict, leadership skills development, career development, and the uniqueness of women in management.[27]

Does such training really help? Joan Harley and Lois Ann Koff have found that it does, especially if given prior to the need.[28] For example, if a woman is about to be promoted into lower-level management and has had inadequate training, she should be given training in supervision. Before she is assigned to make weekly presentations to the department heads, she should possibly be given public speaking training. Such early training offers many benefits, including: (1) the instilling of confidence and self-esteem, (2) prevention of poor starts, (3) ensuring that the women contribute from the start, (4) increasing women's promotability, and (5) rewarding women and giving them recognition.[29]

Academia has also entered the field of training women for management development.

Additionally, academia has recently developed a role for itself in preparing women for management.[30] Many colleges of business are now beginning to offer courses or programs dealing with the special needs of women in management. Some of the topics being covered include strategies for bringing women into management, women in leadership, corporate liberation, issues of equality, and institutional barriers faced by women. An emphasis is also being given to the master's in business administration (MBA). The MBA can help open many doors for today's female manager. This type of training is also useful because it helps women to see how organizations really function. For example, William Doll and his associates recently studied women in the personnel area and compared the views of more successful women with those of less successful women. They found that the "fast-track" females not only had mentors who would help guide their

---

[26]Gary N. Powell, "Career Development and the Woman Manager—A Social Power Perspective," *Personnel*, May–June 1980, pp. 22–32.

[27]Hay, p. 37.

[28]Joan Harley and Lois Ann Koff, "Prepare Women Now for Tomorrow's Managerial Challenges," *Personnel Administrator*, April 1980, pp. 41–42.

[29]Ibid., p. 42.

[30]Rose K. Reha, "Preparing Women for Management Roles," *Business Horizons*, April 1979, pp. 68–71.

TABLE 17-1

Analysis of Career Development Strategies Available to Women Managers

Strategy	Power Bases Emphasized	Advantages	Disadvantages
Use perceptions of feminine characteristics to advantage.	Expert, informational.	Easily assimilated into prevailing masculine culture. Takes advantage of opportunities presently available in socially oriented functions. May be benefactor of increased importance attached to socially oriented functions.	Supports stereotyping of women as unfit for management. Leads to obtaining staff positions typically peripheral to more powerful line positions. May lead to dead-end jobs and career stagnation after initial successes.
Adopt masculine standard of behavior.	Referent.	Easily assimilated into prevailing masculine culture. Precedent established for using this strategy. May succeed if adhered to rigidly.	Supports stereotyping of women as unfit for management. Initially gives up referent power. Leads to conflict between sexual identity and career identity for some women.

careers, but they placed greater emphasis on the need for a mentor than did their less successful counterparts. Those on the fast track also understood that politics is played in the organization, and they placed greater importance on knowing the rules than did those women who were not as successful. In short, successful women have their eyes open, they know what is going on,

TABLE 17-1
continued

Strategy	Power Bases Emphasized	Advantages	Disadvantages
Seek entry into informal networks.	Referent, coercive, rewarding.	More active strategy, reflects less passivity. Complementary to other strategies, may be simultaneously pursued. If successful, power held in both formal and informal systems.	May find resistance to women in "old boy" networks. Results not immediately forthcoming. Maintenance of membership and particular relationship requires energy beyond that devoted to the job. If unsuccessful, may hinder career more than if entry not attempted.

and they adjust to the realities of the situation.[31] One way of acquiring this information, at very low risk, is through formal training and education.[32]

Of course, only time will tell whether business is really going to promote a significant number of women through the management ranks, but it is definitely in the organization's best interests to take advantage of this virtually untapped human resource; and all signs indicate that management intends to do so.

---

[31]William Doll, Dale Sullivan, Jack L. Simonetti, and Jacqueline A. Erwin, "Fast Tracks to Success for Women in Personnel," *Personnel*, May–June 1982, pp. 12–22.

[32]See also Raymond A. Noe, "Women and Mentoring: A Review and Research Agenda," *Academy of Management Review*, January 1988, pp. 65–78.

ECOLOGY

The key word is interrelationship.

In order to grasp fully the importance of the ecological challenge facing business, the reader should understand what is meant by the word *ecology,* which Webster defines as "a branch of science concerned with the interrelationship of organisms and their environments especially as manifested by natural cycles and rhythms, community development and structure, interaction between different kinds of organisms, geographic distributions, and population alterations."[33] The key to understanding ecology rests with the word *interrelationship.* All organisms must relate in some way to their environment. If they cannot coexist with it, change occurs; the environment is altered or the organism dies. When such changes occur in nature's ecological balance, there can be side effects in other areas.

The entire world can thus be viewed as consisting of interlocking and interrelated ecosystems. If people start making changes in these systems, havoc can result. This section of the text will examine some of the ecological challenges facing business today. Some of the current ecological legislation will then be reviewed.

Air Pollution

John Lindsay, a former mayor of New York, once commented that he liked the city's air because he enjoyed seeing what he was breathing. There is no doubt that air pollution has increased dramatically over the past few decades, especially in huge metropolitan areas like New York, Chicago, or Los Angeles. Three of the primary pollutants have been automobiles, industrial smokestacks, and cigarettes.

Automobiles

The automobile is the major cause of air pollution.

The major cause of air pollution in America is the automobile. For some time now, automakers have been trying to control the three main automotive emissions: carbon monoxide, hydrocarbons, and nitrogen oxides. The basic approach has been engine modification. For example, in attempting to limit hydrocarbons and carbon monoxide, the major automakers have turned to higher coolant temperatures and altered valve and retarded-spark timing. For limiting nitrogen oxides, they have given major attention to reducing peak combustion temperatures through water injection or exhaust-gas recirculation and the use of a reducing-type of catalyst for treating exhaust.

Another approach has been to reduce auto weight, thereby decreasing fuel consumption and the accompanying exhaust pollution. A third way is through the development of new auto fuels that give better mileage and lower emissions of harmful gases. Regardless of what is done, however, the United States should witness a reduction in auto air pollution, at least through the 1990s.

---

[33]*Webster's Third New International Dictionary,* s. v. "ecology."

Industrial Smokestacks

Utilities and refineries are also big air polluters.

If one drives into a big city on a cold winter day, smokestack pollution can be seen hanging over the metropolis. Among the worst of the industrial air polluters are the utilities, many of them daily hurling tons of sulphur dioxides into the air. Today experts estimate the amount of air pollutants at hundreds of millions of tons annually, with utilities accounting for a significant percentage of this. Smelting and refining firms are also major contributors.

In an effort to decrease pollutant emission, these firms are beginning to rely on technological advances, such as power plant scrubbers and cyclonic burners. Many power plant scrubbers used today employ pulverized limestone for removing sulfur. In this process, a slurry of rock and water is sprayed into the dirty gas as it moves from the boiler to the scrubber. The limestone combines with the sulfur in the gas to form a liquid, which settles out as sludge waste. The remaining "scrubbed" gas then continues up the smokestack.

Another smokestack antipollution process is the cyclonic burner, which is being used by the lumber industry to dispose of waste products while simultaneously preserving clean air:

> The cyclonic burner is able to achieve near total combustion of solid mill wastes by "grinding them up and suspending the particles on blasts of air in the fire box. The generated heat provides a handy and economical source of energy." Because the system is virtually closed-loop, exhausts are fed back into the smokestack. Two of these systems already in operation illustrate that the heat from the burner can be used to fire kilns in the mill. As a result, it is possible for a mill cutting one million board feet a year to save $115,000 in carting costs and $85,000 on fuel previously needed to fire the kilns.[34]

Technological advances such as these are helping to reduce smokestack pollution. However, a great deal more needs to be done.

Cigarettes

Over the last decade there has been a decline in cigarette consumption. Smoking is now viewed by many as an environmental pollutant, and restaurants, airplanes, and public buildings often have restricted smoking areas—if they allow smoking, at all. Approximately 30 percent of all corporations limit smoking on the job, and the National Center for Health Promotion predicts that the number will leap to 80 percent within a few years. Meanwhile, some firms such as Pacific Northwest Bell and Control Data do not allow smoking at all.[35]

---

[34]Luthans, Hodgetts, and Thompson, p. 423.

[35]Joan O'C. Hamilton et al., "'No Smoking' Sweeps America," *Business Week*, July 27, 1987, pp. 40–46.

There are a number of reasons why firms are moving to limit or ban smoking. One is the high cost. Wayne Cascio estimates the expenditures of the average business per smoker are $2,500 annually.[36] This cost includes sick days, health-care insurance premiums, premature death, and damage to the surrounding environment as evidenced by soot on windows, smoke on walls, and cigarette burns in carpeting. A complementary reason of this anti-smoking attitude of business is the effect of smoking on nonsmokers, who note that their health is being endangered by this habit.

It is likely that smoking in the workplace will be severely curtailed during the 1990s. The most common strategy will be a gradual elimination of this practice. The Blue Cross/Blue Shield of Maryland three-phase approach is a good example.

> Phase I . . . banned smoking in all meetings, conferences, and training sessions, including those in off-site locations. To accommodate smokers as well as nonsmokers, Phase I allowed smoking breaks in meetings lasting longer than one hour.
>
> Phase II . . . made all work areas smoke free, whether private offices, workstations, or open work areas. A committee of smokers and nonsmokers designated smoking areas, but had all cigarette vending machines removed throughout the company.
>
> Phase III . . . prohibited smoking on all company premises. Employees who failed to comply faced the full range of disciplinary action: from warning to suspension and finally termination.[37]

Air pollution from cigarettes will diminish during the 1990s, although it will not be completely eliminated. This current trend will make the workplace a safer and cleaner environment.

Water Pollution

Some firms have used nearby lakes or streams as drainpipes for carrying off industrial production wastes.[38] As a result, some bodies of water, such as the Great Lakes, are said to have been very heavily polluted. In other cases companies have pumped liquid wastes into underground dumps. Unfortunately, sometimes these dumps have leaked, polluting both underground and surface water.

There is also the case of thermal, or warm-water, pollution, often brought about by hydroelectric plants. In order to generate electricity, the utility

---

[36]Wayne F. Cascio, *Costing Human Resources: The Financial Impact of Behavior in Organizations,* 2nd ed. (Boston: PWS/Kent, 1987) p. 82.

[37]Sherry D. Hammond, David A. DeCenzo, and Mollie H. Bowers, "How One Company Went Smokeless," *Harvard Business Review,* November–December 1987, p. 44.

[38]Tom Morgan et al. "Don't Go Near the Water," *Newsweek,* August 1, 1988, pp. 42–47.

brings in cool water from a nearby lake or river. This is converted into steam to turn the plant's turbine engines. The steam is then passed through a condenser, cooled and turned back into water, and then returned to the lake or river. The problem is that often this water is returned at 5 or 10 degrees above its original temperature. The ultimate affect can be a change in the basic ecosystem of the water. The aquatic life, unaccustomed to the warmer environment, may die.

Currently, businesses receive a great deal of pressure to cease any activity that may cause water pollution. This is all part of the national goal of cleaning United States waterways so that the population is guaranteed potable water and the lesser necessities that water affords, such as nontoxic fishing streams. However, it is unlikely that "zero discharge" will become a reality because of the economic problems which that degree of pollution reduction would cause. It is too expensive to totally eliminate all water pollution. But an objective of 80 percent reduction of pollution is feasible.

"Zero discharge" is not feasible.

Some of the major steps business has already taken to fight water pollution include the recycling of water through waste treatment systems and the development of lake restoration projects. General Motors provides a good illustration of the former:

> Water from a foundry is pumped into a large lagoon or settling basin in which the foundry solids gradually settle to the bottom. The clean water is then pumped back into the foundry for use in operations. At the present time General Motors is also looking into a new technique for purifying water to a degree suitable for reuse in any plant process. In essence the purifying process involves passing water through sand filters to remove suspended solids, through activated carbon towers to remove organics, and finally, through reverse osmosis units to reduce dissolved solids.[39]

Meanwhile, in the area of lake restoration, business firms are studying ways to restore already heavily polluted bodies of water. Union Carbide has reported success from its efforts at Lake Waccabuc in New York, the Attica, New York, reservoir, and the Ottoville, Ohio, quarry. All three suffered from oxygen deficiencies that resulted in the growth of algae. By withdrawing water from each, saturating it with oxygen and returning it to the bottom of the lake, Union Carbide eventually overcame the problem.

Noise Pollution

The amount of noise to which the average urban resident is subjected can be quite extreme. Car horns blast, pedestrians shout, and overhead aircraft roar. In the past, little was done about all this. Today, however, with the increased

---

[39]Luthans, Hodgetts, and Thompson, p. 423.

Excessive noise can damage hearing.

numbers of people and noises, steps are being taken to reduce noise pollution. One major cause of concern is medical research, which has established that people who are exposed to prolonged periods of noise at 85 decibels can suffer hearing damage. How loud is 85 decibels? The following provides a framework for answering this question:

Sound	Decibels
Whispering	30
Moderate conversation	35
Light auto traffic from 100 feet	50
Freeway from 50 feet	70
Heavy truck traffic from 50 feet	90
Power mower	95
Riveter	110
Siren	115
Commercial jet takeoff from 200 feet	120
Rocket launch	180

Today the government has established 90 decibels as an acceptable noise level for people in organized workplaces, although numerous groups, including unions, are exerting pressure to reduce this level to 85 decibels.

Noise can also be a source of psychological distress.

Research also indicates that noise can prove to be a source of psychological distress, contributing to symptoms such as instability, headaches, nausea, general anxiety, and sexual impotency.

Business has been taking two approaches in meeting the challenge of noise pollution. First, companies are investigating their environments to find and silence sources of noise. At some automotive plants, for example, noise suppressors are being used to reduce the noise level to 80 decibels. Ceilings and walls at these plants are covered with sound-absorbing materials, and over and around particularly noisy departments there are draft curtains— rigid, wall-like panels stuffed with noise-reducing fiberglass. Meanwhile, in factory areas where power tools are used, firms have attached hoses to the machinery to carry the noise out of the building; and to quiet conveyor systems, plants have slowed down the machines. Other types of manufacturers have used similar approaches, employing shields and padding to stifle plant noise and supplying protective ear devices to workers in areas where the noise level is over 90 decibels.

The second approach is that machine manufacturers are redesigning their equipment so that it makes less noise. For example, the hammer-type riveter is being replaced by an orbital and spin riveter. The riveter head used to be slammed into the ground; now the tool compresses the riveter head with an orbital or revolving motion instead. Attempts are also being made to stifle noise pollution from turbofan or jet engines. The most common method so far has been to redesign the engine by placing sound-absorbing materials on the walls on the inlet duct of the turbofan as well as in the exhaust duct. With these and similar developments, factory, machinery, and aircraft noise is being significantly reduced.

Of course, it is impossible to eliminate all noise pollution. However, a cutback of 10 decibels translates into a 50 percent decrease in a person's awareness of the noise. If procedures of the type discussed continue, the United States should become a quieter place in which to work and live.

Ecological Legislation

Thus far this section has examined the ecological issues facing business. Some of these problems are being handled by means of voluntary action on the part of the business community. Also, many federal and state regulations have been enacted in recent years; these call for specific compliance. The two most important have been the Environmental Policy Act of 1969 and the National Air Quality Standards Act of 1970.

A number of ecological laws directly affecting business have been passed.

The Environmental Policy Act of 1969 established the Council on Environmental Quality. The council's basic duties are to help the president of the United States develop an annual environmental quality report, gather data on environmental trends, and develop recommendations to promote environmental quality. In addition, the act established the Environmental Protection Agency (EPA). The purpose of the agency is to coordinate all major federal pollution control programs for the purpose of achieving environmental quality.

The National Air Quality Standards Act of 1970 is one of the stiffest antipollution bills ever enacted. Some of its provisions follow:

1. All new factories must have the latest pollution control equipment.
2. Auto manufacturers must drastically reduce exhaust and nitrogen oxide emissions.
3. The federal government can set emission standards for ten major pollutants, ranging from soot to sulfur dioxide.

In addition, each state is given the authority to set factory-emission tolerances in accord with federal standards, and if they do not, the EPA, after thirty days' notice to the respective state, can do so itself. Furthermore, the EPA can directly sue polluters; and if the agency is lax in this task, individual citizens have a right to sue both the EPA and the polluter. Violators of the act are subject to maximum fines of $25,000 per day of noncompliance or one year in jail. Finally, it is important to note that the public wants stricter antipollution laws, as seen in Figure 17-1. Helping explain part of this trend, *Business Week* reported:

> What is significant . . . is that the hardening of the public's mood is broad-based and seemingly impervious to . . . economic arguments

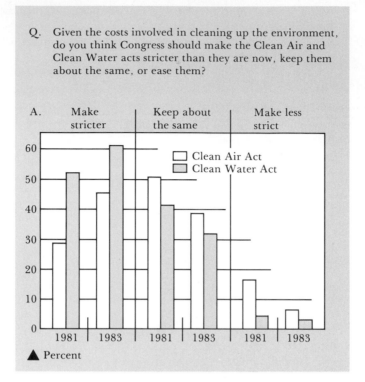

Q.   Given the costs involved in cleaning up the environment, do you think Congress should make the Clean Air and Clean Water acts stricter than they are now, keep them about the same, or ease them?

FIGURE 17-1   Stronger Public Support for Environmental Controls

Source: Reprinted, by permission, from *Business Week,* January 24, 1983, p. 87. By special permission, copyright © 1983 by McGraw-Hill, Inc. Data from Louis Harris & Associates, Inc.

. . . For example, Harris interviewers asked people whether a factory whose air pollution level is dangerous to human health should be granted relief from environmental standards for any reason. . . .

Among the mitigating reasons suggested: that jobs would be saved and that a factory that otherwise would shut down might remain open. By an overwhelming 78% to 17%, the verdict was that no reason is sufficient to grant an exception. And among the most uncompromising were people who identified themselves (or their families) as skilled laborers and union members.[40]

These are only a few of the many environmental control acts now in existence. What does the future hold? From a dollars and cents standpoint, business is going to spend increasing sums for pollution abatement. In

<hr>

[40]"A Call for Tougher—Not Weaker—Antipollution Laws," *Business Week,* January 24, 1983, p. 87.

addition, it has been predicted that the government will eventually set up a system of pollution fee assessments. The greater the amount of air and water pollution caused by a particular company, the greater penalties that company will have to pay.

CONSUMERISM

Since the late 1960s, consumerism has been a major social issue facing business. Phillip Kotler has defined *consumerism* as an organized social movement of concerned citizens and government to enhance the rights and power of buyers in relation to sellers.[41] This enhancement is taking two major forms to date: Buyers are demanding more information about the products and services they are purchasing, and they are insisting on safer products. [42]

Consumer Information and Assistance

It is no surprise that research reveals that many people, when they lack knowledge about a product, tend to equate price with quality. After all, how does one go about deciding which of five brands of aspirin is *really* the best buy? Consumers need more than price guides, and a number of protections and aids for them have sprung up.

Legislative Protection

In recent years, legislation designed to educate the consumer has been enacted. One of these laws is the Truth in Packaging Act, which sets forth the following mandatory labeling provisions:

The Truth in Packaging Act sets forth mandatory labeling provisions.

1. The identity of the commodity shall be specified on the label.
2. The net quantity of contents shall be stated in a uniform and prominent location on the package.
3. The net quantity of contents shall be clearly expressed in ounces [only] and, if applicable, pounds [only] or in the case of liquid measures in the largest whole unit of quarts or pints.
4. The net quantity of a "serving" must be stated if the package bears a representation concerning servings.

A second such consumer protection is the Truth in Lending Act. This bill regulates the extension of credit to individuals and is primarily concerned with ensuring that the person know the charges, direct and indirect,

---

[41]Phillip Kotler, *Marketing Management: Analysis, Planning, and Control*, 5th ed. (Englewood Cliffs, NJ: Prentice-Hall, 1984), p. 85.

[42]See also Steven Waldman, "Dial M for Marketing Fraud," *Newsweek*, May 16, 1988, p. 56.

associated with the loan. To give an example, open-end accounts, such as revolving charges, must provide the holder with the following information on each monthly statement:

1. The amount owed at the beginning of the period.
2. The amount and date of new purchases.
3. Any payments made.
4. The finance charge in dollars and cents.
5. The annual percentage rate.
6. The balance upon which the finance charge is calculated.
7. The closing date of billing and the accompanying unpaid balance.

A third consumer aid is the Consumer Product Safety Act. This act is designed to:

*The Consumer Prod-
uct Safety Act has
four major provisions.*

1. Protect the public against unreasonable risk of injury from consumer products.
2. Assist consumers on evaluating the comparative safety of these products.
3. Develop uniform safety standards for consumer products while minimizing any conflicts with state or local regulations.
4. Promote research and investigation into the causes and prevention of product related injuries, illnesses, or deaths.

In order to carry out these objectives, the act established a Consumer Product Safety Commission consisting of five members appointed by the president of the United States with the advice and consent of the Senate. A primary goal of the commission is to establish and maintain product safety standards. Another is to reduce product-related accidents by demanding safer products.

Business Assistance

*Consumer complaint
departments have
been established.*

The business community has taken action of its own to make the consumer more knowledgeable, and that effort continues. For example, General Foods and Lever Brothers have sponsored consumer clinics in which customers are taught how to use the firms' products. Sears, Roebuck is sponsoring ads designed to improve the consumer's knowledge of its products. Jewel Food Stores and Giant Foods have introduced unit pricing programs. And if something should go wrong, many firms have established departments or offices to help consumers expedite solutions to the difficulty. For example, Whirlpool offers its customers a twenty-four-hour "cool line." An individual with a complaint or question about service can call this toll-free number at any hour of the day or night from any location within the United States. Other companies have established consumer complaint departments which assign a problem to a specific individual, who stays with it until the customer is satisfied. Corning Glass has extended this idea and appointed a manager of consumer interests, whose job it is to represent the consumer and make sure the complaint does not get lost. In this way, the customer has an in-house agent.

Product Safety

Another major issue in consumerism is that of product safety. General product safety, and especially auto and aircraft safety, has received major attention.

Auto Safety

Many new auto safety features are being added.

Ever since consumer advocate Ralph Nader wrote *Unsafe at Any Speed,* auto safety has been an issue of concern. The 1970s were a time of dramatic increases in auto safety legislation. In all fairness to auto manufacturers, however, it must be noted that prior to this public outcry, sales indicated that people were not willing to pay for safety features. Now, of course, much of that has changed.

Some of the new auto-safety features include seat belts, shoulder belts, energy-absorbing steering columns, padded dashboards, and bumpers capable of withstanding minor collisions. In addition, consideration is still being given to the air bag.

Aircraft Safety

While most people are aware that there are more planes in the air today than there were a decade ago and many air traffic controllers are overworked,[43] there is also an air safety problem stemming from improper aircraft maintenance. One of the major reasons is the large number of bogus parts that are being sold as new or properly reconditioned, when in fact they are of poor quality and may not function correctly. Substandard and counterfeit parts are becoming more commonplace, and it can be difficult to tell the difference between them and the genuine item.

In an effort to deal with these problems, many aircraft firms buy only from reputable dealers and suppliers with whom they have had a long-standing relationship. However, this does not ensure that a counterfeit part will not slip in, from time to time.

Additionally, the government is now beginning to crack down hard on maintenance fraud. The government has succeeded in putting the president of Execuair Corp., a parts supplier in Canoga Park, California, behind bars. A federal court in Oklahoma convicted Laurence Manhan, the president, of selling counterfeit actuators—parts designed to cut off the flow of fuel to prevent a fire—to the U. S. Air Force for its C-141 personnel carrier. Execuair

---

[43]Richard Witkin, "Air Traffic Errors Lead F.A.A. to Cut Flights at Chicago," *New York Times,* October 6, 1988, pp. 1, 46.

passed off 56 actuators to the military as originals made by Whittaker Controls, a legitimate manufacturer. Manhan is now serving a five-year prison term.[44]

General Product Safety

Many firms, spurred on by government legislation and the possibility of costly lawsuits, are placing great emphasis on product safety. Some are establishing product safety committees to evaluate current products. Others are providing safety tips, pointing out certain potentially dangerous consumer errors that should be avoided. For example, the Hoover Company makes it a practice to tell the operator not to pick up puddles of water with the vacuum. This would warn anyone who might confuse the capabilities of a household vacuum with those of the industrial-style shop vacuums.

Legal Aspects

In recent years, liability laws have undergone drastic changes. Two areas of particular importance for business have been negligence and strict liability.

Privity of contract has been pushed aside.

Under old English law, businesses were liable for negligence only to the person who bought the good; this doctrine is known as privity of contract. Today the courts have pushed privity of contract aside, and an individual does not have to prove a direct contractual relationship. Persons who buy defective cars need not sue their dealers first; they can sue the automakers directly. This means that manufacturers are now much more vulnerable to suit than before.

Most states have strict liability laws.

Strict liability means that a manufacturer can be held responsible for products that injure the buyer or user; direct negligence need not be proved. If a company places a product on the market, it must take responsibility for it.[45] Today most states have enacted strict liability laws.

The burden sometimes is on the manufacturer.

Another recent development that extends the liability of manufacturers is the "market share liability" ruling by the California Supreme Court and upheld by the U. S. Supreme Court. In *Sindell v. Abbott Laboratories* (1980) the plaintiff was injured as a result of a synthetic, anti-miscarriage drug known as DES which was on the market twenty years earlier. The drug was produced generically and sold through pharmacies, thus it was impossible to identify the specific manufacturer of the drug which did the damage. The Court ruled that this was not necessary. Since five manufacturers accounted for a substantial share of the market, the burden of proof rested on them to prove they did not manufacture the DES which injured the plaintiff. Otherwise, they are jointly liable in relation to the share of the market they

---

[44]Anna Cifelli Isgro, "The Hidden Threat to Air Safety," *Fortune*, April 13, 1987, p. 82.

[45]For more on this area, see William L. Trombetta, "Products Liability: What New Court Rulings Mean for Management," *Business Horizons*, August 1979, pp. 67–72.

held at the time. The essence of this law is to turn the drug companies into insurers of their own products.[46] However, there is some good news on the horizon as far as business firms are concerned. To date over one-third of the states have passed laws which limit the time period during which a suit can be brought. In most cases this is ten years from the time of sale to the first consumer. There is also growing support for legislation to hold manufacturers liable for knowledge and improvements that were available at the time of production and not at the time of trial. For the time being, however, product liability remains a major concern for manufacturers.

Safety Checklist

With the courts making it easier to sue manufacturers for damages, many firms are finding it necessary to review the entire area of product safety. Carl Clark, Chief of The National Commission Task Group on Industry Self-Regulation, was quoted as suggesting that manufacturers use the following safety checklist:

A manufacturer's safety checklist.

1. Review working conditions and competence of key personnel.
2. Predict ways in which the product will fail and the consequences of these failures at the design stage.
3. Select raw materials that are either pretested or certified as flawless.
4. Make use of trade association research and analyses concerning product safety.
5. Insist that all product safety factors be tested by an independent laboratory.
6. Document any production changes that might later affect safety problems.
7. Encourage the product safety staff to review advertising or safety aspects.
8. Inform salesmen of the product's safety features and under what conditions they will fail.
9. Provide information to the consumer on product performance.
10. Investigate every consumer complaint.[47]

This list can be valuable to manufacturers in light of the fact that more consumers have been suing—and winning—product liability suits. The percentage of juries ruling in favor of the plaintiff and the amounts of the awards have been rising for some time.

---

[46]Terry Dworkin, "Enterprise Liability—Increasing the Manufacturer's Burden," *Business Horizons*, May–June 1981, pp. 77–82.

[47]"Consumerism: The Mood Turns Mean," *Sales Management*, July 15, 1969, p. 40.

THE FUTURE OF SOCIAL RESPONSIBILITY

Is the concern for social responsibility a passing fad, or is it here to stay? In this chapter, strong arguments have been made which indicate that this interest will endure. Numerous reasons in support of this view can be cited. One is that many stockholders are demanding that their businesses exhibit a greater sense of social responsibility. This has resulted in shareholder resolutions being presented to a number of boards for votes of adoption.

Other commonly cited reasons for business's concern with social responsibility include (1) enhanced corporate reputation and goodwill, (2) a strengthening of the social system in which the corporation functions, (3) a strengthening of the economic system in which the corporation functions, (4) greater job satisfaction among all employees, and (5) avoidance of government regulation. Two other major developments, worth of special consideration, are ethics and employee assistance programs.

Ethics

Ethics is the study of right and wrong conduct, and businesses today are showing a great deal of interest in the subject. In fact, it has now become a practical necessity for management. The public often demands ethical consideration; the law requires it in many cases; and managers themselves think ethical practice is good business[48] (see Ethics in Action: Redlining Reappears). Some researchers, such as Harold Johnson, not only agree with this last statement, but point out that firms with the highest ethical standards are often the most profitable in their industry.[49] Furthermore, with the development of modern communication techniques, news of unethical practices can be carried via newspapers, magazines, radio, and television to virtually every corner of the globe. So it is in the best interests of business to develop specific codes of ethical behavior and to enforce sanctions against those members who violate these codes.

> In summary, a new age of instant information and public insistence on ethical behavior has transformed business ethics from an ideal condition to a reality, from a luxury to a practical necessity for the survival and success of organizations. The central instrument for making ethics operational and real in an organization is a written code of ethics which is specific . . . is based upon general ethical standards, and is enforceable by appropriate sanctions.[50]

---

[48]Darrell J. Fasching, "A Case for Corporate and Management Ethics," *California Management Review*, Summer 1981, pp. 62–76; and Sir Adrian Cadbury, "Ethical Managers Make Their Own Rules," *Harvard Business Review*, September–October 1987, pp. 69–73.

[49]Harold L. Johnson, "Ethics and the Executive," *Business Horizons*, May–June 1981, pp. 53–59.

[50]James Owens, "Business Ethics: Age-Old Ideal, Now Real," *Business Horizons*, February 1978, p. 30.

Many firms now have codes of ethics in place. For example, Bernard White and Ruth Montgomery surveyed over 600 businesses and found that 77 percent of them had codes of conduct.[51] Some of the specific areas addressed in these codes included: (1) compliance with laws, (2) the misuse of corporate assets, (3) observance of moral and ethical standards of society, (4) use of inside or confidential information, (5) antitrust compliance, (6) equal employment opportunity, and (7) procedures for implementing the particular code.[52] In these statements, companies are setting forth a moral tone to which they expect all of the personnel to adhere. Consider the following, drawn from the *Cummins Practice on Ethical Standards:*

For Cummins, ethics rests on a fundamental belief in people's dignity and decency. Our most basic ethical standard is to show respect for those whose lives we affect and to treat them as we would expect them to treat us if our positions were reversed. This kind of respect implies that we must:

1. Obey the law.
2. Be honest—present the facts fairly and accurately.
3. Be fair—give everyone appropriate consideration.
4. Be concerned—care about how Cummins' actions affect others and try to make those effects as beneficial as possible.
5. Be courageous—treat others with respect even when it means losing business. (It seldom does. Over the long haul, people trust and respect this kind of behavior and wish more of our institutions embodied it.)[53]

Codes are being institutionalized.

Many firms are doing this via a three-step process. First, a code is developed. Second, an ethics committee is created. This committee's job is to enforce disciplinary measures for unethical conduct and reward personnel for ethical actions. Third, an ethics training program is offered to all of the personnel so they are aware of how the company expects them to act.[54] This three-step process is very useful in institutionalizing ethical codes and making them a part of everyone's daily plan of operation.

---

[51]Bernard J. White and B. Ruth Montgomery, "Corporate Codes of Conduct," *California Management Review,* Winter 1980, pp. 80–87.

[52]For more on corporate ethics statements see: Robert Chatov, "What Corporate Ethics Statements Say," *California Management Review,* Summer 1980, pp. 20–29; and Donald R. Cressey and Charles A. Moore, "Managerial Values and Corporate Codes of Conduct," *California Management Review,* Summer 1983, pp. 53–77.

[53]Reported in Oliver F. Williams, "Business Ethics: A Trojan Horse?" *California Management Review,* Summer 1980, p. 20.

[54]James Weber, "Institutionalizing Ethics in the Corporation," *MSU Business Topics,* Spring 1981, pp. 47–52.

ETHICS
IN
ACTION:
Redlining
Reappears

One of the hottest ethical topics during the 1960s and 1970s was "redlining," a process whereby banks identified certain ethnic neighborhoods as undesirable loan risks. Quite often these were black neighborhoods, and potential homeowners found it difficult, if not impossible, to get a mortgage on these properties.

In recent years redlining has again become an issue. The *Atlanta Journal and Constitution* newspaper recently reported that local banks were discriminating against blacks. Computer data analysis revealed that whites were five times more likely to be given mortgages and home improvement loans than were blacks, and Atlanta was not alone. Similar investigative methods found redlining in Baltimore, Chicago, Denver, and Washington, D.C.

What is being done about this? One is that many banks are reviewing their lending practices to ensure that there is indeed equal opportunity lending. A second is that cities and other municipalities are threatening to withdraw deposits from banks that discriminate. A third is that neighborhood activists are using the Community Reinvestment Act (CRA) to discourage redlining. The CRA's original objectives were to stop banks from redlining, but there were few enforcement powers to ensure that the law was followed. As a result, the law sat quietly on the books. However, as bank mergers began to increase, social activists found that they could file objections to mergers under the conditions of the CRA. Aware that these objections could result in the merger being slowed up or rejected by the regulatory agency, banks now often approve the loans to low-income neighborhoods. In fact, private agreements reached under the threat of such filings outnumber formal complaints by a four to one ratio. Some bankers complain about this practice, but it has proven effective. *Business Week* reports:

> . . . banks—fearing bad publicity as much as negative rulings—have coughed up sizable funds. They have pledged more than $5 billion, mainly in loans for low-income housing, over the past three years. By contrast, federal funding for low-income housing—rent assistance and construction subsidies—is now about $8 billion per year. "Without CRA, low-income housing development would be almost impossible," says Barry Zigas, president of the National Low Income Housing Coalition.

Source: John Schwartz and Frank S. Washington, "The Return of 'Redlining'," *Newsweek*, May 16, 1988, p. 44; and Catherine Yang, Michael Oneal, and Richard Anderson, "The 'Blackmail' Making Banks Better Neighborhoods," *Business Week*, August 15, 1988, p. 101.

Aside from adhering to a company code of ethics, in what other ways can business people ensure that they are being ethical? Laura Nash recommends that managers also ask themselves the following 12 questions:

1. Have you defined the problem accurately?
2. How would you define the problem if you stood on the other side of the fence?
3. How did this situation occur in the first place?
4. To whom and to what do you give your loyalty as a person and as a member of the corporation?
5. What is your intention in making this decision?
6. How does this intention compare with the probable results?
7. Whom could your decision or action injure?
8. Can you discuss the problem with the affected parties before you make your decision?
9. Are you confident that your position will be as valid over a long period of time as it seems now?
10. Could you disclose without qualm your decision or action to your boss, your CEO, the board of directors, your family, society as a whole?
11. What is the symbolic potential of your action if understood? If misunderstood?
12. Under what conditions would you allow exceptions to your stand?[55]

These questions can help the manager decide what to do. Additionally, notes Nash, "The situations for testing business morality remain complex. But by avoiding theoretical inquiry and limiting the expectations of corporate goodness to a few rules for social behavior that are based on common sense, we can develop an ethic that is appropriate to the language, ideology, and institutional dynamics of business decision making and consensus. This ethic can also offer managers a practical way of exploring those occasions when their corporate brains are getting warning flashes from their noncorporate brains."[56]

Personnel Assistance

EAPs help deal with alcohol and drug problems.

Another recent area of interest by business has been that of personnel assistance. Many people who work in organizations today suffer from problems such as alcoholism or drug abuse. Modern organizations are aware of these problems and, in many cases, are working to deal with them. In a large number of cases this is being done through the use of employee assistance programs (EAPs). The purpose of these programs is to identify,

---

[55]Laura L. Nash, "Ethics without the Sermon," *Harvard Business Review*, November–December 1981, p. 81.

[56]Ibid., p. 90.

refer, and counsel individuals with personal problems that affect work output. Figure 17-2 shows how a typical EAP works.

Some of the firms that currently have EAPs include Kennecott Copper, Employers Insurance Company of Wausau, Illinois Bell Telephone, General Motors, Great Northern Railway Company, and Gates Rubber. In many cases the results have been impressive. Consider the following:

> Kennecott Copper: after a little more than a year, attendance was up 5.2 percent, indemnity costs were down 74.6 percent and surgical costs had decreased by 55.4 percent.[57]
>
> General Motors: during the first year that its EAP was in place, lost time was reduced by 40 percent, grievances and disciplinary actions were down 50 percent and sickness and accident benefits had fallen by 60 percent.
>
> Great Northern Railway Company: among employees in the plan, absenteeism fell 52 percent and grievances decreased by 78 percent.[58]
>
> Gates Rubber: at the end of the first year absenteeism had fallen from 11,174 hours to 4,106 hours for a savings of $56,000, medical visits to the company clinic fell from 321 to 182, and since this year things have continued to get better.[59]

The development of EAPs illustrates that many enterprises are trying to combine business with social responsibility. The fact that these firms are able to attach cost savings to the programs also shows that human resource accounting techniques are becoming more popular. Aware of the benefits of personnel assistance, it is likely that we will see EAPs continue to grow in both number and services provided.

In summary, then, it is accurate to say social responsibility will continue to be a business concern during the 1980s. This is why so many firms are now incorporating it into their overall strategy (see Figure 17-3). Social responsibility is becoming an integral part of the enterprise's plan. It is a challenge management intends to meet.

■ SUMMARY

Social responsibility is a continuing challenge to modern business. Realizing that business is actually serving its own long-run interests by aiding the

[57]Julian L. Carr and Richard T. Hellan, "Improving Corporate Performance through Employee-Assistance Programs," *Business Horizons*, April 1980, p. 59.

[58]Richard J. Tersine and James Hazeldine, "Alcoholism: A Productivity Hangover," *Business Horizons*, November–December 1982, p. 72.

[59]Edwin J. Busch, Jr., "Developing an Employee Assistance Program," *Personnel Journal*, September 1980, pp. 710–11.

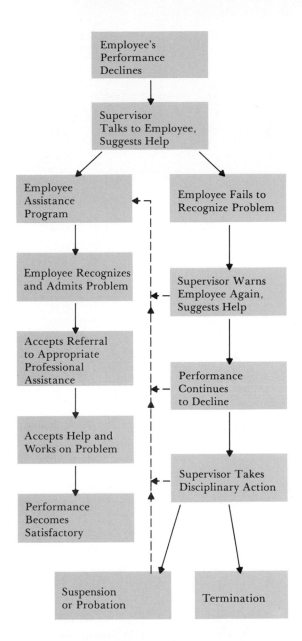

FIGURE 17-2   Employee Assistance Program: The Supervisor's Role

Source: Edwin J. Busch, Jr., "Developing an Employee Assistance Program," reprinted with permission from *Personnel Journal*, Costa Mesa, California. Copyright September 1980. All rights reserved.

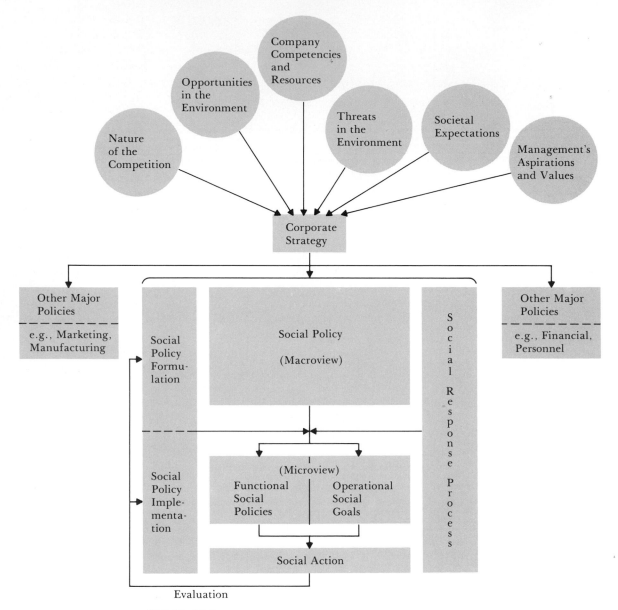

FIGURE 17-3   Corporate Strategy and the Social Policy Process

Source: Reprinted, by permission, from the *Journal of Business Strategy*, Vol. 4, No. 3, Winter 1984. Copyright © 1984, Warren, Gorham & Lamont Inc., 210 South Street, Boston, MA 02111. All rights reserved.

community, many firms today are actively meeting the three major social challenges of the day: equal opportunity, ecology, and consumerism.

The Equal Pay Act of 1963, the Civil Rights Act of 1964, and the Age Discrimination in Employment Act of 1967 were all landmarks in helping ensure equal opportunity in the workplace. However, business has also played a key role in helping find work for minorities and the handicapped, and many firms have also helped minority capitalists by providing them with both technical assistance and business contracts.

Yet in these areas, and particularly in the area of discrimination against women, a great deal remains to be done. Many working women today, despite the law, are subjected to sexual harassment and often do not receive equal pay for equal work. Nor are their chances for management promotion as good as those of their male counterparts. Fortunately, many companies are aware of these conditions and are taking steps to rectify them.

The second major area of consideration in this chapter was ecology, with concerns ranging from air pollution to water and noise pollution. In each instance, demands on business firms have resulted in attempts to respond positively to the challenge.

Finally, today's consumers want to know what they are buying and what they are getting for their dollar. Such legislation as the Truth in Packaging Act and the Truth in Lending Act has helped provide consumers with some important information and assistance. Yet the consumer movement is more than just a need for more data. Consumers also want product safety; and when it is overlooked by manufacturers, lawsuits are likely. As a result more and more companies have begun in recent years to pay close attention to liability laws and the development of safety checklists that help ensure the requisite quality in their products.

The future of social responsibility was discussed in the last part of this chapter. Recent evidence, in the form of codes of conduct and employee assistance programs, indicates that the challenge of social responsibility is going to be here indefinitely. Further, all signs indicate that business is both willing and able to respond to it.

■ REVIEW AND STUDY QUESTIONS

1. What is the doctrine of enlightened self-interest?
2. In what way has the Equal Pay Act of 1963 been of value in promoting equal opportunity?
3. In what way has the Civil Rights Act of 1964 been of value in promoting equal opportunity? The Age Discrimination in Employment Act of 1967 as modified by recent guidelines?
4. How has the Vocational Rehabilitation Act of 1973 affected business's hiring of the handicapped? Explain.

5. How has the business community helped promote minority capitalism? Give two examples, and make your answer as specific as possible.

6. What are the three most common forms of discrimination against working women? Explain each; give specific examples.

7. How can business help ensure equal opportunity for women in the workplace?

8. Explain the word "ecology" in your own terms.

9. What is the major cause of air pollution in America, and what is business doing about it?

10. Why is "zero discharge" considered unrealistic? Explain.

11. Does noise pollution have any effects on people? Give an example.

12. What are the major provisions of the Environmental Policy Act of 1969?

13. What are the major provisions of the National Air Quality Standards Act of 1970?

14. How does the Consumer Product Safety Act help the average consumer?

15. What is meant by the term "consumerism"?

16. What are the major provisions of the Truth in Packaging Act? The Truth in Lending Act?

17. Are any changes occurring in liability laws? What effects are they having on business? Explain.

18. Is the social responsibility of business a fad, or is it here to stay? Explain, being sure to incorporate into your answer a discussion of codes of conduct and employee assistance programs.

■ SELECTED REFERENCES

Baron, Alma S. "What Men Are Saying about Women in Business." *Business Horizons,* January–February 1982, pp. 10–14.

Bloom, Anthony H. "Managing against Apartheid." *Harvard Business Review,* November–December 1987, pp. 49–56.

Bunke, Harvey C. "Should We Teach Business Ethics?" *Business Horizons,* July–August 1988, pp. 2–8.

Busch, Edwin J., Jr. "Developing an Employee Assistance Program." *Personnel,* September 1981, pp. 708–11.

Carroll, Archie B. "In Search of the Moral Manager." *Business Horizons,* March–April 1987, pp. 7–15.

Carroll, Archie B., and Frank Hoy. "Integrating Corporate Social Policy into Strategic Management." *Journal of Business Strategy,* Winter 1984, pp. 48–57.

Chusmir, Leonard H. "Job Commitment and the Organizational Woman." *Academy of Management Review*, October 1982, pp. 595–602.

Cochran, Philip L., and Robert A. Wood. "Corporate Social Responsibility and Financial Performance." *Academy of Management Journal*, March 1984, pp. 42–56.

Coles, Robert. "Storytellers' Ethics," *Harvard Business Review*, March–April 1987, pp. 8–14.

Collins, Eliza G. C., and Timothy B. Blodgett. "Sexual Harassment . . . Some See It . . . Some Won't." *Harvard Business Review*, March–April 1981, pp. 76–95.

Cressey, Donald R., and Charles A. Moore. "Managerial Values and Corporate Codes of Ethics." *California Management Review*, Summer 1983, pp. 53–77.

Drucker, Peter F. "The New Meaning of Corporate Social Responsibility." *California Management Review*, Winter 1984, pp. 53–63.

Dworkin, Terry. "Enterprise Liability—Increasing the Manufacturer's Burden." *Business Horizons*, May–June 1981, pp. 77–82.

Dwyer, Paula et al. "The Defense Scandal." *Business Week*, July 4, 1988, pp. 28–33.

Epstein, Edwin M. "The Corporate Social Policy Process: Beyond Business Ethics, Corporate Social Responsibility, and Corporate Social Responsiveness." *California Management Review*, Spring 1987, pp. 99–114.

Forbes, J. Benjamin, and James E. Piercy. "Rising to the Top: Executive Women in 1983 and Beyond." *Business Horizons*, September–October 1983, pp. 38–47.

Freedman, Sara M., and Robert T. Keller. "The Handicapped in the Workforce." *Academy of Management Review*, July 1981, pp. 449–58.

Goldberg, Leonard D., and Kenneth D. Walters. "No-Fault Criminal Liability for Executives." *California Management Review*, Summer 1982, pp. 25–32.

Goodpaster, Kenneth E., and John B. Matthews, Jr. "Can a Corporation Have a Conscience?" *Harvard Business Review*, January–February 1982, pp. 132–41.

Greenlaw, Paul S., and John P. Kohl. "Age Discrimination in Employment Guidelines." *Personnel Journal*, March 1982, pp. 224–28.

Johnson, Harold L. "Ethics and the Executive." *Business Horizons*, May–June 1981, pp. 53–59.

Kronenberger, George K., and David L. Bourke. "Effective Training and the Elimination of Sexual Harassment." *Personnel Journal*, November 1981, pp. 879–83.

Lawrence, Melanie. "Social Responsibility: How Companies Become Involved in Their Communities." *Personnel Journal*, July 1982, pp. 502–10.

Luthans, Fred, Richard M. Hodgetts, and Kenneth R. Thompson. *Social Issues in Business*, 5th ed. New York: Macmillan, 1987.

Mintzberg, Henry. "The Case for Corporate Social Responsibility." *Journal of Business Strategy*, Fall 1983, pp. 3–15.

Noe, Raymond A. "Women and Mentoring: A Review and Research Agenda." *Academy of Management Review,* January 1988, pp. 65–78.

Novit, Mitchell S. "Employer Liability for Employee Misconduct: Two Common Law Doctrines." *Personnel,* January–February 1982, pp. 12–19.

Powell, Gary N. "Sexual Harassment: Confronting the Issue of Definition." *Business Horizons,* July–August 1983, pp. 24–28.

Rosen, Benson, Mary Ellen Templeton, and Karen Kichline. "The First Few Years on the Job: Women in Management." *Business Horizons,* November–December 1981, pp. 26–29.

Rowe, Mary P. "Dealing with Sexual Harassment." *Harvard Business Review,* May–June 1981, pp. 42–46.

Saul, George K. "Business Ethics: Where Are We Going?" *Academy of Management Review,* April 1982, pp. 269–76.

Sethi, S. Prakash. "Corporate Political Activism." *California Management Review,* Spring 1982, pp. 32–42.

Seymour, Sally. "The Case of the Willful Whistle-Blower." *Harvard Business Review,* January–February 1988, pp. 103–109.

Terpstra, David E., and Douglas D. Baker. "Outcomes of Sexual Harassment Charges." *Academy of Management Journal,* March 1988, pp. 185–94.

Tersine, Richard J., and James Hazeldine. "Alcoholism: A Productivity Hangover." *Business Horizons,* November–December 1982, pp. 68–72.

Trombetta, William L. "Products Liability: What New Court Rulings Mean for Management." *Business Horizons,* August 1979, pp. 67–72.

Weber, Joseph. "The 'Last Minority' Fights for Its Rights." *Business Week,* June 6, 1988, p. 140.

Williams, Oliver F. "Business Ethics: A Trojan Horse." *California Management Review,* Summer 1982, pp. 14–24.

Wilson, Glenn T. "Solving Your Ethical Problems and Saving Your Career." *Business Horizons,* November–December 1983, pp. 16–20.

■ CASE: It's Inevitable

Is concern for social responsibility a fad, or will it be a fundamental and lasting impetus in United States business? Many people tend to believe the latter. They feel that decades ago there was only a slight difference between business's and society's lifestyles. Today, however, the incongruity is quite obvious.

Financial income and security used to dominate lifestyles in the United States. Business, as an economic institution, helped meet the needs of the lifestyle and, in spite of cyclical rises and declines in public favor, its goals were compatible with those of the average person. But modern times have seen a shift toward more socially oriented desires; the pure economic mission of business is now out of step with societal values:

The incongruence between business's lifestyle and society's lifestyle requires intelligent, creative actions to dispel differences and reduce tensions. From a practical point of view it may be assumed that the social environment is the independent variable and business is the dependent variable. The major burden for adaptation, therefore, is upon business. Eventually it must change to meet society's expectations, and not the other way around. There may be minor adaptations by society as it comes to understand business better, but the major change surely will be required of business.[60]

Finally, advocates of social responsibility envision only a limited number of options available to business. First, it can withdraw and refuse to face the issue. Second, it can take a legalistic approach by dragging its feet and fighting long, expensive legal battles against social progress. Third, it can bargain or negotiate with those pressure groups making claims on it. Fourth, it can solve the problems by making a genuine study of society's and business's values and needs and attempt to reconcile them in constructive ways. Social responsibility advocates consider the latter the most viable strategy.

Questions

1. Is there really a growing incongruence between the lifestyles of business and society in this country? Explain.

2. Is the social responsibility factor really here to stay? Cite some illustrations to support your answer.

3. If business does choose the fourth alternative above, namely problem solving, what are some steps it should take? Be specific in your answer.

■ CASE: Mary's Job

Mary Watkins has been with her company for over a year and a half. She came to the firm straight out of college and was hired as a management trainee. This title is common for new lower-level management people in the organization. It means, in the main, that management has not yet made up its mind where the individual will finally be placed in the hierarchy. During her first six months, Mary had to assert herself continually in order not to be stereotyped. For example, she noticed that whenever she was present at a meeting, she was expected to perform secretarial chores such as seeing that everyone had coffee. Whenever a higher-level manager had to write a note or have some papers taken from the meeting room, Mary was asked to do it.

---

[60]Ibid., p. 15.

Realizing that she was being stereotyped as a "gofer," Mary called the fact to the attention of her boss. She noticed that after her short meeting with the latter, people were more careful about what they asked her to do.

Mary also is aware that all of the trainees who came into the organization with her are still at the same level of the hierarchy as she is. She thinks, however, that some of them are getting more money. For example, three months ago she was having coffee with a few of them when one said, "I hope I get a 15-percent raise again next year." Mary received a 9-percent raise this year, and she was led to believe that all of the other people who entered the firm with her were also getting the same amount of money, since all of them received the same performance evaluations.

Last week the management trainees completed their eighteen-month program and were given their first full-time assignments. Some will be staying at headquarters while others will be going into the field. All of the women in the program have been assigned jobs at headquarters. Thirty percent of the men will be going into the field. When she asked her boss about this, he said, "You have real management potential. We want to keep our eye on you, and we can do this better from the home office than from the field." Mary is unsure whether she would be better off in the field or at the home office. She knows that every one of the top managers have had some experience in the field, and she has plenty of time to get this experience later. On the other hand, she is also concerned that the failure to move her into the field right now may be a sign that the organization does not intend to promote women as fast as men. On this latter point, however, she also admits that her conclusion is not backed up with any hard evidence.

Questions

1. In your own words, how does Mary's organization view women? Explain.

2. Is Mary being paid less than some of the men? Are her opportunities for promotion less than those of men? In each case, be sure to defend your answer.

3. What recommendations would you give to Mary? Be complete in your answer.

■ CASE: Quiet in the Home

Conversations about noise pollution usually center around the more noticeable offenders, such as airplanes, locomotives, buses, and heavy machinery. However, a quick look around the average house or apartment is likely to uncover many other polluters, including dishwashers, blenders, garbage disposals, and vacuum cleaners. Most of the noise from these household items goes unnoticed by the average person, although recent government studies show that 16 million Americans suffer from some degree of hearing loss caused directly by noise. Since most people spend a large amount of time at home, noisy appliances quite possibly are causal factors in poor hearing.

One reason that many people are unconcerned about noise pollution from appliances is that they equate noise with power. If a machine makes a lot of noise, it is considered to be getting the job done. If it is too quiet, it is often perceived as ineffective. For example, a while back a quiet vacuum cleaner was introduced into the marketplace. It promptly flopped because consumers thought it lacked power. Similarly, when engineers at another vacuum manufacturer were bothered by a clicking sound in one of their vacuums, a consumer survey found that the noise did not disturb the users, who felt it indicated that the vacuum was working.

Nevertheless, the Environmental Protection Agency (EPA) intends to crack down on noise from home appliances. One of its proposals is to require manufacturers to label household appliances to show how much noise they emit. Another is to use a color-coding or numbering system to allow shoppers to compare noise levels of competing appliances and decide which is most tolerable for them.

EPA administrators admit that it will cost more to make appliances quieter and expect implementation to be gradual. Despite such problems, however, noise labeling is meeting with very little industry resistance.

Questions

1. List six home appliances that you believe make sufficient noise to qualify them as noise pollutants, and try to discover their decibel levels.

2. Why do people associate appliance noise with appliance power?

3. What difficulties will the EPA confront as it attempts to reduce noise in home appliances? Why?

■ CASE: Cleaning Up Their Act

The stock market crash of October 1987 has had a major effect on the way customers view their brokers and the services being provided by brokerage houses. Even today some investors distrust brokerage offices and some individuals have lawsuits pending because of the way they were treated both before and during the horrendous selling spree that saw stock prices plummet. Here are two events that were reported in *Business Week*:

■ The investor, in his late 20s, had ridden the boom. Using risky, highly leveraged trading strategies, he had built up his brokerage account at Quick & Reilly Group Inc. to a $700,000 balance. Now, two weeks after the crash, he sat in the office of Leslie C. Quick III, president of the discount brokerage, nearly in tears. His new balance: a margin debt that may reach $200,000.

■ Since 1979 a retired West Coast couple had invested their money and the funds of two grown children with a broker at Apple Financial Corp., a small New York brokerage. Three days after the crash the family's broker told them forced liquidation of their $1.6 million account left them owing $875,000. Now the family is suing the broker and Apple Financial for $2.5 million plus $5 million in punitive damages. The suit charges that the broker was not available to give advice and accurate quotes as the family's investments crashed, and that improper liquidation of the account increased their losses. The defendants deny the allegations.

At the same time, a number of Wall Street brokers and brokerages have been charged with insider trading. Many of these individuals were present at meetings in which they were asked to help finance the purchase of one firm by another. Aware of the impending acquisition, they bought stock in the firm about to be acquired even though they knew that trading on inside information is illegal. Some brokerages were charged with defrauding clients and manipulating the stock prices, and their top executives were indicted by federal grand juries.

These actions have led many investors to wonder about the ethics of Wall Street. Is the average investor treated fairly or do brokerages take advantage of the individual, while they, the brokerage firms, reap large profits? Regardless of the answer, one thing is certain: during the 1990s Wall Street is going to have to clean up its act.

Questions

1. What responsibilities does a stockbroker have to a client?
2. Is it fair to expect brokers not to trade on insider information? After all, is it not human nature to want to take advantage of useful information?
3. What actions could stock brokerages take to ensure more ethical behavior by their people? Offer two recommendations.

Sources: Stephen Labaton, "Drexel Bid to Remove Judge Fails," *New York Times,* October 7, 1988, pp. 33, 38; and Mark N. Vamos et al. "Wall Street's Credibility Gap," *Business Week,* November 23, 1987, pp. 92–99.

■ SELF-FEEDBACK EXERCISE: What Do You Know about the Current Status of Social Responsibility?

Read and circle the correct answer to each statement. Answers are provided at the end of the quiz.

T F   1. The number of women in top management is increasing.

T F   2. Sexual harassment remains a major problem for women in organizations.

T F   3. Most people believe that business ethics is on the rise.

T F   4. Business is helping to fight illiteracy by training people to read.

T F   5. Research shows that women's salaries in the period from 1980 to 1988 increased dramatically.

T F   6. America is becoming a quieter place in which to work.

T F   7. Water pollution continues to be a major ecological challenge.

T F   8. Auto pollution is worse now than it was in the 1960s.

T F   9. Of the three major social issues—equal opportunity, ecology, and consumerism—equal opportunity is now receiving the greatest attention.

T F 10. Today's consumer is better informed than the consumer of the 1970s.

T F 11. Consumer fraud is on the rise.

T F 12. Companies can now require a test for AIDS before hiring a job applicant.

T F 13. If a theft occurs in the company, any employee refusing to take a lie detector test can be fired.

T F 14. A person failing a lie detector test can be refused employment.

T F 15. A research-based university can refuse to hire a professor who does not have a Ph.D. degree.

T F 16. If a person can do a job, he or she can successfully sue if they are not seriously considered for the job.

T F 17. Air safety is becoming a major social responsibility issue.

T F 18. Government contractors must alter their facilities so as to accommodate the physically handicapped.

T F 19. Many companies have a bill of rights that spells out the protections that are accorded to the personnel.

T F 20. Fortunately, recent research shows that insider stock trading has finally been stamped out.

Answers

1. True. The number is going up although the percentage is remaining the same.
2. True.
3. False. It is just the opposite.
4. True. They are spending millions of dollars to do so.

5. False.

6. True.

7. True.

8. False.

9. False. It is consumerism.

10. True.

11. True.

12. False. In most cases they cannot require such a test.

13. False. In some cases they can, but in most cases they cannot.

14. False. If a person fails the polygraph, there must be supporting evidence to support the decision; it cannot rest solely on the result of the lie detector test.

15. True. This is considered a bona fide occupational requirement in a research-based university and those without such a degree can be turned down.

16. False. In some cases this is not sufficient. For example, a church can refuse to hire a preacher who is not a member of that particular religion or denomination; a movie producer can refuse to hire a female impersonator to play the role of a leading lady.

17. True.

18. True.

19. True.

20. False. The practice appears to be continuing, albeit at a much reduced rate.

CHAPTER 18

International Management: Challenges and Opportunities

For two reasons, the United States is the most important nation in the international arena. First, it does more exporting and importing than any other country in the world; there is virtually no geographic area with which it does not have at least some trade. Second, many of its largest business firms, including Boeing, Caterpillar Tractor, General Electric, General Motors, Eastman Kodak, Ford, Mobil Oil, and IBM, earn a substantial percentage of their annual sales in the overseas market. Today's U. S. business executive is thus concerned not only with domestic management but international management as well.

This chapter will focus attention on what managers from U. S. firms need to know about managing overseas operations. The discussion draws upon and applies much of what has been presented in previous chapters; for to a large extent, the basic ideas are the same. The challenge of international business is in modifying the applications to fit the new environment.

The first goal of this chapter is to examine the possible advantages and disadvantages of going international. The second objective is to analyze the methods used in organizing, controlling, and staffing these overseas operations. The third goal is to scrutinize the role of the multinational corporation in the international economic arena.

When you have finished this chapter, you should be able to:

1. Explain why a U. S. business firm will consider entering a foreign market.

2. Discuss the possible advantages and disadvantages of going overseas.

3. Tell how a joint venture works.

4. Describe the various forms of organization structure used in foreign operations.

5. Define the degrees of control that a parent company can exercise over a subsidiary.

6. Explain how a business firm attempts to staff its overseas operations.

7. Discuss some of the incentives used in motivating employees to accept overseas assignments.

8. Discuss the economic power and international responsibility of the multinational corporation.

ENTERING FOREIGN MARKETS

Why do U. S. businesses enter foreign markets? The numerous answers include: (1) a high-level executive pushes for it, (2) an outside group approaches the firm with a proposal such as an overseas joint venture, (3) a domestic competitor's expansion into certain areas abroad leads the firm to join the bandwagon, (4) strong domestic competition makes foreign expansion desirable, and (5) there is a potentially profitable overseas market for the firm's goods or services. Regardless of which reason(s) explain why a particular firm decides to go international, one thing is certain: the possible advantages outweigh the possible disadvantages. The following examines both of these.

Possible Advantages

Expansion into a foreign market can have many advantages. Three of the most common are profit, stability, and the gaining of a foothold in the Common Market or some similar economic union.

Profit

Profit is important.

One of the biggest attractions in going international is the possibility of increased profit. Research shows that profit as a percentage of sales is usually higher in international markets than in the United States. This helps explain why many firms are going international. (See Table 18-1.)

TABLE 18-1
The Ten Leading
United States Business
Exporters in 1987

Company	Product Line	Exports (in $ millions)	Exports as a Percentage of Sales
General Motors	Motor vehicles, motor parts, locomotives	8,731.3	8.6
Ford Motor	Motor vehicles, motor parts	7,614.0	10.6
Boeing	Aircraft	6,286.0	40.9
General Electric	Generating equipment, aircraft engines	4,825.0	12.3
International Business Machines	Information-handling systems, equipment and parts	3,994.0	7.4
Du Pont de Nemours (E.I.)	Chemicals, fibers, polymer products, petroleum, coal	3,526.0	11.6
McDonnell Douglas	Aircraft, space systems, missiles	3,243.4	24.7
Chrysler	Motor vehicles and parts	3,052.3	11.6
Eastman Kodak	Photographic equipment and supplies	2,255.0	17.0
Caterpillar Tractor	Construction equipment, engines	2,190.0	26.8

Source: *Fortune*, July 18, 1988, p. 71. © 1988 Time, Inc. All Rights Reserved.

A second profit feature is the favorable tax rate imposed by certain foreign countries; this is at times in rather great contrast to tax rates in the United States. Though the U. S. firms still must pay their U. S. taxes, the lower tax rates abroad, combined with the fact that some countries' workers accept lower wages than what the U. S. firms would have to pay at home, make overseas ventures highly promising.

Stability

A second major advantage of foreign expansion is stability. Many firms are capable of manufacturing far more units than they can sell domestically, and a foreign market provides a source of demand for the goods. This demand can be met through direct export to an agent abroad or through an overseas

A foreign source of demand can aid the firm's stability.

branch or subsidiary. A third common approach, brought on by rising nationalism, is to set up operations abroad and attempt to stabilize sales and production by working directly in both the foreign and domestic markets. An excellent example is provided by the Ford Motor Company in Europe, Nissan in Great Britain, and Toyota in the United States.[1]

Common Market and Other Economic Unions

Foreign production, especially in some parts of Europe, can be beneficial also because it gives the company a foothold in the European Economic Community (EEC). The *Common Market,* as it is most frequently called, was created in 1957 by France, West Germany, Italy, the Netherlands, Belgium, and Luxembourg. Its goal is to reduce trade barriers among the members. By 1967 duties charged on industrial goods circulating within the Common Market were only 20 percent of their previous levels, and by mid-1968 they were entirely eliminated. Today there are 12 nations in the EEC including Denmark, Great Britain, Greece, Ireland, Portugal, and Turkey.

The EEC has helped its member countries improve their standards of living and, by 1992 all internal commercial, financial, and customs barriers will be eliminated.[2] The result should be a united European market that can compete successfully with U. S. firms, which, in turn, can take advantage of these developments by entering the Common Market.

The basic idea of economic competition is not limited to the Common Market. Other economic unions have been formed for similar reasons, including the Central American Common Market (Costa Rica, Guatemala, Nicaragua, Honduras, and El Salvador), and the Latin American Free Trade Association (most of the South American countries and Mexico). U. S. firms doing business in these countries can profit from such unions.

Possible Disadvantages

Some possible disadvantages are also associated with going international. They include: (1) the need to understand foreign customs and culture, (2) the necessity of fostering company-government relations and unusual red tape, and (3) risk, expropriation, and the pressure, especially in underdeveloped countries, to bring in foreign partners.

Culture and Customs

Culture is made up of the socially transmitted behavior patterns, beliefs, and values of a society. Customs are the ways in which people in a country act and carry on their business and daily lives. Culture helps dictate custom;

---

[1]David B. Tinnin, "Ford Is on a Roll in Europe," *Fortune,* October 18, 1982, pp. 182–91; and Alex Taylor III, "Japan's Carmakers Take on the World," *Fortune,* June 20, 1988, pp. 67–76.

[2]Steven Greenhouse, "Europe's Big 1992 Goal: Truly Common Market," *New York Times,* March 14, 1988, pp. 21, 25.

Customs and culture may be major stumbling blocks.

since cultures in one area of the world are often different from those in another area, firms that do not know much about the country and the people where they are doing business are at a distinct disadvantage. Some of the most important questions a business should be able to answer about the culture and customs of the country include: What are the religious beliefs of the people, and how do they affect popular moral and ethical standards? What about the family? Is the country basically a matriarchal or patriarchal society? Are the people well educated or virtually illiterate? What are the social relationships and the value systems to which the people subscribe?

If a U. S. company is going to do business in another country, it needs to familiarize itself with the culture, for there are many differences between the way things are done in the United States and the way they are done elsewhere.[3] For example, German managers commonly use a much less participative leadership style than that of the average U. S. executive. As a result, many newly arrived American managers in Germany are seen as soft or weak in dealing with their German subordinates. In Japan a new firm finds a fierce employee loyalty to the company. But it also learns that there is a quid pro quo: Many workers are guaranteed lifelong employment. There is no such thing as firing the poorest workers in a department that fails to meet its production quota. In mideastern countries (see Table 18-2), there also are very distinct differences between the way managers operate and the way Americans are accustomed to handling their subordinates. These cultural norms must be understood by U. S. firms operating there (see Communication in Action: Avoiding Surprises).

This learning process can pose a time problem to a firm in a hurry. The last thing an entering firm wants to do is to violate social customs or culture. But the managers of such firms are also under pressure to get action. U. S. business people can find themselves frustrated in a country like Japan, where negotiations customarily move very slowly. This kind of problem is not merely an interesting point about travel and cross-cultural lifestyles: Some firms have cancelled plans to expand into overseas markets because they have been unable to adapt to the norms and customs of doing business in a foreign country. Yet this need not be the case. If business people prepare themselves properly before attempting to enter foreign countries, many of their culture and custom problems can be sidestepped.

Company–Government Relations

In many countries, especially those in the process of developing themselves industrially, the entering company must show the government that its proposed business venture will be beneficial to both parties. If the government has a master plan (and many do) and if another business firm is already manufacturing the good or providing the proposed service, the company may

---

[3]See, for example, Joel Dreyfuss, ''How to Deal with Japan,'' *Fortune*, June 6, 1988, pp. 107–18.

	Managerial Function	Mideastern	Western
TABLE 18-2 Differences in Mideastern and Western Management	Organizational design	Highly bureaucratic, over-centralized with power and authority at the top. Vague relationships. Ambiguous and unpredictable organization environments.	Less bureaucratic, more delegation of authority. Relatively decentralized structure.
	Patterns of decision making	Ad hoc planning, decisions made at the highest level of management. Unwillingness to take high risks in decision making.	Sophisticated planning techniques, modern tools of decision making, elaborate management information systems.
	Performance evaluation and control	Informal control mechanisms, routine checks on performance. Lack of vigorous performance evaluation systems.	Fairly advanced control systems focusing on cost reduction and organizational effectiveness.
	Manpower policies	Heavy reliance on personal contacts and getting individuals from the "right social origin" to fill major positions.	Sound personnel management policies. Candidates qualifications are usually the basis for selection decisions.
	Leadership	Highly authoritarian tone, rigid instructions. Too many management directives.	Less emphasis on leader's personality, considerable weight on leader's style and performance.
	Communication	The tone depends on the communication. Social position, power, and family influence are ever-present factors. Chain of command must be followed rigidly. People relate to each other rightly and specifically. Friendships are intense and binding.	Stress usually on equality and a minimization of differences. People relate to each other loosely and generally. Friendships are not intense and binding.
	Management methods	Generally old and outdated.	Generally modern and more scientific.

Source: M. K. Badaway, "Styles of Mideastern Management," Copyright © 1980 by the Regents of the University of California. Reprinted from *California Management Review*, Vol. XXII, No. 2, p. 57, by permission of the Regents.

If an American wants to work for a foreign firm, what does the individual need to know in order to succeed? The first thing is to learn the language. Many international firms designate English as the primary language, but if the company is headquartered in a non-English-speaking country top managers are likely also to communicate in their native tongue. Managers who cannot do this are systematically excluded from the conversation. *Fortune* magazine notes:

> U. S. executives who are eager to get ahead buckle down and learn fast. Max J. Garelick, who runs the U. S. branch of Rodier, a Paris fashion house, practices his French from the minute he gets in a cab after landing at Orly airport. "I can see from the reaction of my French colleagues that they are pleased I am making the effort," says the no-nonsense Garelick. Jim Bostik learned Italian while working for Iveco in Turin. He needed it to speak to employees below the level of first-line manager. "I knew I made a major breakthrough," he says, "when I gave a 20-minute speech in Italian to a group of engineers and received thundering applause."

A second communications-related guideline is that many overseas executives do not communicate the way Americans do. In the U. S. managers tend to be explicit in their instructions. Japanese, on the other hand, are more implicit. They rarely give advice, never say no, and seldom provide feedback on a person's performance. Individuals who want to know how well they are doing on a week-by-week basis quickly find themselves dissatisfied with these conditions and often leave the firm. Self-motivators who flourish in an ill-structured environment do extremely well.

A third communication-related guideline is to learn what managers mean when they give out praise. Many Americans fail to realize that culture greatly influences meaning and what they hear is not what the manager said. For example, in England and on the European continent there is much less concern for equal employment than there is in the United States. Women who are hired by these firms need to understand that they are unlikely to be promoted into senior-level positions, no matter how often they are praised or told that they are doing a good job. Moreover, for Americans at large, there is a limit as to how far they will go in a foreign firm. Many Japanese companies make it clear that the presidency of the firm will always be held by a Japanese.

The overall communication lesson is simple. Before going to work for a foreign firm, Americans should understand the company's philosophy and mode of behavior and know how they will fit in. If they can do this, there are unlikely to be any surprises.

Source: Faye Rice, "Should You Work for a Foreigner," *Fortune*, August 1, 1988, pp. 123–24.

not be allowed to start up. This can be true even if the firm that the government has already licensed is less efficient than the one seeking entry into the market.

Furthermore, even if an initial proposal appears feasible, the company *Government red tape* must often fight its way through a mass of red tape. The finance minister *may be too great.* wants to know how much money the firm will bring into the country and how operations will affect the nation's balance of payments. The minister of power wants to know how much electricity will be needed by the proposed plant. Bringing all of these government officials together and obtaining final permissions for the proposed project may take so much time that the company will simply abandon the undertaking. Additionally, many countries including the U. S. are enacting trade laws designed to give the government a stronger hand in trade negotiations[4] and to encourage countries to open their trade doors as is happening with the U. S. food industry in Japan.[5]

Risk, Expropriation, and Foreign Partners

If it does proceed, the U. S. company may find that the foreign government has the authority to set the price of the good and adjust it as it sees fit, allowing the firm a "reasonable" return but no more. Many companies dislike this idea because they feel the return does not justify the risk associated with the investment and the possibility of expropriation. There are numerous illustrations of rising nationalism leading to the takeover of U. S. businesses with plants in foreign countries. Takeovers can usually be fitted into one of five major categories:

1. Formal expropriation or nationalization, in which the use of the firm's property is seized with or without compensation;

2. Intervention, in which case the government assumes managerial control without actually getting legal ownership;

Major categories of 3. Requisition, in which case the government takes temporary control of *takeovers.* the business for a specific public purpose;

4. Coerced sale, in which case the government induces the owners to sell all or a part of their properties to a government entity or to private citizens of the country at or below book or market value;

5. Forced renegotiation of contracts, in which case the government insists that the old arrangement be abandoned and one more favorable to the host country be put in its place.[6]

---

[4]Barnaby J. Feder, "New Trade Law: Wide Spectrum," *New York Times,* August 24, 1988, pp. 27, 30.

[5]Barbara Buell, Jonathan B. Levine, and Lois Thierren, "American Food Companies Look Yummy to Japan," *Business Week,* June 20, 1988, pp. 61–62.

[6]Don R. Beeman and Sherman A. Timmins, "Who *Are* the Villains in International Business?" *Business Horizons,* September–October 1982, p. 9.

One of the most effective ways of reducing the chances of expropriation or government renegotiation is through the use of political risk assessment. When applied to foreign direct investment, there are three major climates that warrant study:

Domestic climate. The level of national violence as measured by tendencies toward subversions, rebellion, or political turmoil. Among the many variables one might consider here are levels of political violence, the existence of extremist tendencies among political parties, or recurring governmental crises.

Political risk assessment climates.

Economic climate. An overall assessment of the foreign investment climate. Among the relevant factors are the likelihood of government intervention in the economy, the rate of inflation, persistent balance of payments deficits, external debts levels, and the rate of gross fixed capital formation.

Foreign relations. The extent to which a nation manifests hostilities toward another. Among the relevant variables here are the size of the defense budget, the evidence of an arms race, and the incidence of conflict with its neighbors.[7]

Of course, political risk assessment does not guarantee that a company's assets will not be expropriated. Even if a firm tries very hard to assess its political risk, it might still make a serious mistake and find the investment taken over by the government.[8] One way in which business firms try to hedge their bets is through use of a joint venture strategy.

Joint Ventures

When a firm establishes a *joint venture*, it takes in local partners who provide money and/or managerial talent. In a number of countries where U. S. firms have been establishing themselves, nationalistic pressure, coupled with the desire of local capitalists who are eager to profit from industrial growth, has led to an increase in the use of this organizational form.

Joint venture strategies take a number of different forms. One is known as the "spider's web" strategy, as represented by firms such as Volvo of Sweden. This firm has established a network of joint ventures with other firms including:

[7]Joseph V. Micallef, "Political Risk Assessment," *Columbia Journal of World Business,* Summer 1981, p. 48.

[8]For more on this topic of risk assessment, see: Thomas L. Brewer, "Political Risk Assessment for Foreign Direct Investment Decisions: Better Methods for Better Results," *Columbia Journal of World Business,* Spring 1981, pp. 5–11; Alan C. Shapiro, "Managing Political Risk: A Policy Approach," *Columbia Journal of World Business,* Fall 1981, pp. 63–69; and Kenneth D. Walters and R. Joseph Monsen, "The Spreading Nationalization of European Industry," *Columbia Journal of World Business,* Winter 1981, pp. 62–72.

1. Teaming up with Garret, Mack Trucks, and KHD of Germany to manufacture gas turbine engines;

2. Starting a joint venture with Peugeot and Renault in France to produce auto parts and provide auto service;

3. Joining with International Harvester in the production of tractor parts.

There are numerous joint venture strategies.

A second common strategy is known as "go together and split" venture. Under this arrangement two or more companies form a joint venture for a specified number of years, after which the organization is liquidated or reorganized. This strategy is commonly used by enterprises that are concerned with meeting a common competitive threat, are seeking to engage in exploratory activities in untested markets, and/or are seeking assistance in obtaining external resources. A third common joint venture strategy is that of "successive integration." Under this arrangement there is a weak interpartner relationship at the start of the venture but it grows progressively stronger as the venture matures. In some cases, this strategy results in the eventual merger of the two firms.[9]

Foreign partners can be useful.

On the positive side, the joint venture combines U. S. technical expertise with nationals' understanding of how to cut government red tape and market the product. Many companies have used this approach, including Du Pont, which holds a 49 percent interest in a Mexican chemical plant, and Merck, which has a 50 percent interest in an Indian pharmaceutical operation.

However, loss of control can be dangerous.

On the negative side, however, are the issues of control and culture. Some countries insist that their people hold at least a 51 percent interest in the venture. This idea is not agreeable to many U. S. firms, including IBM, and there are some very valid reasons for opposing joint ventures. First, the local partners are sometimes more interested in their short-run profit than in the company's long-term gains. Second, the nationals may lack managerial skills necessary to particular enterprises but, as controlling partners, make decisions that may prove quite costly to the firm. Third, the partners may disagree over policy. Fourth, custom or culture may dictate that the nationals find jobs for their families in the company. Fifth, there is the problem of hammering out a jointly agreeable contract. The way Americans go about negotiating such an agreement differs markedly from, for example, the Japanese way. Americans are accustomed to trying to get the best deal and have it agreed to in writing; the Japanese, on the other hand, do not operate this way.

The formal contract itself is viewed differently by the managers in these two business cultures. U. S. managers generally take the position that, given the likelihood of some misunderstanding between the two partners, the contract should provide for every conceivable contingency. Japanese managers do not believe that the contract, mere words on paper, can assure the

---

[9]Endel-Jakob Kolde, *Environment of International Business,* (Boston: Kent Publishing Company, 1982), pp. 246–47.

success of the venture. In fact, the provision of a formal dispute-settling mechanism, such as binding arbitration, augurs the breakdown of mutual trust.[10] In all these instances, the firm stands to suffer. As a result, many U. S. businesses accept joint ventures only when they are forced to do so. Other firms simply stay out of countries where this form of organization is required.

There are three basic control approaches.

Despite the disadvantages, U. S. businesses find that joint ventures are becoming more common today than ever before. Because of this growing prevalence, many firms are not asking whether they should opt for a joint venture, but rather what options are available for them when they use a joint venture. Approached from this standpoint, there are three basic control approaches that can be used: dominant partner, shared management, and independent. Under dominant partner arrangements, one partner essentially runs the joint venture and the other stays on the sidelines. Under a shared management approach, both contribute approximately equal amounts of time and effort to the undertaking. Under an independent arrangement, both firms allow the joint venture organization to operate free of interference by either parent. Killing reports that, based on thirty-seven examples, he found the shared partner arrangement to be least successful and the independent arrangement to produce the best overall results.[11] In the final analysis, however, every venture has to be judged on its own merits. Each of the three arrangements mentioned above can prove successful.

Making the Final Decision

Size of the market affects the decision.

After evaluating the pros and cons, the company's top-level managers will make the final decision as to whether to go international and under what circumstances. Naturally, the major criterion is going to be profit, but many qualitative judgments will be reflected in the decision. First, how large is the market? (See Technology in Action: Adjusting to Foreign Markets on page 690.) Domestic consumers are very different from foreign ones. In the United States, a large percentage of the population is middle class. In England, the largest group is the working class, whose incomes would put them in the upper-lower or lower-middle levels in the United States. In India, most people are at the lowest levels of the income scale (less than $2,000). The question of economic growth and stability is thus of obvious importance.

Political stability is a determinant.

A major, perhaps second, consideration is whether the other country's government is stable or more disrupted by political upheavals than not. It takes time to recoup any investment, and the company must forecast such developments in the political arena. Some areas of the world are considered very risky.

---

[10]Richard B. Peterson and Justin Y. Shimada, "Sources of Management Problems in Japanese-American Joint Ventures," *Academy of Management Review*, October 1978, p. 799.
[11]J. Peter Killing, "How to Make a Global Joint Venture Work," *Harvard Business Review*, May–June 1982, p. 122.

INTERVIEW WITH PAT CHOATE

Pat Choate is vice-president for policy and analysis at TRW, Inc., and is a leading expert on Japanese trade and its ramifications for the United States. A well-known writer and advisor to key members of Congress, he is a staunch advocate of effective international trade strategy.

Q. *Your writings, speeches, and testimony on Capitol Hill all indicate that you see Japan as a powerful American competitor. Is this right?*

A. It sure is both here in the U. S. as well as abroad. For example, between 1980 to 1987 Japanese investment in the U. S. increased by 600 percent. By 1991 they will be the third largest investor in this country behind the British and the Dutch. And during the decade of the 1990s their investment will quadruple. Japan is going to be a major competitor in the U. S.

Q. *Can't we turn the tables and invest in Japan? Isn't this a viable strategy?*

A. It's not as easy as you suggest. When doing business in Japan there are four things you have to do. First, you must have a superior product in terms of price, quality, service, and innovation. Second, you need to penetrate the Japanese distribution system. Third, you almost always need to take a Japanese partner and put this individual up front so it appears that the firm is Japanese-run.

Marketing channels must be advantageous.

Third, if the market and political conditions look favorable, is the company going to export goods to the country or set up facilities there? If it is going to export, it must establish marketing channels. If it is going to set up facilities in the foreign country, it must choose a plant site by matching the needs of the firm with the locations available. Perhaps the company needs to be located near a river or a source of raw materials. In any event, one site will be more advantageous than the others, and the company will want to select it as the final choice.

A review of market investment is the final decision-making necessity.

Finally, the firm must review the market investment. How much money will this venture entail, and how long will it take to reach the break-even point? Also, if there are local partners, will they be putting up any of the money, or will the venture be financed entirely by the firm? The answers to these questions will determine the ultimate fate of the project, which will become a question of risk versus reward.

This entire process is basically one of scanning the international environment just the way one would in evaluating a stateside venture. Particular

Fourth, you need to develop a relationship with the U. S. government so if you are treated unethically or illegally, you can seek government assistance. The Japanese market is tough to crack. You've got to have a good game plan going in. Otherwise, you'll find yourself spending a lot of time and money and have very little to show for it.

Q.   *Many American firms have superior products. Why isn't this enough to ensure their success in the Japanese market?*

A.   The primary answer is "patent flooding." The Japanese government supports new technology efforts. This means that if you introduce a high-tech product, Japanese companies will reverse engineer it to find out how you built it. Armed with this information they will begin getting patents for similar products and if you contest their patent, you might end up in a 10-year court battle. Or you might agree not to contest their patents if they agree not to contest yours. It's really not much of a deal, but unless you're willing to engage in a long court battle, you have no choice. Patent flooding is a typical Japanese strategy designed to undermine competition, and what's worse, the Japanese government supports this practice.

Q.   *How then do we deal with the Japanese?*

A.   The best way is through high-level government negotiations. We have to show them that if they intend to keep the United States as their major trade partner, they have to open up Japanese markets to us. It can't be a one-way street any longer.

attention must be given to the social, political, economic, and technological environments.[12] Having done this, if the company decides to go ahead, it must then focus attention on the management of the enterprise.[13] What type of organization structure will be best? What kind of control will the company want to exercise? How should the company go about staffing the operation?[14]

MANAGEMENT OF FOREIGN OPERATIONS

Organizationally, the simplest way for a company to handle its foreign operations is by exporting the goods to agents and distributors abroad. But sometimes, because of strong nationalistic feelings, import restrictions, and foreign exchange problems, the company is forced to become more deeply

---

[12]Jeremiah J. O'Connell and John W. Zimmerman, "Scanning the International Environment," *California Management Review,* Winter 1979, pp. 15–23.

[13]Andrew Kupfer, "How to Be a Global Manager," *Fortune,* March 14, 1988, pp. 52–58.

[14]For additional considerations see Stephen C. Harper, "Now That the Dust Has Settled: Learning from Japanese Management," *Business Horizons,* July–August 1988, pp. 43–51.

TECHNOLOGY
IN
ACTION:
Adjusting
to
Foreign
Markets

How can American firms be more competitive in their efforts to penetrate international markets? One way is by adapting their technology to the specific market. Many firms are finding that this is not as difficult it might seem. Boeing is a good example.

When Boeing introduced the 737 a number of U. S. airlines purchased the plane. However, sales then began to taper off. Several factors accounted for this including the fact that the 737's primary competitor, McDonnell Douglas's DC-9, had come to the market three years earlier and was a superior product. How could Boeing generate additional demand for its aircraft? The answer was found in the underdeveloped countries of the Mideast, Africa, and South America. These countries could profit from this plane, but it had to be redesigned for their geographic regions. Most runways in underdeveloped countries are shorter than those in the U. S., and they are made of asphalt not concrete. So the 737's wings had to be redesigned to allow for shorter landing and engine thrust had to be increased to allow for faster takeoffs. After traveling overseas to watch how pilots flew, Boeing engineers also realized that aviators brought their planes in hard and the craft tended to bounce on the runway. When this happened the brakes would be less effective in slowing up the plane. So Boeing redesigned the landing gear and installed low-pressure tires so that the plane would stay on the runway once it landed, and the brakes could bring it to a fast stop. The technological changes paid off. Boeing found an overseas market for the 737.

IBM has also found that technological product changes can help it capture overseas sales. When the firm develops a product for worldwide distribution, it also identifies the specific customer requirements in the various geographic areas. For example, to accommodate different languages, the company makes dozens of different keyboards.

Dow Chemical provides another example. Using computerized linear programming the firm is able to determine all the factors that will add cost to the product. These extend from production costs to transportation expenses to tax rates. Because of this computer approach, the company can determine which of its overseas factories to use in producing its various chemicals.

Thanks to technology, American firms are finding it easier to sell in international markets.

Source: Andrew Kupfer, "How to Be a Global Manager," *Fortune,* March 14, 1988, pp. 52–58.

The firm may decide to export or license.

involved. For those wishing to keep involvement at a minimum, licensing may be the answer. Under a licensing agreement, a manufacturer will permit a product on which it holds patents or trademarks to be produced in a foreign country. In turn, the licensee will make royalty payments to the company for each unit it manufactures. To ensure that the product is made correctly, many firms will train the licensee in production methods and manufacturing management. There is thus some involvement on the part of the company.

Overseas assembly of U. S.–made goods is possible.

Another approach, which entails still more involvement, is to manufacture the goods at home and then ship them overseas for assembling. Many firms have used this approach, but in time it is common to find them turning more and more to foreign manufacture. In the final stage, it is likely that the entire product will be manufactured overseas and the firm will begin exporting to nearby countries.

Organization Structure

Many types of organization structure can be employed in the management of foreign operations. In essence, structure depends on the firm's degree of involvement and its desire for control.

Branch Organizations and Subsidiaries

The simplest form is the *branch organization,* which is an integral part of the company structure. In essence, a branch is simply an outpost or detachment that is placed in a specific location for the purpose of accomplishing certain goals on a local level. It is quite common to find branch offices responsible primarily for selling, with the branch manager acting as a sales manager who supervises salespeople, handles orders, and resolves local problems. There is great disparity in the area of control. Some branch offices are highly autonomous and others are under close supervision of the parent company.

A branch organization is an integral part of the company structure.

A *subsidiary* differs from a branch in that it is a separate company, organized under the laws of the foreign country for the purpose of carrying out tasks assigned by the parent firm. By definition, a subsidiary is controlled (at least 51 percent ownership) by the parent, although it is possible that the parent will not completely own the subsidiary.

A subsidiary is a separate company.

Some subsidiaries are highly dependent on the parent for operating instructions. Subsidiary department heads, for example, might report directly to their functional counterpart in the home office, the plant manager to the vice-president of manufacturing, the head of sales to the vice-president of marketing. Although those in the home office may not be best equipped to make decisions for the subsidiary a thousand miles away, the organization structure normally is designed so that it does provide for close coordination of foreign and domestic operations.

On the other hand, many subsidiaries are highly autonomous. Some, for example, have a free hand in conducting small local operations or carrying out narrow functions in a limited market. Others are full-scale companies with a great deal of autonomy across a wide area. When this latter condition exists, the operations of the subsidiary are no longer subordinated to those of the domestic divisions; an international subsidiary company (see Figure 18-1) comes into existence. Management's big challenge now becomes one of coordinating the efforts of the domestic and international divisions. One way

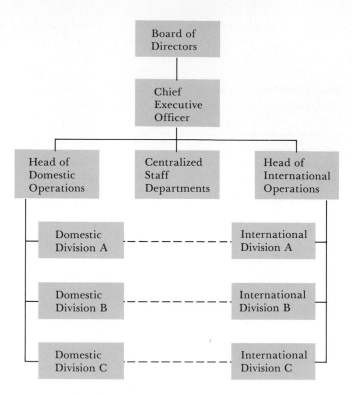

— — — — Synchronization and coordination of effort.

FIGURE 18-1   Model of an International Subsidiary Company

in which this coordination is often accomplished is by having one or two contact people, usually vice-presidents, sit on the boards of both the parent company and the international subsidiary. The important thing to remember, however, is that the latter operates highly independently of the parent.

World Companies

A worldwide view is taken.

Some firms have become so international in scope that they have gone beyond the international subsidiary organization structure. Many of these companies use what can be called a world company structure. These designs take many different forms. Figure 18-2 illustrates one which is area-based. This structure does not differentiate between domestic and foreign divisions; everything is viewed from the standpoint of area of the world. The staff departments provide functional and product assistance. The line managers use the assistance of these individuals in their respective areas of the globe. Commenting on the philosophy behind the world company, Kolde notes:

The world company model compels headquarters executives to view their management responsibilities from a global perspective and to

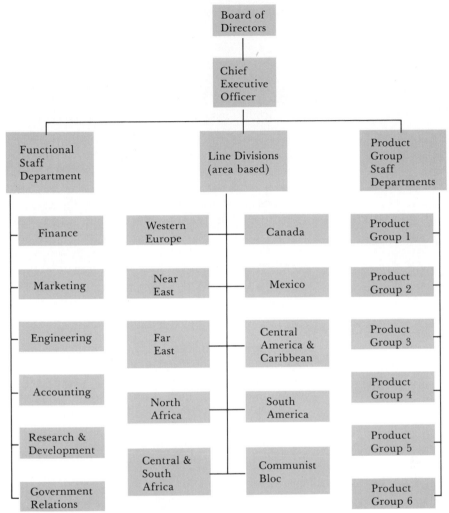

FIGURE 18-2   Model of an Area-centered World Company

cultivate structures and objectives that enable maximum growth and profitability to occur in a worldwide context. The headquarters of the world company is, thus, concerned not just with national or international affairs, but with world affairs. Its orbit is the globe and, in the future, conceivably also the moon and outer space. Management problems peculiar to individual countries or to certain groups of countries belong primarily to lower level jurisdictions. In theory, there is no nation centeredness at all at the top management level. However, since under existing political realities the headquarters of a company must be domiciled in some country, there is always, in fact, a home country whose environmental constraints are an inescapable reality to the headquarters managers of a world company.[15]

Control

One of the major issues that still confronts firms doing business overseas is: How much control should the foreign subsidiaries be given? The issue of control applies especially to those firms that want to create a global organization. Davidson and Haspeslagh put it this way:

> If you asked top executives . . . what is their major problem with international operations, they probably wouldn't say floating exchange rates or recalcitrant foreign governments. Rather, they would say it's how best to organize and coordinate the diversity inherent in these operations. On the one hand, they don't want to kill the local entrepreneurial spirit needed to gain market share abroad. On the other, they must make sure that the activities of individual subsidiaries do not deviate from the long-term, presumably more widely focused, strategy of the parent company.[16]

Hout and his colleagues echo these sentiments, pointing out that organization design continues to remain the Achilles heel of global companies.

> Organizational structure and reporting relationships present subtle problems for a global strategy. Effective strategic control argues for a central product-line organization; effective local responsiveness for a geographic organization with local autonomy. A global strategy demands that the product-line organization have the *ultimate* authority, because without it the company cannot gain systemwide benefits. Nevertheless, the company still must balance product and area needs. In short, there is no simple solution.[17]

When examined from an overall basis, there are three degrees of control a parent firm can exercise: heavy, intermediate, and light. Each has advantages and limitations.

Heavy Control

A parent firm can exercise heavy, intermediate, or light control over a subordinate.

When a subsidiary is required to keep the home office aware of all operations and activities and seek permission before undertaking any important actions, the parent is exercising heavy control. An advantage of heavy control is that it ensures that the subsidiary will operate in accord with home office policies.

---

[15]Kolde, pp. 234–35.

[16]William H. Davidson and Phillippe Haspeslagh, "Shaping a Global Product Organization," *Harvard Business Review*, July–August 1982, p. 125.

[17]Thomas Hout, Michael E. Porter, and Eileen Rudden, "How Global Companies Win Out," *Harvard Business Review*, September–October 1982, p. 107.

In addition, this approach makes it easier for the parent to integrate and coordinate its worldwide operations. If a problem arises, the home office is in a good position to help solve the issue because it understands, through continual monitoring of operations, what is going on.

On the negative side, heavy control can be expensive and far less effective than the home office would like. In addition, costly delays can occur while the parent company ponders a decision. Also, the subsidiary manager and the staff may quit or ask to be transferred home, feeling that they are merely rubber stamps who are not allowed to exercise any personal initiative.

Intermediate Control

When the subsidiary submits continued reports to the home office but has the freedom to make important decisions without obtaining permission in advance, the parent is exercising intermediate control. The main advantages of intermediate control are that the reporting system helps the home office monitor activities and provide assistance to the subsidiary, and the freedom to make decisions helps the subsidiary manager and the staff deal quickly with operational problems. This freedom of action can be a great morale booster for the overseas staff.

On the negative side, the manager is expected to be an operating executive and a paperwork specialist, and it may be difficult to find an individual who is qualified to fill both roles. Also, the home office may be setting the goals for the subsidiary, expecting the manager to attain them. There may be difficulty here, however, because the subsidiary is not being allowed sufficient input into the plan.

Light Control

When a subsidiary is allowed virtually complete freedom, having to provide the home office with only a minimum of information, the parent is exercising light control. Light control has several advantages. First, the manager can devote full attention to running the subsidiary and making money for the firm. Second, when the paperwork is decreased, the number of employees can be cut back and the overhead cost reduced. Third, morale is likely to be high when the overseas people realize that the home office is relying on their judgment to get the job done right.

Light control also has its disadvantages. First, it may be difficult to find a manager who is qualified to handle such a demanding job. Second, the home office gives up any chance to fully coordinate and integrate worldwide operations. Third, if a problem arises, the parent company may not learn of it until a great deal of damage already has been done.

Experience shows that heavy control is often too inflexible, whereas light control is too lacking in checks and balances. For this reason, many companies use some variation of intermediate control. The manager makes decisions at the local level but continually reports to the home office on subsidiary operations. Guvence C. Alpander, after surveying sixty-four multinational corporations, reported that 17 percent used heavy control, 67 percent employed intermediate control, and 16 percent opted for light control.[18]

Staffing

In addition to organizing and controlling foreign operations, a company must concern itself with staffing the enterprise. Who should head up the subsidiary? What qualifications will the overseas employees need?

Choosing the Right People

Careful staff selection is necessary.

The company can answer many of the questions about staffing when it decides whether to set up a branch, a subsidiary, or a world company organization. Other questions will be resolved when the issue of control over operations is determined. Of those questions remaining, some can be handled quite easily. For example, if the firm that has been exporting to a foreign country decides to set up a subsidiary there, the export manager may be the natural choice for subsidiary head. If the company has an operation in Venezuela and decides to open one in Colombia, it may simply transfer staff. The people at the Venezuelan site probably speak Spanish and know a great deal about South American culture and custom. Their skills are thus transferable.

Many firms that must staff subsidiaries in underdeveloped countries have formulated guidelines based on past experience. For example, many like to employ unmarried people who have learned to make quick and easy personal adjustments to transfers and who will not have families to worry about. On the other hand, one U. S. oil company operating in the Middle East considers the middle-aged men with grown children the best risks. Economic conditions of the country and the specific operations of the firm can have an effect on who is most suitable for the job. So too can the geography. Companies with desert surroundings find that people from Texas or Southern California tend to be better risks than those from New England. By employing such guidelines, the firm can often pick those most suitable for the job.[19]

However the company hires, not all staff will be Americans. Many firms realize that unless they recruit some nationals, their firms may encounter very rough going. Not only are there cultural and social problems, but there is also the issue of nationalism. Host governments may insist that the

---

[18]Guvence C. Alpander, "Multinational Corporations: Homebase-Affiliate Relations," *California Management Review,* Spring 1978, pp. 47–56.

[19]For more on this subject, see Jeffrey L. Blue and Ulric Haynes, Jr., "Preparation for the Overseas Assignment," *Business Horizons,* June 1977, pp. 61–67.

company hire local people. In fact, notes one international management expert, "Before headquarters launches a search (at home) for an appropriate individual to fill an overseas job, it should consider if the job in question could be filled by a local national."[20] Her selection staffing process is presented in Figure 18-3. For both of these reasons, it is common to find multinational firms attempting to recruit local people, preferably those with good business judgment and/or political connections.

Firms are also beginning to develop procedures for getting people ready for international work. Some of the most common include:

1. A previsit to the country and/or an audio-visual presentation during which the manager is given a visual frame of reference.

2. Training in that country's language and communication, including informal and nonverbal communication.

3. Detailed study in the specific cultural attitudes, heritage, politics, social structure, economics and religion of the area.

Useful procedures for getting ready to go international.

4. A country-specific handbook that could be entitled "Everything You Ever Wanted to Know about (name of country)," which provides a wealth of practical information, including how to use a telephone, how to get clothes dry cleaned, what to do in an emergency.

5. In-company counseling on company or tax-related matters, contract terms, career path decisions, and the acculturation issues that are so important when an executive's family is also going.

6. Meetings with managers who have recently returned from the country, including a spouse's viewpoint of what to know about the area.[21]

This type of orientation is extremely helpful in overcoming some of the common pitfalls and problems faced by managers, especially those taking overseas assignments for the first time.

Another recent development has been the formulation of selection criteria for choosing personnel for overseas assignments. No longer is a willingness to accept an overseas assignment regarded as the most important criterion. Businesses are beginning to realize that age, sex, initiative, management talent, experience, and technical knowledge are also vitally important.[22]

---

[20]Rosalie T. Tung, "Selection and Training of Personnel for Overseas Assignments," *Columbia Journal of World Business,* Spring 1981, p. 78.

[21]Michael G. Harvey, "The Multinational Corporation's Expatriate Problem: An Application of Murphy's Law," *Business Horizons,* January–February 1983, p. 72.

[22]For more on this subject see: Nicholas Sleveking, Kenneth Anchor, and Ronald C. Marston, "Selecting and Preparing Employees," *Personnel Journal,* March 1981, pp. 197–202; and Yosup Lee and Laurie Larwood, "The Socialization of Expatriate Managers in Multinational Firms," *Academy of Management Journal,* December 1983, pp. 657–65.

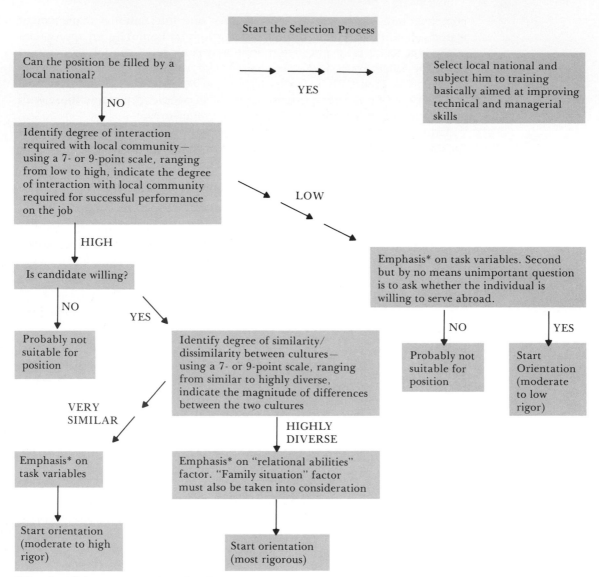

Start the Selection Process

Can the position be filled by a local national?

YES

Select local national and subject him to training basically aimed at improving technical and managerial skills

NO

Identify degree of interaction required with local community— using a 7- or 9-point scale, ranging from low to high, indicate the degree of interaction with local community required for successful performance on the job

LOW

Emphasis* on task variables. Second but by no means unimportant question is to ask whether the individual is willing to serve abroad.

HIGH

Is candidate willing?

NO

Probably not suitable for position

YES

Identify degree of similarity/ dissimilarity between cultures— using a 7- or 9-point scale, ranging from similar to highly diverse, indicate the magnitude of differences between the two cultures

NO

Probably not suitable for position

YES

Start Orientation (moderate to low rigor)

VERY SIMILAR

HIGHLY DIVERSE

Emphasis* on task variables

Emphasis* on "relational abilities" factor. "Family situation" factor must also be taken into consideration

Start orientation (moderate to high rigor)

Start orientation (most rigorous)

*"Emphasis" does not mean ignoring the other factors.
It only means that it should be the dominant factor.

FIGURE 18-3   Flow Chart of the Selection-Decision Process

*Emphasis does not mean ignoring the other factors. It only means that it should be the dominant factor.

Source: Rosalie L. Tung, "Selection and Training of Personnel for Overseas Assignments," Reprinted with permission from *The Columbia Journal of World Business,* Spring 1981, p. 78. © 1981 by the Trustees of Columbia University in the City of New York.

Women Executives

Another area that has begun to receive a lot of attention is that of women executives in overseas subsidiaries. In the United States, there are numerous stereotypical profiles of working women, including the belief that they are less ambitious and rational than men, and more emotional, dependent, conforming, and passive than their male counterparts. In the international arena, women find additional stereotypes, perhaps best summed up by the cliche "these guys over here have never taken orders from women; if anything, they give orders to women." Izraeli and his associates recently investigated the subject of women executives in overseas subsidiaries and found that over 60 percent of managers in their survey thought that a woman could successfully head and manage a subsidiary there. These percentages, broken down by country, were: Belgium (75 percent), West Germany (68.4 percent), France (56.2 percent), Holland (53.8 percent), and the United Kingdom (53.1 percent).[23] On the other hand, when the researchers dug further into the issue through the use of personal interviews, the responses changed dramatically. With few exceptions, the managers were apprehensive about assigning a woman to a position as a senior executive in an overseas subsidiary. Some of their responses were as follows:

> In most cases, it is desirable that the number one person in the subsidiary be a man. But if there is a woman who is outstandingly capable, she could be the number two. (England, banking.)
>
> A woman could well be a manager in a branch, but not the general manager of the subsidiary. (France, industrial products.)
>
> You could place a woman as manager of sales, but not in a representative function and certainly not as subsidiary chief executive. (Germany, tourism and transportation.)
>
> It is possible for a woman to be a senior manager, but not the top manager in the branch. (Holland, agricultural products.)[24]

Responses such as these indicate the growing importance of selection, training, and assignment of women in overseas operations. Researchers and business firms are currently working to develop a series of guidelines that will ensure equal opportunity in overseas assignments. Some of the most recent recommendations include:

1. Women selected for overseas managerial positions should have both managerial experience in the firm and a record of accomplishment. These will help smooth the way for their acceptance as "qualified."

2. Women should be in midcareer so that if they do well overseas they can be promoted even higher in the hierarchy.

---

[23]Dafna N. Izraeli, Moshe Banai, and Yoram Zeira, "Women Executives in MNC Subsidiaries," *California Management Review*, Fall 1980, p. 58.

[24]Ibid., p. 59.

3. Women need to be made aware of any sex role stereotypes that exist in the country to which they are being assigned and should be coached and counseled regarding the most effective ways of dealing with these problems.

Guidelines for creating a pool of international female managers.

4. If the firm is just beginning the assignment of female managers to overseas operations, it is often wisest to assign them to host countries where there are other women in senior executive positions. If male managers there have had experience doing business with high-level women, the transition for the new manager is easier.

5. Before sending a woman to head an overseas subsidiary, the home office should make the personnel in the overseas office aware of the decision and work to establish a positive climate of opinion among them.

6. Since it takes a long time to train a senior level manager, businesses can create a large pool of female talent in their overseas subsidiaries by placing women in number two roles. In this way they gain important overseas experience and as the top cadre of male managers begin to retire or come back to the states, there is a large pool of qualified female managers ready to take their places.

Realistically speaking, the placement of female managers in overseas operations continues to be a problem for many international businesses. However, it is a problem that will have to be addressed. The above guidelines are a good starting point on the road to developing a corps of women executives in overseas subsidiaries.

Monetary Incentives

Once the right people have been chosen in the United States, a firm has the problem of getting them to accept overseas assignments. In addition to travel, many firms offer monetary incentives. Besides their base salary, these people may be given housing subsidies and basic allowances to keep up with the cost of living overseas. In recent years, these extras have risen dramatically, which helps explain why many firms will hire local managers when possible. Not only can they save on these high fringe expenditures, but the pay scale for foreign managers is often much lower. For example, a French manager running a French subsidiary will receive less than an American doing the same job. Such discrepancies have long been a source of dispute with many foreign managers. The situation can become even more difficult if one considers the French student who comes to the United States, receives a degree in business administration, and then takes a job in New York City with a multinational firm. The person in this capacity will receive an equivalent U. S. salary. However, if two years later the individual is sent to France to assist the manager in running the subsidiary there, this person will leave New York earning more money than the French office superior. What should the company do?

Foreign managers are paid less.

The entire area of wages and compensation is under current examination. Multinational firms have established various schemes for resolving the problems. However, the answer still seems to depend on an individual analysis of the merits of the particular situation. Quite often, paying a competitive wage seems to be the only satisfactory solution.

Upward Mobility

Rapid promotion is possible.

Another advantage in going overseas is rapid promotion. Most executives admit that the person overseas can move up the subsidiary ranks much faster than it is possible to move up the ranks at home, because although many Americans will stay overseas for two or three years, most prefer to get back to the home office, having done their job in the field. This opens up opportunities for the lower-level managers to advance. Thus, for the individual who is adaptable to other countries and who can deal with the emotional strains of going international, the promise of upward mobility is a likelihood.

However, it should be noted that such promotions will undoubtedly not come at the expense of capable local management talent. A trend toward prohibiting expatriate managers from getting such favorable treatment is currently strong. This is best seen in the United States. In recent years Americans have been filing lawsuits against multinational firms that continue to bring in top managers from the home country while bypassing local personnel for such promotions. Some firms, well aware of this problem, make it a point to put an American as head of the facility from the very start. Others, concerned about the potential backlash that might accompany cries of "employee discrimination," try to move them up the line as quickly as possible.

In one recent case the Supreme Court ruled that a Japanese firm had indeed discriminated against Americans by systematically excluding them from top management positions in an American subsidiary. This type of ruling scares overseas firms. For all of these reasons, all international managers now have to temper their desire for promotion with the reality of the local situation. There is upward mobility, but it is limited to some degree by the need to accommodate local management talent.

The Multinational Corporation

A good deal of attention has recently been focused on the *multinational corporation,* or *MNC,* as it is sometimes called. The multinational corporation is the subject of some controversy, part of which is a disagreement over how to apply the term. Some people say an MNC is, quite simply, a company that operates in more than one country. Others employ more criteria including:

1. The company must do business in many countries.
2. The foreign subsidiaries must be more than mere sales organizations. There must be some services, such as R&D and manufacturing, carried on.

Criteria for defining multinationalism.

3. Nationals should be running the local companies since they understand the people and the environment better than anyone else.

4. There must be a multinational headquarters staffed by people from many different countries.

5. The company's stock must be owned by people in many different countries.[25]

Most people are inclined to accept far less rigid criteria and would tend to agree with the group of researchers who identified a multinational company as "any firm that has a large portion of its operations devoted to activity that is not limited to one country."[26] This definition allows for various interpretations while conveying the most widely accepted meaning of the term.

U. S. firms have international economic power.

U. S. firms have invested large sums in foreign lands (see Table 18-3). These investments have made the multinational U. S. firm a power in the international economic arena. Giant U. S. companies have significant economic control everywhere. In fact, more than 20 years ago, U. S. MNCs in France already controlled virtually two-thirds of the country's farm machinery, telecommunications equipment, and film photographic paper production, in addition to 40 percent of the nation's petroleum market. In the whole of Europe they controlled 15 percent of all consumer goods then being manufactured, 50 percent of all semi-conductors, 80 percent of all computers and 95 percent of the integrated circuits market. Other countries from England, France, and West Germany to Japan,[27] Korea,[28] and China[29] are becoming increasingly active in the international arena. MNCs now operate in every corner of the globe.

Becoming Truly International

With economic power comes responsibility.

With economic power comes responsibility. As the multinational corporations grow ever larger, they face the problem of rising nationalism. Is U. S. business trying to dominate other countries? Some people think so and believe that the challenge of the next decade will be one of integrating nationals into the top ranks of these giant organizations so that management's point of view becomes international in focus. Kenneth Simmonds has stated it this way:

---

[25]Gene E. Bradley and Edward C. Bursk, "Multinationalism and the 29th Day," *Harvard Business Review*, January–February 1972, p. 39.

[26]Richard D. Hays, Christopher M. Korth, and Manucher Roudiani, *International Business: An Introduction to the World of the Multinational Firm* (Inglewood Cliffs, NJ: Prentice-Hall, 1972), p. 260.

[27]William J. Holstein and Amy Borrus, "Japan's Clout in the U. S.," *Business Week*, July 11, 1988, pp. 64–66.

[28]Louis Kraar, "Korea: Tomorrow's Powerhouse," *Fortune*, August 15, 1988, pp. 75–81.

[29]Dori Jones Yang and Maria Shao, "China's Reformers Say: Let a Thousand Business Bloom," *Business Week*, April 11, 1988, pp. 70–71.

TABLE 18-3	Country	1960	1970	1980	1986
Direct Foreign Investment by Select Countries (including reinvested earnings in $ millions)	United States	$2,940	$7,589	$19,220	$28,050
	Japan	79	355	2,385	14,480
	West Germany	139	876	4,180	8,999
	Britain	700	1,308	11,360	16,691
	Canada	52	302	2,694	3,254
	France	347*	374	3,138	5,230
	Italy	−17*	111	754	2,661

*1961 data

Source: Fortune, March 14, 1988, p. 46. © 1988 Time Inc. All Rights Reserved.

Ensuring that top corporate management in the international corporations does become truly international requires planned action. There are many ways to start. Noteworthy steps include: international executive development programs that concentrate on top management problems, rotation of younger foreign executives through corporate headquarters, decentralization of staff functions to foreign sites, or adoption of policies that treat all executives as internationalists regardless of origin.[30]

Statistics reveal that this action is indeed beginning to occur. For example, Randolph A. Pohlman and two associates surveyed a large sample of American firms operating overseas and found the following percentage of the foreign subsidiaries' top management to be citizens of the countries in which the subsidiaries were located:

Percentage Native Born	Percentage of Firms in Category[31]
0–10	6
11–20	0
21–30	13
31–50	16
51–60	9
61–80	6
81–90	13
91–100	31
"Major"[a]	6

[a]"Major" is an unspecified number, considered of significance by respondents.

---

[30]Kenneth Simmonds, "Multinational? Well, Not Quite," *Columbia Journal of World Business*, Fall 1966, p. 122.

[31]Randolph A. Pohlman, James S. Ang, and Syed I. Ali, "Policies of Multinational Firms: A Survey," *Business Horizons*, December 1976, p. 17.

Pohlman, Ang, and Ali also found that most firms felt that a recruitment policy of "hiring a maximum number of nationals" was most effective. Some of these companies said that United States citizens were used initially, but they were eventually replaced by local people. Furthermore, when Americans are used, greater care is devoted to training those individuals to fit into the host country organization.[32] It thus appears that more and more U. S. firms doing business overseas are becoming multinational in the fullest true sense of the word.

■ SUMMARY

This chapter has examined areas of international management. U. S. firms account for a significant percentage of all international business. The student of management thus needs a working knowledge of this area.

In deciding whether or not to go international, a firm must evaluate many factors. It can begin analyzing the possible advantages and disadvantages associated with such an undertaking. On the positive side are profit, stability, and the possibility of a foothold in an economic union, of which the European Common Market is a famous example. On the negative side are unfamiliar customs and cultures, delicate company-government relations, risk, expropriation, and the possibility of having to bring in foreign partners, which, for many businesses, constitutes the biggest drawback. In an effort to hedge their risks, many firms are turning to joint ventures.

If a company decides to go ahead with a foreign operation, it must find an appropriate organization structure, which will depend, of course, on the amount of involvement it is willing to undertake. For some firms a branch organization will do; for others a subsidiary is necessary.

The next question is one of control. Which is best: heavy, intermediate, or light? Most firms opt for intermediate. Then comes staffing, which entails identifying qualified people and offering them sufficient monetary incentive and upward mobility to get them to go abroad.

The last section of this chapter examined the multinational corporation. Most multinational firms are American, and they carry a good deal of economic power in the international arena. However, with this power comes responsibility, and one of the challenge of the 1990s will be to continue incorporating foreign nationals into the upper ranks of management. In so doing, the multinational firms will become truly international in nature.

■ REVIEW AND STUDY QUESTIONS

1. Why do business firms choose to go international? Identify and describe at least three reasons.

---

[32]Yoram Zeira and Ehud Harari, "Host-Country Organizations and Expatriate Managers in Europe," *California Management Review,* Spring 1979, pp. 40–50.

2. What are some of the possible advantages associated with going international? For most firms, which one of these advantages is more important?

3. What are some of the possible disadvantages associated with going international? For most firms, which one of these disadvantages is more important? Explain.

4. How great is the risk of expropriation? Is this risk, speaking on a worldwide basis, becoming greater or is it diminishing? Defend your answer.

5. How does a joint venture work? In your answer be sure to discuss some of the typical joint venture strategies used by international firms.

6. What are some of the advantages associated with heavy control of foreign subsidiaries? With loose control?

7. Why do most firms use intermediate control with their overseas subsidiaries? Explain.

8. How does an international subsidiary company differ from a world company? Use Figures 18-1 and 18-2 to help you compare and contrast the two.

9. How can business firms go about getting their people ready for an overseas assignment? What are some of the procedures that would be most helpful? Identify and describe three.

10. What are some things a firm should look for in the people it chooses for overseas operations?

11. How great are the opportunities for women in overseas managerial positions? How can their chances for assignment to these jobs be improved? Explain.

12. What is a multinational corporation? Put it in your own words.

13. How powerful are U. S. multinational corporations in the international economic arena? Defend your answer.

14. How international are the top management ranks of multinational corporations? Explain your answer.

■ SELECTED REFERENCES

Anastos, Dennis, Alexis Bedos, and Bryant Seaman. "The Development of Modern Management Practices in Saudi Arabia." *Columbia Journal of World Business,* Summer 1980, pp. 81–92.

Brewer, Thomas L. "Political Risk Assessment for Foreign Direct Investment Decisions: Better Methods for Better Results." *Columbia Journal of World Business,* Spring 1981, pp. 5–11.

Buss, Martin D. J. "Managing International Information Systems." *Harvard Business Review,* September–October 1982, pp. 153–62.

Contractor, Farok J. "The Role of Licensing in International Strategy." *Columbia Journal of World Business*, Winter 1981, pp. 73–83.

Das, Ranjan. "Impact of Host Government Regulations on MNC Operation: Learning from Third World Countries." *Columbia Journal of World Business*, Spring 1981, pp. 85–90.

Davidow, Joel. "Multinationals, Host Governments and Regulation of Restrictive Business Practices." *Columbia Journal of World Business*, Summer 1980, pp. 14–19.

Davidson, William H., and Phillippe Haspeslagh. "Shaping a Global Product Organization." *Harvard Business Review*, July–August 1982, pp. 125–32.

Doz, Yves L. "Strategic Management in Multinational Companies." *Sloan Management Review*, Winter 1980, pp. 27–45.

Doz, Y. L., and C. K. Prahalad. "How MNC's Cope with Host Government Intervention." *Harvard Business Review*, March–April 1980, pp. 149–57.

Drake, Rodman L., and Lee M. Caudill. "Management of the Large Multinational: Trends and Future Challenges." *Business Horizons*, May–June 1981, pp. 83–91.

Dreyfuss, Joel. "How to Deal with Japan." *Fortune*, June 6, 1988, pp. 107–18.

Graham, John L. "A Hidden Cause of America's Deficit with Japan." *Columbia Journal of World Business*, Fall 1981, pp. 5–12.

Greenhouse, Steven. "The Emerging Elite." *New York Times*, July 17, 1988, Section 3, pp. 1, 8.

Harper, Stephen C. "Now That the Dust Has Settled: Learning from Japanese Management." *Business Horizons*, July–August 1988, pp. 43–51.

Hout, Thomas, Michael E. Porter, and Eileen Rudden. "How Global Companies Win Out." *Harvard Business Review*, September–October 1982, pp. 98–108.

Hoy, Harold J., and John J. Shaw. "The United States' Comparative Advantage and Its Relationship to the Product Life Cycle Theory and the World Gross National Product Market Share." *Columbia Journal of World Business*, Spring 1981, pp. 40–50.

Izraeli, Dafna N., Moshe Banai, and Yoram Zeira. "Women Executives in MNC Subsidiaries." *Columbia Journal of World Business*, Fall 1980, pp. 53–63.

Killing, J. Peter. "How to Make a Global Joint Venture Work." *Harvard Business Review*, May–June 1982, pp. 120–27.

Kline, John M. "Entrapment or Opportunity: Structuring a Corporate Response to International Codes of Conduct." *Columbia Journal of World Business*, Summer 1980, pp. 6–13.

Kupfer, Andrew. "How to Be a Global Manager." *Fortune*, March 14, 1988, pp. 52–58.

Micallef, Joseph V. "Political Risk Assessment." *Columbia Journal of World Business*, Summer 1981, pp. 47–52.

Prahalad, C. K., and Yves L. Doz. "An Approach to Strategic Control in MNCs." *Sloan Management Review*, Summer 1981, pp. 5–13.

Shao, Maria. "Laying the Foundation: For the Great Mall of China." *Business Week,* January 25, 1988, pp. 68–69.

Shapiro, Alan C. "Managing Political Risk: A Policy Approach." *Columbia Journal of World Business,* Fall 1981, pp. 63–69.

Takamiya, Makoto. "Japanese Multinationals in Europe: Internal Operations and their Public Policy Implications." *Columbia Journal of World Business,* Summer 1981, pp. 5–17.

Taylor III, Alex. "Japan's Carmakers Take on the World." *Fortune,* June 20, 1988, pp. 67–76.

Teece, David J. "The Multinational Enterprise: Market Failure and Market Power Considerations." *Sloan Management Review,* Spring 1981, pp. 3–15.

Thal, N. L., and P. R. Cateora. "Opportunities for Women in International Business." *Business Horizons,* December 1979, pp. 21–27.

Tung, Rosalie. "Selection and Training of Personnel for Overseas Assignments." *Columbia Journal of World Business,* Spring 1981, pp. 68–78.

■ CASE: Getting Prepared

A large multinational corporation headquartered in the United States had been having trouble keeping its overseas staff happy. Especially when a new executive arrived, the company could always expect some critical problem. In an effort to deal with the difficulty, the company hired a consulting firm to study its overseas assignments and put together a report to help the company select and prepare people for overseas jobs. Although it took almost six months for the consultants to compile their recommendations, the chairman of the board believes now that the corporation got its money's worth. The consulting firm made the following recommendations, which the chairman considered particularly valuable:

1. If there is time, send the executive, with spouse, to the country for an early visit. This will allow a firsthand view of the situation.

2. If English is not spoken there, give the executive couple some training in the language of the country before they leave. Even twenty to thirty hours is preferable to putting the new people through a crash course after they arrive in the new place.

3. Give arriving individuals a booklet containing information about such things as the specific culture, attitudes, religious beliefs and practices, and customs of the people of the host country. Also include in this booklet instructions on how to handle such company policy matters as travel allowances, medical plans, compensation, and vacations.

4. Where possible, have the executive visit with people in the firm who have been in the relevant country and now are stateside. These people can provide a lot of important information to the ones about to depart.

5. When new people arrive, have someone meet the plane and help them get through the first couple of weeks. If possible, have a spouse committee take care of some of this burden while the personnel office handles the rest.

Questions

1. Overall, what do you think of the consultants' suggestions?
2. Which of the five do you think are most important?
3. Would you add any other suggestions to the list? What are they? Explain your answer in detail.

■ CASE: A Matter of Control

When Jusaf, Inc. first decided to go international, the management's primary concern was profit. "Will we make enough money to justify the risk?" the board chairman asked the chief executive officer. Assured that the company would indeed make a reasonable return, the board gave its approval. That was five years ago. Since then the overseas branch has grown dramatically, and today it is a full-fledged subsidiary. The first small sales office in downtown Rio de Janeiro has now been replaced by a ten-story building. The sales manager no longer has to hurry to the airport or to the docks to ensure that shipments of products from the States are on time. The company produces all of its products for the Argentinian and other South American markets in or around Rio. The board chairman likes to reminisce about the day when the board was unsure whether the South American investment would be successful. Now he admits, "Profit is no longer a concern about our operations down there. Other questions now occupy my attention."

The Chairman is referring to the relationship between the subsidiary and the home office. Over the last two years sales in South America have climbed from $35 million to $75 million and profit/sales have risen from 12 percent to 19 percent. The subsidiary is the most profitable division the firm has. The problem currently being encountered is that the head of South American operations wants more autonomy for the subsidiary. He thinks that it takes too long to get business deals cleared through the home office. On the other hand, the home office thinks that it must have the final say on what goes on in its overseas operations. "The right hand needs to know what the left hand is doing," is the way the chairman explained it to the head of the subsidiary.

At the present time the home office is exercising what might be called heavy/intermediate control over operations. Initially heavy control was used, but over the last two years this has changed. The subsidiary head would like the firm to switch to light control and give him even more autonomy. His argument with the president is this, "We've proven we can operate profitably in South America. Most of our decisions are not related to U. S. operations and can be made by us. If you give us more control over our own sphere of operations, we can increase sales and profits even further. This would free you to look at the other areas of the world where Jusaf could set up operations. We have to start thinking in larger terms than just the U. S. market or the U. S. and South American markets. We have the potential to be a world corporation. All I'm asking is that you let me assume the responsibility for South America while you put your time in on more important matters."

Questions

1. What is the current relationship between the subsidiary and the home office? Be sure to include the issue of control in your answer.

2. What are the benefits of giving the South American manager more control? What are the drawbacks associated with such action? Be complete in your answer.

3. What does the manager mean by a world corporation? How would this type of an organization change the way Jusaf's top management currently operates? Include a discussion of Figure 18-2 in your answer.

■ ## CASE: Management in China

Many U. S. firms want to sell their goods in overseas markets; a new opportunity is selling the training that leads to production. Some U. S. organizations are going international by helping to train the work force of other nations. The Chinese, in particular, are interested in buying such training.

During the Cultural Revolution the government of the People's Republic of China claimed that anyone could be a manager. As a result, many business managers were sent to the country to work on farms, while people who were in political step with the government, but had not necessarily had any managerial training, took over the factories and the other administrative positions.

Today China realizes that the country badly needs managerial talent. Only around 15 percent of the country's managers have had any formal managerial training. In an effort to make up lost time, the country is putting on crash courses in management for its people.

Some Chinese colleges have started offering courses in management; the government is also sending some of its young people to study management in colleges in the United States, West Germany, and Japan; and the China Business Management Association is offering short courses at branches all over the country. Topics include how to modernize factories, how to use the behavioral sciences in management, how to employ consultants, and how to conduct market forecasts. In some cases the government brings in U. S. business professors. During the summer of 1980 a U. S. government team, headed by a former dean of a business school, offered a pilot executive management program for a hundred Chinese managers and twenty college professors.

Questions

1. Are the management ideas taught in a basic management course in the United States the same as those needed by Chinese managers? Explain.

2. Can management information be marketed? Can a company offering international management programs actually succeed in the international arena? Explain.

3. Do you think China will ever have multinational corporations? Explain your answer.

■ CASE: Here Come the Japanese

At the rate things are going, it appears that the Japanese will be the world's largest auto producers by the turn of the century. From 1977 to 1987 North American auto production declined by 23 percent while that in Western Europe dropped off by about 15 percent before recovering this loss. During this same decade the Japanese increased their auto production by almost 60 percent. Industry analysts estimate that by 1992 North America will produce around 9.22 million cars, Western Europe will account for 9.69 million autos, and Japan will make 9.14 million cars. This means that from 1977 to 1992 inclusive the net changes in auto production will be: North America, down 26 percent; West Europe, up 5 percent; and Japan up 70 percent.

How are the Japanese managing to do so well? After all, the decline in the value of the dollar during the late 1980s made American goods much more price competitive. So why has demand for Japanese cars not plummeted? The answer is that the Japanese have managed to greatly reduce the cost of building their cars and they have cut their profit margins, so they can still sell inexpensive autos. At the same time, the Japanese have been extending their product line into costlier vehicles with more accessories and convenience features. This top-end of the market is less price conscious and offers higher profit margins. The Japanese are also placing a greater emphasis on new technology introduction and improved quality. Honda, for example, employs 50 percent more engineers per car than does GM. Additionally, Honda builds only 10 model lines as opposed to 47 for GM. The result is engineering talent is more directly focused, which shows up in the finished product. Recent data reveal that American cars have an average of 87 assembly defects per 100 autos in contrast to Japanese cars sold in the U. S. which average 44 assembly defects per 100 cars.

Nor are the Japanese limiting their efforts to the American market. They currently sell 1.2 million cars in Europe and plan to increase this market share during the 1990s. The new Nissan plant in England has an annual capacity of 200,000 cars.

These data indicate that the Japanese are going to be a major power in worldwide auto sales. Unless U. S. and Europe carmakers are able to slow down this competitor, Japan will be the major player in this market by the first decade of the next century.

Questions

1. Why are the Japanese interested in going international? Offer and explain two reasons.

2. Some American auto firms are entering into joint ventures with Japanese firms. Is this a wise decision? Why?

3. In what way is staffing likely to be a problem for the Japanese auto firms? Explain.

Source: Alex Taylor III, "Japan's Carmakers Take on the World," *Fortune*, June 20, 1988, pp. 67–75.

■ SELF-FEEDBACK EXERCISE: How Well Do You Know International Management Practices?

Read and circle the correct answer to each statement. Answers are provided at the end of the exercise.

T F 1. Individual incentive plans have been more effective in motivating personnel in Japan than they have in the United States.

T F 2. Germans are less likely than Americans to bypass the hierarchical chain of command in getting things done.

T F 3. Japanese tend to be more emotional in their approach to human relations than are Americans.

T F 4. In Italy most managers believe that it is important to have precise answers to questions that subordinates may raise about their work.

T F 5. Managers in Mexico tend to have more power than those in the United States.

T F 6. In Japanese auto factories the work focus is on quality of work life while in Scandinavia it is on efficiency.

T F 7. The business culture of South Africa is closer to that of the United States than it is to the business culture of Spain.

T F 8. The business culture of the United States is closer to that of Mexico than it is to the business culture of Italy.

T F 9. The business culture of the United States is closer to that of Kuwait than it is to that of Saudi Arabia.

T F 10. The French see the Americans as very industrious.

T F 11. The Japanese see the Americans as very honest.

T F **12.** The West Germans see the Americans as intelligent.

T F **13.** The British see the Americans as very sophisticated.

T F **14.** The Brazilians see the Americans as self-indulgent.

T F **15.** The Mexicans see the Americans as very lazy.

T F **16.** Indians see Americans as in a perpetual hurry.

T F **17.** Ethiopians feel that Americans are too implicit in their communications.

T F **18.** Colombians feel that Americans put too much emphasis on work and not enough on leisure.

T F **19.** Surprisingly, Japanese are more motivated by money than are Americans.

T F **20.** Quality of work life is more important to the Americans than it is to the Dutch.

Answers

1. False. Japanese prefer group incentive plans.
2. True.
3. True.
4. True.
5. True.
6. False. It is the opposite.
7. True.
8. False. The United States's business culture is closer to that of Italy.
9. False. The U. S. business culture is closer to that of Saudi Arabia.
10. True.
11. False. This is not one of the traits that ranks high on their list of American traits.
12. True.
13. False. This is not one of the traits that ranks high on their list of American traits.
14. False. This is not one of the traits that ranks high on their list of American traits.
15. False. They see Americans as very hardworking.
16. True.
17. False. They feel Americans are too explicit.
18. True.
19. True. Research shows that the Japanese are highly economic-driven.
20. False. It is the opposite.

CHAPTER
19

Management
in
the
Future

Because past and present developments in the field of management have already been discussed, it is possible now to forecast what the future will probably hold. The first goal of this chapter, however, is to synthesize what has already been covered, for the future is at least partly determined by the past. The second goal of the chapter is to review developments in modern management theory, and the third is to examine developments on the horizon that will continue to gain importance over the next twenty years.

When you have finished this chapter, you should be able to:

1. Review the contributions of early classic management theory.
2. Recapitulate the major concepts contained in each of the three major schools of management thought.
3. Discuss current developments in management theory.
4. Describe some major trends in management today, including the continued focus on key result areas, the challenge of managing talent in a work force, and the continuing trend toward professionalism in management.

THE PAST IS PROLOGUE

In management theory, as in history, events of the past help determine events of the future; what has gone before sets the stage for what will follow. The first section of this book examined early management thought. It noted that scientific management, administrative management, and the human relations movement all made major contributions to the development of modern management theory. Although early classical theorists had their shortcomings, they did help uncover some important principles and theories that are still useful today. Two prominent theorists, Alan C. Filley and Robert J. House, have said this:

> In our review, many critical propositions derived from classical management theory have stood the test of research evaluation rather well. They suffer not so much from what they say as from what they fail to say. For example . . . the principle of unity of command is pragmatic convenience, not a necessity. Similarly, optimum spans of supervision do exist, but their determination depends upon a number of variables which are only now becoming clear.[1]

Three distinct schools of thought have emerged.

The classical theorists thus made lasting contributions to management. There was, however, much more to be learned about the field. As research increased and the boundaries of management knowledge expanded, three distinct schools of thought emerged. The first, representing a continuation and expansion of Henri Fayol's work, is the management process school. Chapters 4, 5, 6, and 7, which examined planning, organizing, and controlling, established the basic framework for this school of thought. The second school, often traced directly to Frederick W. Taylor and his scientific management associates, is the quantitative school. Chapters 8, 9, 10, and 11 which examined the fundamentals of decision making and some of the techniques being employed by the modern manager in choosing among alternatives, as well as the role of information systems, introduced the basic philosophy of this school. The third school of thought, which is concerned with applying psychosociological concepts in the workplace, is the behavioral school. Chapters 12 to 15 which examined the areas of communication, motivation, leadership, and human resources development, presented the concepts subscribed to by the advocates of this school. Management theory today can be represented as in Figure 19-1.

THE FUTURE OF MODERN MANAGEMENT THEORY

Modern management theory is advancing on a number of fronts, including (1) continued emphasis on systems theory, (2) the development of modern organization structures, (3) increased research on human behavior in organizations, and (4) greater attention to the management of change.

New developments in systems theory were examined in Chapters 6, 10, 11, and 15. Some individuals believe that systems are a separate new school

---

[1]Alan C. Filley and Robert J. House, *Managerial Process and Organizational Behavior* (Glenview, IL: Scott, Foresman, 1969), p. 483.

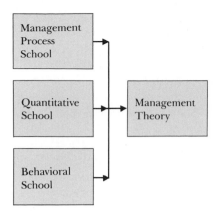

FIGURE 19-1   Modern Management Theory

Modern management theory is advancing on a number of fronts.

of managerial thought because a systems perspective is capable of synthesizing, from a pragmatic standpoint, the views of all other management schools. These people see systems management as the application of systems ideas to the management of organizations. Their approach calls for synthesis and pragmatism for the purpose of achieving maximum operational efficiency.

At present, however, managerial systems theory seems to be less a base for a school of management thought than an integrative concept for the manager to employ in carrying out various types of jobs. Managers today are more likely to view organizations as open systems, subject to the dynamism of the external and the internal environments; and that view is one of the ways in which systems theory has been of use in management. Another is in the way that systems work has made it possible to bring computers into broad applicability in the organization. However, the impact of the computer has not been so drastic as many writers had predicted. Rather, such external developments as changing technology, increasing competition, and megatrends (Chapter 5) have had more severe effects, because they have forced many organizations to abandon their mechanistic structures for more practical, organic ones.

Modern organization structures are flexible and responsive.

The result, as shown in Chapter 6, has been the development of modern organization structures. In contrast to their mechanistic-bureaucratic counterparts, modern organization structures are less predictable and less orderly. On the other hand, they are very well suited to meet the needs of modern businesses.

Management is increasingly concerned with human behavior research.

Management is also finding that, in order to manage its human assets, it has to focus increased attention on the demands of the employees for meaningful work and increased responsibility. These demands, as well as their effect on the national and international arenas, were examined in Chapters 15, 17, and 18. Today, the business organization is more than a profit-making institution, and its responsibilities cannot be limited solely to that function. It is an environment in which individuals come together and, in a give-and-take process, interact with each other and the organization itself (formal objectives, plans, policies, procedures, and rules) in producing a good or providing a service to some segment of society. In an attempt to achieve the necessary coordination and cooperation of its employees, management is trying to understand the needs and values of its people through increased research on human behavior in organizations. This research is reflected in such techniques as management by objectives, job enrichment, transactional analysis, and behavior modification. The future will hold more of the same as behaviorists attempt to answer the question of how the work force and the organization can be brought together in a harmonious, meaningful, and rewarding relationship.

The management of change is actually part and parcel of the three areas that have just been described. With the business environment in a continual state of flux, organizations have discovered that they have to live with change on a daily basis. As noted earlier in the book, change frightens many people. In overcoming this problem, management takes a systems approach to bringing together the people and the work. During the 1990s, management will continue to develop new techniques and tools for effectively adapting to and incorporating change.

How will management theory accomplish this? Many people feel the answer is to be found in a contingency theory of management, in which the manager draws on functional, quantitative, behavioral, and systems concepts as needed. Certainly this is the direction in which modern management theory seems to be moving. It should be realized, however, that despite what the contingency theory advocates say about a "new" school of thought, contingency is really nothing more than the formalization of very old managerial thinking. In summary, the systems and contingency schools may emerge on their own, but their basic thinking is already contained in management theory. Effective administrators are already using both systems and contingency concepts in attaining organizational objectives. Thus, a better term for this type of management theory may well be *eclectic*. The manager, having no exclusive allegiance to any of the schools, draws the best features from each and employs them pragmatically.

OTHER DEVELOPMENTS ON THE HORIZON

Although the previous section synthesizes much of what has been said in this book and provides insight into what can be expected to occur over the next few decades, three other developments, before now only alluded to in this text, merit closer examination. They are: (1) continued focus on key result areas, (2) the current challenge of managing personnel talent, and (3) the continuing trend toward the professionalism of management.

Continued Focus on Key Result Areas

Each chapter in this book has two boxed-in stories related to major developments that are occurring in key result areas: social responsibility, ethics, intrapreneurship, technology, internationalism, and communications. These areas that will continue to be of importance to management during the 1990s.

Social Responsibility

Social responsibility deals with business's obligation to its stockholders and work force and to the public at large. This responsibility can take a variety of forms, and the industry and operations of each particular organization will dictate the necessary responses. Certainly equal opportunity, ecology, and consumerism will continue to be three of the major considerations in the foreseeable future. Additionally, it is likely that equal opportunity will become a more important issue than it has been in recent years. One reason is that minorities are finding that while they have been successful, they still are not on an equal basis with their counterparts. For example, the upward mobility gap between blacks and whites continues to exist (see Social Responsibility in Action: Signs of Stagnation).

Social responsibility will continue to be an important issue.

Ethics

Ethics will receive ever-increasing attention over the next decade, especially in light of such revelations as the insider stock trading scandals of the late 1980s. There will also be greater attention focused on personal decisions by managers who, in the view of many, are personally enriching themselves but are not enhancing the well-being of the company at large. A good example is the golden parachute, a contractual arrangement that provides an executive with a large financial settlement (often running over $1 million) if certain things happen. Three of the most common include: (1) the individual leaves the company, (2) the person is fired, or (3) the firm is purchased by an outside buyer. This arrangement is quite lucrative for the executive and often can help attract top talent to an enterprise. However, it appears that golden parachutes are often used too widely and companies end up paying more for executive talent than they should. Moreover, those arrangements that allow the executive to collect the money even if he or she voluntarily leaves the enterprise are highly suspect. They constitute nothing more than a parting bonus that is payable at the option of the manager. Stockholders certainly seem to have a strong position when they challenge the ethics of this financial arrangement.

Ethics will receive ever-increasing importance.

Intrapreneurship

The rapid growth of small enterprises is making it clear that entrepreneurial drive is widespread in the population. Moreover, large firms are beginning to realize that small enterprises are often able to produce goods and services faster or more cheaply than their giant competitors. The result is that big companies are now attempting to create an environment in which entrepreneurial drive is encouraged and rewarded. These intrapreneurial efforts are changing the way many firms are being organized and managed. Some of the most successful examples are IBM, 3M, and Bell Laboratories. On the other

Intrapreneurship will be encouraged.

SOCIAL
RESPONSIBILITY
IN
ACTION:
Signs
of
Stagnation

How well are blacks in America doing? On the one hand, there has been quite a bit of progress. For example, a couple of presidents of large corporations are black. Another is a three-star general who heads the National Security Council. And everyone knows that the biggest TV star of the 1980s was Bill Cosby. Moreover, while only 13 percent of blacks were in the middle class in 1960, one-third of all black families were earning between $25,000 to $50,000 by 1988.

On the other hand, for many blacks the American dream remains elusive. In particular, blacks are more financially vulnerable than whites. Their wages and salaries trail those of whites in virtually every occupation. When there is a downturn in the economy, blacks are out of work longer and more often than whites; and more of them depend on two incomes to maintain the family's standard of living. And the mobility gap between the two groups is only somewhat better than it was in 1910. At the end of the first decade of this century approximately 21 percent of whites were employed as professionals, civil servants, managers, administrators, or sales and clerical workers. A mere 1 percent of blacks held these jobs. In 1984, the last year for which data are available, approximately 55 percent of whites held these jobs in contrast to 39 percent of blacks. The percentage gap during this 64-year period has declined from 21 to 16 percent. Moreover, while 11.8 percent of managers in the work force in 1987 were white only 5.7 percent were black.

During the 1990s management will have to make a more concerted effort to ensure that blacks and other minorities are provided an equal opportunity for promotions. This will not be an easy chore given the fact that many firms are cutting back the number of people in upper management. *Business Week* put it this way:

> As jobs become scarcer, the willingness to share them diminishes. "Affirmative action becomes harder and more controversial with a small pie," comments Xerox CEO Kearns. If he is correct, the tiny number of blacks at the pyramid's top will symbolize unfilled promise for the black middle class—and for the millions who aspire to join it.

Management's social responsibility strategy of the 1990s will have to address these types of challenges—and figure ways of solving them.

Source: James E. Ellis, "The Black Middle Class," *Business Week,* March 14, 1988, pp. 62–70.

hand, many firms have been unable to make the transition to an intrapreneurial environment. Intrapreneurship in Action: Making It Happen explains two of the major reasons for this problem.

INTRAPRENEURSHIP

IN

ACTION:

Making

It

Happen

If intrapreneurship is a good idea, why don't more companies develop and encourage it? The major reason is that they are unable to overcome or live with the two problems that accompany an intrapreneurial environment.

First, a truly intrapreneurial environment is one in which creative people are allowed to exist and thrive. Unfortunately, many managers find creative people to be a pain in the neck. These individuals always want to do things their own way. They like to come in late, leave early, and circumvent organizational regulations. They do not like to be tied down with red tape or procedures. This type of behavior is often disconcerting to managers who prefer the personnel to play by the rules. As a result management tends to discourage intrapreneurial behavior.

A second problem is that the organization does not redesign its reward system so that those who are successful intrapreneurs are given most of the raises and promotions. Instead the firm continues to reward people based on the old scheme under which those who are regarded as team players tend to be given more than those who are mavericks—regardless of how successful the latter are. Again the result is management discouraging intrapreneurial behavior.

Simply put, a decision to become intrapreneurial requires more than just a verbal commitment on the part of management. It also calls for changes in the management philosophy and the reward system. Management has to alter its approach in dealing with personnel and face the fact that an intrapreneurial environment requires a big change in the way things are done. It is *not* "business as usual." To the extent that management can accept these new conditions, an intrapreneurial environment can be created. To the extent that these conditions are not acceptable, management will find itself unable to generate the interest and enthusiasm that is critical to the creation and nurturing of a successful intrapreneurial organization.

Source: W. Jack Duncan, Peter M. Ginter, Andrew C. Rucks, and T. Douglas Jacobs, "Intrapreneurship and the Reinvention of the Corporation," *Business Horizons*, May–June 1988, pp. 16–21.

Technology

Technology is a critical factor in effective management because it influences both the products and services that are sold and the organization design that is used in coordinating enterprise effort. For some firms technology will be a lead variable because their research and development labs will provide them materials and processes with which to develop new products. Pharmaceutical firms, computer companies, and auto manufacturers are good examples. Most firms, however, will continue to view technology as a lag variable in the sense that they will have to respond to these new products by adapting their

Technology will play an important role.

INTERVIEW WITH DONALD FRAZIER

Donald Frazier is president of his own consulting firm, based in McLean, Virginia near Washington, D.C. Don's background in dealing with the introduction and management of organizational change is extensive and includes public service with the Executive Office of the President and the U. S. Nuclear Regulatory Commission as well as a wide variety of Fortune 100 companies. Don is particularly interested in helping organizations identify and deal with needed change, including the introduction and use of intrapreneurial principles.

Q.   *How important will intrapreneurship be in the future?*

A.   It is going to be fundamental to both public and private sector enterprise, because every employee will have to become more intrapreneurial as a way of doing business. Fundamental shifts in the way business is done are making intrapreneurship essential. For example, in the past five years many companies have downsized or restructured to become more efficient. In turn, the average employee of the 1990s will have to assume greater responsibility and control for his or her area of operations than did the preceding generation of workers. Individuals are going to have to become more intrapreneurial in order to have their companies survive, let alone prosper.

Q.   *Isn't this asking a lot? After all, why should the employees be willing to do more work just because the organization has downsized and is trying to increase its own efficiency and profit? What's in it for the employees?*

current offerings or reducing their prices in order to remain competitive. In either event, technology will continue to be a major variable in the workplace and marketplace, and managers will have to remain abreast of those changes that affect their firm.[2]

Internationalism

More and more firms are going to earn part of their revenue in overseas markets. Recent research reveals that a majority of small- and medium-size firms forecast that during the 1990s their sales to overseas customers will

---

[2]For an excellent discussion of this area see Gene Bylinsky, "Technology in the Year 2000," *Fortune*, July 18, 1988, pp. 92–100.

A. For one thing, the employee's job is on the line. There will be little room for the old-style worker who has little interest in continually upgrading his or her capabilities and performance. The firm must adapt and become more competitive as a way of life—continually—not just as a one-shot upgrading. This cannot be done by the front office alone. As a way of life, intrapreneurship, change management, "ownership," must permeate the way everyone in the company does business. Companies which cannot do this will fall behind.

Q. *A lot of what you say implies that company loyalty is going to increase. Yet many observers believe that such loyalty is now quite low. Will company loyalty improve during the 1990s?*

A. Yes, but it will be a different kind of company loyalty than our parents and grandparents knew. This is because the basic social compact or agreement between employer and employee is changing. The old loyalty was based on paternalism. The head of a company would assume a parental role and everyone in the organization was taken care of the way they would be in a family. In particular, job security was ensured. As a result, a firm might have two or three generations of employees of the same family working for it at the same time.

    The new loyalty will be based on mutual interest between the company and the employee. Not "time-for-pay" or "security for loyalty," but "ownership-type rewards *to* the employee for ownership attitudes/work habits *by* the employee" will be the basis for loyalty. Loyalty will rest on a foundation built of cooperation, teamwork, a sharing of responsibility, and a sharing of rewards.

    People will be loyal to the organization because it will provide them enriched, meaningful work and fair rewards; the organization will be loyal to the personnel because the latter will provide them with high quality output that allows the firm to succeed in a competitive environment. It will be a win-win situation for both.

International sales will increase.

increase every year. There are a number of reasons why managers will be particularly interested in this market. One is because the dollar has weakened in the international market, making American goods more competitive. So more and more foreign customers will be buying from us. Second, many American businesses have never attempted to tap the international market, and as they do they are going to find many market niches that are willing to buy their products. Third, the world business community is becoming so interdependent that an increasing percentage of many business revenues will come from international sales. This is particularly true for American firms that are looking for lower cost sources of supply in order to maintain their profit margins. Buying from outsiders (outsourcing) is often a more profitable method than making the goods in-house. In fact, outsourcing is one of the primary reasons why many large firms are moving away from vertical integration, under which they owned all sources of materials and supplies for their product lines.

Communications

Communication is critical to every enterprise. Unless the personnel can convey information back and forth to each other and to outside customers and clients, the enterprise will cease to exist. During the 1990s managers will have to become more effective communicators. There are a number of reasons for this. First, the amount of information that will be received and examined by the average manager will increase, so he or she will have to be able to read, analyze, write, and speak more effectively. Computers will help in this process,[3] but managers will also have to improve their communication skills. During the decade it is likely that more and more managers will find themselves attending tailor-made courses that help them write briefer, more effective memos and letters. They will also learn how to write and arrange both short and long reports. Public speaking will also become a popular offering as managers learn how to speak from a prepared manuscript as well as to give short, extemporaneous talks. The world of education has not really prepared managers to communicate as well as they must. This is one area where the business world will begin taking the steps necessary to correct this deficiency.

Managers will have to become better communicators.

Managing Personnel Talent

During the 1990s new demands will be placed on the way employees are managed. Some of the specific areas that will be addressed will include: increasing loyalty among the workers, designing more effective compensation policies, and helping personnel deal with job-related stress.

Increasing Loyalty of the Personnel

Many articles report that worker loyalty has declined over the last decade. William Werther notes that: (1) employee turnover at 231 Silicon Valley employers averages 27 percent annually; (2) Du Pont's early-retirement program has attracted twice as many takers as the company anticipated; and (3) turnover at AT&T since the breakup of the Bell System has more than tripled.[4] Moreover, Werther reports:

Loyalty is declining.

> Interviews with more than 50 executives confirm the obvious: all agree that loyalty is important. Each of these executives believes that those who report *directly* to him or her are loyal. Doubts quickly surface, however, when the interview topic shifts from the executive suite toward young workers and union members. As one corporate founder

---

[3]Peter H. Lewis, "Righting English Become Easier," *New York Times,* March 6, 1988, p. 11.

[4]William B. Werther, Jr., "Loyalty at Work," *Business Horizons,* March–April 1988, pp. 28–35.

expressed his assessment, "Some of our young people aren't loyal, and they probably won't amount to much around here." Executives repeatedly stressed how important loyalty is to everyone—the executive, the organization, and the employees. But they typically added, ". . . but loyalty remains low." In the words of James Wall, marketing vice-president at the Stanton Corporation, "There's absolutely no doubt that corporate loyalty is lower today than it has ever been."[5]

During the decade of the 1990s this problem will be addressed in a number of different ways. These can be explained in terms of six steps: awareness, vision, involvement, sponsorship, monetary rewards, and nonmonetary rewards.

There are ways of increasing loyalty.

- **First.** Managers must be aware of the lack of loyalty among the workers. This will be particularly important for those at the upper levels, many of whom do not know of these problems because they are shielded from them by their immediate subordinates.

- **Second.** Managers will have to learn how to share the vision of the firm with their personnel. The latter must learn what the company stands for, what its long-range objectives are, and what the organization intends to do both for its personnel and for the community and country at large. This approach provides the personnel with a basis for feeling proud of the organization.

- **Third.** The personnel must become involved in the company's efforts. They must feel that they are an integral part of the plan and that the company relies on them.

- **Fourth.** The firm must get them involved by giving them important tasks and making it clear that these jobs are critical to the success of the enterprise. When this happens, workers "buy in" to the organization's efforts.

- **Fifth.** The enterprise must financially reward those who are loyal. Across-the-board salary raises must be replaced with larger salaries for those who are committed to the company, and smaller (or no) salary raises for those who are not.

- **Sixth.** Finally, the organization must give recognition and other forms of nonmonetary rewards. People must be praised for good ideas, encouraged to work harder, and made to see themselves as important members of the work force.

When these six ideas are properly implemented, loyalty increases and remains high.

---

[5]Ibid., pp. 28–29.

Compensation Policies

Compensation policies
will be reformulated.

One major approach that seems likely to gain support during the 1990s is the reformulation of compensation policies. The reward packages that are used to motivate people will have to be reconfigured. First, money will continue to remain an important motivator but it will have to be more heavily complemented by psychological rewards. Research shows that most working people lost purchasing power during the 1980s. So salary raises will have to continue to keep up with inflation, if not increase slightly faster. Second, the 1987 Tax Reform Act has changed the tax rates and reduced the income tax bite for many people. This also points to the importance of a well-designed monetary package that pays people well. Third, nontaxable benefits will continue to be a major way of supplementing the financial package. Life and medical insurance programs, company contributions to retirement programs, company cars, and other forms of benefits will remain important.

Organizations will also have to formulate a strategy to deal with the motivational effects of salary compression. As newly hired people are brought in at ever-higher salaries and current personnel are given small raises, the wage differential between the experienced personnel and the recent hires will continue to diminish. People with five-years experience often find themselves making only $1,000 more than someone hired last month. The ultimate result of this salary compression is that experienced people leave for jobs with competitive firms where their incoming salary is much higher. If organizations are to maintain the services of experienced personnel, wage differentials based on experience and contribution must be maintained.

Stress Management Assistance

Another area in which management is current focusing a lot of attention is that of stress management. Research shows that more and more executives are burning out due to overwork.[6] In an effort to deal with this problem, many companies have begun developing formal health programs and encouraging their people to follow basic principles of "wellness." Some of these principles include the following:

1. **Learn to control situations.** For example, do not set unrealistic deadlines; work within your own limits. Do not try to be everything to everyone.

2. **Pace yourself.** Have a plan for the day and work your way through it; however, do not try to control every minute of your time. Switch from

---

[6]For more on this topic see: Oliver L. Niehouse, "Burnout: A Real Threat to Human Resources Managers," *Personnel*, September–October 1981, pp. 25–32; and Harry Levinson, "When Executives Burn Out," *Harvard Business Review*, May–June 1981, pp. 73–81.

one thing to another if this reduces tension and keeps you alert and motivated. Also, try not to do two things at the same time.

3. **Communicate with others.** Talk to your boss, your colleagues, and others with whom you can share your frustrations and problems. They probably have similar concerns and you will learn that you are not alone.

4. **Exercise.** Choose a physical activity that will help you stay in good shape. If possible, get a friend to go with you so that the activity is more enjoyable. Examples include jogging, bike riding, tennis, racquetball, and so on. Do not push yourself too hard; exercise at your own pace. Jogging a mile four times a week is usually just as healthful as jogging three miles a day every day.

5. **Watch your diet.** Limit your intake of sugar and caffeine. Have vegetables at lunch and/or dinner. Keep down your consumption of red meat by substituting fish and fowl. Also remember that the most important meal of the day is breakfast, so do not skip it.

6. **Learn to relax.** Put aside a half hour every work day for quiet time. Sit back in your chair, close your eyes, and focus on relaxing your whole body. Keep a positive mental attitude and tell yourself that you are going to shut out all of the problems around you. It will take some time for you to become good at this, but you will find that you can teach yourself to relax.

There are many things that can cause stress, including organizational design variables, interpersonal variables, and career variables (see Figure 19-2 on page 727). What managers need to do is to take things in stride and not let the pressures "get to" them, but this is more easily said than done. Many of them have climbed the organizational ladder through hard work and the shouldering of heavy responsibility. Now they are being told that excess stress is bad for them and they are going to have to change their way of doing things because it can prove to be life threatening.[7]

In particular, many of them are "Type A" individuals, a term which refers to people who are always doing things in a hurry. In fact, they hate to slow down. As soon as they have finished one assignment they rush pell mell to the next. Their lives seem to be constant struggles to do more and more in less and less time. The ultimate result, unfortunately, is often a heart attack or some other physically impairing calamity.[8] Today many firms are working with psychologists and other professionals to develop programs that can help

---

[7]Manfred F. R. Kets de Vries, "Organizational Stress: A Call for Management Action," *Sloan Management Review*, Fall 1979, pp. 3–13.

[8]John M. Ivancevich, Michael T. Matteson, and Cynthia Preston, "Occupational Stress, Type A Behavior, and Physical Well Being," *Academy of Management Journal*, June 1982, pp. 373–91.

their personnel effectively cope with stress. Business is beginning to realize that stress is not just a personal matter, it is an organizational concern. By helping people extend their careers, management as well as personnel ultimately benefit.[9]

Continuing Trend Toward Professionalism

A trend toward the professionalization of management began some years ago and continues today. Although many definitions have been given to the word *profession*, the following is one of the most comprehensive:

> A profession is a vocation whose practice is founded upon an understanding of the theoretical structure of some department of learning or science, and upon the abilities accompanying such understanding. This understanding and these abilities are applied to the vital practical affairs of man. The practices of the profession are modified by knowledge of a generalized nature and by the accumulated wisdom and experience of mankind, which serve to correct the errors of specialism. The profession, serving the vital needs of man, considers its first ethical imperative to be altruistic service to the client.[10]

Five criteria are necessary for a profession.

The major criteria for a profession are knowledge, competent application, social responsibility, self-control, and community sanction.[11] It should be noted before these are discussed that management differs from many of the other professions, especially the traditional ones of theology, law, and medicine, in that one cannot rigidly apply a set of conditions. With this qualification in mind, it is possible to show that management is indeed moving toward professionalism.

Management Knowledge

Throughout this book, evidence of a tremendous increase in management knowledge over the last twenty-five years has appeared. As Kenneth Andrews points out, "No responsible critic . . . will deny that management practice now rests on a developing body of knowledge being systematically extended by valid research methods."[12] Thus, management meets this first criterion.

---

[9]For more on this area of stress see Jerry E. Bishop, "Prognosis for the 'Type A' Personality Improves in a New Heart Disease Study," *Wall Street Journal*, January 14, 1988, p. 29; John M. Ivancevich, Michael T. Matteson, and Edward P. Richards III, "Who's Liable for Stress on the Job?" *Harvard Business Review*, March–April 1985, pp. 60–72; and Charles R. Stoner and Fred L. Fry, "Developing a Corporate Policy for Managing Stress," *Personnel*, May–June 1983, pp. 66–76.

[10]Reported in Kenneth R. Andrews, "Toward Professionalism in Business Management," *Harvard Business Review*, March–April 1969, p. 50.

[11]Ibid., pp. 50–54.

[12]Ibid., p. 52.

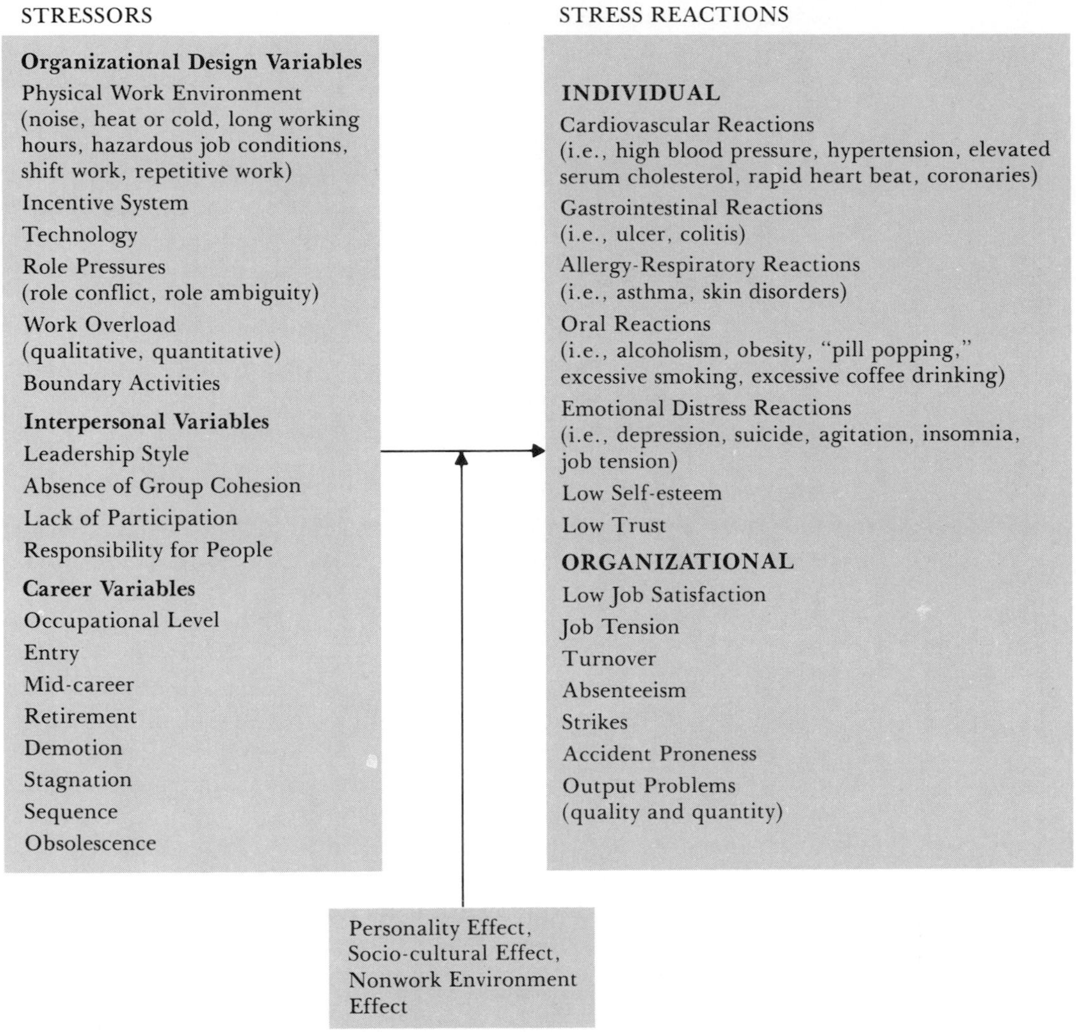

STRESSORS

STRESS REACTIONS

Organizational Design Variables

Physical Work Environment
(noise, heat or cold, long working
hours, hazardous job conditions,
shift work, repetitive work)

Incentive System

Technology

Role Pressures
(role conflict, role ambiguity)

Work Overload
(qualitative, quantitative)

Boundary Activities

Interpersonal Variables

Leadership Style

Absence of Group Cohesion

Lack of Participation

Responsibility for People

Career Variables

Occupational Level

Entry

Mid-career

Retirement

Demotion

Stagnation

Sequence

Obsolescence

INDIVIDUAL

Cardiovascular Reactions
(i.e., high blood pressure, hypertension, elevated
serum cholesterol, rapid heart beat, coronaries)

Gastrointestinal Reactions
(i.e., ulcer, colitis)

Allergy-Respiratory Reactions
(i.e., asthma, skin disorders)

Oral Reactions
(i.e., alcoholism, obesity, "pill popping,"
excessive smoking, excessive coffee drinking)

Emotional Distress Reactions
(i.e., depression, suicide, agitation, insomnia,
job tension)

Low Self-esteem

Low Trust

ORGANIZATIONAL

Low Job Satisfaction

Job Tension

Turnover

Absenteeism

Strikes

Accident Proneness

Output Problems
(quality and quantity)

Personality Effect,
Socio-cultural Effect,
Nonwork Environment
Effect

FIGURE 19-2   Factors Contributing to Stress

Source: Reprinted from "Organizational Stress: A Call for Management Action," by Manfred R. R. Kets deVries, *Sloan Management Review*, Vol. 22, No. 2, p. 7, by permission of the publisher. Copyright © 1979 by the Sloan Management Review Association. All rights reserved.

Competent Application

Many professions, such as medicine and law, ensure competent application by certifying their members for practice. Although this is not the case in management, the surveillance of junior managers by higher-level executives serves the same purpose. Furthermore, "the diversity of business practice, the market mechanism rewarding successful and penalizing unsuccessful entrepreneurship, and the organization means for supervising competence in management all make it impracticable and unnecessary to erect educational requirements in imitation of the formality of law, medicine, and the ministry.[13]

Social Responsibility

Today, more than ever before, business is aware of the importance of its own social role. Profit is certainly not a dirty word. Even so, business is making it increasingly clear that it is pursuing multiple objectives, with profit only one of them.

Other objectives are the provision of goods and services to the customer and the integration of the firm into the everyday life of the community. In recent years many businesses have been formulating social responsibility philosophies by way of meeting this criterion.

Emergence of Self-Control

Federal and state agencies have been established to regulate business and ensure compliance to prescribed norms. At the national level, for example, are the Federal Drug Administration, the Federal Trade Commission, and the Antitrust Division of the Department of Justice. It should be realized, however, that business also exercises degrees of self-control as reflected by industry codes of conduct. For example, the National Association of Purchasing Agents has an extensive code, one of its standards being "to buy and sell on the basis of value, recognizing that value represents the combination of quality, service and price which assures greatest ultimate economy to the user." The American Association of Advertising Agencies has an analogous set of standards, one of them being "Advertising shall tell the truth and shall reveal material facts, the concealment of which might mislead the public." Codes like these will undoubtedly increase in number in the foreseeable future. Why? The answer is twofold. First, the public is demanding higher ethical standards. Second, business managers not only believe that ethics are good for business but also feel that an industry code can have many additional advantages.

For example, an industry code is a useful aid when business people want to refuse an unethical request impersonally. A manager who has been approached unethically may be said by the would-be influencer to be hiding behind the industry code. In fact, though, this manager is simply taking advantage of a freedom from risk that the business has provided. Such a code would also help businesspeople define the limits of acceptable conduct and, where severe competition existed, reduce cutthroat practices. There is thus the emergence of self-control.

---

[13]Ibid., p. 53.

Community Sanction

The final attribute of a profession, community sanction, also exists in management today, even though many business groups are not held in esteem by the public. Electricians who are called in to install a new outlet and then charge the home owner $88.50 do little to win community acceptance. Plumbers who fix a sink in five minutes but have a minimum house-call fee of $37.50 leave people angry and disillusioned. Fortunately, however, the management profession does not suffer from such stigmas. In fact, in many areas of social distress the public realizes that U. S. management has the technical skill and the organizational expertise to help overcome the problems; management can, for example, hire and train the hard-core unemployed, build housing of decent quality for low-income groups, and ease the problems of personal poverty and a stagnant economy by developing jobs, given sufficient capital. If anything, community sanction of management is stronger than ever.

Future Developments

Despite its gains, management still has a way to go before it will fully qualify as a profession. However, significant steps have been taken, and this decade will see even greater progress. In particular will be the continuing development of academic management curricula, including: (1) the growth of new methods of quantitative analysis associated with the computer; (2) the study of organizational behavior; (3) better concepts for analyzing, understanding, and reacting responsibly to the social, economic, technical, and political environment of business; and (4) the study of policy formulation.[14] This, in turn, will lead to more sophisticated management practices, better self-regulation, and more attention to people problems in both the domestic and international arenas.

JUST A BEGINNING

Managerial knowledge is a good beginning.

The purpose of this text has been to identify, define, and place in perspective the concepts most important to the modern manager. This knowledge alone will not solve all problems for an organization, but it will provide a basis for formulating intelligent approaches to dealing with each specific situation. From here on, managers have to employ the method that they believe will work best. As J. Paul Getty, the oil billionaire, noted:

> To argue that business management is a science, in the sense that chemistry is a science, is to misunderstand the functions of management and to disregard its most significant element: people.

---

[14]Ibid., p. 59.

Management—the fine art of being boss—is nothing less than the direction of human activities, obtaining results through people. Formal business education can only form a basis on which man can build. . . . But no theory in the world holds that a man with one, two or even three degrees in business administration can repair a cracking corporate structure merely because he has a collection of sheepskins hanging on his office wall.[15]

Coupling this perspective with the facts that modern organizations are in a state of flux and the environment promises to become more, not less, dynamic, management may appear to be a profession that should be pursued only by the most daring (or foolhardy). On the other hand, much information is available to the manager proceeding through the maze of modern organizational problems, and the rewards and challenges promise to make it an exciting career for those who have the potential and the desire. For example, Dalton McFarland puts it this way:

Although management alone cannot solve the world's problems, managers and organizations will continue to play a central role in changing social institutions. Thus the field of management stands at the brink of an enormous challenge. If society's problems are centered in organizations and social institutions rather than inherent in human nature, management theory and practice can provide ample scope for the advancement of an enduring civilization.[16]

A CAREER IN MANAGEMENT

Now that the basic field of management has been examined, it is time to ask the reader a personal question: Do you think you might like a career in management? You might well think you do not yet know enough about the overall field to be sure whether it would offer you the type of challenge you would like. However, it is not too early to examine the subject of career planning. The first place to begin is with an evaluation of yourself.

Know Thyself

No matter how much you know about management, in order to be an effective manager you must have a desire or willingness to work with others. Can you usually interact well with people, especially in a supervisory or

---

[15]J. Paul Getty, "The Fine Art of Being the Boss," *Playboy,* June 1972, p. 146.

[16]Dalton E. McFarland, "Management, Humanism, and Society: The Case for Macromanagement Theory," *Academy of Management Review,* October 1977, p. 622.

managerial way? Or are you the type of person who prefers to work alone or with one or two people at most? Successful managers must be able to get things done through others.

Second, what kind of a job would appeal to you? Your answer to this question can help you pinpoint the type of organization where you can begin your search.

You must know how you deal with pressure.

Third, how well do you take pressure? Are you the type of person who likes to be involved in a lot of activity and feels no pressure when time demands are placed on you? Or are you the kind of individual who likes to work at a leisurely pace and does not function well in a high pressure situation? Depending on your answer to this question, you can eliminate certain types of industries or jobs because of the amount of pressure they have or do not have. People and pressure need to be well matched.

While these are only three of the many questions that you should ask yourself in getting a personal profile, they are important because they help point out your likes and dislikes. Remember, to be effective as a manager, you are going to have to like the job. Very few people are successful doing things they do not like. So begin with an analysis of yourself.

The Interviewing Process

Once you have identified the type of job or organization in which you want to work, the next step is getting hired. Today, virtually no firm will hire you without first having interviewed you. And many people fail to get a job with the organization of their choice because they do not know how to come across well during the interview. Interviews frustrate or frighten some people for a surprising reason: There is not a great deal that one needs to do in preparing for the interview. You should dress properly, be courteous, and try to answer the recruiter's questions as accurately and completely as possible. Otherwise, there is little else you need to know, although some experts recommend that if you are interviewing with a national firm you should look through the company's annual reports and learn a little about the firm. This, they feel, helps prove to the interviewer that you are indeed interested in the job. Certainly, it helps distinguish you from most, if not all, of the individuals the person will interview that day; and it will probably create a positive image in the interviewer's mind. Be sure, though, not to try to lecture on the company.

Possibly the best way to prepare for the interview is to be aware of some of the typical questions that the individual is likely to ask you. Some people have tried role-playing with friends to simulate the situation and the questions, some of which will be:

1. Tell me a little about yourself. What is your background?
2. Why are you interested in working for our organization?

Some typical inter-viewer questions.

3.   What did you major in at school? What are your favorite subjects? Which did you like least? Why?

4.   What do you feel are your biggest strengths? Your biggest weaknesses?

5.   What are your career objectives? How do you hope to achieve them?

6.   Why do you feel we should hire you?

These, of course, are not the only questions the interviewer is likely to ask you; but they represent the general, most commonly used, approach.

Forewarned Is Forearmed

Once you get that all-important first job, you know that you will be expected to perform well. You should also know that there is more to this job than just performance requirements. A whole new world of work faces you, and you should be aware of some of the common pitfalls and problems that confront the new young employee embarking on a career. In this way you will be forewarned and prepared to deal with them.

Young managers' early expectations are very high.

One of the first things you should realize is that most young people who are starting out have very high expectations. They believe that their job will be extremely interesting, challenging, and personally rewarding. Actually, while the salary may be good, the work itself is often boring, routine, or simply monotonous. The real excitement will come later as you move up the hierarchy. Expect your enthusiasm to be replaced with the cold reality that the work will not be up to your level of expectation. Many times you will find yourself doing menial tasks that seem to have no real benefit. Nevertheless, this is part of the job.

Their anxiety level is also high.

Additionally, new employees, especially those on first jobs, feel a great deal of anxiety about these jobs. Many people are so anxious to be successful that they read every comment from the boss as being personal praise or admonishment. Actually, the boss will probably give you little feedback on your performance except to encourage you to keep trying hard and point out any big mistakes you have made so that you can avoid them in the future. However, you will not have such a significant job that a mistake will be catastrophic for the organization. You will, at best, make little mistakes. So relax and try to master the job as quickly as possible.

A positive attitude is necessary.

Third, maintain a positive attitude and show the boss that even when you do not know what you are supposed to be doing, or when you have done something wrong, you are prepared to keep going. At this early stage of your career, enthusiasm and drive are often as important as actual job perfor-mance because there is so little of the latter on which you can be evaluated.

A mentor can be helpful.

Fourth, remember that every boss has an "in group" that he or she is looking after. The boss may recommend everyone in the department for a cost-of-living raise, but there are some who will be recommended for more.

Try to get into this special group. One way of doing this is by proving to the boss that you are trustworthy and hardworking. You can be counted on. In fact, where possible, try to be not just reliable but indispensable to the boss. As soon as this individual realizes that you are an important part of the team, your status will go up; and your superior will take care of you. After all, you have shown that your boss cannot afford to be without you. Furthermore, as you begin to move up the hierarchy, try to develop a mentor, someone who will look after you and guide you a bit. Many up-and-coming managers are taken under the wing of a higher-ranking executive who makes sure that they move up the organization together. In this way, the mentor takes care of you and you, in turn, reciprocate. Today, many individuals report that part of their success can be traced directly to their mentor. It may be regrettable, but this is particularly true for women in large organizations. Without a mentor to ensure that they are given a fair deal, many of them find themselves sidetracked or shunted into dead-end jobs.

Develop a Career Plan

When you first start out, it is difficult to develop a career plan. After all, you really do not know what type of career track is available to you. Nor do you have any idea of how fast the organization is going to promote you. And many other such unknowable variables will face you. However, after you have been pursuing your career for three to five years, you should consider setting long-range career objectives. Here are some illustrations:

1. By the time I am thirty, I will be making $40,000 a year.
2. I will develop a sponsor within eighteen months.

Set personal objectives.

3. I will receive a promotion every two years for the next eight years or leave the firm and find employment elsewhere.
4. I will be an upper-middle manager at the end of ten more years.
5. I will be in charge of a major department or division by the time I am forty-five.

Keep in mind that these goals are only set forth as examples of typical career objectives. They are not meant to apply to all people; nor are they intended to be inflexible. The important thing is to have a plan of action.

Also keep in mind that many businesses offer help to their personnel in career planning. Some of the most common forms include assigning mentors who provide assistance and guidance to young up-and-coming managers; coaching and counseling by one's immediate superior; and training and development programs designed to provide one the necessary experience for moving up the ladder. Additionally, many organizations offer career guidance by trained personnel for the purpose of helping managers clarify their career goals and decide how to attain them. If these goals are too ambitious, the manager is offered help in trimming them back; if they cannot be attained with the current company, the manager is provided assistance in moving to a firm where these objectives are attainable.[17]

■ SUMMARY

Management has come a long way since the days of the early classical theorists. It has received contributions from many people in many fields including psychology, sociology, and anthropology. Thus management thought has not developed in one basic direction. Rather, it has branched out into three schools: management process, quantitative, and behavioral.

What does the future hold? In one respect it will be more of the same: continued emphasis on system theory; the development of modern organization structures; increased research on human behavior in organizations; and greater attention to the management of change. Other developments on the management horizon include a continued focus on key result areas, the management of employee talent, and the continuing trend toward professionalism.

Managers of the future will need to be aware of these developments. However, this knowledge, in and of itself, is no guarantee of success. The challenges of management are too great to be solved by simple knowledge of effective management processes and practices. On the other hand, for those who have the ability and the desire to study and to work and continue to learn, the opportunities and rewards in the field of management promise to be very great indeed.

The last part of the chapter offered some suggestions for those who feel they might like a career in management. The first step is a personal evaluation. Second, the individual should prepare for interviews by thinking of responses to questions typically asked during such meetings. Third, before taking a job, the individual should realize some of the common pitfalls and problems that confront new, young employees. Fourth, young managers should eventually develop a career plan. For the person who is very effective in this overall career planning process, all kinds of rewards are available. The sky is the limit.

---

[17]For more on this subject see: Albert R. Griffith, "Career Development: What Organizations Are Doing about It," *Personnel*, March–April 1980, pp. 63–69; Kathy E. Dram, "Phases of the Mentor Relationship," *Academy of Management Journal*, December 1983, pp. 608–25; Barbara S. Lawrence, "The Myth of the Midlife Crisis," *Sloan Management Review*, Summer 1980, pp. 35–49; Janet P. Near, "The Career Plateau: Causes and Effects," *Business Horizons*, June 1980, pp. 53–57; and Joe Thomas, "Mid-Career Crisis and the Organization," *Business Horizons*, November–December 1982, pp. 73–78; and Dennis C. Sweeney, Dean Haller, and Frederick Sale, Jr., "Individually Controlled Career Counseling," *Training and Development Journal*, August 1987, pp. 58–61.

■ REVIEW AND STUDY QUESTIONS

1. What contributions did the classical theorists make to management theory?
2. What are the three major schools of management theory? Briefly describe each.
3. What is the contingency school of thought?
4. How are the systems and contingency approaches eclectic in nature?
5. What are the six key result areas that will be of importance to management in the 1990s? Identify and briefly describe each.
6. Is corporate loyalty on the decline? Explain.
7. How can management increase loyalty of the personnel? Explain.
8. How will management need to reform its compensation policies during the 1990s?
9. How is management helping personnel cope with personal problems such as stress? Explain.
10. What does the term "profession" mean?
11. What are the major criteria for a profession? Explain.
12. Is management a profession? Give your reasoning.
13. How can a person prepare for a job interview? What are some questions the recruiter will be likely to ask?
14. What are some of the common pitfalls and problems that face individuals just starting their careers?
15. How important are career objectives? List some.
16. Explain in your own words what some of the rewards for successful managers are.

■ SELECTED REFERENCES

Abdel-Halim, Ahmed A. "Effects of Role Stress-Job Design-Technology Interaction on Employee Work Satisfaction." *Academy of Management Journal*, June 1981, pp. 260–73.

Andrews, Kenneth R. "Toward Professionalism in Business Management." *Harvard Business Review*, March–April 1969, pp. 49–60.

Arnone, William. "Preretirement Planning: An Employee Benefit That Has Come of Age." *Personnel Journal*, October 1982, pp. 760–63.

Benfari, Robert C., and Harry E. Wilkinson. "Intelligence and Management." *Business Horizons*, May–June 1988, pp. 22–28.

Bernstein, Paul. "The Work Ethic: Economics, Not Religion." *Business Horizons*, May–June 1988, pp. 8–11.

Brenner, S. N. A., and E. A. Molander. "Is the Ethics of Business Changing?" *Harvard Business Review*, January–February 1977, pp. 57–71.

Byron, W. J., S. J. "The Meaning of Ethics in Business." *Business Horizons*, December 1977, pp. 31–34.

Duncan, W. J. "Transferring Management Theory to Practice." *Academy of Management Journal*, December 1974, pp. 724–38.

Duncan, W. Jack, Peter M. Ginter, Andrew C. Rucks, and T. Douglas Jacobs. "Intrapreneurship and the Reinvention of the Corporation." *Business Horizons*, May–June 1988, pp. 16–21.

Gettings, Lisa, and E. Nick Maddox. "When Health Means Wealth." *Training and Development Journal*, April 1988, 81–85.

Glicken, Morley D., and Katherine Janks. "Executive under Fire: The Burnout Syndrome." *California Management Review*, Spring 1982, pp. 67–72.

Gutteridge, Thomas G., and Fred L. Otte. "Organizational Career Development: What's Going on Out There?" *Training and Development Journal*, February 1983, pp. 22–26.

Ivancevich, John M., Michael T. Matteson, and Edward P. Richards III. "Who's Liable for Stress on the Job?" *Harvard Business Review*, March–April 1985, pp. 60–72.

Jackson, Susan E., and Randall S. Schuler. "Preventing Employee Burnout." *Personnel*, March–April 1983, pp. 58–68.

Kreitner, Robert. "Personal Wellness: It's Just Good Business." *Business Horizons*, May–June 1982, pp. 28–35.

Korman, Abraham K., Ursula Wittig-Berman, and Dorothy Lang. "Career Success and Personal Failure: Alienation in Professionals and Managers." *Academy of Management Journal*, June 1984, pp. 342–60.

Pearson, Andrall E. "Tough-Minded Ways to Get Innovative." *Harvard Business Review*, May–June 1988, pp. 99–106.

Richman, Louis S. "Tomorrow's Jobs: Plentiful, But . . ." *Fortune*, April 11, 1988, pp. 42–56.

Steffy, Brian D., and John W. Jones. "Workplace Stress and Indicators of Coronary-Disease Risk." *Academy of Management Journal*, September 1988, pp. 686–98.

Sweeney, Dennis C., Jr., Dean Haller, and Frederick Sale, Jr. "Individually Controlled Career Counseling." *Training and Development Journal*, August 1987, pp. 58–61.

Taylor, III, Alex. "Tomorrow's Chief Executives." *Fortune*, May 9, 1988, pp. 30–42.

Veiga, John F. "Plateaued versus Nonplateaued Managers: Career Patterns, Attitudes, and Path Potential." *Academy of Management Journal*, September 1981, pp. 566–78.

Waters, James A. "Managerial Assertiveness." *Business Horizons*, September–October 1982, pp. 24–29.

Werther, William B., Jr., "Loyalty at Work," *Business Horizons*, March–April 1988, pp. 28–35.

■ CASE: Worlds Apart

Is there a gap between management research and management practice? Many people seem to think so. For example, some management professors claim that their research is ignored by practitioners. One senior-level professor had his graduate students investigate whether recommendations from management studies in the literature were actually implemented by managers in those firms that were investigated. He found they were not. Supporting this argument, many managers admit that while their firms may subscribe to various business journals and periodicals, they seldom read the management literature.

On the other hand, practicing managers argue that there is a big gap between the way management scholars say things happen and the way in which they actually occur. Most contend that management research is simplistic, devoted to attacking nonexistent or unlikely problem areas, or that it addresses issues that simply do not warrant the manager's time.

How can this gap between research and practice be narrowed? One suggestion has been the establishment of closer rapport between individual firms and schools of business by having managers work in academia for short periods of time, while professors go off to industry for similar periods. In this way, each would gain insights into what the others do. Business people would obtain new appreciation for the academic world, and professors of management would get a clearer idea of the problems facing the practicing manager and how they should be addressed.

Questions

1. How much of the research done by professors in business schools do you think is really applied by practicing managers? Give reasons for your opinion.
2. In addition to the suggestions given in this case, how else can the gap between theory and practice be reduced?
3. Realistically speaking, how much progress toward narrowing the gap between theory and practice do you believe can be expected between now and 2000? Why?

■ CASE: Who Really Succeeds?

Career development planning is important to everyone who is interested in a working career. However, many people believe that regardless of career planning, certain individuals have a better chance of making it to the top than others. Some of the most commonly cited success factors include: a college degree, participation in extracurricular activities in college, and a high grade point average. Do these factors have any real effect on success? Recent shows that the first two do but the last does not.

A survey of 243 major CEOs shows that 99 percent of them attended college and 91 percent graduated. In the U. S. population at large, only 33 percent have at least one year of college. The largest percentage of those polled (44 percent) had undergraduate degrees in business administration. Additionally, in some industries researchers found a large percentage of the CEOs had graduate degrees. Here are some examples:

Industry	Percentage of CEOs with Graduate Degrees
Medical products	100%
Transportation	67
Service industries	56
Utilities	56
Food products	50
Retailing	46
Wholesaling	40
Manufacturing	34
Banking	30

The most common advanced degree was the MBA. Law degrees were the second most common.

Many CEOs have also participated in sports or held college offices in a club, fraternity, or campus organization. Here is a breakdown of college sports participation.

Industry	Percentage of CEO Participants				
	Baseball	Football	Basketball	Other*	Total
Transportation	30%	20%	10%	20%	80%
Wholesaling	—	20	60	—	80
Manufacturing	7	11	7	21	46
Service industries	10	20	2	14	46
Banking	7	9	2	18	36
Retailing	6	6	17	6	35
Food products	18	9	—	—	27
Utilities	2	7	5	12	26
Medical products	—	—	—	—	—

*Other intercollegiate sports mentioned include track/cross country, hockey, soccer, golf, and tennis.

In addition, over 50 percent of all CEOs in the above industries held a college office.

On the other hand, not all of the CEOs were "A" students. In fact, only 38 percent were. Of the remainder, 55 percent were "B" students and 7 percent were "C" students.

Questions

1. How important is an undergraduate college education for management success? Why?

2. What are the benefits of having played college sports or held office in a college-affiliated organization? Cite and explain two.

3. Why were all the CEOs not "A" students? Are CEOs not highly intelligent? Explain.

Source: Louis E. Boone, David L. Kurtz, and C. Patrick Fleenor, "CEOs: Early Signs of a Business Career," *Business Horizons,* September–October 1988, pp. 20–24.

■ CASE: The Key Is in Training

The decade of the 1980s was one during which small businesses grew rapidly. Between now and the end of the century, this trend will continue to hold true. In particular, growth in services sector will be vigorous. Here are some of the forecasts regarding how employment will change between 1986 to 2000.

Industries	Employment in 1986 (in millions)	Employment Forecasted for Year 2000 (in millions)
Business, health, social, and other services	24	34
Wholesale and retail trade	24	30
Finance, insurance, and real estate	6	8
Transportation, communications, and public utilities	5	5.5
Manufacturing, construction, and mining	25	25
Agriculture, forestry, and fishing	3	2.7

The American economy will produce far more jobs than those in other geographic regions of the world. The big problem for many firms, however, will be to give the workers the types of training that they need to get the job done. Jobs will be changing because of both rapid technological advancement and competitive strategies. Many of these jobs will occur in areas that require postsecondary education. Unfortunately, for many firms this is bad news. As *Fortune* magazine has reported, "a dishearteningly large number of workers lack the basic skills the job market increasingly requires—and for many, matters are getting worse." This will be particularly troubling for those who are already in the job market, because they will need a lifelong commitment to training. Every year or two, they will need to get additional training if they are to keep up with the demands of the workplace.

Industry analysts forecast that by the year 2000 only 27 percent of all jobs will require low-level skills compared to 40 percent in 1986. Medium-level skills will still be needed for about 35 percent of all jobs, about the same percentage as in 1986. The big change will be in jobs requiring higher level-skills. In the year 2000 approximately 40 percent of all jobs will require high-level skills compared to 25 percent in 1986.

Questions

1. Where are the greatest number of career opportunities likely to occur between now and the turn of the century? Explain.

2. What challenges will American business face with regard to training its work force? Explain.

3. Why will more training be needed for jobs between now and the turn of the century? Identify and describe two reasons.

Source: Louis S. Richman, "Tomorrow's Jobs: Plentiful, But . . ." *Fortune,* April 11, 1988, pp. 42–56.

■ SELF-FEEDBACK EXERCISE: Are You a Type A or Type B Personality?

Some people are basically Type A personalities; others are Type B; still others are a mix of the two. Which are you? Answer the following ten pairs of statements and decide best describes you, statement A or statement B. Then give yourself a score on each set of statements by using the following scale:

If statement A is totally descriptive of you, give yourself 5 points.

If statement A is much more descriptive of you than statement B, give yourself 4 points.

If statement A is a little more descriptive of you than statement B, give yourself 3 points.

If statement B is a little more descriptive of you than statement A, give yourself 2 points.

If statement B is much more descriptive of you than statement A, give yourself 1 point.

If statement B is much totally descriptive of you, give yourself 0 points.

1. **A.** You work at a very hectic pace.
   B. You work at a very leisurely pace.

2. **A.** You like to talk.
   B. You like to listen.

3. **A.** You try to be always doing something.
   B. You like to spend time just relaxing and doing nothing.

4. **A.** You love to work.
   B. You love to spend time with your family and friends.

5. **A.** You eat very fast.
   B. You eat at a relaxed pace.

6. **A.** When you play games, you like to win.
   B. You enjoy the social and fun sides of playing games; you don't feel you have to win.

7. **A.** You manage your time very closely.
   B. You have fairly good control of your time.

8. **A.** When people talk slowly, you want to finish their sentences.
   B. When people talk slowly, you patiently wait for them to finish.

9. **A.** You tend to measure your progress in terms of time and performance.
   B. You try to get things done in an agreed upon time without putting heavy pressure on yourself.

10. **A.** You like to be respected for what you do.
    B. You like to be respected for who you are.

Place your answers below and then add them up. An interpretation of your score is provided below.

    1. _____
    2. _____
    3. _____
    4. _____
    5. _____
    6. _____
    7. _____
    8. _____
    9. _____
   10. _____
Total _____

Interpretation

Compare your total to the key below. Most people are a mixture of Type A and Type B personalities. However, highly successful sales types and many up-and-coming managers are moderate Type A types.

0–10   You have a strong Type B personality.

11–20   You have a moderate Type B personality.

21–30   You have a mixture of Type A and Type B personalities.

31–40   You have a moderate Type A personality.

41–50   You have a strong Type A personality.

■ COMPREHENSIVE CASE: **What Makes for Success?**

One overriding question for the remaining years of this decade appears certain to continue as a major issue that executive decision makers must face: How can an organization achieve excellence in management? Many organizations have attempted to respond to this query, and a recent report by the management consulting firm of McKinsey & Company may have provided the answer.

After conducting an analysis of almost forty firms that are often pointed to as examples of well-run organizations, the consulting group focused its attention on ten: IBM, Procter & Gamble, 3M, Johnson & Johnson, Texas Instruments, Dana, Emerson Electric, Hewlett-Packard, Digital Equipment, and McDonald's.

None of these organizations is a holding company; all are operating firms. And all of them succeed because their management adheres closely to the eight characteristics which this case will discuss. Interestingly, none of these characteristics requires the use of sophisticated management tools or gimmicks. None calls for the specific expenditure of funds. Rather, all that is needed is a commitment on the part of management to devote the necessary time and effort to ensuring that these eight characteristics exist within the firm.

First: Be Prepared to Move to Action

Successful firms do not spend a great deal of time analyzing and reanalyzing problem areas or marketing opportunities. They look the situation over, determine the best course of action, and get on with the process of implementing the plan. Sometimes, of course, the plan does not work well. When that happens, this kind of company sets about adjusting the plan and trying it again.

In particular, successful companies avoid long or complicated procedures for developing new ideas. They realize that their plans may not be perfect; but plans can always be fixed up. Furthermore, as these firms begin to develop this philosophy of action, they become better and better at avoiding typical pitfalls into which other, more hesitant, firms fall.

The 3M Company, which demands that proposals for new product ideas be written in five pages or less, is a good example of these firms' action orientation. Procter & Gamble is another such company, with a one-page memo more the rule than the exception there.

Furthermore, in order to keep their action plans simple, many of these organizations set forth only one or two objectives. For example, in getting an advertising program off the ground, a company manager would pursue a goal of "Have the entire advertising program implemented by June 30." The statement of the goal is simple and to the point, though a timid manager probably would find its latitude frightening.

When it comes to dealing with problems, the action orientation of these firms is basically the same. Once a problem is identified, someone is put in charge of attaining a solution. If a task-force approach is used, a time period is set; and an answer must be forthcoming by this date.

Second: Keep the Organization Structure Simple

All of these successful firms believe one thing—a small structure is better than a big one. Even though all of these corporations are quite large, they get around typical bureaucratic problems by breaking the company into small entrepreneurial units. For example, Hewlett-Packard keeps its division size at no more than 1,000 people. And where possible, each is autonomous, functioning independently of the others in all possible ways. Texas Instruments, where there are 90 product customer centers, each functioning independently of the others, is another such example.

TI uses this same basic approach within each of the units. Small, manageable groups are formed and, to the extent possible, work independently of the others. This, in turn, helps keep the overall corporate bureaucracy to a minimum.

Third: Stay Close to the Customer

Technology is important to many successful firms. However, they examine technology in terms of the customer. How will new developments help the purchaser? What is in it for the buyer? By concentrating on these types of questions, the firms keep their emphasis on the marketing side of the business equation.

One way in which they do this is by soliciting ideas from customers. Instead of working out new product ideas in the lab, believing that the product is really very interesting and a sure customer appeal, these firms go out and ask the purchaser: What modifications would you like to see in our products? What other types of products would help you do your work more easily or more efficiently?

McKinsey & Company found that some firms have their top managers in the field as many as thirty days a year for the purpose of talking to customers and getting new product ideas. Companies like IBM, for example, believe that this hands-on approach is important; and in most cases, they do not leave people in staff positions for more than three years. They want these people out in the mainstream where they can interact regularly with customers. In fact, regular staff, such as individuals in R&D or finance, are sent out to the field on occasion to get a feel for the customer's perspective on the product line and to assess how the firm can be more effective in improving customer relationships.

Another way of getting market information is through customer-satisfaction surveys. Also, some of these firms hire individuals in "assistant to" positions to senior executives, with the assistant's sole responsibility being the handling of customer complaints within twenty-four hours of the time they are received.

Fourth: Improve Productivity through Increased Motivation

One of the easiest ways to improve productivity is to bring in new machinery. However, this method is limited by the fact that the competition can do the same thing and offset any real edge the firm is hoping to gain. McKinsey & Company found that the companies in its study tried to improve productivity simultaneously with motivation. One of the primary ways of doing this was to give the individuals increased autonomy. In production settings, shop floor teams set their own pace for production, the only stipulation being that they meet the agreed upon output target. Managers report that this approach often leads workers to setting ambitious but attainable objectives.

In firms where new product development is the principal goal, it is common to find a product group. In this group will be individuals from all of the necessary areas: marketing, technology, finance, and production. The group then operates on a self-sufficient basis and remains intact from the inception of the new product until its national introduction. The team spirit and morale that develop with this approach more than offset any costs associated with its use.

Finally, while many behavioral theorists frown upon such hygiene factors as recognition awards like plaques, badges, pins, and medals, these well-managed firms use them with success. However, monetary rewards are not the only form of recognition. In some companies a successful production team would be given an intrinsic reward, such as an invitation to describe its success to the board of directors.

Fifth: Use Autonomy to Encourage Entrepreneurship

Autonomy fosters independence and creative thinking. Firms of the sort under discussion find that individuals respond better when they work in a loose-control environment. This is why the organization encourages its managers to act like entrepreneurs. In plants, the head managers are free to make purchasing decisions and start productivity programs as they see fit. Does this approach really pay off? McKinsey & Company has found that it does, reporting that among such groups the grievance rate tends to be lower than the average for similar firms in the industry.

Furthermore, while the top staff may offer general direction, it does not force lower-level managers to make decisions that are not in accord with their personal judgment. Certainly, marketing analysis is used to help pinpoint target areas and develop product promotion campaigns; but these firms also realize that the manager is the one who must be sold on the success of the campaign. If this individual thinks the whole thing is a bad idea, or that it is a good idea but poorly timed, the firm usually listens to this manager.

Additionally, while many managers like to develop large numbers of successful products and make their organizational divisions ever larger, it is common in successful companies to find the product being pushed out of the division to stand on its own, while rewarding the manager for the product's success. Entrepreneurship is encouraged and nurtured. TI, for example, charges special groups with assessing new product ideas. IBM has a Fellows Program that serves essentially the same purpose.

Sixth: Emphasize Key Business Factors

One or two business factors in each of these firms are the keys to success. Keeping the emphasis on these factors, the company improves its chances for growth and profitability. For example, Dana's top management focus was on cost reduction and productivity improvement; in seven years the firm doubled its productivity. At TI, where the focus is on product development, the chairman of the firm made it a point every evening on the way home to drop in at a development laboratory. At IBM, even after his retirement, Thomas Watson, Jr., continued to write memos to the staff on the topic of calling on customers, even going so far as to discuss the proper way to dress for such calls.

As the firm begins to emphasize key business factors, they become a basis for daily action. For example, at Hewlett-Packard the operational review is focused on new products, while a minimal amount of time is devoted to financial projections or results. The company is convinced that if new product plans are properly implemented, finances will take care of themselves.

As managers who have been shaped in these experiences move up the line, they serve as role models for those who take their place. In this way, a firm ensures that these key business values permeate the organization. Everyone eventually begins to stress the same key business factors, with the result being an increase in efficiency, teamwork, and profits.

Seventh: Lead from Strength

All of these firms adhere to one basic principle—they stick to what they know best. They never acquire a business that they do not know how to run.

They have identified their particular strengths, and they try to develop strategy around them. Some of the strengths possessed by the group McKinsey & Company studied follow: (1) IBM—customer service; (2) Dana—productivity improvement; (3) Hewlett-Packard and 3M—new product development; (4) Procter & Gamble—product quality; and (5) McDonald's—customer service, including value, quality, and cleanliness.

Eighth: Employ the Proper Combination of Tight and Loose Controls

Some controls have to be tightly applied. The rest can be used flexibly and loosely. For example, at the 3M Company return on sales is one of the tight controls. Management watches this statistic closely. In most other things, such as control of day-to-day operations, however, the lower-level manager has a lot of leeway. At Dana all divisions report costs and revenues on a daily basis, while other controls are used flexibly.

These eight characteristics have enabled these ten firms to achieve better-than-average growth. One reason for this is that following these eight basic rules allows the companies to concentrate their attention on the external environment—the competition, industry changes, and customer needs. Internal considerations, such as profit and loss, efficiency, cost reduction, and staffing, are taken care of in the process. The external focus helps ensure internal effectiveness at the same time that it helps the firm succeed in its external environment.

Successful firms during the 1990s will find that their progress can be attributed less to sophisticated control techniques and more to the basics of effective management. Succinctly stated, these are service to the customer, productivity improvement, innovation, low-cost manufacturing, and risk taking. Current research indicates that these criteria will continue to separate well-run organizations from their mediocre counterparts.

Questions

1. How difficult it is to follow the eight guidelines in this case? Why is it that more firms do not follow them?

2. During the 1990s, which of the eight guidelines will be hardest for most firms to implement? Why?

3. How can the material in this book help the management practitioner become more effective in implementing these eight guidelines? Explain, using specific applications where possible.

Glossary

This glossary contains definitions of many of the concepts and terms used in the book. For the most part, the terms correspond to those given in the text, and their definitions are followed by the numbers of the chapters in which they appear.

Absoluteness of responsibility   The concept that managers cannot avoid responsibility for the activities of their subordinates. They may delegate authority to their people, but they cannot delegate all responsibility. (Chapter 3)

Acceptance   The third step in the communication process, implying a willingness on the part of the receiver to comply with the message. (Chapter 12)

Acceptance theory of authority   Popularized through the writings of Chester I. Barnard, this theory states that the ultimate source of authority is the subordinate, who chooses either to accept or to reject orders issued by a superior. (Chapter 2)

Action   The last step in the communication process, entailing the implementation of the communication. (Chapter 12)

Activity   An operation required to accomplish a particular event in a PERT network. (Chapter 7)

Adaptive mechanism   A mechanism that, through its acceptance of dynamism, encourages responses to external and internal environments. (Chapter 16)

Ad hoc committee   A committee that is appointed for a specific purpose and disbanded upon completion of the job. (Chapter 5)

Administrative costs   Expenses associated with ordering inventory. *See* Clerical costs. (Chapter 9)

Adult ego state   In transactional analysis, an ego state characterized by attention to reasonable fact gathering and objective analysis. (Chapter 15)

Age Discrimination in Employment Act of 1967   An act, amended in 1978 and extended since then, which protects persons 40 years or older from employment discrimination based on age. (Chapter 18)

Aggression   A frustration reaction that consists of attacking, either physically or symbolically, whatever barriers may prevent goal attainment. (Chapter 10)

Alternative budget   A budgetary approach in which budgets are set up on the basis of the level of operations: high, medium, or low. (Chapter 7)

Analog computer   A measuring machine used principally by engineers in solving job-related problems. (Chapter 10)

Attention   The first step in the communication process; it involves getting the receiver to listen to whatever is being communicated. (Chapter 12)

Authority   The right to command and the power to make oneself obeyed. (Chapter 2)

Authority of knowledge   The right to command that is held by the person who knows the most about the situation and is therefore put in charge of its operation. (Chapter 5)

Authority of the situation   The right to command that is held by a person on the basis of the need for immediate action, as in a crisis in which a leader emerges. (Chapter 5)

Automation   The technique of making an apparatus, a process, or a system operate automatically. (Chapter 10)

Autonomy   The degree of control a worker has over a job. (Chapter 15)

Avoidance   A frustration reaction that consists of withdrawal from a situation that the individual considers too personally thwarting to endure. (Chapter 10)

Balance theory   A theory used in the study of communication to explain how people react to change. The theory places primary attention on the consideration of three relationships: (1) the attitude of the receiver toward the sender; (2) the attitude of the receiver toward the change; and (3) the receiver's perception of the sender's own attitude toward the change. (Chapter 12)

Basic decisions   Long-range decisions, often involving large expenditures of funds and carrying a high degree of importance. (Chapter 8)

Basic socioeconomic purpose   The reason for an organization's existence. (Chapter 4)

Behavioral school   A modern school of management thought propounded by those persons who view management as a psychosociological process. Advocates of this school are particularly concerned with such topics as needs, drives, motivation, leadership, personality, behavior, work groups, and the management of change. (Chapter 3)

Benevolent-authoritative leadership style   A basic leadership style in which management acts in a condescending manner toward subordinates and decision making at the lower levels occurs only within a prescribed framework. (Chapter 14)

Black box concept   The inner workings that take place between input and output. As applied to human behavior, the concept may involve such things as the introduction of a new wage incentive payment scheme (input) and a 10 percent increase in productivity (output). The reason for the change may be the wage plan, but it may also be something else. The black box, or transformation process between input and output, is said to contain the answer. (Chapter 2)

Brainstorming   A creative thinking technique that involves the encouragement of imagination, freewheeling, and the combination of ideas in the generation of alternatives for solving problems. (Chapter 8)

Branch organization   Often employed in a firm's operations in other countries, it is simply an overseas office set up by the parent company. (Chapter 18)

Break-even point   The volume of sales sufficient to cover all fixed and variable expenses but providing no profit. (Chapter 7)

Budget   A plan that specifies anticipated results in numerical terms and serves as a control device for feedback, evaluation, and follow-up. (Chapter 7)

Bureaucracy   A highly structured organization which has a clear-cut division of labor, a hierarchy of offices, a consistent system of abstract rules and standards, a spirit of impersonality, and employment based on technical qualifications and protected from arbitrary dismissal. (Chapter 6)

Carrying costs   Costs associated with keeping inventory on hand, including sundry expenses, such as storage space, taxes, and obsolescence. (Chapter 9)

Causal variables   Independent variables that determine the results that will be attained. Examples include management decisions, business strategies, and leadership behavior. (Chapter 15)

Centralization   A system of management in which major decisions are made at the upper levels of the hierarchy. (Chapter 2)

Certainty decisions   Decision situations in which the manager knows all possible alternatives and the outcome of each. (Chapter 8)

Change process   A three-step process entailing the unfreezing of old ways, the introduction of new behaviors, and the refreezing of a resulting new equilibrium. (Chapter 15)

Child ego state   In transactional analysis, an ego state that is made up of all the impulses learned in infancy and early childhood. (Chapter 15)

Civil Rights Act of 1964   Federal legislation that forbids discrimination against individuals or groups when the discrimination is based on race, color, religion, sex, or national origin. The act provides an agency, the Equal Employment Opportunity Commission, for dealing with employment-related discrimination complaints and charges. (Chapter 17)

Clerical and administrative costs   Expenses associated with ordering inventory. *See* Administrative costs. (Chapter 9)

Closed system   A system that does not interact with its external environment. (Chapter 7)

Closed-loop system   A system that does not receive inputs from the external environment. (Chapter 7)

Cluster chain   An informal communication chain in which information is passed on a selective basis. (Chapter 12)

Coercive power   Power based on the manager's ability to control rewards that are valued by subordinates as well as to punish those who do not comply with directives and formal procedures. (Chapter 5)

Commanding   The art of leadership coupled with the goal of putting an organization into motion. (Chapter 2)

Common Market   A European economic community formed in 1957 by France, West Germany, Italy, Holland, Belgium, and Luxembourg. Today Great Britain, Denmark, Ireland, Portugal, Turkey, and Greece are also members. (Chapter 18)

Communication process   The conveying of meaning from sender to receiver. (Chapter 12)

Complementary transaction   In transactional analysis, a transaction that is appropriate and expected; it follows the natural order of healthy human relationships. (Chapter 15)

Completed staff work   Staff work whose completed recommendation or solution can either be approved or disapproved by a line executive without the necessity for any further investigation. (Chapter 5)

Comprehensive budgeting   A budgeting process that covers all phases of operations. (Chapter 7)

Comprehensive planning   Planning that incorporates all levels of the organization: top, middle, and lower. (Chapter 4)

Compulsory staff service   A concept developed centuries ago by the Roman Catholic Church, requiring superiors to solicit the advice of specified subordinates before making any decisions. (Chapter 2)

Computer program   A set of instructions that tells a computer what to do. (Chapter 10)

Conditional value   The payoff that occurs if a particular strategy proves successful. (Chapter 8)

Consideration   Behavior indicative of friendship, mutual trust, respect, and warmth in the leader-staff relationship. (Chapter 14)

Consultative-democratic leadership style   A basic leadership style in which management has confidence and trust in subordinates and a great deal of decision making is carried out at the lower levels. (Chapter 14)

Consumer Product Safety Act of 1970   A federal law designed to develop uniform safety standards for consumer products and to protect the public against unreasonable risk of injury from such products. (Chapter 17)

Consumerism   Attempts by concerned citizens and government units to enhance the rights and powers of buyers in relation to sellers. (Chapter 17)

Contingency model of leadership effectiveness   A leadership model, developed by Fred Fiedler, that postulates that a leader's effectiveness is determined by three variables: (1) how well the leader is accepted by subordinates; (2) the degree to which subordinates' jobs are routine and spelled out (in contrast to vague and undefined); and (3) the formal authority provided for in the position the leader holds. (Chapter 14)

Contingency organization design   Organization structures that are designed after taking the forces in the task, the managers, the subordinates, and the environment into consideration. (Chapter 15)

Controlling   The managerial function of seeing that everything is done in accord with adopted plans. (Chapter 2)

Controlling process   The process of determining that everything is going according to plan. In essence, the process consists of three steps: (1) the establishment of standards; (2) the comparison of performance against standards; and (3) the correction of any deviations that occur. (Chapter 7)

Coordinating   The managerial function used in attaining the necessary unity and harmony to attain organizational goals. (Chapter 2)

Corporate culture   The behaviors, actions, attitudes, and expectations of the organizational personnel. (Chapter 14)

Creative thinking process   A four-step process used in arriving at novel or unique approaches to problems; it involves preparation, incubation, illumination, and verification. (Chapter 8)

Critical path   The longest path in a PERT network; it begins with the first event and ends with the last one. *See also* Event; Program evaluation and review technique. (Chapter 7)

Crossed transaction   In transactional analysis, a transaction that occurs when a response is not appropriate or expected. (Chapter 15)

Decentralization   A system of management in which a great deal of decision-making authority rests at the lower levels of the hierarchy. (Chapter 5)

Decision making   The process of choosing from among alternatives. (Chapter 8)

Decision support systems   The linking of computers and people so as to allow them to communicate with each other, the result being more effective decision making. (Chapter 10)

Decision tree   An operations research tool that permits: (1) the identification of alternative courses of action in solving a problem; (2) the assignment of probability estimates to the events associated with these alternatives; and (3) the calculation of the payoffs corresponding to each act-event combination. (Chapter 9)

Delegation of authority   The managerial process used to distribute work to subordinates. (Chapter 5)

Delphi technique   A method of forecasting future developments, especially technological discoveries. (Chapter 8)

Departmentalization   The process of grouping jobs on the basis of some common characteristic—for example, function, product, territory, customer, process. (Chapter 5)

Departmentalization by equipment or process   The organization of employees on the basis of the equipment they operate or the process they perform. (Chapter 5)

Departmentalization by simple numbers   The organization of employees on the basis of numbers of people working. (Chapter 5)

Departmentalization by time   The organization of employees on the basis of work time schedules (for example, day, swing, and graveyard shifts). (Chapter 5)

Derivative departments   Departments formed through the subdivision of major departments. For example, derivative production departments could include manufacturing and purchasing. (Chapter 5)

Diagonal communication   Communication that involves the flow of information across departments or people on different levels of the hierarchy. It allows for messages to be transmitted directly instead of emanating from the bottom up to the top and down again. (Chapter 12)

Differential piece-rate system   An incentive wage system, formulated by Frederick W. Taylor, that paid a fixed rate per piece for all production up to standard and a higher rate for all pieces if the standard was met. (Chapter 2)

Digital computer   A counting machine which, by use of electrical impulses, can perform arithmetic calculations far in excess of human capacity. This was one of the most widely used of the early computers in business. (Chapter 10)

Distributed data processing   A computer term which means that at least some portion of the computing function is carried on outside a centralized location. (Chapter 10)

Division of work   Breaking down a job into simple, routine tasks so that each worker becomes a specialist in handling one particular phase of an operation. Often results in increased production efficiency. (Chapter 2)

Domestic system   The stage of a materially productive civilization in which individuals, assured of their own survival, begin to specialize in areas (for example, fabricating textiles) in order to sell the goods at local fairs for whatever price they will bring. Predominant system in England in the early eighteenth century. (Chapter 2)

Downward communication   Communications used to convey directives from superiors to subordinates. (Chapter 12)

Ecology   A scientific study area concerned with the interrelationships of organisms and other environments, especially as manifested by natural cycles and rhythms, community development and structure, interaction between different kinds of organisms, geographic distributions, and population alterations. (Chapter 17)

Econometrics   A mathematical approach used in economic forecasting. (Chapter 4)

Economic man   A term used to identify someone who makes decisions that maximize the person's economic objectives. (Chapter 2)

Economic order formula   An economic order quantity model useful to the manager in the determination of how many units to order in replenishing inventory. (Chapter 9)

Electronic data processing (EDP)   The processing of information through the use of electronic equipment such as computers and calculators. (Chapter 10)

End-result variables   Outcomes brought about by causal variables (for example, earnings, productivity, and costs). (Chapter 15)

Enlightened self-interest   A doctrine that business actually serves its own long-run interests by helping out its community. (Chapter 17)

Entropy   The tendency of a closed system to move toward a chaotic random, or inert state. (Chapter 16)

EOQ formula   *See* Economic order formula.

Equal Pay Act of 1963   Federal legislation designed to correct the existence of wage differentials based on sex; applies to industries engaged in commerce or in the production of goods for commerce. (Chapter 17)

Equity or social comparison theory   The contention that people are motivated not only by what they receive but also by what they see, or believe, others receive. According to this theory, individuals compare their rewards with those of others in judging whether their own renumeration is equitable. (Chapter 13)

Esteem needs   A person's need to feel important and receive recognition from others that supports feelings of personal worth; fourth level in Maslow's hierarchy. (Chapter 13)

Ethics   The study of right and wrong conduct. (Chapter 18)

Event   A point in time when an activity starts or ends. *See also* Activity; Program evaluation and review technique. (Chapter 7)

Exception principle   The belief that managers should concern themselves with exceptional, not routine, cases and results. (Chapter 7)

Expectancy   The probability that a specific action will be followed by a particular first-level outcome. (Chapter 13)

Expectancy theory   A theory of motivation that holds that individuals will be high-level performers when they: (1) see a high likelihood that their efforts will lead to high performance; (2) see a high probability that high-level performance will lead to specific outcomes; and (3) view these outcomes as personally desirable. (Chapter 13)

Expectancy–valence theory   A motivation theory, formulated by Victor Vroom, that states that motivation is equal to the summation of valence times expectancy. *See also* Instrumentality; Expectancy; Valence. (Chapter 13)

Expected time   A time estimate for each activity in a PERT network; it is calculated by means of the following formula:

$$t_E = \frac{t_o + 4t_m + t_p}{6}$$

$$\begin{aligned} where \ t_E &= \text{Expected time} \\ t_o &= \text{Optimistic time} \\ t_m &= \text{Most likely time} \\ t_p &= \text{Pessimistic time} \end{aligned}$$

(Chapter 7)

Expected value   The result of the multiplication of a conditional value by its success probability. (Chapter 8)

Expert power   Power based on task-relevant knowledge as perceived by the subordinates. (Chapter 5)

Exploitative-authoritative leadership style   A basic leadership style in which management has little confidence in its subordinates. Decision making tends, therefore, to be highly centralized. (Chapter 14)

Exploratory forecast   A technological forecasting technique that assumes that future technological progress will continue at its present rate. This technique moves from the present to the future and considers technical factors more heavily than other variables. (Chapter 4)

External audit   An audit conducted by an outside accounting firm. (Chapter 7)

Extinction   A learning strategy in which the individual is not reinforced for a specific behavior, thereby reducing the likelihood that he or she will perform the same act again in the future. (Chapter 13)

Extrapolation   The simplest form of economic forecast, consisting of the straightforward projection of current trends into the future. (Chapter 4)

Factory system   The final stage in the evolution of a materially productive civilization; characterized by the introduction of power-driven machinery. Workers come to one central site, where the machinery is located (that is, the factory) rather than working at home. *See also* Domestic system; Putting-out system. (Chapter 2)

Feedback   The amount of information that an individual receives in regard to how well the work is being performed. (Chapter 15)

First-level outcome   A factor that brings about a second-level outcome; for example, productivity (first-level outcome) leads to promotion (second-level outcome) in many companies. (Chapter 13)

First wave of change   Changes that occurred as a result of the agricultural revolution. (Chapter 1)

Fixed costs   Costs that will remain constant, at least in the short run, regardless of operations (for example, property taxes and administrative salaries). (Chapter 7)

Flat organization structure   A unit structure characterized by a wide span of control, with only a small number of levels in the hierarchy. *See also* Tall organization structure. (Chapter 5)

Flextime   A work schedule that management makes flexible enough to allow employees some decision-making authority over when they begin and end their workdays. (Chapter 15)

Forecasting   A method of projecting future business conditions for the purpose of establishing goals and budgets. (Chapter 4)

Formal organization   The officially designated jobs and relationships in an organization as seen on the organization chart and in the job descriptions. (Chapter 5)

Free-form organization structure   *See* Organic organization structure.

Functional authority   Authority in a department other than one's own, as in the case of a comptroller who can order production workers to provide cost-per-unit data directly to the finance department. (Chapter 5)

Functional departmentalization   Organization of a department along the lines of major activities. In a manufacturing firm so organized, it is not uncommon to find marketing, production, and finance departments reporting directly to the president. (Chapter 5)

Fusion process   The process by which an individual and an organization, when they come together, tend to influence each other's objectives. (Chapter 5)

Game theory   Theory used in operations research to study conflict-of-interest situations. (Chapter 9)

Gangplank principle   Developed by Henri Fayol, a principle holding that individuals at the same hierarchical level should be allowed to communicate directly, provided that they have permission from their superiors to do so and that they tell their respective chiefs afterward what they have agreed to do. The purpose of the principle is to cut red tape while maintaining hierarchical integrity. (Chapter 2)

Gantt chart   A chart on which progress on various parts of an undertaking is compared with time. (Chapter 7)

GNP *See* Gross national product.

Gordon technique A creative thinking technique widely used in handling technical problems. (Chapter 8)

Gossip chain An informal communication chain in which one person passes information along to the rest. (Chapter 12)

Grapevine The informal communication channel in an organization. (Chapter 12)

Graphic rating scale A performance evaluation instrument that allows the manager to evaluate employee performance on a number of different factors. (Chapter 7)

Grass-roots method A sales forecasting method that relies on input from salespeople in the field. (Chapter 4)

Gross national product (GNP) The value of goods and services produced within a country in a year. (Chapter 4)

Group behavior branch A branch of the behavioral school that is interested in the study of groups and organizational behavior. (Chapter 3)

Hawthorne effect Behavior that is differentiated by people's awareness of being under observation. Named after this phenomenon as first described by the Hawthorne researchers. (Chapter 2)

Hawthorne studies Studies conducted at the Western Electric plant in Cicero, Illinois, that provided the impetus for the human relations movement. The research had four major phases: (1) illumination experiments; (2) relay assembly test room experiments; (3) massive interviewing program; and (4) the bank wiring observation room study. (Chapter 2)

Heuristic programming An operations research technique that employs both rules of thumb and the use of trial and error. (Chapter 9)

Hierarchy of objectives The interrelationship of objectives within an organization; short-term objectives are related to intermediate-range objectives, which are in turn related to long-range objectives. (Chapter 4)

Human relations philosophy A philosophy that holds that the business organization is a social system and that employees are largely motivated and controlled by the human relationships in that system. (Chapter 2)

Human resources accounting A recent development in management whose purpose is: (1) to view the acquisition of organizational employees as an investment of the firm and (2) to obtain a regular evaluation of these assets. (Chapter 15)

Human resources philosophy A philosophy that holds individuals want not only to be treated well but to be able to contribute creatively to organizational solutions to problems. For contrast, *see* Human relations philosophy. *See also* Theory Y. (Chapter 2)

Hygiene factors   Factors, identified by Frederick Herzberg in his two-factor theory of motivation, that will motivate people by their absence but not by their presence (for example, money, security, and good working conditions). (Chapter 13)

Identity of the task   The degree to which a job allows for completion of a whole or identifiable piece of work. (Chapter 15)

Industrial psychology   A subfield of psychology concerned with applying psychological knowledge to the selection, training, and development of an organization's employees. (Chapter 2)

Inference   A view of reality held by a person in response to implied data. (Chapter 12)

Informal group norms   Sentiments to which individuals must adhere in order to win acceptance and maintain membership in a group. Observed in the Hawthorne bank wiring observation room, for example, they included these dicta: (1) you should not turn out too much work; (2) you should not turn out too little work; (3) you should not tell a superior anything to the detriment of an associate; (4) you should not attempt to maintain social distance or act officious; and (5) you should not be noisy, self-advancing, or anxious for leadership. (Chapter 2)

Informal organization   The unofficially designated relationships in an organization; not shown on organization charts and often not reflected in job descriptions. (Chapter 5)

Information design   A process of filtering the number and kinds of reports and other data being sent to managers; the purpose is to prevent managers from being inundated with irrelevant reading. (Chapter 7)

Information system   An organized method of providing past, present, and projected information related to internal operations and external intelligence. (Chapter 10)

Initiating structure   The leader's behavior in delineating the relationship between leader and work group and the leader's work toward establishing well-defined patterns of organization, channels of communication, and procedural methods. (Chapter 14)

Institutional level   Upper level of the organization; concerned with relating the overall organization to its environment. (Chapter 16)

Institutional managers   Top-level managers whose concern is surveying the environment and developing cooperative and competitive strategies that will ensure the organization's survival. Such managers tend to adopt philosophical viewpoints. (Chapter 16)

Instrumentality   The relationship an individual perceives between a first-level and second-level outcome. *See also* Expectancy-valence theory; First-level outcome; Second-level outcome. (Chapter 13)

Intermediate-range planning The setting of subobjectives and substrategies that are in accord with the long-run objectives and strategies of the overall plan. (Chapter 4)

Internal audit An audit conducted by the organization's own staff specialists. (Chapter 7)

Interpersonal behavior branch A behavioralist school that is heavily oriented toward the individual, especially in regard to motivations. (Chapter 3)

Intervening variables Internal, unobservable, psychological processes that account for human behavior. These variables cannot be measured directly but instead must be inferred; motivation is one example of such a variable. (Chapter 15)

Intrapreneurship Entrepreneurial activity that occurs inside an enterprise.

JIT inventory A hand-to-mouth approach that calls for purchasing or producing just in time for use. (Chapter 11)

Job characteristics model A model that helps explain how jobs can be redesigned so as to become more motivational in nature. (Chapter 15)

Job enlargement An attempt to make work more psychologically rewarding; consists of increasing the number of tasks being performed by a given worker. (Chapter 15)

Job enrichment An attempt to make work more psychologically rewarding; consists of building motivators into jobs in order that the worker can satisfy some personal higher-level needs. Popularized by M. Scott Myers. *See also* Motivational factors. (Chapter 15)

Joint venture An enterprise undertaken by two or more parties. In international trade, it often consists of a foreign corporation, such as a U. S. business firm, and a host-country partner. (Chapter 18)

Jury of executive opinion A sales forecasting method that relies on input from the organization's executives. (Chapter 4)

Key area control A control technique by which a firm measures its performance in a number of vital areas. At General Electric, for example, key areas include profitability, market position, productivity, product leadership, personnel development, employee attitudes, public responsibility, and integration of short-range and long-range objectives. (Chapter 7)

Lag indicators Series of economic indicators that often follow changes in the economic cycle. (Chapter 4)

Laplace criterion A basis for decision making; using it, the manager applies equal probabilities to all states of nature. (Chapter 8)

Lateral communication Communication that takes place among departments or people on the same hierarchical level. (Chapter 12)

Law of triviality   Formulated by C. Northcote Parkinson, a law stating that the time spent on any agenda item will be in inverse proportion to the monetary sum involved. (Chapter 5)

Lead indicators   Series of economic indicators which often precede changes in the economic cycle. (Chapter 4)

Leader behavior description questionnaire (LBDQ)   A questionnaire designed for gathering information on how a leader carries out leadership activities. (Chapter 14)

Leadership   A process of influencing people to direct their efforts toward the achievement of some particular goal or goals. (Chapter 14)

Leading from strength   A rule of strategy holding that an organization should draw on its strong points in fashioning its strategy. (Chapter 4)

Legitimate power   Power that is vested in the manager's position and is given to all who hold that particular position. (Chapter 5)

Line authority   Direct authority, as in the case of a superior who can give orders directly to a subordinate. (Chapter 5)

Line department   A department concerned with attaining the basic objectives of the organization. In a manufacturing firm, production, marketing, and finance would be line departments. (Chapter 5)

Linear programming   A mathematical technique for determining optimum answers in cases in which a linear relationship exists among the variables. (Chapter 9)

Maintenance mechanism   A mechanism that attempts to stop a system from changing so rapidly that it is thrown out of balance. (Chapter 16)

Management   The process of setting objectives, organizing resources to attain them, and then evaluating the results for the purpose of determining future action. (Chapter 1)

Management audit   An evaluation of the management's success in operating the organization. Criteria often employed in this evaluation include production efficiency, health of earnings, fairness to stockholders, and executive ability. (Chapter 7)

Management by objectives (MBO)   A process in which superior and subordinate jointly identify common goals, define the subordinate's areas of responsibility in terms of expected results, and then use these measures as guides in operating the unit and in evaluating the subordinate's contribution. (Chapter 15)

Management functions   The activities managers perform in carrying out their jobs. Planning, organizing, and controlling are the most commonly accepted ones. (Chapter 3)

Management information system (MIS)   An organized method of gathering and providing information to managers for use in decision making. (Chapter 10)

Management process school   Modern school of management thought whose adherents believe that the way to study management is through a systematic analysis of the managerial functions—planning, organizing, and controlling. (Chapter 3)

Management science   *See* Operations research.

Management systems   Basic leadership styles identified by Rensis Likert. In essence, there are four: exploitative-authoritative, benevolent-authoritative, consultative-democratic, and participative-democratic. (Chapter 14)

Managerial grid   A two-dimensional leadership model that permits simultaneous consideration of concern for production and concern for people. (Chapter 14)

Marginal analysis   Analysis that concerns the extra output attainable by adding an extra unit of input. (Chapter 8)

Marginal cost   The costs incurred by selling one more unit of output. (Chapter 8)

Marginal physical product   The extra output obtained by adding one unit of input while all other factors are held constant (for example, the extra output obtained by adding one unit of labor while holding all other inputs constant). (Chapter 8)

Marginal revenue   The additional revenue obtained by selling one more unit of output. (Chapter 8)

Material requirements planning   A systematic, comprehensive manufacturing and controlling technique that increases the efficiency of both purchasing and inventory control. (Chapter 11)

Matrix structure   A hybrid form of organization containing characteristics of both project and functional structures. (Chapter 6)

Maximax criterion   A decision-making basis. The manager determines the greatest payoff for each strategy and then chooses the one that is most favorable, thus maximizing the maximum gain. (Chapter 8)

Maximin criterion   A decision-making basis. The manager determines the most negative payoff for each strategy and then chooses the one that is most favorable, thus maximizing the minimum gain. (Chapter 8)

Mechanistic organization structure   An organization structure that is often effective in a stable environment where technology is not very significant. (Chapter 6)

Microchronometer   A clock with a large sweeping hand capable of recording time to 1/2000 of a minute. Developed by Frank and Lillian Gilbreth, the clock is still of use today in photographing time-and-motion patterns. (Chapter 2)

Milestone scheduling   A scheduling and controlling procedure that employs bar charts to monitor progress. In essence, it is very similar to a Gantt chart, but its use is not restricted to production activities. (Chapter 7)

MIS   *See* Management information system.

MNC   *See* Multinational corporation.

Monte Carlo technique   An operations research technique that makes use of simulation and random numbers in arriving at optimal solutions. (Chapter 9)

Motion study   The process of analyzing work in order to determine the preferred motions for completing the job most efficiently. (Chapter 2)

Motivational factors   Identified by Frederick Herzberg in his two-factor theory of motivation, the term refers to those factors that will build high levels of motivation and job satisfaction. Some of the motivational factors Herzberg identified are recognition, advancement, and achievement. (Chapter 13)

Multidimensional matrix   A matrix design that combines a number of different variables such as product, function, and geographic, this structure is most widely used by multinational manufacturers. (Chapter 6)

Multinational corporation (MNC)   Any firm that has a large percentage of its operations devoted to activities in more than one country. (Chapter 18)

Need hierarchy   A widely accepted framework of motivation, developed by Abraham Maslow. In essence, the theory makes three major statements: (1) The five levels of needs, in order of importance, are physiological, safety, social, esteem, and self-actualization. (2) Only those needs not yet satisfied influence behavior. (3) When one level of needs has been satisfied, the next higher level emerges as dominant and influential. (Chapter 13)

Negative reinforcement   Reinforcement that increases the frequency of a behavior while bringing about the termination of some condition. (Chapter 13)

Net present value (NPV)   The statement of future cash flows in terms of current dollars. (Chapter 8)

Nonprogrammed decisions   Important decisions, novel and unstructured in nature. (Chapter 8)

Non-zero-sum games   Games in which gains by one side do not automatically result in equal losses to the other side. (Chapter 9)

Normative forecasting   A technological forecasting technique that begins with the identification of some future technological objective and works back to the present, identifying problem areas that will have to be surmounted along the way. Although it is a technological technique, normative forecasting considers both technological and nontechnological factors. (Chapter 4)

NPV   *See* Net present value.

Ombudsman   An individual who handles complaints by making inquiries and investigating problem areas. (Chapter 19)

On-line processing   A computer term; it means that transactions are fed into a computer as they occur. (Chapter 10)

Open system   A system that is in constant interaction with its external environment. (Chapter 16)

Open-loop system   A system that receives input from the outside environment. (Chapter 7)

Operational planning   The setting of short-run goals and targets that are in accord with the subobjectives and substrategies of the intermediate-range plan. (Chapter 4)

Operations management   The process of designing, operating, and controlling a production system that takes physical resources and transforms them into goods and services. (Chapter 11)

Operations research (OR)   The application of mathematical tools and techniques to the decision-making process. (Chapter 9)

Optimistic time   *See* Expected time.

Optimization   The combining of elements in just the right balance, often to secure maximum profit. (Chapter 3)

OR   *See* Operations research.

Organic functions   Activities that the organization must carry out to remain in existence (examples in a manufacturing firm are marketing, production, and finance). (Chapter 5)

Organic organization structure   Structure that is most effective in a dynamic environment especially where technology plays a significant role; since the structure can take any design, it is also known as free-form structure. (Chapter 6)

Organization chart   A diagram of an organization's departments and their relationships to each other. (Chapter 5)

Organizational decisions   Decisions made by executives in their role as managers. (Chapter 8)

Organizational level   Middle level of a company, concerned with coordinating and integrating work performance at the technical level. (Chapter 16)

Organizational managers   Middle managers whose goal is to coordinate the technical and institutional levels of the firm in some harmonious fashion and who tend to assume a political or mediating viewpoint. (Chapter 16)

Organizing   The structuring of activities, materials, and employees for accomplishing assigned tasks. (Chapter 2)

Organizing function   The assignment of duties and coordination of efforts among all employees to ensure maximum efficiency in the attainment of predetermined objectives. (Chapter 5)

Paired comparison   A performance evaluation technique that entails comparing each worker in a unit to every other worker and ranking them from best to poorest. (Chapter 7)

Parent ego state   An ego state containing the supervisory attitudes and behaviors that children perceive in their parents and later replicate in supervisory situations. (Chapter 15)

Participative-democratic leadership style   A basic leadership style in which management has complete confidence and trust in the subordinates and in which decision making is highly decentralized. (Chapter 14)

Path–goal theory of leadership   A theory which holds that the leader's job is: (1) to help the subordinates by increasing their personal satisfactions in work–goal attainment and (2) to make the path to these satisfactions easier. (Chapter 14)

Payback period   The time it takes for an investment to pay for itself. (Chapter 8)

Perception   A person's view of reality. (Chapter 12)

Performance evaluation   A process in which individual performance is evaluated and decisions made regarding salary increases, promotions, additional training, transfers and/or separation. (Chapter 7)

Personal decisions   Decisions that relate to the manager as an individual, not as a member of the organization. (Chapter 8)

Personal power   Informal authority that is created or sustained by such factors as experience, drive, association with the right groups, and education. (Chapter 5)

PERT   *See* Program evaluation and review technique.

Pessimistic time   *See* Expected time.

Physiological needs   Physical needs (for example, food, clothing, and shelter); the first level in Maslow's hierarchy. (Chapter 13)

Planning   A forecast of events and, based on the forecast, the construction of an operating program; one of the three most basic managerial functions. (Chapter 2)

Planning function   The formulation of objectives and the steps that are employed in attaining them. (Chapter 4)

Planning organization   An organization specifically designed to help a company develop a comprehensive and logical approach to planning at all the hierarchical levels. (Chapter 4)

Plural executives   Committees having the authority to order that their recommendations be implemented. (Chapter 5)

Policy   A general guide to thinking and action. (Chapter 8)

Primacy of planning   The principle that, at least initially, planning precedes all the other managerial functions. (Chapter 3)

Principles of management   General guidelines (in the case of the classical theorists, they were basically inflexible) useful to the manager in carrying out the practice of management. (Chapter 3)

Principles of scientific management Set forth by Frederick W. Taylor, principles that include the following four points: (1) Develop a science for each element of an employee's work, thus replacing the old rule-of-thumb method. (2) Scientifically select and then train, teach, and develop the employee, as contrasted with the earlier practices of letting a worker individually pick up whatever knowledge was available. (3) Heartily cooperate with the workers to ensure that all work is being done in accord with the principles of scientific management. (4) Divide work almost equally between management and employees, with the difference from the past being that managers take over managerial tasks, whereas these formerly fell generally on the employees. (Chapter 2)

Probability The likelihood that a particular outcome will occur. (Chapter 8)

Probability chain An informal communication chain in which information is passed on a random basis. (Chapter 12)

Procedure A guide to action that relates the chronological steps entailed in attaining some objective, such as allowing a person to return faulty merchandise. (Chapter 8)

Product departmentalization The organization of a department, particularly one belonging to a large corporation, along product lines. (Chapter 5)

Product-function matrix A matrix structure used to manage a product line, this design is popular among consumer products companies. (Chapter 6)

Product-region matrix A matrix structure used to achieve product market emphasis, this design is most commonly employed by multinational manufacturers. (Chapter 6)

Productivity Output/input. (Chapter 11)

Profession A vocation whose practice is founded on an understanding of some department of learning or science or upon the abilities accompanying such understanding (for example, physician, attorney, professor, priest). Major criteria include: (1) knowledge, (2) competent application, (3) social responsibility, (4) self-control, and (5) community sanction. (Chapter 19)

Profit The remainder after expenses are deducted from revenues. (Chapter 7)

Program evaluation and review technique (PERT) A sophisticated time-event network series that permits a manager to evaluate and control the progress of a complex undertaking. *See also* Activity; Event. (Chapter 7)

Programmed decisions Routine decisions often handled in the implementation of predetermined policies. (Chapter 8)

Project authority Authority exercised by project managers over personnel assigned to them for a project. This authority, which flows horizontally, contrasts with functional authority. (Chapter 6)

Project matrix   A matrix structure used for accomplishing a particular project, this design is popular in the aerospace industry. (Chapter 6)

Project organization   An organization that is created for the attainment of a particular objective and disbanded on its completion. (Chapter 6)

Projection   A frustration reaction that involves blaming others for one's own shortcomings. (Chapter 10)

Putting-out system   The second stage in the evolution of a materially productive civilization initially characterized by an entrepreneur's agreement to take all the output an individual (or family) can produce at a fixed price. This stage later progressed to the stage where the entrepreneur provided the workers with the raw materials and paid them on a piece-rate basis for finished goods. *See also* Domestic system; Factory system. (Chapter 2)

Quality control circle   A small group of volunteers who do similar work and meet on a regular basis to identify, analyze, and solve problems related to the work area. (Chapter 11)

Quantitative school   A modern school of management thought consisting of theories on management as a system of mathematical models and processes. Advocates of this school are greatly concerned with decision making. The genesis of the school is scientific management. (Chapter 3)

Queuing theory   An operations research technique used for balancing waiting lines and service. (Chapter 9)

Real time   A computer term; it means that files are updated as new information is received. (Chapter 10)

Referent power   Power based on the followers' identification with the leader. (Chapter 5)

Responsibility   The obligation of a subordinate to perform assigned tasks. (Chapter 2)

Return on investment (ROI)   A control technique used to determine how well a firm is managing its assets. In essence, the ROI computation is:

$$\frac{\text{Earnings}}{\text{Sales}} \times \frac{\text{Sales}}{\text{Total investment.}}$$

(Chapter 7)

Revery   Used by Elton Mayo to refer generally to an individual's entire outlook on life. (Chapter 2)

Reward power   Power that is based on the manager's ability to reward those who comply with orders and/or do their jobs well. (Chapter 5)

Risk decisions   Decision situations in which the manager has some information on the outcomes of each alternative and can formulate probability estimates based on the knowledge. (Chapter 8)

Routine decisions   Decisions that are often repetitive in nature and have only a minor impact on the firm. (Chapter 8)

Saddle point   A term used in game theory to identify an ideal strategy. (Chapter 9)

Safety needs   The need for such things as economic security, job security, and an orderly environment; second level in Maslow's hierarchy. (Chapter 13)

Sales forecast   A method of projecting future sales. Some common techniques include survey of current sales information, the jury of executive opinion, the grass-roots method, and user expectation. (Chapter 4)

SBU   *See* Strategic business unit.

Scalar chain   The chain of command that runs from the top of an organization to its lowest ranks. (Chapter 2)

Scientific management   A system of management popularized by Frederick W. Taylor and others in the early twentieth century that sought to develop: (1) ways of increasing productivity by making work easier to perform and (2) methods for motivating workers to take advantage of these labor-saving devices and techniques. (Chapter 2)

Scientific method   A logical problem-solving process used in identifying the problem, diagnosing the situation, gathering preliminary data, classifying the information, stating a tentative answer to the problem, and testing the answer. (Chapter 2)

Second-level outcome   The effect brought about by a first-level outcome— for example, a promotion (second-level outcome) brought about by productivity (first-level outcome). (Chapter 13)

Self-actualization needs   The need to realize one's full potential; highest level in Maslow's hierarchy. (Chapter 7)

Self-audit   An evaluation of organizational performance which is carried out by individuals working in the enterprise. (Chapter 7)

Sensitivity training   A form of training designed to make managers more aware of their own feelings and those of others. (Chapter 15)

Sensory reality   Physical reality, such as a house or a chair. (Chapter 12)

Significance of the task   The degree to which a job has an impact on the lives or work of other people. (Chapter 15)

Simulation   As used in a business setting, mathematical models designed to provide answers to "what if" questions. (Chapter 10)

Single strand   An informal communication chain in which information is passed from one person to another, through a line of recipients. (Chapter 12)

Situational theory   View of leadership as multidimensional, consisting of the leader's personality; the requirements of the task; the expectations, needs, and attitudes of the followers; and the environment in which they operate. (Chapter 14)

Slack   The time difference between scheduled completion and each of the paths in a PERT network. (Chapter 7)

Social needs   The need for acceptance, friendship, and affection; third level in Maslow's hierarchy. (Chapter 13)

Social responsibility   The obligations of business to society, especially in the areas of equal opportunity, ecology, and consumerism. (Chapter 17)

Span of control   The number of subordinates who report to a given superior. (Chapter 5)

Staff authority   Auxiliary authority as seen in the case of individuals who advise, assist, recommend, or facilitate organizational activities (for example, the company lawyer who advises the chief executive officer on the legality of contract matters). (Chapter 5)

Staff department   A department that provides assistance and support to line departments in attaining basic objectives of the organization. In a manufacturing firm, purchasing and accounting would be staff departments. (Chapter 5)

Staff independence   A concept developed centuries ago by the Roman Catholic Church whereby advisors are neither appointed by the person they advise nor removable by that person; the yes-man pitfall is avoided by this concept. (Chapter 2)

Staffing   The recruiting, selecting, training, and developing of individuals for organizational purposes. (Chapter 16)

Standing committee   A committee, often advisory in nature, that exists for an indefinite period of time. (Chapter 5)

Status   Attributes that rank and relate individuals in an organization. (Chapter 12)

Strategic business unit (SBU)   A unit within the overall organization which has a single business, a distinct mission, competitors, and a responsible manager. (Chapter 4)

Strategic planning   The determination of an organization's major objectives and the policies and strategies that will govern the acquisition, use, and disposition of resources in achieving these objectives. (Chapter 4)

Suboptimization   Using less than the total of each input in order to maximize the total output or profit. (Chapter 3)

Subsidiary   A company that is owned in part or fully by another firm. (Chapter 18)

Supplemental monthly budget   A budgetary approach in which the firm determines a minimum operational budget and prior to the beginning of each month provides the units with additional funds to supplement this minimum. (Chapter 7)

TA   *See* Transactional analysis.

Tall organization structure   An organization structure in which there is a narrow span of control with a large number of levels in the hierarchy. *See also* Flat organization structure. (Chapter 5)

Technical level   Low organizational level concerned primarily with the production and distribution of goods and services. (Chapter 16)

Technical managers   Low-level managers concerned with turning out goods and services as economically as possible. These managers tend to have an engineering point of view. (Chapter 16)

Territorial departmentalization   Organization of a department along the lines of geographic location. An example is found in a company with four major divisions: eastern, midwestern, western, and foreign. (Chapter 5)

Theory X   A set of assumptions that holds that people: (1) dislike work; (2) have little ambition; (3) want security above all else; and (4) must be coerced, controlled, and threatened with punishment in order for them to produce. (Chapter 13)

Theory Y   A set of assumptions that holds that: (1) if conditions are favorable, people will not only accept responsibility but will seek it; (2) if people are committed to organizational objectives, they will exercise self-direction and self-control; and (3) commitment is a function of the rewards associated with goal attainment. (Chapter 13)

Therblig   A term used in time-and-motion study to identify a basic hand motion (for example, "grasp" or "hold"). The word is formed by spelling Gilbreth backward, transposing the *t* and *h*. (Chapter 2)

Time sharing   A common characteristic of larger computers; the term means that more than one person can use the machine at the same time. (Chapter 10)

Time study   A method of determining the time it takes to perform a particular task. The procedure often involves the use of a stopwatch for timing all the various elements associated with the task (for example, the time for picking up a piece of material, positioning it, or inserting it into the machine). Time study was widely used by the scientific managers in determining a fair day's work and is still employed in industrial settings. (Chapter 2)

Time–event analyses   Control techniques that permit the manager to monitor and evaluate elapsed time and attained progress on an undertaking. (Chapter 7)

Trait theory   A theory of leadership that attempts to relate success to an individual's personal characteristics or traits. (Chapter 14)

Transactional analysis (TA)   A technique designed to help managers communicate with and understand their people through an analysis of their own behavior as well as that of the subordinates. (Chapter 15)

Transformation process   *See* Black box concept.

Two-dimensional leadership model   A leadership model that addresses the importance of two factors: (1) task orientation and (2) relationship orientation. (Chapter 14)

Two-way communication Transmission of information and ideas both up and down the hierarchy. (Chapter 12)

Ulterior transaction A complex transaction involving more than two ego states with the real message often disguised under a socially acceptable transaction. (Chapter 15)

Uncertainty decisions Decision situations in which managers feel they cannot develop probability estimates because they have no way of gauging the likelihood of the various alternatives. (Chapter 8)

Understanding The second step in the communication process; it involves ensuring that the receiver grasps the essentials of the message. (Chapter 12)

Unity of command A management principle that states that a subordinate should report to only one superior. (Chapter 2)

Unity of direction *See* Unity of management. (Chapter 2)

Unity of management One of Henri Fayol's classical principles, calling for one manager and one plan for all operations having the same objective. Also called unity of direction. (Chapter 2)

Upward communication Communications channels which provide a route for subordinates to convey information to superiors. (Chapter 12)

User expectation A sales forecast that is constructed after conducting a consumer survey or some other form of consumer research. (Chapter 4)

Valence A person's preference for a first-level outcome. *See also* Expectancy; Expectancy-valence theory; First-level outcome; Instrumentality. (Chapter 13)

Variable costs Costs that change in relation to output (for example, salaries and cost of materials). (Chapter 7)

Variable expense budget A budget in which expenses and allowances are computed for different levels of activity, then adjusted following the budget period in accord with a predetermined formula. (Chapter 7)

Variety of skill The degree to which a job calls for activities involving different talents and skills. (Chapter 15)

Vocational Rehabilitation Act of 1973 A federal law that requires businesses with contracts or subcontracts with the federal government to hire the handicapped. (Chapter 17)

Whole-brain thinking The use of left brain (analytical, logical, sequential) and right brain (emotional, creative, holistic) thinking; it encourages managers to employ both sides of their brain. (Chapter 8)

Zero-base budgeting A budgeting technique in which all organizational activities or projects are broken into decision packages, then cost estimated, and finally ranked by priority; no unit is assumed to automatically receive any sum above $0 in the initial process. (Chapter 7)

Zero-sum games Games in which gains by one side are offset by losses to the other side. (Chapter 9)

NAME INDEX

SUBJECT INDEX

Abstraction, 427
Acceptance, 419
Acceptance theory of authority, 49–51
Activity, 240
Adaptive mechanism, 605–606
Adaptive organization structures
  bureaucracy, 182–83
  configurations, 182
  continuous process production and, 188–89
  free-form organizations, 206–10
  large batch production and, 188–89
  and mass production, 188–89
  matrix designs, 194–206
  mechanistic designs, 185–91
  organic designs, 185–91
  project organizations, 191–206
  pure project structures, 193–94
  small batch production and, 188–89
  technology and, 183–91
  unit production and, 188–89
Adaptive organization systems, 608–10
Age Discrimination in Employment Act of 1967, 635
Air pollution, 648–50
  automobiles, 648
  cigarettes, 649–50
  industrial smokestacks, 649
Attention, 419
Auditing
  external, 249
  internal, 249
  management, 249–51
Authority
  acceptance theory of, 49–51, 151
  Chester Barnard and, 49–51
  decentralization of, 158–61
  delegation of, 161–64
  formal theory of, 151
  functional, 156–58
  improving line-staff problems of, 155
  line, 152
  line-staff problems of, 153–55
  of the situation, 151
  of knowledge, 151
  power and, 166–70
  project, 196, 198–200
  sources of, 150–52

staff, 152–53
  zones of indifference and, 50–51
Automation, 349
Autonomy, 558

Balance theory, 442–43
Basic decisions, 271
Basic socioeconomic purpose, 99–101
Behavioral school
  group behavior, 79–80
  interpersonal behavior, 79
  nature of, 78–79
  overview and contributions, 80–81
Brainstorming, 290–91
Break-even point, 234–35
Budgeting
  avoiding inflexibility in, 233–34
  comprehensive, 231–32
  zero-base, 232–33
Bureaucracy, 182–83

Centralization, 6–7, 39
Certainty, 275
Civil Rights Act of 1964, 634–36
Classical management
  shortcomings, 54–56
  theory, 36–41
Cluster chains, 434–35
Committees
  advantages of, 144–45
  disadvantages of, 145–47
  effective use of, 147
Common Market, 678
Communication
  abstraction, 427
  acceptance, 419
  action, 421
  attention, 419
  balance theory, 442–43
  barriers, 421–29
  channels, 429–36
  commandments of, 448–49
  diagonal, 433–34
  downward, 431–32
  face-to-face, 440
  inference, 427–28
  informal, 434–36

  interpersonal, 418–21
  language, 427
  lateral, 433–34
  listening and, 443–48
  logic, 427
  media selection, 441
  normative reality, 423–26
  oral, 437–38
  perception, 421–23
  process, 418
  protecting credibility of, 442–43
  repetitive language, 440–41
  resistance to change and, 429
  satisfaction with MBA skills, 17
  sensitivity and, 439
  sensory reality, 423–26
  skills, 17
  status, 428–29
  steps in process, 419–20
  toward effective, 438–39
  two-way, 439
  understandable, 440–41
  understanding, 419
  upward, 432–33
  written, 436–37
Completed staff work, 155
Compulsory staff service, 30
Computers
  airline reservations and, 357
  automatic bank teller, 358
  data banks, 357–58
  drawbacks to, 361–62
  electronic office, 358–59
  inventory control and, 357
  micros, 351–55
  minis, 351–55
  modern, 350–51
  performance and cost, 351
  programming of, 355–56
  simulation, 359–61
  uses, 357–61
Concentration, 6
Contingency-organization design
  influencing forces, 210–12
  matter of "fit," 212–14
Controlling
  auditing, 249–51
  basic process, 226–29